MANAGING AND LEADING SOFTWARE PROJECTS

IEEE computer society

IEEE

MANAGING AND LEADING SOFTWARE PROJECTS

RICHARD E. (DICK) FAIRLEY

IEEE computer society

WILEY

A JOHN WILEY & SONS, INC., PUBLICATION

Published by John Wiley & Sons, Inc., Hoboken, New Jersey.
Published simultaneously in Canada.

For general information on our other products and services please contact our Customer Care Department within the United States at (800) 762-2974, outside the United States at (317) 572-3993 or fax (317) 572-4002.

Wiley also publishes its books in a variety of electronic formats. Some content that appears in print may not be available in electronic formats. For more information about Wiley products, visit our web site at www.wiley.com.

Library of Congress Cataloging-in-Publication Data is available.

ISBN: 978-0-470-29455-0

MIX
Paper from responsible sources
FSC www.fsc.org FSC® C013604

CONTENTS

PREFACE

Too often those who develop and modify software and those who manage software development are like trains traveling different routes to a common destination. The managers want to arrive at the customer's station with an acceptable product, on schedule and within budget. The developers want to deliver to the users a trainload of features and quality attributes; they will delay the time of arrival to do so, if allowed. Sometimes the two trains appear to be on the same schedule, but often one surges ahead only to be sidetracked by traffic of higher priority while the other chugs onward. One or both may be unexpectedly rerouted, making it difficult to rendezvous en route and at the final destination.

Managers traveling on their train often wonder why programmers cannot just write the code that needs to be written, correctly and completely, and deliver it when it is needed. Software developers traveling on their train wonder what their managers do all day. This text provides the insights, methods, tools, and techniques needed to keep both trains moving in unison through their signals and switches and, better yet, shows how they can combine their engines and freight to form a single express train running on a pair of rails, one technical, the other managerial.

By reading this text and working through the exercises, students, software developers, project managers, and prospective managers will learn why

> managing a large computer programming project is like managing any other large undertaking—in more ways than most programmers believe. But in many ways it is different—in more ways than most professional managers expect.[1]

Readers will learn how software projects differ from other kinds of projects (i.e., construction, agricultural, manufacturing, administrative, and traditional engineering projects), and they will learn how the methods and techniques of project management must be modified and adapted for software projects.

[1] *The Mythical Man-Month, Anniversary Edition*, Frederick P. Brooks Jr., Addison Wesley, 1995; pp. x.

Those who are, or will become managers of software projects, will acquire the methods, tools, and techniques needed to effectively manage software projects, both large and small. Software developers, both neophyte student and journeyman/journeywoman professional, will gain an increased understanding of what managers do, or should be doing all day and why managers ask them to do the things they ask/demand. These readers will gain the knowledge they need to become project managers. Those students and software developers who have no desire to become project managers will benefit by gaining an increased understanding of what those other folks do all day and why the seemingly extraneous things they, the developers, are asked to do are important to the success of their projects.

This text is intended as a textbook for upper division undergraduates and graduate students as well as for software practitioners and current and prospective software project managers. Exercises are included in each chapter. Practical hints and guidelines are included throughout the text, thus making it suitable for industrial short courses and for self-study by practitioners and managers.

Chapters 1 through 3 provide the context for the remainder of the text: Chapter 1 provides an introduction to software project management; Chapter 2 covers process models for developing software-intensive systems; Chapter 3 is concerned with establishing the product foundations for software projects.

Chapters 4 through 10 cover the four primary activities of software project management:

- Planning and estimating is covered in Chapters 4 through 6.
- Measuring and controlling is covered in Chapters 7 and 8.
- Managing risk is covered in Chapter 9.
- Leading, motivating, and communicating are covered in Chapter 10.

Chapter 11 covers organizational issues and concludes the text with a summary of 15 guidelines for organizing and leading software engineering teams.

For each topic covered, the approach taken is to present the full scope of activities for the largest and most complex projects and to show how those activities can be tailored, adapted, and scaled to fit the needs of projects of various sizes and complexities.

Learning objectives are presented at the beginning of each chapter and each concludes with a summary of key points from the chapter. Occasional sidebars elaborate the material at hand. An appendix to each chapter relates the topics covered in that chapter to four leading sources of information concerning management of software projects:

1. CMMI-DEV-v1.2 process framework
2. ISO/IEC and IEEE/EIA Standards 12207
3. IEEE/EIA Standard 1058
4. PMI's Body of Knowledge (PMBOK®)

The text is consistent with the guidelines contained in PMBOK and ACM/IEEE curriculum recommendations.

Presentation slides, document templates, and other supporting material for the text and for term projects are available at the following URL:
computer.org/book_extras/fairley_software_projects

Terms used throughout this text are defined in the Glossary at the end of the text. Topics, schedule, and a template for term projects follow the Glossary and included are some hypothetical projects that can be used as the basis for term projects in a course or as examples that practitioners and managers can use to gain experience in preparing software project management plans. Schedule and templates for deliverables for the hypothetic projects are also provided; electronic copies of templates and some software tools are provided at the URL previously cited. Alternatively, practitioners and managers can apply the templates and tools to a past, present, or future project.

A continued example for planning and conducting a project to build the software element of an automated teller system is presented to motivate and explain the material contained in each chapter.

As is well known, one learns best by doing. I strongly recommended that the exercises at the end of each chapter be completed and that progress through the material be accompanied by an extended exercise (i.e., a term project) to develop some elements a project plan for a real or hypothetical software project. The planning exercise can be based on an actual project that the reader has been, is currently, or will be involve in; or it can be based on one of the hypotheticals at the end of the text; or it can be based on a project assigned by the instructor. A week-by-week schedule for completing the term project on a quarter or semester basis is provided. Completion of the planning exercise will result in a report that contains elements similar to those presented in IEEE/EIA Standard 1058 for software project management plans.

The material can be presented in reading/lecture/discussion format or by assigned readings followed by classroom or on-line discussions based on the exercises and the term project.

I am indebted to the pioneers who surveyed the terrain, prepared the roadbed, laid down the tracks, and drove the golden spike so that our project trains can proceed to their destinations. Those pioneers include Fred Brooks, the intellectual father of us all; Winston Royce, who showed us systematic approaches to software development and management of software projects; Barry Boehm, who was the first to address issues of software engineering economics, risk management, and so much more; Tom DeMarco, the master tactician of software development, project management, and peopleware; and the many others who prepared the way for this text. I accept responsibility for any misinterpretations or misstatements of their work. My apologies to those I have failed to credit in the text, either through ignorance or oversight.

Thanks to Mary Jane Fairley, Linda Shafer, and the other reviewers of the manuscript for taking the time to read it and for the many insightful comments they offered. Special thanks to the many students to whom I have presented this material and from whom I have learned as much as they have learned from me.

Teller County, Colorado RICHARD E. (DICK) FAIRLEY

1

INTRODUCTION

In many ways, managing a large computer programming project is like managing any other large undertaking—in more ways than most programmers believe. But in many other ways it is different—in more ways than most professional managers expect.[1]

—Fred Brooks

1.1 INTRODUCTION TO SOFTWARE PROJECT MANAGEMENT

When you become (or perhaps already are) the manager of a software project you will find that experience to be one of the most challenging and most rewarding endeavors of your career. You, as a project manager, will be (or are) responsible for (1) delivering an acceptable product, (2) on the specified delivery date, and (3) within the constraints of the specified budget, resources, and technology. In return you will have, or should have, authority to use the resources available to you in the ways you think best to achieve the project objectives within the constraints of acceptable product, delivery date, and budget, resources, and technology.

Unfortunately, software projects have the (often deserved) reputation of costing more than estimated, taking longer than planned, and delivering less in quantity and quality of product than expected or required. Avoiding this stereotypical situation is the challenge of managing and leading software projects.

There are four fundamental activities that you must accomplish if you are to be a successful project manager:

[1] *The Mythical Man-Month, Anniversary Edition*, Frederick P. Brooks Jr., Addison Wesley, 1995; p. x.

1. planning and estimating,
2. measuring and controlling,
3. communicating, coordinating, and leading, and
4. managing risk.

These are the major themes of this text.

1.2 OBJECTIVES OF THIS CHAPTER

After reading this chapter and completing the exercises, you should understand:

- why managing and leading software projects is difficult,
- the nature of project constraints,
- a workflow model for software projects,
- the work products of software projects,
- the organizational context of software projects,
- organizing a software development team,
- maintaining the project vision and product goals, and
- the nature of process frameworks, software engineering standards, and process guidelines.

Appendix 1A to this chapter provides an introduction to elements of the following frameworks, standards, and guidelines that are concerned with managing software projects: the SEI Capability Maturity Model® Integration CMMI-DEV-v1.2, ISO/IEC and IEEE/EIA Standards 12207, IEEE/EIA Standard 1058, and the Project Management Body of Knowledge (PMBOK®). Terms used in this chapter and throughout this text are defined in a glossary at the end of the text. Presentation slides for this chapter and other supporting material are available at the URL listed in the Preface.

1.3 WHY MANAGING AND LEADING SOFTWARE PROJECTS IS DIFFICULT

A *project* is a group of coordinated activities conducted within a specific time frame for the purpose of achieving specified objectives. Some projects are personal in nature, for example, building a dog house or painting a bedroom. Other projects are conducted by organizations. The focus of this text is on projects conducted within software organizations. In a general sense, all organizational projects are similar:

- objectives must be specified,
- a schedule of activities must be planned,
- resources allocated,
- responsibilities assigned,

- work activities coordinated,
- progress monitored,
- communication maintained,
- risk factors identified and confronted, and
- corrective actions applied as necessary.

In a specific sense, the methods, tools, and techniques used to manage a project depend on the nature of the work to be accomplished and the work products to be produced. Manufacturing projects are different from construction projects, which are different from agricultural projects, which are different from computer hardware projects, which are different from software engineering projects, and so on. Each kind of project, including software projects, adapts and tailors the general procedures of project management to accommodate the unique aspects of the development processes and the nature of the product to be developed.

Fred Brooks has famously observed that four essential properties of software differentiate it from other kinds of engineering artifacts and make software projects difficult[2]:

1. complexity,
2. conformity,
3. changeability, and
4. invisibility of software.

1.3.1 Software Complexity

Software is more complex, for the effort and the expense required to construct it, than most artifacts produced by human endeavor. Assuming it costs $50 (USD) per line of code to construct a one-million line program (specify, design, implement, verify, validate, and deliver it), the resulting cost will be $50,000,000. While this is a large sum of money, it is a small fraction of the cost of constructing a complex spacecraft, a skyscraper, or a naval aircraft carrier.

Brooks says, "Software entities are more complex for their *size* [emphasis added] than perhaps any other human construct, because no two parts are alike (at least above the statement level)."[3] It is difficult to visualize the size of a software program because software has no physical attributes; however, if one were to print a one-million line program the stack of paper would be about 10 feet (roughly 3 meters) high if the program were printed 50 lines per page. The printout would occupy a volume of about 6.5 cubic feet. Biological entities such as human beings are of similar volume and they are far more complex than computer software, but there are few, if any, human-made artifacts of comparable size that are as complex as software.

The complexity of software arises from the large number of unique, interacting parts in a software system. The parts are unique because, for the most part, they are encapsulated as functions, subroutines, or objects and invoked as needed rather

[2] *Ibid*, pp. 182–186.
[3] *Ibid*, p. 182.

than being replicated. Software parts have several different kinds of interactions, including serial and concurrent invocations, state transitions, data couplings, and interfaces to databases and external systems. Depiction of a software entity often requires several different representations to portray the numerous static structures, dynamic couplings, and modes of interaction that exist in computer software.

A seemingly "small" change in requirements is one of the many ways that complexity of the product may affect management of a project. Complexity within the parts and in the connections among parts may result in a large amount of evolutionary rework for the "small" change in requirements, thus upsetting the ability to make progress according to plan. For this reason many experienced project managers say there are no small requirements changes. Size and complexity can also hide defects that may not be discovered immediately and thus require additional, unplanned corrective rework later.

1.3.2 Software Conformity

Conformity is the second issue cited by Brooks. Software must conform to exacting specifications in the representation of each part, in the interfaces to other internal parts, and in the connections to the environment in which it operates. A missing semicolon or other syntactic error can be detected by a compiler but a defect in the program logic, or a timing error caused by failure to conform to the requirements may be difficult to detect until encountered in operation. Unlike software, tolerance among the interfaces of physical entities is the foundation of manufacturing and construction; no two physical parts that are joined together have, or are required to have, exact matches. Eli Whitney (of cotton gin fame) realized in 1798 that if musket parts were manufactured to specified tolerances, interchangeability of similar (but not identical) parts could be achieved.

There are no corresponding tolerances in the interfaces among software entities or between software entities and their environments. Interfaces among software parts must agree exactly in numbers and types of parameters and kind of couplings. There are no interface specifications for software stating that a parameter can be "an integer plus or minus 2%."

Lack of conformity can cause problems when an existing software component cannot be reused as planned because it does not conform to the needs of the product under development. Lack of conformity might not be discovered until late in a project, thus necessitating development and integration of an acceptable component to replace the one that cannot be reused. This requires unplanned allocation of resources and can delay product completion. Complexity may have made it difficult to determine that the reuse component lacked the necessary conformity until the components it would interact with were completed.

1.3.3 Software Changeability

Changeability is Brooks's third factor that makes software projects difficult. Software coordinates the operation of physical components and provides the functionality in software-intensive systems.[4] Because software is the most easily changed element (i.e., the most malleable) in a software-intensive system, it is the most frequently changed element, particularly in the late stages of a project. Changes may occur because customers change their minds; competing products change; mission objectives change; laws, regulations, and business practices change; underlying hardware and software technology changes (processors, operating systems, application packages); and/or the operating environment of the software changes. If an early version of the final product is installed in the operating environment, it will change that environment and result in new requirements that will require changes to the product. Simply stated, now that the new system enables me to do A and B, I would like for it to also allow me to do C, or to do C instead of B.

Each proposed change in product requirements must be accompanied by an analysis of the impact of the change on project work activities:

- what work products will have to be changed?
- how much time and effort will be required?
- who is available to make the changes?
- how will the change affect your plans for schedule, budget, resources, technology, other product features, and the quality attributes of the product?

The goal of impact analysis is to determine whether a proposed change is "in scope" or "out of scope." In-scope changes to a software product are changes that can be accomplished with little or no disruption to planned work activities. Acceptance of an out-of-scope change to the product requirements must be accompanied by corresponding adjustments to the budget, resources, and/or schedule; and/or modification or elimination of other product requirements. These actions can bring a proposed out-of-scope requirement change into revised scope.

A commonly occurring source of problems in managing software projects is an out-of-scope product change that is not accompanied by corresponding changes to the schedule, resources, budget, and/or technology. The problems thus created include burn-out of personnel from excessive overtime, and reduction in quality because tired people make more mistakes. In addition reviews, testing, and other quality control techniques are often reduced or eliminated because of inadequate time and resources to accomplish the change and maintain these other activities.

1.3.4 Software Invisibility

The fourth of Brooks's factors is invisibility. Software is said to be invisible because it has no physical properties. While the effects of executing software on a digital computer are observable, software itself cannot be seen, tasted, smelled, touched, or heard. Our five human senses are incapable of directly sensing software; software is thus an intangible entity. Work products such as requirements specifications, design documents, source code, and object code are representations of software, but

[4] Software-intensive systems contain one or more digital devices and may include other kinds of hardware plus trained operators who perform manual functions. Nuclear reactors, modern aircraft, automobiles, network servers, and laptop computers are examples of software-intensive systems.

they are not the software. At the most elemental level, software resides in the magnetization and current flow in an enormous number of electronic elements within a digital device. Because software has no physical presence we use different representations, at different levels of abstraction, in an attempt to visualize the inherently invisible entity.

Because software cannot be directly observed as can, for example, a building under construction or an agricultural plot being prepared for planting, the techniques presented in this text can be used to determine the true state of progress of a software project. An unfortunate result of failing to use these techniques is that software products under development are often reported to be "almost complete" for long periods of time with no objective evidence to support or refute the claim; this is the well-known "90% complete syndrome" of software projects. Many software projects have been canceled after large investments of effort, time, and money because no one could objectively determine the status of the work products or provide a credible estimate of a completion date or the cost to complete the project. Sad but true, this will occur again. You do not want to be the manager of one of those projects.

1.3.5 Team-Oriented, Intellect-Intensive Work

In addition to the essential properties of software (complexity, conformity, changeability, and invisibility), one additional factor distinguishes software projects from other kinds of projects: *software projects are team-oriented, intellect-intensive endeavors*. In contrast, assembly-line manufacturing, construction of buildings and roads, planting of rice, and harvesting of fruit are labor-intensive activities; the work is arranged so that each person can perform a task with a high degree of autonomy and a small amount of interaction with others. Productivity increases linearly with the number of workers added; the work will proceed roughly twice as fast if the number of workers is doubled. Although labor-saving machines have increased productivity in some of these areas, the roles played by humans in these kinds of projects are predominantly labor-intensive.

Software is developed by teams of individuals who engage in creative problem solving. Teams are necessary because it would take too much time for one person to develop a modern software system and because it is unlikely that one individual would possess the necessary range of skills. Suppose, for example, that the total effort to develop a software product or system[5] results in a productivity level of 1000 lines of code per staff-month (more on this later). A one million line program would require 1000 staff-months. Because effort (staff-months) is the product of people and time, it would require 1 person 1000 months (about 83 years) to complete the project.

A feasible combination of people and time for a 1000 staff-month project might be a team of 50 people working for 20 months but not 1000 people working for 1 month or even 200 people working for 5 months. The later proposals (1000×1 and

[5] Software *products* are built by *vendors* for sale to numerous customers; software *systems* are built by *contractors* for specific customers on a contractual basis. The terms "system" and "product" are used interchangeably in this text unless the distinction is important; the distinction will be clarified in these cases.

200×5) are not feasible because scheduling constraints among work activities dictate that some activities cannot begin before other work activities are completed: you can't design (some part of a system) without some corresponding requirements, you should not write code without a design specification for (that part of) the system, you cannot review or test code until some code has been written, you cannot integrate software modules until they are available for integration, and so on.

Adding people to a software development team does not, as a rule, increase overall productivity in a linear manner because the increased overhead of communicating with and coordinating work activities among the added people decreases the productivity of the existing team. To cite Fred Brooks once again, the number of communication paths among n workers is $n(n-1)/2$, which is the number of links in a fully connected graph. Five workers have 20 communication paths, 10 have 45 paths, and 20 have 190. Increasing the size of a programming team from 5 to 10 members might, for example, might increase the production rate of the team from 5000 lines of code per week to 7500 lines of code per week, but not 10,000 lines of code per week as would occur with linear scaling. In *The Mythical Man-Month*, Brooks described this phenomenon as Brooks's law[6]:

Adding manpower to a late software project makes it later.

Brooks's law is based on three factors:

1. the time required for existing team members to indoctrinate new team members,
2. the learning curve for the new members, and
3. the increased communication overhead that results from the new and existing members working together.

Brooks's law would not be true if the work assigned to the new members did not invoke any of these three conditions.

A simile that illustrates the issues of team-oriented software development is that of a team of authors writing a book as a collaborative project; a team of authors is very much like a team of software developers. In the beginning, requirements analysis must be performed to determine the kind of book to be written and the constraints that apply to writing it. The number and skills of team members will constrain the kind and size of book that can be written by the available team of authors within a specified time frame. Constraints may include the number of people on the writing team, knowledge and skills of team members, the required completion date, and the word-processing hardware and software available to be used.

Next the structure of the book must be designed: the number of chapters, a brief synopsis of each, and the relationships (interfaces) among chapters must be specified. The book may be structured into sections that contain several chapters each (subsystems), or the text may be structured into multiple volumes (a system of systems). The dynamic structure of the text may flow linearly in time or it may move backward and forward in time between successive chapters; primary and

[6] *Ibid*, pp. 25 and 274.

secondary plot lines may be interleaved. An important constraint is to develop a design structure that will allow each team member to accomplish some work while other team members are accomplishing their work so that the work activities can proceed in parallel. Some books are cleverly structured to have multiple endings; readers choose the one they like.

Design details to be decided include the format of textual layout, fonts to be used, footnoting and referencing conventions, and stylistic guidelines (use of active and passive voice, use of dialects and idioms). Writing of the text occurs within a predetermined schedule of production that includes reviews by other team members (peer reviews) and independent reviews by copy editors (independent verification). Revisions determined by the reviews must be accomplished. The goal of the writing team is to produce a seamless text that appears to have been written by one person in a single setting.

A deviation from the planned narrative by one or more team members might produce a ripple effect that would require extensive revision of the text. If the completed book were software, a single punctuation or grammatical error in the text would render the book unreadable until the writers or their copy editor repaired the defect. An editor determines that each iteration of elements of the text satisfy the conditions placed on it by other elements (verification). Finally, reviews by critics and purchases by readers will determine the degree to which the book satisfies its intended purpose in its intended environment (validation).

The various development phases of writing (analysis, high-level design, detailed design, implementation, peer review, independent verification, revision, and validation) are creative activities and thus rarely occur in linear, sequential fashion. Conducting analysis, preparing and revising the design of the text, and production, review, and revision of the various parts may be overlapped, interleaved, and iterated. Team members must each do their assigned tasks, coordinate their work with other team members, and communicate ideas, problems, and changes on a continuous basis. The narrative above depicts a so-called Plan-driven approach to writing a book and, by analogy, to developing software. An alternative is to pursue an Agile approach by which the team members start with a basic concept and evolve the text in an iterative manner. This approach can be successful:

- if the team is small, say five or six members (to limit the complexity of communication);
- if all members have in mind a common understanding of the desired structure of the text (i.e., a "design metaphor");
- if there is a strict page limit and a completion date (the project constraints);
- if each iteration occurs in one or a few days (to facilitate ongoing revisions in structure; known as "refactoring"); and
- if a knowledgeable reader (known as the "customer") is available to review each iteration and provide guidance for the contents of the next iteration.

In some cases, the team members may work in pairs ("pair programming") to enhance synergy of effort.

In reality, most software projects incorporate elements of a plan-driven approach and an agile approach. When pursuing an agile approach, the team members must understand the nature of the desired product to be delivered, a design metaphor must be established, and the constraints on schedule, budget, resources, and technology that must be observed; thus some requirements definition, design, and project planning must be done. Those who pursue a plan-driven strategy often pursue an iterative (agile) approach to developing, verifying, and validating the product to be delivered; frequent demonstrations provide tangible evidence of progress and permit incorporation of changes in an incremental manner.

The approach taken in this text is to present a plan-driven strategy, based on iterative development, that is suitable for the largest and most complex projects, and to show how the techniques can be tailored and adapted to suit the needs of small, simple projects as well as large, complex ones. Process models for software development are presented in Chapter 2.

Over time humans have learned to conduct agricultural, construction, and manufacturing projects that employ teams of workers who accomplish their tasks efficiently and effectively.[7] Because software is characterized by complexity, conformity, changeability, and invisibility, and because software projects are conducted by teams of individuals engaged in intellect-intensive teamwork, we humans are not always as adept at conducting software projects as we are at conducting traditional kinds of projects in agriculture, construction, and manufacturing. Nevertheless, the techniques presented in this text will help you manage software projects efficiently and effectively, that is, with economical use of time and resources to achieve desired outcomes.

Your role as project manager is to plan and coordinate the work activities of your project team so that the team can accomplish more working in a coordinated manner than could be accomplished by each individual working with total autonomy.

1.4 THE NATURE OF PROJECT CONSTRAINTS

Many of the problems you will encounter, or have encountered, in software projects are caused by difficulties of management and leadership (i.e., planning, estimating, measuring, controlling, communicating, coordinating, and managing risk) rather than technical issues (i.e., analysis, design, coding, and testing). These difficulties arise from multiple sources; some you can control as a project manager and some you can't. Factors you can't control are called *constraints*, which are limitations imposed by external agents on some or all of the operational domain, operational requirements, product requirements, project scope, budget, resources, completion date, and platform technology. Table 1.1 lists some typical constraints for software projects and provides brief explanations.

The *operational domain* is the environment in which the delivered software will be used. Operational domains include virtually every area of modern society, including health care, finance, transportation, communication, entertainment, business, and manufacturing environments. Understanding the operational domain in which the software will operate is essential to success. *Operational requirements* describe the

[7] To be *efficient* is to accomplish a task without wasting time or resources; to be *effective* is to obtain the desired result.

TABLE 1.1 Typical constraints on software projects

Constraint	Explanation
Operational domain	Environment of the users
Operational requirements	Users' needs and desires
Product requirements	Functional capabilities and quality attributes
Scientific knowledge	Algorithms and data structures
Process standards	Ways of conducting work activities
Project scope	Work activities to be accomplished
Resources	Assets available to conduct a project
Budget	Money used to acquire resources
Completion date	Delivery date for work products
Platform technology	Software tools and hardware/software base
Business goals	Profit, stability, growth
Ethical considerations	Serving best interests of humans and society

users' view (i.e., the external view) of the system to be delivered. Some desired features, as specified in the operational requirements, may be beyond the current state of scientific knowledge, either at large or within your organization. *Product requirements* are the developers' view (i.e., the internal view) of the system to be built; they include the functional capabilities and quality attributes the delivered product must possess in order to satisfy the operational requirements.

Process standards specify ways of conducting the work activities of software projects. Your organization may have standardized ways of conducting specific activities, such as planning and estimating projects, and measuring project factors such as conformance to the schedule, expenditure of resources, and measurement of quality attributes of the evolving product. In some cases the customer may specify standards and guidelines for conducting a project. Four of the most commonly used frameworks for process standards are the Capability Maturity Model Integration (CMMI), ISO/IEEE Standard 12207, IEEE Standard 1058, and the Project Management Body of Knowledge (PMBOK). Elements of these standards and guidelines are contained in appendixes to the chapters of this text.

The *scope* of a project is the set of activities that must be accomplished to deliver an acceptable product on schedule and within budget. *Resources* are the assets, both corporate and external, that can be applied to the project. Resources have both quality and quantity attributes; for example, you may have a sufficient number of software developers available (quantity of assets), but they may not have the necessary skills (quality of assets). The *budget* is the money available to acquire and use resources; the budget for your project may be constrained so that resources available within the organization cannot be utilized. The *completion date* is the day on which the product must be finished and ready for delivery. In some cases there may be multiple completion dates on which subsets of the final product must be delivered. The constrained delivery date(s) may be unrealistic.

Platform technology includes the set of methods, tools, and development environments used to produce or modify a software product. Examples include tools to develop and document requirements and designs, compilers and debuggers to generate and check the code, version control tools to track evolving versions of a project's work products, and testing tools to aid in verify the software. Platform technology also includes the hardware processors and operating systems on which the software is developed and on which it will operate (which may be the same or different). One or more aspects of the platform technology may be obsolete or otherwise inappropriate for the work to be done.

Business goals may constrain your project to complete the product as soon as possible (to maximize short-term revenue), or to produce the highest possible quality (to maintain credibility with existing customers). *Ethical considerations* may constrain your project from delivering a product with known defects or from incorporating knowledge of a competitor's product gained by unethical methods.

Some of the most difficult problems you will encounter in managing software projects arise from establishing and maintaining a balance among the constraints on project scope, budget, resources, technology, and the scheduled delivery date:

1. scope: the work to be done;
2. budget: the money to acquire resources;
3. resources: the assets to do the job;
4. technology: methods and tools to be used; and
5. delivery date: the date on which the system must be ready for delivery.

The initial balance among these factors is established in your initial project plan. The scope of your project may change during project execution because of changes to product requirements or other factors such as the budget or delivery date. The constraints on your budget, resources, and schedule may change because of internal factors in your organization, changes in the operational environment of the product to be delivered, or competitive pressures. Changes in project scope must always be accompanied by corresponding changes in schedule, budget, resources, and (perhaps) technology.

The constraints listed in Table 1.1 reduce the conceptual space available in which to plan and conduct your project. For example, it may not be possible to deliver a satisfactory product using 10 people for 12 months, but it might be possible if the schedule were extended to 15 months or if the number of people were increased from 10 to 15, or if the requirements for the product were reduced to the functionality that can be delivered with acceptable quality by 10 people in 12 months. In addition to the constraints listed in Table 1.1, there may be political and sociological factors that you cannot control.

Some of the first things you must do in managing a software project are:

1. establish the success criteria for your project,
2. clarify the constraints on the project and the product, and
3. determine whether there is a reasonable chance of meeting the success criteria within the constraints.

Constraints should be clarified to determine whether there is any flexibility or possibility of trade-offs among the constraints because fewer or looser constraints increase the options for planning and executing your project. There may be priorities among the success criteria of delivering an acceptable product on schedule and within budget; for example, delivering on schedule may be more important than the number of features delivered, or features delivered may be more important than cost. There may be additional success criteria, such as establishing a working relationship with a new customer, or developing a product architecture that provides a basis for developing future products, that is, developing a product-line architecture that consists of base elements and configurable elements.

Factors you will have (or should have) some influence over include:

1. establishing the success criteria,
2. negotiating the project constraints,
3. obtaining consensus among project stakeholders on an initial set of operational requirements, and
4. obtaining consensus among project stakeholders on an initial set of product requirements.

Factors you will have responsibility for include:

5. making initial estimates and plans;
6. maintaining a balance among requirements, schedule, and resources as the project evolves;
7. measuring and controlling the progress of the work;
8. leading the project team and coordinating their work activities;
9. communicating with stakeholders; and
10. managing risk factors that might interfere with, or prevent achieving a successful outcome.

The major activities of project management are planning and estimating, measuring and controlling, communicating and leading, and managing risk factors. Planning and estimating are concerned with determining the scope of activities that must be accomplished, estimating effort and schedule for the overall project, and developing estimates and plans for each major work activity. Planning for measurement involves establishing a data collection and reporting system that will be used to determine and report the actual status of work activities and work products on a continuing basis. Controlling involves applying corrective actions when actual status, as indicated by the measurements, does not agree with planned status.

Communicating involves establishing and maintaining adequate communication channels among all involved parties so that everyone is aware of progress and problems, and so that they are constantly reminded of the goals and success criteria for the project. Leading is concerned with providing direction to, removing roadblocks for, and maintaining the morale of project personnel.

Risk management is concerned with identifying risk factors (potential problems), both initially and on a continuing basis; monitoring identified risk factors; and engaging in risk mitigation activities such as preparing contingency plans and executing them when necessary.

1.5 A WORKFLOW MODEL FOR MANAGING SOFTWARE PROJECTS

The primary objective of a software project is to develop and deliver one or more acceptable work products within the constraints of required features, quality attributes, project scope, budget, resources, completion date, technology, and other factors. The work products to be delivered (e.g., object code, training materials, and installation instructions) result from the flow of intermediate work products that are produced by and flow through the work processes (requirements, design, source code, and test scenarios).

The model of project workflow used in this text is presented in Figure 1.1. All models, including the one in Figure 1.1, are abstractions of real situations that emphasize some aspects of interest and suppress details that are unimportant to the purposes of the model. Important details may be expressed in subordinate models. Subordinate models to Figure 1.1 are presented throughout this text.

Figure 1.1 indicates some of the processes that support the primary activity of Product Development; they include Verification and Validation (V&V), Quality Assurance of work processes and work products (QA), Configuration Management (CM), and others. Some supporting processes and their purposes are listed in Table 1.2. Each supporting process must be accomplished in accordance with a well-defined model for accomplishing the work activities of that process.

The model in Figure 1.1 is called a *process model* because it emphasizes work activities and the flow of work products among work activities. Each work activity in a process model produces one or more work products that provide inputs to subsequent work activities. By *work product* we mean any document produced by a software project (including the source code). Some work products are delivered to the customer (called deliverable work products), while others are intermediate work products developed to advance the creative problem-solving process in an orderly manner. Some of the work products of software projects are listed in Table 1.3.

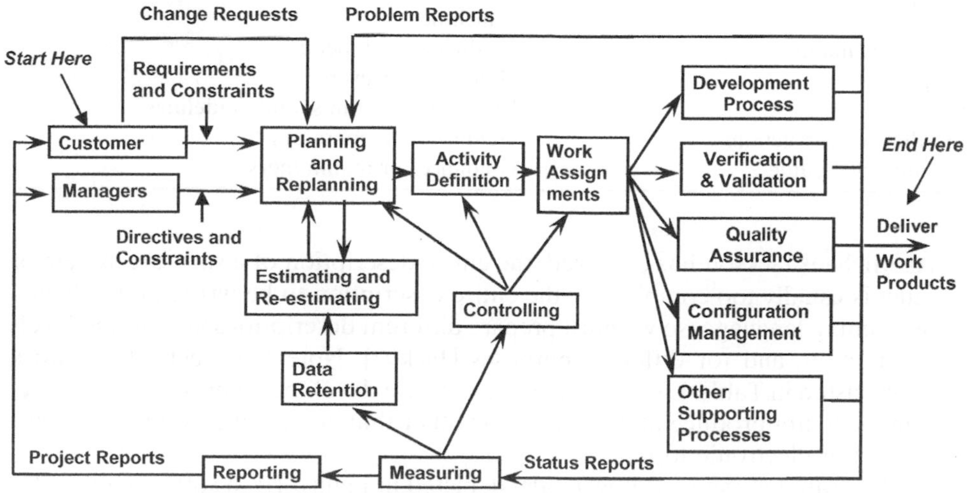

FIGURE 1.1 A workflow model for managing software projects

TABLE 1.2 Some supporting processes for software development

Supporting Process	Purpose
Configuration management	Change control, baseline management, product audits, product builds
Verification	Determining the degree to which work products satisfy the conditions placed on them by other work products and work processes
Validation	Determining the degree of fitness of work products for their intended use in their intended environments
Quality Assurance	Determining conformance of work processes and work products to policies, plans, and procedures
Documentation	Preparation and updating of intermediate and deliverable work products
Developer training	Maintaining adequate and appropriate skills
User and operator training	Imparting skills needed to effectively use and operate systems

TABLE 1.3 Some work-product documents produced by software projects

Document	Content of Document
Project plan	Roadmap for conducting the project
Status reports	State of progress, cost, schedule, and quality
Memos and meeting minutes	Issues, problems, recommendations, and resolutions
e-Mail messages	Ongoing communications
Operational requirements	User needs, desires, and expectations
Technical specification	Product features and quality attributes
Architectural design document	Components and interfaces
Detailed design specification	Algorithms, data structures, and interface details of individual modules
Source code	Product implementation
Test plan	Product verification criteria, test scenarios, and facilities
Reference manual	Product encyclopedia
Help messages	Guidance for users
Release notes	Known issues, hints, and guidelines
Installation instructions	Guidance for operators
Maintenance guide	Guidance for maintainers

As Michael Jackson has observed, the entire description of a software system or product is usually too complex for the entire description to be written directly in a programming language, so we must prepare different descriptions at different levels of abstraction, and for different purposes [Jack02]. Note that each of the work products listed in Table 1.3 is a document; software developers and software project managers do not produce physical artifacts other than documents, which may exist in printed or electronic form.

As illustrated in the workflow model depicted in Figure 1.1, a software project is initiated by customer and managers. A *customer* is the person or organization that provides the requirements for and accepts the deliverable work products. Customers may place constraints on a project, such as specifying a required database interface (a product constraint) or the date when the delivered system must be available for use (a process constraint). Managers include your management and you, the project manager. Managers specify constraints and directives. A process constraint from your manager might place a limit on the number of people available to conduct the project; a management directive might require that all software projects in the organization perform a design activity. You, the project manager, might issue directives requiring that the design be documented using UML (the Universal Modeling Language) and that one or more design reviews be held.

Requirements, constraints, and directives provide the inputs to the planning process, which is (or should be) a group activity led by you, the project manager. You should involve the customer, selected members of the development team, and other primary stakeholders in the planning process. Planning involves estimation. Factors to be initially estimated include a schedule for conducting the major work activities; kinds and numbers of resources needed, when they will be needed, and for how long; and the project milestones (points in time when progress is assessed). Estimation is best accomplished by using historical data from a data repository. Data at the completion of your project can be placed in a repository to aid in estimation of future projects. Intermediate data can be retained to assess progress and prepare completion estimates, which may result in replanning.

The output of your planning process will include identification of the roles to be played in conducting the project, which results in assignment of personnel to those roles. During initial planning, the major work activities to be planned include software development and the various supporting processes such as configuration management, process and product quality assurance, verification, validation, user training; plus other necessary activities that constitute the scope of your project. Detailed plans for these activities will evolve as the project evolves.

During execution of the project, data are collected and status reports are prepared on a periodic basis by you and your staff. The status reports will be used by you (the project manager), your customer, your managers, support groups, and other project stakeholders. Status reports compare planned progress to actual progress; they may cause you and your customer, working together, to revise plans and requirements, or you might, for example, reassign some personnel to different project roles (e.g., a software designer might be moved to the independent validation team). Status data are also used to provide a basis for estimating future progress based on progress to date (which may result in replanning), and is retained to provide a basis of estimation for future projects.

Problem reports are generated to document defects discovered in work products that must be reworked. Status reports, new requirements, and changes to requirements, constraints, directives, and problem reports provide the data needed to continually update, elaborate, and revise your project plan.

Every organization that develops and maintains software, including yours, should have one or more workflow models of software development that depicts the major work activities and flow of work products. Each member of the organization should be familiar with the workflow model(s) and understand the ways in which their work activities and work products fit into the model(s). Everyone in your software development organization should be able to sketch and describe the workflow model(s) used in the organization. If there is more than one workflow model, everyone should understand the kinds of projects for which the various models are appropriate.

1.6 ORGANIZATIONAL STRUCTURES FOR SOFTWARE PROJECTS

Projects are one-time, transient events that are initiated to accomplish a specific purpose and are terminated when the project objectives are achieved (and are sometimes cancelled before achieving the objectives). A project exists within the context of the organization in which it is conducted; each project must adhere to the structural model of the organization. Departments that conduct engineering projects, including software projects, are typically organized in one of four ways: functional structure, project structure, matrix structure, or hybrid structure.

1.6.1 Functional Structures

As the name implies, workers in a functional organization are grouped by the functions they perform. Functional groups can be process-oriented or product-oriented. One process-oriented functional group might, for example, specialize in requirements engineering, another in design of user interfaces, another in design and implementation of code, another in product validation, and yet another in user training. When organized by product specialty, one group might specialize in data communication, another in database systems, another in user interfaces, and yet another in numerical algorithms. Figure 1.2 illustrates a process-oriented functional organization, and Figure 1.3 illustrates a product-oriented functional group.

Each functional group has a functional manager whose job is to acquire and maintain the quantity and quality of workers needed to support the projects within the organization, train them as necessary, provide the necessary tools, and coordinate their work activities on various projects. Different group members apply their

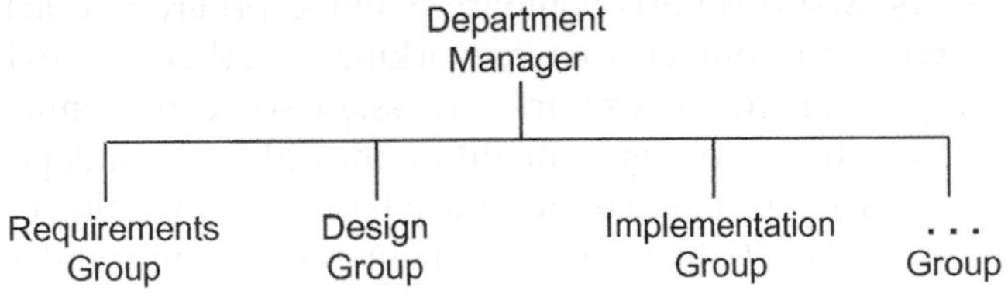

FIGURE 1.2 A process-oriented functional organization

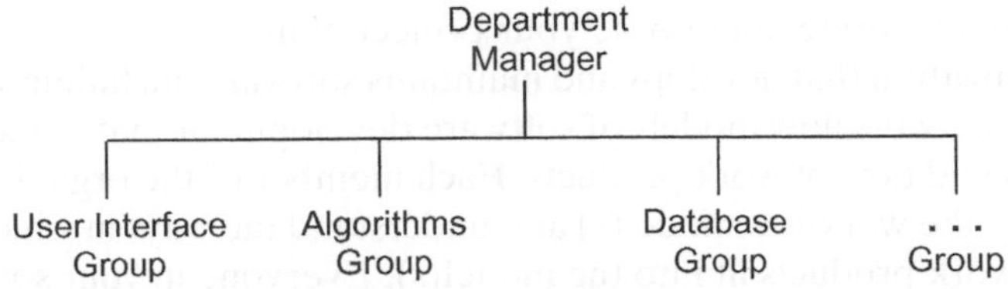

FIGURE 1.3 A product-oriented functional organization

expertise to different projects as needed. As a project manager in a functional organization, responsible for delivering an acceptable product on schedule and within budget, your ability to successfully conduct your project will depend on your skill in working with the functional managers and their team members to complete the various work activities and develop the various work products for your project.

1.6.2 Project Structures

In a purely project-structured organization, you, as project manager, have full authority and responsibility for managing budget and resources. You acquire the kinds of workers you need to conduct your project and all project members report directly to you; you might acquire your workers from functional groups or you might hire them from outside. You, the project manager, have the authority to acquire staff members within the constraints of your budget and to remove them when they are no longer needed or are not performing up to your expectations. Your ability to successfully conduct your project depends on acquiring the quantity and quality of workers needed, training them as necessary, providing the necessary tools, and coordinating their work activities. A project-structured organization is illustrated in Figure 1.4.

1.6.3 Matrix Structures

The goal of a matrix organization is to obtain the advantages of both functional and project structures; functional specialists are assigned to projects as needed and work for you, the project manager, while applying their expertise to your project. When their tasks are completed, they return to their function groups and are assigned, as needed, to other projects. Workers in a matrix organization thus have two bosses: their functional manager and their project manager.

An example of a matrix organization is illustrated in Figure 1.5. The functional groups might be, for example, a user interface group, an algorithms group, a database group, and a communications protocol group. The numbers in the matrix indicate the number of workers of each functional type assigned to each project; for example, project #1 has 10 members: 2 of functional type #1 (user interface), 5 of functional type #3 (database), and 2 of functional type #4 (communications). Project #3 is the largest; it has 23 members. Currently 6 members of the user interface group are assigned to this project, 8 from the algorithms group, 2 from the database group, and 7 from communications.

Matrix organizations can be characterized as weak or strong, depending on the relative authority of the functional managers and the project managers. In a strong

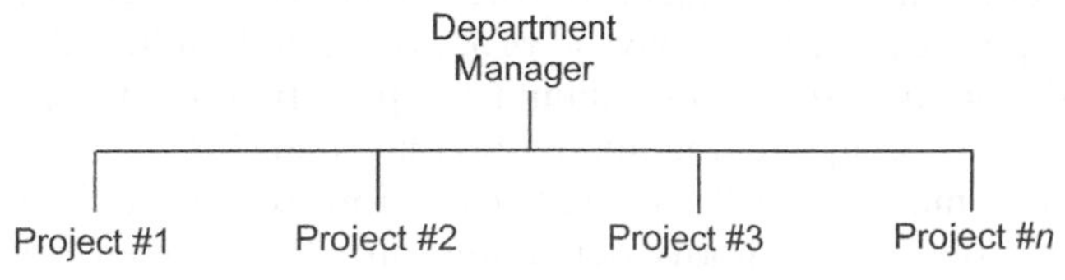

FIGURE 1.4 A project-oriented organization

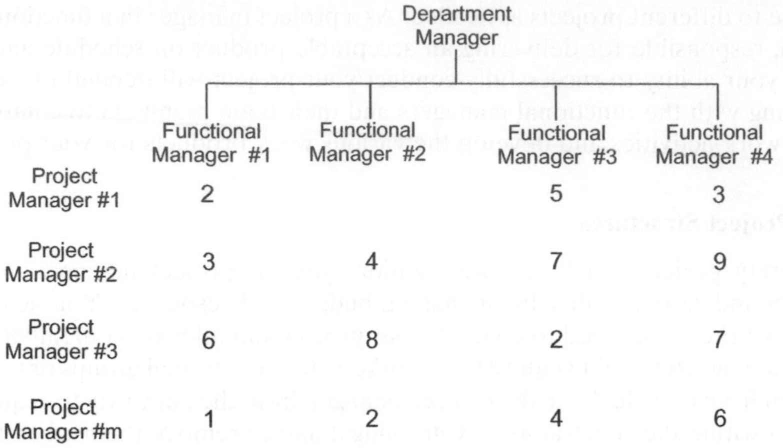

FIGURE 1.5 A matrix-structured organization

matrix, the functional managers have authority to assign workers to projects, and project managers must accept the workers assigned to them. In a weak matrix, the project manager controls the project budget, can reject workers from functional groups and hire outside workers if functional groups do not have sufficient quantities or qualities of workers.

When a matrix organization performs as intended, functional workers apply their specialties to different projects, under the direction of project managers, over time while retaining membership in a group of like-minded experts. Two problems that can occur in matrix organizations are (1) conflicts between functional managers and project managers over the allocation of worker resources (which puts the workers in untenable situations), and (2) frequent shifting of workers from project to project as crises occur (know as "firefighting" mode).

1.6.4 Hybrid Structures

Few, if any, organizations are purely functional, project, or matrix in nature. In a purely functional organization, there would be no project managers; a coordinator at the department level would assign tasks to the functional groups and work products would be passed from group to group as they become available. In a purely project organization, the project would be an entirely separate organization. The project manager would be responsible for physical facilities, janitorial service, human resources (i.e., hiring, firing, payroll, health insurance, and conflict resolution), and other organizational functions. Similarly projects organized in matrix format do not operate in isolation but are dependent on other functional elements of the organization to provide physical facilities, payroll processing, and janitorial service. Figure 1.6 illustrates the organizational continuum from pure function to pure project with matrix organizations occupying the middle region [Youk77].

You, as project manager, will have fewer or more responsibilities and more or fewer constraints on your authority depending on whether your organization has predominantly a functional, matrix, or project structure.

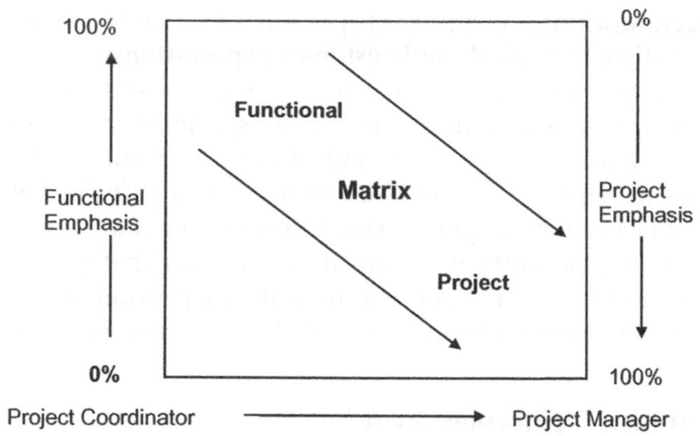

FIGURE 1.6 The organizational continuum [Youk77]

1.7 ORGANIZING THE PROJECT TEAM

The way in which your organization is structured determines the way in which you acquire your project members. It is your job to organize your project team, and to participate, as appropriate as a member of other teams such as the system engineering team.

1.7.1 The System Engineering Team

The responsibilities of systems engineers include:

- defining the operational requirements;
- specifying system requirements;
- developing the system design;
- allocating system requirements to system components;
- integrating the system components as they become available;
- verifying that the system to be delivered is correct, complete, and consistent with respect to its technical specifications; and
- validating operation of the system with its intended users in its intended operational environment.

System engineering, when it exists as a separate entity, is typically a specialty function in an organization. System engineers may be assigned to projects from a functional group within a matrix organization, or they may provide internal consulting to projects while remaining in their functional group. System engineers must be experts in their customer domains and knowledgeable of their organization's capabilities; they are more likely to be long-term organizational members than to be hired from outside the organization by a project manager.

Note that system engineers are not component specialists; they are generalists who understand (must understand) the operational domains of their customers and users and the capabilities of their organizations to develop systems for those domains.

System engineers work with component specialists to specify collections of components that will satisfy user needs and customer expectations.

A system engineering team for a complex, software-intensive system should include hardware, software, and human factors specialists as appropriate for the various kinds of hardware, software, and manual operations of the envisioned system. You, as manager of the software project for a software-intensive system, should be (must be) a member of the system engineering team. In addition the lead technical person on your software team (if you are not that person) and a representative of the group that will maintain the software portion of the system (if that is not your team) should also be members of the system engineering team.

1.7.2 The Software Engineering Team

Every software project, whether stand-alone or a subproject of a system-level program, should include a project manager, a lead designer/software architect, and one or more small development teams, each with a designated team leader. On a small project (up to 10 members), the roles of team leader, project manager, and lead designer may be played by a single individual (you). Or, a project manager may be assigned on a part-time basis with another individual playing the roles of lead designer and team leader. For intermediate-size projects (11 to 20 members), there will be (must be) separate people playing the roles of lead designer and full-time project manager. On large projects (more than 20 members), there may be a design team with a designated chief architect, staff members to support the project manager, and multiple development teams.

Figure 1.7 illustrates a hierarchical model for organizing software projects that can be expanded or contracted to accommodate various sizes of software projects.

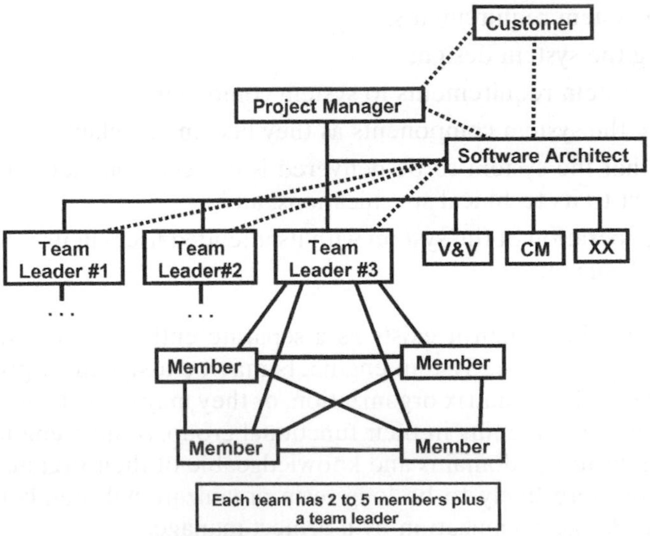

V&V: Verification and Validation
CM: Configuration Management
XX: other supporting processes

FIGURE 1.7 An organizational model for software projects

A very small project (5 or fewer members) may have only one team whose leader is the project manager and software architect; a project having 5 to 10 members may include two teams and a project manager/software architect. Intermediate-size projects will have one individual playing the role of project manager and another as lead designer; a project having 20 software developers might have 4 teams of 5 members, with one member of each team playing the role of team leader. For projects of more than 50 members, the team leaders depicted in Figure 1.7 will be subsystem managers and subsystem designers with team leaders and their teams reporting to them; a project having 100 software developers might be decomposed into 4 subsystems with, for example, 5 teams of 5 assigned to each subsystem.

A hierarchical project structure, as depicted in Figure 1.7, thus provides a flexible model that can be expanded and contracted as the needs of various projects dictate. The purpose of hierarchical structures is not to restrict the flow of communication within the project but rather to provide well-defined work activities, roles, authorities, and responsibilities at each level in the hierarchy that minimizes the need for communication among different groups. Communication paths among teams are not restricted to the hierarchy; the communication paths are informal networks that are dynamically established and disbanded as appropriate.

To facilitate communication, a fundamental principle of software analysis and design is that the requirements must be partitioned and the design structured so that the work of each small team can proceed concurrently with the work of other teams. The reason for limiting the size of each team is to control the number of intensive communication paths among software developers who are engaged in closely coordinated work activities. As previously mentioned, communication paths can be modeled as links in a fully connected graph where each team member is a node in the graph. The number of links in a fully connected graph of n nodes is $n(n-1)/2$. Five members thus have 10 paths; 10 members have 45.

The need to partition the work into well-defined work activities for multiple teams either by process function (e.g., design, coding, testing) or product function (e.g., database, algorithms, user interface) is particularly important if the team members reside in functional groups or are geographically distributed. In these cases the work to be done must be partitioned so that each functional group or geographic group can proceed with their work activities with a large degree of autonomy from the other groups.

1.8 MAINTAINING THE PROJECT VISION AND THE PRODUCT VISION

Every software project, large or small, simple or complex, must maintain the process vision (the project roadmap) and the product vision (the goals for the product) from beginning to end; otherwise, it is easy to lose sight of vision and goals in the midst of the daily work activities of a project. You, as the project manager, are the keeper of the process vision, which is documented in the project plan (and is updated as the project evolves). The software architect is the keeper of the product vision, which is documented in the requirements and architectural design specifications (and is updated as the product evolves).[8]

The project manager can be likened to a movie producer and the software architect to a movie director. The producer has overall responsibility for schedules, budgets, resources, customer relations, and delivery of a satisfactory product on time and within budget. The director is responsible for the content of the product. Producer and director must work together to maintain and constantly communicate the process vision and the product vision to the cast of developers and supporting personnel as well as all other project stakeholders.

Fred Brooks observes that producer and director can be the same person on a small project (five to seven developers), but they must be different individuals on larger projects because of the differing skills required and the number of tasks to be performed. As Brooks points out, if you, as project manager (producer) are not also the director (i.e., lead designer), you must "proclaim the director's technical authority. . . . For this to be possible, the producer and director must see alike on fundamental technical philosophy; they must talk out the main technical issues privately, before they really become timely; and the producer must have a high respect for the director's technical prowess."[9] We should add that, conversely, the director must have a high respect for the producer's managerial prowess.

1.9 FRAMEWORKS, STANDARDS, AND GUIDELINES

A *process framework* is a generic process model that can be tailored and adapted to fit the needs of particular projects and organizations. An *engineering standard* is a codification of methods, practices, and procedures that is usually developed and endorsed by a professional society or independent agency. *Guidelines* are pragmatic statements of practices that have been found to be effective in many practical situations.

Some well-known frameworks, standards, and guidelines for software engineering and the associated URLs are:

- the Capability Maturity Model® Integration for development (CMMI-DEV-v1.2) [www.sei.cmu.edu/cmmi/models];
- ISO/IEC and IEEE/EIA Standards 12207 [www.iso.org], [standards.ieee.org/software];
- IEEE/EIA Standard 1058 [standards.ieee.org/software]; and
- the Project Management Body of Knowledge (PMBOK®) [www.pmibookstore.org].

Elements of these models that are relevant to managing and leading software projects are presented in appendixes to the chapters of this text, including Appendix 1A to this chapter.

[8] *Ibid*, pp. 79–83.
[9] *Ibid*, p. 79.

1.10 KEY POINTS OF CHAPTER 1

- A project is a coordinated set of activities that occur within a specific time frame to achieve specific objectives.
- The primary activities of software project management are planning and estimating; measuring and controlling; communicating, coordinating and leading; and managing risk.
- Software projects are inherently difficult because software is complex, changeable, conformable, and invisible.
- Software projects are conducted by teams of individuals who engage in intellect-intensive teamwork.
- Project constraints consist of limitations imposed by external agents on some or all of the operational domain, operational requirements, product requirements, project scope, budget, resources, completion date, and platform technology.
- A workflow model depicts the work activities and the flow of work products among work activities in a software project.
- The entire description of a software system or product is usually too complex for the entire description to be written directly in a programming language, so we must prepare different descriptions at different levels of abstraction, and for different purposes.
- Organizations that conduct software projects use functional, project, weak matrix, and strong matrix structures.
- Software projects organized in a hierarchical manner provide well-defined work activities, roles, authorities, and responsibilities at each level in the hierarchy; hierarchies can expand and shrink to fit the needs of each project.
- Requirements must be allocated and the design structured so that the work of each small team can proceed concurrently with the work of other teams.
- The project manager maintains the project vision, as documented in the project plan, and the software architect maintains the product goals, as documented in the requirements and architectural design.
- A software process framework is a generic process model that can be tailored and adapted to fit the needs of particular projects and organizations.
- A software engineering standard is a codification of methods, practices, and procedures, usually developed and endorsed by a professional society or independent agency.
- SEI, ISO, IEEE, and PMI provide process frameworks, standards, and guidelines that contain information relevant to managing software projects (see Appendix 1A to this chapter).

1.11 OVERVIEW OF THE TEXT

This text is organized into 11 chapters. The first 3 chapters present the context in which software projects are conducted. This chapter provides an overview of and an introduction to managing software projects. Chapter 2 presents commonly used process models for software development and the project management considerations for each of the models. Chapter 3 describes product and process foundations for software projects. Product foundations include operational requirements, system requirements and system design, design constraints, and software requirements. Process foundations include the workflow model, the software development model, the contractual agreement, and the project plan.

Chapters 4, 5, and 6 are concerned with planning and estimation. Chapter 4 describes the planning process and the format and contents of project management plans. Chapter 5 presents planning techniques, including work breakdown structures, work packages, activity networks (critical paths and PERT), Gantt charts, and resource-loading histograms. Chapter 6 is concerned with estimation techniques, including pragmatic, theory-based, and regression-based techniques.

Chapter 7 presents an introduction to measures and measurement, and measurement and control of work products, including techniques to measure and analyze software defects. Chapter 8 presents measurement and control of work processes, including techniques for measuring and controlling schedule, budget, progress, and risk. Chapter 9 covers risk management, including risk identification, analysis and prioritization, mitigation strategies, action plans and action items, contingency plans and contingent actions, and crisis management.

Chapter 10 covers teamwork, motivation, personality styles, and leadership styles. Chapter 11 covers organizational issues; it concludes with 15 guidelines for organizing and leading software engineering teams.

Each chapter provides exercises; completing them will further your understanding of the topics covered in the chapter. An appendix to each chapter of this text includes relevant topics, keyed to that chapter, from the SEI Capability Maturity Model® Integration CMMI-DEV-v1.2, ISO/IEC and IEEE/EIA Standards 12207, IEEE/EIA Standard 1058, and the PMI Project Management Body of Knowledge (PMBOK®).

Appendix A to this text provides a glossary of terms used throughout the text. Appendix B describes some topics for term projects and a schedule of assignments for a term project to develop a software project management plan. Presentation slides for each chapter and other supporting material are available at the URL listed in the Preface.

REFERENCES

[Brooks95] Brooks, F. P. *The Mythical Man-Month*. Addison Wesley, 1995.

[CMMI06] SEI. *CMMI® Models and Modules*. http://www.sei.cmu.edu/cmmi/models/, 2006.

[IEEE1058] IEEE Std 1058™—1998 *IEEE Standard for Software Project Management Plans*. IEEE Press, New York, 1998. Also in Engineering Standards Collection. IEEE Product: SE113. Institute of Electrical and Electronic Engineers, August 2003.

[IEEE12207] *Industry Implementation of International Standard ISO/IEC 12207:1995 Standard for Information Technology–Software Life Cycle Processes*. IEEE/EIA 12207.0/.1/.2-1996 (March), IEEE Press, New York, 1996. Also in Engineering

Standards Collection. IEEE Product: SE113. Institute of Electrical and Electronic Engineers, August 2003.

[Jack02] Jackson, M. *Descriptions in Software Development.* Lecture Notes in Computer Science. Springer Verlag, 2002.

[PMI04] PMI, *A Guide to the Project Management Body of Knowledge*, 3rd ed. (PMBOK® Guide). Project Management Institute, 2004.

[Youk77] Youker, R. Organizational alternatives for project managers. *Project Management* Quarterly, Vol. VIII, No. 1, (March 1977).

URLs

SEI Capability Maturity Model Integration (CMMI®) [www.sei.cmu.edu/cmmi/models].

ISO/IEC Standard 12207–1995 [www.iso.org].

IEEE/EIA Software Engineering standards, including IEEE/EIA Standard 12207–1996 and IEEE/EIA Standard 1058 [standards.ieee.org/software].

PMI Project Management Body of Knowledge (PMBOK® Guide), 3rd Ed., 2004 [www.pmibookstore.org].

EXERCISES

1.1. A project is a collection of coordinated work activities conducted within a specific time frame that utilizes resources to achieve specified objectives.

a. Briefly describe a project from your personal life that you have recently completed. State the nature of the project, the initial objectives, and planned the starting and ending dates and the actual starting and ending dates of the project. List any resources used (money, tools, materials, labor).

b. List and compare the outcome of your project to the initial objectives.

1.2. Different kinds of projects tailor and adapt the generic techniques of project management (planning, estimating, measuring, controlling, communicating, coordinating, leading, managing risk) to fit the needs of the projects. For each of the following kinds of projects, list some factors that would influence the way you would plan, estimate, measure, control, communicate, coordinate, lead, and managing risk those projects:

a. Building construction

b. Restaurant kitchen

c. Fruit picking

c. Handcrafting of race cars

1.3. A 1,000,000 line of code program, when printed at 50 lines per page, results in stack of paper about 10 feet high (3 meters). Show the calculation of this result. List any assumptions made.

1.4. In the text *The Mythical Man-Month*, Fred Brooks differentiates accidental difficulties from essential difficulties in software engineering. Accidental difficulties are those that arise because of the current state of our knowledge, processes, tools, and technology. Essential difficulties arise from the inherent complexity, conformity, changeability, and invisibility of software.

a. List and briefly describe five accidental difficulties that make software development difficult.

b. Compare and contrast the current state of your five accidental difficulties to the state of those difficulties in 1960.

1.5. Describe a circumstance in which adding more people to a software project would not invoke Brooks's law; that is, a situation where the 3 factors listed in the text would not apply.

1.6. The text describes the ways in which a team of people writing a book is like a team of people writing software. Read the description and develop a two-column table in which the activities of writing a book are listed in the first column and comparable activities of writing software are listed in the rows of the second column.

1.7. Describe three ways in which a team effort to develop software is not similar to a team effort to write a book.

1.8. Describe a circumstance in which a software team would be:

a. efficient but not effective and

b. effective but not efficient.

1.9. Briefly describe an example of each kind of constraint listed in Table 1.1.

1.10. In an example in the text, it is stated that the project discussed might be successfully completed by 10 developers in 12 months if the 10 were outstanding *team members*. List five attributes of an outstanding team member; include some individual and some team membership skills.

1.11. Table 1.2 lists some supporting processes for software development. List and briefly describe three additional supporting processes that might be needed for some software projects.

1.12. Authority and responsibility are major issues for project managers.

a. Briefly state what is meant by authority.

b. Briefly state what is meant by responsibility.

c. Can authority be delegated? If not, why not? If so, give an example.

d. Can responsibility be delegated? If not, why not? If so, give an example.

e. Briefly explain why authority must be commensurate with responsibility.

1.13. Briefly describe the work environment of a software developer working in a software department organized as:

a. a functional organization

b. a project organization

c. a matrix organization

1.14. Figure 1.3 illustrates an organizational model for software projects. List the kind of work each of the three teams might do if the project is organized:

a. by process component
b. by product component

1.15. In the text, software project managers are compared to movie producers and software architects to movie directors. Briefly explain the roles comparable to project manager and software architect if software projects are compared to:

a. symphony orchestras
b. sports teams (baseball, soccer)
c. an army platoon

1.16. ISO and IEEE standards 12207 include five activities for managing software projects: initiation and scope definition, planning, execution and control, review and evaluation, and closure. Consult a copy of either ISO 12207 or IEEE 12207 and briefly summarize the topics included in each of these five activities.

1.17. The seven processes included in level 2 of the staged representation of CMMI-DEV-v1.2 are some of the most important processes for managing software projects. Access CMMI-DEV-v1.2 at www.sei.cmu.edu/cmmi/models.

a. Briefly summarize, in your own words, the purpose of each of these seven processes.
b. Briefly summarize, in your own words, the Introductory Notes for each of these seven processes.
c. Briefly summarize, in your own words, the related process areas for each of these seven processes.
d. Briefly explain why and how the related process areas are important for the purposes of managing software projects.

APPENDIX 1A

FRAMEWORKS, STANDARDS, AND GUIDELINES FOR MANAGING SOFTWARE PROJECTS

1A.1 THE CMMI-DEV-v1.2 PROCESS FRAMEWORK

CMMI process frameworks are developed and supported by the Software Engineering Institute, which is an affiliate of Carnegie Mellon University [CMMI06]. As stated on the home page for CMMI [http://www.sei.cmu.edu/cmmi/general/general.html]:

> Capability Maturity Model® Integration (CMMI) is a process improvement approach that provides organizations with the essential elements of effective processes. It can be used to guide process improvement across a project, a division, or an entire organization. CMMI helps integrate traditionally separate organizational functions, set process improvement goals and priorities, provide guidance for quality processes, and provide a point of reference for appraising current processes.

This text is not primarily focused on process improvement. However, understanding the goals and adopting the specific practices of the process areas for project management in the CMMI frameworks will improve your ability, and your organization's ability to manage software projects. Thereby your chances of delivering acceptable products on schedule and within budget will be enhanced.

Version 1.2 of CMMI is structured as a framework from which various "constellations" can be derived. CMMI-DEV-v1.2 is the first constellation; see www.sei.cmu.edu/cmmi/models. CMMI-ACQ-v1.2 for acquisition processes has just been released at the time of writing this text. Other constellations of the version 1.2 framework are under development. It is important to note that the v1.2 constellations are not process models but rather frameworks for developing and improving processes that satisfy the goals of the CMMI frameworks.

This text is primarily concerned with the process areas related to managing software and systems projects in CMMI-DEV-v1.2, which contains 22 process areas. Both staged and continuous representations are provided. The staged representation places each process area into one of five *maturity levels* numbered 1 through 5 and the continuous representation provides *capability levels* for each process area on a scale of 0 to 5. In the staged representation each higher level adds more processes. The maturity levels and their names are listed in Table 1A.1.

The 22 process areas in the staged representation of CMMI-DEV-v1.2 are illustrated in Figure 1A.1. The purposes of each process in Figure 1A.1 are listed in Table 1A.4 of this appendix. In the continuous representation of CMMI-DEV-v1.2 a capability level is determined for each individual process area selected for assessment. All the CMMI processes or any subset of them can be assessed and improved, as determined by business needs of the organization. There are six capability levels, numbered 0 through 5 and named as indicated in Table 1A.2.

In the continuous representation the CMMI processes are grouped into four categories. Categories are not levels; they are a way of grouping related process areas. The process areas in each category are as follows:

TABLE 1A.1 CMMI maturity levels

Maturity Level	Name
Level 1	Initial
Level 2	Managed
Level 3	Defined
Level 4	Quantitatively managed
Level 5	Optimizing

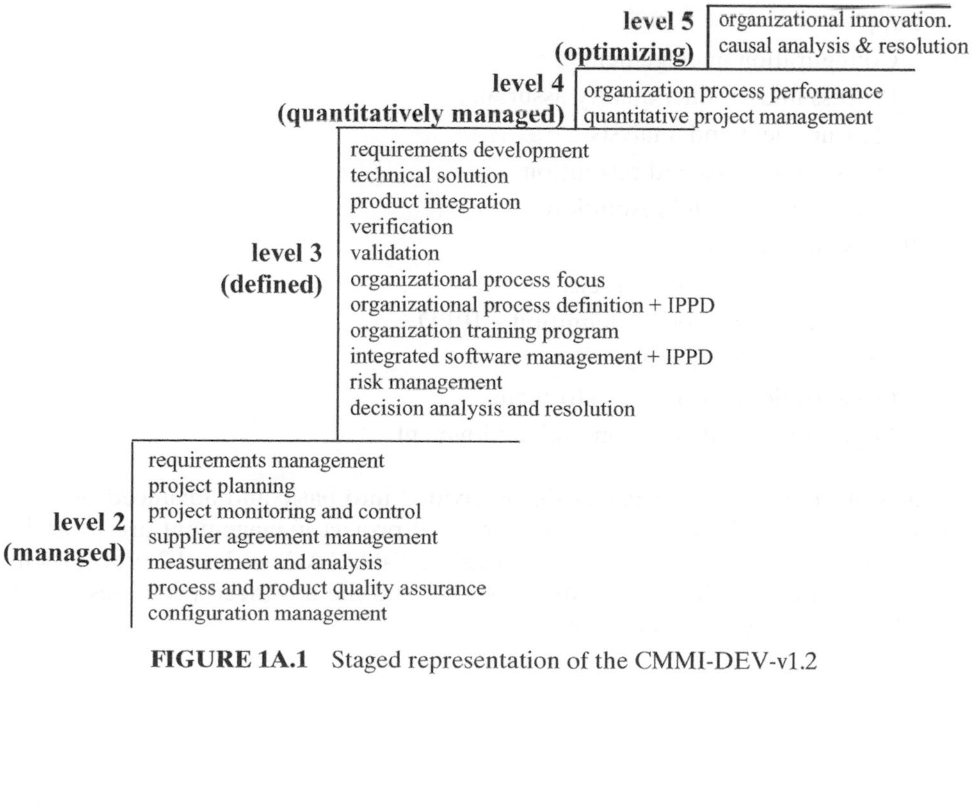

FIGURE 1A.1 Staged representation of the CMMI-DEV-v1.2

TABLE 1A.2 Capability levels in the CMMI continuous representations

Capability Level	Name
Level 0	Incomplete
Level 1	Performed
Level 2	Managed
Level 3	Defined
Level 4	Quantitatively managed
Level 5	Optimizing

- Project management
  - Project planning
  - Project monitoring and control
  - Supplier agreement management
  - Integrated project management + IPPD
  - Risk management
  - Quantitative project management
- Engineering
  - Requirements development
  - Requirements management
  - Technical solution
  - Product integration
  - Verification
  - Validation
- Support
  - Configuration management
  - Process and product quality assurance
  - Measurement and analysis
  - Decision analysis and resolution
  - Causal analysis and resolution
- Process management
  - Organizational process focus
  - Organizational process definition + IPPD
  - Organizational training
  - Organizational process performance
  - Organizational innovation and deployment

Each of the four process categories is divided into basic and advanced process areas. The basic and advanced process areas of project management are listed in Table 1A.3. Note that the basic process areas in Table 1A.3 are level 2 processes in the staged representation of CMMI-DEV-v1.2 and the advanced processes are at level 3 in the staged representation.

Each of the 22 process areas in CMMI-DEV-V1.2 has:

- generic and specific goals (required components),
- generic and specific practices (expected components), and
- informative components, which include typical work products, examples, notes, and references

TABLE 1A.3 Process areas for project management in the continuous representation of CMMI-DEV-v1.2

Basic process areas for project management	• Project planning • Project monitoring and control • Supplier agreement management
Advanced process areas for project management	• Integrated project management + IPPD • Risk management • Quantitative project management

The generic goals and specific goals for a given level, plus all of the goals for lower levels, must be satisfied to reach that level. It is expected that the generic and specific practices will be implemented unless you can demonstrate that you are using equivalent or superior processes. Informative components are illustrative in nature; they are neither required nor expected.

Generic goals and generic practices apply to each process area; their purpose is to institutionalize the process areas so that they are embedded in the corporate memory and corporate procedures. Generic goal 2 (GG2), for example, must be satisfied for level 2 (managed) processes. The generic practices of GG2 are as follows:

GG 2 Institutionalize a managed process
- GP 2.1 Establish an organizational policy
- GP 2.2 Plan the process
- GP 2.3 Provide resources
- GP 2.4 Assign responsibility
- GP 2.5 Train people
- GP 2.6 Manage configurations
- GP 2.7 Identify and involve relevant stakeholders
- GP 2.8 Monitor and control the process
- GP 2.9 Objectively evaluate adherence
- GP 2.10 Review status with higher level management

Satisfying GG3 for a process area assumes that a standard organizational process exists and that you have tailored it to suit the needs of your project. At level 3 (managed) each process is documented (at the organizational level) to specify:

- purpose
- inputs
- entry criteria
- activities
- roles
- measures
- verification steps
- outputs
- exit criteria

At level 2, each project can satisfy the generic and specific goals using different practices, but at level 3, all projects in an organization implement the process areas in a uniform manner so that consistent data can be collected from projects across the organization. Levels 4 and 5 are concerned with analyzing process and product data and using the results to make improvements in processes and technology.

Specific goals and specific practices are, as the name implies, specific to each process area. For example, the specific goals and specific practices of project planning are as follows:

SG 1 Establish estimates
- SP 1.1 Estimate the scope of the project
- SP 1.2 Establish estimates of work product and task attributes
- SP 1.3 Define project life cycle
- SP 1.4 Determine estimates of effort and cost

SG 2 Develop a project plan
- SP 2.1 Establish the budget and schedule
- SP 2.2 Identify project risks
- SP 2.3 Plan for data management
- SP 2.4 Plan for project resources
- SP 2.5 Plan for needed knowledge and skills
- SP 2.6 Plan stakeholder involvement
- SP 2.7 Establish the project plan

SG 3 Obtain commitment to the plan
- SP 3.1 Review plans that affect the project
- SP 3.2 Reconcile work and resource levels
- SP 3.3 Obtain plan commitment

The purpose of the quantitative project management (QPM) process area (a level 3 process in the staged representation) is to quantitatively manage the project's defined process to achieve the project's specified quality and process-performance objectives, namely to manage projects "by the numbers." This involves defining measures for each project phase and each kind of work process, collecting quantita-

TABLE 1A.4 Purposes of the CMMI-DEV-v1.2 processes

Process Area	Purpose
Requirements management	Control requirements and maintain consistency of requirements with plans and work products
Project planning	Establish and maintain the plans that define the project work activities
Project monitoring and control	Compare progress to plans and apply corrective actions as needed
Supplier agreement management	Manage acquisition of product elements from vendors and subcontractors
Measurement and analysis	Supply status information needed to support decisions
Process and product quality assurance	Evaluate processes and work products to identify areas of noncompliance
Configuration management	Establish and maintain control of work products
Requirements development	Obtain, analyze, and develop customer, product, and product-component requirements
Technical solution	Design, develop, and implement solutions that satisfy requirements
Product integration	Integrate components, validate overall functionality, and deliver the product
Verification	Ensure that selected work products meet their specified requirements
Validation	Ensure that selected work products satisfy their intended use when placed in their intended environments
Organizational process focus	Plan and implement organizational process improvement
Organizational process definition + IPPD	Establish and maintain a usable set of organizational process assets
Organizational training	Develop skills and knowledge so that people can perform their jobs efficiently and effectively
Integrated project management + IPPD	Develop and use an integrated and defined set of processes that are tailored from the organization's set of standard processes
Risk management	Identify potential problems; develop and implement strategies and techniques for mitigating them
Decision analysis and resolution	Identify possible decisions using a formal evaluation process that evaluates alternatives against established criteria
Quantitative project management	Use quantified data to manage each project's quality and process-performance objectives
Organizational process performance	Provide process performance data and quantitative models to understand the organization's standard processes
Organizational innovation and deployment	Select and deploy incremental and innovative improvements that measurably improve the organization's processes and technologies
Causal analysis and resolution	Identify causes of defects and other problems and take action to prevent them from occurring in the future

tive data, performing statistical analyses, and comparing results to plans and expectation on an ongoing basis.

A staged maturity level cannot be attained until all of the generic and specific goals of all processes at lower levels plus the generic and specific goals for the processes in that level are satisfied. A higher capability level for an individual process cannot be attained until all of the generic and specific goals of the lower levels plus the generic and specific goals for that level have been attained for that process.

In general, staged representations provide a systematic approach to building process maturity, level by level. Continuous representations allow different organizations to choose the processes to be improved according to the priorities established by those organizations.

Note that levels 4 and 5 in both the staged and continuous representations are termed "quantitatively managed and optimizing." Quantitatively managed process areas are those for which uniformly defined and measured data are collected from all projects across an organization and analyzed for strengths and weaknesses. At level 5 the results of level 4 data analysis are used to improve process areas and to introduce new technologies in support of the process areas. Level 5 is "optimizing" and not "optimized." The latter term (optimized) implies that the organization's processes are as good as possible. In contrast, the former term (optimizing) implies that the organization's processes are being continuously improved but are not optimum; there is always room for improvement.

The purpose of each of the 22 processes in CMMI-DEV-v1.2 is briefly summarized in Table 1A.4. Relevant elements of CMMI-DEV-v1.2 are presented in appendixes to the chapters of this text.

1A.2 ISO/IEC AND IEEE/EIA STANDARDS 12207

ISO/IEC Standard 12207 is a framework for organizing and conducting software life cycle processes. ISO/IEC 12207 was published in 1995 and amended in 2002 and 2004. Amendments 1 and 2 revise 12207 to incorporate lessons learned in using 12207 and to more closely align it with ISO Standard 15504, which is a standard for assessing the software processes within an organization to determine areas of strength and weakness.

ISO/IEC Standard 12207 provides a comprehensive set of life cycle processes for acquisition, supply, development, operation, and maintenance of software. It includes 17 processes:

- 5 primary life cycle processes,
- 8 supporting processes, and
- 4 organizational processes.

The five primary processes are:

- acquisition,
- supply,
- development,

- operation, and
- maintenance.

The acquisition and supply processes are concerned with the relationships between a customer and a supplier. In ISO/IEC 12207, the development process consists of 13 activities:

1. Process implementation
2. System requirements analysis
3. System architectural design
4. Software requirements analysis
5. Software architectural design
6. Software detailed design
7. Software coding and testing
8. Software integration
9. Software qualification testing
10. System integration
11. System qualification testing
12. Software installation
13. Software acceptance support

The eight supporting processes in ISO/IEC 12207 are:

- documentation,
- configuration management,
- quality assurance,
- verification,
- validation,
- joint review,
- audit, and
- problem resolution.

The four organizational life cycle processes are:

- management,
- infrastructure,
- improvement, and
- training.

The management process in ISO/IEC 12207 includes five activities for managing software projects:

- initiation and scope definition,
- planning,

- execution and control,
- review and evaluation, and
- closure.

ISO/IEC 12207 is packaged in three volumes:

- 12207.0, software life cycle processes;
- 12207.1, life cycle data; and
- 12207.2, implementation considerations.

ISO/IEC 12207.0 is the primary document; in addition to specifying primary life cycle processes, supporting processes and organizational life cycle processes, it includes appendixes that provide guidance for tailoring the various processes to fit particular situations.

ISO/IEC 12207.1 (life cycle data) includes generic guidelines for 7 types of documents (e.g., plans, descriptions, records) and specific guidelines for 30 kinds of documents (e.g., project management plans, software design descriptions, software quality assurance records).

ISO/IEC 12207.2 (implementation considerations) provides guidance, based on industry experiences, for implementing the life cycle processes in 12207.0.

The IEEE/EIA version of ISO/IEC Standard 12207 was developed by the Software and Systems Engineering Standards Committee of the IEEE Computer Society [IEEE12207]. Simply stated, IEEE/EIA 12207 is ISO/IEC 12207 with modifications and clarifications of wording and the addition of some appendixes. It is the umbrella standard for the IEEE's suite of approximately 40 standards for software engineering documents and processes [standards.ieee.org/software]; each of those standards is (is intended to be) harmonious with IEEE/EIA 12207.

According to the abstract in IEEE/EIA Standard 12207.0–1996, the standard includes clarifications, additions, and changes accepted by the Institute of Electrical and Electronics Engineers (IEEE) and the Electronic Industries Association (EIA). The goal of the standard is to provide better understanding of and a basis for software practices in both national and international business. According to the Foreword to IEEE/EIA 12207.2, it summarizes the best practices of the U.S. software industry in the context of the process structure provided by ISO/IEC 12207. Relevant elements of the ISO and IEEE Standards 12207 are presented in appendixes to the chapters of this text.

1A.3 IEEE/EIA STANDARD 1058

Project management plans based on IEEE Std 1058™–1998 IEEE Standard for Software Project Management Plans will include plans for [IEEE1058]:

- managerial processes,
- technical processes,

- supporting processes, and
- additional processes.

Plans for managerial processes include:

- a startup plan,
- a work plan,
- a control plan,
- a risk management plan, and
- a closeout plan.

Plans for technical processes include plans for a development process model; methods, tools, and techniques; infrastructure; and product acceptance. Supporting process plans include plans for the eight supporting processes in IEEE/EIA Standard 12207; namely configuration management, verification and validation, documentation, quality assurance, reviews and audits, problem resolution, subcontractor management, and process improvement.

Plans for additional processes include plans for other processes such as user training, installation, or ongoing maintenance and support that may not be required on some projects.

An overview of IEEE/EIA Standard 1058 is presented in Chapter 4 of this text. A template for preparing project management plans based on IEEE/EIA Standard 1058 is contained in Appendix 4B to Chapter 4 of this text; an electronic copy of the template can be accessed at the URL for the text, which is listed in the Preface. Relevant elements of IEEE/EIA Standard 1058 are presented in appendixes to the chapters of this text.

1A.4 THE PMI BODY OF KNOWLEDGE

The PMI Body of Knowledge was developed by the Project Management Institute, which is a nonprofit organization that promotes the profession of project management by sponsoring chapters, special interest groups, and affiliations with colleges and universities [www.pmi.org]. PMI has more than 200,000 members worldwide. PMI's activities include education and knowledge acquisition, professional development and networking, career advancement and professional standards, and products and services. PMI offers a certificate examination by which one can become a certified project management professional.

The Guide to the PMI Body of Knowledge (PMBOK®) covers five process groups [PMI04]:

- project initiation,
- project planning,
- executing a project,
- monitoring and controlling a project, and
- closing a project.

TABLE 1A.5 Chapters in the PMBOK® Guide

Chapter 1	Introduction
Chapter 2	Project Life Cycle and Organization
Chapter 3	Project Management Processes for a Project
Chapter 4	Project Integration Management
Chapter 5	Project Scope Management
Chapter 6	Project Time Management
Chapter 7	Project Cost Management
Chapter 8	Project Quality Management
Chapter 9	Project Human Resource Management
Chapter 10	Project Communication Management
Chapter 11	Project Risk Management
Chapter 12	Project Procurement Management

These five process groups include 44 management processes. PMBOK also includes 34 key competencies for project managers. Titles of the chapters in *A Guide to the Project Management Body of Knowledge*, 3rd ed. (PMBOK® Guide) are listed in Table 1A.5; they indicate the scope of topics addressed by PMBOK [PMI04]. Relevant elements of PMBOK are presented in appendixes to the chapters of this text.

2

PROCESS MODELS FOR SOFTWARE DEVELOPMENT

process A series of operations performed in the making or treatment of a product.
—*American Heritage College Dictionary*, Third Edition

2.1 INTRODUCTION TO PROCESS MODELS

Management of software development and modification is accomplished by decomposing high-level work activities into lower-level work activities in a hierarchical manner. The lowest level work activities subject to management planning and accountability are called *tasks; activities* are thus aggregations of tasks and subordinate activities.[10] Systematic accomplishment of a task typically involves following a set of procedures and using a set of tools and techniques (i.e., performing a process).

Process engineering is concerned with developing and constantly improving the workflow within and among tasks to make software development more efficient and more effective; that is, to accomplish tasks without wasting time, effort, or resources (i.e., efficiently) and to achieve the desired results (i.e., effectively). Improved work processes raise the productivity and morale of software developers, the quality attributes of work products, and satisfaction of users and customers.

The basis tenets of process engineering are as follows:

1. Better work processes result in better work products, where "better work products" means enhanced features, improved quality, less rework, and easier modifications.

[10] The terms "activity" and "task" will be used interchangeably in this text unless the difference is important to the topic under discussion, in which cases, the distinction will be made.

Managing and Leading Software Projects, by Richard E. Fairley

2. Work processes must be designed with the same care used to design work products; work processes must be designed to satisfy process requirements and process constraints, fit the needs of individual projects, and make the work processes efficient and effective.
3. Work processes for each project should be derived from a process framework. A process framework is a generic process model that can be tailored to meet the needs of a variety of situations. The tailoring of a framework involves adding, deleting, and modifying elements to adapt the framework to the needs of particular projects.
4. Process design and process improvement result in shorter schedules, higher quality, lower costs, happier users and customers, and happier workers and managers.
5. Process improvement seldom happens spontaneously. Investment in process engineering saves more time, effort, and cost than is invested. A positive ROI (return on investment) requires an ongoing investment of time, effort, and resources.

Many organizations have established frameworks for project management, for software development, for software product lines, for business processes, for process improvement, and many other situations. Some organizations have developed pretailored process models for various kinds of software projects, derived from the organization's process framework. In these cases you, as a project manager, would select an appropriate process model from an inventory of models and, if necessary, further tailor it to meet the specific needs of your project.

A process framework (i.e., a workflow model) for software projects was introduced in Chapter 1; it is illustrated in Figure 1.1 and repeated here as Figure 2.1*a*. Like all models the workflow model emphasizes aspects of relevance to its purposes and suppresses other aspects, which can be elaborated in subordinate models; Figure 2.1*b* is a subordinate model for the box in the upper right corner of Figure 2.1*a* (i.e., development process). This chapter presents additional models of the software development process depicted in the upper right corner of Figure 2.1*a*. Other chapters of this text elaborate other elements of the workflow model in Figure 1.1 and examine their relevance to the tasks of managing and leading software projects.

A process model for software development emphasizes:

- the work activities to be performed in making a software product;
- the order in which the work activities and tasks are to be performed;
- the ways in which work activities and tasks can be overlapped and iterated; and
- the work products that result from, and flow among, the various work activities.

The development process you use to develop your work products exerts a strong influence on the techniques you will use during your projects to:

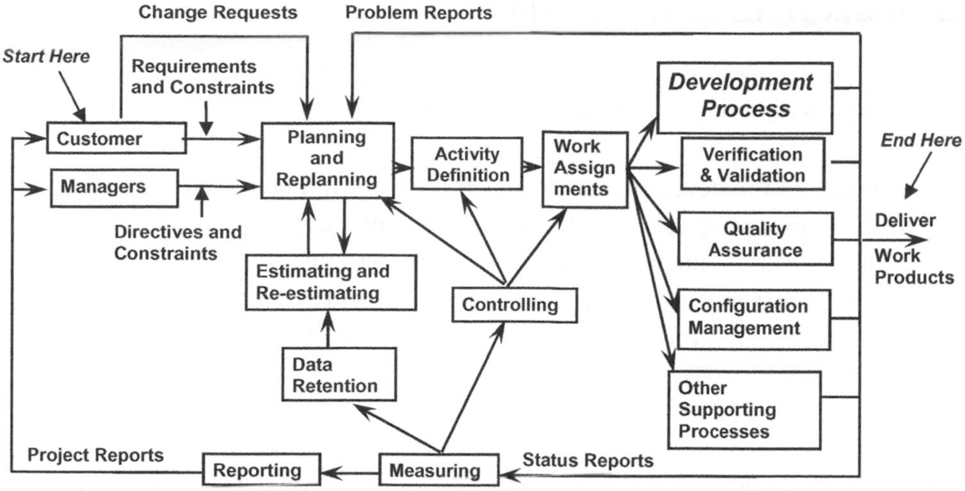

FIGURE 2.1A A workflow model for managing software projects.

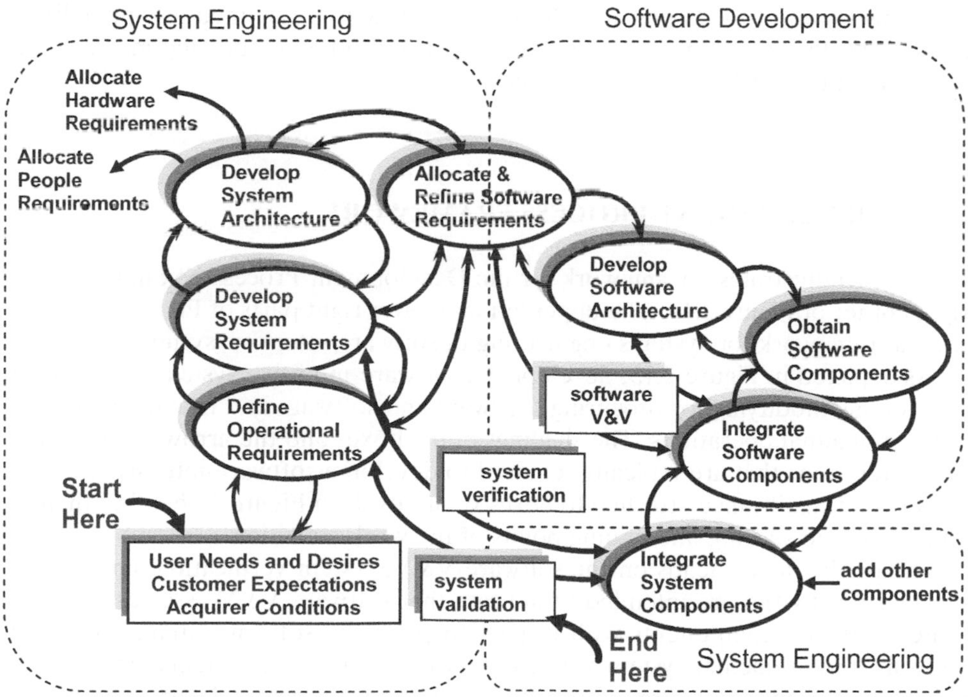

FIGURE 2.1B A process framework for developing software-intensive systems

- plan and estimate,
- measure and control,
- communicate, coordinate, and lead, and
- manage risk.

2.2 OBJECTIVES OF THIS CHAPTER

This chapter presents process models for software development. After reading this chapter and completing the exercises you should understand:

- elements of the development process framework in Figure 2.1*b*;
- distinctions among users, customers, and acquirers;
- tailoring of the framework for software-only systems;
- several commonly used process models for software development;
- ways in which the various development process models influence management of software projects; and
- an example of process design.

Appendix 2A to this chapter covers the elements of CMMI-DEV-v1.2, ISO/IEC and IEEE/EIA Standards 12207, IEEE/EIA Standard 1058, and the of PMI Body of Knowledge that are relevant to software development processes. Appendix 2B includes guidelines for choosing among iterative development models.

Terms used in this chapter and throughout this text are defined in Appendix A to the text. Presentation slides for this chapter and other supporting material are available at the URL listed in the Preface.

2.3 A DEVELOPMENT-PROCESS FRAMEWORK

Figure 2.1*b* illustrates a framework for the Development Process box in the upper right corner of Figure 2.1*a*. The upper left and lower right parts of Figure 2.1*b* illustrate a framework for systems engineering of software-intensive systems.

As depicted in Figure 2.1*b*, developing a software-intensive system may involve developing, modifying, or procuring hardware and software and training people to perform manual operations. The shadings of the boxes and the arrows indicate the many iterations that are typically required to develop a software-intensive system. There is no significance attached to boxes versus ovals in Figure 2.1*b*, other than to emphasize the starting and ending points of the work activities.

The double arrowheads on the software V&V, system verification, and system validation activities are intended to indicate that software V&V assesses the integrated software components with respect to (wrt) the software architecture and software requirements, system verification wrt system requirements, and system validation wrt operational requirements. *Verification* is concerned with determining the extent to which a work product is correct, complete, and consistent with respect to other work products and work processes. *Validation* is concerned with determining that a work product is suitable for its intended purpose in its intended environment.

Hardware may include computing hardware and other devices to be built, modified, or procured. Software may include existing software to be used as is, software to be developed and/or modified by your project personnel, and software to be procured. People to be trained may include end users, system operators, and operational support personnel.

Some software-intensive systems are *embedded systems*. An embedded system is a system contained within another system. For example, computers and software are embedded within consumer products such as DVD players, game machines, microwave ovens, cellular telephones, and automobiles and within complex systems such as nuclear reactors, communication networks, and spacecraft. Users of embedded systems interact with the interfaces of the larger system rather than directly with the computer hardware and software. The direct users of the software are thus hardware and other software.

The elements of the framework depicted in Figure 2.1*b* are *development phases*. A development phase is a set of related work activities that produce one or more work products. Phases can be interleaved, overlapped, and iterated as specified by the development process being used. The arrows and shadings in Figure 2.1*b* indicate some of the many iterative paths and ongoing revisions to, and enhancements of, work products that attempt to accurately portray the nonlinear processes of creativity and innovation that occur when teams of individuals work collaboratively to develop complex software-intensive systems.

Elements of the process framework depicted in Figure 2.1*b* are presented in the following sections:

- Users, customers, and acquirers are covered in Section 2.3.1.
- Operational requirements are covered in Chapter 3, as is the topic of requirements engineering for the software components of systems.
- System requirements and system design are covered in Section 2.3.2.
- Developing the software architecture and obtaining the software components are covered in Section 2.3.3.
- Verification and validation are covered in Section 2.3.4.

Tailoring of the framework in Figure 2.1*b* for software-only projects and commonly used process models for software development are presented in subsequent sections of this chapter.

2.3.1 Users, Customers, and Acquirers

Projects are initiated because of unsatisfied needs, desires, expectations, and conditions. The starting point (lower left corner of Figure 2.1*b*) may involve users, customers, an acquirer, as well as other stakeholders. In many cases user, customer, and acquirer are the same person or organization, but in other cases they are distinct entities. In addition there may be a "project sponsor" who is distinct from users, customers, and acquirer, and who controls the resources for development of the system. Users are those individuals (or other systems, as in the case of embedded systems) that will utilize the delivered software to accomplish their work activities or pursue recreational pastimes. Customers are those who specify requirements and constraints, and accept the deliverable work products of a project. Your customer might be another person or group in your department, another department in your organization (e.g., a system engineering or marketing group), or an external organization (e.g., a manufacturing company, a financial institution, or a government agency).

The customer is called the acquirer in situations where the contractual agreement between customer and developer is a legally binding contract; in these cases the development organization is called the supplier. In some cases the acquirer may be a third-party agent who represents one or more customers or user communities and who provides the communication interface between the supplier and the customers/users.

You, as a software developer, may be your own customer. Organizations sometimes develop software-intensive systems in a speculative manner without having a specific customer or user group in mind. In some cases, the marketing department plays the role of surrogate customer. In other cases, a research and development (R&D) team may, by introspection, build a prototype or demonstration version of a product they would want if they were the customer/user. Whatever the situation, every software project has a customer; otherwise, there are no needs to be satisfied, no one to specify the requirements and constraints, and no one to accept the delivered work products.

Customers, users, and acquirer may be one and the same, as illustrated in Figure 2.2 (designated as Customer), or they may be distinct entities, as illustrated in Figure 2.3.

Figure 2.2 illustrates an important point: *every software project is two or more projects.* At minimum, a software project includes the customer's project to acquire a system and the developer's project to develop and deliver the system. There are activities that each party must accomplish separately and activities they must do together. The customer must, for example, determine, specify, and prioritize user needs, state constraints (e.g., schedule and budget), and accept (or reject) the system or product; the developer must develop and deliver an acceptable product; together, customer and developer must negotiate requirements and constraints and periodically review progress and resolve problems.

In the general case, users, customers, and acquirer are distinct entities. Users are those who will use the system or product to their work activities or to recreational activities; customers are those who specify the requirements and constraints and

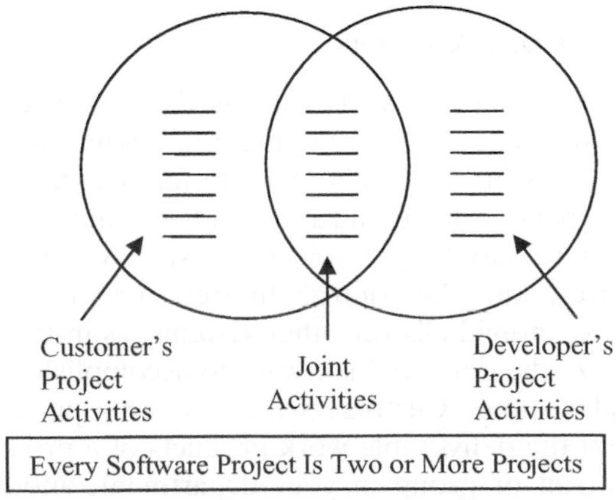

FIGURE 2.2 A simple customer–developer relationship

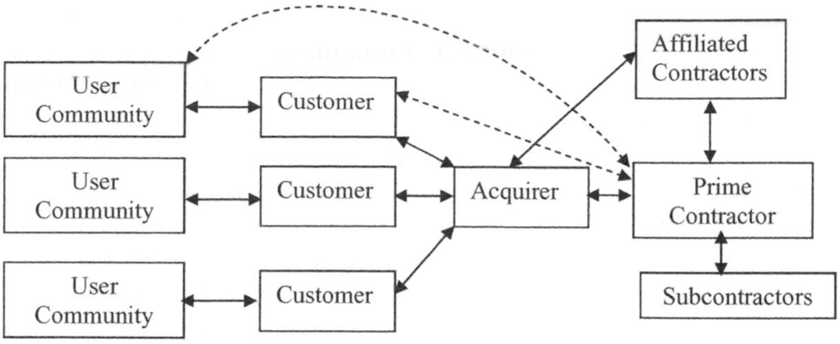

FIGURE 2.3 Relationships among project stakeholders

accept the product on behalf of the users; an acquirer is the agent of one or more customers or user groups.

Customer and users might be different, with no formally designated acquirer. For example, a marketing department or an aerospace department internal to your company might be the customer who represents a user community of teenage game players in the former case and astronauts in the latter case.

As illustrated in Figure 2.3, an acquirer is the agent of one or more customers.[11] An individual customer, such as a financial institution, might employ a knowledgeable acquirer to procure a new data-processing system for their organization, or several customers might collaborate to acquire a software-intensive system for shared usage. In the latter case an airline, a rental car agency, and a hotel chain might ban together to acquire a comprehensive reservation and sales system. One of the three companies might be the designated acquirer, or they might employ a separate individual or organization to serve as their customer representative to the system supplier (designated as the Prime Contractor in Figure 2.3). The supplier might use one or more subcontractors to develop one or more parts of the system. Other contractors might be working on related projects that require communication with you, the prime contractor. Or, you might be a subcontractor; in this case your customer is the prime contractor.

There may be additional relationships as portrayed in Figure 2.3, for example, direct contact between the Prime Contractor and various Customers and User Communities, with the interactions(s) being coordinated by the Acquirer.

An important aspect of project planning is to identify all of the project stakeholders and to establish well-defined communication paths among them. Stakeholders include users, customers, and acquirer plus those individuals and organizations that affect a project or will be affected by the outcomes of the project. The impact of the new or modified system on stakeholders' work activities must be taken into consideration, as in the case of workers who must learn to follow new accounting procedures and use the software for a new financial transaction system.

Note that the term "customer" is relative to the context: for example, users are the customers of the marketing department, organizations that collaborate to acquire a system are the customers of the acquirer, the acquirer is the customer of

[11] Some acquirer organizations are termed *system integrators*; they procure and integrate components and deliver the resulting systems to customers.

the prime contractor, and the prime contractor is the customer of subcontractors if it uses subcontractors. The term "supplier" (as in the acquirer–supplier relationship) is also context dependent. Subcontractors are suppliers to the prime contractor, the prime contractor is the supplier to the acquirer, and the acquirer is the supplier to customers and customers are suppliers to users. The development group is a supplier to the independent testing group; the independent testing group is a customer of the development group.

In this text the term "customer" is used to denote the individual or organization that specifies requirements and constraints and accepts the resulting system or product; "developer" denotes the group that is responsible for delivering an acceptable system or product on schedule and within budget. The terms "customer," "acquirer," "supplier," and "developer" will be clarified when the meanings are not clear from the context of usage.

2.3.2 System Requirements and System Design

As illustrated in Figure 2.1*b*, the first phase of system development involves identifying the project stakeholders and establishing lines of communication among them. The next phases[12] of system development involve developing the operational requirements, the system requirements, and the system architecture. Operational requirements document the external view of the system; they specify the needs, desires, expectations, and constraints of the users, customers, acquirers, and other stakeholders. It is important that all stakeholders be identified and their interests be accounted for in the operational requirements.

The system requirements are derived from the operational requirements; they specify the features and quality attributes the system must provide in order to satisfy the operational requirements. For example, the operational requirements might state that the system must have acceptable response time. Feasibility studies, demonstrations of prototypes, and discussions might result in a system requirement that specifies response time of less than 1 second for Type A queries and less than 5 seconds for Type B queries when the system is running at 70% load capacity (where the details of Type A and Type B queries are also specified).

Operational requirements are sometimes vague and imprecise, but system requirements must be quantified to the extent possible because system requirements are the basis for design, implementation, and acceptance of the system. It is, of course, necessary to verify that the system requirements, if satisfied, will result in a system that satisfies the operational requirements. Traceability, prototyping, and joint reviews between customer(s) and developer are techniques that can be used to verify that the system requirements are correct, complete, and consistent with respect to the operational requirements. Details of requirements engineering are presented in Chapter 3.

The next phase of system development in Figure 2.1*b* is development of the system architecture. The top-level architecture of a software-intensive system is typically represented as a block diagram that illustrates the primary hardware, software, and people elements plus the interconnections among them plus their con-

[12] A development phase is a set of related work activities that produce one or more work products. Phases can be interleaved, overlapped, and iterated as determined by the development process being used.

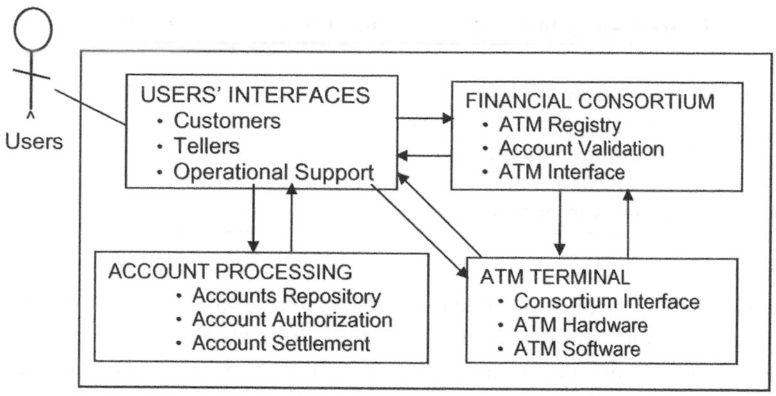

FIGURE 2.4 A system-level block diagram for an Automated Teller System

nections to the environment of the system. Functional requirements and quality attributes are allocated to the various hardware, people, and software elements in the figure. Each functional requirement is allocated to an individual element of the system, while quality attributes may apply to one, some, or all of the system components.

In addition the specifications for the hardware components, the skills required for manual operations to be performed by the people elements, and design constraints on the hardware and software elements are specified. A system-level block diagram for an Automated Teller System is illustrated in Figure 2.4. As illustrated, a block diagram shows the major system components, information flows among system components, the boundary between the system and its environment (its context), and the information flows across the system boundary.

System-level requirements are allocated to the hardware, software, and manual elements of the system. Additional requirements may be derived to support the higher level requirements allocated to the components.

2.3.3 Software Requirements, Architecture, and Implementation

System requirements allocated to software should be reviewed, revised, and elaborated to sufficient detail so that:

1. hidden complexities are exposed (i.e., the job to be done is understood);
2. opportunities for reuse of existing software components can be identified;
3. the necessary hardware resources such as computer memory and processor speed can be estimated (which may result in revision of the hardware requirements); and
4. estimates of effort, required skills, and schedule needed to develop the software can be made.

Requirements engineering is covered in Chapter 3 of this text.

Architectural design of software, as depicted in Figure 2.1*b*, is concerned with specifying the major software components, their interrelationships, and their

TABLE 2.1 Some ways to obtain software components

- Implement in-house
- License from a vendor
- Procure from a subcontractor
- Reuse from another system
- Reuse from a library
- Obtain from open source

connections to the environment of the software. There are several kinds of interrelationships among software components; they include structural, functional, behavioral, and data relationships. As a result different representations (different views) may be used to specify the different kinds of relationships among components and the connections of components to the environment [Bass03].

In former times, software components were obtained by writing the code for most, if not all, of the components. Some software routines from a math library or an I/O library might have been incorporated, but most of the software for each product was written by the software developers. Currently software components are obtained using a variety of techniques, as listed in Table 2.1.

Implementation of software involves performing detailed design, coding, and unit-level V&V. Detailed design is concerned with specifying the details of interfaces, algorithms, data structures, and other aspects of the components specified at the architectural level. Coding involves writing the software and unit-level V&V is concerned with determining that each unit of software (i.e., each software module) satisfies the conditions placed on it by the requirements and the design (verification) and that each unit is suitable for its intended use in its intended environment (validation).

Different approaches to obtaining software components require different approaches to managing the project. For example, developing components in-house requires:

- detailed planning for numbers and skills of the software developers,
- organizing the development team(s),
- allocating requirements to the teams,
- specifying project metrics to be collected,
- monitoring of progress, and
- applying corrective actions when actual progress does not agree with planned progress.

Licensing of components involves:

- evaluating candidate components;
- selecting appropriate components; and
- negotiating terms, conditions, and delivery dates for the selected components.

Procurement of components involves selecting a subcontractor and negotiating a contract that includes items such as:

- the scope of work to be performed by the subcontractor;
- work products to be delivered to the subcontractor (e.g., requirements, design documentation, source code to be tested);
- work products to be delivered by the subcontractor (e.g., source code, test cases, test results);
- the delivery date and cost of the subcontractor's project;
- metrics to be reported and frequency of reporting by the subcontractor's project;
- schedule of joint meetings and reviews; and
- penalties, and rights in data (i.e., who owns what).

Reuse involves:

- specifying the features and quality attributes of components to be reused;
- locating candidate components;
- evaluating their features, quality attributes, and interfaces; and
- modifying them as necessary.

Obtaining components from open sources involves:

- locating components;
- evaluating their features, quality attributes, and interfaces; and
- determining access rights and liabilities.

Software projects typically use more than one of these techniques to obtain the necessary components. For example, some of the components may be developed in-house, some reused from a library of components, and some may be obtained from a subcontractor, a vendor, or an open source.

Regardless of how the software components are obtained, the following activities must be performed: verifying that each component is complete, correct, and consistent with respect to the architectural design and software requirements for that component; integrating the components; verifying that the integrated components are correct, complete, and consistent with respect to the architectural design and the software requirements; and validating that the integrated components will satisfy their intended purpose when used in their intended operating environment. Iterative development processes support incremental implementation, verification, and validation of software as it is being built.

Obtaining, verifying, and integrating software components are best accomplished in an iterative manner by which each component is systematically added to the growing product. Project plans based on an iterative approach must incorporate plans for iterative development, incremental verification and validation, and ongoing revisions of and enhancements to work products because these activities do not occur in a linear sequence of steps when teams of individuals engage in the creative and innovative work activities of iterative software development.

For example, prototyping of the user interface during analysis of software requirements may indicate the need to revise the requirements for the tasks to be performed by the human elements of the system (e.g., manual operations performed by the operators of nuclear reactors, pilots of fighter aircraft, or users of iPods). Prototyping of software components during the software design activity may indicate that performance requirements for a particular component cannot be achieved in software. In this case the functionality to be provided by that component might be re-allocated to a hardware component (e.g., data encryption and decryption will require a special-purpose chip). In similar fashion some of the requirements for hardware and/or manual functions may be re-allocated to software.

2.3.4 Verification and Validation

Verification is concerned with determining the degree to which a work product fulfills the requirements and conditions placed on it by other work products and work processes. A verified work product is complete, correct, and consistent with respect to the requirements and conditions for that work product. Thus the specification of a system's functional requirements and quality attributes can be verified with respect to the operational requirements; the design can be verified with respect to the operational requirements, the functional requirements, and the quality attributes; the code can be verified with respect to other work products, including the requirements and the architectural and detailed designs.

Verification techniques include:

- traceability,
- reviews,
- prototyping,
- analysis, demonstrations, and
- functional testing.

Traceability establishes logical links between two work products, for example, in establishing that all requirements allocated to a segment of the design are covered in that segment. Reviews are an acceptable verification procedure to determine, for example, that technical specifications are complete, correct, and consistent with respect to the operational requirements. Prototyping can be used, for example, to determine that the user interface will be complete, correct, and consistent with respect to user needs when it is implemented in the delivered product. Analysis of software involves establishing certain logical properties of software using formal reasoning techniques, for example, establishing the absence of deadlock or race conditions in concurrent software using state-based techniques. Functional testing can be used to verify that the deliverable software is complete, correct, and consistent with respect to its functional requirements and quality attributes when the software is operated in the test environment.

Validation is closely related to verification, but it is a distinct concept. In general, validation of a work product is concerned with determining the degree to which the work product satisfies its intended purpose when placed in its intended environment. Validation, like verification, is a general process that can be and should be applied to all work products, both intermediate and deliverable, throughout the product development cycle. Thus validation of the design is concerned with determining that the design is a suitable basis for implementation (construction, review, testing, and integration of the code) when the design specification is placed in the environment of the software developers and testers. Similarly validation of the software/system test scenarios is concerned with determining that the test scenarios will adequately test the software/system when it is operated in the operational environment.

Verification is often phrased as: "Did we construct the work product correctly?"

Validation is often phrased as: "Did we construct the correct work product?"

It is entirely possible for a work product to be verified but not validated. For example, an architectural design specified in UML might be verified to be correct, complete, and consistent with respect to the requirements (constructed correctly), but it would not be a valid document for the implementers and testers if they were unfamiliar with UML (not a correct work product for them) because the design description would not satisfy its intended purpose when placed in its intended environment (the environment of the implementers and testers who are unfamiliar with UML).

Verification of a system to be delivered (end-item verification) is concerned with determining that the system is correct with respect to its technical specifications; that is, does it perform the specified functions, and does it have the specified quality attributes (was it built correctly)? Planning for verification occurs (or should occur) during development of the system requirements and software requirements.

End-item validation of a system is concerned with determining that the system satisfies its intended purpose when placed in the environment of its intended users; that is, does it satisfy user needs (is it the correct product)? Developing plans and procedures for verification and validation of deliverable work products are important activities that occur (or should occur) during development of the operational requirements, system requirements, and software requirements.

Validation techniques for deliverable work products include:

- reviews,
- operational testing, and
- demonstrations.

Reviews are an acceptable validation procedure for certain deliverable work products, such as test plans, test results, training materials, and installation instructions. Operational testing and demonstrations can be used to validate that the software satisfies its intended purpose when operated by the intended users in the intended environment(s).

Planning for operational tests involves specifying input data and other environmental conditions *plus* the required results of the tests; for example, a mathematical function should return the correct mathematical result under all conditions except for those that violate the range of inputs (e.g., numbers for which squaring the input value would result in overflow) and invalid operational environments (e.g., hardware failure of the math coprocessor). Additional tests should be planned and conducted to determine that exception handling for out-of-range input values and faulty operational environments is performed correctly.

A demonstration differs from a test in that the acceptability of the results cannot be predicted with certainty. For example, a demonstration of the user interface to knowledgeable users may reveal deficiencies from their point of view, even though the interface provides the specified features and quality attributes. Another example: it may not be possible to predict the sequence of moves a chess-playing program will make (testing), but experts (chess masters) can determine the level at which the program is playing by observing demonstrations of the moves made by the program.

Unfortunately, it sometimes occurs that a deliverable system is verified (was built correctly in that it satisfies its technical specifications) but is not valid (is not correct in that it does not satisfy user needs). This can occur because the operational requirements from which the technical specifications were generated were incorrect, or because the correct operational requirements were not correctly translated into technical specifications, or because the correct technical specifications were incorrectly translated into design and code. In these cases a system such as a satellite launch vehicle can veer off course and have to be destroyed, or a user-intensive system may be rejected by the users because it does satisfy their needs.

Planning for verification and validation of deliverable work products (V&V) during development of requirements is also useful to determine the degree of understanding of the various requirements by the system engineers and software developers (i.e., operational requirements, functional specifications, and quality attributes). Inability to specify objective criteria for V&V indicates that the associated requirements may be vague, ambiguous, or incomplete. The need for further elaboration of the requirements is thus indicated.

2.4 TAILORING THE SYSTEM ENGINEERING FRAMEWORK FOR SOFTWARE-ONLY PROJECTS

Figure 2.1*b* illustrates a process framework for developing software-intensive systems that include hardware, software, and people elements. Many software projects are concerned with developing applications software for which the hardware and operating system are provided by an off-the-shelf computer, and no special training is required for users, operators, or operational support personnel. The hardware/software platform may be specified as a design constraint or it may be selected as part of the analysis process.

It may be, for example, that your project will develop software that must work in conjunction with existing software that is implemented on existing computers that are used throughout the customer's organization. Thus the hardware/software platform is specified as a design constraint.

Figure 2.5 illustrates tailoring of the development framework in Figure 2.1*b* for these software-only projects; the system-level elements have been deleted from Figure 2.1*b* and a Specify Hardware/Software Platform activity has been added. For software-only projects, operational requirements provide the basis for developing the software requirements. The operational requirements provide the external, user-

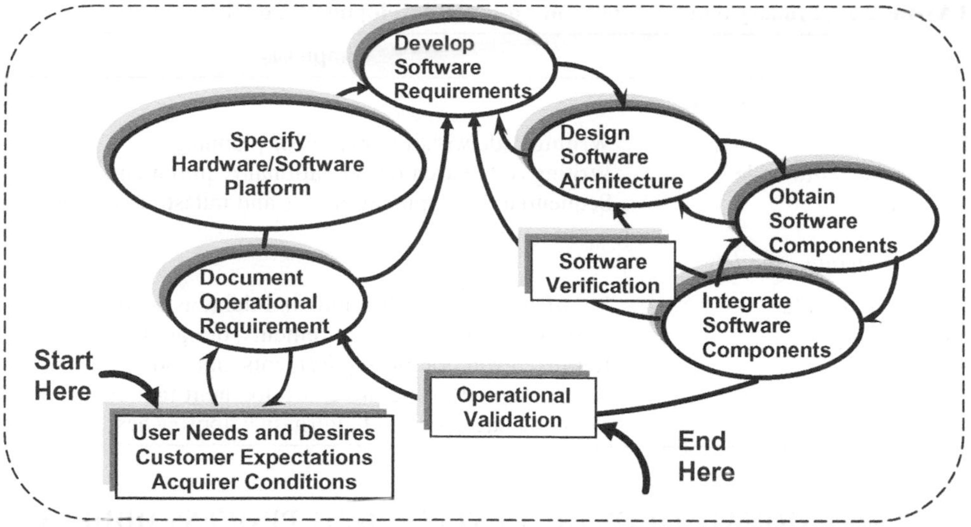

FIGURE 2.5 A development framework for software-only projects

oriented specification of the system; the software requirements are the internal, developer-oriented specification of the system. As before, the arrows and shadings in Figure 2.5 depict some of the many iterative paths and revisions for software projects.

For the most part, this text concentrates on managing software-only projects for which the major development processes are depicted in Figure 2.5. Various ways of tailoring Figure 2.5 for commonly used software-development process models are presented in the following section.

A fundamental tenet of software engineering is:

the processes used to develop a software system or product must be designed with the same care that is used to design the product.

Product design is best accomplished by starting with an architectural framework (or architectural style) and tailoring it to fit the needs of the product. In a similar manner process design is best accomplished by starting with a process framework and tailoring it to fit the needs of the project. Tailoring of a framework involves adding, deleting, and modifying elements of the framework to meet the needs of specific situations.

The framework for software development in Figure 2.5 can be tailored to depict the process models most frequently used to develop software. These development models, in turn, can be tailored to fit the needs of your projects. The following sections of this chapter are concerned with these models.

Like all models, software development models emphasize aspects of interest and suppress details that are not important to the aspects being modeled. And, like all models, the details can be elaborated in subordinate models. Table 2.2 lists the software development models presented in this chapter and the aspects of software development that are emphasized by those models.

TABLE 2.2 Primary emphases of some software development models

	Emphasis
Traditional models	
Hacking	Writing code without analysis or planning
Requirements-to-code	Writing code based on operational requirements
Waterfall	Sequential development phases and milestone reviews
Iterative models	
Incremental-build	Iterative coding, verification, and demonstration cycles
Evolutionary	Iterative evolution of requirements, design, and code
Agile	Iterative evolution of requirements and code
Spiral	A meta-model for iterative development that emphasizes risk management and alternative approaches

2.5 TRADITIONAL SOFTWARE DEVELOPMENT PROCESS MODELS

This section presents the traditional software development process models that have been, and in some cases continue, to be used.

2.5.1 Hacking

In software engineering, the term "hacking" has two meanings:

1. to surreptitiously gain access to systems and data in an unauthorized manner; and
2. writing code without any preplanning.

It is the second meaning to which we refer; a hacking development "process" involves writing code without first understanding or documenting user needs and technical requirements, developing a design description, or preparing a test plan. Hacking is characterized by the cartoon that depicts a project manager telling the software developers, as he walks out the door, "You start coding and I'll go find out what they want."

Aside from these problems, hacking prematurely forces the mental processes involved in developing software to an inappropriate level of detail before higher level concerns are understood. The coder is simultaneously attempting to envision the requirements, design, and testing considerations and express them in the syntax and semantics of the programming language. As mentioned in Chapter 1, the entire description of a software product is usually too complex for the entire description to be written directly in a programming language [Jack02], so we must prepare different descriptions at different levels of abstraction, and for different purposes.

To portray the Hacking model, tailoring of the framework in Figure 2.6 degenerates to eliminating all elements of the framework except Obtain Software Components and rephrasing it as Write the Code. However, we should not spend time tailoring the framework in Figure 2.6 to accommodate hacking (i.e., tailoring the model out of existence). A better approach is: *Do not allow your software developers to hack the code!*

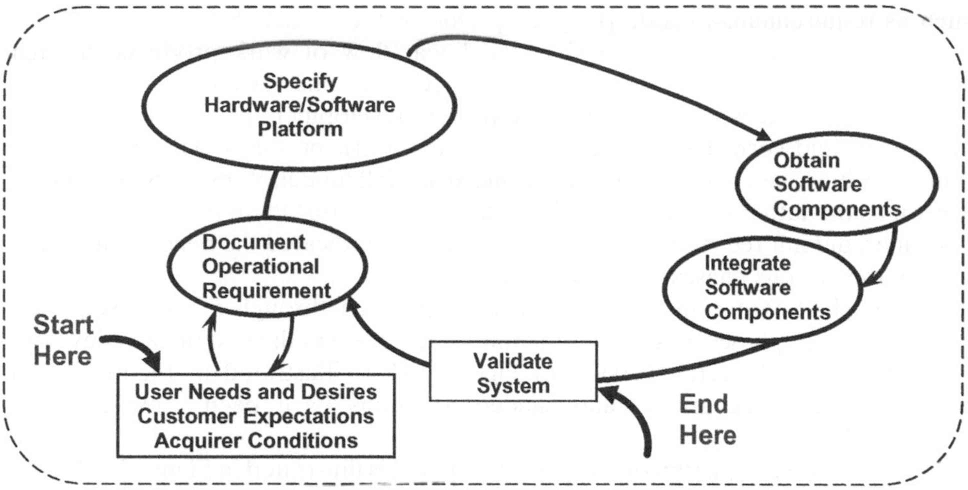

FIGURE 2.6 The Requirements-to-code development model

2.5.2 Requirements-to-Code

Compared to Hacking, Requirements-to-code development has the virtue of developing an understanding of the needs to be satisfied by new or modified software before implementing the software. In a Requirements-to-code process, operational requirements are elicited and may or may not be documented, but technical specifications for the software requirements are not developed and a design specification is not generated. Depending on the rigor with which the model is implemented, the operational requirements may or may not be placed under version control and a validation plan based on those requirements may or may not be developed. A Requirements-to-code process might be used to develop "throw-away" prototype code to demonstrate a mock-up of a user interface.

Omitting the design phase results in failure to systematically identify the system components, the interconnections among them, and their connections to the environment. Consequently requirements are not systematically allocated to components, and opportunities for reuse of existing components are not systematically identified. As with the Hacking model, these higher level considerations, if considered at all, are accounted for at an inappropriate level of detail in the syntax and semantics of the programming language.

For a Requirements-to-code process, tailoring the process framework in Figure 2.5 involves removing the Develop Software Requirements, and Design Software Architecture, phases and the Software Verification activity from the framework, as illustrated in Figure 2.6. Note also that the iterative feedback loops and shaded iterations in Figure 2.5 have been removed in Figure 2.6.

2.5.3 The Waterfall Development Model

In his seminal paper "Managing the Development of Large Software Systems: Concepts and Techniques," published in 1970, Winston Royce presented several approaches to software development to illustrate the shortcomings of approaches such as requirements-to-code [Royce70]. One of the models he presented was a feed-forward model that emphasizes the linear flow of work products through various development phases and the associated milestone reviews whose purpose is to verify that the work products of the various development phases are complete, consistent, and correct with respect to previous work products. That model, not named by him, has come to be known as the Waterfall model; Winston Royce is thus known as the father of the Waterfall model. This is unfortunate because Royce, in his paper, did not recommend the model; he clearly indicated the need for iteration among the various phases of software development.

The goal of Waterfall development is to proceed through a linear sequence of development phases that includes a milestone review at the end of each development phase. A Waterfall version of Figure 2.1*b* is illustrated in Figure 2.7, in which the feedback arrows and shaded iterations have been removed from Figure 2.1*b*.

The traditional depiction of the Waterfall model is illustrated in Figure 2.8; Figure 2.7 has been "unwound" to highlight the linear work phases and associated milestones. The model is termed a Waterfall because work products are supposed to cascade from phase to phase in a smooth progression, as water cascades down a Waterfall.

The purpose of a milestone review is to verify that the work products under review are complete, consistent, and correct with respect to (wrt) other work products; that is, to verify the operational requirements wrt user needs, to verify the software requirements wrt the system requirements and operational requirements, and so forth. A successful milestone review results in the reviewed work products

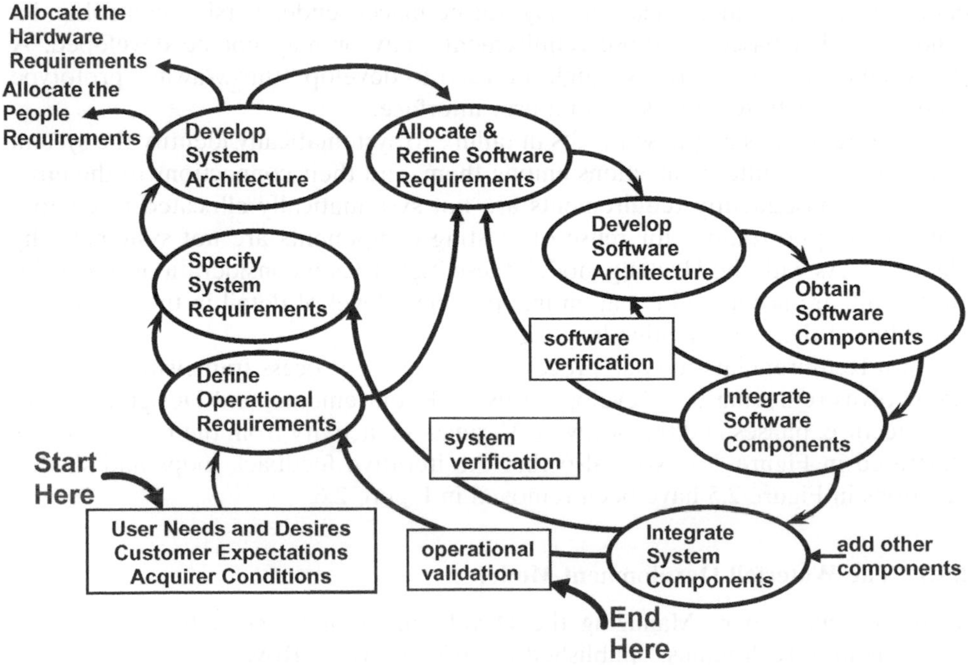

FIGURE 2.7 Waterfall tailoring of Figure 2.1*b*

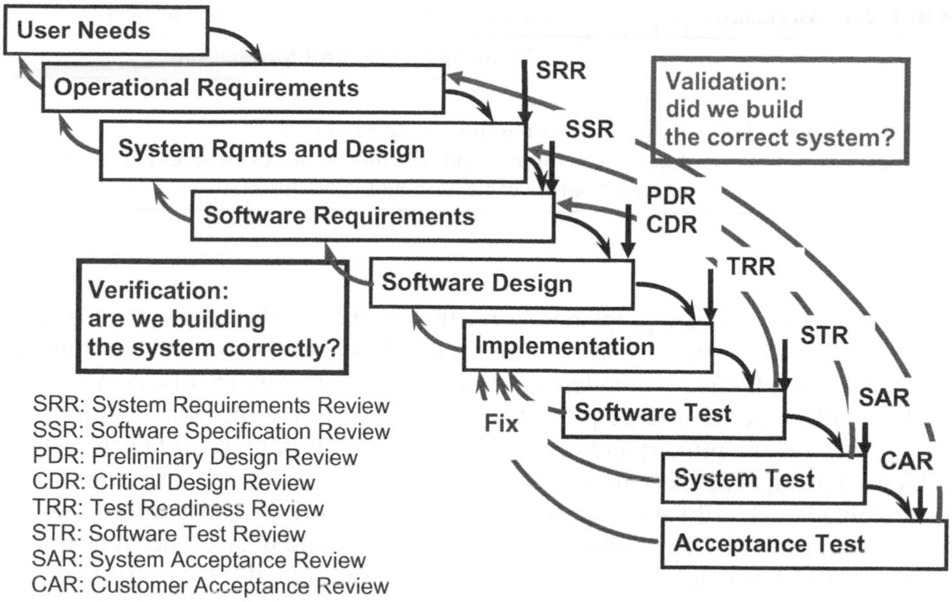

FIGURE 2.8 Traditional depiction of the Waterfall model with milestones

being placed under version control to provide a baseline (a foundation) for further work. A successful milestone review at the end of the design phase, for example, would result in a design baseline that has been verified to be correct, complete, and consistent with respect to requirements and user needs, and that then provides the basis for software implementation. Subsequent changes to baselined work products must be approved by those authorized to make the changes (i.e., a change control board).

Milestone reviews are sometimes referred to as "control gates," meaning that the gate will not be opened to proceed to the next phase until the problems identified during a milestone review are corrected. Or the gate might be partially opened to let some work proceed while problems are corrected in other areas.

The goal of the Waterfall model is to develop a system in a single pass but, as Royce states in describing the Requirements-to-code model: "This sort of very simple implementation concept is in fact all that is required if the effort is sufficiently small and if the final product is to be operated by those who built it…"[13]. The same could be said of the Waterfall model.

Planning a Waterfall project involves determining a schedule of phases and reviews and identifying the resources needed to conduct each phase of the work. Often a constraint on the duration of the project dictates the time available for each development phase and scheduling of the milestone reviews. A schedule determined in this way (a dictated schedule) may or may not be adequate. Milestone reviews are the primary mechanism of monitoring the progress of a Waterfall project. The primary mechanism of control is the "control gate" aspect of the reviews.

The Waterfall model has many shortcomings as a model for the creative, intellect-intensive nature of software development; for example, iterative revisions

[13] Proceedings, IEEE WESCON, August, 1970, page 1.

TABLE 2.3 Mechanisms of planning and controlling traditional software projects

Development Model	Planning and Control Mechanisms
Hacking	None
Requirements-to-code	Requirements baseline, code validation
Waterfall	Linear development phases, milestone reviews, baselines, change control board, verification and validation

of work products are not preplanned and thus represent disruptions to planned work activities when they become necessary (as they always do). Other shortcomings include use of infrequent milestone reviews as progress indicators. A Waterfall development phase for a large project can take several months. Relying on milestone reviews as the primary indicators of progress (or lack thereof) fails to detect problems that might have occurred, and could have been fixed, much earlier. Another shortcoming is delayed validation of the deliverable work products until the final phase of the project. This results in expensive rework and delayed delivery if it is found that the deliverable work products cannot be validated (i.e., the system will not satisfy its intended purpose when operated by its intended users in its intended environment).

The fundamental problem of the Waterfall development process is linear sequencing of the project phases (analysis, design, implementation, validation). Iterative development models overcome these problems by systematic interleaving and overlapping the work activities of the development phases in various ways.

2.5.4 Guidelines for Planning and Controlling Traditional Software Projects

Table 2.3 summarizes the primary mechanisms for planning and controlling projects for traditional software development models (Hacking, Requirements-to-code, Waterfall).

2.6 ITERATIVE-DEVELOPMENT PROCESS MODELS

Developing and modifying software involves creative processes that are subject to many external and changeable forces. Long experience has shown that it is impossible to "get it right" the first time, and that iterative development processes are preferable to linear development processes such as the Requirements-to-code and Waterfall models. In iterative development, each cycle of the iteration subsumes the software of the previous iteration and adds new capabilities to the evolving product to produce a next, expanded version of the software.

Iterative development processes provide the following advantages:

- continuous integration, verification and validation of the evolving product;
- frequent demonstrations of progress;
- early detection of defects;
- early warning of process problems;

- systematic incorporation of the inevitable rework that occurs in software development; and
- early delivery of subset capabilities (if desired).

Iterative development takes many forms in software engineering:

- iterative prototyping can be used to evolve a user interface or explore a technical issue;
- an Incremental-build process can be used to produce weekly builds of increasing product capabilities;
- Agile development can be used to closely involve a prototypical customer in an iterative process that may repeat on a daily basis;
- an Evolutionary Spiral model can be used to confront and mitigate risk factors encountered in developing the successive versions of a product based on evolving requirements.

Each of these models is described below.

2.6.1 The Incremental-Build Model

Delaying validation until the final phase of software development is a major shortcoming of the Waterfall model. Problems that might have been found earlier are not found until near delivery time, and problems found last are the most expensive to fix. As illustrated in Figure 2.9, finding and fixing a requirements defect during system testing may cost 100 times more to fix than fixing it during the requirements phase; similarly finding a design defect during system testing may cost 50 times as much to fix as finding it and fixing it during design [BOEHM81].

The relative cost thus increases in an exponential manner because more work products of increasing levels of detail and volumes of content have been generated in successive phases of development. Fixing a requirements defect during a requirements review may involve changing a few words, such as correcting "the ATM *will not* allow multiple transactions per session" to "the ATM *will* allow multiple transactions per session." Fixing this defect during validation testing of the deliverable

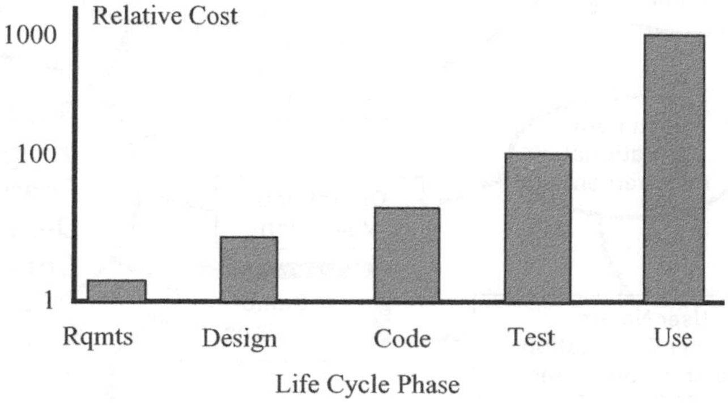

FIGURE 2.9 Relative cost to find and fix a software defect

system may require changes to the code in several different places plus rewriting and rerunning the associated validation tests. This correction, which would have taken less than a minute during a requirements review, could take much more than 100 minutes during validation testing. The effort required to correct a defect when the system is installed in multiple locations (i.e., "fielded") is even greater because the software must be reinstalled in each location (i.e., each ATM terminal).

The Incremental-build model is a build–test–demonstrate model of iterative development in which frequent demonstrations of progress and verification and validation of work to date are emphasized. Figure 2.10 is a tailoring of Figure 2.5 for an Incremental-build process. Note, in particular, that a design partitioning phase has been added. Requirements are allocated to various elements of the software architecture, and the architecture is partitioned into a prioritized sequence of builds. Each build adds new capabilities to the incrementally growing product. Figure 2.10 has been further tailored by subsuming the Obtain Software Components and Integrate Software Components into a Build and Integrate Features Set i activity. Also a Demo Version i link has been added. The development process ends when version *N* (the final version) is verified, validated, demonstrated, and accepted by the customer.

Figure 2.11 is an "unwound" depiction of Figure 2.10 that illustrates the details of the build–verify–validate–demonstrate cycles in the Incremental-build process. A "build cycle" includes detailed design, implementation, integration, review, and testing by the developers. In cases where code is to be reused without modification, some or all of an Incremental-build may consist of review, integration, and test of the base code augmented with the reused code. Builds of demonstrable, running versions of the system are produced frequently, typically on a weekly or bi-weekly basis, weekly being the norm.

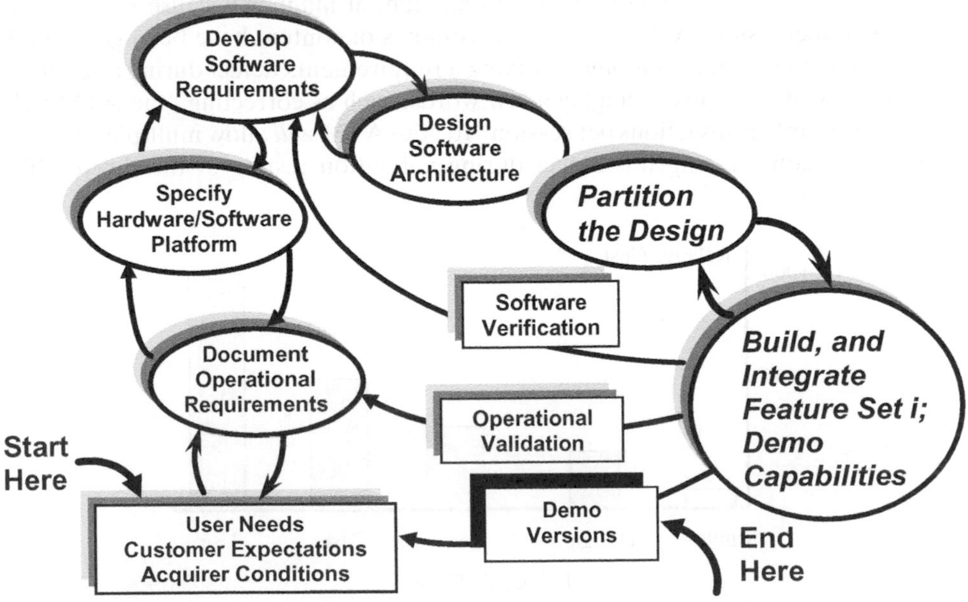

FIGURE 2.10 Tailoring of Figure 2.5 for the Incremental-build process

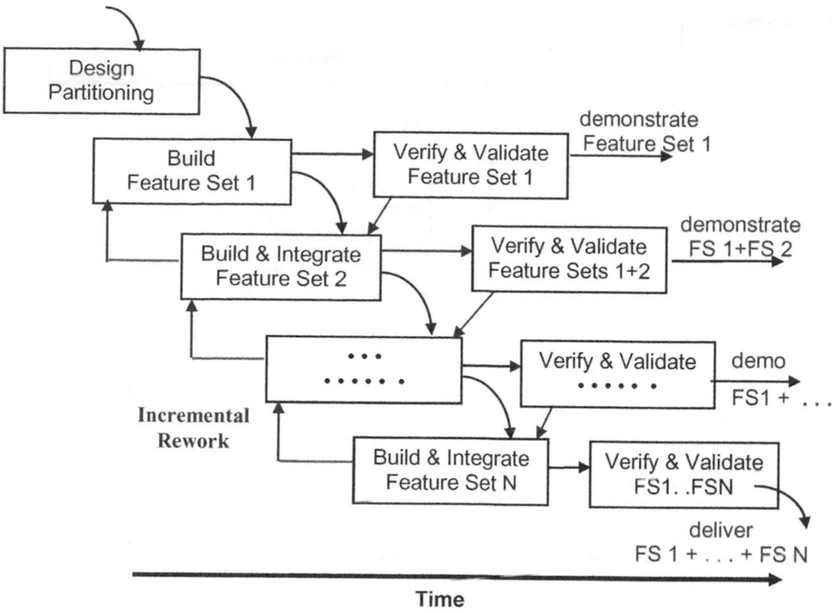

FIGURE 2.11 Incremental build–verify–validate–demonstrate cycles

Verifying a build is concerned with determining the degree to which the build is complete, correct, and consistent with respect to the requirements and design for the current build (which incorporates requirements, design, and code for all prior builds). Validating a build is concerned with determining the degree to which the demonstrated build will satisfy its intended purpose in its intended environment. Verifying and validating may result in rework of previously developed components to better accommodate the new components being integrated, or to fix defects in previously developed components exposed by addition of the new components, or to fix defects in the new components.

Some (perhaps all) of the builds in an Incremental-build process are typically demonstrated to validate progress-to-date for user representatives, customer(s), and/or the acquirer. Other builds may be demonstrated for you (the project manager), your development team, and perhaps for your managers to provide concrete evidence that the project is (or is not) proceeding according to plan. In any case, frequent demonstrations of progress (or lack thereof) are a major benefit of an Incremental-build development process.

Figure 2.12 illustrates the milestone chart for a six-month project to build a compiler using the Incremental-build model. The first 2 months are allocated to analysis and design followed by 8 bi-weekly build–verify–validate–demonstrate cycles. The software developed for each increment is added to the growing base. The design is partitioned so that each build provides the interfaces and functionality needed by the next build.

Figure 2.12 illustrates another advantage of the Incremental-build process, namely the ability to gracefully make trade-offs among product features, resources, and the delivery schedule. If, for example, the compiler is not ready for delivery as scheduled

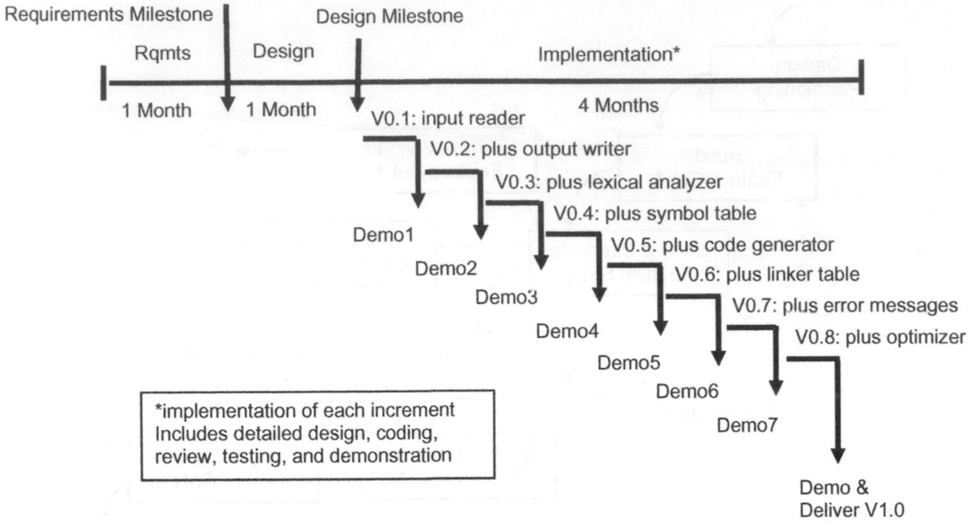

FIGURE 2.12 An Incremental-build example

at the end of six months, a choice can be made between delivering a first version of the compiler without the optimizer, or extending the schedule to allow completion of the project. Because of the frequent demo milestones, early warning of slippage in the delivery schedule is provided and offers the option to add more or better developers to the project to meet the delivery date (being mindful of Brooks's law, as described in Chapter 1). Because of the detailed history of progress, it should be possible to accurately estimate the amount of time needed to deliver the final version of the compiler in case of a schedule delay.

A large project may involve tens or even hundreds of incremental cycles, many of which may be performed by different teams working in parallel. In these cases planning is also incremental. The initial project schedule contains the major activities to be completed and the schedule milestones for completing them; detailed plans are developed in an incremental manner. Incremental planning is discussed in Chapter 4.

Monitoring and controlling Incremental-build projects are based on milestone reviews for requirements and architectural design and on the frequent demonstrations of progress that occur during the build–verify–validate–demonstrate cycles. In some cases the project plan may incorporate early delivery of subset capabilities for operational use while the remaining iterations are completed. If, for example, the compiler depicted in Figure 2.13, is for a new programming language, then v0.7 (error messages) could be implemented following v0.4, and the subset could be delivered to users of the compiler so they could learn to write syntactically correct programs while the compiler is being completed.

Incremental verification, validation, and demonstration as illustrated in Figures 2.11 and 2.12 overcome two of the major problems of a Waterfall approach: (1) problems are exposed early and can be corrected as they occur; (2) minor in-scope changes to requirements that occur as a result of incremental demonstrations can be incorporated in subsequent Incremental-builds.

The Incremental-build process works well when each team consists of two to five developers plus a team leader (who is also a technical contributor). Team members may work as individuals or in pairs. Each individual or pair may produce unofficial builds on a daily basis using a copy of the current official version as a test bed. An official build that integrates, verifies, validates, and demonstrates progress made by all developer teams is produced on a weekly or bi-weekly basis.

The Incremental-build model can be scaled up for large projects by partitioning the architecture into well-defined subsystems and allocating requirements and interfaces to each subsystem. The subsystems can be independently tested and demonstrated, perhaps using stubs and drivers for the subsystem interfaces, or perhaps using early incremental versions of other evolving subsystems. System integration can proceed incrementally as intermediate versions of the various subsystems become operational.

Figure 2.11 illustrates that it may be possible to overlap, in time, successive builds of the product. It may be possible, for example, to start a detailed design of the next version while the present version is being validated. Three factors determine the degree of overlap that can be achieved:

1. availability of sufficient personnel to concurrently pursue multiple activities,
2. adequate progress on the previous version to provide needed capabilities for the next version, and
3. the risk of significant rework that must be accomplished if verification and validation of the previous build reveals problems that invalidate the work accomplished on the next overlapped build.

Significant changes to requirements, design constraints, or environmental factors (e.g., changes to middleware APIs or hardware features) may require significant rework of the design and existing code in an Incremental-build process (which is true of all development process models).

A significant advantage of an Incremental-build process is that features built first are verified, validated, and demonstrated most frequently because subsequent builds incorporate the features of the earlier builds. In building the software to control a nuclear reactor, for example, the emergency shutdown software could be built first. Operation of emergency shutdown (scramming) would then be verified and validated in conjunction with the features of each successive build.

Planning an Incremental-build project involves planning for analysis and design plus planning the number of and frequency of iterative versions to be built and demonstrated. The number of iterations is determined by the partitioning of the design. Table 2.4 lists some partitioning criteria for incremental development. Itera-

TABLE 2.4 Some partitioning criteria for incremental builds

Kind of System	Partitioning Criteria
Application package	Essential features first; prioritized desirables next
Safety-critical systems	Safety features first; prioritized others next
User-intensive systems	User interface first; prioritized others next
System software	Kernel first; prioritized utilities next

tions should be planned for durations of one work-week for each. One-week increments and the number of developers available to work on the project determine the number of features that can be included in each Incremental-build. This in turn determines the overall schedule.

Frequent demonstrations of the growing system provide an objective mechanism for monitoring progress in an Incremental-build process. Indicators of problems include:

1. failure to implement the planned number of features in a given cycle,
2. inadequate performance or excessive use of computing resources in a build–verify–validate–demonstrate cycle, and
3. excessive rework of previous versions to accommodate the current build.

Corrective actions can be taken before problems result in a crisis situation. Corrective action should be taken, for example, if the rework to fix defects exceeds 20% of the effort on each of two successive build cycles. Corrective actions might include revising the requirements, reworking the design, fixing the code, acquiring a new testing tool, providing refresher training on peer reviews, or revising the Incremental-build schedule to allow more time to do an adequate job.

In summary, the Incremental-build model, like all iterative models, provides the advantages of continuous integration and validation of the evolving product, frequent demonstrations of progress, early warning of problems, early delivery of subset capabilities, and systematic incorporation of the inevitable rework that occurs in software development.

2.6.2 The Evolutionary Model

The term "evolutionary" in an Evolutionary development process refers to the systematic evolution of requirements, design, and code. The Incremental-build model can tolerate some minor changes (in-scope changes) to requirements and design without renegotiating schedule and budget; in contrast, an Evolutionary model is appropriate in cases where the requirements and software architecture cannot be (mostly) specified in advance or when they are likely to undergo significant changes during development. An Evolutionary model may be appropriate for the initial phases of a new kind of project for which no corporate history exists.

Figure 2.13 illustrates tailoring of Figure 2.5 for an Evolutionary development process. As illustrated in Figure 2.13, each iteration of an Evolutionary process is a mini-Waterfall that involves:

- evolving the operational requirements and software requirements,
- designing the software for that iteration,
- obtaining and integrating the components,
- verifying and validating the resulting software, and
- evaluating the outcome.

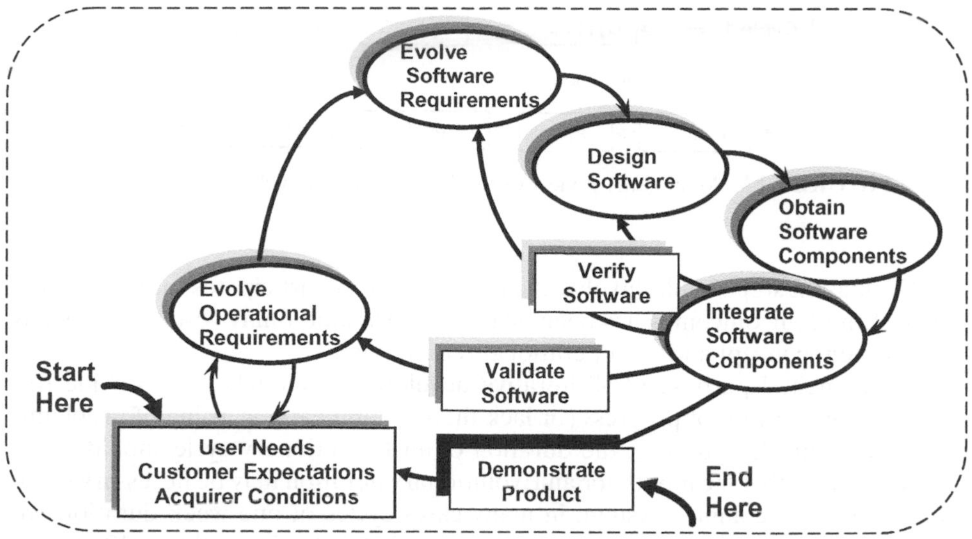

FIGURE 2.13 Tailoring of Figure 2.5 for the Evolutionary development process

Each cycle in an Evolutionary development process should be limited to not more than one month to prevent the mini-Waterfall from becoming a maxi-Waterfall.

At the end of each development cycle, an evaluation of the outcome, based on verification, validation, and demonstration will reveal one of several possible next steps:

1. the chosen approach for this iteration is satisfactory and provides insight for conducting the next cycle of analysis, design, implementation, and evaluation;
2. the outcome of analysis, design, and implementation for this iteration is not satisfactory, and an alternative approach must be attempted;
3. sufficient knowledge has been gained on this iteration (and previous iterations) to specify the remaining requirements, complete the design, partition it, and finish the project using an Incremental-build approach; or
4. the project should be canceled, perhaps because the state of knowledge or technology cannot support the system concept.

Figure 2.14 illustrates the Evolutionary development process as viewed by you, the project manager. Each iterative cycle involves:

- analyzing the current situation and deciding which of the 4 possible next steps to pursue,
- planning for the chosen course of action,
- developing the software, provided alternative 4 above is not chosen, and
- evaluating the results.

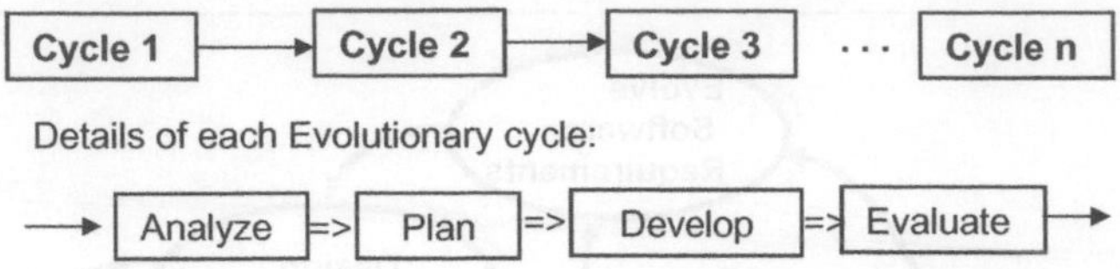

FIGURE 2.14 Management view of the Evolutionary development process

The Evaluation step should involve the customer, who participates in determining which of the four outcomes has been achieved. Evaluation may result in revisions to the system concept and the operational requirements.

A fundamental purpose of all iterative development models is to provide frequent demonstrations of progress (or lack thereof) and early warning of problems. In keeping with this purpose, the duration of an Evolutionary cycle should never exceed one month. One month for an Evolutionary iteration may be necessary when evolving a large, complex system; in many cases cycles of one week duration are appropriate. In any case, you do not want to wait 3 months, 6 months, or 12 months to find out that the design and implementation do not satisfy requirements and user needs, or that the requirements were incorrectly stated, or that it is not feasible to satisfy the requirements within the current state of technology. Each of these outcomes can happen when using a Waterfall development process or an Evolutionary cycle of extended duration.

Using an Evolutionary development process indicates a high-risk endeavor; otherwise, an Incremental-build process, based on stable requirements and architecture, would be used. Planning must proceed in an evolutionary manner because some or all of the requirements are unstable or unknown. The evaluation step of each evolutionary cycle determines what to do next. A time constraint may be placed on the overall undertaking, as in "we will pursue an Evolutionary approach for not more than 3 months; a major re-evaluation will be conducted if the requirements and design are not stable by then."

2.6.3 Agile Development Models

Agile development models are also evolutionary, in that the requirements evolve during implementation, but they differ from the Evolutionary model in that the Evolutionary model is appropriate when the system concept is unclear or the feasibility of the project is in question. Agile develop is best suited to small applications projects that are conducted in the presence of a knowledgeable customer/user who has a clear understanding of the needs to be satisfied by the system that is being built. There are several variations on the Agile theme, but most Agile-process models emphasize the following aspects [Agile]:

1. continuously involving a representative customer/user;
2. developing test cases and test scenarios before implementing the next version of the product;
3. implementing and testing the resulting version;
4. demonstrating each version of the evolving product to the customer;

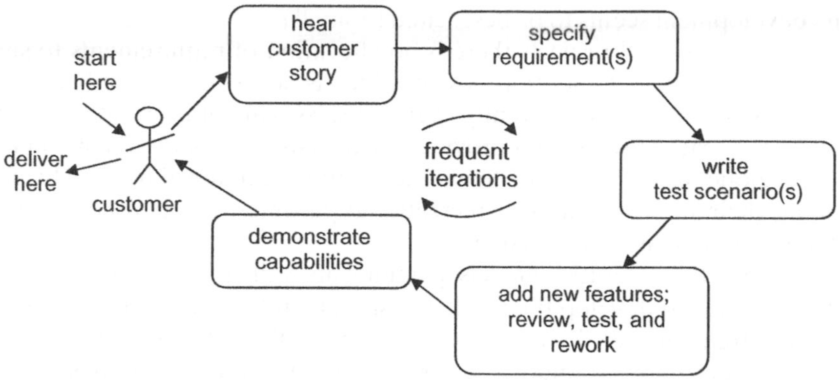

FIGURE 2.15 An Agile development process

5. eliciting the next requirement(s) from the customer; and
6. periodic delivery into the operational environment.

The customer's roles are to provide the "story line" that determines the requirements, to review demonstrated capabilities, and to specify the next chapter of the story line for the next iteration. An iterative process model for agile development is depicted in Figure 2.15. "Story cards" are sometimes used to record elements of story chapters. They can be sorted by the customer to reflect priorities; estimates of effort can be written on them, and actual effort can be recorded and compared to estimates.

As indicated in Figure 2.15, there is no explicit design step and no design documentation in an Agile development process. This is compensated for by a design "metaphor" that is shared among the developers. A design metaphor might be based on an architectural style; for example, the system may be based on a layered style (e.g., a 3-tier architecture) or a separation-of-concerns architecture (e.g., a *m*odel–*v*iew–*c*ontrol architecture). Lack of explicit design requires that the developers be highly skilled; otherwise, "agile" becomes a euphemism for hacking. Other development processes are sometime characterized as "Plan-driven," in contrast to the intentional lack of emphasis on written requirements specifications, design documentation, and V&V plans in the Agile models.

In many versions of the Agile process, the software developers produce a next version of a running system within time periods not longer than one work-day. Some Agile models use pair-programming, in which pairs of developers share one computer terminal and develop software together. Experience with Agile models indicates that the resulting products are rated low in defect levels and high in user satisfaction. However, user satisfaction is critically dependent on having a knowledgeable and prototypical user as the customer in the iterative development loop. Some critics have raised the concern that an Agile process may result in a functionally structured product that lacks design documentation, thus making the system hard to modify in the future. This problem can be minimized if the software developers share a common design metaphor and common coding and code documentation practices.

Agile development seems to be best suited to small projects that develop applications software.[14] In small projects there is no allocation of requirements to subsystems and partitioning of an a priori design, which is necessary if members of large project teams are to work concurrently. Agile processes are appropriate for applications projects because user-stories provided by the customer and design metaphors used by developers, are best suited to end-item software that will be used by people in pursuing their work activities or recreational pastimes, as opposed to complex embedded and mission-critical systems.

In common with all iterative models, planning an Agile project involves working with the customer to develop the product vision, plan the frequency of iterations, and plan the frequency of delivery of evolving capabilities to users. In contrast to other iterative development models, a design metaphor must be established by the developers, and the particular version of an Agile process to be used must be reviewed and accepted by the project stakeholders. During project execution, it is especially important to review with customers, developers, and other stakeholders, on a weekly basis, factors such as the current state of the evolving product, scheduled releases, product vision and the design metaphor, quality factors, and plans for the next two or three months (or until the expected end of the project if less than two or three months). Differences between the planned and actual state of affairs must be evaluated and reconciled on an on-going basis.

In summary, Agile development processes are suitable for projects that develop applications software, require fewer than 10 developers, have a knowledgeable on-site customer (user representative), have highly skilled developers who share a common design metaphor, have continuity of development staff; and for a product that will undergo frequent releases and periodic deliveries into the operational environment.

The text *Balancing Agility and Discipline* by Boehm and Turner contrasts Plan-driven and Agile approaches to software development and presents a middle-ground approach to achieving a balance than incorporates aspects of both approaches, based on the particular situation [BOEHM04].

2.6.4 The Scrum Model

The Scrum model is a framework for planning and conducting software projects based on the principles of Agile development (the term "scrum" is from the game of rugby) [Schwab04]. The project manager/leader is termed the "ScrumMaster." The customer (user representative) is termed the "Product Owner" and the software developers are the "Team." Teams include up to 10 software developers. The Product Owner writes User Stories, prioritizes them, and places them in the "Product Backlog."

Development iterations are termed "sprints," which are typically of 30 days duration. These result in a set of features that can be delivered to the users, if desired. The features to be implemented in a sprint are determined during a sprint planning meeting; the features to be included are derived from the Product Backlog and placed in a "Sprint Backlog." Brief (15 minute) stand-up meetings are held each day during a sprint to review work accomplished the previous day and to plan the work

[14] A small project is considered to be one that involves 10 or fewer software developers.

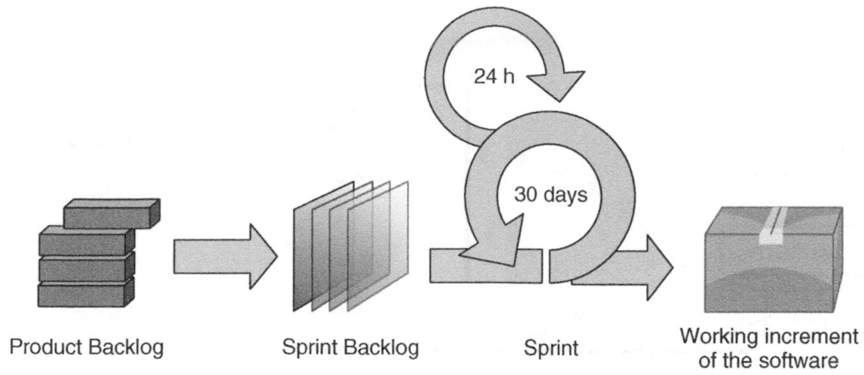

FIGURE 2.16 The Sprint development process [Wiki]

for the present day. The daily meetings allow the ScrumMaster to determine the rate of task completions and to anticipate and confront potential problems before they become real problems (i.e., to manage risk factors).

Each sprint is followed by a meeting (a "sprint retrospective") during which the Team reviews the sprint and determines how they can improve their work processes in future sprints. The Sprint process is illustrated in Figure 2.16 [Wiki].

2.6.5 The Spiral Meta-Model

Originally the Spiral model was presented as a development model [Boehm88]. In recent times it has come to be regarded as a meta-model (i.e., a development process framework) from which various iterative models can be derived. As illustrated in Figure 2.17, each cycle of a Spiral process involves:

1. analyzing objectives, identifying alternative approaches, and establishing constraints for the next process cycle;
2. planning the next cycle by evaluating alternative approaches, identifying the risk factors of each approach, and selecting an approach;
3. implementing the selected alternative; and
4. evaluating the outcome and deciding what to do next.

What-to-do-next depends on the particular instantiation of the Spiral meta-model. In an Evolutionary–Spiral model the next cycle may involve trying a different approach; in an Incremental-build–Spiral model the next cycle involves building and integrating the next set of features. Figures 2.18 and 2.19 illustrate Evolutionary and Incremental-build instantiations of the Spiral meta-model. The duration of a Spiral cycle might range from one day for an Agile Spiral to one month for an Evolutionary Spiral.

Although systematic evaluation of risk is a major theme of Spiral models, it should not be inferred that you should always choose the lowest risk approach. High-risk endeavors, if successful, often result in high payoffs. You might decide to spin off a parallel investigation of a high-risk approach while implementing a lower

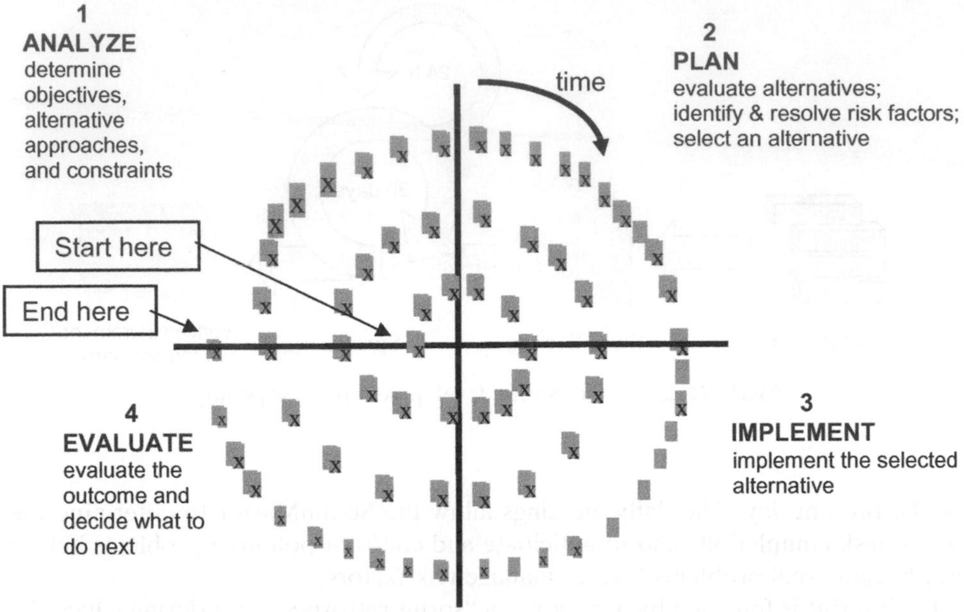

FIGURE 2.17 The Spiral meta-model

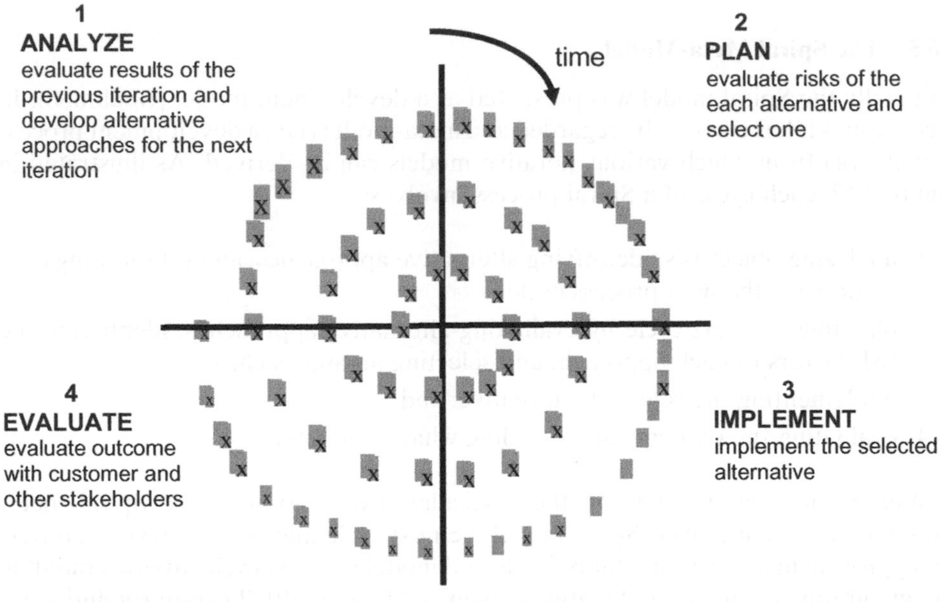

FIGURE 2.18 A Spiral depiction of the Evolutionary development process

risk alternative. The evaluation step would then weigh both outcomes, and provide information for the next cycle.

In summary, the concepts of the Spiral meta-model can be integrated into all iterative process models; the Spiral meta-model adds the dimensions of systematically generating alternative approaches for the next iteration, evaluating the risk of

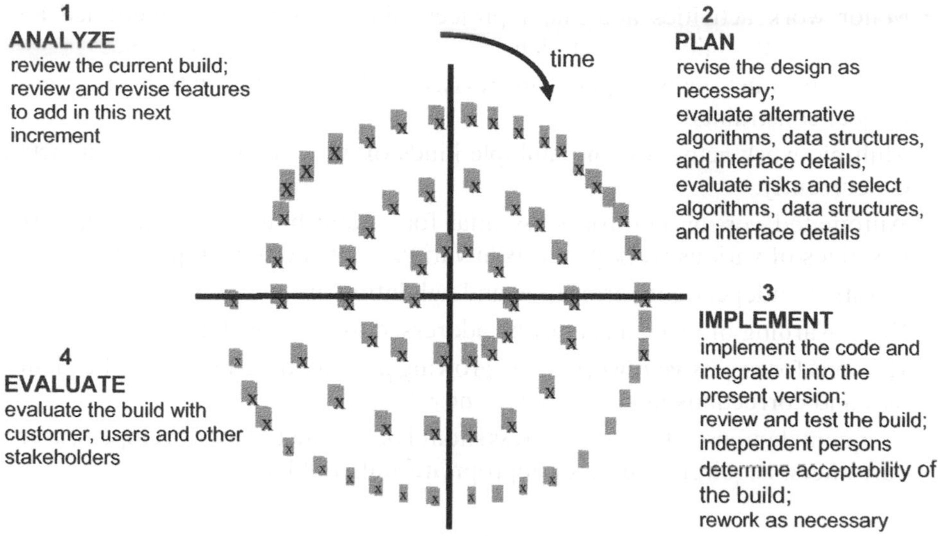

FIGURE 2.19 A Spiral depiction of the Incremental-build process

each, selecting an alternative for implementation, and evaluating the outcome. Alternatively, the Spiral meta-process provides a framework for generating iterative development models.

TABLE 2.5 Primary mechanisms for planning and controlling iterative projects

Development Model	Planning and Control Mechanisms
Incremental-build	Frequency and content of builds, frequent build–verify–validate–demonstration iterations, version control
Evolutionary	What-to-do-next decisions based on evaluation of outcomes; limited duration cycles, version control
Agile	User stories, design metaphors, periodicity of iterations, frequency of deliveries, version control
Spiral	Systematic evaluation of alternative approaches and resolution of risk factors on each cycle, version control

Table 2.5 summarizes the primary mechanisms of planning and controlling for different iterative development models.

2.6.6 Guidelines for Planning and Controlling Iterative-Development Projects

The following guidelines are useful when planning and conducting an iterative development project:

- The initial project plan must specify the kind of iterative model to be used; it must be tailored to meet the needs of the project.
- The duration of each iteration must be specified in the initial project plan.

- Major work activities and major project milestones must be identified and included in the initial project plan.
- As the product evolves, plans are revised and elaborated within the overall project constraints.
- Multiple work activities, and multiple kinds of work activities, are conducted concurrently.
- Automated version control is essential for establishing and maintaining the baselines of various work products in various stages of development.
- Iterative, independent verification and validation are necessary.
- Early warning of problems must be addressed as soon as detected.
- Reasons for excessive rework of the growing product baseline should be identified and corrections made as soon as possible.
- Frequent demonstrations of progress should be conducted for developers, users, customers, acquirer, and other appropriate stakeholders.

2.7 DESIGNING AN ITERATIVE-DEVELOPMENT PROCESS

Software designers use architectural styles, design patterns, and idioms to guide the design choices they make. In the same way you, as designer of the development process for your project, can use the development framework in Figure 2.1*b* or Figure 2.5, or one of the development process models described above as your starting point. The processes you use to develop a software product should be designed with the same care you use to design the product. Process design, like software design, is facilitated by the availability of guidelines and document templates for tailoring of process frameworks. Your organization may have internal consultants who can help you design your development process model.

In general, design, whether it be design of software, computer hardware, automobiles, spacecraft, or buildings, is always concerned with making choices among alternatives to optimize certain design criteria within the limits of the design constraints. A software product might be designed to optimize performance, safety, security, or ease of future modification. Because some criteria may be in conflict (e.g., maximizing performance and minimizing memory usage), it is often necessary to prioritize design criteria.

In the case of a software project, your goal might be to minimize schedule while maintaining quality; this might require increased staffing and omission of some desired product features. Alternatively, your goal might be to maximize features and quality, which would increase the schedule and/or the staffing level. A goal of minimizing schedule and resources while simultaneously maximizing features and quality attributes is overly constrained and probably unachievable.

An example of a process designed for a specific project is illustrated in Figure 2.20. Project attributes included:

- Criteria to be optimized were frequent demonstrations of progress and earliest possible delivery of a specified subset capability.
- The most severe product constraint was the requirement that the system intercommunicate with a system for which no interface documentation existed.

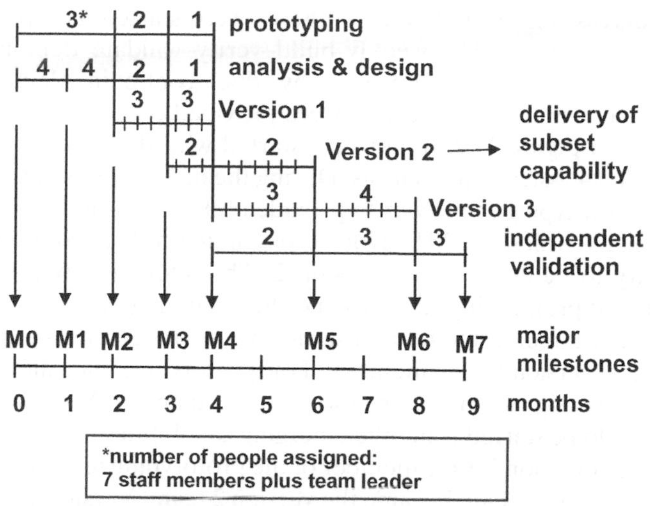

FIGURE 2.20 A tailored development process

- The product constraint was accompanied by a process constraint that the developers were not able to communicate with anyone who understood the other system.
- The schedule constraint required a fixed delivery date 12 months after the start of the project.
- An additional process constraint was a limitation on the development staff of seven developers plus a team leader/project manager.

As depicted in Figure 2.20, the development process that was designed involved:

- prototyping (to understand the interface to the other system and to prototype the user interface for the system under development),
- analysis and design (to specify the requirements and the major components of the system),
- incremental development (for frequent demonstrations of progress, early warning of problems, and delivery of the subset capability), and
- independent verification and validation (by developers other than those who implemented each version).

The design was partitioned into three major versions with weekly incremental builds within each version. Development of the three versions was overlapped in time. Version 2 subsumed and incorporated version 1; version 3 subsumed and incorporated version 2. Version 2 provided the early subset capabilities delivered to users. The numbers in the figure indicate the number of personnel assigned to each task at each point in time.

The project had seven major milestones (eight including the starting milestone M0). The major milestones were points in time where development phases were completed, progress was evaluated, new phases were started, and personnel were assigned to different tasks. The weekly build–verify–validate–demonstrate cycles provided minor milestones for the project, by which continuing demonstrations of progress and early warning of problems were provided on a weekly basis.

As illustrated in Figure 2.20, the project started with three developers assigned to prototyping and 4 assigned to analysis. During the first four months of the project, the role of the prototyping effort was to provide answers to questions posed during analysis and design. Milestone M1 involved baselining of the requirements for the subset capability to be delivered as version 2. The interval between M1 and M2 involved continued prototyping, analysis and the beginning of design. At M2, it was determined that the requirements and design were sufficiently stable to support implementation of version 1. One member of the prototyping team and two members of the analysis and design team became the version 1 team. At M3 it was determined that version 2 could be started using the emerging capabilities of version 1 as a basis for development of version 2. One member of the prototyping team and one member of the analysis and design team became the version 2 team. Version 1 was completed at M4. The remaining prototyping and analysis and design members became the independent verification and validation (V&V) team for version 1 plus the emerging capabilities of version 2. The three developers of version 1 became the development team for version 3.

As planned, the subset capabilities of version 2 were delivered to users at milestone 5. The weekly builds and incremental V&V of the weekly builds made it possible to complete version 2, perform the final validation reviews, tests, and demonstration, and deliver version 2 within the same week. One member of the version 2 team was then assigned to version 3, and the other member was assigned to V&V. This development process allowed completion of the project and delivery of the product in 9 months, 3 months ahead of the committed delivery date of 12 months.

Details of the incremental development process illustrated in Figure 2.20 were elaborated as the project evolved. The initial plan incorporated prototyping, analysis and design, incremental development of three versions, independent validation of each version, and delivery of the early subset capability. The major milestones included in Figure 2.20 were included in the initial plan; the timing of the milestones and the content of the weekly builds were adjusted as the project evolved. As noted, the system was completed in 9 months; 3 months ahead of the required delivery date.

Considerations for selecting an iterative-development process model based on the characteristics of the requirements, the project team, the user community, and project type and risk factors are presented in Appendix 2B of this chapter.

2.8 THE ROLE OF PROTOTYPING IN SOFTWARE DEVELOPMENT

In software engineering a prototype is a mock-up of the desired functionality of some part of the system. This is in contrast to physical systems, where a prototype is usually a first full functionality version of a system. Software prototypes are constructed to investigate a situation or to evaluate a proposed approach to solving a technical problem. A prototype of a user interface, for example, might be constructed to promote dialogue with users and to thus better understand their needs and concerns. A prototype implementation of an algorithm might be undertaken to study the performance or security aspects of the algorithm.

Prototypes are not constructed with the same attention to architectural structure, interfaces, documentation, and quality concerns as is devoted to product components. Prototypes may be built using different tools than are used to build production systems. For example, a prototype of a user interface might be rapidly developed in Visual Basic, but the production version of the interface might be implemented in C to provide the required performance and compatibility with other system components.

Many problems have been created by incorporating prototype software into production systems. Prototyping is a useful technique that should be employed whenever appropriate; however, prototyping is not a process model for software development. Some organizations use the term "prototyping," in conjunction with other terms such as "structured" or "rapid" to describe their software development model. In many cases this is a euphemism for chaotic hacking.

Prototyping is a technique that can be used in conjunction with all software development process models. Prototyping must be planned, monitored, and controlled; it must not be used as an excuse for uncontrolled hacking. Guidelines for prototyping include setting specific and limited objectives for each of the prototyping iterations, limiting the duration of iterations to 1 week or less, and using the evaluated results as the basis for the next step. Although this sounds like the Evolutionary approach, the distinction is that the iterations of Evolutionary development follow a systematic process within a larger context; prototyping is a technique to study a specific problem within a limited context.

When building a prototype, we keep the knowledge we have gained but we do not use the code in the deliverable version of the system

> *unless we are willing to do additional work to develop production-quality code from the prototype code.*

In many cases it is more efficient and more effective to build the production code "from scratch" using the knowledge gained by prototyping than to re-engineer the prototype code.

When using an Evolutionary approach, we keep the knowledge we have gained in each cycle of the iteration, and we may, or may not, use the code we have written in the deliverable version of the system, depending on the evaluation of results. When using the Incremental-build model, the goal is to keep the code we write in each build as the next element of the deliverable system.

2.9 KEY POINTS OF CHAPTER 2

- The development process for each software project must be designed with the same care used to design the product.
- A development-process framework is a generic process model that can be tailored and adapted to fit the needs of various projects.

- Process design is best accomplished by tailoring and adapting well-known development process models and process frameworks, just as product design is best accomplished by tailoring and adapting well-known architectural styles and architectural frameworks.
- There are several well-known and widely used software development process models, including Waterfall, Incremental-build, Evolutionary, Agile, and Spiral models.
- There are various ways to obtain the needed software components; different ways of obtaining software components require different mechanism of planning, measurement, and control.
- The development phases of a software project can be interleaved and iterated in various ways.
- Iterative development processes provide the advantages of continuous integration, iterative verification and validation of the evolving product, frequent demonstrations of progress, early detection of defects, early warning of process problems, systematic incorporation of the inevitable rework that occurs in software development, and early delivery of subset capabilities (if desired).
- Depending on the iterative development process used, the duration of iterations range from one day to one month.
- Prototyping is a technique for gaining knowledge; it is not a development process.
- The mechanisms of planning, measurement, and control used in a software project are strongly influenced by the development process used.
- SEI, ISO, IEEE, and PMI, provide frameworks, standards, and guidelines relevant to software development process models (see Appendix 2A to this chapter).

REFERENCES

[Bass03] Bass, L., P. Clements, and R. Kazman. *Software Architecture in Practice*, 2nd ed. Addison-Wesley, 2003.

[Boehm04] Boehm, B., and R. Turner. *Balancing Agility and Discipline*. Addison Wesley, 2004.

[Boehm81] Boehm, B. *Software Engineering Economics*. Prentice Hall, 1981, p. 40.

[Boehm88] Boehm, B. A Spiral model of software development and enhancement. *Computer*, May 1988, IEEE.

[CMMI06] SEI. *CMMI® Models and Modules*, http://www.sei.cmu.edu/cmmi/models/, 2006.

[IEEE1058] IEEE Std 1058™—1998 *IEEE Standard for Software Project Management Plans*. Engineering Standards Collection. IEEE Product: SE113. Institute of Electrical and Electronic Engineers, August 2003.

[IEEE12207] IEEE/EIA 12207.0/.1/.2. *Industry Implementation of International Standard ISO/IEC 12207:1995 Standard for Information Technology—Software Life Cycle Processes*. Engineering Standards Collection. IEEE Product: SE113. Institute of Electrical and Electronic Engineers, August 2003.

[PMI04] PMI. *A Guide to the Project Management Body of Knowledge*, 3rd ed. (PMBOK® Guide). Project Management Institute, 2004.

[Royce70] Royce, W. Managing the development of large software systems: Concepts and techniques. *IEEE WESCON, 1970*; reprinted in the *Proceedings of the 9th International Conference on Software Engineering*, Monterey, CA. ACM Press, 1987.

[Schwab04] Schwaber, Ken. *Agile Project Management with Scrum*. Microsoft Press, 2004.

URLs

[Agile] www.agilealliance.com/intro

[Wiki] en.wikipedia.org/wiki/Scrum_(development)

EXERCISES

2.1. Briefly compare and contrast the disciplines of system engineering and software engineering. How are they similar? How are they different?

2.2. CMMI-DEV-v1.2 lists five related process areas for the Technical Solution process area: requirements development, verification, decision analysis, requirements management, and organizational innovation and deployment.

Access the CMMI Web site at http://www.sei.cmu.edu/publications/documents/06.reports/06tr008.html. Review the Technical Solution process area, and briefly explain how each of the five related process areas is related to Technical Solution.

2.3. Briefly explain the different roles played by users, customers, and acquirers in software development projects.

2.4. Identify five different kinds of stakeholders in a project to develop an Automated Teller System, such as the one illustrated in Figure 2.4. Briefly explain the roles played by each kind of stakeholder.

2.5. Briefly explain the roles played in a software-intensive systems project by operational requirements and software requirements. How are they similar? How are they different?

2.6. Derived requirements are included in software requirements to add details to an operational requirement allocated to software, to elaborate a system-level requirement, or to provide features that are not visible to end-users but must be present to support features that are visible to end users.

Provide two examples of derived requirements for an Automated Teller System. For each example, first state the system-level requirement or operational requirement from which the derived requirement is derived.

2.7. Provide an example of each of the following:

a. A structural relationship between two software components.

b. A functional relationship between two software components.

c. A behavioral relationship between two software components.

d. A data relationship between two software components.

2.8. For the Automated Teller System illustrated in Figure 2.4, give an example of some software that might be obtained from each of the six sources of software components listed in Table 2.1.

2.9. Briefly compare and contrast the mechanisms of planning and control used in a Waterfall development project and those used in iterative development projects.

2.10. Briefly explain the distinctions between the Incremental-build process and the Evolutionary development process.

2.11. There are several different versions of Agile development. Investigate and briefly describe three different Agile process models. Explain how they are similar and how they are different. *Hint*: Do an internet search to find your three models.

2.12. Briefly compare and contrast the Evolutionary development process, the Agile development process, and the prototyping technique. How are they similar? How are they different?

2.13. Sketch a comparable workflow diagram to Figures 2.18 and 2.19 for the Agile development model illustrated in Figure 2.15. Briefly describe the attributes of your figure.

APPENDIX 2A

FRAMEWORKS, STANDARDS, AND GUIDELINES FOR SOFTWARE DEVELOPMENT PROCESS MODELS

2A.1 THE CMMI-DEV-v1.2 TECHNICAL SOLUTION PROCESS AREA

The purpose of the CMMI models is to provide frameworks that can be elaborated and tailored to improve the efficiency and effectiveness of software projects and organizations that conduct software projects [CMMI06]. Software development activities are covered by the Technical Solution process in CMMI-DEV-v1.2.

As stated in the CMMI-DEV-v1.2 report[15]:

> The purpose of Technical Solution (TS) is to design, develop, and implement solutions to requirements. Solutions, designs, and implementations encompass products, product components, and product-related life cycle processes either singly or in combination as appropriate.

The specific goals and specific practices of the Technical Solution process area in CMMI-DEV-v1.2 are:

SG 1 Select product component solutions
- SP 1.1 Develop alternative solutions and selection criterias
- SP 1.2 Select product component solutions

SG 2 Develop the design
- SP 2.1 Design the product or product component
- SP 2.2 Establish a technical data package
- SP 2.3 Design interfaces using criteria
- SP 2.4 Perform make, buy, or reuse analyses

[15] CMU/SEI-2006-TR-008, page 456.

SG 3 Implement the product design
- SP 3.1 Implement the design
- SP 3.2 Develop product support documentation

As the report states, the criteria used to select, design, and implement components may vary significantly across products, depending on product type, operational environment, performance requirements, support requirements, and cost or delivery schedules. The task of selecting the final solution makes use of the specific practices in the Decision Analysis and Resolution process area.

The related process areas and topics relevant to the Technical Solution are:

- Requirements development
  - Allocation of system requirements
  - Development of the operational concept
  - Interface requirement definition
- Verification
  - Peer reviews
  - Verification that product and product components meet requirements
- Decision analysis and resolution
  - Formal evaluation
- Requirements management
  - Specific practices of requirements management are performed interactively with those in the Technical Solution process area
- Organizational innovation and deployment
  - Improving the organization's technology

2A.2 DEVELOPMENT PROCESSES IN ISO/IEC AND IEEE/EIA STANDARDS 12207

The development process specified in the ISO/IEC and IEEE/EIA Standards 12207 consists of 13 activities [IEEE12207]:

1. Process implementation,
2. System requirements analysis,
3. System architectural design,
4. Software requirements analysis,
5. Software architectural design,
6. Software detailed design,
7. Software coding and testing,
8. Software integration,
9. Software qualification testing,
10. System integration,
11. System qualification testing,

12. Software installation, and
13. Software acceptance support.

Section 5.3 of 12207.0 states that the development process typically includes work activities for requirements analysis, design, coding, integration, testing, and installation and acceptance of software products. The development process may also contain system related activities if appropriate and if specified in the contractual agreement.

2A.3 TECHNICAL PROCESS PLANS IN IEEE/EIA STANDARD 1058

IEEE/EIA Standard 1058 for Software Project Management Plans (SPMPs) states that the Technical process plans will be contained in clause 6 of an SPMP. Items to be specified include:

- the development process model,
- the technical methods, tools, and techniques to be used,
- plans for establishing and maintaining the project infrastructure; and
- the product acceptance plan [IEEE1058].

2A.4 THE PMI BODY OF KNOWLEDGE

The PMBOK® Guide (*A Guide to the Project Management Body of Knowledge*) presents an overview of project management processes that are generally applicable to management of all kinds of project [PMI04].

As stated in Appendix D of the Guide, Application Area Extensions provide additions to the core material that may include new or modified material, elaborations of existing processes, different ways for processes to interact, addition elements or modifications of common process definitions, or special inputs, tool and techniques, and/or outputs for existing processes.

At this time (2009) there is no application area extension in the PMI Body of Knowledge for managing the various development process models of software engineering.

APPENDIX 2B

CONSIDERATIONS FOR SELECTING AN ITERATIVE-DEVELOPMENT MODEL[16]

The following tables indicate considerations for choosing among the Incremental-build, Evolutionary, Agile, and Spiral development process models based on characteristics of the requirements, the project team, the user community, the project type, and the risk factors. A "yes" indicates that the model would be a good choice based on the characteristic in question. A "no" indicates that the model would not be a good choice for that characteristic. For example, an Incremental-build model would be appropriate if the requirements are easily defined or well known (yes); an Evolutionary model would be not be appropriate in this case (no) because Incremental-build is more appropriate. An Agile model might be appropriate, depending on the desire for daily interactions with the customer (yes). In all cases a Spiral element can be (should be) added to systematically evaluate alternatives and risk factors on each iteration of the chosen process model.

[16] The tables in this appendix are based on material in *Quality Software Project Management* by R. Futrell, D. Shafer and L. Shafer; Prentice Hall, 2002, pp. 147–152.

TABLE 2B.1 Considerations based on characteristics of the requirements

Requirements	Incremental-build	Evolutionary	Agile
If the requirements are well known or easily defined	Yes	No	Yes
If the requirements can be defined early in the development cycle	Yes	No	No
If the requirements are likely to change often during the development cycle	No	Yes	Yes
If demonstrations are needed to develop the requirements	No	Yes	Yes
If a proof of concept is needed to determine feasibility	No	Yes	No
If the requirements indicate a large and complex system	Yes	Yes	No
If early delivery of limited functionality is desired	Yes	Yes	Yes

TABLE 2B.2 Considerations based on characteristics of the project team

Project Team	Incremental-build	Evolutionary	Agile
If most of the team members are new to the problem domain for the project	No	Yes	No
If most of the team members are new to the technology domain for the project	No	Yes	No
If most of the team members are unfamiliar with the tools to be used on the project	No	Yes	No
If some team members will likely be reassigned during the project development cycle	Yes	Yes	No
If the team members will be required to interact with a customer representative on a daily basis	No	No	Yes
If the team's progress will be closely tracked by managers and customer	Yes	No	Yes

TABLE 2B.3 Considerations based on characteristics of the user community

User Community	Incremental-build	Evolutionary	Agile
If availability of user representatives will be limited during the development cycle	Yes	Yes	No
If user representatives are new to the concepts of requirements definition	No	Yes	No
If user representatives are experts in the problem domain	Yes	No	Yes
If user representatives want to be involved in all phases of the development cycle	Yes	No	Yes
If the customer wants to closely track progress	Yes	No	Yes

TABLE 2B.4 Considerations based on characteristics of project type and risk factors

Project Type and Risk	Incremental-build	Evolutionary	Agile
If the project is a new area for the organization	No	Yes	No
If the project involves system integration	Yes	No	No
If the project involves enhancing an existing system	Yes	No	Yes
If funding is expected to be unstable during the development cycle	No	Yes	Yes
If high reliability, safety, or security of the product is essential	Yes	No	No
If the schedule is constrained	Yes	No	Yes
If external interfaces to other systems are unstable	No	Yes	No
If reusable components are available	Yes	No	No
If resources (people, tools, money) are scarce	Yes	No	Yes

3

ESTABLISHING PROJECT FOUNDATIONS

The problem is that we started in the middle. We had to go back and start over at considerable cost, effort, and pain.

—from a consulting client

3.1 INTRODUCTION TO PROJECT FOUNDATIONS

Getting started on a software project is sometimes called the initiation phase of the project. A project to develop or modify a software-intensive system is conceived, initiated, and conducted in the belief that the benefits of the resulting system or product will offset the cost of the project. Sometimes the benefit is calculated as a cost/benefit ratio that accounts for the present value of money, opportunity costs, and anticipated rate of return on the investment, or as the breakeven point for number of sales at a stated price. In other instances the benefits are less tangible; they may involve considerations of safety, security, or convenience for a specific population or for society at large. Financial considerations provide the motivation for projects undertaken by vendors that develop products for sale to the general public. Considerations of national security are the basis of projects undertaken by governmental agencies such as the U.S. Department of Defense.

Sometimes projects are initiated as the result of a bidding process by potential contractors and award of a contract by an acquirer; sometimes they are based on a business plan that is consistent with the mission of the organization. At other times the benefits may be speculative or they may be based on political considerations. In any case, the perceived benefits, determined by some criteria, must outweigh the estimated cost of a project.

Managing and Leading Software Projects, by Richard E. Fairley

TABLE 3.1 Foundation elements of software projects

	Concerned with
Product foundations	
Operational requirements	External view; users' view of the system
System requirements and system architecture	Hardware, software, and people elements; interconnections among elements; interfaces to the environment
Software requirements	Internal view; developers' view of the software to be developed or modified
Design constraints	Predetermined design decisions
Process foundations	
Contractual agreement	Statement of understanding between a developer and customer
Workflow model	Managerial work activities and work products
Development model	Technical work activities and work products
Project plan	The project roadmap

Successful software projects, like earthquake-resistant buildings, are built on strong and flexible foundations; establishing the foundation elements is thus an important activity during project initiation. Foundation elements for software projects include foundations for both the product to be delivered and the process by which it will be developed or modified. The workflow model for software projects, depicted in Figure 1.1, has inputs of Requirements and Constraints from the customer and Directives and Constraints from managers. Project foundations are derived from these inputs.

As indicated in Table 3.1, there are four kinds of product foundations and four kinds of process foundations. Product foundations include operational requirements, system requirements and architecture, software requirements, and design constraints. An overview of product foundations was presented in Chapter 2; they are elaborated in this chapter.

Process foundations include a contractual agreement, a model of workflow for managing the project, a process model for software development, and a project plan. The contractual agreement is presented in this chapter. The workflow model for software projects was presented in Chapter 1. Selecting and tailoring of software development models were presented in Chapter 2. Project planning and the format and contents of project plans are presented in Chapter 4.

3.2 OBJECTIVES OF THIS CHAPTER

After reading this chapter and completing the exercises, you should understand:

- the nature of requirements engineering,
- determining the scope of a project, and
- establishing a contractual agreement.

Appendix 3A to this chapter presents the relevant elements of CMMI-DEV-v1.2, ISO/IEC and IEEE/EIA Standards 12207, IEEE/EIA Standard 1058, and the of PMI Body of Knowledge.

Terms used in this chapter and throughout this text are defined in Appendix A to the text. Presentation slides for this chapter and other supporting material are available at the URL listed in the Preface.

3.3 SOFTWARE ACQUISITION

Contracting for software is addressed by the field of software acquisition, which is distinct from software project management; acquisition is concerned with the legally binding issues involved in contracting with an external customer (the acquirer). An overview of contractual issues is presented in this section, but these issues are not considered in detail in this text.

A contract typically specifies the scope of a project and legal clauses such as liabilities and penalties for breach of contract. It will likely include a rights-in-data clause or an intellectual property agreement that specifies exactly what the customer is paying for and what will be delivered to, and owned by, the customer. This may range from object code only, to source code, to code plus design documentation, to code design documentation, test scenarios and test cases, or to all of the above plus a copy of the software tools used to develop the software and control its configuration. Rights-in-data is a particularly important issue for open source software and software licensed from a vendor.

There are several kinds of contracts; for example:

- fixed price,
- time and materials,
- cost plus fixed fee, or
- cost plus incentive fee.

A fixed price contract is an agreement by which the customer will pay a specified amount of money for a system or product containing specified features and quality attributes. The money may be paid in lump sum upon final delivery of the contracted work products or it may be paid in increments upon satisfactory achievement of specified milestones. Because projects to develop or modify software-intensive systems are high risk endeavors, a fixed price contract should include a substantial contingency reserve in the price and the schedule. The contract should also contain a clause that permits renegotiation of price and schedule when the requirements are changed by the customer.

A time and materials contract is an agreement to reimburse the supplier at a fixed rate for the effort and resources expended in conducting a project. Different skill categories may be reimbursed at different rates, and there may be a ceiling placed on the total amount to be expended. These contracts are sometimes used for projects to maintain a system on an annual basis.

A cost plus fixed fee contract reimburses the cost of conducting the project plus a fee to cover the cost of expenditures that may be necessary in areas such as the supplier's infrastructure, acquisition of equipment, or training. In addition the fee typically includes a specified profit margin for the supplier.

A cost plus incentive fee contract awards the supplier for exceeding the requirements and/or developing or modifying a software-intensive system at less cost and in less time than specified in the contract. Many contractors who do business with governmental agencies rely on incentive fees to provide a margin of profit.

For more information on acquisition topics, see the CMMI-ACQ-v1.2 process model that has been developed and released by the Software Engineering Institute [ACQ07]. CMMI-ACQ-v1.2 "focuses on acquirer processes and integrates bodies of knowledge that are essential for successful acquisitions." Additional information on software and systems acquisition can be found in other references, such as [SACMM02] and [CMMIAM05].

3.4 REQUIREMENTS ENGINEERING

Requirements provide the basis for all that follows on a software project. Therefore it is important that you, the project manager, understand the nature of requirements engineering and be involved in the requirements engineering process. Product foundations in CMMI-DEV-v1.2, for example, include requirements development and requirements management [CMMI06].

Requirements development encompasses the following kinds of activities:

- *elicitation:* understanding user needs, customer expectations, and acquirer's conditions and documenting them in a Concept of Operations document
- *analysis:* translating user needs, customer expectations, and acquirer's conditions into technical requirements for hardware, software, and people elements
- *allocation:* allocating requirements to the hardware, software, and people elements of the system
- *specification:* documenting technical requirements in standard notations and formats; recorded in a Technical Specifications document
- *verification:* determining that the Technical Specifications are correct, complete, and consistent with respect to the Concept of Operations
- *negotiation:* give-and-take discussions among stakeholders to achieve consensus views
- *acceptance:* commitment to a requirements baseline, by all involved stakeholders, that accounts for the constraints of schedule, budget, resources, technology, and risk factors

Requirements management is concerned with managing the evolving requirements baseline during system development. An important aspect of requirements management is *impact analysis*, which is concerned with assessing the need for and making necessary changes to schedules, budgets, resources, technology, and risk factors commensurate with changes to baselined requirements.

If your project involves specifying hardware requirements and requirements for manual operations (i.e., those performed by people) in addition to the software requirements, as in a complex software-intensive system, you and your lead designer (software architect) should be members of the system engineering team. If the project is software-only, you may be responsible for developing the requirements, or the requirements may be developed by a system analyst (or an analysis team) and provided to you as the starting point for your project.

In general, there are several kinds of product requirements, as illustrated in Figure 3.1 and discussed in the following sections. A process-flow diagram for requirements engineering is depicted in Figure 3.2; work activities are indicated in italics and work products in bold.

3.4.1 Requirements Development

As illustrated in Figure 3.2, requirements development consists of requirements elicitation, requirements analysis, and requirements acceptance. Users' needs and customer's expectations that include desired product features and quality attributes provide the inputs to requirements elicitation. The operational requirements

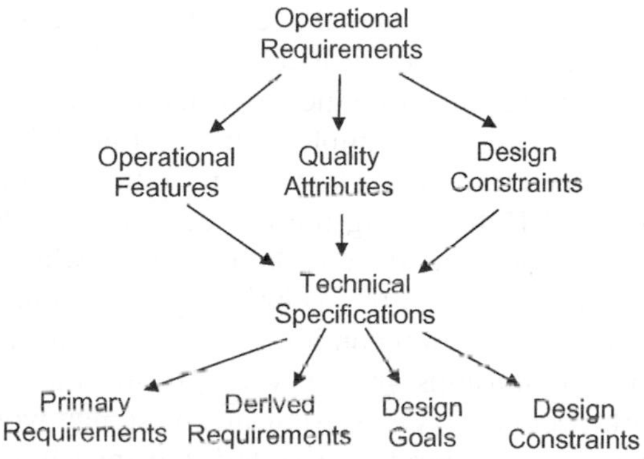

FIGURE 3.1 A taxonomy of product requirements

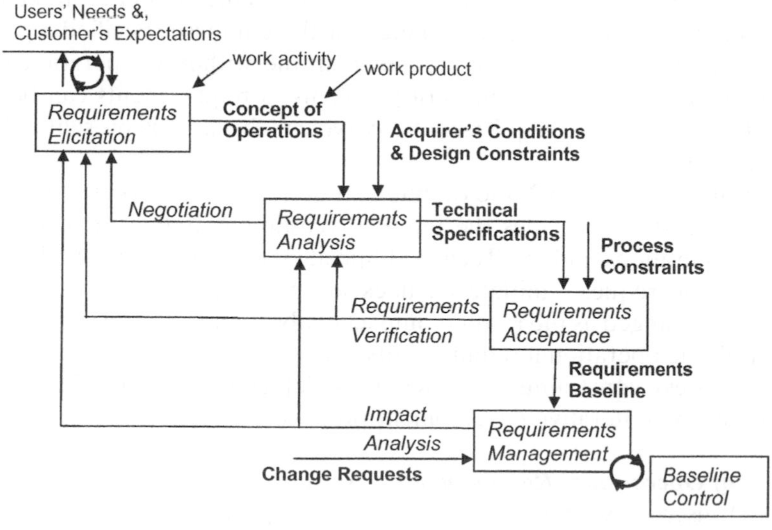

FIGURE 3.2 Process-flow of requirements engineering

that result from requirements elicitation are documented in a Concept of Operations that, along with the acquirer's conditions and the design constraints, provide the input to requirements analysis.

Elicitation and analysis typically require negotiation with users and customer. The analysis activity produces the technical specifications, which, along with the process constraints, provide the input to requirements acceptance. As illustrated in Figure 3.1, technical specifications include primary requirements, derived requirements, design goals, and design constraints. Distinctions among the four categories of technical specifications are described in Section 3.4.3.

Requirements verification determines the degree to which the technical specifications are correct, complete, and consistent with respect to the operational requirements and process constraints; it is a necessary activity of requirements acceptance. Completeness of technical specifications is determined by showing that they cover all of the operational requirements; traceability matrices that document the correspondences of operational requirements to technical specifications are often used for this purpose.

Verification of work products requires that each work product not only cover the work products completely from which it is derived but also covers them correctly and consistently. Determining the correctness of operational requirements requires expertise in the users' domain; for example, is it true that debits and credits must always balance in a financial transaction system or are there some conditions under which they may disagree? Determining the correctness of technical specification would include answering questions such as: Is the way in which debits and credits are to be handled correctly stated in the technical specifications?

Consistency (the third verification condition) requires that there be no external inconsistencies in the relationships among work products and no internal inconsistencies within work products. An external inconsistency would be detected if, for example, the operational requirements stated that the server in an Automated Teller System must be available at all times (24×7) and the technical specifications stated the ATS server shall provide an availability rating of 0.9, thus allowing the system to be unavailable 10% of the time. An internal inconsistency in the requirements would exist if an interface parameter for the database specified a parameter in dollars while the corresponding parameter in the withdraw operation specified the parameter in euros. Taxonomies of problems in requirements can be used as checklists for verifying the requirements. A typical checklist is presented in Table 3.2 [HAYES03].

As illustrated in Figure 3.2, the output of requirements acceptance is a requirements baseline, which provides the input to requirements management (i.e., the Concept of Operations and the Technical Specifications are placed under baseline control). Change requests initiate changes to the requirements baseline, which should only be changed as the result of impact analysis and appropriate adjustments to some or all the operational requirements, design constraints, technical specifications, and process constraints. The activities depicted in Figure 3.2 may occur multiple times in an iterative development process.

Elicitation of Operational Requirements As illustrated in Figure 3.2 (and Figures 2.1 and 2.5), users have needs, customers have expectations, and acquirers have conditions. Users of Automated Teller Machines (you and I, the end users of ATMs)

TABLE 3.2 Taxonomy of requirements problems and examples

Problem Category	Examples
Incorrect	Incorrect statement of an operational requirement
	Incorrect translation of an operational requirement into a technical specification
	Incorrect value or variable in a requirement
	Incorrect external constants
	Overstating or understating the computing resources assigned to a requirement
	Incorrect description of initial system state
Incomplete	Omitted requirement
	Incomplete decomposition of a requirement
	Incomplete description of a requirement
	Failure to fully describe system input or output
	Failure to specify the initial state
	Incomplete description of initial system state
Inconsistent	Requirements that are pairwise inconsistent
	Requirements for concurrent processes, when taken pairwise, are incompatible
Ambiguous	Meaning of requirement is unclear
	Requirements stated in a manner that is difficult to understand
Infeasible	Requirement impossible to achieve given the state of technology
	Requirement impossible to achieve given the current science of algorithms
	Requirement impossible to achieve given the current skills of our software developers
	Requirement impossible to achieve given other system factors such as processor speed or available memory
Difficult to achieve	Requirement that will be difficult to implement with available resources, schedule, and technology
	Requirement that will be difficult to achieve given the current skills of our software developers
Overspecified	Requirement exceeds operational needs, causing additional cost
Overly constrained	Constraints on performance and reliability excessive for the operational need, causing additional cost
Not traced	Requirement has not been traced to previous or subsequent phases
	Requirement cannot be traced to previous or subsequent phases
Not verifiable	Completeness, correctness, and consistency of the requirement cannot be verified by any reasonable verification method
Cannot be validated	Requirement not stated in a manner that provides validation criteria for implemented software
Misplaced requirement	Requirement belongs in another section of the document
Redundant requirement	Requirement specified elsewhere in the specification
Inappropriate information	Schedule, budget, training plans, and other items that belong in other documents

have needs that range from obtaining cash at convenient times and locations to making deposits and transferring funds between accounts. Customers (the financial institutions that acquire ATM systems) may have expectations of increased customer satisfaction for their customers (you and me), fewer operational personnel, and less paperwork associated with customer accounts. End users (you and I) may be well-pleased with the ATM system but the financial institution may find they need more operational personnel and have more paperwork than before. It is thus possible to satisfy user needs and not satisfy customer expectations, and vice versa. An acquirer (who also may or may not be the customer, who also may or may not be a user) typically has conditions that specify constraints on process factors such as schedule and budget.

The needs and expectations of stakeholders other than end users and customers must also be taken into consideration. Other stakeholders include those who affect or are affected by the proposed system. Operations personnel for an ATM system, for example, are stakeholders. They include bank tellers, other personnel who work in the financial institution, and those who provide operational support for the machines, including the personnel who configure the machines, load money into them, check the operation of the machines, and repair them when they malfunction.

These operations personnel (tellers and operations support) are not classified as end users of the system because they are under control of the customer; they can be recruited, trained, supervised, and dismissed by the customer. In this sense they are part of the system and not part of the operational environment of the system. Users of an ATM system (you and I) are not under control of the customer; we are thus elements of the operational environment.

The process of determining user needs and customer expectations is known as requirements elicitation. There are many techniques for eliciting operational requirements. Some of the more widely used techniques include the following:

- introspection: what would I want/need/desire if I were a user of the proposed system?
- brainstorming: free association and generation of ideas for the proposed system
- Post-It notes and white board: create, modify, group, and rearrange statements of needs and desires
- paper prototypes and storyboards: construct interfaces and operational scenarios.
- questionnaires: which of the following features do you need/desire?
- observation: watch people performing their work tasks
- open-ended interviews: tell me how you would use the proposed system
- focus groups: please tell us what you would want/need/desire in the proposed system
- operational walkthroughs: development of scenarios by interacting with users
- demonstrations: how to you like this interface? what should be added/removed/changed?
- protocol analysis: document the tasks users perform and the features they would need in the proposed system

- business case analysis: what features are needed to support the operations of our business?
- JAD (joint application development) sessions: facilitated meetings with users

More information on requirements elicitation can be found in the following references: [LEFF03], [ROBERT06] [WEIGER03].

The Concept of Operations (ConOps) The document in which operational requirements are recorded is termed the Concept of Operations (ConOps). Other names for this document include Operational Concepts Document (OCD) and Vision Statement. The format and contents of Concept of Operations documents are specified in IEEE Standard 1362™–1998 *IEEE Guide for Information Technology–System Definition–Concept of Operations (ConOps) Document* [IEEE1362].

Contents of a ConOps include the following:

- needs and expectations that motivate development of a new system or modification of an existing system
- an operational vision for the proposed system
- modes of operation for the proposed system
- user classes and characteristics
- kinds of and characteristics of operations personnel
- operational requirements
- operational scenarios
- prioritized system features and quality attributes
- impact of the proposed system on the development, operational, and maintenance environments

User needs and customer expectations provide the impetus for undertaking a software project. The ConOps should include a description of the deficiencies in the existing system or situation that provides the motivation for modifying an existing system or developing an automated system to replace or augment manual operations.

An operational vision of the proposed system includes a narrative overview of the system in its operational environment. This information is sometimes contained in a mission statement or a marketing proposal; it may be fully contained in the ConOps or summarized in the ConOps and fully described in a referenced document. Different modes of operation provide different sets of behaviors for different situations and different kinds of users. An ATM, for example, might have an on-line–normal mode, and on-line–assisted mode, on-line–degraded mode, an off-line–configuration mode, and an off-line–diagnostic mode.

Different modes of operation are often associated with different classes of users and operational personnel. The on-line–degraded mode might allow limited usage of an ATM when the communication link to the server is unavailable; for example, accepting deposits for later posting to an account or limiting cash dispensation to $50 USD or less during periods of communication outage. The on-line–assisted mode of an ATM might be specified to support users who need augmented support to see or hear when operating the machines. The off-line–configuration mode might be specified to allow operational maintainers to load money into the bins of the ATM and record the amount of money loaded into each bin. Diagnostic mode would check the operation of the system, including the communication link and the peripheral devices such as the camera, printer, card reader, and money dispenser.

Operational requirements and operational scenarios are the heart of a ConOps; they express the desired system features and quality requirements from the external viewpoint of users' needs and customer's expectations. Each operational scenario is a description of a step-by-step sequence of interactions for a transaction between a class of users or operational personnel and a software-intensive system. Examples of transactions include a user withdrawing money from an ATM or a bank teller setting up a new user account. Depositing money is a different scenario than withdrawing money because these are distinct user tasks.

Operational scenarios describe step-by-step interactions between an external agent (i.e., a user) and internal elements of a system. Operational scenarios should include scenarios for normal operation of the system by its intended users, plus scenarios for exception handling, degraded responses, generation of reports, reconciliation of data, and maintenance activities, as appropriate. Techniques for documenting operational scenarios include numbered lists of sequential interactions, sequence diagrams, and state diagrams [RUMB98].

Use cases are often used to document operational scenarios; a template for, and an example of a use case is provided in Table 3.3. Additional details concerning use cases are presented in the sidebar "Assessing Use Cases" in Chapter 7 of this text. Quality requirements that apply to a use case can be documented in the *Comments* section, for example, "good response time" during User Logon.

Quality requirements, as expressed by users and customers, are often vague, imprecise, and ambiguous. Users may, for example, express a desire for a system that is highly reliable and easy to use. During requirements analysis these statements

TABLE 3.3 Use case template and example

Use case ID: ATM #34
Use case name: User Logon
Actor that initiates the use case: Bank customer
Other actors, if any: none
Statement of the purpose of this use case:
 this use case documents the way bank customers log onto an ATM
Preconditions (must be true before this use case can be "executed"):
 customer has a valid bank card and PIN (personal identification number)
Primary scenario (to describe the main action of the use case):
 can be documented using a sequence diagram, state diagram, or narrative
Post-conditions (what *must be true* after this use case "executes"):
 customer is logged on OR customer has received a sorry message
Alternative scenarios (exception handling):
 invalid bank card; incorrect PIN; invalid account number; ATM is off-line
Comments: this use case belongs to Initiate Transaction. The ATM should have good response time during User Logon.

must be translated into technical specifications from which objective verification and validation criteria for the deliverable system can be derived; however, users and customers should be encouraged to express quality attributes in whatever terms are meaningful to them because their quality statements express, however imprecisely, user needs and customer expectations. Failure to satisfy their perceived needs and expectations can result in rejection of the delivered system by the customer or failure of users to adopt the product when it is installed in the operational environment.

As an example of the distinction between operational requirements and technical specifications, an operational requirement might be expressed as:

3.6 The ATM terminals in the Automated Teller System shall provide good response time.

This operational requirement, as expressed by the customer may be, after considerations of user satisfaction, project schedule, effort, cost, and technology translated into the following technical specification:

3.6 The ATM terminals in the Automated Teller System shall provide:

- an average response time of 2 seconds and a maximum response time of 5 seconds for transaction initiation and balance inquiries
- an average response time of 5 seconds and a maximum response time of 10 seconds for withdrawal and deposit requests.

Average and maximum response times shall be determined for a 1 hour period of operation during which a random mix of 3000 balance inquiries, withdrawal requests, and deposit requests are processed.

These response times shall be measured when 50 terminals are concurrently active and the server is running at an average load factor of 80%.

A prototype of the ATM user interface that provides the indicated response times could be built to demonstrate the response times to user representatives and the customer so that an agreement can be reached that the specified response times would be acceptable.

Establishing priorities among system features and quality attributes is an important step because users, customers, and other stakeholders will typically have more needs, expectations, and desires than can be implemented within the constraints of time, money, resources, and technology. One way to prioritize operational requirements is to first itemize them and then place each requirement in the category of Essential, Desirable, or Optional. Each itemized requirement should be a simple declarative statement that contains no “ands,” “ors,” “ifs,” or “buts.”

Essential requirements are those features and quality attributes that must be provided if the system is to satisfy basic user needs and customer expectations. Essential requirements for an ATM system might include the following:

E1: allow bank tellers to create user accounts

E2: provide a secure mechanism for users to access their accounts

E3: allow users to withdraw money from their accounts

All essential requirements must be implemented; prioritization of essential requirements provides a basis for iterative development.

Desirable requirements are those that add value to the system. They are implemented in decreasing order as time, resources, and technology permit. Examples for an Automated Teller System, in priority order, might provide users with the ability to:

D1: deposit money into an account

D2: access both savings and checking accounts

D3: access credit card accounts

D4: have pre-authorized credit limits for overdrafts

Optional requirements might include the ability to:

O1: purchase postage stamps through the ATM interface

O2: pay utility bills through the ATM interface

Techniques for developing priorities among operational requirements include the Delphi approach [Boehm81], Quality Function Deployment (QFD) [COHEN95], and the Analytical Hierarchy Process (AHP) [MIND95], [SAATY05].

Your initial project plan must provide sufficient schedule, budget, and resources to implement the Essential requirements and as many of the Desirable ones as can be accommodated within the project constraints (subject to negotiation with and agreement of the customer). Optional requirements are those that might be implemented if there is sufficient time and resources and/or if they are easy to incorporate. An important role for Optional requirements is to document ideas for features that might be included in future versions of the system and ideas that are too "far out" for today's users and technologies. Requirements triage is another technique for determining which requirements a product should satisfy given the time and resources available to develop the product [DAVIS03].

It is also important to document in the ConOps the impact of the proposed system on the development, operational, and maintenance environments. The developers of the new or modified system may have to maintain the old system while developing the new one. The customer and user representatives will have to allocate time to meet with the developers, to try out proposed user interfaces, to view demonstrations, and to critique the evolving system. New operational facilities may have to be constructed, as in physical locations for ATM machines or control rooms for nuclear reactors or spacecraft. Operational impacts might include setting up new help desks and training of support personnel for applications packages or, in the case of ATMs, hiring and training of operations support personnel and training of bank tellers. Impacts on the maintenance environment for the system may include acquisition of maintenance equipment, construction of maintenance facilities, and hiring and training of maintenance personnel.

3.4.2 Requirements Analysis

You may find that the operational requirements for your project are stated in a vague, imprecise, and/or ambiguous manner. Such statements are termed "design goals." The process of requirements analysis is concerned with clarifying operational requirements and restating them in terms that provide objective criteria that can be used to verify and validate that the specified system, when it is ready for delivery, will be complete, correct, and consistent with respect to the objectively stated requirements (verification) and that it will satisfy its intended purpose in its intended environment (validation).

You, the project manager, must not accept design goals as binding requirements. To avoid this, you and your customer might agree, for example, that "user friendly" means the system should be easy to learn and easy to use for a certain class of users. You and your customer might further agree that "user friendly" will be established by conducting experiments with a population of typical users to assess whether they can learn to perform, and repeatedly perform, specified tasks within specified periods of time.

For example, an experiment might involve selecting, at random, 30 typical users of a point-of-sale system such as those used in supermarkets and discount stores. It could be agreed that the "user friendly" criterion would be satisfied if 27 of 30 users can, after a 4 hour training course, successfully complete a set of specified operations within 30 minutes and can successfully complete the operations again one week later after a 20 minute refresher class. The experiment might be conducted with an early prototype of the user interface to provide feedback to the software developers and again when verifying and validating the delivered system. In this manner the design goal of "user friendly" has been converted into a requirement that can be validated by objective means. It may be possible to specify objective criteria for many of the operational requirements in a similar manner.

Some operational requirements describe functionality to be provided; for example:

> 3.4 The Automated Teller Terminals must provide a mechanism for authorizing access to individual customer accounts.

and

> 3.5 ATM terminals must provide a quick cash option.

The method of authorizing customers' access to their accounts (e.g., thumb print, retinal scan, voice recognition, or ATM card and PIN) would be determined by prototyping, feasibility studies, and discussions with the customer and user representatives. Operational requirement 3.4 might be restated as a primary requirement in the technical specifications:

> 3.4 ATM cards and PINs shall be the mechanism used to authorize access to individual customer accounts.

Or, the requirement might be stated more precisely as:

> 3.4 ATM cards having the physical dimensions of a credit card and PINs consisting of six alphanumeric symbols will be the mechanism used to authorize access to individual customer accounts.

Details concerning the information to be encoded on an ATM card would also be stated.

Operational requirement 3.5 might be restated as:

3.5 ATM terminals shall provide a "quick cash" withdrawal option that provides $100 USD in denominations of $20 USD. Multiple transactions will not be allowed in quick cash withdrawals.

Note that more precise statements of technical specifications restrict the design space from which solutions can be synthesized but, at the same time, provide more specific expressions of users' needs and customer's expectations. They also provide more specific guidance to the system developers and provide objective validation criteria.

It may not be possible to restate every design goal in an objective manner. For example, it may not be practical or even possible to objectively establish that the delivered system is the "world's best financial transaction system" or the "most realistic flight simulator ever built." In these cases the design goals, while not stated in an objective manner, may nevertheless influence design decisions and other factors such as schedules, budgets, and the features and quality attributes of the product. If, for example, "best" is taken to mean "has more user features than comparable systems," this would indicate that number of features to be implemented is of higher priority than cost or schedule; given design alternative A or B, the alternative that provides the larger number of features would be chosen. Design goals can thus influence the development of a system, but they are not, and must not be, binding requirements.

3.4.3 Technical Specifications

As illustrated in Figure 3.1, there are three kinds of operational requirements and 4 kinds of technical specifications for software. The operational requirements include:

- operational features,
- quality attributes, and
- design constraints.

The technical specifications, which are derived from the operational requirements, include:

- primary requirements,
- derived requirements,
- design goals, and
- design constraints.

Each of the four kinds of technical specifications (primary requirements, derived requirements, design goals, and design constraints) should be separately identified and listed within their own category.

Primary requirements are operational features that have been translated into objectively stated specifications; they include both functional requirements and quality requirements. The second versions of requirements 3.4 and 3.5 (above) are examples of primary requirements. Some operational requirements may be stated in an objective, verifiable manner; those operational requirements become primary requirements or design constraints without further translation.

As another example of the distinction between operational requirements and technical specifications, the operational requirements for a driving system simulator might specify that the simulator should be capable of simulating a variety of driving conditions, including clear and dry conditions as well as rain, ice, snow, and fog conditions. The corresponding technical specifications might state that the coefficient of friction in the vehicle stability equations must be variable between 0.0 and 1.0, that visual acuity in the simulated field of vision must be variable between 3 feet and infinity, and that both variables must be controllable from an instructor's console.

Both statements are necessary. In this example, the external view (operational requirement) states, for users, customers, acquirer, developers, and other stakeholders, the operational characteristics of the system to be built. The internal view (technical specification) provides the foundation for design, implementation, and verification that the deliverable system is complete, correct, and consistent with respect to its technical specifications, design documentation, and code. The operational requirement (capable of simulating a variety of driving conditions, including clear and dry conditions or rain, ice, snow, and fog conditions) provides validation criteria for determining the degree to which the system will satisfy user needs and customer expectation when placed in the operational environment.

In many cases requirements engineers attempt to use one document to specify both the external (operational) and internal (technical) requirements. This often results in a document that is too technical for users and customers to understand or too vague to be of use to the developers. Experience has shown that it is more efficient and more effective to develop two distinct documents for two distinct purposes: the Concept of Operations to document the operational requirements and the Requirements Specification to document the technical requirements. Of course, the correspondences between the two documents must be established and maintained. Traceability matrices are often used for this purpose (see Table 3.6).

Figure 3.3 illustrates tracking of the translation process from operational features to primary requirements. An operational requirement may translate into more than one primary requirement. In this case the operational feature should be decomposed so that each operational feature is translated to one and only one primary requirement. Otherwise, some elements of some operational features may be implemented more than once by different developers or development teams, and some elements may be omitted if the mapping of an operational requirement to multiple primary requirements is not complete and one to one. Satisfaction of this condition may require some reorganization and decomposition of the operational requirements. Figure 3.3 indicates that some operational requirements do not have corresponding primary requirements; perhaps the translation process is not completed or perhaps the translation process is completed and those operational requirements that do not have corresponding primary requirements are design goals.

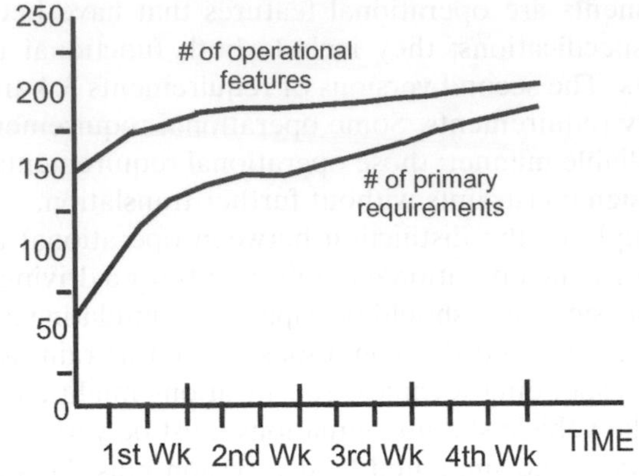

FIGURE 3.3 Operational features and primary requirements

Translating operational features into primary requirements requires some time and effort; research, analysis, and prototyping may be required to understand the effort, schedule, technical feasibility, cost, and levels of acceptability to users of different levels of quantification of requirements. In a similar manner, translating design constraints from operational requirements to technical specifications may require some effort to determine acceptable trade-offs between levels of quantification and effort, schedule, technical feasibility, cost, and user acceptance. Some operational requirements may remain as design goals for an extended period of time until acceptable, quantified values of the corresponding technical specifications can be determined. Translation of operational requirements into technical specifications may be an ongoing process.

Note also that the number of operational features continues to grow over time in Figure 3.3; this may be caused by:

- decomposition of the operational requirements to finer levels of detail, or
- "scope creep" in which requirements are increasing without corresponding adjustments to schedule, budget, and/or resources (bad), or
- ongoing redefinition of project scope, schedule, budget, and resources to meet changing user needs or market conditions, which is acceptable, as long as stakeholders are in agreement.

Derived requirements (the second kind of technical specification) are requirements for system features and quality attributes that are not visible to users but are necessary to support the operational requirements. Derived requirements are included in the technical specifications for two reasons:

1. to decompose high-level operational requirements into detailed technical specifications, and
2. to provide additional capabilities needed to satisfy operational requirements.

An extreme example of the first situation (decomposition of high-level operational requirements) would be derivation of the technical specifications for an Automated Teller System based on a single operational requirement:

3.0 The Automated Teller System shall provide the features, performance, and quality attributes typically provided by such systems.

Or, famously, the single operational requirement stated by U.S. President Kennedy in 1961:

to put a man on the moon and return him safely to the Earth by the end of this decade.

As an example of providing a derived capability to satisfy an operational requirement, the operational requirement might state:

2.9 Each ATM transaction shall provide to the user a printed receipt containing a record of the transaction that includes the date and time of the transaction.

A derived requirement must be added to the technical specifications to specify a clock function that will be accessed when printing customer receipts. The derived requirement would specify a clock function having the necessary resolution and allowable drift (e.g., a resolution of 1 millisecond and drift of not more than 5 milliseconds per day). The derived clock requirement might be allocated as a hardware requirement, as a software requirement, or it might result in specification of the hardware and software required to obtain accurate time from an external source such as a central server, a universal time standard, or the GPS satellite system.

As mentioned previously, requirements stated in a manner that does not support objectively stated verification and validation criteria are classified as design goals. Design goals are thus operational requirements that have not yet been, or cannot be, translated into objectively stated technical specifications. Each design goal should be examined for possible translation into one of the other three categories (primary requirement, derived requirement, or design constraint). It may be possible to translate some design goals, as in the previous example of "user friendly", into objective specifications. Other requirements such as "world's best financial transaction system" may not be quantifiable and will thus remain as design goals. Those that cannot be translated must not be binding requirements used to determine acceptability of the delivered product.

It may not be possible to translate design goals into technical specifications during the initial stages of requirements development because of uncertainties about the cost, schedule, and feasibility of implementing various levels of quantification. For example, prototyping and feasibility studies may reveal that achieving an average response time of 2 seconds and a maximum response time of 5 seconds for balance inquiries in the Automated Teller System when 50 terminals are active and the server is running at 80% load capacity will require expensive technology (i.e., CPUs in the terminals, communication bandwidth, server capacity, speed of access to the customer-accounts database); however, an average response time of 4 seconds and a maximum response time of 8 seconds could be achieved for much less cost. Given the trade-off between cost and performance, the customer may agree to the less stringent performance parameters. The more expensive performance option might be chosen if the system were a mission critical system such as an air traffic control system for communication between air traffic controllers and pilots, rather than an automated teller system.

As stated above, it may never be possible to translate some design goals into quantified requirements. Suppose, for example that an operational requirement states:

4.1 The order processing system *shall* be the best in the world.

The problem with this requirement is that it is not feasible to study all order processing systems in the world and quantify "best in the world" and as a result, the requirements engineer should not accept the contractually binding "shall" in the statement. Nevertheless, this design goal expresses a desired outcome and should be accepted as a nonbinding requirement that will determine the priorities among cost, schedule, features, design options, and the technology to be utilized. Or, this design goal may be dropped when the reality of the cost and schedule to build a system that approximates "the world's best" are presented to the customer.

Design constraints are the fourth category of technical specification. A design constraint is a design decision stated in the requirements and for which no flexibility in design or implementation is allowed, as for example:

3.12 The merge-sort algorithm shall be used to reconcile customer-account data on a daily basis.

Imprecisely stated design constraints must be clarified. For example, which customer data are to be reconciled? Reconciled with what? Why must the mergesort algorithm be used? Is it important to state the time of day when the data are to be reconciled?

Design constraints may also specify operations that the system must not do, for example:

3.17 Withdrawals from each customer account shall not exceed $500 USD in any 24 hour period.

Failure to incorporate this feature in the design of the system could result in significant rework to incorporate it during verification and validation of the delivered system. Design constraints, as stated in the operational requirements, may be vague, imprecise, and/or overly restrictive, but in the technical specifications they must be stated in a manner that is achievable and that permits objective verification of the technical specifications.

A (questionable) design constraint might be stated as follows:

7.3 The customer-transaction database will be updated between 12:00 and 1:00 AM each day, using the merge-sort algorithm.

This design constraint is questionable on several counts:

- First, the operational detail of precisely when the data are sorted does not belong in the requirements documentation; it should be stated in an operations manual. It should also be questioned as to the necessity of the time constraint of 12:00 to 1:00 AM when the Ops manual is reviewed by operations personnel.

- Second, the feasibility of completing the data sort in a 1 hour period when the server is (presumably) running with a small number of active terminals and a low percentage of CPU usage (i.e., late night) must be determined.
- Third, "small number of active terminals" and "low percentage of CPU usage" must be quantified, perhaps after some analysis, and specified in primary requirements that corresponds to operational requirement 7.3 above.
- Fourth, the necessity of using the merge-sort algorithm should be clarified.

On the other hand, a design constraint of the following form may be necessary to provide a required interface of an Automated Teller System:

4.4 The bank-teller interface shall provide an SQL query capability for accessing the customer-accounts database.

Each design constraint restricts the design space available to the software designers and may result in a suboptimal design of the system.[17] Design constraints should therefore:

- be identified as such,
- have their necessity justified,
- provide flexibility, if any, and
- be restated in an objective manner.

During the design phase, alternative approaches to satisfying the constraint, if they exist, should be identified and analyzed. The derived requirement for a clock function in the ATM machines, for example, does not restrict alternative approaches to providing that functionality. If, however, the requirement were stated as a design constraint that required the date and time of transactions to be obtained from a universal time standard, it would preclude the options of obtaining time from the ATS server, the internal clock of the ATM's CPU, from GPS satellites, or from another source. One of these options might be a better design choice within the context of the ATS client-server software architecture.

In some cases (e.g., a Web-based user-intensive system), the operational requirements, when translated into primary requirements, may provide an adequate basis for building a software-intensive system. But often you will find it necessary to include derived requirements and quantified design constraints to facilitate implementation of the directly translated operational requirements and design constraints and to, for example, ensure interoperability of your system with other systems. In other cases, you may receive high-level operational requirements and design constraints from a marketing, system engineering, or hardware group. In these cases you will find it is necessary to decompose and quantify the operational requirements, add derived requirements, and clarify the design constraints in order to provide an

[17] An optimal system design achieves the best possible balance among prioritized features and quality attributes. A suboptimal design is one that optimizes particular features or quality attributes at the expense of others.

adequate basis for developing and implementing plans to accomplish software design, implementation, and verification and validation.

Documenting Technical Specifications The categories listed in Table 3.4 can be used to organize and document technical specifications.

IEEE Standard 830™–1998 is a "Recommended Practice for Software Requirements Specifications" [IEEE830]. Table 3.5 lists the specific requirements to be documented in section 3 of a Software Requirements Specification that conforms to IEEE 830.

As indicated in Table 3.5, performance requirements are to be stated in quantitative terms. Static performance requirements include items such as the number of terminals to be supported; for example, "the system shall support 50 user terminals." This is similar to the "capacities" category in Table 3.3. Dynamic performance requirements specify factors such as the number of transactions to be processed in a given time period; for example "90% of transactions shall complete in less than 1 second when 50 user terminals are concurrently active," which would be classified as a design constraint using the categories in Table 3.3.

The categories of technical specifications in Tables 3.4 and 3.5 can be organized in various ways in a requirements specification document. Technical specifications for a scientific data processing system might be organized by listing the input–output functions the system must perform at the top level with other categories, such as interfaces, behavior, and performance specified for each input–output function; a user-intensive system might be organized by specifying windows, menus, and

TABLE 3.4 Categories of technical specifications

Category	Description
Interfaces	To the environment and other subsystems
Functions	Stimulus–response pairs
Performance	Response time; throughput
Behavior	Sequences of system states over time
Capacities	Data; communication; memory
Design constraints	Predetermined design decisions
Quality attributes	Safety; security; reliability; others

TABLE 3.5 Specific requirements in IEEE Standard 830–1998

Specific Requirements	Description
External interfaces	Inputs into and outputs from the software system
Functions	Actions taken in accepting and processing inputs and generating outputs
Performance requirements	Static and dynamic quantified requirements
Logical database requirements	Requirements for information to be placed into a database
Design constraints	Constraints imposed by conformance to standards, hardware limitations, etc.
Software system attributes	Reliability; availability; security; maintainability; portability

modes of interaction for each user interface with other categories of requirements subordinated within the interface specification; the technical specifications for a real-time system might be organized by behaviors. Annex A of IEEE Standard 830™–1998 provides several alternative ways of organizing the information in Tables 3.4 and 3.5.

3.4.4 Requirements Verification

In general, verification is concerned with determining the degree to which a work product satisfies the conditions and constraints placed on it by other work products and work processes. This means the work product must be complete, correct, and consistent with respect to other work products and work processes. There are three distinct areas of requirements verification:

1. determining the internal completeness, correctness, and consistency of each of operational requirement and each technical specification;
2. determining that each operational requirement and each of the technical specifications is externally complete, consistent, and correct with respect to the other requirements and related work products such as test plans and test scenarios; and
3. determining the internal completeness, correctness, and consistency of related test plans, test scenarios and other mechanisms of end-product verification and validation.

Techniques for verifying the internal properties of requirements and related documents include analysis, reviews, and walkthroughs. Traceability is the primary technique for establishing external completeness, correctness, and consistency among these four documents: (1) operational requirements (design goals and operational design constraints), (2) technical specifications, (3) end-product verification plans, and (4) end-product validation plans.

Table 3.6 is an example of a traceability matrix used to establish correspondences between prioritized operational features and the primary requirements in a techni-

TABLE 3.6 Traceability of operational features to primary requirements

Primary Requirements	→					
Operational Features ↓	[P1]	[P2]	[P3]	[P4]	[P5]	[P6]
[E1]	X					
[E2]			X			
[E3]				X		
[E4]						
[D1]					X	
[D2]		X				
[D3]						
[D4]						X

cal specification. Primary requirements are often stated as functional input–output specifications. For example, the balance inquiry function accepts a user account number and returns the amount of money in the account; a withdrawal request accepts a user account number and a requested amount and returns a "yes" or "no" response (after invoking the balance inquiry function, which would be implemented first in an iterative development process).

In Table 3.6 operational feature [E3], for example, is covered by primary requirement [P4]; operational features [E4] and [D3] do not yet have corresponding primary requirements. Note that in Table 3.6 each operational feature is allocated to one, and only one, primary requirement; otherwise, an operational feature might be implemented multiple times in the system. Operational features E4 and D3 do not have corresponding primary requirements; this may be because the work is in progress, or it may be an oversight that must be corrected. Quality attributes (e.g., security of user accounts) may apply to one, several, or all features of the system. Other traceability matrices can be used to depict the allocation of quality attributes to technical specifications.

Because technical specifications provide the foundation for all that follows in a software project, it is important that they be complete, consistent, and correct with respect to the operational requirements, and that the technical specifications provide objective criteria for verifying and validating that each technical requirement is satisfied by the code of the deliverable system. Matrices similar to Table 3.6 can be used to illustrate the correspondence between operational requirements and validation plans and between technical specifications and verification plans, as well as between primary requirements and derived requirements. Derived requirements must also have objective verification and validation plans for which traceability matrices are necessary.

3.4.5 Requirements Management

The goal of requirements development is to establish an initial baseline of operational requirements and technical specifications, as indicated in Figure 3.2. Requirements management is concerned with managing subsequent changes to the operational requirements and technical specifications and keeping those changes in balance with schedule, budget, resources, technology and other project factors.

Depending on the scope of your project you may or may not be responsible for developing the initial set of requirements; they may be developed and given to you as the starting point for your project. But you will certainly be responsible for managing changes to operational requirements and technical specifications as the project evolves. Requirements may be changed by addition, modification, and deletion of operational requirements, design constraints, and technical specifications. Each change to requirements must be accompanied by an impact analysis to determine the effect of the change on schedule, budget, resources, quality attributes, technology, and other factors. Impact analysis may determine that the proposed change is in scope, meaning that it can be handled without changes to other project factors or the change may be out of scope, meaning that the proposed change to the requirements cannot be accepted without compensating changes to other project factors.

Baselines and Change Control Boards Baselines and change control boards are the primary mechanisms used to managing requirements. A *baseline* is a work product that is placed under version control and may not be further modified with the approval of a change control board (CCB). A CCB consists of one or more individuals who have the authority to make changes to the requirements and make the corresponding adjustments to schedule, budget, resources, and/or technology as necessary.

On a small project, you (as project manager and lead developer) and your customer may be the only members of the CCB. On a large project, the CCB may include you, an acquirer who represents a group of customers (or perhaps a marketing manager), and representatives of your analysis and design team, the implementation and validation teams, the support and maintenance teams, and other concerned stakeholders.

On a system-level project or program, your CCB may be subordinate to the system CCB. In that case you and your chief software architect should be members of that control board. To be efficient and effective, CCB membership should include those individuals who have the authority to make changes and who are directly responsible for delivering an acceptable system on time and within budget.

A process-flow diagram for a software development CCB is illustrated in Figure 3.4. The initial baseline of a work product (e.g., the technical specifications) is established by a review and acceptance process that determines (at least, some of) the requirements are a suitable basis (a baseline) for further work activities.

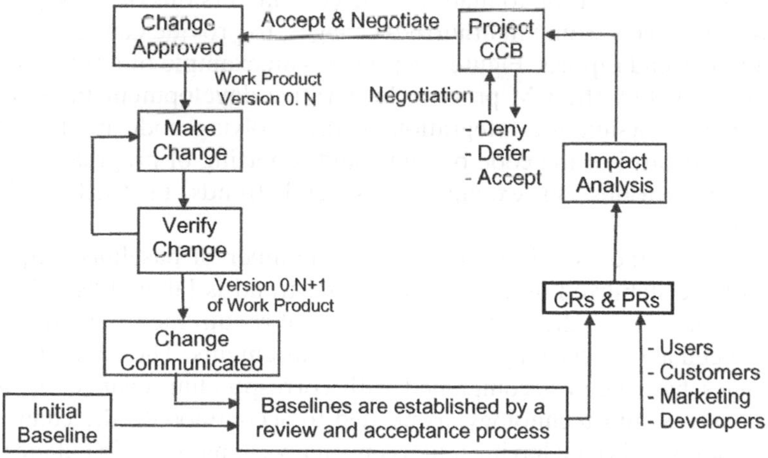

FIGURE 3.4 Process flow for a software development CCB

Once established, a baseline is changed for one of two reasons:

1. because of a requested change to the work product or
2. because of a defect in the work product.

Requested changes are submitted as CRs (Change Requests). Defects in a work product are documented in PRs (Problem Reports). As indicated in Figure 3.4, a CR or DR can be submitted by any concerned stakeholder.

The first activity during impact analysis is to determine whether the submitted request has already been received. In this case the submitter is notified of the status of the requested change. Impact analysis for a new CR or PR is conducted to determine whether the proposed change is in scope or out of scope; in the latter case an estimate of effort and resources to implement the change is developed. In both cases a recommended priority for the change is provided.

The CCB (which includes you, the project manager as a member and perhaps chair) must have the authority to accept the proposed change with a priority designation, defer the request (perhaps to the next release of the product), or to deny the request. Deferral or denial of a change request may involve negotiation with the submitter of the request. Acceptance of the change request may involve some negotiation with the developers, who must incorporate the change into their work activities if the request is in scope or modify their schedules of work activities, with your concurrence, if the change is out of scope. Major out-of-scope changes may require major replanning of the project.

If the request is accepted and the change negotiated, the work is assigned, the change is made and verified to be complete, correct, and consistent, and a new baseline version of the work product is generated. The final step is to ensure that all affected parties are notified of the work product's new baseline and the changes that resulted from processing of the change request.

The CCB relies on a configuration management (CM) process, which involves use of a version control tool, to maintain the current versions of work products, to protect work products from unauthorized changes, to provide configuration audits, and to provide trend reports. Figure 3.5 provides an example of a trend report that might be provided by the CM process. In iterative development the CM process may also involve systematic integration of the evolving code modules into the growing base, control of the code baseline, and reporting of progress.

Figure 3.5 provides an example of several trends in tracking baselined requirements:

First, note that the "stable profile" for the number of baselined requirements appears to have stabilized at 200; however, the trend is labeled "stable profile?" because, as can be seen, the cumulative number of requirements changes indicates there have been about 65 changes to the 200 requirements. The concern is whether these changes have been accompanied with corresponding changes in schedule, budget, resources, and technology, as needed to accommodate the changes. If so, the requirements, although having undergone many changes, are in balance with the current requirements baseline. If not, the project is in serious trouble because the schedule, budget, resources, and technology are based on an outdated set of requirements.

Second, note that the "unstable profile" is also questioned. Again, the question is whether appropriate changes to other project variables have been made (i.e., schedule, budget, resources, and technology). If so, the project is stable; if not, the project is unstable.

Third, note that in the beginning 150 requirements were labeled as design goals, meaning that no objective verification or validation mechanisms were associated

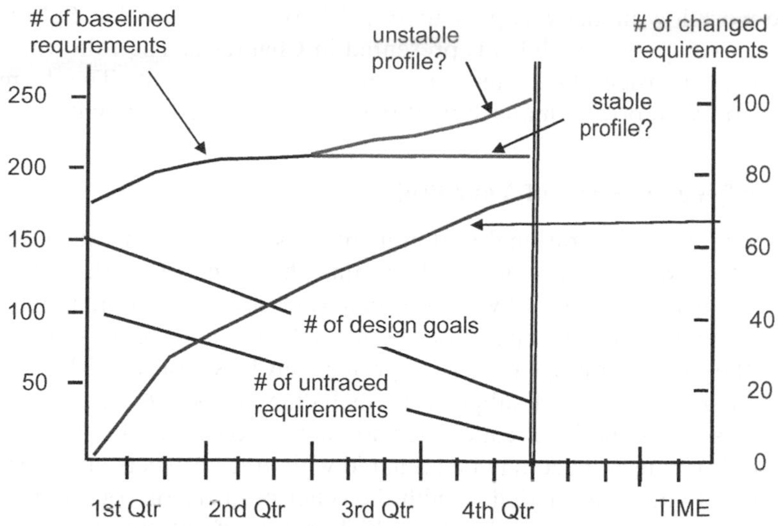

FIGURE 3.5 Trend report for baselined requirements

with those requirements. As can be seen, about 100 design goals have been converted to objectively stated requirements; however, 50 remain to be converted. As discussed above, it may not be possible to convert all of these design goals into objectively stated requirements, for example, as the operational requirement for "the world's best inventory system."

Fourth, the number of untraced requirements has decreased from 100 to 25. The trends indicate that conversion of design goals and traceability are ongoing processes.

In summary, a CCB:

- identifies the work products to be placed under version control;
- approves initial baselines of those work products;
- evaluates proposed changes to baselines, approves, defers, or denies change proposals;
- adjusts schedule, budget, resources, and technology to accommodate approved changes;
- schedules and tracks changes to completion;
- analyzes change trends and responds as appropriate; and
- has the authority to accomplish these tasks.

Version control, change control boards, and trend analysis have been presented in the context of requirements management; however, the same processes apply to configuration management of all baselined work products.

3.5 PROCESS FOUNDATIONS

As indicated in Table 3.1, process foundations for software projects include the workflow model, the development model, the contractual agreement, and the project plan. The workflow model was presented in Chapter 1, Figure 1.1. Selecting and tailoring a development model was presented in Chapter 2. The following section presents scope considerations and the contractual agreement. The format and content of software project management plans are presented in Chapter 4.

3.5.1 Specifying the Scope of Your Project

Product foundations (operational requirements, system requirements, design constraints, and software requirements) determine the scope of work to be accomplished in a project. The scope of your project may involve development of hardware and software and training of operations personnel, or it may be a "software-only" project. In the former case, your software project may be subordinated to a systems-level project that has several subprojects, including yours (system-level development projects are sometimes called development programs). In the latter case (software-only), your project may be affiliated with other projects and thus require coordination of your work activities with the other projects, or your software-only project may be a "stand-alone" that has a high degree of autonomy.

Even in the case of autonomous software-only projects the overall system requirements must be determined. At minimum, the delivered software will operate on a hardware platform and, in most cases, in the environment of system software (e.g., I/O drivers and a process scheduler, or a full-feature operating system). The hardware and software environment for development may differ from the environment of operation, for instance, if you are developing embedded software using a host computer and downloading the software to a target computer. The hardware and software to be used in developing a system may be stated as design constraints (most likely) or you may have the freedom to choose the best development and operating environments for the system (less likely).

The scope of some software-only projects involves working with users, customers, acquirer, and other stakeholders to develop the project foundations, construct a software solution, deliver and install the resulting system, train the users, and provide ongoing support for a specified period of time. Other projects may start after the requirements have been established and end with acceptance validation of the delivered product. Still others may involve modification of an existing version of a system to produce a next release.

3.5.2 The Contractual Agreement

Project scope can be documented in a contractual agreement. In general, a contract is a statement of understanding between two parties. The agreement may be formal or informal. A formal agreement is a legal contract between your organization and the acquirer's organization. An informal agreement is a statement of understanding between you, the project manager, and an internal customer. Informal contractual agreements for software projects are documented in Memos of Understanding (MOUs). MOUs are appropriate for in-house projects when the software project is performed for other units of your organization or perhaps for others within your unit.

Formal contracts are legally binding documents that include legally enforceable consequences to both parties if either party should violate the terms of the contract.

They are appropriate when your organization and the acquiring organization are distinct entities and money is to be paid to the supplier (your organization) by the acquiring organization. In this case the elements of a contractual agreement are appended to a formal contract in the form of a Statement of Work (SOW). The agreed-to operational requirements and technical specifications are appended to, and are thus are part of, a formal contract; however, only the technical specifications should be legally binding. In cases where the technical specifications have not been developed, the contract must contain a caveat that operational requirements are not binding and that technical specifications based on the operational requirements will be negotiated and accepted by acquirer and supplier.

Items typically contained in a contractual agreement include:

- scope of work
- deliverable work products
- delivery date(s)
- customer/user and developer join review schedule
- change request procedures
- development constraints
- product acceptance criteria
- additional items, as appropriate

The scope of work includes all of the major work activities that must be accomplished to deliver a satisfactory product, for example, project management, analysis, design, implementation, verification, and validation; activities such as user training, providing support for evolution of the system after delivery, and similar work activities would be included as appropriate. The deliverable work products may include object code only, or object code plus reference and training materials, or may also include source code and test suite, as negotiated between customer and developer (or acquirer and supplier).

There may be more than one agreed-to delivery date as, for example, in the case of early delivery of one or more subset capabilities to be followed by delivery of the full system. Delivery dates can be specified as calendar dates or elapsed time from the start of the project, the former being preferable because it sounds more definite. Joint reviews between customer/user and developer (or acquirer and supplier) can range from major milestone reviews in a Waterfall development process, to frequent reviews in an Incremental-build process, to daily interactions in an Agile process.

Because change is inevitable in software projects, a mechanism such as the workflow diagram for change requests illustrated in Figure 3.4 and a CCB as described in Section 3.4.5 above must be agreed to by customer and developer (or acquirer and supplier). Development constraints may include process constraints imposed by the customer, such as use of an Incremental-build process that incorporated frequent demonstrations of progress and early delivery of subset capabilities, or product constraints such as the hardware platform, operating system, or database facility to be used. The product acceptance criteria must be stated in an objective manner so that both parties can agree when the product has been satisfactorily completed.

Additional items (e.g., a schedule for user training) may be included as appropriate. In cases of formal relationships between acquirer and supplier, items such as price, payment schedule, rights in data, and consequences of failure to satisfy the contractual terms will be stated in the formal contract. The items listed above will be included in the Statement of Work, which will be an element of the contract.

Every software project must have a contractual agreement in the form of a Memo of Understanding (MOU) for informal contractual agreements or a Statement of Work (SOW) for formal contracts. Some elements of a contractual agreement may be project constraints, for example, the delivery date(s) and development constraints. Other items may be completed only after an initial planning phase, for example, the scope of work and the product acceptance criteria. The MOU or SOW would be amended at that point.

Some organizations use project authorization forms (sometimes called "project work orders" or "project charters") to officially launch a software project. The MOU or SOW should be part of the project authorization document if there is one.

3.6 KEY POINTS OF CHAPTER 3

- Software projects have four kinds of product foundations and four kinds of process foundations.
- Software requirements include operational requirements and technical specifications.
- Operational requirements include operational features, quality attributes, design constraints.
- Technical specifications include primary requirements, derived requirements, design goals, and quantified design constraints.
- Design goals are operational requirements that have not been, or cannot be, translated into technical specifications.
- The primary activities of requirements development are elicitation of operational requirements, analysis, translation into technical specifications, and acceptance baselining of the technical specifications.
- Requirements management is concerned with baseline control of requirements and with maintaining consistency among requirements, effort, schedule, budget, and technology.
- Configuration management, which includes version control, a change control board (CCB), and status reporting, is the primary mechanism of requirements management.
- Technical specifications can be categorized in various ways, and typically include interfaces, functions, performance, behavior, capacities, design constraints, and quality attributes
- A contractual agreement includes items such as the scope of work to be accomplished, deliverable work products, development constraints, and product acceptance criteria

- Every project must have a contractual agreement. Informal contractual agreements are called Memos of Understanding (MOUs). Formal contractual agreements are called Statements of Work (SOWs)
- SEI, ISO, IEEE, and PMI provide frameworks, standards, and guidelines relevant to establishing project foundations (see Appendix 3A to this chapter)

REFERENCES

[ACQ07] *CMMI for Acquisition, Version 1.2 Model.* http://www.sei.cmu.edu/publications/documents/07.reports/07tr017.html.

[Boehm81] Boehm, B. *Software Engineering Economics*. Prentice Hall, 1981.

[CMMI06] *CMMI® Models and Modules.* http://www.sei.cmu.edu/cmmi/models/, 2006.

[CMMIAM05] *CMMI Acquisition Module (CMMI-AM), Version 1.1.* http://www.sei.cmu.edu/publications/documents/05.reports/05tr011.html.

[CMMSA02] *Software Acquisition Maturity Model, Version 1.03*, http://www.sei.cmu.edu/arm/SA-CMM.html, 2002.

[COHEN95] Cohen, L. *Quality Function Deployment*. Prentice Hall, 1995.

[DAVIS03] Davis, A. *The art of requirements triage. IEEE Computer*, March 2003.

[HAYES03] Hayes, J. Building a requirement fault taxonomy: Experiences from a NASA verification and validation research project. *Proceedings of the IEEE International Symposium on Software Reliability Engineering (ISSRE)*. Denver, CO, November 2003 IEEE Computer Society.

[IEEE830] IEEE Std 830™–1998. *IEEE Recommended Practice for Software Requirements Specifications*. IEEE Software Engineering Standards Collection. IEEE Product SE113. Institute of Electrical and Electronic Engineers, August 2003.

[IEEE1362] IEEE Std 1362™–1998. *IEEE Guide for Information Technology–System Definition–Concept of Operations (ConOps) Document.* Software Engineering Standards Collection. IEEE Product SE113. Institute of Electrical and Electronic Engineers, August 2003.

[IEEE12207] IEEE/EIA 12207.0/.1/.2. *Industry Implementation of International Standard ISO/IEC 12207:1995 Standard for Information Technology—Software Life Cycle Processes*. Engineering Standards Collection. IEEE Product SE113. Institute of Electrical and Electronic Engineers, August 2003.

[LEFF03] Leffingwell, D., and D. Ledwig. *Managing Software Requirements: A Use Case Approach*. Addison-Wesley, 2003.

[MIND95] The Delphi Method, Mindtools, 1995. http://www.mindtools.com/pages/article/newTMC_95.htm.

[PMI04] PMI. *A Guide to the Project Management Body of Knowledge*, 3rd ed. (PMBOK® Guide). Project Management Institute, 2004.

[ROBERT06] Robertson, S., and J. Robertson. *Mastering the Requirements Process*. Addison-Wesley, 2006.

[RUMB98] Rumbaugh, J., I. Jacobson, and G. Booch. *The Unified Modeling Language Reference Manual*. Addison-Wesley, 1998.

[SAATY05] Saaty, T. *Theory and Applications of the Analytic Network Process: Decision Making with Benefits, Opportunities, Costs, and Risks*. RWS Publications, 2005.

[WEIGER03] Weigers, K. *Software Requirements*. Microsoft Press, 2003.

EXERCISES

3.1. CMMI-DEV-v1.2 lists the following related process areas for the Requirement Development and Requirements Management process areas:

Project Planning
Technical Solution
Product Integration
Verification process
Validation process
Project Monitoring and Control
Configuration Management
Risk Management

Access the CMMI Web site at http://www.sei.cmu.edu/publications/documents/06.reports/06tr008.html. Review the Requirements Development and Requirements Management process areas, and briefly explain how each of the related process areas is related to Requirements Development and Requirements Management.

3.2. Briefly explain why it is important that each operational requirement be stated as a simple declarative statement that contains no "ands," "ors," "ifs," or "buts."

3.3. Given a set of operational requirements, briefly describe the techniques you would use to determine which requirements to place in each of the categories: Essential, Desirable, and Optional.

3.4. Briefly explain why it is desirable to categorize technical specifications using the categories in Table 3.4 or 3.5.

3.5. Briefly indicate how you would organize the categories of technical specifications in Table 3.4 for an object-oriented development project.

3.6. Briefly give some reasons why it might be preferable to use elapsed time rather than calendar dates in a contractual agreement.

3.7. Each operational feature should map to one and only one primary requirement. Quality attributes may apply to one, some, or all primary requirements. Provide an example of:

a. a quality attribute that maps to only one primary requirement in an Automated Teller System. State the quality attribute and the corresponding primary requirement.

b. a quality attribute that maps to some, but not all primary requirements in an Automated Teller System. State the quality attribute and the corresponding primary requirements.

c. a quality attribute that maps to all primary requirements in the technical specifications for an Automated Teller System.

For each of the following exercises, form a small team (three or four members). Conduct these exercises alone if it is not possible to form a team.

A Home Control Unit (HCU) consists of a server, a user-friendly interface, and numerous peripheral devices of various kinds. An HCU can include various facilities, such as surveillance, security, and programmable control of entertainment and communication devices, kitchen appliances, and sprinkler systems.

3.8. Conduct a brainstorming exercise to develop 10 operational features and 5 quality attributes for an HCU.

3.9. Identify three kinds of stakeholders for a Home Control Unit and briefly describe how they would interact with, or be affected by, individual HCUs and introduction of HCUs into the local community.

3.10. State five operational requirements for an HCU that would always be design goals; that is to say, it is not likely they could be, or would be, converted into technical specifications.

APPENDIX 3A

FRAMEWORKS, STANDARDS, AND GUIDELINES FOR PRODUCT FOUNDATIONS

3A.1 THE CMMI-DEV-v1.2 PROCESS AREAS FOR REQUIREMENTS DEVELOPMENT AND REQUIREMENTS MANAGEMENT

The CMMI-DEV-v1.2 process framework includes requirements development as a level-3 staged process and requirements management as a level-2 staged process [CMMI06]. The purpose, specific goals, and related processes of requirements development, as stated in CMMI-DEV-v1.2, are:

> The purpose of Requirements Development (RD) is to produce and analyze customer, product, and product component requirements.
>
> SG 1 Develop Customer Requirements
> SP 1.1 Elicit Needs
> SP 1.2 Develop the Customer Requirements
> SG 2 Develop Product Requirements
> SP 2.1 Establish Product and Product Component Requirements
> SP 2.2 Allocate Product Component Requirements
> SP 2.3 Identify Interface Requirements
> SG 3 Analyze and Validate Requirements
> SP 3.1 Establish Operational Concepts and Scenarios
> SP 3.2 Establish a Definition of Required Functionality
> SP 3.3 Analyze Requirements
> SP 3.4 Analyze Requirements to Achieve Balance
> SP 3.5 Validate Requirements
> Related process areas:
> Requirements Management
> Technical Solution
> Product Integration
> Verification process
> Validation process

Risk Management
Configuration Management

The term "customer" in CMMI includes both customer and users as those terms are used in this text.

The purpose, specific goals, and related processes of requirements management, as stated in CMMI-DEV-v1.2, are:

The purpose of Requirements Management (REQM) is to manage the requirements of the project's products and product components and to identify inconsistencies between those requirements and the project's plans and work products.

SG 1 Manage Requirements
SP 1.1 Obtain an Understanding of Requirements
SP 1.2 Obtain Commitment to Requirements
SP 1.3 Manage Requirements Changes
SP 1.4 Maintain Bidirectional Traceability of Requirements
SP 1.5 Identify Inconsistencies Between Project Work and Requirements

Related process areas:
Requirements Development
Technical Solution
Project Planning
Configuration Management
Project Monitoring and Control
Risk Management

3A.2 PRODUCT FOUNDATIONS IN ISO/IEC AND IEEE/EIA STANDARDS 12207

The 12207 standards emphasize the relationship between acquirer and supplier, as well as the acquirer's role and the supplier's role in a contractual relationship [IEEE12207]. As illustrated in figure 2 of IEEE/EIA Standard 12207.2–1997, the acquirer must develop:

- the system requirements,
- the acquisition plan,
- the acceptance criteria, and
- a request for proposals (RFP).

Potential suppliers must make a bid decision and prepare a response; if selected, the supplier then prepares a project plan.

As stated in Section 5.3 of 12207.0, activities related to establishing the technical foundations of the supplier's project include:

- system requirements analysis,
- system architectural design, and
- software requirements analysis.

3A.3 IEEE/EIA STANDARD 1058

This chapter is predominantly concerned with establishing the product foundations for a software project. The format and contents of the 1058 standard for software project management plans (a process foundation) are presented in Chapter 4.

3A.4 THE PMI BODY OF KNOWLEDGE

Section 1.3.3, of A Guide to the Project Management Body of Knowledge (Projects and Strategic Planning) [PMI04] states that projects are typically conducted to achieve strategic goals and are typically authorized as a result of:

- a market demand,
- an organizational need,
- a customer request,
- a technological advance, or
- a legal requirement.

Other elements of PMBOK that relate to project initiation include developing a project charter and a statement of project scope. The project charter is the authorization document for the project. The project scope defines, at a high level, the project work activities and deliverable work products, the methods to be used in controlling the project, and methods of product acceptance.

4

PLANS AND PLANNING

A plan in the mind of a man is not a plan.
—Richard H. Thayer

4.1 INTRODUCTION TO THE PLANNING PROCESS

By definition, every project of every kind is an endeavor of limited duration that uses resources to achieve stated objectives. A project plan specifies, among other things, the duration of the project, the resources needed, and how the resources will be applied to achieve the stated objectives. Software requirements (discussed in Chapter 3) provide the objectives for the product to be developed or modified. The planning process is concerned with developing the various elements of a project plan and documenting the plan in a specified format.

Your software project management plan must be a written document; otherwise, various stakeholders in the project will have differing interpretations of how the project will be conducted, and there will be no documentation of plans for effort, cost, schedule, resources, and supporting activities. The project plan also provides a vehicle for trade studies and for negotiating trade-offs among cost, schedule, and requirements, both initially and as changes occur. Baseline control of the written project plan supports systematic updating of the plan and communication of changes.

In the best case, your planning process will begin with tailoring of your organization's standard processes to fit the management, software development, and supporting processes of your project. In that case the information in this chapter can be used as a checklist against which you can compare your organization's planning processes and document templates.

Managing and Leading Software Projects, by Richard E. Fairley

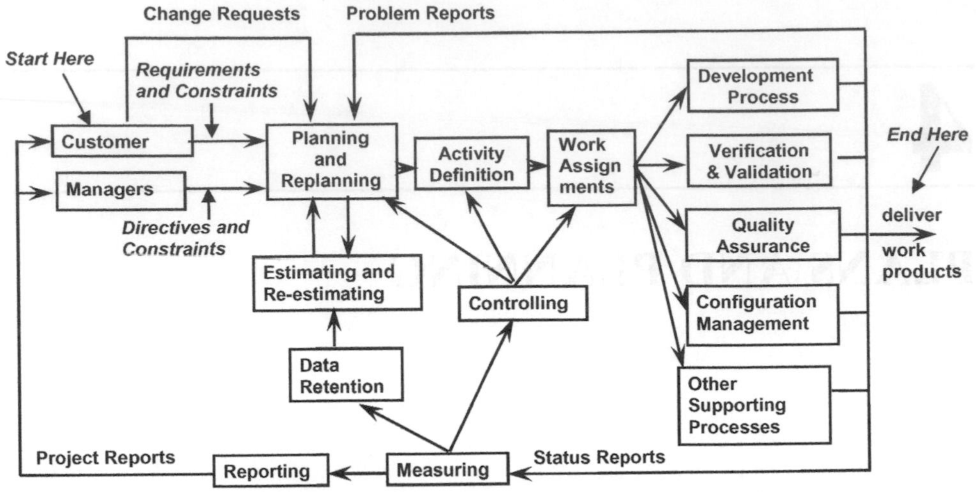

FIGURE 4.1 A workflow model for software projects

In the worst case, you will have to develop your project plan without any organizational structures or guidelines. In the absence of organizational structures and guidelines, the workflow model for managing software projects presented in Figure 1.1 (repeated here as Figure 4.1), the system engineering model presented in Figure 2.1*b*, and the development models and supporting processes described in Chapter 2, plus the information in this chapter can provide a tailorable framework for planning and executing software projects.

Project planning, like all elements of software development, is best accomplished in an iterative manner; details are added as understanding grows.

4.2 OBJECTIVES OF THIS CHAPTER

After reading this chapter and completing the exercises, you should understand:

- the planning process for software projects
- the project planning process area of CMMI-DEV-v1.2
- an approach to planning Agile projects
- a template for software project management plans (SPMPs)
- tailoring the SPMP template
- techniques for preparing a SPMP

The planning process presented in this chapter is informed by the Project Planning process area of the CMMI-DEV-v1.2 process framework, the planning elements of ISO and IEEE Standards 12207, IEEE Standard 1058, and the PMI Body of Knowledge. These elements are described in Appendix 4A to this chapter. An annotated version of IEEE Standard 1058 is presented in Appendix 4B.

An electronic copy of the annotated version of IEEE Standard 1058, presentation slides for this chapter, and other supporting material are available at the URL listed in the Preface to this text. Terms used in this chapter and throughout this text are defined in the Glossary at the end of the text. Mechanisms and techniques of project planning and estimation are presented in Chapters 5 and 6 of this text.

4.3 THE PLANNING PROCESS

As depicted in the workflow model of Figure 1.1 in Chapter 1 of this text, repeated here as Figure 4.1, inputs to planning include the customer's requirements and constraints as well management directives and constraints. The system requirements, system design, and software requirements may also be available or they are developed during project initiation. As discussed in Chapter 3, customer's requirements include operational features, quality attributes, and design constraints for the envisioned product. Constraints imposed by the customer may include both product and process constraints.

A product constraint might require that the system be developed using a specified version of an operating system or that the new or modified system provide an SQL interface to an existing database. A process constraint might require that the system be delivered in a staged sequence of increasing capabilities or that the source code for the deliverable software plus the requirements and design documentation be delivered to an independent agent for final verification and validation.

Management directives may include a policy statement that all projects must produce design documentation and verify it for completeness, correctness, and consistency using peer reviews. A management constraint might limit your project resources to a staffing level of 10 software developers.

Some of your first tasks as project manager are to establish a pattern of ongoing communication with the designated customer representative (your primary point of contact), and to clarify with him/her/them the operational requirements, development constraints, and success criteria for the project.

As stated in Chapter 3, each operational requirement must be prioritized as Essential, Desirable, or Optional to facilitate achievement of a balance among requirements, schedule, and budget. Sufficient time and resources must be provided to implement all of the Essential requirements and as many of the Desirable requirements as desired by the customer.

Depending on the nature and scope of your project, clarifying the operational requirements and developing the system requirements, system architecture, and software requirements may be your task. Alternatively, you may delegate it to one or more members of your planning team, or they may be provided as the starting point for your planning process.

Your understanding of the operational requirements and development constraints will influence your choice of the development model to be used and the procedures to be followed. Considerations include:

- Development of a user-intensive system may require prototyping to clarify the operational requirements and to provide information for design of the user interface.
- Development of the software for an embedded system may require the participation of you and your technical leader on the system engineering team.

- Development of staged delivery of system capabilities based on stable requirements and a stable architecture may indicate that an incremental build strategy is appropriate.
- Development of a first-of-its-kind system may require an evolutionary development strategy.
- An Agile process may be appropriate for development and ongoing enhancement of a Web-based application or in cases where the requirements are evolving or changing rapidly.

Development models are presented in Chapter 2.

An external customer (an acquirer) will typically specify the amount of money and the time available for the project, which may have to be negotiated to achieve a balance with the requirements. An internal customer may or may not provide money and/or resources for the project but will undoubtedly specify a schedule constraint for completion of the project, which may have to be negotiated. In any case, a contractual agreement in the form of a Statement of Work or a Memo of Understanding that contains items such as those listed in Section 3.3.2 of this text should be negotiated and accepted by you and your customer. Other planning activities include establishing an initial baseline of requirements, preparing estimates, and negotiating constraints to obtain a balance among requirements, cost, and schedule.

According to IEEE Standard 12207.1, every kind of plan, whether it is a project plan, a configuration management plan, a quality assurance plan, a training plan, or other kind of plan should contain the following information [12207]:

- needs to be satisfied
- success criteria
- work activities to be accomplished
- schedule, budget, and resources
- quality control measures
- change procedures and tracking of project history
- interfaces to relevant stakeholders
- roles to be played
- responsibilities and authorities
- resource acquisition plan
- skills acquisition plan, as needed

In addition every kind of plan must undergo a formal review and be accepted by the appropriate stakeholders, including the initial version of and subsequent changes to the plan.

In conjunction with preparing the generic information listed above, planning the specifics of a software project should include the activities contained in Tables 4.1 and 4.2.

Although the activities in Tables 4.1 and 4.2 are in sequential order, it should be understood that they, like most activities in software engineering, are best accomplished in an iterative manner. It should also be understood that the planning

TABLE 4.1 Preplanning activities for software projects

Preplanning activities

- Establish a working relationship with your customer/acquirer and other project stakeholders
- Develop and/or clarify operational requirements and development constraints
- Prioritize operational requirements
- Establish the initial baseline of operational requirements
- Develop system requirements and system architecture, as appropriate
- Develop technical specifications for the software requirements
- Establish traceability among operational requirements, system requirements, and software requirements
- Obtain commitment to an initial version of the requirements by customer/acquirer and other appropriate stakeholders
- Establish an initial baseline of operational requirements and technical specifications
- Identify the resources needed and a schedule for developing the initial version of the project plan

TABLE 4.2A Comprehensive scope of planning activities for software projects (part 1)

Planning activities

- Plan for ongoing interactions with the customer in reviews, demonstrations, approvals, and acceptance of the delivered product
- Plan for ongoing interactions with the user community in requirements elicitation, prototype demonstrations, and operational evaluations
- Prepare a preliminary estimate of effort, cost, and schedule to determine feasibility of the project within the constraints on those factors
- Refine the technical specifications for the system or product
- Specify a development process and supporting processes
- Develop an architecture decomposition view (ADV) of the product architecture and allocate requirements to the elements of the ADV
- Specify the interfaces among modules in the ADV and the interfaces between modules and the external environment
- Develop a work breakdown structure that includes work elements for the ADV modules
- Develop work packages for the tasks in the work breakdown structure (WBS)
- Define a schedule of objectively measurable milestones
- Prepare a schedule network and identify the critical path(s)
- Prepare a PERT (Program Evaluation and Review Technique) estimate of project duration
- Identify numbers and kinds of resources needed, when they will be needed, and for how long
- Prepare an estimate of optimal effort, cost, schedule, and resources
- Negotiate with the customer to obtain a balance among requirements, cost, resources, and project duration that satisfies the project constraints
- Finalize a contractual agreement with the customer that provides a balance among requirements, schedule, resources, and cost

TABLE 4.2B Comprehensive scope of planning activities for software projects (part 2)

Planning activities
• Define the organizational structure of the project team and specify roles, responsibilities, and authorities
• Establish the engineering environment to include standards, procedures, and tools for software development, verification, and validation
• Specify a version control process and a version control tool
• Establish a change control board for the project
• Identify work products to be placed under version control
• Establish a change control process that includes an impact analysis process
• Specify objective acceptance criteria for placing new and modified work products under version control
• Plan for verification and validation of work products
• Develop a measurement plan to measure and report quantity and quality of work products, effort, cost, progress, defects and other quality measures
• Develop a risk management plan to identify and confront risk factors on an on-going basis
• Develop plans, as appropriate, for the following kinds of activities:
◦ management of subcontractors and vendors
◦ coordination with associated projects and programs
◦ coordination with the Independent (big "I") verification and validation organization
◦ information security, including security clearances and access to information within various organizational entities
◦ approvals as required by regulations, licensing agreements, and rights-in-data
◦ installation, user training, and transition
◦ ongoing maintenance activities
◦ management of computing resources, facilities management, physical security
◦ backup protection of product and process data
• Prepare a plan for updating the project plan on a periodic basis and as events dictate
• Document the project plan using the organization's standard format, a tailored format based on IEEE Standard 1058 [IEEE1058], or the format in Table 4.4 of this text
• Review the project plan with the customer, higher level managers, and other appropriate stakeholders; revise as needed
• Obtain commitment to the plan by the appropriate stakeholders
• Place the plan under version control, thus establishing the initial baseline of the plan

activities in Tables 4.1 and 4.2 may be more comprehensive than necessary for your project; they should be tailored to fit the needs of the project.

The items tagged "as appropriate" in Table 4.2 may not apply to your project; all other items in the list should be addressed at a level of detail appropriate for the nature and scope of your project and the criticality of the system or product to be developed. Items in Table 4.2 that are not included in your planning activities should be noted in the project plan, and brief justifications should be provided for not including them.

If you are fortunate to work in a well-managed organization most of the activities Tables 4.1 and 4.2 will have standard processes, procedures, and tools that will require little, if any, tailoring for your project. For example, the configuration management and independent testing processes may be standardized; there may be a set of development process models to choose from; there may be organizational units that have trained personnel, procedures, and tools for most or all of the supporting processes; and there may be internal consultants to assist in tailoring a template and preparing the project plan.

If you are not so fortunate, the planning process can require a large amount of effort. In this case it is tempting to circumvent most of the planning activities listed above. The risk to project success must be assessed for the items that are not planned; for example:

- What risks are incurred if you don't have a process for managing changes to requirements?
- What risks are incurred if you don't have a process for assessing the impact of changes to requirements, cost, schedule, or technology?
- What risks are incurred if you don't have a schedule with objective milestones?
- What risks are incurred if you don't have a process for measuring effort and defects?
- What risks are incurred if you don't practice risk management?

These issues and other aspects of project risk are presented in Chapter 9.

Of course, the level of detail in your plan should be appropriate to the scope and criticality of your project. The plan may consist of a few pages for a small project or many pages for a large project. An additional consideration is that the planning activities listed above may not be accomplished in the order listed. For example, some elements of the contractual agreement may be specified in a legally binding contract before you, the project manager, become involved in the project.

Planning activities should occur in a manner that fits the needs of the situation; for example, some planning activities may occur in an evolutionary manner, as in situations where requirements evolve and schedule milestones indicate that a working version of the system is to be demonstrated to the customer on a weekly basis. In these situations planning what to do next will evolve as the situation evolves.

4.4 THE CMMI-DEV-V1.2 PROCESS AREA FOR PROJECT PLANNING

According to CMMI-DEV-v1.2, the purpose of the project planning process is to establish and maintain plans that define project activities. Other CMMI-DEV-v1.2 process areas related to project planning include:

- requirements development,
- requirements management,
- risk management, and
- the technical solution process areas.

Specific goals of project planning in CMMI-DEV-v1.2 include establishing estimates, developing a project plan, and obtaining commitment to the plan. Specific practices related to these specific goals are listed in Table 4.3. The nature of those

TABLE 4.3 CMMI-DEV-v1.2 specific goals and practices of project planning

	Specific Practices	Chapters of This Text
	SG 1 establish estimates	
SP 1.1-1	Estimate the scope of the project	Chapter 3
SP 1.2-1	Establish estimates of work product and task attributes	Chapter 5
SP 1.3-1	Define project life cycle	Chapter 2
SP 1.4-1	Determine estimates of effort and cost	Chapter 6
	SG 2 develop a project plan	
SP 2.1-1	Establish the budget and schedule	Chapter 6
SP 2.2-1	Identify project risks	Chapter 9
SP 2.3-1	Plan for data management	Chapters 7 & 8
SP 2.4-1	Plan for project resources	Chapter 5
SP 2.5-1	Plan for needed knowledge and skills	Chapter 5
SP 2.6-1	Plan stakeholder involvement	Chapter 2
SP 2.7-1	Establish the project plan	Chapter 4
	SG 3 obtain commitment to the plan	
SP 3.1-1	Review plans that affect the project	Chapter 4
SP 3.2-1	Reconcile work and resource levels	Chapter 6
SP 3.3-1	Obtain plan commitment	Chapter 4

specific practices is discussed here. Techniques for accomplishing these practices are presented in subsequent chapters, as indicated in the third column of Table 4.3.

An estimate of effort, schedule, and resources based on requirements and constraints is an essential element of a project plan; stated differently, it is not possible to develop a plan without estimates, and it is not possible to develop estimates without requirements. The CMMI-DEV-v1.2 process areas of requirements development and requirements management (presented in Chapter 3) are thus closely related to the project planning process area.

Estimating the scope of a project is concerned with identifying all of the work activities to be accomplished. A work breakdown structure is typically used to document the scope of a project; work breakdown structures are presented in Chapter 5. Product size and complexity are the primary factors typically used to determine the amount of effort that will be required to develop a software product. Other factors include required performance, reliability, safety, and security. Therefore establishing estimates of product attributes such as size and complexity is a specific practice of specific goal SG 1 (SP 1.2-1). Other factors that will impact effort and schedule should also be considered.

An appropriate development model for a software project depends on the scope of work to be accomplished, the attributes of the product, and the phases of development to be included. SP 1.3-1 is concerned with defining a software development model that includes a set of development phases appropriate for the project scope and product attributes. Based on the outcomes of specific practices 1.1-1, 1.2-1, and

1.3-1, an estimate of effort and cost is developed using historical data, expert judgment, and other techniques presented in Chapter 6 of this text.

Achieving specific goal SG 1 in Table 4.3 provides the foundation for achieving SG 2, Develop a Project Plan. A project plan that satisfies SG 2 will contain a schedule and a budget that satisfy the effort and cost estimates developed in satisfying SG 1; said another way, effort, schedule, and cost estimates provide constraints that cannot be exceeded in the project plan.

Because effort is the product of people and time, a schedule can be derived from an effort estimate; for example, 54 person-months of effort might be scheduled as 6 persons for 9 months. The schedule specifies the predecessor tasks that must be completed, and the work products produced by those tasks that must be available, before subsequent tasks can begin; the schedule also specifies the successor tasks that can be performed after each task is completed. Sequencing constraints among work activities are thereby specified, and opportunities for concurrent work activities are identified. The budget is then allocated to each of the tasks to be accomplished.

A risk is a potential problem that (should it become a problem) will adversely impact a successful outcome of delivering an acceptable product on time and within budget. Risk factors should be identified in the project plan and appropriate mitigation actions planned. Risk management for software projects is presented in Chapter 9.

SP 2.3-1 in Table 4.3 involves developing a plan for management of project data, which includes all of the data in all areas of the project (project management, development processes, and supporting processes). The plan should specify the project data to be collected, a schedule for collecting and validating the data, report formats and distribution lists, and any requirements for privacy and security of project data.

SP 2.4-1 and SP 2.5-1 are concerned with identifying and planning for the resources necessary to perform a project. Resources include quantities of people and required skill levels, software tools, computing hardware, facilities, travel budget, and all other resources needed to conduct a project (SP 2.4-1). Because people are typically the most important resource for a software project, it is important to identify the knowledge and skill levels needed to perform a project (SP 2.5-1).

Stakeholders are people whose involvement in a project is necessary or desirable to ensure a successful outcome. Different kinds of people may have different kinds and amounts of involvement during different phases of a project. For example, involvement of user representatives is more important during requirements definition and product acceptance than during detailed design and coding. SP 2.6-1 is concerned with planning for involvement of identified stakeholders.

Achievement of SG 2 in Table 3.1 culminates in SP 2.7-1 (Establish the Project Plan). Format and contents of a software project management plan are presented and discussed in the following section of this chapter.

Obtain Commitment to the Plan (SG 3) includes three specific practices. SP 3.1-1 involves reviewing all plans that affect the project to understand project commitments. For example, documentation of requirements, plans for some or all of the supporting processes, and plans for activities such as installing the delivered system and training of users are typically developed and documented separately, and referenced in the project plan.

SP 3.2-1 (Reconcile Work and Resource Levels) is concerned with reconciling differences between estimates and available resources. An estimate might, for example, indicate that 10 people having specified skills will be needed to complete a project in the required 12 months. Perhaps the budget will support only 7 people at the requisite skill level.

Acceptable options for reconciling differences between the work to be done, resources, and available time include:

- reducing the requirements (de-scoping),
- increasing the quantity of resources (and the corresponding budget),
- using more productive resources, and
- extending the schedule.

Unacceptable options for achieving a balance among the work to be done, resources, and available time (i.e., requirements, effort, and schedule) in the project plan include descoping plans for measurement and control, peer reviews, and verification and validation; and planning for overtime.

The final step in the CMMI® Project Planning process area is obtaining commitment to the plan by the stakeholders who are responsible for performing and supporting execution of the plan. Commitments to each work activity identified in SP 1.1-1 should be obtained from the relevant stakeholders internal to your project as well as any external stakeholders such as senior management, external customer, and associated projects. Organizational interfaces and technical interface specifications should be specified and commitments must be obtained from the appropriate stakeholders to participate in maintaining the interfaces. At minimum, stakeholders will include you, your software architect, the quality assurance group, your manager, and a customer representative (e.g., the marketing department, or an external customer).

The approach to project planning indicated in Tables 4.1 and 4.2 and by the Project Planning process area of CMMI-DEV-v1.2 is the basis of the so-called plan-driven approach to managing software projects. It must be emphasized that the comprehensive set of tasks in Tables 4.1 and 4.2 and the specific goals and practices of CMMI-DEV-v1.2 are sufficient for the largest and most complex software projects. They must be tailored and adapted to fit the needs of each project. Unfortunately, some people misinterpret the plan-driven approach and reject it as being too cumbersome and bureaucratic without understanding that a plan must be tailored and adapted to the needs of each situation. The plan-driven approach to project planning is appropriate in two situations:

1. when there is a formal contractual agreement between an acquirer and a supplier, and/or
2. for large, complex projects internal to an organization.

4.4.1 Planning Agile Projects

An Agile approach may be appropriate for small projects (e.g., 10 or fewer software developers) when formal contractual conditions do not apply and in cases where the requirements are evolving or changing on a continuing basis and frequent delivery of evolving capabilities are to be delivered to users, for example, in a web-based application. The Agile development process is described in Section 2.5.3. As related there, planning for an Agile project involves:

- working with the customer to develop the product vision,
- determining project duration and level of effort to be applied,
- obtaining the commitment of a knowledgeable customer representative for ongoing involvement in the project,
- establishing the development environment,
- planning the frequency of iterations, and
- planning the frequency of delivery of evolving capabilities to users.

In addition a design metaphor must be established by the developers and the particular version of an Agile process to be used must be adopted and accepted by the project stakeholders; the Scrum version of Agile development is discussed in Section 2.5.3. A plan for ongoing reviews with customers, developers, and other stakeholders must be established, as must plans for periodically reviewing the planned and actual state of affairs and for reconciling differences. As with all software projects, initial assessment of risk factors and plans for ongoing risk management must be established. Planning an Agile project thus involves:

- developing the product vision;
- determining the project duration and level of effort;
- obtaining commitment of a knowledgeable customer representative;
- establishing the development environment;
- planning the frequency of iterations;
- planning the frequency of deliveries;
- establishing a design metaphor;
- adopting a version of Agile development;
- planning for ongoing reviews by the stakeholders;
- planning for periodic reviews of project status;
- conducting an initial risk assessment and risk mitigation; and
- planning for ongoing risk assessments and mitigation activities.

4.4.2 Balancing Agility and Discipline

As related in Chapter 2, the text *Balancing Agility and Discipline* by Boehm and Turner contrasts plan-driven and Agile approaches to software development and presents a middle-ground approach to achieving a balance that incorporates aspects of both approaches based on each particular situation [BOEHM04].

4.5 A MINIMAL PROJECT PLAN

At minimum, a plan for a software project, whether plan-driven or Agile, must include the following information:

- a statement of the purpose and objectives of the project
- identification of stakeholders and their objectives
- software development model to be used
- software development environment to be used
- platform technology to be used
- scope of work activities to be completed
- schedule of work activities including periodic, objective milestones
- skill levels and numbers of software personnel needed
- when various numbers and kinds of software personnel will be needed
- resources in addition to software personnel
- a plan for periodically reporting project status
- a risk management plan

As has been repeatedly emphasized, these elements of a project plan must be based on the development model to be used and scaled to the size and complexity of the project. Techniques for developing and documenting these elements of a project plan are presented in subsequent chapters.

The following sections of this chapter provide a template for and a description of the elements of a comprehensive plan-driven plan, an example of tailoring the template, and techniques for reducing the effort required to develop a software project management plan.

4.6 A TEMPLATE FOR SOFTWARE PROJECT MANAGEMENT PLANS

In the absence of a standard format for project plans in your organization, the template presented in Tables 4.4*a*, *b*, and *c* can be used. This template is similar to the format for project plans specified in IEEE/EIA Standard 1058. The template is comprehensive and is intended for the largest and most complex projects. It can be, and should be, tailored to fit the needs of each project; an example of tailoring is presented later in this chapter. The lengthy template is presented in three tables for ease of presentation. The topics in the tables are discussed in numerous places throughout the text; the "Discussed In" column of each table indicates the chapters and sections where the primary discussion of each topic is presented.

An annotated version of the template is contained in Appendix 4B of this chapter. In the appendix a series of questions is posed to assist you in preparing your project plan. An on-line version of the template that provides an easy-to-use outline for preparing project plans can be obtained at the URL listed in the Preface to this text.

An overview of the various elements of the template is presented in the following sections.

4.6.1 Front Matter

There are nine major sections in the template for software project management plans based on IEEE Standard 1058 plus the "front matter," which includes a title

TABLE 4.4A Template for a Software Project Management Plan (part 1)

Contents	Discussed In
Front matter	Section 4.4.1
Title Page	
Revision History	
Preface	
Table of Contents	
List of Figures	
List of Tables	
Project summary	Section 4.4.2
1. Project Summary	
1.1 Purpose, Scope, and Objectives	
1.2 Assumptions	Section 4.4.2
1.3 Constraints	
1.4 Project Deliverables	Chapter 1
1.5 Schedule and Budget Summary	
Evolution, references, definitions	Section 4.4.3
2 Evolution of the Plan	
3 References	
4 Definitions	
Project organization	Section 4.4.4
5. Project Organization	
5.1 Project Interfaces	
5.2 Project Structure	Chapter 1
5.3 Roles and Responsibilities	Chapter 8

page, a revision history, a preface, and perhaps a table of contents, a list of figures, and a list of tables. The title page should contain:

- the project name,
- the version number of the plan,
- the date of issue,
- the name of the responsible party (you),
- your organization, and
- your contact information (telephone numbers, e-mail address).

Your project plan must be placed under version control as soon as commitment to it is obtained from the appropriate stakeholders.[18] As the plan evolves, the revision history will include an entry for each prior version of the plan. Each entry should include:

[18] see Section 3.2.5 for a discussion of version control

- the version number,
- date of release,
- sections changed, and
- the nature of the changes made.

In some situations it may be appropriate that each version of the plan (including the initial version) include the names, signatures, and titles of the persons who are authorized and responsible for approving the initial plan and changes to the plan. This person might be an external customer (the acquirer), or you, the project manager, in the case of an internal project.

The Preface should address the following issues:

- the purpose of the project,
- the context in which the project will occur, and
- the intended audience of the plan

Depending on the scope and formality of your project plan, it may be appropriate to include a table of contents, a list of figures, and a list of tables.

4.6.2 Project Summary

Section 1 of a software project management plan provides a summary of the project (sometimes referred to as the "executive summary"). The summary, as indicated in Table 4.4*a*, includes the purpose, scope, and objectives of the project.

Purpose, scope, and objectives of your project plan should address the following issues:

- purpose: the reason your organization is doing the project and the business needs or contractual agreements to be satisfied by the outcomes of the project
- scope: the scope of the project specifies the major work activities to be conducted and the relationship of this project to other projects and other ongoing activities
- objectives: the success criteria for the project; the objectives that must be satisfied to ensure an acceptable outcome; the work products to be delivered; and methods to be used in determining that the objectives have been satisfied
- exclusions: scope and objectives that are explicitly excluded from this project and/or from the resulting work products

The purpose should present the motivation for conducting the project, which might be, for example, to replace an existing system, to upgrade an existing system, to provide an automated system to replace a manual process, or to conduct a feasibility study and build a prototype of a future product. The purpose of the ATM project, for example, might be to replace or upgrade an existing ATM system, to provide a first-time ATM system for a financial institution, or to conduct a feasibility study and build a prototype of an advanced user interface for an ATM system. The prototype might involve using thumb prints, RFID cards, retinal scans, facial scans, or voice recognition and spoken commands for the user interface.

The scope of work activities for a project (e.g., the ATM system) might include refinement of the operational requirements, development of the technical specifications, design and implementation of the software, validation by an independent group, training of users, installation of the software at multiple sites. Or, it might be limited to modifying the design of an existing product and re-implementing some features, which would result in a new version of the product.

The objectives of your project should specify, as clearly as possible, the success criteria for the project. It may be that the delivery date is the most critical success factor, even if fewer features than desired are included in the delivered product. Or, it may be that developing an architectural structure for a family of products (a product line) that will maximize reuse of components in future systems is of high priority even if it means extending the schedule beyond the planned completion date.

In some cases it is important to clearly state what activities are excluded from the scope of your project. It might be, for example, that based on sensitivity of the customer's data, your project will not include testing of the system in the users' environment. Or, because your project involves improving the performance of some elements of a customer's operational system, and because the users must not be impacted by the changes, the user interface must not be modified.

Assumptions are conditions on which your project plan is based that you have not verified or are unable to verify at this time. You might assume, for example, that sufficient numbers of personnel who have the necessary skills will be available when needed. Or, you might assume that product complexity will not be a problem because you expect to have software developers who are familiar with this kind of system. Section 1.2 should list the factors and conditions that you assume will be true.

Constraints (section 1.3 of the management plan) are externally imposed conditions that your project must satisfy. Constraints are categorized as design constraints and process constraints. A design constraint might require reuse of existing components or building specified interfaces to another system. A process constraint might limit the money, resources, and/or time available to conduct the project.

Section 2.3 should thus state limitations that have been imposed on factors such as:

- schedule,
- budget,
- resources,
- software to be incorporated,
- technologies to be used, and
- interfaces of the product to other systems.

Project deliverables should specify the following items:

- work products to be delivered to the customer (see section 1.3)
- when and where they will be delivered,

- quantities and media of delivery,
- any special packaging and handling instructions.

Project deliverables may be limited to object code and a users' manual or they might include source code, design documentation, and test suite, all under version control using a specified version control tool, perhaps because the customer intends to maintain and evolve the delivered work products. The deliverables listed in the project plan should reflect those listed in the contractual agreement (MOU or SOW) and other contractual documents. A reference to those documents should be included.

The final item in the executive summary (section 1.5) is a summary of the schedule and budget for the project. Topics to be addressed in section 1.5 include:

- the time frame for this project (stated in elapsed time or by start and end dates),
- the major milestones and when are they scheduled to occur (by elapsed time from start or by dates of occurrence),
- the overall cost (in dollars or staff-hours), and
- costs and schedules for supporting processes and additional plans that are not included in this plan, with references to the documentation for those plans.

The duration of the project can be stated in elapsed time (e.g., six months) or by start and end dates (e.g., 3/15/20xx to 9/15/20xx). Start and end dates are preferable because they make the plan more specific. Cost may be stated in monetary units or total units of effort (e.g., staff-months). The latter measure may be preferable because of organizational sensitivities. Major milestones, such as customer reviews and demonstrations that involve the user community, or planned deliveries of subset versions of the final system or product, should be included in the project summary.

Costs and schedules for supporting processes such as subcontractor management or verification and validation by an independent organization, and additional plans for the "as appropriate" activities listed in Table 4.4*a*, (user training, etc.) that are not contained in this project plan should be listed.

Because of the nature of the information in the project summary, this section is typically completed last.

4.6.3 Evolution, Definitions, and References

Section 2 of a project plan (evolution of the Plan) describes the plan for updating the project plan on a periodic basis and as events dictate. The following issues should be addressed:

- the planned schedule for periodic updating of the plan,
- conditions and events for which unscheduled updates will be made
- method of controlling changes to the plan, and
- methods used to issue updates to the appropriate stakeholders

You might, for example, plan to update the project plan on a monthly basis and, with the customer's involvement, revise the cost, schedule, and/or requirements when a customer's change request is out of scope for the current plan. Changes to the plan should be controlled by a (small) group of authorized individuals (the project CCB; see Section 3.2.5) and tracked using a version control tool. As explained in Section 3.2.5, the CCB should be scaled to fit the needs of the project; on a small project, the CCB may consist of you, the project manager, and the customer. Although it may not be thought of in this way, you and the customer are the (informal) CCB if your project uses an Agile development model.

On a large system-level program that involves multiple coordinated projects, there may be several CCBs; you may be a member of the large program control CCB in addition to being the chair of the software CCB. In any case, updated plans and a brief explanation of the changes made to the project plan must be communicated to appropriate stakeholders; notifications of changes might be distributed to an e-mail distribution list.

Section 3 of the template in Table 4.4*a* provides references to related documents. This section should list the documents that are related to the plan, such as the Concept of Operations and the Technical Specifications, and indicate where they can be found. As always, related documents (and the project plan) should be scaled to fit the needs of the project. The ConOps, for example, may be a vision statement of a few pages or a small set of use cases. The Technical Specifications may be a document of comparable size. On the other hand, the ConOps and Technical Specifications may each be large documents if the envisioned system is large and complex.

Documents to be referenced should include the product and process foundation documents listed in Table 3.1 (operational requirements, system requirements and architecture, software requirements, design constraints, and the contractual agreement). References should be provided for other applicable documents, such as additional contractual documents, and also references to plans for associated projects. References to organizational policies and procedures, and applicable standards and guidelines to be followed should be listed.

Note, in particular, that requirements documentation and the project plan should be cross-referenced and maintained for consistency among requirements, schedule, budget, resources, and risk factors; however, they should be separate documents because they address different issues and are intended for different audiences. Requirements documents should not contain any information related to schedules, budgets, resources, or facilities required to conduct the project. Similarly the project plan should not contain any product information other than a brief overview of the product to be developed or modified and a reference to the requirements documentation. Traceability matrices can be used to cross-reference the project plan and related documents (see Section 3.2.4). Physical locations where the related documents can be found should be provided and path names and passwords for accessing electronic files should be provided.

Section 4, definitions, provides explanations of terms and acronyms used in the plan that may not be familiar to the intended audience of the plan. The definitions section should indicate the meanings of terms and acronyms and include references to other documents that contain terminology needed to understand this plan (e.g.,

IEEE Standard 610.12™—IEEE Standard Glossary of Software Engineering Terminology).

4.6.4 Project Organization

Section 5 of the plan is concerned with the way in which the project is organized. It describes the project's communication interfaces, the organizational structure for the project, and the roles and responsibilities for those who will conduct the project work activities.

Project interfaces (section 5.1 of the SPMP) should indicate the organizational entities with which you and your project members will interact and the individuals who will be the points of contact in those organizations.

Project interfaces may exist between your project and supporting entities within your organization such as an independent testing group and the parent organization, and to external entities such as the acquiring organization, subcontractors, vendors, and affiliated projects. You can use organizational charts and diagrams to depict your project's organizational interfaces. Names, titles, phone numbers, and e-mail addresses should be listed for those with whom you will interact.

Section 5.2, project structure, addresses the following issues:

- how the development team will be organized;
- how the development team will interact with supporting entities such as configuration management, quality assurance, and verification and validation; and
- the points of contact and the lines of communication within the project.

In particular, section 5.2 of your project plan should indicate the ways in which you (the project manager), the software architect (who may be you), the team leaders, and the software developers will interact. Graphical devices such as organizational charts or diagrams can be used to illustrate the lines of authority, responsibility, and communication within the project. An example of an organization structure for a software project is depicted in Figure 1.3 of this text.

Section 5.3, roles and responsibilities, specifies:

- the roles that must be played to accomplish the various development activities and supporting processes,
- the organizational units that will play the roles, and
- the persons responsible for playing those roles within the organizational units.

This section should specify the job titles and necessary skills of individuals and organizational units that are responsible for the various work activities and supporting processes. The individuals whose names are known (perhaps now, perhaps later) can be assigned to the responsibilities. But first, the roles to be played in conducting the project are identified. A role (e.g., the designer role) may be played by one or more individuals. One individual may play multiple roles, concurrently and/or sequentially. For example, an individual may be a designer first and later become a programmer; an individual may concurrently be a tester and the keeper of evolving product versions on a small project. One or more matrices that trace roles to development activities and supporting processes can be used to depict project roles and responsibilities.

4.6.5 Managerial Processes

Section 6 of a software project management plan, managerial processes, is the essence of a project plan. It contains the start-up plan, the work plan, the project control plan, the risk management plan, and the closeout plan, as listed in Table 4.4*b*.

The start-up plan for your project (section 6.1) is concerned with developing a plan for making initial estimates, doing the estimates, and developing a staffing plan, a plan for acquiring other necessary resources, and a training plan for the project team (if needed). Depending on the size and scope of the project, these plans may be incorporated directly into the project plan, or the project plan may contain reference to other documents and electronic files that contain the start-up plans.

The project estimation plan (section 6.1.1) should address the following issues:

- the plan for making initial and ongoing estimates (who will do them?, when will they be done?, who will approve them?);
- the tools and techniques that will be used to make estimates;
- how the estimates will be documented;

TABLE 4.4B Template for a Software Project Management Plan (part 2)

Contents	Discussed In
Managerial processes	Section 4.4.5
6. Managerial Processes	
6.1 Start-up Plan	
6.1.1 Project Estimation	Chapter 6
6.1.2 Staffing Plan	Chapter 5
6.1.3 Resource Acquisition Plan	
6.1.4 Project Staff Training Plan	
6.2 Work Plan	
6.2.1 WBS and Work Packages	Chapter 5
6.2.2 Schedule Dependencies	Chapter 5
6.2.3 Resource Allocation	Chapter 5
6.2.4 Budget Allocation	Chapter 5
6.3 Project Control Plan	
6.3.1 Requirements	Chapters 3 and 7
6.3.2 Schedule	Chapter 8
6.3.3 Budget	Chapter 8
6.3.4 Quality	Chapter 7
6.3.5 Metrics Plan	Chapter 8
6.3.6 Reporting Plan	Chapters 7 and 8
6.4 Risk Management Plan	Chapter 9
6.5 Closeout Plan	

- plans for periodic re-estimation of cost, schedule, staffing, and other resources required to complete the project;
- frequency of re-estimation; and
- the plan for re-estimating when requirements or other project conditions change.

When an estimate is prepared, the following items should be documented:

- person(s) who made the estimate;
- methods, tools, and techniques used to make the estimate;
- historical data used as the basis of estimation; and
- the estimator's level of confidence in the estimate.

Estimation methods, tools, and techniques are presented in Chapter 6 of this text.

In some cases an estimate of cost, duration, and resources might be completed and commitments made before you develop the project plan at the level of detail indicated in Table 4.4*b*. In those cases you must still validate the estimate. If you think the estimate is not valid, you must re-negotiate requirements, schedule, and budget; otherwise, you risk failure before you start.

The staffing plan (section 6.1.2) should indicate:

- the kinds of skills required;
- the numbers of people needed who have those skills;
- when they will be needed;
- for how long;
- how they will be obtained; and
- the person, or persons, responsible for acquiring the necessary personnel.

Tools such as resource Gantt charts, resource histograms, spreadsheets, and tables can be used to depict the staffing plan by skill level, by project phase, and by aggregations of skill levels and project phases. These techniques are discussed in Chapter 5.

The resource acquisition plan (section 6.1.3) should address the following issues:

- resources, in addition to personnel, that will be needed;
- quantities of each kind of resource needed;
- when the resources will be needed;
- the person, or persons, responsible for obtaining the resources; and
- approvals needed.

The resources may include items such as computer hardware and software, service contracts, transportation, facilities, and administrative services.

The resource acquisition plan should specify the points in the project schedule when the various acquisition activities should occur. Constraints on acquiring the necessary resources should be specified. This section can be expanded into additional subsections (labeled as 6.1.3.x, etc.) to accommodate acquisition plans for the various types of resources to be acquired. References to resource acquisition plans contained in separate documents should be included here.

The project staff training plan (section 6.1.4) indicates the kind and extent of training needed to ensure that the necessary skill levels, in sufficient numbers, will be available to successfully conduct the software project.

The need for special training may depend on the nature of the product to be developed and the skills needed to do the work. If training is required, a training plan should include:

- the types of training to be provided,
- numbers of personnel to be trained,
- entry and exit criteria for training, and
- the training methods to be used (e.g., lectures, consultations, mentoring, or computer-assisted training).

As in all plans, the staff training plan should include:

- schedule,
- budget,
- milestones, and
- responsible parties.

The training plan should include training needed in both technical and managerial skills.

The work plan (section 6.2) describes the work activities and the details of schedules, resources, and budget for your software project. The four subsections contain the work breakdown structure (WBS) and work packages, the work activities to be performed, schedule dependencies, resource allocation, and budget allocation.

Section 6.2.1 (WBS and work packages) documents:

- the scope of work activities included in this project plan,
- partitioning of the work activities,
- the level of detail provided in the plan, and
- documentation of the work activities.

The scope of work activities and the partitioning of that work are specified at the top level of the WBS. A WBS is a hierarchical decomposition of work activities; it is a fundamental tool for planning and controlling software projects. During project planning an initial version of the WBS should be developed. Work activities in the initial WBS should be decomposed so that:

- accurate estimates of resource requirements and schedule duration for each major work activity can be made,

- opportunities for reuse of software components can be identified, and
- the project's risk factors are exposed (both technical and managerial).

The level of decomposition for different work activities in the work breakdown structure may be different depending on factors such as the quality of the requirements, familiarity of the work, novelty of the technology to be used, and software components to be reused.

Work packages are used to specify, for each work activity, factors such as:

- the resources needed,
- estimated duration,
- work products to be produced,
- acceptance criteria for the work products,
- predecessor and successor work activities, and
- risk factors for the work activity.

Techniques and guidelines for constructing work breakdown structures and preparing work packages are presented in Chapter 5.

Schedule dependencies (section 6.2.2) indicate:

- tasks must be completed before subsequent tasks can begin;
- tasks that can be accomplished concurrently with other tasks; and
- schedule constraints imposed by dependencies on external factors such as vendor-supplied equipment and software, subcontractor-supplied software, and interfaces to other system components.

Tasks are the lowest level work activities in a WBS hierarchy; they are also the elements of the schedule. The project schedule should include frequent milestones that can be assessed for attainment using objective indicators to assess the scope and quality of work products completed at those milestones. Techniques that can be used to specify scheduling relationships include milestone charts, activity lists, schedule networks, critical path networks, PERT charts, activity Gantt charts, and resource Gantt charts. Examples and illustrations are provided in Chapter 5.

Resource allocation (section 6.2.3) documents, for each work activity in the work breakdown structure, the following:

- kinds and numbers of resources needed (people and other resources),
- when they are needed, and
- for how long.

Resources to be allocated include personnel by skill level, and may include hardware elements, software tools, travel budget, testing and simulation facilities, and administrative support. A table that documents, for each task, the resources required and when the task is scheduled to occur should be provided, plus an inverse table that shows, for each resource, the tasks to which it is allocated and when the task is scheduled to occur. The necessary data for these tables can be obtained from the work packages and the schedule network.

Budget allocation (section 6.2.4) documents the budget components allocated to each work activity and task in the WBS. The task-by-task budget should include the estimated cost for personnel by skill level to accomplish each task (in monetary units or staff-hours) and may include, as appropriate, costs for items such as travel, meetings with customer and users, computing resources, software development tools, testing tools, and administrative support for each work activity.

Budgets for higher level activities in the WBS (the sum of budgets for lower level activities and tasks in the WBS) should be documented. The total budget for each type of resource and their sum (the overall project budget) should be provided. The budget allocation can be developed in tabular form using a spreadsheet.

Section 6.3 of the project management plan (the project control plan) specifies the control procedures to be used in meeting product requirements, schedule, budget, and the quality standards of work processes and work products. Also, a plan for collecting project data and a reporting plan must be developed. Each element of the control plan should be consistent with your organization's standards, policies, and procedures for controlling software projects and should satisfy any contractual agreements for project control.

The requirements control plan (section 6.3.1) should address the following issues:

- how the requirements will be initially accepted as a product baseline;
- control mechanisms that will be used to measure, report, and control changes to the requirements baseline; and
- how the impact of requirements changes on product scope and quality, and project schedule, budget, resources, and risk factors will be assessed.

Configuration management mechanisms for controlling the requirements should include change control procedures, a version control tool, and a change control board. Techniques that can be used to measure and control requirements include traceability, prototyping, impact analysis, and reviews. These and other techniques are discussed in Chapter 3 of this text.

The schedule control plan (section 6.3.2) indicates the techniques that will be used to:

- measure and report the progress of work completed at the major and minor project milestones,
- compare actual progress to planned progress at the milestones, and
- implement corrective action when actual progress does not conform to planned progress.

Achievement of schedule milestones should be assessed using objective criteria to measure the quantity and quality of work products completed at each major and minor milestone.

The budget control plan (section 6.3.3) is concerned with:

- how the cost of completed work is to be determined,
- how comparisons of budgeted costs to actual costs will be made,
- how the cost of corrective action will be tracked, and
- tools and techniques that will be used to track and control the budget.

The budget plan should include frequent milestones that can be assessed for achievement using objective indicators to assess the quantity and quality of work products completed at those milestones. Mechanisms such as binary tracking and earned value reporting should be used to measure and report schedule progress and the cost of work completed versus work planned for completion. These mechanisms are described in Chapter 8.

The quality control plan (section 6.3.4) documents the mechanisms that will be used to measure and control the quality of the work processes and the evolving work products. Quality control mechanisms may include audits of work processes, verification and validation of work products, reviews, root cause analysis, and process assessments. Technical performance measurement can be used to track technical parameters that are allocated to individual elements of the system or product, such as actual versus allocated memory bytes and execution time cycles. Details are provided in Chapters 7 and 8.

The metrics plan (section 6.3.5) addresses the following issues:

- process and product data to be collected;
- how the data will be collected and validated;
- who will collect and validate project data;
- methods, tools, and techniques to be used;
- frequency of collecting the various types of metrics data;
- mechanisms for validating the metrics data; and
- how will the data be retained for future use.

Process and product metrics to be collected and validated should be consistent with the needs of the project and the reporting plan.

The reporting plan (section 6.3.6) documents:

- the mechanisms, report formats, and information flows that will be used to communicate the status of requirements, schedule, budget, scope, quality, and other status metrics;
- the kinds of reports that will be prepared;
- who will prepare and distribute the reports;
- frequency of preparing and distributing each type of report;
- formats to be used;
- methods, tools, and techniques that will be used; and
- individuals who will receive copies.

The nature of and frequency of reporting project status should be consistent with the project scope, criticality, risk, visibility, organizational policies, and contractual requirements. Metrics and reporting are discussed in Chapters 7 and 8.

Section 6.4 of the plan contains the risk management plan for your project. A risk is a potential problem that, if it materializes, will have a negative impact on your project. The risk management plan documents the following topics:

- mechanisms that will be used to identify, analyze, and prioritize project risk factors;
- mechanisms for developing action plans and contingency plans;
- staff members who will implement the plans;
- methods to be used to track the identified risk factors, evaluate changes in the levels of risk factors, and respond to those changes;
- staff members who will be responsible for monitoring risk factors; and
- how risk factors will be continuously identified, assessed, and mitigated on an ongoing basis during the project.

The kinds of risk factors that should be considered include:

- risks in the acquirer-supplier relationship;
- contractual risks;
- technological risks;
- risks caused by the size and complexity of the product;
- risks in the development and target environments;
- risks in personnel acquisition, skill levels, and retention;
- risks to schedule and budget;
- risks in vendor and subcontractor relations; and
- risks in achieving customer and user acceptance of the product.

Risk management is covered in Chapter 9.

The project closeout plan (section 6.5) documents:

- conditions and events that will indicate completion of the project;
- postmortem meetings and lessons-learned briefings that will be held;
- how lessons learned and analysis of project objectives achieved (and not achieved) will be documented, distributed, and archived;
- the plan for archiving project work materials; and
- how project members will be reassigned.

The remaining elements of the template for software project management plans (technical processes, supporting processes, additional plans, appendices, and index) are listed in Table 4.4*c* and discussed in the following sections.

4.6.6 Technical Processes

Section 7 of the plan (technical processes) documents the development processes to be used. This is the section where you specify the technical methods, tools, and

TABLE 4.4C Template for a Software Project Management Plan (part 3)

Contents	Discussed In
Technical processes	Section 4.4.6
7. Technical Processes	
7.1 Development Process Model	Chapter 2
7.2 Methods, Tools, and Techniques	
7.3 Infrastructure Plan	
7.4 Product Acceptance Plan	
Supporting processes	Section 4.4.7
8. Supporting Processes	
8.1 Configuration Management	Chapter 3
8.2 Verification and Validation	Chapter 2
8.3 Documentation	Chapter 1
8.4 Quality Assurance	Chapter 1
8.5 Reviews and Audits	Chapter 2
8.6 Problem Resolution	Chapter 1
8.7 Subcontractor Management	Chapter 1
8.8 Process Improvement	
Additional plans, appendixes, index	Section 4.4.8
9. Additional Plans	
Appendices	
Index	

techniques to be used; plans for establishing and maintaining the project infrastructure; and the product acceptance plan.

Section 7.1 (development process model) specifies:

- the development process model that will be used to develop the software product, and
- tailoring of the process model for this project.

The development process model should be described in sufficient detail to document:

- the relationships among major development activities and supporting processes (by specifying the flow of information and work products among activities and tasks),
- sequencing constraints among work products to be generated,
- reviews to be conducted,
- major milestones to be achieved,
- baselines to be established,

- project deliverables to be completed, and
- required approvals that span the duration of the project.

A combination of graphical and textual notations can be used to describe the development model. Any tailoring of an organization's standard process model should be indicated in this section. Development process models are described in Chapter 2 of this text.

Methods, tools, and techniques to be used to develop or modify the software are specified in section 7.2. The issues that should be addressed in this section are:

- development methods, techniques, software tools, and programming languages and other notations that will be used to specify, design, build, test, integrate, document, deliver, and modify and maintain the work products;
- technical standards, policies, procedures, and guidelines that will be used to govern development and/or modification of work products; and
- government regulations and laws, if any, that must be observed.

The infrastructure plan (section 7.3) addresses:

- the plan for establishing and maintaining the development environment (hardware, operating system, network, software utilities); and
- facilities, policies, procedures, and standards.

Infrastructure resources may include workstations, local area networks, desks, office space, and provisions for physical security, administrative personnel, and janitorial services.

The product acceptance plan (section 7.4) documents:

- how user and customer acceptance of the deliverable work products will be obtained;
- objective criteria to be used in determining acceptability of the deliverable work products;
- technical processes, methods, and tools that will be used in obtaining product acceptance; and
- if appropriate, the formal agreement for the acceptance criteria to be prepared and signed by representatives of the development organization and the acquiring organization during initial planning.

Validation methods such as testing, demonstration, analysis, and inspection should be specified. The relationship among the requirements, requirements-based test plans, and the list of required deliverable work products should be indicated. Traceability matrices can be used for this purpose.

4.6.7 Supporting Processes

Section 8 of a project management plan contains plans for the supporting processes that span the duration of the software project. These plans may include, but are not limited to those listed in Table 4.4*c* (configuration management, verification and validation, software documentation, quality assurance, reviews and audits, problem resolution, and subcontractor management). The eight supporting processes in Table 4.4*c* are those specified in IEEE Standard 12207; tailoring of the template for project plans may result in deletion or modification of some supporting processes. Additional processes may be added as appropriate.

Plans for supporting processes should be developed to a level of detail consistent with the other sections of the plan. In particular, the plan for each supporting process plan should include:

- roles,
- responsibilities,
- authorities,
- schedule,
- budget,
- resource requirements,
- risk factors, and
- work products.

The nature of, and types of supporting processes required may vary from project to project. However, the absence of a configuration management plan, verification and validation plan, quality assurance plan, joint customer-developer review plan, or problem resolution plan should be explicitly justified in any software project management plan that does not include them.

Plans for some supporting processes may be separately developed by the organizational entities that will provide the support. Those plans may be incorporated directly into your software project management plan or incorporated by reference. Referenced plans are considered to be part of the project plan. Supporting plans may be based on the organization's standard support processes, which can be included by reference.

The configuration management plan (section 8.1 of the SPMP) addresses the following issues:

- work products to be placed under version control;
- how readiness of work products for baselining (placement under version control) will be determined;
- how change requests and problem reports will be handled (logged, analyzed, and tracked);
- change control procedures to be used;
- members of the change control board;
- how stakeholders will be notified of changes to baselines;
- who will track changes in work products and analyze change trends;
- automated tools to be used for version control; and
- methods, tools, and conventions that must be used to satisfy your organization's policies, the contractual agreement, and post-release product support requirements

The verification and validation plan (section 8.2) addresses:

- who will do verification and validation (V&V);
- scope of activities that will be included;
- methods, tools, and techniques that will be used;
- the degree of independence between the development entities and the V&V entities of the project;
- automated tools to be used for V&V; and
- How will interactions with an Independent V&V organization be coordinated, if applicable.

Verification planning should result in plans for techniques such as traceability, milestone reviews, progress reviews, peer reviews, prototyping, simulation, and modeling. Validation planning should result in plans for techniques such as testing, demonstration, analysis, and inspection.

The documentation plan (section 8.3) should indicate:

- nondeliverable and deliverable documents that will be generated;
- templates or standard formats that will be used;
- responsible individuals for providing the necessary information, generating the various documents, reviewing them, and accepting them;
- documents that will be placed under version control;
- when review copies and initial baseline versions will be required; and
- who will get copies of the review and baselines versions of the documents.

Nondeliverable documents may include:

- requirement specifications;
- design documentation;
- source code;
- traceability matrices;
- test plans, meeting minutes;
- review reports;
- action items;
- change requests; and
- defect reports.

Deliverable work products may include:

- source code,
- object code,
- users' manual,
- on-line help system,
- regression test suite,

- configuration library,
- principles of operation,
- maintenance guide, and
- any other items specified in section 1.4 of the project plan (project deliverables).

The quality assurance plan (section 8.4) addresses:

- how assurance will be provided that the software project is fulfilling its commitments to the planned software processes and work products as specified in the requirements, software project management plan, supporting plans, and any policies, standards, procedures, or guidelines to which the process or the product must adhere;
- who will be responsible for process and product assurance; and
- the authorities, responsibilities, and lines of communication for those who will be responsible for process and product assurance.

Quality assurance procedures may include analysis, reviews, audits, and assessments. The quality assurance plan should indicate the relationships among the quality assurance, verification and validation, review, audit, configuration management, and assessment processes. The quality assurance plan must be developed and executed by an organizational entity (or entities) independent of you, the project manager, and incorporated by reference into your project plan.

The plan for reviews and audits (section 8.5) documents:

- the kinds of reviews and audits that will be conducted;
- who will conduct them; and
- schedules, resources, methods, and procedures that will be used to conduct project reviews and project audits.

This plan should include plans for joint customer-developer reviews, management reviews, developer peer reviews, quality assurance audits, and customer audits. Elements of this plan should be consistent with organizational policies, the project's contractual agreement, and other contractual documents.

The problem resolution plan (section 8.6) indicates:

- how problems in the work processes and work products will be reported, analyzed, prioritized, and resolved;
- how problems will be tracked to closure;
- the roles of organizational entities such as development, configuration management, the change control board, verification and validation, and quality assurance in problem resolution;
- how the relationship between problem resolution and risk management (section 5.4) will be managed; and

- how effort devoted to problem reporting, analysis, and resolution will be separately reported so that rework can be tracked and needed process improvements identified.

Subcontractor management plans (section 8.7) address:

- how subcontractors will be selected;
- who will be responsible for preparing subcontractor management plans;
- who will be responsible for providing the technical and managerial interfaces to subcontractors; and
- mechanisms of measurement, reporting, and control that will be used.

Plans for subcontractor management should include the items necessary to ensure successful completion of each subcontract. In particular, plans for:

- requirements management,
- monitoring of technical progress,
- schedule and budget reporting,
- product acceptance criteria, and
- risk management procedures

should be included in each subcontractor plan. Additional topics should be added as needed for successful completion of each subcontract. A reference to the official subcontract and prime contractor/subcontractor points of contact should be provided.

A plan for process improvement (section 8.8) documents:

- the frequency of assessment to determine areas for improvement,
- who will do the project assessments,
- who will develop and implement improvement plans, and
- who will implement improvement plans.

The process improvement plan should be closely related to the risk management and problem resolution plans. For example, root cause analysis of recurring problems may lead to simple process improvements that can significantly reduce rework during the remainder of the project. Proposed improvements should be carefully examined to identify those processes that can be improved without serious disruptions to your ongoing project and to identify those processes that can best be improved by process improvement initiatives at the organizational level.

4.6.8 Additional Plans, Appendixes, Index

Section 9 provides additional plans that should be included in your software project management plan, as appropriate. The following issue should be addressed:

- additional plans needed to satisfy product requirements, organizational policies, and contractual terms;
- who will prepare them; and
- who will execute them.

Additional plans for a particular project may include plans for:

- assuring that special safety or security requirements for the product are met,
- special facilities or equipment,
- product installation,
- user training,
- system integration,
- data conversion,
- system transition,
- product maintenance, or
- product support plans.

Appendixes may be included in a project plan to provide supporting details that would detract from the plan if included in the body of the plan. An index to the key terms and acronyms used throughout the project plan is optional, but is recommended to improve the usability of the plan.

Details of the mechanisms used to prepare and execute a project plan are provided in subsequent chapters of this text.

4.7 TECHNIQUES FOR PREPARING A PROJECT PLAN

Preparing a software project management plan using the template presented in Tables 4.4*a, b*, and *c* and described in Section 4.4 will be overwhelming if you, alone, are faced with developing all of the elements of the plan for a large project. Several factors should reduce the time and effort you will have to invest in preparing a project plan.

4.7.1 Tailoring the Project Plan Template

Tailoring is concerned with adding, deleting, and modifying elements of the template for your project plan. If you are planning a project for an internal customer in a familiar and well-defined development environment using a small team of experienced software developers and a standard set of supporting processes your tailoring of Tables 4.4*a, b*, and *c* might result in the tailoring indicated by deleting the indicated elements:

Title Page
Revision History
~~Preface~~
~~Table of Contents~~

~~List of Figures~~
~~List of Table~~
1 Project Summary
    1.1 Purpose, Scope, and Objectives
    1.2 Assumptions and Constraints
    1.3 Project Deliverables
    1.4 Schedule and Budget
~~2 Evolution of the Plan~~
3 References
~~4 Definitions~~
~~5 Project Organization~~
    ~~5.1 Project Interfaces~~
    ~~5.2 Project Structure~~
    5.3 Roles and Responsibilities
6 Managerial Processes
    6.1 Start-Up Plan
        6.1.1 Project Estimation
        ~~6.1.2 Staffing Plan~~
        ~~6.1.3 Resource Acquisition Plan~~
        ~~6.1.4 Project Staff Training Plan~~
    6.2 Work Plan
        6.2.1 WBS and Work Packages
        6.2.2 Schedule Dependencies
        ~~6.2.3 Resource Allocation~~
        ~~6.2.4 Budget Allocation~~
    6.3 Project Control Plan
        6.3.1 Requirements
        ~~6.3.2 Schedule~~
        ~~6.3.3 Budget~~
        ~~6.3.4 Quality~~
        ~~6.3.5 Metrics Plan~~
        ~~6.3.6 Reporting Plan~~
    6.4 Risk Management Plan
    ~~6.5 Closeout Plan~~
~~7 Technical Processes~~
    ~~7.1 Development Process Model~~
    ~~7.2 Methods, Tools, and Techniques~~
    ~~7.3 Infrastructure Plan~~
    7.4 Product Acceptance Plan
~~8 Supporting Processes~~
    ~~8.1 Configuration Management~~
    ~~8.2 Verification and Validation~~
    ~~8.3 Documentation~~
    ~~8.4 Quality Assurance~~
    ~~8.5 Reviews and Audits~~
    ~~8.6 Problem Resolution~~
    ~~8.7 Subcontractor Management~~
    ~~8.8 Process Improvement~~

9 Additional Plans
~~Appendices~~
~~Index~~

The tailored plan would have the resulting format:

Title Page
Revision History
1 Project Summary
  1.1 Purpose, Scope, and Objectives
  1.2 Assumptions and Constraints
  1.3 Project Deliverables
  1.4 Schedule and Budget
3 References
  5.3 Roles and Responsibilities
6 Managerial Processes
    6.1.1 Project Estimation Plan
    6.2.1 WBS and Work Packages
    6.2.2 Schedule Dependencies
    6.3.1 Requirements Control Plan
  6.4 Risk Management Plan
  7.4 Product Acceptance Plan

Tailoring is not meant to imply that the deleted elements are unimportant but that they will be conducted in the usual, familiar way (e.g., configuration management, verification and validation) and do not need to be documented in the project plan, or that they are not applicable to this project (e.g., there is no subcontractor plan because there are no subcontractors). Cases where elements would not be deleted are, for example, cases where the process to be used (e.g., for CM or QA) differs from the standard organizational process.

To maintain consistency among project plans within your organization, you should retain the numbering scheme from the template for project plans.

4.7.2 Including Predefined Elements

Your organization may have policies, procedures, checklists, document templates, one or more standard process models, tailoring guidelines, and examples that you can use to guide your preparation of the initial version of your project plan. This can significantly reduce the time and effort required.

4.7.3 Using Organizational Support

Your organization may have internal consultants and experts who can help you with areas such as requirements definition, tailoring the organization's standard development process, cost and schedule estimation, risk management, configuration management, tailoring and preparing project plans, and specialty disciplines such as human factors, safety, security, and reliability.

4.7.4 Leading a Planning Team

Small projects have small plans because the number of work activities to be planned and coordinated is small and because the projects often occur in stable, well-defined environments; large projects have correspondingly large plans. If you are the project manager of a large project your primary planning activity may involve coordinating the efforts of a planning team and integrating their work into a comprehensive project management plan. Members of the team may include specialists in areas such as those mentioned above (requirements engineering, tailoring the organization's standard development process, cost and schedule estimation, risk management, configuration management, tailoring and preparing project plans, and specialty disciplines such as human factors, safety, security, and reliability).

In the cases of large, complex projects you may need a "plan for planning." Like all plans, a plan for planning should include items such as:

- roles,
- responsibilities,
- authorities,
- schedule,
- budget,
- resources,
- risk factors, and
- work products.

4.7.5 Incremental Planning

Your initial project plan should be sufficiently comprehensive to include all of the work activities within the scope of your project. The level of detail in your initial plan should satisfy the following criteria:

1. the scope of the plan includes all of the major work activities to be accomplished
2. opportunities for reuse of existing components are identified;
3. effort, schedule, and resources for each identified work activity can be estimated with confidence;
4. predecessor and successor activities for each work activity are specified and a schedule is determined; and
5. complexities and risk factors are identified.

Different work activities may be decomposed to different levels. Familiar work activities and components identified for reuse in the product may satisfy the criteria at a high level; unfamiliar work, risk factors based on uncertainties, and use of new technologies may indicate the need to incorporate prototyping and feasibility studies in the plan.

During project execution the plan is updated and elaborated as specified in section 2 of your plan (evolution of the plan). For example, you may plan to update your project plan on a monthly basis or when external factors such as changes in the customer's requirements, difficulties with subcontractors, or delays in delivery of hardware components dictate the need for replanning.

4.8 KEY POINTS OF CHAPTER 4

- Operational requirements, technical specifications, and process constraints provide the basis for project planning.
- A software project management plan is a baseline-controlled written document. Appendix 4B to this chapter provides a template for developing software project management plans based on IEEE Standard 1058; an electronic copy is available at the URL listed in the Preface to this text.
- The comprehensive template for software project management plans presented in Tables 4.4*a*, *b*, and *c* can be, and should be, tailored to fit the needs of each project, as in the example of tailoring.
- Developing a software project management plan, like all software engineering processes, is best accomplished in an iterative manner. The initial version of the plan should be updated on a periodic basis and as events require.
- The level of effort devoted to project planning, and the level of detail in a project plan, both initially and ongoing, are determined by the risk factors created by not doing more.
- The level of detail in your initial project plan should satisfy the following criteria: effort, schedule, and resources for each identified work activity can be estimated with confidence; predecessor and successor activities for each work activity can be determined; opportunities for reuse of existing components are identified; and complexities and risk factors are identified.
- Acceptable options for obtaining a balance among effort, schedule, and requirements in your project plan include descoping the requirements, increasing the quantity of resources, using more productive resources, extending the schedule, and combinations of these options.
- Unacceptable options for achieving a balance among effort, schedule, and requirements include descoping the plans for measurement and control, peer reviews, verification and validation, and planning for overtime effort.
- SEI, ISO, IEEE, and PMI provide frameworks, standards, and guidelines for project planning (see Appendix 4A to this chapter)

REFERENCES

[BOEHM04] Boehm, B., and R. Turner. *Balancing Agility and Discipline*. Addison Wesley, 2004.

[CMMI06] SEI, *CMMI® Models and Modules*. http://www.sei.cmu.edu/CMMI/models/, 2006.

[IEEE1058] IEEE Std 1058™–1998. *IEEE Standard for Software Project Management Plans*. Engineering Standards Collection. IEEE Product: SE113. Institute of Electrical and Electronic Engineers, August 2003.

[IEEE12207] IEEE/EIA 12207.0/.1/.2. *Industry Implementation of International Standard ISO/IEC 12207:1995 Standard for Information Technology–Software Life Cycle Processes*. Engineering Standards Collection. IEEE Product: SE113. Institute of Electrical and Electronic Engineers, August 2003.

[PMI04] *A Guide to the Project Management Body of Knowledge*, 3rd ed. (PMBOK® Guide). Project Management Institute, 2004.

[SACMM02] SEI, *Software Acquisition Capability Maturity Model (SA-CMM), Version 1.03*. http://www.sei.cmu.edu/publications/documents/02.reports/02tr010.html

EXERCISES

4.1. CMMI-DEV-v1.2 lists four related process areas in the project planning process area:

requirements development,
requirements management,
risk management, and
technical solution.

Access the CMMI Web site at http://www.sei.cmu.edu/publications/documents/06.reports/06tr008.html, review the project planning process area, and briefly explain how each of the four related process areas is related to project planning.

4.2. What risk factors are created if a project does not have a written project plan?

4.3. What risk factors are created if a project manager does not maintain baseline control of the project plan?

4.4. Briefly describe the ways in which each of the following provides a basis for project planning:

a. operational requirements
b. software specifications
c. process constraints
d. product constraints

4.5. Briefly explain why identifying opportunities for reuse of existing components is an important aspect of project planning.

4.6. Why is planning for overtime effort an unacceptable option in a project plan?

APPENDIX 4A

FRAMEWORKS, STANDARDS, AND GUIDELINES FOR PROJECT PLANNING

4A.1 THE CMMI-DEV-v1.2 PROJECT PLANNING PROCESS AREA

Project Planning is a level 2 process area in the staged representation of the CMMI-DEV–v1.2 process framework [CMMI06]. According to CMMI-DEV–v1.2:

> The purpose of Project Planning (PP) is to establish and maintain plans that define project activities.

The specific goals and specific practices of project planning are:

SG 1 Establish Estimates
- SP 1.1 Estimate the Scope of the Project
- SP 1.2 Establish Estimates of Work Product and Task Attributes
- SP 1.3 Define Project Life Cycle
- SP 1.4 Determine Estimates of Effort and Cost

SG 2 Develop a Project Plan
- SP 2.1 Establish the Budget and Schedule
- SP 2.2 Identify Project Risks
- SP 2.3 Plan for Data Management
- SP 2.4 Plan for Project Resources
- SP 2.5 Plan for Needed Knowledge and Skills
- SP 2.6 Plan Stakeholder Involvement
- SP 2.7 Establish the Project Plan

SG 3 Obtain Commitment to the Plan
- SP 3.1 Review Plans That Affect the Project
- SP 3.2 Reconcile Work and Resource Levels
- SP 3.3 Obtain Plan Commitment

Related process areas are:

- Requirements Development
- Requirements Management
- Risk Management
- Technical Solution

4A.2 ISO/IEC AND IEEE/EIA STANDARDS 12207

As discussed in Chapter 1, IEEE/IEA Standard 12207–1996 is the Industry Implementation of International Standard ISO/IEC 12207:1995; it is the umbrella standard for software lifecycle processes for the IEEE's suite of software engineering standards. 12207 consists of three documents: 12207.0, Software life cycle processes; 12207.1: Life cycle data; and 12207.2, Implementation considerations [IEEE12207].

Section 5.2 of 12207.1, states that the generic purpose of all plans is to specify the activities to be performed and state when, how, and by whom the activities will be performed.

According to 12207.1, every kind of plan, whether it is a project plan, a configuration management plan, a quality assurance plan, a training plan, or other kind of plan should contain the following generic information:

- needs to be satisfied;
- success criteria;
- work activities to be accomplished;
- schedule, budget, and resources;
- quality control measures;
- change procedures and tracking of project history;
- interfaces to relevant stakeholders;
- roles to be played;
- responsibilities and authorities; and
- resource acquisition plan.

According to 12207.1, the specific contents of a project management plan includes items such as

- software life cycle model;
- project structural relationships;
- authority and responsibility of each organizational unit;
- the engineering infrastructure to be used, including items such as the test environment, standards, procedures, and tools;
- a work breakdown structure;
- scheduling of activities and tasks;
- quality management plan;

- configuration management plan;
- subcontractor management plans, as appropriate;
- verification and validation plans;
- risk management plan;
- tracking and reporting plan;
- plans for involvement of the acquirer and users;
- training plan; and
- security policy.

4A.3 IEEE/EIA STANDARD 1058

IEEE/EIA Standard 1058–1998 is the IEEE Standard for Software Project Management Plans. The format and content of project plans based on 1058 are presented in this chapter [IEEE1058].

4A.4 THE PMI BODY OF KNOWLEDGE

Section 4.3 of A Guide to the Project Management Body of Knowledge [PMI04], Develop Project Management Plan, states that the project management plan integrates and coordinates all subsidiary plans. Subsidiary plans include, but are not limited to:

- project scope management plan,
- schedule management plan,
- cost management plan,
- quality management plan,
- process improvement plan,
- staffing management plan,
- communication management plan,
- risk management plan, and
- procurement management plan.

Each of the subsidiary plans is detailed to the extent required by the specific project. In section 1.1, Purpose of the PMBOK® GUIDE, it is emphasized that the project management team is responsible for determining what is appropriate for any given project.

APPENDIX 4B

ANNOTATED OUTLINE FOR SOFTWARE PROJECT MANAGEMENT PLANS, BASED ON IEEE STANDARD 1058

4B.1 PURPOSE

This outline describes the format and content of software project management plans based on IEEE Std 1058. The standard does not specify the exact techniques to be used in developing a software project management plan, nor does it provide examples of software project management plans. Each organization using this standard should develop a set of practices and procedures to provide detailed guidance for preparing and updating of software project management plans based on the standard. These practices and procedures should take into account the environmental, organizational, and political factors that influence application of the standard.

Not all software projects are concerned with development of source code for a new software product. Some software projects consist of a feasibility study and definition of product requirements. Other software projects terminate on completion of the product design, and some projects are concerned with major modifications to existing software products. The standard is applicable to all types of software projects; applicability is not limited to projects that develop source code for new products. Project size or type of software product does not limit application of this standard. Small projects may require less formality in planning than large projects, but all components of the standard should be addressed by every software project.

Software projects are sometimes component parts of larger projects. In these cases the software project management plan may be a separate component of a larger plan or it may be merged into a system-level or business-level project management plan. Various parts of a project plan may be adaptations of, or direct implementations of the development organization's policies, procedures, and guidelines. In these cases references to those documents can be included with the appropriate tailoring information. For example, the quality assurance procedures for the project may be "the same way we always do it." In that case the QA planning section of the project plan might incorporate a reference to the organization's QA policies, standards, and procedures plus a description of the schedules and resources required for QA on this project.

4B.2 EVOLUTION OF PLANS

Developing the initial version of the software project management plan should be one of the first activities to be completed for a software project. As the project evolves, the nature of the work to be done will be better understood and plans will become more detailed. In addition requirements will change, personnel will come and go, and project conditions will change. Thus the project plan should contain a plan for revising the plan at periodic intervals and on occurrence of unusual events. Each version of the project plan should be placed under version control, and each version should contain a schedule for subsequent updates to the plan.

4B.3 OVERVIEW

The format and typical contents of software project management plans are described in this document. A software project management plan is the controlling document for managing a software project; it defines the technical and managerial processes necessary to develop software work products that satisfy the product requirements.

Some organizations may have generic project plans based on this standard, so that development of a particular project plan will involve tailoring of the generic plan in areas such as the process model, supporting processes, and infrastructure and adding project-unique elements such as schedule, budget, work activities, and risk management plan.

4B.4 FORMAT OF A SOFTWARE PROJECT MANAGEMENT PLAN

The individual or organization responsible for conducting a software project should also be responsible for preparing the software project management plan (the SPMP). The outline of elements in an SPMP is provided in Table 4A1.1.

The ordering of elements presented in Table 4A1.1 is not meant to imply that the sections must be developed in that order. The order of elements is intended for ease of reading, presentation, and use, and not as a guide to the order of preparation of the various elements of a SPMP. The various sections and subsections of a SPMP may be included by direct incorporation or by reference to other plans and documents.

Each version of a SPMP based on this outline should contain a title page, a signature page, and a change history.

TABLE 4A1.1 Format of a Software Project Management Plan

Title Page
Signature Page
Change History
Preface
Table of Contents
List of Figures
List of Tables
1 Overview
  1.1 Project Summary
    1.1.1 Purpose, Scope, and Objectives
    1.1.2 Assumptions and Constraints
    1.1.3 Project Deliverables
    1.1.4 Schedule and Budget Summary
  1.2 Evolution of the Plan
2 References
3 Definitions
4 Project Organization
  4.1 External Interfaces
  4.2 Internal Structure
  4.3 Roles and Responsibilities
5 Managerial Process Plans
  5.1 Start-up Plan
    5.1.1 Estimation Plan
    5.1.2 Staffing Plan
    5.1.3 Resource Acquisition Plan
    5.1.4 Project Staff Training Plan
  5.2 Work Plan
    5.2.1 Work Activities
    5.2.2 Schedule Allocation
    5.2.3 Resource Allocation
    5.2.4 Budget Allocation
  5.3 Control Plan
    5.3.1 Requirements Control Plan
    5.3.2 Schedule Control Plan
    5.3.3 Budget Control Plan
    5.3.4 Quality Control Plan
    5.3.5 Reporting Plan
    5.3.6 Metrics Collection Plan
  5.4 Risk Management Plan
  5.5 Closeout Plan
6 Technical Process Plans
  6.1 Process Model
  6.2 Methods, Tools, and Techniques
  6.3 Infrastructure Plan
  6.4 Product Acceptance Plan
7 Supporting Process Plans
  7.1 Configuration Management Plan
  7.2 Verification and Validation Plan
  7.3 Documentation Plan
  7.4 Quality Assurance Plan
  7.5 Reviews and Audits
  7.6 Problem Resolution Plan
  7.7 Subcontractor Management Plan
  7.8 Process Improvement Plan
8 Additional Plans
Annexes
Index

Title Page

The title page should contain:

project name
version number of the plan
issuing organization

Signature Page

The signature page should contain the signature(s) and title(s) of the persons responsible for approving the SPMP.

Change History

The change history should include a list of all prior versions of the plan:

version number
date of release
sections changed
nature of changes

Preface

The preface of the SPMP should describe:

scope and context of the plan
intended audience
table of contents
list of figures
list of tables

4B.5 STRUCTURE AND CONTENT OF THE PLAN

1 PROJECT OVERVIEW

This section of the SPMP contains the following information: the purpose, scope, and objectives of the project; the major assumptions and constraints, a list of project deliverables, a summary of the project schedule and budget, and the plan for evolution of the SPMP.

1.1 Project Summary

1.1.1 Purpose, Scope, and Objectives (Subclause 1.1.1 of the SPMP)

Purpose: why are we doing this project? What business or system needs are to be satisfied by the outcomes of the project?

Scope: what activities are included in this project? What is the relationship of this project to other projects and ongoing work processes?

Objectives: what outcomes do we desire? What work products are to be delivered? How will satisfaction of objectives be determined?

Exclusions: what scope factors and objectives are explicitly excluded from this project and/or the resulting work products.

1.1.2 Assumptions and Constraints

Assumptions: what are the conditions that we have assumed will be true for this project?

Constraints: what constraints have been imposed on factors such as the schedule, budget, available resources, software to be reused, technology to be employed, and/or interfaces of the product to other products?

1.1.3 Project Deliverables What work products will we deliver to the customer? When and where must we deliver them? In what quantities and on what media? Are there any special packaging or handling instructions? Is there another document, such as a CDRL (Contractor's Data Requirements List) or PPL (Program Parts List), that contains the deliverables list? If so, where can this document be found?

1.1.4 Schedule and Budget Summary What is the time frame for this project? What is the overall cost (in dollars or staff-hours)? When are the major milestones scheduled to occur? What are the major supporting processes and additional plans for the project?

1.2 Evolution of the SPMP

What is the planned schedule for periodically updating the SPMP? Under what conditions will unscheduled updates occur? How will changes to the plan be controlled? What methods will be used to issue updates to the appropriate stakeholders?

2 REFERENCES

Where can additional documents related to this plan be found? (e.g., the Concept of Operations, system requirements specification, software requirements specification, and/or CDRL). Applicable standards and guidelines, such as IEEE or corporate standards for the project plan and supporting processes, should be included. Path names should be provided for access to electronic files.

3 DEFINITIONS

What are the meanings of the terms and acronyms are used in this document? What other documents contain terminology needed to understand this plan (e.g., IEEE Standard 610-12).

4 PROJECT ORGANIZATION

This section of the SPMP identifies interfaces to organizational entities external to the project, describes the project's internal organizational structure, and defines roles and responsibilities for the project.

4.1 External Interfaces

What are the organizational entities external to the project and where are the points of contact between the project and those entities? External interfaces may exist between the project and the parent organization, the acquiring organization, subcontractors, and affiliated projects. Organizational charts and diagrams may be used to depict the project's organizational interfaces.

4.2 Internal Structure

How is the development team organized? How does the development team interact with supporting entities such as configuration management, quality assurance, and verification and validation? Where are the points of contact and what are the lines of communication? Graphical devices such as organizational charts or diagrams can be used to illustrate the lines of authority, responsibility, and communication within the project.

4.3 Roles and Responsibilities

Which organizational units are responsible for the various work activities and supporting processes? A matrix that relates work activities and supporting processes to organizational units can be used to depict project roles and responsibilities.

5 MANAGERIAL PROCESS PLANS

This section of the SPMP specifies the project start-up plan, the risk management plan, the project work plan, the project control plan, and the project closeout plan.

5.1 Project Start-up Plan

Project start-up involves developing an estimation plan and doing estimates, developing a staffing plan, a plan for other necessary resources, and a training plan for the project team. Depending on the size and scope of the project, these plans may be incorporated directly into the SPMP, or the SPMP may contain reference to other documents and electronic files that contain the start-up plans.

5.1.1 Estimation Plan What is the plan for making initial and ongoing estimates? What are the details of the project cost, schedule, staff requirements, and other resources? What methods, tools, and techniques were used to make the estimates? What historical information was used? What is the estimator's level of confidence in the estimate? How will periodic re-estimates be made of cost, schedule, staffing, and other resources required to complete the project? How frequently will re-estimation be done? What is the plan for re-estimating when requirements or other project conditions change?

5.1.2 Staffing Plan What skills are required? How many people having what skill levels are needed? When will they be needed? For how long? How will the people be obtained? Who is responsible for acquiring the necessary personnel? Techniques such as Gantt charts, resource histograms, spreadsheets, and tables can be used to depict the staffing plan by skill level, by project phase, and by aggregations of skill levels and project phases.

5.1.3 Resource Acquisition Plan What resources, in addition to people, are needed? When are they needed? Who is responsible for acquiring them? What approvals are required? The resource acquisition plan may include plans for items such as the equipment, computer hardware and software, service contracts, transportation, facilities, and administrative services. The resource acquisition plan should specify the points in the project schedule when the various acquisition activities will be required. Constraints on acquiring the necessary resources should be specified. This section can be expanded into additional subsections of the form 5.1.3.x to accommodate acquisition plans for the various types of resources to be acquired. References to resource acquisition plans contained in separate documents must be included here.

5.1.4 Project Staff Training Plan What training is needed to ensure that necessary skill levels, in sufficient numbers are available to successfully conduct the software project? The training schedule should include the types of training to be provided, numbers of personnel to be trained, entry and exit criteria for training, and the training methods; for example, lectures, consultations, mentoring, or computer assisted training. The training plan should include needed training in both technical and managerial skills.

5.2 Work Plan

This section of the SPMP describes the work activities, and the details of schedule, resources, and budget for the software project.

5.2.1 Work Activities This section contains the project work breakdown structure. Work activities in the WBS should be decomposed to a level that exposes the project risk factors and allows accurate estimation of resource requirements and schedule duration for each work activity. Work packages should be used to specify, for each work activity, factors such as the necessary resources, estimated duration, work products to be produced, acceptance criteria for the work products, and predecessor and successor work activities. The level of decomposition for different work activities in the work breakdown structure may be different depending on factors such as the quality of the requirements, familiarity of the work, novelty of the technology to be used, and software components to be reused.

5.2.2 Schedule Allocation The allocated schedule provides answers to questions such as: What are the time-sequencing constraints among work activities? Where are the opportunities for concurrent work activities? What schedule constraints are caused by dependencies on external factors such as vendor-supplied equipment and software, interfaces to hardware components, and subcontractor-supplied software? The allocated schedule should include frequent milestones that can be assessed for attainment using objective indicators to assess the scope and quality of work products completed at those milestones. Techniques that can be used to specify schedule relationships include milestone charts, activity lists, activity Gantt charts, activity networks, critical path networks, and PERT charts.

5.2.3 Resource Allocation What resources are allocated to the various work activities in the work breakdown structure and the project schedule? Resources specified may include personnel by skill level and factors such as computing resources, software tools, special testing and simulation facilities, and administrative support. A separate line item should be provided for each type of resource needed. Allocation of resources to activities should be indicated. A summary of resource requirements for the various work activities can be collected from the work packages of the work breakdown structure and presented in tabular form.

5.2.4 Budget Allocation What elements of the budget are allocated to each of the major work activities in the work breakdown structure? The activity budget should include the estimated cost for personnel (in dollars or staff-hours by skill level) to accomplish each activity and may include, as appropriate, costs for factors such as travel, meetings, computing resources, software tools, special testing and simulation facilities, and administrative support. A separate line item should be provided for each type of resource for each activity. The work activity budget may be developed using a spreadsheet and presented in tabular form.

5.3 Control Plan

This section of the SPMP specifies the metrics, reporting mechanisms, and control procedures to be used in measuring, reporting, and controlling the product requirements, the project schedule, budget, and resources, and the quality of work processes and work products. Each element of the control plan should be consistent with the organization's standards, policies, and procedures for controlling software projects and with any contractual agreements for project control.

5.3.1 Requirements Control Plan How will requirements be accepted as product baselines? What control mechanisms will be used to measure, report, and control changes to the requirements baseline? How will the impact of requirements changes on product scope and quality, and project schedule, budget, resources, and risk factors be assessed? Configuration management mechanisms should include change control procedures, version control, and a change control board. Techniques that can be used for requirements control include traceability, prototyping and modeling, impact analysis, and reviews.

5.3.2 Schedule Control Plan What techniques will be used to measure the progress of work completed at the major and minor project milestones, to compare actual progress to planned progress, and to implement corrective action when actual progress does not conform to planned progress? Achievement of schedule milestones should be assessed using objective criteria to measure the scope and quality of work products completed at each milestone.

5.3.3 Budget Control Plan How will the cost of work completed, comparisons of planned cost to budgeted cost, and the cost of corrective action (when actual cost, schedule, scope, or quality does not conform to plans) be accomplished? How frequently will budget/cost information be provided? What tools and techniques will be used? Who will get copies of the information? The budget plan should include frequent milestones that can be assessed for achievement using objective indicators to assess the scope and quality of work products completed at those milestones. A mechanism such as earned value tracking should be used to report the budget and schedule plan, schedule progress, and the cost of work completed.

5.3.4 Quality Control Plan How will the quality of work processes and evolving work products be measured and controlled? Quality control mechanisms may include audits of work processes, verification and validation of work products, joint reviews, root cause analysis, and process assessments. Technical performance measurement should be used.

5.3.5 Reporting Plan What are the reporting mechanisms, report formats, and information flows to be used in communicating the status of requirements, schedule, budget, scope, quality, and other desired or required status metrics? The methods, tools, and techniques of communication should be included in the reporting plan. The frequency and nature of project measurement and control should be consistent with the project scope, criticality, risk, visibility, and contractual requirements.

5.3.6 Metrics Collection Plan How will necessary metrics data be collected, validated, and retained? What methods, tools, and techniques will be used? How frequently will various types of metrics data be collated, analyzed, and reported?

5.4 Risk Management Plan

What mechanisms will be used to identify, analyze, and prioritize project risk factors? How will contingency plans be developed? What methods will be used to track the identified risk factors, evaluate changes in the levels of risk factors, and respond to those changes? How will risk factors be identified, assessed, and mitigated on an ongoing basis during the project? Risk factors that should be considered include risks in the acquirer-supplier relationship, contractual risks, technological risks, risks caused by the size and complexity of the product, risks in the development and target environments, risks in personnel acquisition, skill levels, and retention, risks to schedule and budget, and risks in achieving user, customer, and acquirer acceptance of the product.

5.5 Project Closeout Plan

How will the project be concluded? How will staff members be reassigned? What postmortem meetings and briefings will be held? What is the plan for archiving project work materials? How will lessons learned and analysis of project objectives achieved be documented?

6 TECHNICAL PROCESS PLANS

This section of the SPMP specifies the development process model, the technical methods, tools, and techniques to be used to develop the various work products; plans for establishing and maintaining the project infrastructure; and the product acceptance plan.

6.1 Process Model

What process model will be used to develop the software product? The process model should describe the relationships among major project work activities and supporting processes by specifying the flow of information and work products among activities and functions, the timing of work products to be generated, reviews to be conducted, major milestones to be achieved, baselines to be established, project deliverables to be completed, and required approvals that span the duration of the project. The process model for the project should include project initiation and project termination activities. To describe the process model, a combination of graphical and textual notations may be used. Any tailoring of an organization's standard process model for a project should be indicated in this section.

6.2 Methods, Tools, and Techniques

What development methodologies, tools, techniques, programming languages, and other notations will be used to specify, design, build, test, integrate, document, deliver, and modify and maintain the work products internal to the project and those to be delivered to the customer? In addition, what technical standards, policies, procedures, and guidelines will be used to govern development and/or modification of work products?

6.3 Infrastructure Plan

What are the plan for establishing and maintaining the development environment (hardware, operating system, network, and software), and the policies, procedures, standards, and facilities required to conduct the software project? These resources may include workstations, local area networks, software tools for analysis, design, implementation, testing, and project management, desks, office space, and provisions for physical security, administrative personnel, and janitorial services.

6.4 Product Acceptance Plan

What is the plan for user, customer, and acquirer acceptance of the deliverable work products generated by the software project? What objective criteria will be used to determine acceptability of the deliverable work products? Will a formal agreement for the acceptance criteria be prepared and signed by representatives of the development organization and the acquiring organization? Any technical processes, methods, or tools required for product acceptance should be specified in the product acceptance plan. Validation methods such as testing, demonstration, analysis, and inspection should be specified in this plan. The relationship among the requirements, requirements-based test plans, and the list of required deliverable work products should be indicated—a traceability matrix can be used.

7 SUPPORTING PROCESS PLANS

This section of the SPMP contains plans for the supporting processes that span the duration of the software project. These plans may include, but are not limited to, items such as configuration management, verification and validation, software documentation, quality assurance, reviews and audits, problem resolution, and subcontractor management. Plans for supporting processes should be developed to a level of detail consistent with the other sections of the SPMP. In particular, the roles, responsibilities, authorities, schedule, budgets, resource requirements, risk factors, and work products for each supporting process should be specified. The nature and types of supporting processes required may vary from project to project; however, the absence of a configuration management plan, verification and validation plan, quality assurance plan, joint acquirer-supplier review plan, problem resolution plan, or subcontractor management plan should be explicitly justified in any software project management plan that does not include them. Plans for supporting processes may be incorporated directly into the software project management plan or incorporated by reference to other plans. Referenced plans are considered to be part of the project plan. Supporting plans may be based on the organization's standard support processes, which can be included by reference.

7.1 Configuration Management Plan

What work products will be placed under configuration management (version control)? How will readiness of work products for baselining be determined? How will change requests be handled (logging, analysis, and tracking)? What will be the change control procedures? Who will be the members of the change control board? How will stakeholders be notified of changes to baselines? Who will track changes in progress and analyze change trends? What automated tools will be used for configuration management? What methods, tools, and conventions must be used to satisfy corporate policies and product support requirements?

7.2 Verification and Validation Plan

Who will do verification and validation (V&V)? What scope of activities will be included? What methods, tools, and techniques will be used? What will be the degree of independence between the development entities and the V&V entities of the project? What automated tools will be used for V&V? Verification planning should result in plans for techniques such as traceability, milestone reviews, progress reviews, peer reviews, prototyping, simulation, and modeling. Validation planning should result in plans for techniques such as testing, demonstration, analysis, and inspection. Automated tools to be used in verification and validation should be specified.

7.3 Documentation Plan

The documentation plan should answer the following questions: What documents will be generated? What templates or standards will be used? Who will be responsible for providing the necessary information, generating the documents, reviewing them, and accepting them? Which documents will be placed under version control? When will review copies and initial baseline versions be due? Who will get copies of the review and baselines versions of the documents? Nondeliverable work products may include requirements specifications, design documentation, traceability matrices, test plans, meeting minutes, review reports, action items, change requests, and defect reports. Deliverable work products may include source code, object code, users' manual, on-line help system, regression test suite, configuration library, principles of operation, a maintenance guide, and any other items specified in subclause 1.1.3 of the SPMP.

7.4 Quality Assurance Plan

How will assurance be obtained that the software project is fulfilling its commitments to the planned software processes as specified in the requirements specification, the software project management plan, supporting plans, and any standards, procedures, or guidelines to which the process or the product must adhere? Quality assurance procedures may include analysis, inspections, reviews, audits, and assessments. The quality assurance plan should indicate the relationships among the quality assurance, verification and validation, review, audit, configuration management, system engineering, and assessment processes.

7.5 Reviews and Audits Plan

What schedules, resources, methods, and procedures will be used to conduct project reviews and audits? This plan should include plans for joint acquirer-supplier reviews, management progress reviews, developer peer reviews, quality assurance audits, and acquirer-conducted reviews and audits.

7.6 Problem Resolution Plan

How will problems in the work processes and work products be reported, analyzed, prioritized, and resolved? What will be the roles of organizational entities such as development, configuration management, the change control board, and verification and validation in problem resolution? Effort devoted to problem reporting, analysis, and resolution should be separately reported so that rework can be tracked and process improvement accomplished.

7.7 Subcontractor Management Plans

How will subcontractors be selected and managed? Who will be responsible for preparing subcontractor management plans? Who will be responsible for providing the technical and managerial interfaces to subcontractors? Plans based on this standard should be prepared to include the items necessary to ensure successful completion of each subcontract. In particular, requirements management, monitoring of technical progress, schedule and budget control, product acceptance criteria, and risk management procedures should be included in each subcontractor plan. Additional topics should be added as needed to ensure successful completion of the subcontract. A reference to the official subcontract and prime contractor/subcontractor points of contact should be provided.

7.8 Process Improvement Plan

How and when will the project be periodically assessed to determine areas for improvement? Who will do the project assessments? Who will develop and implement improvement plans? The process improvement plan should be closely related to the problem resolution plan. For example, root cause analysis of recurring problems may lead to simple process improvements that can significantly reduce rework during the remainder of the project. Proposed improvements should be carefully examined to identify those processes that can be improved without serious disruptions to an ongoing project and to identify those processes that can best be improved by process improvement initiatives at the organizational level.

8 ADDITIONAL PLANS

What additional plans are needed to satisfy product requirements and contractual terms by systematically managing the software project? Who will prepare them and execute them? What forms will they have? Additional plans for a particular project may include plans for assuring that special safety, privacy, or security requirements for the product are met, plans for special facilities or equipment, product installation plans, user training plans, integration plans, data conversion plans, system transition plans, product maintenance plans, and product support plans.

APPENDIXES

Appendixes may be included, either directly or by reference to other documents, to provide supporting details that could detract from the SPMP if included in the body of the plan.

INDEX

An index to the key terms and acronyms used throughout the SPMP is optional. An index is nevertheless recommended to improve the usability of the SPMP.

5

PROJECT PLANNING TECHNIQUES

Failing to plan is planning to fail.
—Alan Lakein

5.1 INTRODUCTION TO PROJECT PLANNING TECHNIQUES

Previous chapters of this text have addressed the requirements, constraints, and directives elements of the workflow model in Figure 1.1 of Chapter 1 (repeated here as Figure 5.1), the roles of customer and management, and the nature of plans and planning. This chapter is concerned with the planning, activity definition, and estimating elements highlighted in Figure 5.1. Additional estimation techniques are presented in Chapter 6.

Planning techniques, activity definition, and estimation of effort and schedule includes the following activities, which are a subset of the activities contained in Table 4.1*b* in Chapter 4.

- Develop an architecture decomposition view (ADV) of the product architecture and allocate requirements to the elements of the ADV
- Develop a work breakdown structure that includes work elements for the ADV modules and the allocated requirements for each element of work
- Develop work packages for the tasks in the work breakdown structure (WBS)
- Define a schedule of objectively measurable milestones
- Prepare a schedule network and identify the critical path(s)

Managing and Leading Software Projects, by Richard E. Fairley

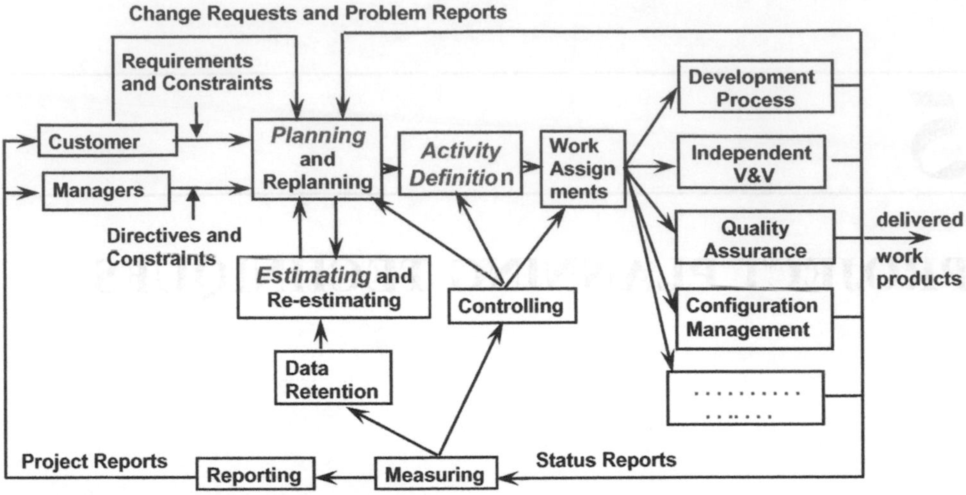

FIGURE 5.1 Project workflow, emphasizing planning, estimating, and activity definition

- Prepare a PERT estimate of project duration
- Identify numbers and kinds of resources needed, when they will be needed, and for how long
- Prepare an estimate of optimal effort, cost, schedule, and resources
- Negotiate with the customer to obtain a balance among requirements, cost, and project duration that satisfies the project constraints

It is self-evident that you cannot prepare a plan for developing a software product if you don't know what product to make. It is equally evident that the more you understand about the product to be made, the more confident you will be in the details of your plan. The initial version of your project plan will be, by necessity, high level and imprecise; however, you can refine the plan as the architectural structure of the product evolves and as your understanding of the project grows based on clarification of the product foundations covered in Chapter 3 of this text (system requirements, system architecture, software requirements, and design constraints). Planning is thus an iterative process; the more you understand about the product the better plan you can make.

5.2 OBJECTIVES OF THIS CHAPTER

After reading this chapter and completing the exercises, you should understand:

- the scope of planning
- rolling-wave planning
- scenarios for developing a project plan
- developing an architecture decomposition view

- developing a work breakdown structure
- developing the project schedule
- developing resource profiles
- resource Gantt charts
- estimating project cost

The planning techniques presented in this chapter are informed by the Project Planning process area of the CMMI-DEV-v1.2 process framework, the planning elements of ISO and IEEE Standards 12207, IEEE Standard 1058, and the PMI Body of Knowledge. These elements are described in Appendix 5A to this chapter.

Terms used in this chapter and throughout this text are defined in the Glossary at the end of the text. Presentation slides for this chapter and other supporting material are available at the URL listed in the Preface.

5.3 THE SCOPE OF PLANNING

The scope of your project may involve developing requirements, negotiating schedule and budget, acquiring facilities and resources, building the software product,[19] installing it, training users, and maintaining the system on an ongoing basis. Or, you may be handed a set of changes to be made along with a schedule and a budget and be given the responsibility of managing a project to make the modifications. Or, your project may fall somewhere between these extremes. In any case, this chapter (and this entire text) considers the full scope of activities that may be required to manage large and complex software projects. As emphasized throughout this text, the activities of project management must be adapted and tailored to fit the needs of each project.

5.4 ROLLING-WAVE PLANNING

Rolling-wave planning acknowledges that it is impossible to develop plans at the level of detail indicated throughout this chapter during the initial planning phase of your software projects. When you are conducting a project, a recommended approach is to augment the high-level master plan with detailed plans for the coming month, for the subsequent month, and for three months hence. Each month the plans are moved forward one month, that is, moved forward in a rolling-wave manner. The plans for the next month should be detailed and specific. The plans for two and three months hence should be as specific as possible. Rolling the three-month plan forward each month provides an opportunity to:

[19] Software *products* are built by *vendors* for sale to numerous customers; software *systems* are built by *contractors* for specific individual customers on a contractual basis. The terms "system" and "product" are used interchangeably in this text unless the distinction is important; the distinction will be clarified in these cases.

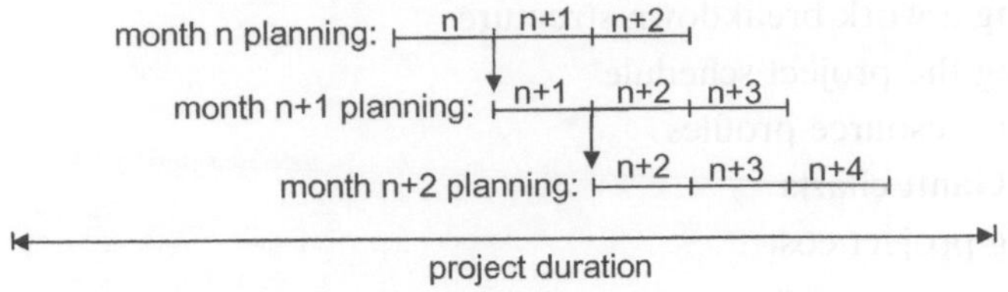

FIGURE 5.2 Rolling-wave updating of detailed plans each month

- have resources available when they are needed,
- clear roadblocks and coordinate work activities, and
- identify and confront risk factors before they become problems.

Rolling-wave planning is illustrated in Figure 5.2.

5.5 SCENARIOS FOR DEVELOPING A PROJECT PLAN

At minimum, you must have some operational requirements for the product or system to prepare the initial version of your plan. Ideally you would have prioritized operational requirements, technical specifications, a functional block diagram, and a decomposition view of the product's architectural structure on which to base your plan. However, this ideal basis is seldom realized when preparing the initial version of a project plan.

Initial planning typically proceeds from one of the following scenarios:

1. You are given a set of operational requirements and constraints on one or more of the schedule, budget, and resources. For example, a system that will have a specified list of operational features and quality attributes must be delivered in 9 months; 6 software developers are available to implement the system. Your first task is to determine whether it is feasible to build the envisioned product (or modify an existing product) within those parameters. This may involve working with the customer to clarify the requirements and using historical data and rules of thumb to determine the feasibility of the project.

If the project is not feasible, with a high probability of success, you and your customer must prioritize the requirements into Essential, Desirable, and Optional categories (which is always a good thing to do). It must be possible to implement all of the Essential requirements, with a very high probability of success, within the development constraints on schedule, budget, and resources. The customer must agree to accept a product that implements all of the Essential requirements and as many of the Desirable requirements as can be implemented within the constraints on schedule, budget, and resources. Or, the development constraints must be relaxed, or some combination of de-scoping the requirements and relaxing the development constraints must be pursued.

2. You may be given a list of features and quality attributes and asked to estimate, and then commit to, the schedule, budget, and resources needed to develop a system

or product having those features and quality attributes. In this case you must first review, clarify, and elaborate whatever product information is available. You should not commit to requirements that are infeasible because of the current state of technology or lack of expertise in your organization; those requirements should be labeled as design goals to be achieved to the extent possible. In this scenario, you should prepare a range of estimates with associated probabilities of success and make a commitment to an estimate having not less than 90% probability of success. The assumptions on which your estimate and commitment are based must be documented and accepted by your customer.

3. You may be given a completion date and a budget and be asked to determine the characteristics of a product that can be built or modified within the constraints of specified time and money. For example, what operational features and quality attributes can you and 6 of your software developers build and deliver in 9 months for a product of a specified kind?

In any case, your initial project plan must achieve a balance among requirements, schedule, budget, resources, and technology. Subsequent revisions of your plan must maintain this balance as requirements and other factors change. In all cases, your first task in developing a project plan is to review, clarify, and further elaborate whatever information is available concerning the product to be built or modified.

For each of the scenarios above, the next step is to refine the requirements to remove areas of uncertainty and to prepare a decomposition view of the product architecture and a work breakdown structure as a basis for preparing a more accurate estimate.

5.6 DEVELOPING THE ARCHITECTURE DECOMPOSITION VIEW AND THE WORK BREAKDOWN STRUCTURE

Architectural design of software is concerned with specifying the software modules, their interrelationships, and their connections to the environment of the software. Several different kinds of views are used to document different kinds of relationships. The views are depicted using notations, such as those illustrated in Figure 5.3, to document structural, functional, and behavioral relationships. Other architectural views are also useful [Bass03].

A partial ADV for ATM software is presented in Figure 5.4. Note that the requirements listed in Table 5.1 are allocated to the leaf nodes of the financial transactions component of the ADV.

Note the use of terms "shall" for Essential requirements, "should" for desirable requirements, and "could" for Optional requirements. "shall" is a contractually binding term; "should" indicates desired but not essential requirements; "could" indicates options that could be included if time, budget, and resources permit.

Figure 5.5*a* illustrates a tree-structured representation of a work breakdown structure (WBS) for the ATM project. An alternative representation (an indented list) is presented in Figure 5.5*b*. The leaf nodes of the tree (or the list) specify tasks. A *task* is a smallest unit of project planning, measurement, and control. The higher level nodes in a WBS are *activities*; activities are composed of subordinate activities

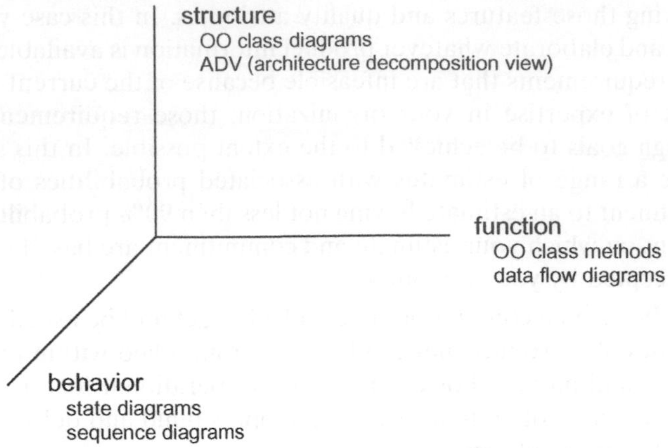

FIGURE 5.3 Three architectural views of software and examples of notations used. The architecture decomposition view (ADV) specifies the hierarchical "is-part-of" relationship among software modules. The ADV is used by project managers (you) to develop the work breakdown structure (WBS)

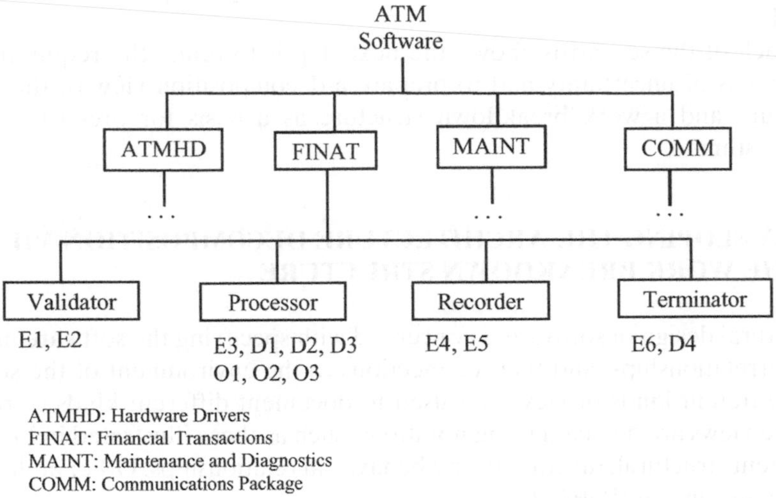

FIGURE 5.4 A partial architecture decomposition view (ADV) of ATM software

and tasks. The relationships among activities and tasks in a WBS are thus containment or "is-part-of" relationships in the same way that the relationships among software module in an architectural decomposition view are "is-part-of" relationships among the modules.

The WBS is a fundamental tool for planning, estimating, measuring, and controlling a software project. The role of a WBS is to partition the activities and tasks of a software project into manageable units with clearly defined roles, responsibilities, and authorities for each unit. In addition a WBS depicts the interfaces and lines of communication among work activities and tasks. One of the primary design criteria

TABLE 5.1 Some prioritized requirements for ATM software

	Essential requirements
E1	Financial transactions shall be authorized by an ATM card and a password
E2	Financial transactions shall be terminated if a customer fails to enter the correct password «settable» times
E3	Financial transaction shall allow quick cash withdrawals
E4	Financial transaction shall provide a printed receipt for each transaction
E5	The ATM shall retain the information listed in the requirements specification, section 3.2.1, for each customer transaction
E6	Financial transaction shall process Terminate requests from customers
	Desirable requirements
D1	Financial transaction should accommodate balance inquiry transactions
D2	Financial transaction should accommodate standard withdrawal transactions
D3	Financial transaction should accommodate deposit transactions
D4	Customers should be allowed to conduct multiple transactions per session
	Optional requirements
O1	Financial transaction could support debit card transactions
O2	Financial transaction could support payment of utility bills
O3	Financial transaction could allow customers to purchase postage stamps which will be disbursed by the ATM hardware

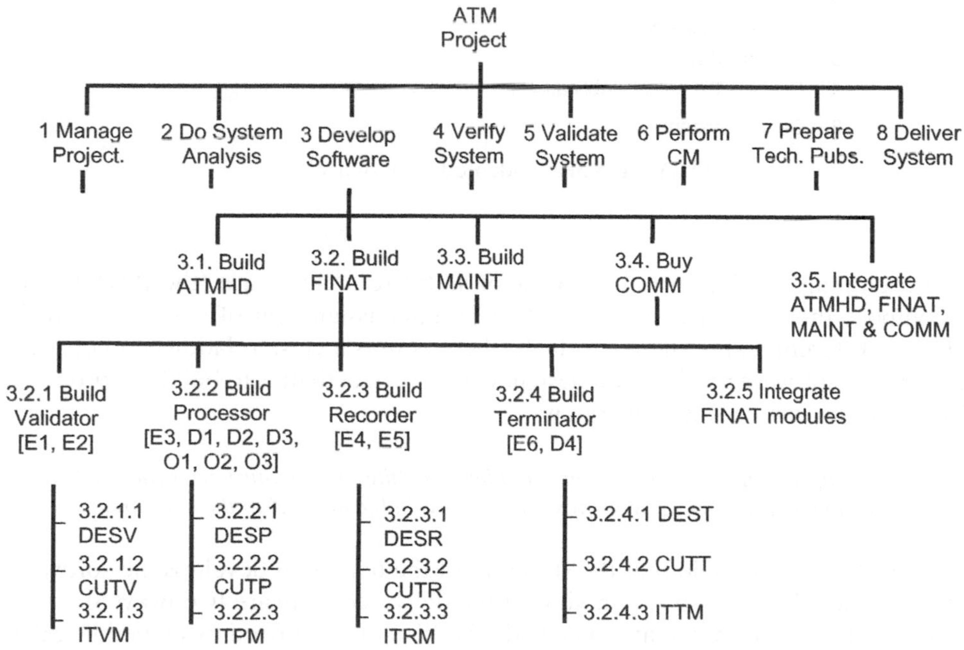

DESx: detailed design of module x; CUTx: coding & unit testing x; ITxC: integrating and testing of x

FIGURE 5.5A Tree-structured form of a WBS

1 Manage Project
2 Do System Analysis
3 Develop Software
3.1 Build ATM Hardware Drivers (ATMHD)
3.2 Build Financial Transaction Handler
3.2.1 Build Validator [E1, E2]
3.2.1.1 Design Validator
3.2.1.2 Code & Unit Test Validator
3.2.1.3 Integrate & Test Validator
3.2.2 Build Transaction Processor (FINAT) [3, S1, D2, D3, O1, O2, O3]
3.2.2.1 Design Transaction Processor
3.2.2.2 Code & Unit Test Transaction Processor
3.2.2.3 Integrate & Test Processor Components
3.2.3 Build Recorder [E4, E5]
3.2.3.1 Design Recorder
3.2.3.2 Code & Unit Test Recorder
3.2.3.3 Integrate & Test Recorder Module
3.2.4 Build Terminator [E6,D4]
3.2.4.1 Design Recorder
3.2.4.2 Code & Unit Test Recorder
3.2.4.3 Integrate & Test Recorder Module
3.2.5 Integrate FINAT Modules
3.3 Build Maintenance & Diagnostic Module (MAINT)
3.4 Buy the Communications Package (COMM)
3.5 Integrate ATMHD, FINAT, MAINT, and COMM
4 Verify System
5 Validate System
6 Perform CM
7 Prepare Technical Publications
8 Deliver System

FIGURE 5.5B Indented form of a WBS

for developing the decomposition view of software architecture (the ADV) is to decompose the product in a manner that permits assignment of concurrent work tasks to different teams and individuals; there is thus a close relationship between designing a software product and designing the work activities to build the product. This criterion can be stated as follows:

> *The decomposition view of software architecture (the ADV) must be structured to provide concurrent work assignments for those available to develop the software.*

Conversely, it can be said that the structure of the team that develops the software will influence the decomposition view of the delivered software [Conway68].

The distinction between an ADV and a WBS is often blurred by embedding the ADV directly into the WBS without rephrasing it. This blurring must be avoided. The elements of an ADV are product modules; they are specified by *noun phrases* that designate things, as in Figure 5.4. Work breakdown structures for software projects are process-oriented, hierarchical decompositions of *work* activities and tasks. The elements of a WBS are specified by *verb phrases* that indicate actions to be taken, as in Figures 5.4*a* and 5.4*b* (e.g., *manage* project, *develop* software, *perform* CM). The elements of an ADV are related to the elements in a WBS by embedding within the WBS the work needed to develop or otherwise obtain the software modules.

The top level of your WBS should include all of the major work activities within the scope of your project; that is, the top level should encompass all work activities necessary to satisfy the requirements, constraints, and contractual commitments for your project (e.g., project management, system analysis, software development, verification and validation, and product delivery). Each node of the WBS in your initial project plan should be decomposed into sublevels until each of the following WBS decomposition criteria are satisfied:

1. hidden complexities are exposed (i.e., the job to be done is understood);
2. opportunities for reuse of existing software components can be identified;
3. the necessary hardware resources, such as computer memory and processor speed, can be specified (which may result in revision of the hardware requirements); and
4. estimates of effort needed to develop the software can be made.

Satisfying criterion 1 is necessary in order to satisfy criterion 2; this may not be possible without prototyping, feasibility studies, and revision of the requirements. Also the estimated effort to find, assess, and modify modules to be reused must be balanced against the effort required to develop new modules. It is much better to confront these issues early in your project rather than later.

The WBS depicted in Figures 5.5*a* and 5.5*b* is partially decomposed. Elements 1, 2, 4 to 8, and 3.1, 3.3, and 3.4 should be expanded as necessary to satisfy the WBS decomposition criteria. For example, decomposition of element 1, Manage Project, might be as follows:

1 Manage Project
- 1.1 Initiate project
  - 1.1.1 Identify stakeholders
  - 1.1.2 Develop/clarify requirements
  - 1.1.3 Prepare initial estimates
  - 1.1.4 Prepare initial project plan
  - 1.1.5 Obtain commitment to the plan
- 1.2 Conduct project
  - 1.2.1 Measure and control project
  - 1.2.2 Lead and direct personnel
  - 1.2.3 Communicate and coordinate
  - 1.2.4 Manage risk
- 1.3 Closeout project
  - 1.3.1 Obtain product acceptance
  - 1.3.2 Conduct postmortem sessions
  - 1.3.3 Prepare and distribute lessons-learned report
  - 1.3.4 Assist in reassigning project personnel

During planning the various paths in your WBS may be decomposed to different levels in order to satisfy the WBS decomposition criteria. Familiar work of low complexity will require less decomposition to permit confident estimates than a new kind of work of uncertain complexity. An identified opportunity for reuse of an existing module will require less decomposition if you are confident the candidate module will be suitable, and more decomposition to assess its suitability if you are less confident in it. The elements of a WBS are typically decomposed to three or four levels during planning; one or two additional levels are typically added during execution of the project.

5.7 GUIDELINES FOR DESIGNING WORK BREAKDOWN STRUCTURES

The work breakdown structure (WBS) is a fundamental tool for planning a software project and for measuring and controlling the progress of a project; it integrates the managerial and technical activities of a software project. A well-designed WBS is thus an essential element of a software project management plan. Fifteen guidelines for designing work breakdown structures are itemized in Table 5.2 and discussed below. Additional guidelines for using the WBS to track the progress of your project are presented in Chapter 11. As indicated by these guidelines, your WBS should be designed and structured with the same care used to design the architectural views of the software system or product.

TABLE 5.2 Fifteen guidelines for designing work breakdown structures

Guideline	Work Breakdown
1:	Use the Architecture Decomposition View (ADV) of the software architecture as the basis for developing the WBS.
2:	Structure the ADV and the WBS to facilitate work assignments.
3:	Develop and use process-oriented work breakdown structures.
4:	Embed the work activities to develop and modify product modules in the WBS.
5:	Partition the scope of the project into not more than 7 or 8 functional areas at the top level of the WBS.
6:	Limit the fan-out of each element (i.e., the scope of each element) in the WBS to seven or less.
7:	Limit the maximum depth of the WBS to six or fewer levels.
8:	Use a decimal numbering system to systematically identify work activities and tasks.
9:	Allocate prioritized requirements to development activities and tasks in the WBS.
10:	Design the WBS top-down, bottom-up, and middle out.
11:	Use work packages to specify project tasks.
12:	Analyze work packages for desired properties.
13:	Derive the schedule network from the work packages.
14:	Determine resource requirements using the work packages and the schedule network.
15:	Revise and elaborate the WBS periodically and as events dictate.

WBS Design Guideline 1: Use the decomposition view of the software architecture (ADV) as a basis for developing the WBS As illustrated in Figure 5.4, the elements of an ADV are denoted by noun phrases; they are things. The work to develop the elements of an ADV is embedded in the WBS by adding appropriate verbs to the noun phrases in the ADV.

WBS Design Guideline 2: Structure the ADV to facilitate work assignments The decomposition view of the software architecture embedded in the WBS should provide opportunities for concurrent work activities. For example, the hardware driver, financial transaction, diagnostics, and communication modules in Figure 5.4 can be developed or otherwise obtained by different teams working concurrently; the COMM package can also be procured concurrently. Similarly the validator, processor, recorder, and terminator modules of the financial transaction module can be developed by individuals or teams working concurrently on the modules.

WBS Design Guideline 3: Develop and use process-oriented work breakdown structures As illustrated in Figures 5.5*a* and 5.5*b*, a WBS specifies work activities, tasks, and the containment relationships among them. Each activity and task is specified by a verb phrase that indicates actions to be taken.

WBS Design Guideline 4: Embed the work activities to develop and modify product modules in the WBS The activities and tasks to develop or otherwise obtain the modules in the decomposition view of the software architecture in Figure 5.4 are embedded in the WBS of Figures 5.5*a* and 5.5*b* by converting the noun phrases in Figure 5.4 to the corresponding verb phrases in Figures 5.5*a* and 5.5*b*.

WBS Design Guideline 5: Partition the scope of the project into not more than seven or eight functional areas at the top level of the WBS The top level of a WBS should partition all the work activities to be accomplished into seven or eight elements, as illustrated in Figures 5.5*a* and 5.5*b*. Limiting the number of activities to seven or eight elements at the top level facilitates management of the intellectual complexity of a project by partitioning it into a small number of work activities to be directly managed by you, the project manager, and by those who report directly to you. Subordinate activities and tasks are assigned to team leaders and team members who are responsible for those activities and tasks.

WBS Design Guideline 6: Limit the fan-out of each element in the WBS to seven or eight The fan-out of a WBS element is the number of branches connecting an element to its immediate subordinate elements. As described above, one role of a WBS is to designate roles, responsibilities, and authorities in a software project. Limiting fan-out has the advantage of controlling the complexity of each work activity by limiting the number of subordinate activities or tasks that must be managed to accomplish that work activity; intellectual manageability of a project is thus obtained. This advantage is not dissimilar to the advantage gained by limiting the fan-out of product modules in the architecture decomposition view of software architecture.

WBS Design Guideline 7: Limit the depth of the WBS to six or fewer levels The depth of a WBS is the length of the longest path(s) in the WBS; in Figures 5.5*a* and 5.5*b* the depth is 4, which is indicated by the number of digits in the lowest level task designators. Limiting the depth of each path in a WBS to six or fewer levels has similar advantages to limiting fan-out in controlling intellectual manageability of a project. Decomposing a path more than six levels to satisfy the WBS decomposition criteria of exposing complexity and risk factors indicates areas of the product and/or process architecture that must be studied in greater detail and reconfigured as appropriate.

Consider a software project that has 10 developers working for 12 months (480 staff-weeks). If each development task represents one staff-week of effort there would be 480 leaf nodes in the software development sub-tree of the WBS. Assuming software development (design, code, test) is 50% of the total effort, and assuming all project tasks are decomposed to a level of one staff-week, the WBS would have 960 leaf nodes. In contrast, a WBS that has 6 levels with a fan-out of 7 at each node (a 6×7 WBS) would have 7^6 leaf node tasks (117,659). Clearly, a 6×7 WBS is sufficient for the largest mega-projects.

Another design consideration: if a node in your WBS has, say, 3 or 4 sub-levels with fan-outs of 5 or 6 at each node, this may indicate the need to "spin off" that segment of the WBS into a separate subproject (a 3×6 WBS has 216 leaf node tasks).

WBS Design Guideline 8: Use a decimal numbering system to specify work activities and tasks in the WBS The numbering system illustrated in Figures 5.5*a* and 5.5*b* provides a systematic way of specifying the containment and sibling relationships among activities and tasks. Task 3.2.4.3, in Figures 5.5*a* and 5.5*b*, for example, is on level 4 of the WBS because there are 4 digits in its identifier; it is the 3th element of the 4th element of the 2nd element of the 3rd element in the WBS. All elements having a 2 in the 2nd position are sibling software work activities (e.g., the Build FINAT activities in Figures 5.5*a* and 5.5*b*). Some organizations specify the numbers to be used in designating the top elements in work breakdown structures. For example, every work element in every WBS that starts with a 3 would designate software work, and elements of work starting with a 6 would denote configuration management. This convention facilitates uniform reporting and accounting practices among projects across an organization.

WBS Design Guideline 9: Allocate prioritized requirements to development activities and tasks in the WBS Each activity and task in a WBS indicates work that must be accomplished and work products that must be produced. Allocating requirements to development activities and tasks, as illustrated in Figures 5.5*a* and 5.5*b*, provides prioritized specifications for the work products to be produced by those activities and tasks. In addition to specifying the features to be provided, the allocated requirements should specify design constraints, capacities, performance, interfaces, and quality attributes, as appropriate.

Product features should be uniquely allocated to tasks so that work assignments for building the modules are clearly defined. Other requirements (design constraints, capacities, performance, interfaces, and quality attributes) may apply to multiple modules, perhaps including the entire system or product, as discussed in

Chapter 3. Those requirements should be allocated to the highest level activity to which they apply and be "flowed down" to the descendents of that activity.

WBS Design Guideline 10: Design the WBS top down, bottom up, and middle out Designing a WBS is best done iteratively by interleaving top-down, bottom-up, and middle-out strategies. In this regard the cognitive processes involved when developing a WBS (i.e., designing a software project) are not unlike those observed in designers of software [Walz93].

Top-down development of a WBS proceeds by partitioning the scope of the project into a set of top-level activities and successively decomposing activities until a set of tasks is specified that satisfy the WBS decomposition criteria listed above. Bottom-up development of a WBS proceeds by identifying a set of tasks that must be performed and grouping related tasks into activities. Middle-out development of a WBS proceeds by identifying a mid-level activity that must be performed, decomposing it into tasks and/or subordinate activities, grouping it with similar activities, and connecting the related set of activities to a higher level activity.

WBS Design Guideline 11: Use work packages to specify development tasks Work packages are specifications for the activities and tasks in a WBS. Tasks are the lowest level elements in the WBS. Work packages for activities are aggregations of work packages for subordinate activities and tasks.

A work package should contain:

- the corresponding WBS number and name,
- a brief description of the task,
- estimated duration,
- resources needed,
- predecessor and successor tasks,
- work products to be produced,
- work products that will be placed under version control (baselined),
- risk factors (i.e., potential problems that might interfere with successful completion of the work package), and
- objective acceptance criteria for the work products generated by the task.

A template for work packages is illustrated in Table 5.3*a*; an example is provided in Table 5.3*b*.

WBS Design Guideline 12: Analyze work packages for desired properties The attributes of work packages, and collections of work packages, can be analyzed to determine various project factors. For example, the estimated cost of personnel to execute a work package can be determined from the numbers and kinds of people specified and the estimated duration of the task. In Table 5.3*b*, the cost of personnel is the loaded salaries (i.e., pay plus overhead) for 10 staff-weeks of senior designer effort. The cost of other resources can be similarly determined: the workstation and software tools in Table 5.3*b* may be available at no cost, or a cost to be borne by this task, or the cost may be amortized across this task and other tasks that will use

TABLE 5.3A Template for work packages

Task identifier:	«WBS number and name»
Task description:	«brief description»
Estimated duration:	«days or weeks»
Resources needed:	
Personnel:	«numbers of people needed to complete this task»
Skills:	«personnel skills needed to complete this task»
Tools:	«software and hardware needed»
Travel:	«to where? for how long?»
Other:	«other resources needed to complete this task»
Predecessor tasks:	«to be completed before this task can begin»
Successor tasks:	«to start after this task is completed»
Work products:	«outputs of this task»
Baselines:	«work products to be placed under version control»
Risk factors:	«potential problems for this task»
Acceptance criteria:	«for the work products of this task»

TABLE 5.3B A work package example

Task identifier:	3.2.2.1 Design transaction processor
Task description:	Specify internal architecture of the transaction processor module
Estimated duration:	2 weeks
Resources needed:	
Personnel:	2 senior telecom designers
Skills:	Designers must know UML
Tools:	One workstation running Rapsody
Travel:	Three day design review in San Diego for 2 people
Predecessor tasks:	3.2.1 Develop system architecture
Successor tasks:	3.3.2.2 Implement transaction processor
Work products:	Architectural specification for transaction processor and test plan
Baselines created:	Architectural specification for transaction processor and text plan
Risk factors:	Designers not identified
Acceptance criteria:	Successful design inspection by peers and approval of transaction processor design by the software architect

those resources; the cost of travel can be determined and included in the cost of executing the work package (in Table 5.3*b*, two round trips to San Diego and 3 days travel support for 2 people).

The estimated costs for a collection of work packages can be aggregated (i.e., rolled up) to determine the elements of cost for various kinds of activities and to determine the overall cost estimate for the parent activity. Estimated costs of development tasks and activities can be rolled up to provide an estimated cost for software development, which can be used as a basis of estimation for the entire project. For example, a project would be estimated to cost $100,000 USD if software development was estimated to cost $50,000 USD and was estimated to be 50% of overall project cost (50% perhaps determined from historical data within the organization).

If the roll-up of costs results in an estimate that exceeds the constraint on the project budget, you can start at the top level and reallocate portions of the budget to activities and tasks in a top-down manner so that the allocations to the subordinate elements of each activity do not exceed the amount allocated to that activity. This may involve eliminating or simplifying some product requirements and/or incurring greater levels of risk.

WBS Design Guideline 13: Derive the schedule network from the work packages A schedule network for a set of tasks can be constructed from the durations, predecessors, and successors of the work packages for those tasks, as explained in the following section of this chapter. Constructing the schedule network may reveal discontinuities, circularities, and other inconsistencies among predecessor and successor tasks that can be resolved by iterative refinement of the work package specifications.

WBS Design Guideline 14: Determine resource requirements using the work packages and the schedule network Knowing the time in the schedule when various tasks are planned to occur permits determination of the dates when various kinds of resources will be needed and the durations for which they will be required; for example, the need date for the unidentified senior designers in Figure 5.5*b* can be determined from the development schedule. If the need date is three months hence, there is adequate time to acquire the designers; if the need date is next week, you are probably in big trouble because failure to complete the work package on schedule will delay subsequent tasks and might delay completion of the project. Resource profiles for the various kinds of resources needed can be produced by summing up the resource requirements across the schedule, as illustrated later in this chapter.

WBS Design Guideline 15: Revise and elaborate the WBS periodically and as events dictate The elements of the initial WBS are decomposed to levels that satisfy the WBS decomposition criteria. As the project evolves, understanding grows and circumstances change; increased detail can be added to facilitate work assignments to individuals and teams. Additional work elements may be identified and others revised. The WBS should be updated each month in a rolling-wave manner. Also events such as major changes to requirements, schedule, and resources must be reflected in a revised WBS. The WBS must be placed under version control to clearly identify the current version and to provide a historical record of the evolution of the WBS.

An alternative approach is to interchange the order of guidelines 11, 12, 13, and 14 by first developing the schedule network and resource estimates for each task in the schedule network (guidelines 13 and 14) and then using the schedule network and resource estimates to specify and analyze the work packages (guidelines 11 and 12). In any case, as will be shown in Chapter 8, work package specifications for the WBS elements are essential for allocating the work to development teams and tracking the progress of their work.

5.8 DEVELOPING THE PROJECT SCHEDULE

The work packages for your tasks specify the estimated durations of the tasks and their predecessor and successor tasks. Given a collection of work packages, a task list such as that in Table 5.4 can be developed using the predecessor and successor information contained in the work packages. Alternatively, you can first construct a task list as an initial step in specifying the WBS and work packages. A task list can be portrayed as a schedule network such as the one in Figure 5.6; the figure contains the information in Table 5.4 but conveys it in a different representation. Note that only the tasks (lowest level elements) in Table 5.4 are shown in Figure 5.6. In addition Figure 5.6 illustrates the two critical paths in the schedule (see the following section).

A well-formed schedule network, such as the one in Figure 5.6, is an acyclic directed graph. The arrows are annotated with the corresponding WBS (and work package) numbers and the task durations. The numbers in the nodes of the graph are project milestones. The representation in Figure 5.6 is a task-on-arrow diagram. Complementary representations that place the tasks in the nodes of the graph are sometimes used; in this case the milestones are implicitly represented by the arrowheads because a subsequent task cannot begin until the immediately preceding tasks have been completed.

Note in Figure 5.6 that external event 2.1 must occur before the project can begin. Some of your projects may have other external events (i.e., events that are not in your control) that must occur at intermediate milestones before the project can continue; for example, availability of an interface specification or delivery of needed hardware. These external events are depicted by arrows connected to the appropriate milestones, as in the case of event 2.1.

TABLE 5.4 A task list

Activity number	Description	Predecessors	Duration	Staff number
2.1	Receive approval to proceed	—	—	—
3.1	Analyze requirements	2.1	1	2
3.2	Design			
3.2.1	Redesign existing components	3.1	6	4
3.2.2	Design new components	3.1	3	1
3.2.3	Design interfaces	3.2.2	1	2
3.3	Implement code			
3.3.1	Implement new code	3.2.2	6	2
3.3.2	Modify existing code	3.2.1, 3.2.3	5	1
3.4	Finish implementation			
3.4.1	Develop integration plan	3.2.2	2	2
3.4.2	Finish unit testing	3.3.1, 3.3.2	2	2
3.4.3	Update documentation	3.3.1, 3.3.2	2	3
3.5	Integrate and test			
3.5.1	Develop integration tests	3.4.1	1	3
3.5.2	Perform integration tests	3.4.2, 3.4.3, 3.5.1	1	2
3.6	Perform acceptance tests	3.5.2	1	1

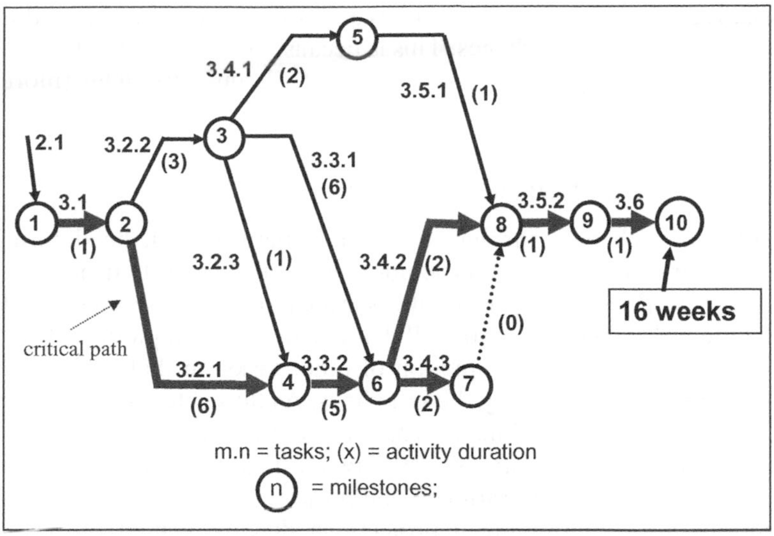

FIGURE 5.6 A critical-path activity network

TABLE 5.5 Milestones for the schedule network in Figure 5.6

Event	Description
1	Project initiation
2	Requirements analysis completed
3	Design of new components completed
4	Existing components redesigned; interfaces to new components designed
5	Integration plan completed
6	New code implemented; existing code modified
7	Documentation updated
8	Unit testing completed; documentation updated; integration tests ready
9	Integration tests completed
10	Acceptance tests completed

Also note the "dummy" task of zero duration connecting milestones 7 and 8. Inserting milestone 7 and a task of zero duration permits separate reporting of task completions for tasks 3.4.2 and 3.4.3. Because these tasks are on critical paths (see the following section), it is important to know when each task has been completed and, if milestone 8 is not reached as planned, which task has been delayed. Additional milestones and dummy tasks can be inserted into a schedule network, as desired, to improve the granularity of progress reporting.

The numbers in the circles are *project milestones* that are used as progress indicators during project execution. Achievement of a milestone is determined by verifying that all of the tasks along the path leading to that milestone have been successfully completed. A task is successfully completed by satisfying the acceptance criteria for the work products produced by that task, as specified in the task's work package. The milestones for Figure 5.6 are listed in Table 5.5.

Tasks 3.2.1, 3.3.1, and 3.3.2 (and perhaps 3.2.2) should be decomposed into subtasks with associated work packages. This is because overruns in the long durations of these tasks would not provide early warning of schedule problems (more on this in Chapter 8).

5.8.1 The Critical-Path Method

The duration of each path through a schedule network can be determined by summing the durations of the tasks along that path. A path that has the longest duration is a *critical path.* A critical path is critical in the sense that any delays in completing the tasks along that path will delay scheduled completion of the project unless compensated by early completion of other tasks on that path. The critical paths in Figure 5.6 are denoted by the bold lines. As illustrated, there may be more than one critical path in a schedule network. The critical path (or paths) determines the overall schedule. The durations of the two critical paths in Figure 5.6 are 16 weeks. This is the estimated duration of the project.

This approach to determining a project schedule is termed the critical-path method (CPM). Any schedule overruns for any tasks on a critical path will extend the entire schedule unless other tasks on that critical path are finished in less time than estimated to compensate for the overruns.

Each path in a CPM network that is not critical has associated nonzero *slack time.* For example, summing the task durations along the top-most path in Figure 5.6 (denoted by milestones 1, 2, 3, 5, 8) indicates that milestone 8 can be reached in 7 weeks. However, the project cannot continue until tasks 3.4.2 and 3.4.3 also reach milestone 8 at week 14. The top-most path therefore has 7 weeks of slack time between milestones 0 and 8. Slack time can be used to adjust the scheduling of noncritical tasks. For example, task 3.4.1 might be scheduled for weeks 8 and 9 if the resources are not available to execute the task in weeks 5 and 6 (the earliest start time for task 3.4.1). Slack time is also known as float. Tasks on a critical path have zero float.

5.8.2 The PERT Method

The critical-path method provides an estimated schedule for a project but does not provide any indication of the probability of meeting that schedule. For example, what is the probability that the project depicted in Figure 5.6 can be completed in the estimated 16 weeks? Is 16 weeks overly optimistic, about right, or overly pessimistic?

The PERT method provides probability distributions for achieving project milestones on schedule, based on the probability of completing each task along the path to that milestone. To use the PERT method, three numbers are specified for each task, as illustrated in Figure 5.7: an optimistic (shortest probable) estimated duration, the 50% probably estimated duration, and a pessimistic (longest probable) estimated duration. The three estimates for each task are used to compute the expected value and standard deviation of a probability function for each task. The expected values and standard deviations of the probability functions for the tasks along a path to a milestone are used to compute the probability distribution of achieving that milestone at various times (see the PERT sidebar for the PERT

CALCULATING CRITICAL PATHS AND SLACK TIMES

Critical paths can be found by summing the durations of the tasks on each path through a schedule network and selecting the longest paths (or the longest one in the case of a single critical path). An algorithmic approach to determining critical paths and slack times for tasks not on a critical path involves calculating the following quantities associated with each task: EST, EFT, LST, and LFT.

EST (Earliest Start Time)

EST is the earliest time a task can be started. The EST of a task is the EST of the preceding task plus the duration of that preceding task. If multiple tasks immediately precede the starting milestone of the task for which the EST is being computed, the preceding task having the largest EST plus the duration of that task must be used. The duration of the project is the EST of the nonexistent task that would follow the project completion milestone (i.e., the EST associated at the final milestone). The EST at milestone 10 of Figure 5.6 is 16 weeks.

EFT (Earliest Finish Time)

EFT is the earliest time at which a task can be completed. EFT is EST plus the duration of the task.

LST (Latest Start Time)

LST is the latest time at which a task can be started without delaying completion of the project. LST is computed by setting the LST at the final milestone equal to the EST at that milestone. The LST of each preceding task is computed by subtracting the duration of the subsequent task from the LST of the subsequent task. For example, the LST of task 3.6 in Figure 5.6 is 15 (16 – 1). If multiple tasks emanate from the milestone on which a task terminates, the one having the smallest LST is used. In Figure 5.6 the LST associated with task 3.2.2 is 3 because the LSTs of tasks 3.3.1, 3.2.3, and 3.4.1 are 6, 6, and 11, respectively, and 6 (the smallest LST) minus 3 (the duration of task 3.2.2) equals 3.

LFT (Latest Finish Time)

LFT is the latest time a task can be finished without delay completion of the project. LFT for each task is LST plus the task duration.

The slack time, or float, associated with each task is EST – LST (or EFT – LST). Tasks on a critical path have zero slack time. *Free float* is the slack time available to a task when all preceding tasks and all subsequent tasks start as early as possible (EST). *Total float* for a task is the slack time available when all preceding tasks on the path of that task start as early as possible (EST) and all subsequent tasks start as late as possible (LST). Slack time available to a task is bracketed by total float minus free float; however, using the entire total float available to a task will make all subsequent tasks on that path critical because all of those tasks will then start as late as possible.

CPM can also be used to track the progress of a project. Each milestone can be checked off as it is reached; failure to achieve a milestone as scheduled provides early warning of risk to completing the project on schedule. Critical paths can be, and should be, recalculated as the project evolves.

A historical Note

The critical-path method was developed in the late 1950s by M. R. Walker of E.I. DuPont de Nemours and Co. and J. E. Kelly of Remington Rand as a mechanism for scheduling the construction and refurbishing of chemical plants.

formulas). Computing the probability distribution for the final milestone provides a range of estimated project durations at various levels of probability.

A straightforward approach to computing the probability of completing a project in time T_s or sooner, $P(t \leq T_s)$, is to compute the mean value μ and standard deviation σ of the probability density function for the final milestone based on the probability functions of the tasks on a critical path to the final milestone. The mean value μ is the sum of the mean values along the critical path. The standard deviation σ is the square root of the sum of the squares of the standard deviations along the critical path (see the PERT sidebar for the PERT formulas). Critical paths can be computed using the 50% probable estimates for each task.

Various values of $P(t \leq T_s)$ can be obtained using a standard Z-distribution table and the formula: $t = \sigma Z + \mu$, where $t \leq T_s$.

The probability is obtained by reading the value of P corresponding to the value of Z in the Z-distribution table.

If, for example, the mean value is $\mu = 12$ and the standard deviation is $\sigma = 3$ for milestone 10 in Figure 5.7, the probability $P(t \leq T_s)$ of completing the project at the indicated times t or in less time are listed in Table 5.6. Other values of P can be

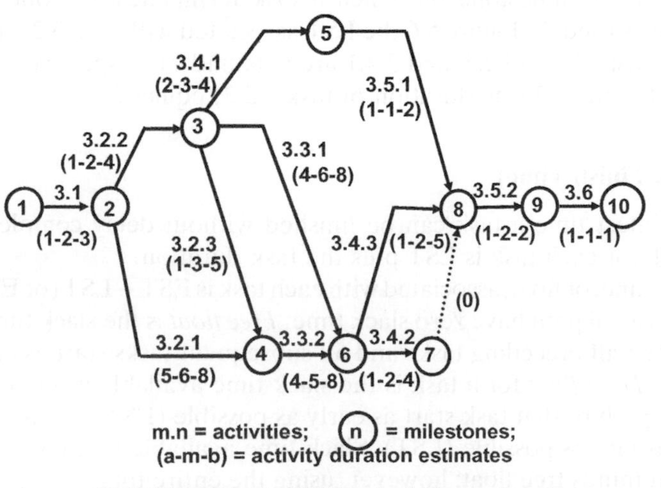

FIGURE 5.7 A PERT scheduling network

TABLE 5.6 Probability of completing a project in time t or less when $\mu = 12$ and $\sigma = 3$

Z	$P\ (t \le T_s)$	t
0	50%	12 weeks
1	84%	15 weeks
2	97.7%	18 weeks

obtained using the formula and a Z-distribution table. For example, it is 90% probable the project can be completed in roughly 16 weeks or less if $\mu = 12$ and $\sigma = 3$.

5.8.3 Task-Gantt Charts

There are two kinds of Gantt charts: task Gantts and resource Gantts. A task-Gantt chart (the most commonly used of the two) is a plot of tasks versus the times in which the tasks are scheduled to occur (resource Gantt charts are discussed subsequently). The task-Gantt chart in Figure 5.8 is derived from the CPM network in Figure 5.6. Note that the vertical axis depicts the WBS structure. Note also that only tasks (lowest level elements of the WBS) are shown in Figure 5.8; the schedules for higher level activities are indicated by arrows that span the extent of the tasks that are subordinate to the activities.

The cross-hatched tasks are those on the critical paths. Note that those tasks are sequenced consecutively on the time line. The noncritical tasks (in the scheduling sense) are shown with earliest start times (EST) and earliest finish times (EFT) indicated. The extent of the "box" for each noncritical task indicates the latest finish time (LFT) for that task based on scheduling constraints. The difference between the EFT and LFT is the free float for each of the tasks based on the EST for each task (see the sidebar on calculating critical paths and slack times).

Figure 5.9 is an augmented version of Figure 5.8; it contains only the tasks. The numbers associated with the tasks in Figure 5.9 are the number people needed to perform the tasks; they were obtained from Table 5.4. The numbers along the x axis are the sums of the people needed to perform all tasks in the indicated time periods. They are obtained by summing the numbers in each column.

Simplicity of representation is the primary advantage of task-Gantt charts. The primary disadvantage is that schedule dependencies among noncritical tasks are not explicitly represented. To overcome this problem, you can insert links in a Gantt chart to show the dependencies, as in Figure 5.10, or you can refer to the schedule network to see the dependencies.

5.9 DEVELOPING RESOURCE PROFILES

A task-Gantt chart annotated with resource requirements, as in Figures 5.9 and 5.10, is a convenient tool for developing the resource profiles for your project. The resulting staffing profile, based on earliest start times for all tasks, is illustrated in Figure 5.11. The numbers associated with the cross-hatched areas indicate resources needed for tasks on the critical paths. The other numbers indicate resources needed for noncritical tasks scheduled at their earliest start times.

PERT (PROGRAM EVALUATION AND REVIEW TECHNIQUE)

In the PERT approach, three estimates are provided for each task:

a: the shortest estimated duration (optimistic)
m: the 50% probable estimated duration
b: the longest estimated duration (pessimistic)

If beta probability distributions are assumed for the tasks, the three values can be used to calculate the mean of the probability density function for each task.

The mean *m* is computed as

$$m = \frac{a + 4m + b}{6}.$$

The square of the standard deviation σ is computed as

$$\sigma^2 = \frac{b - a}{x}.$$

The value of x varies, depending on the probability levels used to assign values to *a* and *b*. If *a* and *b* are assigned at the 5% (optimistic) and 95% (pessimistic) levels of probability the formula is

$$\sigma^2 = \frac{b - a}{6} \qquad \text{(i.e., } x = 6\text{)}.$$

If *a* is assigned at the 20% level of probability (optimistic) and *b* is assigned at the 80% level (pessimistic) the formula is

$$\sigma^2 = \frac{b - a}{3.2} \qquad \text{(i.e., } x = 3.2\text{)}.$$

Beta distributions are reasonable choices for the probability functions because they are defined on finite intervals and can be skewed or symmetrical, depending on the values of *a* and *b* in relation to *m*.

The mean of the cumulative probability density μ for the tasks along a path to a project milestone is the sum of the means of the probability densities for the tasks on the path to that milestone. The standard deviation σ of the probability density function at the milestone is the square root of the sum of the squares of the individual deviations.

Nontrivial scheduling networks have multiple paths. Comprehensive determination of the probability functions for the completion milestone of a project would involve calculating μ and σ for each path in the network. A simple and effective approach is to calculate the probability distribution function for the tasks on the (or *a*) critical path, where the critical path is determined using the most likely (*m*) values of the tasks.

A Historical Note

PERT was developed in the late 1950s for the POLARIS missile program by the Program Evaluation Branch of the Special Projects office of the U.S. Navy, with the assistance of the Lockheed Missile Systems division and the consulting firm of Booz-Allen and Hamilton. Because the Polaris program was a research and development project involving numerous contractors and numerous technologies, the large number of uncertainties in conducting the program resulted in the probabilistic approach to schedule estimation.

Although most software projects are not as large and complex as was the POLARIS program, they are nevertheless characterized by many uncertainties. The PERT method is thus applicable. The biggest problem in using PERT is estimating three durations for each task. "What-if" analysis (trying different values to see the consequences of "what if") can be used in the absence of solid data on which to base the estimates.

PERT methods are further discussed in Chapter 6 (Estimation Techniques) and Chapter 9 (Risk Management) of this text.

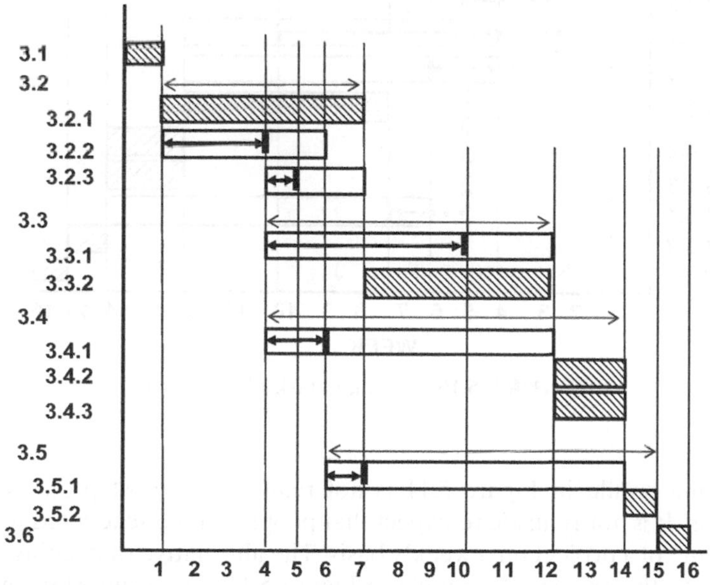

FIGURE 5.8 Task-Gantt chart corresponding to Figure 5.6

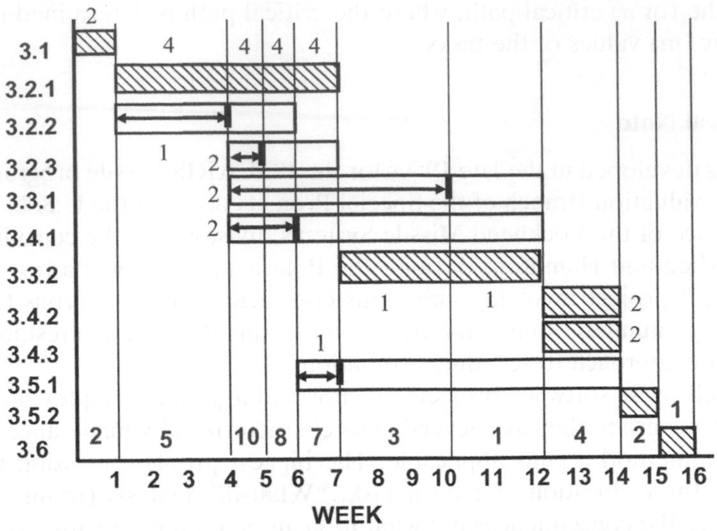

FIGURE 5.9 An augmented task-Gantt chart

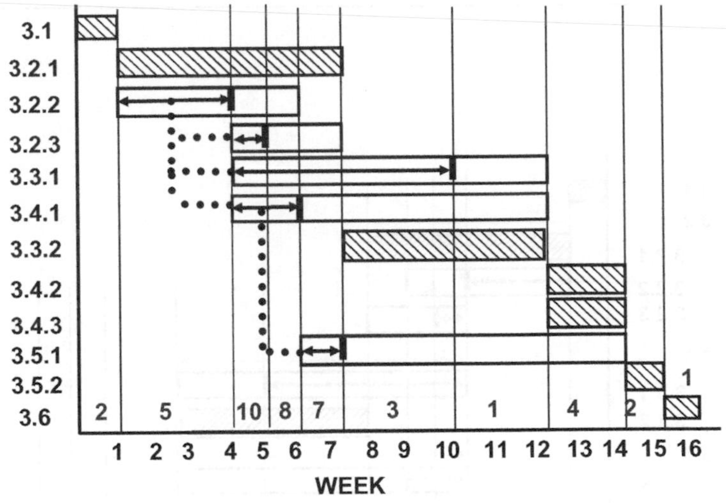

FIGURE 5.10 A linked task-Gantt chart

The staffing profile in Figure 5.11 is not realistic for most projects and most organizations. It is not realistic to expect that people can be scheduled to "drop in" and "drop out" of a project on a weekly basis. The alternative of keeping peak staffing assigned to the project (10 people in Figure 5.11) and using staff members as they are needed is also not realistic. What do they do the rest of the time? Stay home? Interfere with the work of others? Go to the movies? Go fishing? Go skiing? And what is the impact of paying staff for unproductive time? They might work on other projects, but scheduling resources for multiple projects at this level of granularity is not practical.

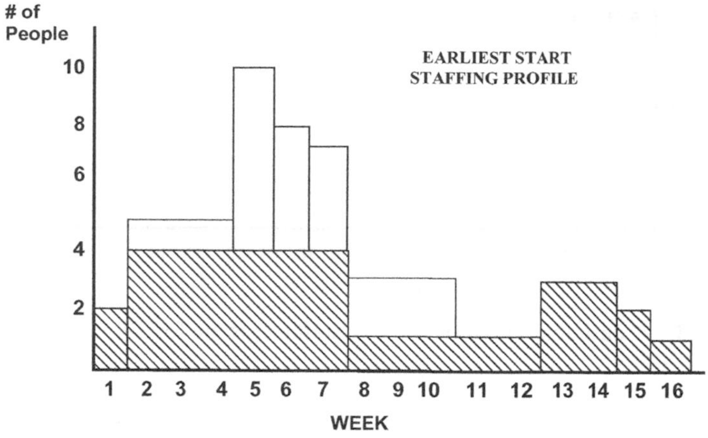

FIGURE 5.11 Staffing profile for earliest start times for all tasks

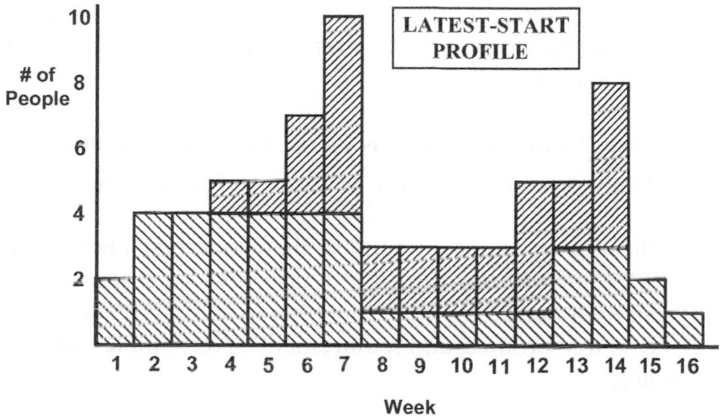

FIGURE 5.12 Staffing profile for latest start times for all tasks

The slack times illustrated in Figures 5.8, 5.9, and 5.10 can be used to adjust the staffing profile in an attempt to obtain a more feasible staffing profile. If, for example, you were to schedule all noncritical tasks at their latest start times, the staffing profile in Figure 5.12 would result. This profile is not realistic for two reasons:

1. the peaks and valleys in the profile and
2. the cross-hatching indicates all paths in the schedule network are critical because starting all tasks as late as possible means a delay in completing any task will delay the overall schedule.

In Figure 5.12 the cross-hatching for the original critical path is shown slanting as in Figure 5.11; the cross-hatching on the upper part of Figure 5.12 depicts the criticality of the other paths. If you try various combinations of scheduling for the noncritical tasks in Figure 5.6, you will find that it is not possible to obtain a flat staffing profile, such as the one illustrated in Figure 5.13. The schedule/resource

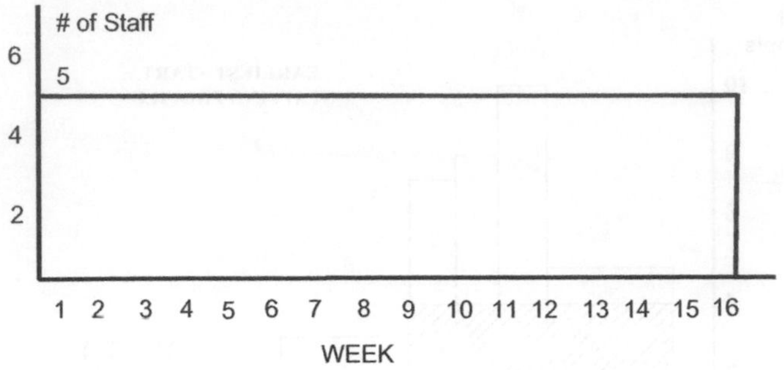

FIGURE 5.13 A desirable but unobtainable staffing profile for Table 5.4 and Figure 5.6

allocation problem in this example is caused by the large number of software developers needed in weeks 4, 5, and 6, as indicated in Figures 5.9 and 5.10.

The resource allocation problem is further complicated when there are multiple kinds of resources to be allocated to the schedule (e.g., designers, coders, testers, safety and security specialists, technical writers). Other factors that complicate the allocation of resources include:

- lack of sufficient resources of various kinds, when needed, and
- sharing of resources among multiple projects and programs.

Despite these difficulties it is recommended that your first pass at developing a project schedule proceed without regard to constraints on resources and resource allocation. You can then iterate on the initial plan to achieve an acceptable balance among schedule, resource profiles, and requirements. Acceptable options for achieving a balance include:

- rearranging the tasks so that fewer resources are needed in peak weeks,
- extending the schedule so that fewer resources are needed in peak weeks,
- adding more resources to maintain the schedule,
- using more productive resources so that fewer numbers are needed, and
- descoping the requirements so that fewer resources and less time are needed.

Combinations of these options may be used to achieve an acceptable balance.

Unacceptable options include:

- producing an unrealistic plan that has no chance of being successfully implemented;
- planning for overtime; and
- reducing or eliminating quality control activities such as inspections, reviews, and testing

Unfortunately, the unacceptable options are often chosen. Planning for overtime is a particularly bad choice because people will become tired and demotivated. Also

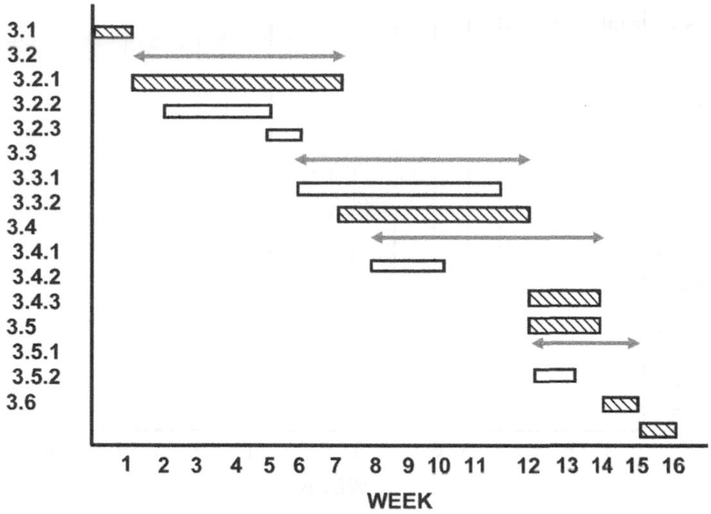

FIGURE 5.14 A WBS-Gantt chart for a project schedule

most software projects hit periods when short bursts of overtime are needed. Planned overtime leaves no reserve for those periods.

The representations of Gantt charts in Figures 5.8, 5.9, and 5.10 can be used to plan the project schedule and develop the resource profiles. When the scheduling decisions have been made for tasks with associated slack times, a combined WBS-Gantt chart for that schedule can be prepared, as in Figure 5.14. As before, the cross-hatch bars indicate critical path tasks, and the open bars indicate tasks for which slack time exists. Also note that only the tasks are scheduled; the schedule for each activity spans the extent of the subordinate task schedules.

5.10 RESOURCE-GANTT CHARTS

Resource-Gantt charts can be used to depict the tasks assigned to various resources. The grid-filled tasks in Figure 5.15 are those for which the expertise of Joe Hotshot is needed and the time in which they have been scheduled; the tasks as scheduled in Figures 5.8, 5.9, and 5.10 to which Joe is not assigned have been deleted from Figure 5.15. Figure 5.16 depicts the hours per week that will be required of Joe to complete those tasks. This is clearly unworkable; each resource must be allocated within the constraints of availability.

5.11 ESTIMATING PROJECT EFFORT, COST, AND SCHEDULE

Total effort for the tasks listed in Table 5.4 is 68 staff-weeks; total effort is determined by multiplying duration by the number of people for each task and summing the products. If loaded salary per staff-week is X and the tasks in Table 5.4 represent 50% of project cost, the estimated cost is $2 \times X \times 68$. If, for example,

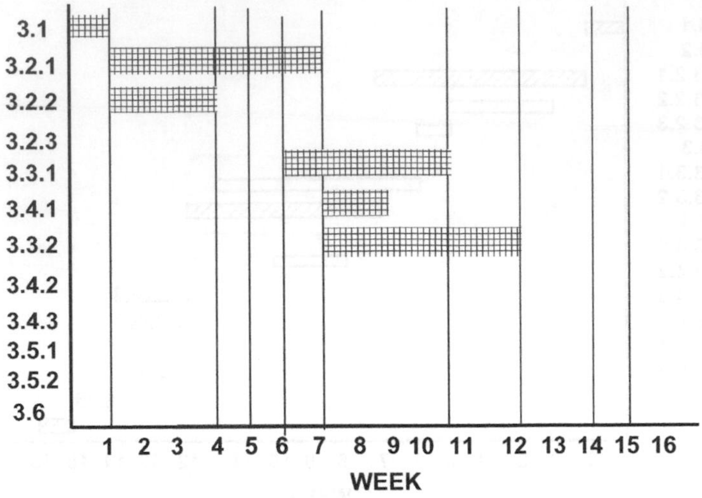

FIGURE 5.15 Resource-Gantt chart for Joe Hotshot

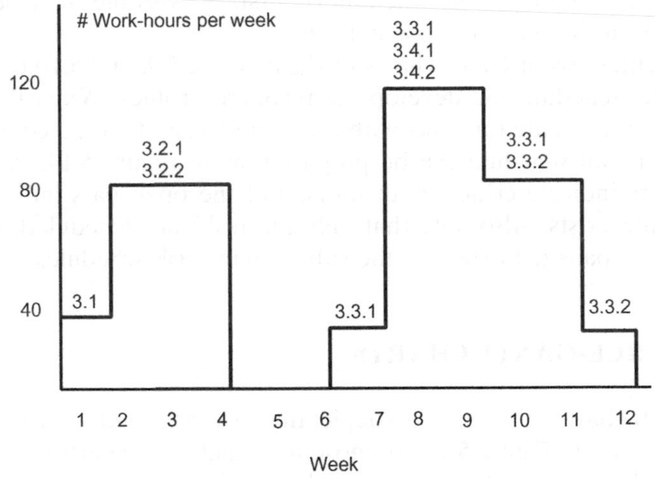

FIGURE 5.16 Resource profile for Joe Hotshot

loaded salaries are $2500 USD per week, the cost of the project is estimated to be $340,000 USD. The critical path approach indicates that the project will require 16 weeks or more (e.g., more to account for scheduling constraints of scarce resources such as Joe Hotshot). The PERT example indicates that the project can be completed in 15 weeks or less at 85% probability, subject to resource availability constraints.

Additional techniques for estimating effort, schedule, resources, and cost are presented in Chapter 6.

5.12 KEY POINTS OF CHAPTER 5

- Project plans must be consistent with product requirements; you cannot prepare a plan for developing a software product if you don't know what product to make.
- The more you understand about the product to be made, the more confident you will be in the details of your plan.
- A project plan must be updated periodically and as events dictate using a rolling-wave approach.
- Your initial plan and subsequent plans must maintain a balance among requirements, schedule, budget, and resource availability.
- Essential elements of a project plan include a WBS, an activity network, resource profiles for the various kinds or resources, and strategies for dealing with identified risk factors.
- The work breakdown structure (WBS) is a fundamental tool for planning, tracking, and controlling a software project.
- The architecture decomposition view (ADV) of the software architecture provides the basis for developing a WBS.
- The ADV is product-oriented; noun phrases are used to specify things.
- The WBS is process-oriented; verb phrases are used to specify activities and tasks.
- Using the guidelines for designing a WBS will ensure that the WBS is designed with the same care that is used to design the product.
- Your initial WBS should be decomposed to satisfy the WBS decomposition criteria.
- Work packages are the specifications for tasks and activities in the WBS.
- Work packages for activities are aggregations of work packages for subordinate tasks and activities.
- The schedule network, resource requirements, cost estimates, and risk factors can be derived from work packages.
- The critical path method (CPM) can be used to determine the minimum estimated duration of a project and the slack times associated with noncritical tasks.
- The Program Evaluation and Review Technique (PERT) can be used to determine the times, at various levels of probability, required to reach project milestones, including the final milestone.
- A task-Gantt chart can be used to depict the critical path, illustrate slack times for noncritical tasks, and determine resource profiles for the various kinds of resources.
- A resource-Gantt chart can be used to depict the resource loading for various resources.
- Acceptable options for reconciling schedule/resource conflicts include reconfiguring the schedule network, extending the schedule so that fewer resources are needed in peak weeks, adding more resources to maintain the schedule, using more productive resources so that fewer numbers are needed, descoping

the requirements so that fewer resources and less time are needed, and combinations of the above.

- Unacceptable options for reconciling schedule/resource conflicts include producing an unrealistic plan that has no chance of being successfully implemented; planning for overtime; and reducing or eliminating quality control tasks such as inspections, reviews, and testing.
- Resource profiles can be used to calculate effort and the costs of the various resources; project schedule can be determined from the critical path or from PERT calculations.
- SEI, ISO, IEEE, and PMI provide frameworks, standards, and guidelines for project planning techniques (see Appendix 5A to this chapter).

REFERENCES

[Bass03] Bass, L., P. Clements, and R. Kazman. *Software Architecture in Practice*, 2nd ed. Addison Wesley, 2003.

[CMMI06] SEI, *CMMI® Models and Modules*. http://www.sei.cmu.edu/cmmi/models/, 2006.

[Conway68] Conway, M. E. “How Do Committees Invent?” *Datamation* (April 1968). Vol. 14, No. 4, pp. 28–31.

[IEEE1058] IEEE Std 1058™–1998. *IEEE Standard for Software Project Management Plans*. Engineering Standards Collection. IEEE Product: SE113. Institute of Electrical and Electronic Engineers, August 2003.

[IEEE12207] IEEE/EIA 12207.0/.1/.2. *Industry Implementation of International Standard ISO/IEC 12207:1995 Standard for Information Technology–Software Life Cycle Processes*. Engineering Standards Collection; IEEE Product: SE113. Institute of Electrical and Electronic Engineers, August 2003.

[PMI04] PMI. *A Guide to the Project Management Body of Knowledge*, 3rd ed. (PMBOK® Guide). Project Management Institute, 2004.

[Walz93] Walz, D. B., J. Elam, and B. Curtis. Inside a software design team: Knowledge acquisition, sharing, and integration. Communications of the ACM, 36 (October 1993). pp. 63–67.

EXERCISES

5.1. List and briefly explain three factors that might prevent you, as the project manager, from preparing a project estimate that has a 90% or greater probability of success.

5.2. The assumptions on which your estimate and your commitment are based must be documented and accepted by your manager and your customer. List and briefly explain five (relevant and reasonable) assumptions you might make in preparing an estimate that would be accepted.

5.3. The architecture decomposition view depicts the hierarchical “is-part-of” containment relationship among software modules. List and briefly explain the desirable attributes of software modules in an ADV.

5.4. Assume that a WBS has a depth of M with a fan-out of N at each level.

a. State the formula for the number of leaf nodes (i.e., number of tasks) in the WBS.

b. How many tasks are there in a WBS of depth 4 with a fan-out of 5 at each level?

5.5. Refer to Figures 5.5*a* and 5.5*b*, and assume the following:

- Assume that tasks 3.2.1.1, 3.2.3.1, and 3.2.4.1 each require 1 person for 2 weeks.
- Assume that task 3.2.2.1 will require 2 persons for 4 weeks.
- Assume that tasks 3.2.1.2 and 3.2.1.3, 3.2.3.2 and 3.2.3.3, and 3.2.4.2 and 3.2.4.3 and will each require 1 person for 1 week.
- Assume that tasks 3.2.2.2 and 3.2.3.3 will require 2 persons for 2 weeks.
- Assume that task 3.2.5 will require 2 persons for 2 weeks.

a. Prepare a schedule network for the 13 tasks, showing sequential and concurrent activities and milestones.

b. Prepare a list of the 13 tasks. List the EST, LST, EFT, and LFT for each task.

c. List the tasks on the critical path using the ESTs and LSTs.

d. Using the critical path, list the time needed to complete the 13 tasks.

e. Prepare a staffing profile for the 13 tasks using the EST for each task.

5.6. Calculate and list the slack time for each of the tasks between milestones 0 and 8 for each of the noncritical paths in Figure 5.6. Show your work.

5.7. Using the template for work packages in Table 5.3*a*, design work packages for 5 of the 12 tasks in Table 5.4 and Figure 5.6. You will have to "invent" some of the missing information; be creative but not ridiculous.

5.8. In the text it is stated that 68 staff-weeks of effort is required to complete the tasks in Table 5.4. Perform the calculations and verify this statement. Show your work.

5.9. Assuming you have access to a scheduling tool such as Microsoft Project, use the tool to accomplish the following:

a. Replicate the task list in Table 5.4 as a combined WBS and Gantt chart.

b. Replicate the critical-path network in Figure 5.6.

c. Observe and print a list of the slack times associated with each task.

d. Replicate the PERT network in Figure 5.7. Observe and print the probability distribution for milestone 10.

e. Add staff resources to each task, using the staff numbers in Table 5.4. Observe and print a staffing profile for the project.

f. Observe and print the resource-Gantt charts for each staff member.

g. Briefly describe how you would attempt to resolve the resource conflicts in your resource-Gantt chart.

5.10. Consult a Z-distribution table and complete the calculations for the values of time t shown in Table 5.6. Also find the Z value that corresponds to $P(t \leq T_s) = 90\%$ and compute the corresponding time t.

APPENDIX 5A

FRAMEWORKS, STANDARDS, AND GUIDELINES FOR PROJECT PLANNING TECHNIQUES

5A.1 SPECIFIC PRACTICES OF THE CMMI-DEV-v1.2 PROJECT PLANNING PROCESS AREA

The CMMI process framework CMMI-DEV-v1.2, [CMMI06] include specific practices SP 2.1 (Establish the Budget and Schedule) and SP 2.4 (Plan for Project Resources) under specific goal SG 2 (Develop a Project Plan) in the project planning process area. Typical work products of SP 2.1 are:

1. project schedules
2. schedule dependencies
3. project budget

Subpractices of SP 2.1 (Establish the Budget and Schedule) include:

1. identify major milestones
2. identify schedule assumptions
3. identify constraints
4. identify task dependencies
5. define the budget and schedule
6. establish corrective action criteria

Typical work products of SP 2.4 (Plan for Project Resources) include:

1. WBS task dictionary
2. WBS work packages
3. staffing requirements based on project size and scope
4. critical facilities/equipment list

5. process/workflow definitions and diagrams
6. program administration requirements list

Subpractices of SP 2.4 include:

1. determine process requirements
2. determine staffing requirements
3. determine facilities, equipment, and component requirements

5A.2 ISO/IEC AND IEEE/EIA STANDARDS 12207

Section 7.1 of ISO & IEEE Standards 12207.0 covers the management process [IEEE12207]. Section 7.1.2 covers planning; section 7.1.2.1 states that the following items must be included in plans for the management processes:

- schedules
- effort estimates
- adequate resources
- allocation of tasks
- assignment of responsibilities

Section 6.11.3 of 12207.1 indicates that a work breakdown structure must be included in the project management plan.

5A.3 IEEE/EIA STANDARD 1058

Project management plans based on IEEE Std 1058™–1998 IEEE Standard for Software Project Management Plans [IEEE1058] will include clause 5.2 (Work Plan), which contains the following items:

- work activities
- schedule allocation
- resource allocation
- budget allocation

According to 1058, a work breakdown structure is used to show the work activities and the relationships among them. Work packages can be used to specify the work activities. 1058 states that techniques such as milestone charts, activity lists, activity Gantt charts, activity networks, critical path networks, and PERT can be used to specify schedule relationships. The various kinds of resources needed to accomplish the project should be allocated to elements of the WBS and documented in the work packages.

5A.4 THE PMI BODY OF KNOWLEDGE

A Guide to the Project Management Body of Knowledge, 3rd ed. (i.e., the PMBOK® Guide) [PMI04], includes sections that are relevant to the contents of this chapter:

5.3 Create WBS
6.5 Schedule Development
9.1 Human Resource Planning

6

ESTIMATION TECHNIQUES

Predictions are hard; especially about the future.
—paraphrase of a quote variously attributed to Samuel Goldwyn and Yogi Berra

6.1 INTRODUCTION TO ESTIMATION TECHNIQUES

The goal of estimation is to determine a set of parameters that provide a high level of confidence you will be able to deliver an acceptable product within the bounds of the project constraints. The parameters and constraints to be considered are:

- product features,
- quality attributes,
- effort,
- other resources,
- schedule,
- budget, and
- technology.

Some of these parameters are specified as constraints and others are estimated. For example, you may be given a set of requirements and a technology base (the constrained parameters are thus: features and quality attributes, hardware platform and operating system), and asked to estimate how much time, effort, other resources, and budget will be needed (the estimated parameters); you should also indicate your level of confidence in the estimate. Or, you may be given a schedule, budget, and resources and asked to estimate the set of features and quality attributes that can be developed within those constraints. Other combinations are possible.

Experience has shown that developing realistic estimates for software projects is an error-prone process. After the fact, project attributes such as actual effort, schedule, resources, cost, product features, and quality attributes are often quite different than the estimated parameters. There are several reasons for this unfortunate situation:

- the initial estimate of effort and schedule might have been based on vague and changing requirements,
- the initial estimate was not updated as knowledge was gained and as understanding increased,
- the basis of estimation might not have been appropriate for the project being estimated,
- the method or tool used to make the estimate might not have been appropriate,
- the recall of experts consulted might have been incorrect or biased,
- the finished product might have been larger or more complex than assumed when making the estimate,
- the schedule and/or resources might have been reduced without adjusting the requirements for product features and quality attributes,
- the requirements for product features and quality attributes might have been increased without adjusting the schedule and resources,
- the number of available software developers and their skill levels might not have been as assumed when making the estimate, and
- external factors such as unanticipated changes in hardware and software interfaces or late completion of work by a subcontractor might have delayed completion of the project.

The goal of this chapter is to provide methods, tools, and techniques that can reduce the probability of making bad estimates.

6.2 OBJECTIVES OF THIS CHAPTER

After reading this chapter and completing the exercises you should understand:

- the role of estimation in the workflow model for software projects;
- three fundamental principles of estimation;
- size measures and size measurement;
- how to develop a size measure;
- some pragmatic, theory-based, and regression-based estimation techniques;
- how to develop, calibrate, and evaluate the acceptability of regression-based estimation models;
- capabilities of estimation tools;

- an estimation procedure; and
- a format for documenting estimates.

The four sets of standards and guidelines for managing projects presented in this text; namely the CMMI-DEV-v1.2 process framework, the ISO/IEEE standard 12207, IEEE standard 1058, and the PMI Body of Knowledge address estimation issues to varying degrees. Aspects of estimation in these documents are presented in Appendix 6A to this chapter.

Terms used in this chapter and throughout this text are defined in Appendix A to the text. Presentation slides for this chapter and other supporting material are available at the URL listed in the Preface.

6.3 FUNDAMENTAL PRINCIPLES OF ESTIMATION

Three fundamental principles of estimation are presented and discussed in this section. The first fundamental principle of estimation for software projects is stated as follows:

Estimation Principle 1 A project estimate is a projection from past experiences to the future, adjusted to account for differences between past and future.

Three things are apparent from this principle:

1. you must have some past experiences to draw upon (known as the *basis of estimation*),
2. you must know something about the future (requirements for the system or product you will develop or modify, and
3. you must make adjustments to account for the differences between past and future (known as the adjustment factors).

All estimation techniques for software projects incorporate, in varying ways and to varying degrees, past experiences, knowledge of the future, and adjustment factors. Past experiences might, for example, have resulted in a rule of thumb (a guideline) that states software productivity in your organization, for your kind of project, is typically 500 delivered source lines of code per staff-month (500 DSLOC/SM). If you have estimated that the future product will be 50,000 lines of code (based on the requirements and past experiences) and if the future project is thought to be similar to past projects (no adjustments), it will require an estimated 100 staff-months of effort (50,000/500).

In the absence of adjustment factors, you might plan the project for 10 months using 10 software developers. If you think the product to be developed will be more complex than past products, you might increase you effort estimate to 120 staff-months and plan the project for 12 months using 10 software developers; conversely, you might lower the effort estimate if you think the product will be less complex than past products and/or you think the software developers have gained familiarity with this type of product building similar products.

Historical data based on past experiences might also indicate that the number of defects found prior to product release is typically 10 per thousand lines of delivered source lines of code (10D/KDSLOC) and the number found by users during the first 6 months of operation are 1 per KDSLOC. You could then estimate that 500 defects should be found prior to product release (50×10) and 50 will be reported by users during the first 6 months of operation.

In making these estimates, you might have assumed several things (either explicitly or implicitly). For example, you might have assumed that the product will be similar in complexity to the typical ones built in the past; therefore you have not applied a complexity adjustment factor. You might have assumed that the developers of the future product will be similar in ability to those on which the productivity rule of thumb is based (500 DSLOC/SM); otherwise, you would include an adjustment factor to increase or decrease the estimate based on your assumption of how the productivity of your developers will differ from productivity in the past.

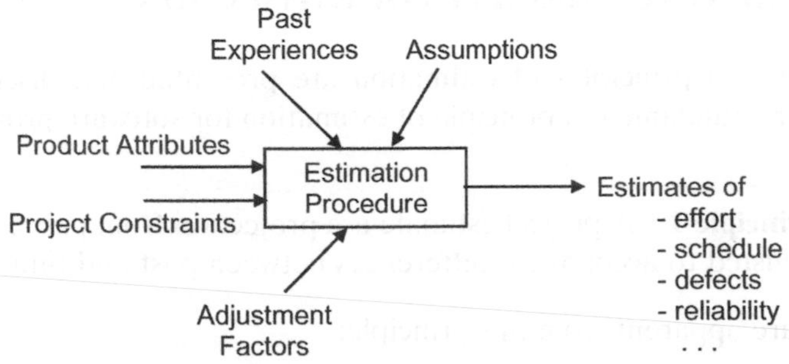

FIGURE 6.1 The estimation process

Figure 6.1 illustrates the roles played by attributes of the product to be developed or modified, the project constraints, past experiences, assumptions, and adjustment factors. Figure 6.1 is related to the workflow model for software projects in Figure 1.1, repeated here as Figure 6.2:

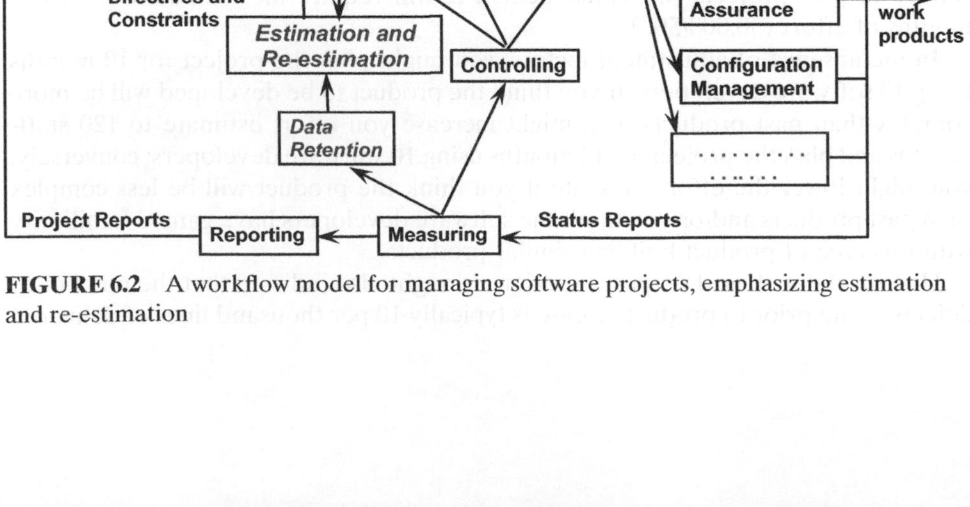

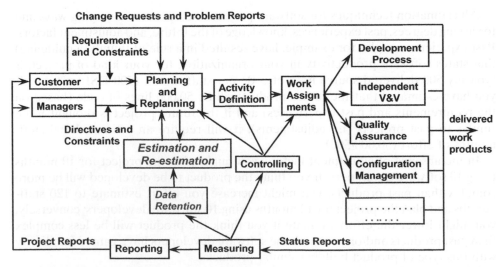

FIGURE 6.2 A workflow model for managing software projects, emphasizing estimation and re-estimation

A comparison of Figures 6.1 and 6.2 shows that product attributes are derived from the customer requirements. Project constraints include customer constraints and management directives and constraints. Past experiences are summarized by the data retention element Figure 6.2; these experiences may be summarized in a database of local completed projects, in the heads of experts, in local rules of thumb, in industry averages, or in folklore. Adjustment factors are applied to account for your understanding of the requirements and how they differ from past experiences, as well as differences in project parameters such as skill levels, availability of resources, and schedule constraints.

Assumptions are based on factors you believe to be true or that you believe will be true. Replanning typically involves re-estimation, which is based on changes to requirements, directives, and constraints, and as required by problem reports. Continuing the (simple) example above:

- the attributes of the future product are summarized in the size estimate of 50,000 DLOC (derived from the requirements);
- past experiences are summarized by the productivity rule of thumb (500 DSLOC/SM) and the pre-release and post-release defect densities; and
- if no adjustment factors are applied, it is assumed that the future project will be similar in every way to the past projects on which the estimate is based; adjustment factors are applied to account for differences between past projects and the future one.

Adjustment factors are attributes that cause seemingly similar projects (i.e., seemingly similar products) to differ in effort, schedule, resources, cost, features, quality attributes, and other attributes of interest. Typical adjustment factors include:

- relative complexity of the product,
- skills and abilities of the developers,
- specificity and volatility of the requirements, and
- excessive constraints such as schedule pressure.

Each of these factors (and others) may be better or worse than typical past projects.

Adjustments factors are important in estimating software projects because no two software projects are alike; otherwise, you could make a copy of some existing software and give it to your customer. Stated differently, every software project incorporates unique aspects. The reason you do software projects is to produce software artifacts unlike any others you or your organization have developed.

In this regard software differs from physical entities. A great deal of effort is required to duplicate a building, an automobile, or a computer. When finished, the physical entity will be similar, but not identical, to the original. The goal of manufacturing processes is to produce multiple copies of artifacts that are as nearly alike as possible, within the limits of technology and economic considerations, but the results are never identical. The primary goal of your software project is (or should be) to produce one acceptable copy, on time and within budget. Then you can easily produce as many identical copies of your software as desired, defects and all (witness Microsoft and other software vendors).

In the example above, you might think the product to be built will be more complex than the typical ones in the past, so you might adjust the estimate upward by 20% to account for increased complexity. You might then schedule the project as a 10-month project with an average staffing level of 12 software developers (i.e., 12 full-time equivalents, FTEs). If the schedule duration is constrained to 9 months, linear adjustment of staffing would indicate that approximately 13 FTE software developers are needed:

$$\text{FTE} = \frac{120 \text{ staff-months}}{9 \text{ months}} = 13.3.$$

As will be shown later, linear compensation is not sufficient; more than 13.3 software developers will be needed to compensate for schedule compression because the increased level of communication and coordination required when more people are added.

All estimates are based on assumptions and constraints. An *assumption* is a statement that is taken to be true without verifying, or being able to verify, the truth of the statement. In the example above it is assume that the productivity factor used in your organization (500 DSLOC/SM) and the estimated defect levels (10/KDSLOC and 1/KDSLOC) are appropriate for your project. The estimate was adjusted upward by 20% because it was assumed that increased product complexity would require more effort than typical past projects; the estimate might be adjusted downward based on the assumption that you will have a team of highly skilled software developers who will more than compensate for increased product complexity. Assumptions that later turn out to be false invalidate the estimates based on those assumptions.

A *constraint* is an externally imposed condition that must be observed. In the example above, the schedule might be constrained to 6 months. Completing 120 staff-months of effort in 6 months would require an average staffing level of more than 20 software developers (120/6 = 20); more than 20 because the increased level of communication and coordination required for 20 FTEs[20] compared to 10 FTEs on a 12-month schedule will decrease the individual productivity of each software developer. Also the compressed schedule will likely increase the number of pre-release and post-release defects.

In addition it may not be possible to compress a 12-month schedule to 6 months because some work products have to be completed before other work can begin; you cannot develop software until the requirements are (at least partially) known. You cannot integrate or test the code until it is written. Constraints on factors such as availability of qualified software personnel or delivery of needed hardware or software can also prevent compression of the schedule. Historical data may indicate that no project in your organization has ever succeeded after compressing a pre-planned schedule by 50% (i.e., from 12 months to 6 months).

[20] FTE is an acronym for full-time equivalent personnel. If 20 FTEs are required for a project, and if each person is available to work on your project 50% of their time, you will need many more than 40 developers.

These observations are stated as the second fundamental principle of estimation for software projects:

Estimation Principle 2 All estimates are based on a set of assumptions that must be realized and a set of constraints that must be satisfied.

Said differently, your estimate will be invalid if you fail to satisfy the assumptions made in preparing the estimate; the project will fail to meet its goals if the constraints are violated.

Another way to view the assumptions and constraints on which estimates are based is to regard assumption and constraints as risk factors for your project. A risk factor is a potential problem that, should it become a real problem, will create difficulties in achieving a satisfactory outcome for your project (i.e., delivering an acceptable product on time and within budget). For example, basing an estimate on the assumption of highly skilled developers creates a risk factor that will invalidate the estimate if the software developers are not highly skilled. Attempting to complete the project within the constraints of 6 months using more than 20 people may create problems of communication and coordination that will prevent completion of the project on schedule and/or may result in an unsatisfactory product.

Estimation Principle 3 Projects must be re-estimated periodically as understanding grows and aperiodically as project parameters change.

This principle is a corollary to principle 2. As your project evolves, your understanding of the product under development, the assumptions you have made, and the impact of the constraints will become clear (clearer). For example, the product may be more or less complex than you assumed; your developers may be more or less skilled and more or less motivated than you assumed; the schedule constraint may be more or less severe than you assumed. Better understanding of the product, the validity (or invalidity) of your assumptions, and the impact of the product and process constraints will typically result in re-estimation and refinement of plans, as illustrated in Figure 6.2.

As a rule, re-estimation and re-planning should occur on a monthly basis for projects of less than 12 months duration, and monthly, or perhaps quarterly for project of more than 12 months duration. The longer interval is determined by the stability of the requirements, the resources, the technology, and the development process.

Projects must be re-estimated aperiodically when unanticipated changes occur in project parameters such as:

- a major change in requirements,
- failure of a new technology,
- compression of the schedule,
- reduction of the planned budget, or
- loss of key personnel.

Major re-planning may be required, depending on the magnitude of the unanticipated change.

As stated previously in this text, acceptable ways to accommodate changes in project parameters include:

- re-scoping the requirements,
- extending the schedule,
- adding more resources, and
- utilizing better resources.

Unacceptable ways include:

- excessive overtime,
- reduction in planned verification and validation activities, and
- reduction in planned documentation.

If you are committed to a fixed price-and-schedule contract with rigid requirements (always a bad idea), you must have sufficient reserve in the agreed-upon price and schedule to accommodate changes as understanding grows (projects always become larger and more complex than assumed). The reserve may range from 10% to 50% of estimated cost, depending on your confidence in your original estimate. The contract must also contain a clause stating that the contract will be re-negotiated if there is an unplanned event such as a major change in customer-controlled factors; as for example, changes to requirements, schedule, or funding, namely the out-of-scope changes.

6.4 DESIGNING TO PROJECT CONSTRAINTS

The estimation process illustrated in Figure 6.1 is applicable when product attributes such as size and complexity are used to estimate project attributes such as effort and duration. In this case the product attributes are in fact product constraints. In some cases effort and/or schedule and/or quality attributes are specified as project constraints and used to estimate the attributes of a product that can be developed or modified within those constraints. This approach is termed "designing to project constraints;" it is illustrated in Figure 6.3 (in system engineering this approach is known as "designing to cost").

Suppose, for example, that a project must be completed in 6 months by 5 software developers (30 staff-months of effort). Using the rules of thumb from above, it is estimated that the constrained 30 staff-months of effort will result in 15,000 DSLOC (30×500), and that the number of defects will be 150 pre-release and 15 post-release.

This designing-to-constraints estimate is based a productivity factor that is assumed to be typical of the organization (500 DSLOC/SM). If the future product is estimated to have 20,000 DLOC, the 5-member project team will have to be 33% more productive than the typical project team in the past (20,000/15,000) if they are to complete the project in 6 months.

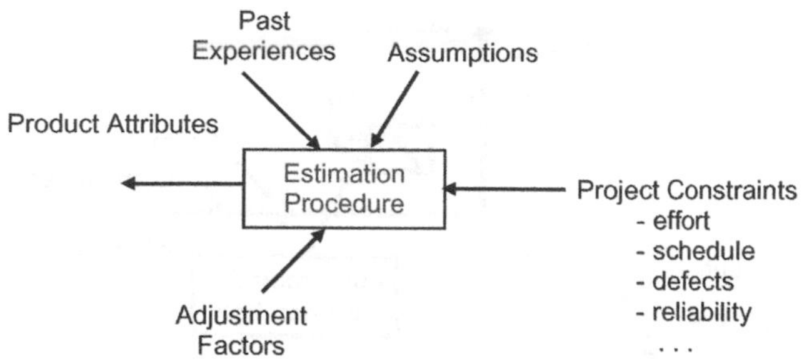

FIGURE 6.3 Design to project constraints

The feasibility of the project depends on specifying one or more *realistic* adjustment factors that can increase productivity by 33%; for example, the project might be feasible if you could utilize 5 of the best software developers in your organization. If you cannot assume that some realistic adjustment factors will be true, with a high level of confidence, there is a correspondingly high risk of project failure (i.e., inability to deliver an acceptable product on time and within budget). If the product size is estimated to be 30,000 DLOC, the project team will have to be twice as productive as the typical team. This is unlikely under any scenario, and indicates that the project, as constrained, is infeasible.

You must be cautious that project constraints do not make it impossible to find feasible values for the estimated factors. There is an old saying: "You can have the software soon, good, cheap; pick any two." If you want your software soon and good it won't be cheap (i.e., it will be expensive); if you want it good and cheap, it won't be soon (i.e., the schedule duration will not be short); if you want your software soon and cheap, it won't be good (i.e., quality will suffer).

The situation is illustrated in Figures 6.4*a* and 6.4*b* as three fundamental parameters of estimation—schedule, resources, and requirements—that must be balanced. As indicated, there may be some flexibility in one or more of the dimensions: there may (or may not) be some contingency reserve in the schedule (i.e., the difference between the estimated schedule and the committed schedule). There will likely be an upper limit on the resources that can be applied to the project. There may be a minimum, in the sense that the project is infeasible unless the minimum resources are available, and, there will be a minimum number of features and quality attributes that must be delivered (i.e., the Essential requirements). The solution box in Figures 6.4*a* and 6.4*b* is the result of projecting the upper and lower constraints on the three dimensions into the three-dimensional space.

The fundamental goal of estimation is to develop and maintain estimates that keep your projects "in the solution box," both initially and as conditions change. Keeping your project in the box means that you will deliver an acceptable product that satisfies all of the Essential requirements (and some of the Desirable and Optional ones) within the constraints of an acceptable schedule and available resources. Finishing your project at any point within the constrained solution box indicates that you delivered an acceptable product on time and within budget (the budget is used to obtain the resources).

If there is no flexibility in the requirements, the box in Figure 6.4*b* becomes the front plane of the box; if in addition there is no flexibility in the schedule, the plane

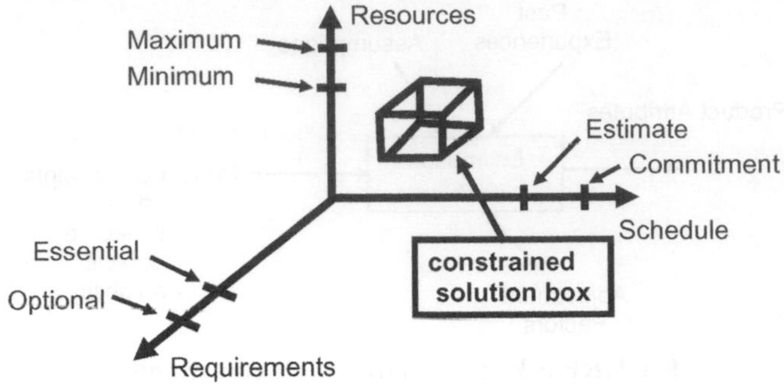

FIGURE 6.4A Three fundamental variables of estimation and the resulting solution box

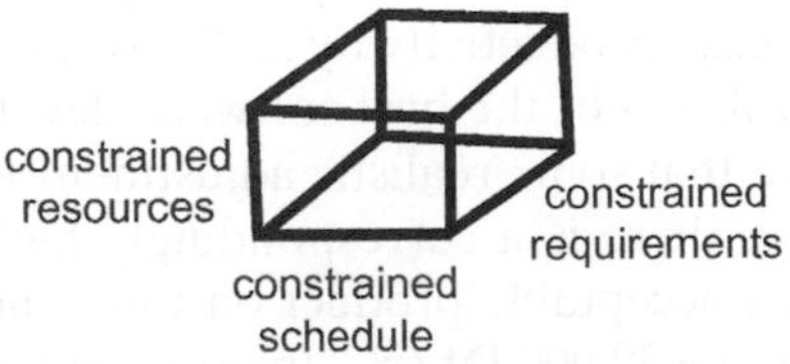

FIGURE 6.4B The constrained solution box in Figure 6.4*a*

becomes a vertical line which indicates some flexibility in the resources. If there is no flexibility in any of the three parameters, the box collapses to a single point.

An overly constrained project is one for which there is no feasible solution in the box or the plane or at the single point. This situation results when the constrained schedule is less than the estimate of time needed, and/or the resources are less than the minimum number and kind required, and/or the number of requirements that can be implemented within the constraints of schedule and resources is less than those in the Essential category. Rigidly constraining 1 or 2 of the 3 fundamental variables requires flexibility in the other 1 or 2 in order to establish feasible solution points. Rigidly constraining all 3 variables is usually a recipe for failure.

Estimates are sometimes "mandated." These "estimates" are the result of overly constrained product and project factors that have no flexibility in the estimation parameters (i.e., your team of 5 developers must develop 60,000 lines of high-quality code in 6 months; it must be good, cheap, and soon). This is not an estimate; it is a disaster waiting to happen, for you, your project, your organization, and your customer.

6.5 ESTIMATING PRODUCT SIZE

As indicated in Figure 6.1, estimates of factors such as effort, schedule, resources, cost, and quality attributes are based on estimated product attributes, project constraints, past experiences, and adjustment factors. Alternatively, Figure 6.3 indicates that project constraints may dictate the attributes of a product that can be built or modified within those constraints.

Most estimation models, tools, and techniques use some measure of size as the fundamental product attribute on which the estimate is based, or in the case of designing to project constraints (Figure 6.3), size is the product attribute that is estimated. Depending on the nature of the product, factors in additional to size, such as product complexity, degree of connectivity, real-time responses needed, or amount of data to be manipulated, may influence the estimates of effort, schedule, resources, quality factors, and cost; additional product factors such as these are included as adjustment factors in most estimation models.

Most estimation methods based on product factors use some measure of product size as the primary factor that drives the estimate because:

1. size has a stronger causal relationship to project attributes such as effort and schedule than do other product attributes;
2. size can be measured more objectively than other product attributes;
3. some measures of size can estimated more accurately from the requirements than can other product attributes; and
4. data for size, effort, schedule, and other project attributes can be collected from completed projects and stored in a database to provide a historical basis of estimation for future projects.

Historically, delivered source lines of code (DSLOC) has been used as the size measure but there are several problems related to using lines of code:

- it is difficult to estimate lines of code early in a project; it is difficult to relate changes to the requirements to changes in estimated lines of code;
- calculating productivity as lines of code generated per programmer-month may encourage programmers to write lots of poor-quality lines of code rather than fewer lines of high-quality code; and
- modern development methods such as model-driven development, object-based programming, reuse of library components, and use of open source components make the relationship between lines of code and project attributes less relevant and less precise than in the past.

Size measures other than lines of code have been developed to overcome the problems of using lines of code. The function point size measure is the best known and historically was the first alternative to lines of code [Albrecht79]. Function points (FPs) are calculated by counting the number of different kinds of inputs, outputs, internal files, queries, and interfaces in a system to be estimated.

These counts are based on objective counting rules, and each unique input, output, internal file, query, and interface is weighted as simple, average, or complex. The function point model is illustrated in Figure 6.5.

The weighted values are summed to provide a total number of unadjusted function points (UFPs). Adjustment factors such as the complexity of processing, transaction rate, and required ease of use are then applied to account for conditions that will require more or less effort than the typical project. Further details and an example of a function point estimate are provided in the accompanying sidebar. As indicated in the sidebar, function point analysis has been generalized to become functional size measurement.

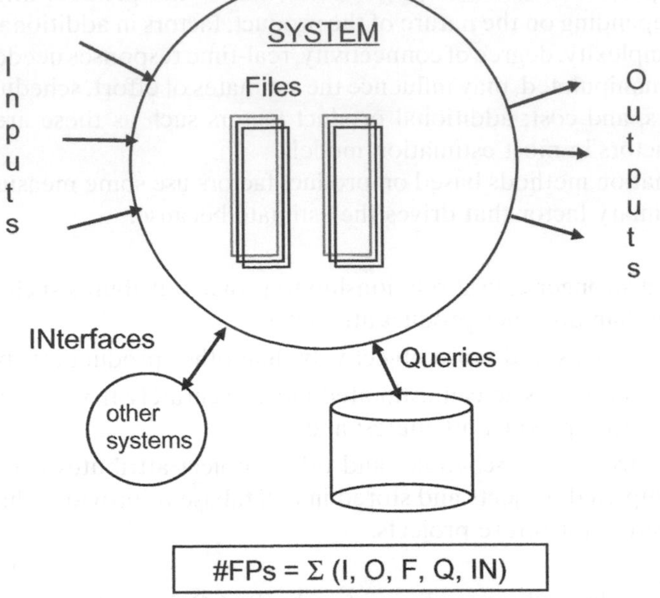

FIGURE 6.5 Function point factors to be counted

An interesting aspect of the function point size measure is that the lines of code required to implement a given number of function points depends on the programming language used to implement the software needed to process the inputs and use the files, interfaces, and queries to produce the outputs. It might be, for a given organization and a particular kind and size of product, that the conversion factor from function points to delivered lines of code is 50 DSLOC/FP for programs written in Java and 300 DSLOC/FP for similar programs written in assembly language. This would indicate that Java is 6 times more expressive than assembly language for this kind and size of product within this organization. If it is assumed that the effort required to write, say, 100 lines of code is independent of the programming language used (a reasonable first-order approximation), it would appear that Java programmers would be 6 times more productive than assembly language programmers as measured by function points implemented per programmer-week or programmer-month.

The qualifier in the previous paragraph "for a given organization and a particular kind and size of product" is important because the ratio of lines of code to function points is different for different kinds of software, for different sizes of software, and for different organizations. Although guidelines have been published to convert function points to lines of code for various programming languages, the conversion factor(s) should be locally derived. Within your organization you might have different conversion factors for different kinds and sizes of software products, and the conversion factors might not be valid in other parts of your company.

Conversion factors between function points and lines of code are useful to:

1. use function points as inputs to estimation tools that are calibrated to lines of code and

FUNCTIONAL SIZE MEASUREMENT

The function point size measure was the first functional size measure (FSM); it was developed by Alan Albrecht in the mid-1970s to measure the "external size" of data processing applications [Albrecht79]. He called the approach "function point analysis" (FPA).

The International Function Point Users' Group (IFPUG; a nonprofit organization) is now the official keeper of FPA. IFPUG maintains the Function Point Counting Practices Manual, holds annual conferences, and sponsors educational seminars and workshops [IFPUG]. IFPUG also provides a professional certification program for Certified Function Point Specialists.

TABLE 6.1 A function point example

Complexity:	Simple	Average	Complex	Total
Inputs	**3** × 3	**2** × 4	**0** × 6	17
Outputs	**4** × 4	6 × 5	**3** × 7	67
Files	**5** × 7	**2** × 10	**0** × 15	55
Queries	**0** × 3	**9** × 5	**4** × 7	73
Interfaces	**0** × 5	**0** × 7	**3** × 10	30
			Total	**242**

Table 6.1 illustrates the function point approach to functional size measurement. The example in the table shows the number of function points for inputs, outputs, files, queries, and interfaces (in bold) and the weighting factors for simple, average, and complex weightings in each case. Note that the weighting factors for files and interfaces are larger than the weights for inputs, outputs, and queries. This indicates that more effort is required to develop the functionality for files and interfaces than for the other three factors.

As indicated in Table 6.1, the number of unadjusted function points (UFPs) for the example is 242. If the composite adjustment factor is 1.13, the number of adjusted function points is approximately 276 (1.13 × 242). If history data for past projects indicates productivity of 6.5 function points per staff-month (6.5 FP/SM) the effort estimate is approximately 42 staff-month (which could be estimated as 6 people for 7 months).

Several other functional size measures have been developed. The function point method counts external factors that are important in data-intensive application; the feature points method adds a count of algorithms for computationally intensive systems [Jones86]. MK II function points improves on the count of function point files to better account for the internals of data-rich applications [Symons88].

In 1998, COSMIC (the Common Software Measurement International Consortium) was formed by a working group of the International Standards Organization (ISO) for the purpose of developing and publishing ISO standards for functional size measurement, which is a generalization of function point analysis. According to the COSMIC Web site [COSMIC1]:

COSMIC-FFP (ISO 19761) is a functional size measurement method which generalizes the measurement process to address management information systems issues, as well as real-time and hybrid software projects. It conforms to the ISO meta-standard on functional size measurement (ISO 12143-1) and uses only FURs (Functional User Requirements) of the software project as inputs to the measurements process.

The advantages of COSMIC-FFP as compared to function points are documented in [COSMIC2].

2. to convert historical data for projects based on lines of code to historical data based on function points.

Table 6.2 lists several examples of size measures in the spirit of FPA. These measures are termed external size measures (ESMs). The generic term for the units of measure is external size units (ESUs). Function points are thus an ESM, and the numbers of function points in a software system or product are ESUs. This terminology is used because ESMs measure factors external to the software to be developed or modified, including:

1. inputs that must be responded to,
2. outputs that must be delivered, and
3. passive interfaces.

TABLE 6.2 Examples of external size measures

Type of System	ESM Factors Counted
Data processing	Inputs, outputs, interfaces, queries, files
Process control	Sensors, valves, actuators
Embedded systems	Interrupts, signals, priority levels
User interfaces	Windows, menus, items per menu
Object-oriented	Classes, associations, methods

These three factors determine the "external size" of the software that, along with conversion factors and adjustment factors, can be used to estimate factors such as amount of effort required, time needed, the densities of pre-release and post-release defects, and reliability. For example, if the productivity rule of thumb, determined from past projects, is 7 function points per staff-month (7 FP/SM), the project depicted in Table 6.1 will require roughly 35 staff-months of effort (242/7).

Based on these considerations, the following conjecture for external size measures is offered:

The ESM Conjecture:

It is always possible to find an External Size Measure that can be used, along with historical data and adjustment factors, to develop estimates of project attributes of interest.

A conjecture is a statement that is believed to be true but cannot be (exhaustively) proven to be true. A conjecture that includes the qualifier "always" can be refuted by a single counterexample; however, this author has not yet encountered that counter example.

That the ESM conjecture should be true is based on the observation that the purpose of software is to process inputs, interact with other systems, and produce outputs. The software to be developed is therefore directly proportional to the numbers and kinds of inputs, outputs, and interfaces to be handled by the software, which are measured by the ESM. The situation is illustrated in Figure 6.6.

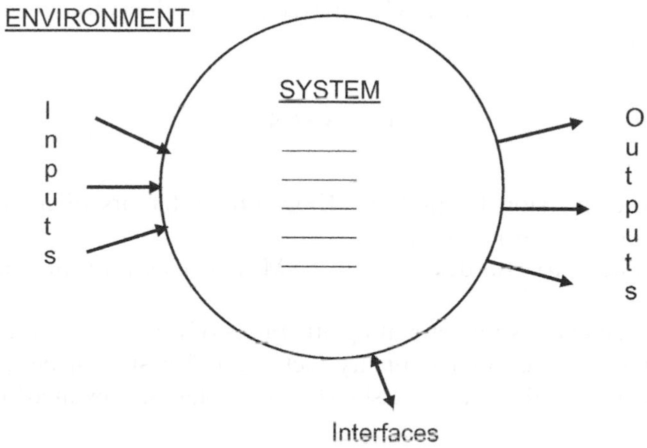

FIGURE 6.6 Elements of external size measures

For example, suppose that you have developed an ESM for building embedded software that uses the following parameters:

Inputs
- number of interrupts, I
- number of priority levels, P

Interfaces
- number of control table entries, E

Outputs
- number of signals, S

Also suppose you have developed the following relationship from historical data:

$$\text{ESUs} = 2*I + 4*P + E + 5*S.$$

The weighting factors indicate the relative effort required to implement the code to process an interrupt, handle priority levels, access control tables, and generate output signals. A system having 5 different interrupts in 3 priority levels, 15 control table interfaces, and 15 different signals would have 112 ESUs.

Suppose further that you have examined past projects and developed the productivity ratio of 2 ESU per staff-month (2 ESU/SM). Then estimated effort for software development would be

$$\text{Effort} = \frac{112}{2} = 56 \text{ staff-months.}$$

The project might be scheduled using 6 software developers for 10 months.

If you are concerned about memory constraints (i.e., the number of object bytes to be loaded into memory), you might analyze past products to develop a relationship of the form:

$$\text{Bytes} = x * \text{ESU},$$

where x is the conversion factor Bytes/ESU. Other factors of interest could be accounted for in a similar manner.

The steps necessary to develop an ESM are listed in the accompanying sidebar.

The various techniques for estimating attributes of interest for software projects (e.g., effort, schedule, resources, quality factors, and cost) can be categorized as pragmatic, theory-based, and regression-based. Pragmatic estimation techniques include:

- rule of thumb
- analogy
- expert judgment
- Delphi
- WBS/CPM/PERT

Theory-based estimation techniques include:

- system dynamics
- SLIM

Regression-based estimation models include:

- COCOMO
- locally derived models

Theory-based and regression-based models use size as the primary estimation input; pragmatic techniques may or may not use a size measure. The nature of these methods and examples of their uses are presented in the following sections.

DEVELOPING AN EXTERNAL SIZE MEASURE

External size measures for similar systems or products can be developed as follows:

1. Analyze some existing systems or products similar to the systems or products to be developed:
   a. identify some candidate ESUs to be counted in the environments of the systems or products and
   b. develop counting rules for the ESUs.
2. Calibrate the ESM as follows:
   c. count ESUs for some existing systems;
   d. develop weighting factors for the ESUs;
   e. apply the weighting factors to produce adjusted ESUs (AESUs);
   f. develop conversion factors from external size units to factors to be estimated, such as effort, cost, lines of code, and defect density;
   g. apply the conversion factors to compute factors to be estimated;
   h. compare estimates to actual values for the past project; and
   i. adjust the weighting factors for the ESUs and develop adjustment factors to account for variations in estimated factors for historical systems having similar ESUs.
3. Iterate steps 1 and 2 until your ESM estimation model satisfies the following criteria:
   a. the ESUs are countable at the requirements and early design phases of your projects,
   b. the ESUs characterize the software to be implemented, and
   c. conversion factors can be derived to convert adjusted ESUs to factors to be estimated.

Criterion 3c should support estimation of factors such as

$$\text{Estimated LOC} = \text{AESUs} \times \left(\frac{\text{LOC}}{\text{ESU}}\right),$$

$$\text{Estimated effort} = \text{AESUs} \times \left(\frac{\text{Effort}}{\text{ESU}}\right),$$

$$\text{Estimated cost} = \text{AESUs} \times \left(\frac{\text{Cost}}{\text{ESU}}\right),$$

$$\text{Estimated defects} = \text{AESUs} \times \left(\frac{\text{Defects}}{\text{ESU}}\right),$$

where

LOC is lines of code;
LOC/ESU, Effort/ESU, Cost/EST, and Defects/ESU are obtained from historical data for past projects; and
AESUs are adjusted ESUs, for the project being estimated, adjusted by the adjustment factors for the project.

6.6 PRAGMATIC ESTIMATION TECHNIQUES

Pragmatic estimation techniques are not based on theoretical models nor on regression analysis. They have been shown to be useful in practice despite having no underlying theoretical or regression basis. Several pragmatic techniques are presented in this section.

6.6.1 Rule of Thumb

A rule of thumb (ROT) is a generally accepted guideline.[21] Because software engineering, unlike other engineering disciplines, does not deal with physical entities, we lack many of the mathematical models on which traditional engineering is based. Therefore we use many rules of thumb, some that are industrywide (e.g., in general, it costs 50 to 100 times more to fix a post-release defect than to fix a pre-release defect) and some that are locally derived (e.g., in our organization it costs 75 times as much to fix a product-interface defect post-release than to fix it pre-release).

The productivity factor used in the example of Section 6.3 (500 DSLOC/SM) might be an industrywide rule of thumb for a particular kind of software (e.g., scientific applications, data processing, or telecommunications) or it might be a local rule of thumb for your organization and your kind of software.

When you use metrics such as 500 DSLOC/SM or 5 FP/SM, you must understand the factors included in the metrics. Productivity metrics, for example, are determined by counting lines of code in past products (or some other size measure), determining the staff-months required to produce those lines and forming the ratio (e.g., 500 DSLOC/SM). You must understand how size was counted and what scope of effort was included to use the productivity metric. Counted lines of code might have included:

- lines of assembly code in the load module of the program;
- source code without comments;
- source code with comments;
- source lines, including comments and library routines;
- all of the code that was written (retained plus discarded);
- all reused, open source, and new code in the final product; or
- all of the above plus all of the test-harness code.

[21] A *rule of thumb* is a method or procedure that comes from practice or experience, without any formal basis.

The effort might have been for coding only, for coding and testing, or for all of software development activities plus project management, system installation, and user training. It might have included all of the software developers' time, including the time they spent in unrelated meetings and maintaining other software. It might have been recorded as 40 hours per week when in fact the developers were working 60 hours per week.

The projects on which the rule of thumb is based might have been data-processing applications, real-time embedded systems, or perhaps web-based e-commerce applications. Those projects might have exhibited similar metrics so that an average of the values from them is a good metric to use or they may have varied widely, thus making their average value an unreliable rule of thumb.

When you apply a productivity rule of thumb (or any other ROT) to make an estimate, you are estimating the same scope of work, for the same kind of projects, that was included in the derivation of the ROT. If, for example, a productivity ROT of 500 DLOC/SM is based on (only the) effort to write the embedded lines of assembly code and the developers were working 60 hours per week, your estimate will be for the amount of effort needed to write the estimated number of embedded assembly lines when the developers are working 60 hours per week. A productivity rule of thumb for developing embedded real-time systems using the C language is probably not applicable to development of business applications using COBOL.

If, on the other hand, the function points counted in deriving the ROT are counted using objective counting rules and the effort includes actual hours worked on the entire project (analysis, design, programming, testing, CM, QA, management), your estimate will be for all of the effort required to develop and deliver software containing the estimated number of function points.

Another caution: you must determine that the ROT is for the same range of product size as your estimated size. Even for similar kinds of products and systems, the conversion factor used to relate size to effort is usually nonlinear. Thus an effort estimate based on a productivity ROT for products that contain 500 function points might have to be increased by a factor of 1.5 or more for products of 1000 function points (more on this later).

Also you must understand the variations in the past experiences used to derive the rule of thumb. If, for example, your ROT is based on 5 past projects whose size and effort, when counted in the same way, produce an average ROT of 5 FP/SM but the productivity ROTs for the 5 past projects range from 3.5 FP/SM to 7 FP/SM, you must understand the factors that resulted in these variations (i.e., the adjustment factors) and use those projects that are most similar to your project.

Despite these caveats, estimates based on rules of thumb are useful to:

- provide rough order of magnitude estimates, and
- they can be used when doing feasibility studies and "what if" scenarios.

However,

- it is a risky endeavor to base a project estimate on rules of thumb alone.

6.6.2 Analogy

Analogy is a widely used technique for estimating project attributes in software engineering and other engineering disciplines. The goal of analogy-based estimation is to find one or more analogous projects for which the attributes of interest are known. The closer the analogy, the more confident you will be in your estimate. A rule of thumb, for example, can be used with greater confidence if it is based on projects that are analogous to the one you are estimating.

Analogy-based estimates can be simple (e.g., a similar project required 5 people for 6 months) or sophisticated. In the latter case, your organization might have a relational database of past projects. Each row in the data schema would contain data for a completed project. Each column would record an attribute of past projects, such as:

- the customer,
- the kind of product,
- the scope of activities included,
- product size and the size measure used,
- adjustment factors used (e.g., product complexity, skill level of the developers),
- the development model used,
- development tools used,
- deliverable products produced,
- estimated and actual project duration,
- estimated and actual effort,
- estimated and actual cost,
- pre-release and post-release defect densities,
- problems encountered, and
- lessons learned.

To make an estimate, you would specify the known characteristics of the project you are estimating. You would then write a query that retrieves a list of projects that match your project within a specified range, for example, all projects that developed products of high complexity and that are within ±10% of your estimated size built by developers of average skill levels using C++ and an Incremental-build model.

The primary strength of analogy-based estimation is that:

- good analogies provided a good basis of estimation for your project.

The primary weakness is that:

- false analogies produce inaccurate estimates.

The estimate is no better or worse than the analogies on which it is based.

6.6.3 Expert Judgment

Expert judgment involves asking one or more experts for their estimates of project attributes such as effort, time, required skill levels, and risk factors. Refering to Figure 6.1 data retention is in the heads of one or more experts. The adjustment factors they apply may include subjective factors such as knowing the people who will do the work and manage the work, the politics of customer relations, and frictions that may exist among internal elements of the organization. Product attributes include whatever information is available for the experts to examine.

Experts might tell you that the requirements are too vague and incomplete for them to render an opinion (which is useful to know). At the other extreme, different kinds of experts may be able to provide estimates for different elements of the architecture decomposition view (ADV) of the envisioned system or product (e.g., the user interface, the database, the communication package, the algorithms).

The primary strengths of expert judgment are that:

- different kinds of experts can provide estimates for different kinds of product components and
- experts can include subjective and political factors that are not typically recorded in databases of past projects.

The primary weaknesses are that:

- experts may be overoptimistic in estimating the time and resources needed for them to do the work rather than the time and resources needed by less expert developers and
- their recall of past experiences may be incorrect or incomplete.

6.6.4 Delphi Estimation

You can use the Delphi technique to obtain composite estimates from different experts.[22] Each expert is given the same information concerning the future product (e.g., operational requirements, technical specifications, architectural views, constraints). Each is asked to provide an estimate of project attributes and a brief justification for their estimate. Each expert can apply rules of thumb, analogies, their expert judgment, or theory-based and regression-based models as they choose in developing their estimates.

You, the coordinator, collate their estimates, provide the composite results back to them (with names removed) plus any additional information they might have requested, and ask them to provide a second estimate. E-mail correspondence, using estimation templates to be completed and returned, is a convenient way to conduct the Delphi process. An example an expert's second-round estimate are provided in Figure 6.7.

The interval between submitted estimates should be one to two days. This gives each expert enough time to reflect on the summary report from the previous round,

[22] The Delphi technique was developed in the 1940s at the Rand Corporation as a forecasting tool. It is named for the Oracle of Delphi whose predictions were sought and relied on by the ancient Greeks.

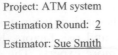

Project: ATM system

Estimation Round: 2

Estimator: Sue Smith

Round 1 estimates from 4 experts

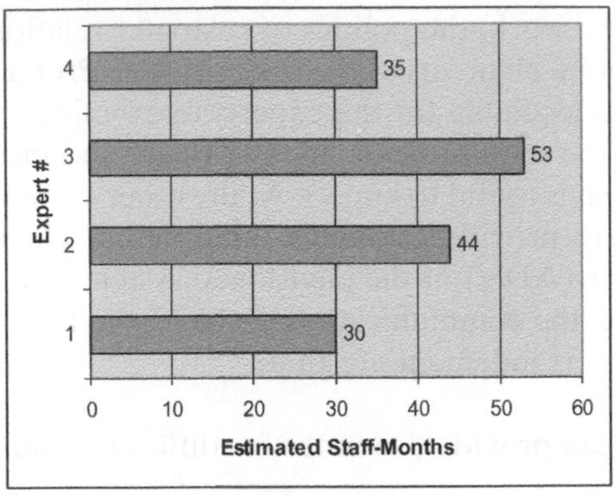

Summary of rationales for round 1 from 4 estimators:

1: I don't see any problems; should be a routine project.

2: The requirements are vague in some areas; could cause problems.

3: The new hardware interface could cause some problems.

4: Our people have lots of experience with these kinds of systems.

Your round 2 estimate: 35 staff-months

Your round 2 rationale:

I don't think the vague requirements will be a problem because our people have lots of experience developing these kinds of systems and have experience working with this customer. I am increasing my estimate from 30 to 35 staff-months because of the new hardware interface mentioned in rationale 3.

FIGURE 6.7 A Delphi report

but not so much time that they forget the details or lose interest in the process. The anonymity of the Delphi approach combines the advantages of multiple expert opinions while avoiding the disadvantage of undue influence or persuasiveness by one or more of the experts.

The estimates may or may not converge after 3 or 4 rounds (3 rounds is typical in the Delphi process). If the estimates converge to a narrow range, a meeting among the experts is convened to confirm their estimates and to record any concerns they might have about the proposed project. If their estimates do not converge, a meeting is held to allow them to justify their estimates and to settle their differences among themselves. If the estimates do not converge during the meeting, the range of estimates can be used to develop a probability density function for the estimates.

An alternative approach is called the wideband Delphi process [Boehm81]. This approach involves convening a meeting of the experts in the beginning to discuss the project, allowing time to reflect and submit anonymous estimates, and holding meetings after each round of estimation to discuss the assumptions and rationale on which their estimates are based. There is some danger that some estimators may unduly influence others by virtue of their personalities or positions of authority, but each estimator is given time to reflect on the discussions and do additional research before submitting their next estimate, which is reported anonymously.

A more radical approach is one where the process is completed in one meeting. Each round of estimation is conducted by secret ballot, with discussion of the estimates between rounds. This can be done efficiently, especially if facilitated by a groupware tool that allows each expert to anonymously enter an estimate and a brief justification from their keyboard. Each expert's estimate and justification is anonymously displayed on a large screen for the group to observe and provides the basis of discussion between estimation rounds. This approach is more efficient than traditional Delphi or wideband Delphi, but it is not recommended because it does not allow sufficient time for the experts to reflect on the results of previous rounds, to perhaps do some research in preparing their next estimate, and to avoid the (perhaps inappropriate) influence of others in the room.[23]

A Delphi process may or may not produce a consensus result. Failure to achieve a consensus may indicate the need for further work to be done with the customer and your management in refining the requirements, examining the design constraints, and assessing the feasibility of the project. Another way to use nonconvergent results is to develop a probability function from the range of estimates and use it to perform a quantitative risk analysis using a probabilistic model.

The primary strengths of a Delphi estimation process are:

- obtaining the combined opinions of experts without undue influence of experts on one another's estimates and
- multiple rounds of estimation in which each expert reflects on the anonymously submitted rationales of others.

Weaknesses of the Delphi process are:

- the time and effort required of the experts,
- the possibility of intransigence by one or more experts, and
- the possibility of undue influence in the wideband Delphi meetings.

6.6.5 WBS/CPM/PERT

The WBS/CPM/PERT approach to estimation is based on the architecture decomposition view embedded in the WBS and the WBS work packages. As discussed in Chapter 5, work packages can be used to provide bottom-up estimates of project attributes by rolling up lower level estimates for activities and tasks. The work package estimates can be based on other pragmatic techniques (rule of thumb, analogy, Delphi, expert judgment) or on theory-based or regression-based estimation models.

[23] I participated in one such meeting in which a participant commented "Who is the idiot that submitted that estimate?" The comment was not conducive to a collegial outcome.

In this regard the WBS/CPM/PERT approach is perhaps the most accurate of the pragmatic techniques because of the increased level of detail at which various estimation techniques can be applied and because positive and negative variations in inaccuracies at lower levels may "average out" when aggregated at higher levels. The PERT approach can be used to provide probability distributions for the schedule durations to reach various milestones and to complete the project.

You might not have sufficient detail to develop an ADV, a WBS, work packages, and a critical-path schedule network early in your project, but developing these items should be a top priority in planning and replanning. Revised estimates based on initial results should be made as soon as possible. The WBS, and the schedule network will become more detailed as understanding grows and as execution of the project progresses. Updated estimates based on the evolving WBS and schedule network should be prepared on an ongoing basis.

The primary strength of the WBS/CPM approach is:

- the increased accuracy of estimates that result from an increased level of detail and the accompanying level of understanding.

The primary weakness is:

- lack of sufficient knowledge or time to prepare the ADV, WBS, work packages, and critical path network in the early planning phase of a software project.

6.7 THEORY-BASED ESTIMATION MODELS

A theory-based estimation model is so called because there is an underlying theory of software projects on which the estimation model is based. Two theory-based models are described herein: system dynamics, which uses difference equations to model project behavior, and the original formulation of the SLIM model, which uses the Putnam software equation and Putnam's version of the Norden–Rayleigh equation to model software projects.

The goal this section is not to fully explain these theory-based models but rather to present the nature of the underlying theories, how the models incorporate the theories, and to caution that before you use a theory-based estimation model, you must understand the nature of the underlying theory to determine whether the model based on that theory is appropriate for your situation.

6.7.1 System Dynamics

System dynamics was invented by Jay Forrester around 1960 [Forrester61]. This approach has been used to model software development processes by [Hamid91] and has been further investigated by Madachy and Boehm [Madachy01]. Theories of how software projects behave are modeled using interacting continuous variables that employ feedback loops with time as the independent variable. Simulation models are implemented using difference equations to model the continuous variables.

A simple model of software production might model the production rate as the productivity for each individual multiplied by the number of personnel, where the number of personnel at any point in time depends on the initial number, the hiring rate (the rate at which personnel are added to the project) and the attrition rate (the rate at which personnel leave the project). Both the hiring rate and attrition rate would be modeled as functions of time. Productivity, as a function of time, might be modeled as gross productivity (e.g., lines of code per staff-week) minus the rework rate (e.g., defective lines of code per staff-week, as a function of time). The corresponding difference equations are as follows:

```
INIT(#_STAFF) = 10
INIT(ATTRITION_FACTOR) = 0.02
INIT(GROSS_PROD_RATE) = 500
INIT(REWORK_FACTOR) = 0.8
INIT(HIRING_FACTOR) = 1.2
HIRING_RATE = HIRING_FACTOR * ATTRITION_RATE
ATTRITION_RATE = ATTRITION_ FACTOR * #_STAFF
NET_HIRING_RATE = (HIRING_RATE - ATTRITION_RATE)
#_STAFF = #_STAFF + NET_HIRING_RATE * Δt
GROSS_PRODUCTION = #_STAFF * GROSS_PROD _RATE * Δt
NET_PRODUCTION = GROSS_PRODUCTION * REWORK_FACTOR
```

Values on the left side of each equation are updated at each time step (Δt) using the values computed on the right side of the equation during the previous time step. The model could, for instance, produce a report that lists (week by week or month by month) deliverable lines of code (or function points or other size unit) produced that week or month and the cumulative total of lines of code produced up to that point in time. An estimate of project duration could be determined by observing how much time is needed to develop the estimated lines of code.

The effects of different theories, including variations in factors such as the hiring rate, attrition rate, and rework factor could be determined by running different simulations with different parameter values. More sophisticated theories would include more project factors in the model, such as the impact of the project manager's experience, the cohesiveness of the development team, effectiveness of version control, an Incremental-build process, and verification and validation processes, such as design inspections.

Iconic representations of system dynamics models can be constructed and the models can be executed using simulation tools such as STELLA, iThink, and DYNAMO (accessible on the Internet).

6.7.2 SLIM

The SLIM estimation model (Software LIfecycle Management) was developed by Larry Putnam in the 1970s and has evolved over time to include variations on the original model that reflect changing practices used to develop software-intensive systems. The theory on which the original model is based is described here [Putnam92].

The original SLIM estimation model is based on two equations in two variables; project effort, E, and schedule duration, T. One of the equations is Putnam's version of the Norden–Rayleigh equation that models the rate of buildup and phase-down of project staff. The other equation is Putnam's software equation.

Simplified forms of the two equations are

$$E \sim \text{MBI} * T^3 \qquad \text{(based on the Norden–Rayleigh equation)},$$

$$E \sim \left(\frac{\text{SLOC}}{\text{PI}}\right)^3 * T^{-4} \qquad \text{(based on Putnam's software equation)}.$$

The parameters of the equations are:

MBI: a manpower buildup index that reflects the estimated rate of staff buildup for the project;

SLOC: estimated product size (expressed in source lines of code, SLOC, or in function points, which are converted by SLIM to lines of code using an internal table of FP/SLOC); and

PI: the productivity index; local data can be used to calibrate the PI parameter, or industry-average values can be used for different types of products.

Simultaneous solution to the two equations results in pairs of values for E (effort) and T (time) that satisfy the equations. The maximum effort, minimum time solution of the equations, for given values of MBI, PI, SLOC, and some other constants occurs at the point of intersection on the log-log scale illustrated in Figure 6.8. Note that the MBI line, from the Norden–Rayleigh equation, has a slope of +3. Also note that the $(\text{SLOC/PI})^3$ line, from the Putnam software equation, has a slope of –4.

As indicated in Figure 6.8, a maximum time constraint can be specified, which results in a minimum effort and maximum time solution. According to Putnam, the point of intersection in Figure 6.8 for the minimum time, maximum effort solution to the simultaneous equations is based on empirical data that indicates no projects have been observed to have successfully finished with effort and time combinations on the PI line above the MBI line; this region is termed the impossible region in SLIM. Combinations of effort and time on the PI line below the MBI line are feasible.

An interesting aspect of the SLIM model, as implemented in the SLIM estimation tool, is the use of Monte Carlo simulation to compute various combinations of effort and schedule at various levels of probability. Estimated size (expressed in function points or lines of code) is specified using the PERT method: smallest estimated size, 50% probable size, and largest estimated size from which the mean and standard deviation of a beta probability function are determined. Size can be specified for the entire system or for the individual elements of the architecture decomposition view. PI and MBI can be specified as fixed or within probability ranges.

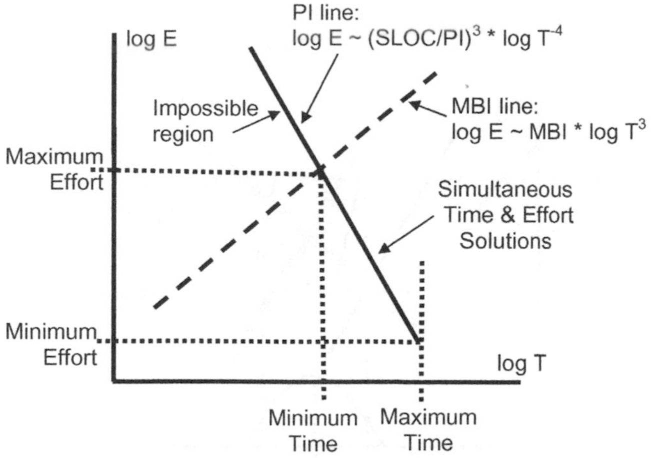

FIGURE 6.8 Simultaneous solution of the SLIM equations

The *Monte Carlo technique* is a simulation method by which random, independent values are selected from each of the inverse probability distributions for size, PI, and MBI. The resulting three numbers (one each for size, PI, and MBI) are used to calculate an effort–time combination. Another random, independent set of input values is then selected from the probability distributions and a second answer is calculated. The calculations are typically repeated a few hundred or a few thousand times. See Section 6.8.2 for a discussion of Monte Carlo simulation.

A conceptual view of the outcome of a SLIM simulation is depicted in Figure 6.9, where each of the "starred" data points is one of the simultaneous solutions to the Norden–Rayleigh and Putnam equations; a few hundred or a few thousand solution points are typically computed. The solutions in Figure 6.9 are bounded by the probability distributions of size, PI, and MBI, by the minimum time solution, and by the constraint (if any) specified for the maximum duration of the project.

Projecting the distribution of those solutions to the time axis provides the probability density function for the project duration; projecting them to the effort axis provides the probability density function for effort, as illustrated in Table 6.3.

Interpolating Table 6.3, with a schedule of 30 months (99.99% probable schedule), it is 87% probable that the project can be completed with 500 staff-months of effort; with 800 SM of effort (99.99% probable), it is 93% probable that the project can be completed in 24 months. The joint probability of completing the project in 24 months with 500 staff-months of effort is roughly $0.87 \times 0.93 = 0.81$ (81%).

The major strengths of the SLIM model are the simultaneous solution of effort, E, and duration, T, and the use of Monte Carlo simulation, which together provide trade-off combinations of effort and schedule at various levels of probability. Alternatively, one of effort or duration can be specified and the corresponding range of values of the other with its associated probabilities can be calculated.

Some people have criticized the Putnam software equation as being too sensitive in modeling the effort–duration relationship as $E \sim T^{-4}$; doubling the schedule would reduce effort to 1/16 the original value.

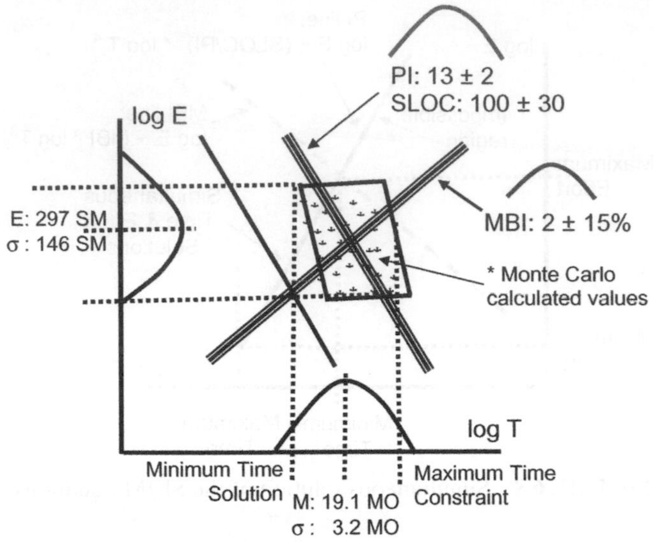

FIGURE 6.9 A conceptual view of a SLIM estimate

TABLE 6.3 Probability ranges for a SLIM estimate

	50% Probable	84% Probable	97.5% Probable	99.7% Probable
Effort, *E*	297 SM	443 SM	589 SM	735 SM
Duration, *T*	19.1 MO	22.3 MO	25.5 MO	28.7 MO

To recap an earlier point: you must understand the theory on which a theory-based model is based to know whether it is an appropriate estimation model for your project. For example, the buildup and phase-down of project staffing incorporated in the original SLIM model would not be appropriate if the staffing profile for your project reflected a constant, fixed value such as 20 people from start to finish. Newer SLIM models are appropriate for various staffing profiles.

6.8 REGRESSION-BASED ESTIMATION MODELS

Regression-based estimation models are based on equations derived from historical data collected from past projects. Constructing equations from the data is known as regression analysis. Equations that incorporate multiple independent variables are derived by a procedure known as multivariate regression analysis. But in most cases of regression-based estimation models for software projects, the primary estimation equation is based on analysis of the relationship between a single independent variable (e.g., size) and a dependent variable (e.g., effort), as in

$$E = a*(S)^b,$$

where E is effort, S is size, and a and b are constants.

For example, if S is size in thousands of delivered source lines of code (KDSLOC) and E is effort in staff-months, the equation might be

SLIM EQUATIONS

Without going into excessive detail, it is interesting to note a few aspects of the original SLIM model, which is based on Putnam's version of the Norden–Rayleigh equation and Putnam's software equation.

The Putnam software equation was derived by Larry Putnam from empirical data collected from several large software projects in the 1970s. It is of the form

$$E \sim \left(\frac{\text{SLOC}}{PI}\right)^3 * T^{-4},$$

where E is effort, SLOC is source lines of code, PI is the productivity index, and T is time.

The Norden–Rayleigh equation is used to model the buildup and phase-down of staffing level in the original SLIM model. It is of the form "t times e to the minus t squared":

$$y' = \left(\frac{K}{t_d^2}\right) t e^{-f(t)},$$

$$f(t) = \frac{t^2}{2t_d^2},$$

where y' is the rate of effort buildup and phase-down, K is the area under the staffing curve from $t = 0$ to ∞, and t_d is the time at which y' achieves its maximum value, as illustrated in Figure 6.10.

The Rayleigh equation is a particular form of a Weibull probability distribution. The equation acquired the name "Norden–Rayleigh" because Lord Rayleigh used a similar equation in the 1800s to model the scattering of sunlight reflected from the earth, which explains why we perceive the sky to be bright blue on a clear sunny day (a different form of light scattering, Mie scattering, explains why the sky looks gray on polluted or overcast days and red at sunrise and sunset).

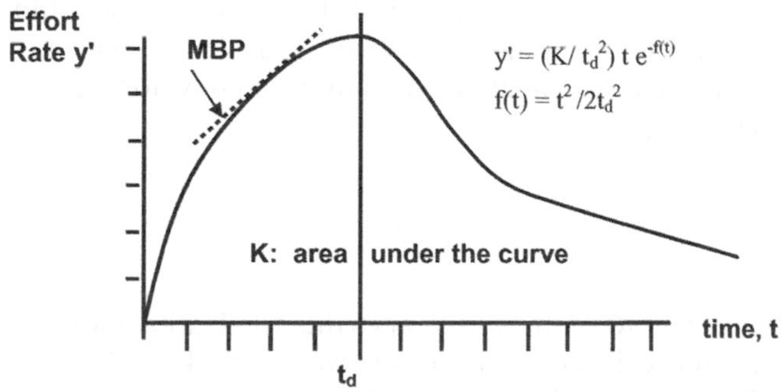

FIGURE 6.10 A Norden–Rayleigh equation and curve

In the 1960s Peter Norden noted regular patterns of staff buildup and phase-down in hardware design projects. He modeled hardware projects as consisting of planning and specification, design, prototyping, and release. He observed that each activity has a buildup and phase-down pattern and found that the Rayleigh equation fit the composite set of these overlapping activities [Norden63]. Putnam used a similar model for software projects consisting of planning, design and implementation, testing, and maintenance.

The manpower buildup parameter (MBP) in Figure 6.10 determines the slope of the Norden–Rayleigh curve (i.e., the derivation of y'). It is expressed as

$$\text{MBP} = \frac{K}{(t_d)^3}.$$

K and t_d in Figure 6.10 determine the size and shape of the Norden–Rayleigh curve. Larger K and smaller t_d values result in a taller and more sharply peaked curve than do smaller values of K and larger values of t_d, that is, larger K and smaller t_d result in larger values of MBP and vice versa.

Based on empirical data from completed software projects, Putnam found that the MBP had a wide range of values, roughly 7 to 233. In the SLIM estimation tool these values are keyed to the manpower buildup index (MBI), which has six discrete values (1, 2,…, 6). MBI values can be selected to reflect staff buildup rates ranging from slow to extremely rapid. The MBI is used, as illustrated in Figure 6.8, to determine the minimum duration of a project for a given value of MBI.

The integral of Putnam's version of the Norden–Rayleigh equation is of the form

$$y(t) = K * (1 - e^{-f(t)}),$$

where K is the total area under the curve and, as before, $f(t) = t^2/2t_d^2$.

The value of $y(t)$, for a particular time T, is the cumulative amount of effort that will be expended from project initiation up to time T. Putnam then observed that many projects release the product at the peak of the curve, t_d, and then enter the maintenance phase, so that K is the total life cycle effort. At time t_d,

$$y(t_d) = 0.39K.$$

This corresponds to the widely used rule of thumb that 40% of life cycle effort goes to software development and 60% to software maintenance.

Another SLIM equation calculates the minimum development time, T_d for a software project as

$$T_d = \left(\frac{K}{C}\right)^{0.33},$$

where T_d is in years, K is in staff-years (the total area under the Norden–Rayleigh curve), and C is a constant in the range of 14 to 15. Converting years to months, staff-years to staff-months, and letting $C = 14.5$ results in

$$T_d = 2.15(E)^{0.33},$$

where T_d is in months and E is effort in staff-months.[24]

The minimum duration for a 120 staff-month project, for example, would be

$$T_d = 2.15(120)^{0.33} \sim 2.15 \times 5 = 10.75 \text{ months.}$$

This effort–development time equation corresponds to the widely used rule of thumb that development time is proportional to the cube root of effort (some organizations use a square root rule).

Additional information on the theory of the original SLIM estimation model can be found in [Putnam92].

$$E = 2.5 * (S)^{1.2}.$$

Thus, $E \sim 40$ when $S = 10$ and $E \sim 91$ when $S = 20$. Note the nonlinear increase in effort when size is doubled.

Size is used as the independent variable in regression-based estimation equations because size can be determined more objectively than other product attributes. Also size measures such as function points can be estimated more accurately than other product attributes in the early phases of a project (and converted to lines of code, if desired).

The exponent b in the equation reflects the typically nonlinear relationship between size and effort. If b is greater than 1, the relationship exhibits diseconomy of scale (i.e., a product of twice the size will require more than twice the effort). If b is less than 1, the relationship exhibits economy of scale (i.e., larger products require disproportionately less effort). And, of course, $b = 1$ indicates a linear relationship between product size and development effort. In most cases b is greater than 1, but not always.

Referring to Figure 6.1, note that it relates to a regression-based estimation model in that:

- Past Experiences are summarized in the regression equation derived from historical data,
- Product Attributes are summarized in the size estimate and some adjustment factors (e.g., complexity), and
- an effort adjustment factor (EAF) is applied as a multiplier in the effort–size equation

$$E_{adj} = a * (S)^b * \text{EAF}.$$

A similar equation can be derived to relate schedule S to effort E:

$$S = c * (E_{adj})^d.$$

[24] [Boehm81], page 470.

In this relationship, the exponent d is typically in the range of 0.3 to 0.5. Similar equations can be developed from historical data to relate, for example, number of defects to product size.

The following sections describe the COCOMO regression-based estimation models and considerations involved in developing a locally derived, regression-based estimation model.

6.8.1 COCOMO Models

COCOMO is an acronym derived from the phrase "constructive cost model." The original set of COCOMO models was developed by Barry Boehm and published in his text *Software Engineering Economics* in 1981 [Boehm81]. The 1981 COCOMO models, later COCOMO models, and COCOMO-like models derived from local historical data (i.e., regression-based) models are the most widely used estimation models.

To distinguish the first COCOMO model from later COCOMO models, we refer to the first one as COCOMO81. There are 3 sets of estimation equations in COCOMO81 that were derived from data collected by Boehm from 63 completed software projects. These projects and the resulting equations are documented in the referenced text. Each set of equations includes an equation to estimate effort as a function of size, where size is measured in thousands of source lines of code (KSLOC) and effort is in staff-months, plus a regression equation that relates schedule in months to effort in staff-months.

There are 3 sets of equations for effort and schedule in COCOMO81 because the data from the 63 projects clustered into 3 groupings. On investigation, Boehm determined that one set of projects required the least effort for a given size. He termed these the "organic" projects, which were projects that typically developed stand-alone applications programs. The set of projects that required the largest amount of effort for a given size were termed "embedded" projects. These were projects that developed real-time software for computers embedded within larger systems. The intermediate projects were termed "semidetached." The products developed by these projects were typically systems programs such as compilers and other software development tools such as debuggers, and database applications; they were semidetached from the operating systems.

For semidetached systems, for example, the values of a, b, c, and d result in the estimation equations

$$E = 3.0(\text{KSLOC})^{1.12}$$

and

$$S = 2.5(E)^{0.35}.$$

Here KSLOC is thousands of source lines of code, E is effort in staff-months, and S is schedule in months.

To explain the variations in effort for projects of the same size within the same data set (i.e, the scatter in the historical data), Boehm and some other experts used the Delphi technique to develop the 15 adjustment factors and the ranges of values listed in Table 6.4.

TABLE 6.4 COCOMO81 cost drivers and effort multipliers

	Ratings					
	Very Low	Low	Nominal	High	Very High	Extra High
Cost drivers			*Effort multipliers*			
PRODUCT ATTRIBUTES						
RELY (required reliability)	0.75	0.88	1.00	1.15	1.40	
DATA (database size)		0.94	1.00	1.08	1.16	
CPLX (product complexity)	0.70	0.85	1.00	1.15	1.30	1.65
COMPUTER ATTRIBUTES						
TIME (execution time constraint)			1.00	1.11	1.30	1.66
STOR (main memory constraint)			1.00	1.06	1.21	1.56
VIRT (virtual machine volatility)		0.87	1.00	1.15	1.30	
TURN (computer turnaround time)		0.87	1.00	1.07	1.15	
PERSONNEL ATTRIBUTES						
ACAP (analyst capability)	1.46	1.19	1.00	0.86	0.71	
AEXP (application experience)	1.29	1.13	1.00	0.91	0.82	
PCAP (programmer capability)	1.42	1.17	1.00	0.86	0.70	
VEXP (virtual machine experience)	1.21	1.10	1.00	0.90		
LEXP (programming language experience)	1.14	1.07	1.00	0.95		
PROJECT ATTRIBUTES						
MODP (use of modern programming practices)	1.24	1.10	1.00	0.91	0.82	
TOOL (use of software tools)	1.24	1.10	1.00	0.91	0.83	
SCED (schedule constraint)	1.23	1.08	1.00	1.04	1.10	

The adjustment factors are called cost drivers; their values are called effort multipliers. Effort multipliers are applied to an estimate produced by the effort estimation equation to account for anticipated differences between past projects and the project being estimated. An effort multiplier value (EM) of 1.0 denotes an assumption that the cost driver will have the same effect on the future project as on typical past projects of the same size. An EM > 1 indicates an assumption that more effort will be required to accommodate that cost driver than on the typical past project; and EM < 1 indicates less effort will be required. Guidance for choosing multiplier values for the mnemonics Very Low, Low, Nominal, High, Very High, and Extra High are provided in the text.

The ranges and relative values of the effort multipliers can be visualized by placing them on a graph, as in Figure 6.11 where a few of the effort multipliers have been plotted. The origin of the graph represents a mnemonic of "Nominal" and an effort multiplier value of 1.0. A Nominal value does not influence the outcome, which is to say that choosing a Nominal value for an effort multiplier indicates that the multiplier will have the same effect as on the "typical project" from the historical

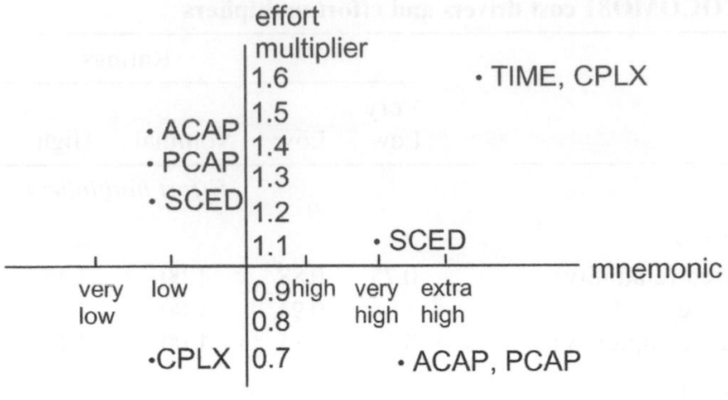

FIGURE 6.11 Ranges of values for some COCOMO81 effort multipliers

data set. A plot of the ranges of all 15 COCOMO81 cost drivers can be found in the Boehm text.[25]

In comparing Table 6.4 and Figure 6.11, it can be seen that the TIME effort multiplier has an Extra High rating of 1.66 and CPLX has an Extra High rating of 1.56. CPLX has a Very Low rating of 0.7. Table 6.4 indicates that TIME has a Nominal effort multiplier value of 1.0 (not shown in Figure 6.11). No effort multiplier values are specified for Low and Very Low ratings of TIME (or STOR). This is because the absence of an execution time constraint (or a memory constraint) will not require less effort provided the typical past project was not time or memory constrained; however, lack of sufficient execution time or memory space will make a project much harder and thus require more effort.

Note further that in Table 6.4 and Figure 6.11 High and Very High ratings for Product Attributes and Computer Attributes (e.g., CPLX) have effort multiplier values greater than 1.0 and values less than 1.0 for ratings of Low and Very Low, whereas effort multiplier values for Personnel Attributes such as ACAP and PCAP have values less than 1.0 for High and Very High ratings and corresponding values greater than 1.0 for Low and Very Low ratings.

Now the Very Low rating of the SCED effort multiplier is 1.23 and the Very High rating is 1.1. SCED has a value of 1.0 for a Nominal rating, as do all other effort multipliers. SCED thus has a "lazy U" shape (as illustrated in Figure 6.14; page 254).

It should also be noted that effort multiplier values other than those corresponding to the mnemonics can be chosen for the cost drivers. The mnemonics are provided as an aid to selecting cost driver values.

The product of a group of effort multipliers is called the effort adjustment factor (EAF). The resulting COCOMO equations are of the form:

$$E_{\text{adj}} = a(\text{size})^b \times \text{EAF}, \quad \text{EAF} = \Pi\,\text{EMs},$$

where E_{adj} is effort computed by the equation, adjusted by the product of the 15 effort multipliers: EAF = Π EMs. Size is measured in lines of code. Most estimation tools based on COCOMO81 permit specification of size in function points that are converted to lines of code by a table in the tool.

[25] *Software Engineering Economics*, Prentice Hall, 1981, p. 124.

As described above, the schedule equation is of the form

$$S = c(E_{\text{adj}})^d.$$

An example of computing an EAF is provided in Table 6.5.

TABLE 6.5 An example of determining the EAF

Cost Driver	Situation	Rating	Effort Multiplier
RELY	Similar to past projects	Nominal	1.00
DATA	Low ratio of data to code	Low	0.94
CPLX	Complex algorithms	Very high	1.30
TIME	80% of available cycles	High	1.11
STOR	70% of available memory	High	1.06
VIRT	Stable system	Nominal	1.00
TURN	Good response time	Nominal	1.00
ACAP	Good senior people	High	0.86
AEXP	Four years	Nominal	1.00
PCAP	Good senior developers	High	0.86
VEXP	Six months	Low	1.10
LEXP	Twelve months	Nominal	1.00
MODP	More than one year	High	0.91
TOOL	Basic	Low	1.10
SCED	As estimated	Nominal	1.00
		EAF (Π15 EMs)	**1.17**

If the effort equation is

$$E_{\text{adj}} = 3.0 * (S)^{1.2} * \text{EAF},$$

and if $S = 20$ and EAF = 1.17, then

$$E_{\text{adj}} = 3.0 * (20)^{1.2} * 1.17 \sim 128 \text{ staff-months}$$

and

$$S = 2.5 * (128)^{0.35} \sim 13.5 \text{ months.}$$

If E_{adj} is in staff-months and S in months, the average staffing level is approximately 9.5 full-time equivalent (FTE) software developers (128/13.5).

Boehm also developed tables for percentage distributions of effort and schedule across the project phases of Product Design (PD), Detailed Design (DD), Coding and Unit Testing (CUT) and Integration and Testing (IT). These tables account for the fact that smaller projects have a greater percentage of total effort devoted to detailed design, coding, and unit testing than do larger projects, where larger percentages of effort and time are spent on analysis, design, and integration and system testing of larger systems.

In addition he developed tables for the percentage distribution of effort across eight kinds of work activities within each phase of software development for different kinds (organic, semidetached, embedded) and sizes of products:

1. requirements analysis,
2. product design,
3. programming (detailed design, coding, and unit testing),
4. test planning,
5. verification and validation,
6. project office,
7. CM/QA, and
8. manuals.

The procedure for making an estimate using COCOMO81 is as follows:

1. determine which set of equations to use (i.e., Is your project "organic?" "semidetached?" or "embedded?");
2. estimate size in thousands of delivered source instructions (KSLOC);
3. select a multiplier value for each of the 15 cost drivers;
4. compute the effort adjustment factor;
5. compute estimated effort;
6. use estimated effort to compute the schedule duration;
7. use the tables provided in [Boehm81] to determine the phase distribution of work activities; and
8. use the tables provided in [Boehm81] to determine the distribution of effort for each of eight kinds of work activities within each phase.

COCOMO81 was developed in the era of mainframe computers and Waterfall development processes. In 1987 Boehm published the Ada-COCOMO estimation model for estimating embedded systems projects. Ada-COCOMO was sonamed because it was developed in conjunction with the Ada process model to estimate projects that use incremental development and other development processes consistent with using the Ada programming language (and similar languages and methods) to develop embedded systems programs [Boehm87].

Ada-COCOMO added some new cost drivers and made adjustments to some of the COCOMO81 effort multipliers. The two most significant enhancements in Ada-COCOMO were:

- incorporation of four scale factors to adjust the exponent of the effort estimation equation for embedded systems, and
- an estimation procedure for incremental development of a software system or product.

The four scale factors introduced to allow adjustment of the exponents in the effort and schedule equations are:

- experience with the Ada process model,
- design thoroughness at PDR (preliminary design review),

- risks eliminated at PDR, and
- requirements volatility.

Values between 0 and 5 are selected for each of the four factors (0 being bad and 5 being good). These values are used in formulas that result in an effort exponent that ranges between 1.04 and 1.24. The effort equation is of the form:

$$E = a*(S)^b,$$

where

$$b = 1.04 + 0.01*\sum \mathrm{SF}_j, \qquad 1 \le j \le 4,$$

and

$$\sum \mathrm{SF}_j, \qquad 1 \le j \le 4,$$

is the sum of the four scale factor values.

Making an estimate for an incremental development project, as in Ada-COCOMO, requires that you specify:

- the size of each increment;
- the start of each increment with respect to the previous increment; and
- the "breakage factor," which is an estimate of the percent of code in previous increments that will be reworked while developing the current increment.

In 1997 Boehm published the COCOMO II model and subsequently updated it in 2000. The model described here is COCOMO II.2000 [Boehm02]. Among the many changes to COCOMO81 and Ada COCOMO in COCOMO II, three major ones are:

1. replacement of the 3 sets of estimation equations in COCOMO81 with two equations, one for estimating effort and one for estimating schedule; each equations has an adjustable exponent. These equations are similar to, but not identical to, those of Ada-COCOMO,
2. replacement of some cost drivers and addition of new cost drivers that resulted in 17 cost drivers and associated multiplier values in COCOMO II, and
3. a nonlinear model for estimating the cost of reusing software.

The effort exponent in COCOMO II is of the form:

$$b = 0.91 + 0.01*\sum \mathrm{SF}_j, \qquad 1 \le j \le 5.$$

The five exponent scale factors in COCOMO II are:

- Precedentedness (PREC): how familiar is this kind of work?
- Flexibility (FLEX): how much flexibility exists in the requirements?

- Resolution (RESL): how thorough is the design at PDR? are risks resolved at PDR?
- Team Cohesion (TEAM): do all stakeholders have a common view? are all stakeholders willing to accommodate other stakeholders' objectives?
- Process Maturity (PMAT): what is the CMMI capability maturity rating at the start of the project?

One of six values is selected for each of the five factors. These values result in an effort exponent that ranges between 0.91 and 1.18. A similar formula is used to compute the schedule exponent. The schedule exponent ranges between 0.28 and 0.33.

The reader is referred to the textbook and URL for additional information on COCOMO II [Boehm02], [USC]. A historical retrospective on the evolution of COCOMO is presented in [Fairley07].

6.8.2 Monte Carlo Estimation

Regression-based estimation models can be used to produce ranges of estimates at differing levels of probability [Fairley02]. The regression equations and cost drivers can be programmed on a spreadsheet. A simulation tool such as Crystal Ball (a tool that incorporates a set of spreadsheet macros) can be used to specify probability functions for the estimated size and effort multipliers in the cells of the spreadsheet, whereby probability distributions are entered rather than single values [Crystal]. The spreadsheet tool uses Monte Carlo simulation to repeatedly sample the probability distributions and compute solutions using those values. If the process is repeated a few hundred or a few thousand times, a histogram of probable effort is generated, as illustrated in Figures 6.13*a* and 6.13*b*.

Note in Figure 6.13*b* that the simulation was run 300 times. If 12 of 300 estimates are computed to have the same value E, the probability that required effort will be E is 0.04 (12/300). The probability that a project can be completed with an amount of effort less than or equal to E is determined by summing up all of the probabilities for values of effort less than or equal to E. In the probability distribution of Figure 6.13*b*, for example, it is 80% probable that the project can be completed with 200 staff-months of effort or less because 80% of the calculated values of effort are at or to the left of 200 SM.

In a similar manner the probability range for project duration can be determined using the probability distribution of effort in a regression equation that relates schedule S to effort E as in the COCOMO models:

$$S = c*(E)^d.$$

The resulting histogram of probability density for the schedule will be similar in concept to that of Figure 6.13*b*.

6.8.3 Local Calibration

Rather than developing a new estimation model, you may be able to recalibrate an existing model to the local situation within your organization. The parameters used

DEVELOPING A REGRESSION-BASED ESTIMATION MODEL

The details of constructing the COCOMO models presented by Boehm in *Software Engineering Economics* have resulted in widespread replication of the process. Many organizations have developed and use locally derived "COCOMO-like" estimation models. COCOMO-like models are also incorporated into commercially available software estimation tools; some tools support entry of local data and derivation of the equations using these data [CoStar].

Figure 6.12 illustrates derivation of an equation that relates development effort E to product size S, where each of the starred data points represents a completed project. If, for example, the linear equation in the log-log domain is of the form

$$\log_{10} \text{effort} = \log_{10} 0.5 + 1.25 * \log_{10} \text{size},$$

then the equation in the real domain is

$$\text{effort} = 3.3 * \text{size}^{1.25}.$$

If a similar equation relating schedule to effort is of the form

$$\log_{10} \text{schedule} = \log_{10} 0.4 + 0.33 * \log_{10} \text{effort},$$

then

$$\text{schedule} = 2.8 * \text{effort}^{0.33}.$$

When the resulting equations are used, an Effort Adjustment Factor (EAF) is applied (in the real domain) to explain the difference in effort required for products of the same size.

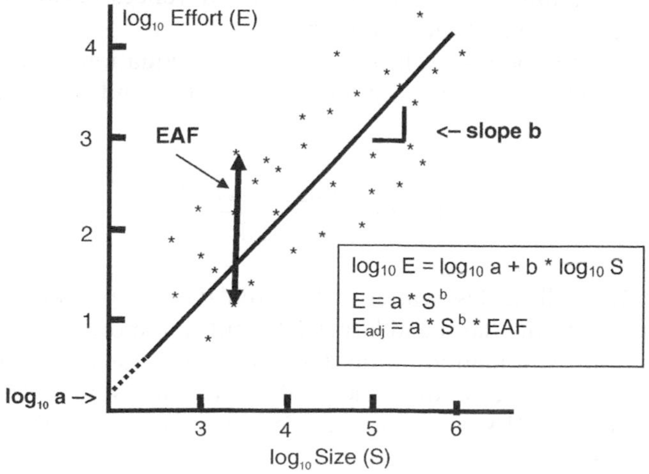

FIGURE 6.12 Derivation of a regression-based estimation model

Software tools such as the free Calico calibration tool from SoftstarSystems can be used to compute the constants and exponents of regression equations using data from past projects, entered by you or some other member of your organization [http://softstarsystems.com/].

Several points should be noted. First, the historical data is transformed to the log-log domain, the equation is derived in the log-log domain, and the result is transformed back to the real domain. This permits the use of linear regression techniques to derive and analyze the (typically) nonlinear relationship between effort and size.

A second factor to be noted in Figure 6.12 is the scatter in the data. If product size were a perfect predictor of required effort, all data points would be on the line of the equation. Said differently, the scatter in the data indicates that factors other than size determine the amount of effort needed. The composite of these other attributes is the effort adjustment factor in the COCOMO models. These are also the adjustment factors in Figures 6.1 and 6.3. As related to those figures:

- past experience is summarized by the regression equations derived from the data for past projects,
- the future product is summarized primarily in the size estimate, and
- other product and process attributes are accounted for by the effort multiplier values of the cost drivers (the adjustment factors).

The goal of regression analysis is to find values of the parameters *a, b, c,* and *d* in the equations $E = a\ (\text{size})^b$ and $S = c\ (\text{size})^d$ that provide best fits to the data, where *E* is effort and *S* is schedule duration. In the log-log domain, as illustrated in Figure 6.12, linear regression analysis is performed to find values of log *a* (the intercept) and *b* (the slope) of the linear equation. A similar process is used to find the values of *c* and *d* for the effort–duration equation. The least squares method is typically used to derive the equations because it is relatively simple and produces good results. It involves finding values of log *a* and *b* (and log *c* and *d*) that minimize the squares of the differences between actual and estimated values for each of the data points.

One measure of goodness of fit for a regression equation is the sum of the relative errors (RE) between each estimated value and each actual value where:

$$\text{each RE} = \frac{|\text{estimate} - \text{actual}|}{\text{actual}}.$$

Thus smaller REs indicate less scatter in the actual data for past projects (a better fit of the equation to the data) and larger REs indicate more scatter in the data (a less good fit of the equation to the data). RE = 0 means that the estimated value and the actual value are the same. If all data points were on the line of the equation, the sum of REs would be zero. In this case size would be a perfect predictor of effort.

The distribution of relative errors between estimated values and actual values can be used to determine the percentage of estimated values that lie within a given percentage of the actual data points. For example, you might find that 80% of the estimated values differ by not more than 20% from the actual values when the actual values are normalized by the adjustment factors for the projects. This is expressed by a PRED (predictor) function for estimation models: PRED(0.8) = 0.2 in the example.

The PRED function is widely accepted as a measure of the efficacy of an estimation model (all estimation models, including regression models). A model that does not achieve PRED(0.8) = 0.2 is usually judged to be too inaccurate for use, meaning there is too much scatter in the underlying historical data.

Another measure of goodness of fit is the correlation coefficient r, which is a measure of the correspondence between estimated and actual values. r varies between 0 and 1; $r = 0$ means there is no correspondence, and $r = 1$ means there is perfect correspondence between estimated and actual values. In the latter case ($r = 1$) all data points would be on the line of the estimation equation, and as stated previously, size would be a perfect predictor of effort.

In principle, development of a regression-based estimation model is simple:

1. collect some data from past projects,
2. use a regression analysis tool to derive some equations, and
3. develop some cost drivers and effort multiplier values to account for differences among seemingly similar past projects.

In practice it is not so simple, of course. The first problem you may encounter is lack of data for past projects that is consistently recorded using consistent units of measurement and consistent ways of counting factors such as size, effort, schedule, and adjustment factors. If you do not have consistent historical data, you or someone in your organization must establish a metrics collection process that will result in the accumulation of data on which to base an estimation model.

The second problem you may encounter is wide scatter in the data, which means the data values for projects of the same size are so widely dispersed that the data do not cluster around the lines of the equations; said differently, the residual error, correlation coefficient, and PRED(0.8) all indicate that past projects are so dissimilar that it is not possible to estimate future projects based on these past experiences. This is an indicator (a symptom) of a deeper underlying problem: *chaotic development processes, namely lack of systematic development and management practices in your organization!* It is impossible to develop a systematic approach to estimating future projects when the past projects are characterized by chaos.

If you succeed in overcoming mismanagement problems, it may still be difficult to find a small set of cost drivers that explain the differences in effort and schedule for projects of the same kind and size. The true cost drivers may be political or social in nature, such as poor customer relations, indifferent management, and/or demoralized software developers. You may be hesitant to include such factors in an estimation model.

It is not impossible to overcome these problems. Many organizations have developed and routinely use locally derived regression-based estimation models. Some organizations have different regression-based estimation models for different kinds of projects; the equations are based on robust repositories of history data. When a project is completed the oldest data set in the repository for that kind of project is removed, data for the just-completed project is entered, and the model is recalibrated (i.e., the equations are re-derived using the new data). There is thus a "sliding window" of historical data that constantly refreshes the data repositories and updates the estimation models.

in most commercial estimation models are calibrated to industry averages (e.g., PI and MBI in the SLIM tool; values of constant multipliers, exponents, and cost drivers in the CoStar tool for COCOMO II). Local calibration allows you to adjust the model parameters.

You can determine if local calibration is warranted by comparing estimated values produced by the model to recorded values for past projects and attempting to find a set of realistic parameters for the model that produces acceptably small variations between estimated values and the known values for completed projects. If this is not possible, the model must be recalibrated.

The SLIM estimation tools, for example, can automatically recalibrate the PI and MBI parameters based on history data from local past projects that you enter into the tool. The constant multipliers a and c in the COCOMO effort and schedule

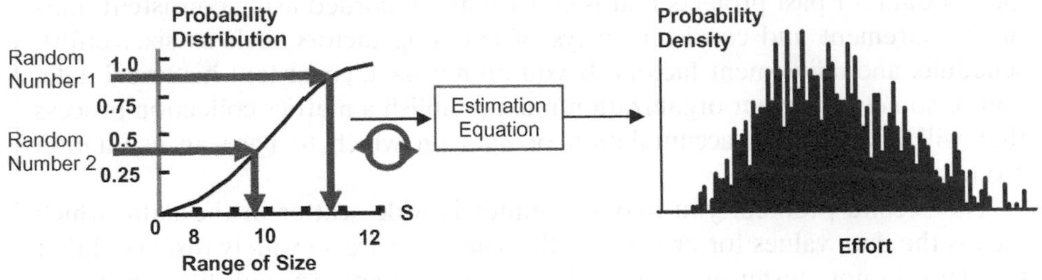

FIGURE 6.13A Sampling using Monte Carlo estimation

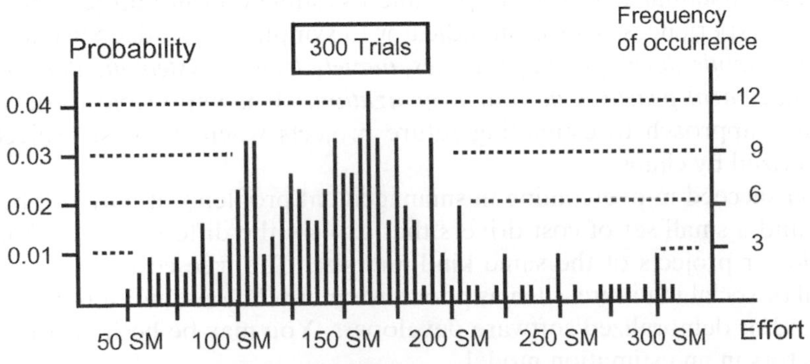

FIGURE 6.13B An effort histogram

equations can be recalibrated using a least squares approximation technique that compensates for differences between the estimated values using the old equations and the actual values; Boehm recommends that data from at least five past projects be used to recalibrate the constant term in a regression equation [Boehm81].

Calibration of both the constant multipliers and exponents in the effort and schedule equations of a regression-based estimation model is more problematic because calculation of both the constant multiplier and exponent (i.e., the intercept and slope of the straight line using linear regression in the log-log domain) is more sensitive to variations in the data than is calculation of the constant multiplier alone. Boehm recommends that consistent data from at least 10 projects that are representative of the projects to be estimated in the future be used [Boehm81].

A final note of caution: in light of the previous discussion, you should not use an estimation model or tool to estimate your projects without checking the agreement of the model to known outcomes of some completed projects in your organization and making the necessary adjustments and recalibrations; whether the tool or model be a COCOMO model, a SLIM model, a locally developed model, or any other estimation model.

6.9 ESTIMATION TOOLS

SLIM and COCOMO are representative of estimation models for which software tools are available to assist you in making estimates. According to Capers Jones, there were around 50 commercially available estimation tools marketed in the United States and 25 or so in Europe in 2002 [Jones02]. In the cited paper, Jones lists the basic capabilities of most estimation tools, additional capabilities provided by some but not all estimation tools, and capabilities provided by only a few, if any, estimation tools. Some of the capabilities in his lists, plus a few other capabilities not mentioned in his paper, are presented in Table 6.6.

Some estimation tools can be purchased, others can be leased, and some are available as freeware. Most of the commercial tool vendors sell or lease additional tools to record and report project metrics, repository tools for storing historical data for completed projects, and calibration tools. Most also provide downloadable evaluation copies of their tools.

As mentioned above, commercially available software tools are usually calibrated to industry-average data. You should check and adjust the calibration before using any software tool to make estimates for your project. As discussed below, you should always use two or more complementary estimation techniques (e.g., WBS/CPM based on expert judgment plus a locally calibrated estimation tool) and reconcile the differences in the estimates provided by the different techniques.

6.10 ESTIMATING LIFE CYCLE RESOURCES, EFFORT, AND COST

Depending on the nature of your project and your organization, you may be asked to provide an estimate of life cycle resources, effort, and costs for developing the software, installing it and training users, providing ongoing support and maintenance, and retiring the software. You may have historical data on which to base your

TABLE 6.6 Capabilities of software estimation tools [Jones02]

Capabilities of most estimation tools
Support for both function points and lines of code (LOC)
Conversion between LOC and function points
Phase-level, activity-level, and task-level estimation
Estimation for incremental development
Support for software reusability of various artifacts
Additional capabilities of some, but not all estimation tools
Support for estimates based on metrics such as object-oriented metrics
Risk and value analysis
Estimation templates derived from historical data
Defect and reliability estimation
Cost-to-complete and time-to-complete estimates
Links to project management tools such as Artemis and Microsoft Project
Currency conversions for international projects
Inflation calculations for long-term projects
Estimates keyed to the SEI capability maturity levels
Capabilities provided by few (if any) estimation tools
Conversion and nationalization costs for international projects
Fees for trademark and copyright searches
Acquisition costs for commercial off-the-shelf software packages
Deployment costs for enterprise resource planning applications
Litigation costs for breach of contract if a project is late or over budget

estimate, you may use some industry averages, or the estimation method/tool you are using may provide estimates of life cycle costs based on industry averages or local data.

Local historical data or industrywide averages may indicate, for example, that development cost is typically 33% of total life cycle cost for your kind of system or product, thus indicating that additional life cycle costs will include an additional factor of twice your estimate for the software development project.

You might have a local rule of thumb that indicates the defect density reported by users is typically 0.1 defects per function point (0.1 D/FP) during the first six months of operation and 0.05 D/FP during the second six months. If your product contains 1000 function points, you should expect users to report 100 defects during the first six months and 50 during the second six. If it takes, on average, 1 staff-week to repair a user reported defect and distribute the updated version of the product, and if you assume there are 25 work-weeks in 6 months, you should plan for 4 software maintainers during the first six months (100/25) and 2 during the second six (50/25). If you must provide telephone and Web site support for users, the costs of personnel and facilities must be estimated.

If you use the Rayleigh profile for effort rate, as in SLIM, the area under the Rayleigh curve represents total life cycle effort. Based on past experiences or other information, you might estimate that 40% of total effort will be required for product development and 60% for maintenance (SLIM uses 39% and 61%; 0.39 being the point on the time axis where effort reaches its maximum value in the Norden–Rayleigh equation).

COCOMO II estimates maintenance effort from a size estimate, Size_M, (size to be added plus size to be modified during the maintenance period) multiplied by a maintenance adjustment factor (MAF) that accounts for programmer unfamiliarity (UNFM) and software understanding (SU). Size_M can be specified in function points or lines of code. Additions and changes are specified for the duration of the maintenance period T_M, which might extend over the lifetime of the software or might be re-estimated on an annual or semi-annual basis. The UNFM and SU factors account for the effect of the condition of the software and its documentation on the effort needed to understand the changes to be made; these are the same factors used in the COCOMO II model for software reuse.

In COCOMO II,

$$\text{Size}_M = (\text{size added} + \text{size modified}) \times \text{MAF},$$

where MAF is the maintenance adjustment factor:

$$\text{MAF} = 1 + \left(\left(\frac{\text{SU}}{100}\right) + \text{UNFM}\right).$$

Size_M is used in the COCOMO II effort estimation equation. As is usual in COCOMO II, an effort adjustment factor (EAF) is applied to the effort estimate determined by the effort estimation equation:

$$\text{PM}_M = a \times (\text{Size}_M)^b \times \text{MAF},$$

where PM_M is estimated programmer months of maintenance effort and MAF is the product of the effort multiplier values of the cost drivers for software maintenance.

The average staffing level for software maintenance is obtained by calculating:

$$\text{FSPM} = \frac{\text{PM}_M}{T_M},$$

where FSPM is full-time staff for program maintenance and T_M is the time period of the maintenance effort.

6.11 AN ESTIMATION PROCEDURE

Estimation, like all software engineering processes, should be conducted in accordance with a well-defined procedure (i.e., a set of steps to be followed). A multi-step estimation procedure is listed and discussed below:

1. Determine the purpose of, and required accuracy of the estimate.
2. Determine the information needed and sources of it.

3. Plan the schedule, resources, and responsibilities for developing the estimate.
4. Develop the requirements in as much detail as possible and as warranted.
5. Verify that the requirements are complete, consistent, and correct, to the extent possible.
6. Develop a top-level architecture decomposition view (ADV) in as much detail as possible and as warranted.
7. If warranted, develop the size, complexity, and required quality attributes for each component in the ADV.
8. Develop a work breakdown structure (WBS) in as much detail as possible and as warranted.
9. Supply any additional factors required by the estimation techniques to be used (*always use more than one estimation technique;* for example, WBS-based expert judgment and a locally calibrated SLIM or COCOMO model)
10. Prepare estimates using the selected estimation techniques.
11. Conduct sensitivity analyses on the estimates.
12. Reconcile differences in the estimates.
13. Document risk factors exposed by the estimation process.
14. Prepare a plan for updating the estimate at periodic intervals and as aperiodic events occur.
15. Prepare and implement a plan for baseline retention of estimation data, the documented estimate, and ongoing updates to the estimate.
16. Document the estimate using a standard template for estimates, to include the information in Section 6.12 of this chapter.

As with all processes, the procedural steps listed above should be tailored to fit the needs of the situation. If step 1 (determine the purpose of, and required accuracy of the estimate) reveals that the estimate is a "ball park" estimate to determine the feasibility of a contemplated project, a quick rule of thumb calculation may be sufficient. If step 1 reveals that the estimate is for the organization's next major product, on which the survival of the company may depend, the estimate should be conducted with great care and may involve feasibility studies, prototyping, and analysis of the competition.

Several steps in the estimation procedure use the phrase "in as much detail as possible and as warranted." Depending on the purpose and criticality of the estimate, development of an ADV and a WBS may or may not be warranted. Depending on the quality of the requirements and the time available, it may not be possible to develop an ADV or WBS without additional work to develop the requirements.

Step 9 indicates that you should always use more than one estimation technique and step 12 calls for reconciling the difference in the estimates produced by multiple techniques. Again, depending on the purpose of the estimate and the information available for making the estimate, use of multiple estimation techniques may not be warranted; however, you should use multiple techniques if you are preparing to commit yourself and your project team to a project based on the estimates. It is recommended that one of the techniques be based on expert judgment or local history of effort, duration, skills, and resources needed to complete the work package tasks in the WBS. If it is available, the second choice should be a locally calibrated estimation tool. A third estimate might involve use of a pragmatic estimation technique such as rule of thumb, analogy, or Delphi.

To reconcile differences produced by different estimates, step 11 in the estimation procedure calls for conducting a sensitivity analysis on each resulting estimate. Sensitivity analysis is concerned with determining the sensitivity of variations in the estimated outputs based on variations in the estimation inputs. Large variations in estimated outputs that result from small variations in the inputs indicate that the estimation technique is sensitive to those input parameters. Knowing that the estimated values are sensitive to certain input values may result in closer examination of those inputs and may help explain why two estimates produced by two different techniques do not agree.

For example, product size is the most sensitive input parameter for most estimation tools because it is the primary variable. In COCOMO II the combined effect of the Personnel effort multipliers is the second most sensitive parameter. The combined effect of the range of values Personnel effort multipliers, as specified in the COCOMO II text, can cause variations of approximately 10:1 in effort estimates, which is consistent with the observations of others [Sack68], [DeMarco99].

In addition the TEAM rating used to adjust the exponent in the COCOMO II effort estimation equation exerts a strong, non-linear effect on estimated effort as a function of product size; for example, varying the team rating from Very Low to Very High results in a 20% change in estimated effort for small projects. Because of the nonlinear effect of the effort equation exponent, larger sizes will result in larger variations in estimated effort based on the TEAM value.

Another sensitivity factor to consider when using a COCOMO-like model is the nonlinear trade-off between effort and schedule. In the various COCOMO models, for example, the relationship between effort and schedule is of the form

$$S = c * (E_{\text{adj}})^d,$$

where S is schedule in months, E_{adj} is effort in staff-months (calculated using the effort equation and effort multipliers), c and d are constants in COCOMO81, and c is a constant and d is calculated in Ada-COCOMO and COCOMO II.

Constant c is in the range of 2.5 to 3.0 for the various COCOMO models and exponent d is on the order of 0.33 (the cube root of effort). If $c = 2.5$ and $d = 0.33$ in the schedule equation, a project estimated to require 120 staff-months of effort would require a schedule of approximately 12.5 months which results in an average staffing level of approximately 10 FTE staff members (120/12.5).

The squareroot rule of thumb is another way to estimate schedule and average staffing level for a given amount of effort [Jalote02]. If, for example, a project is estimated to require 120 staff-months of effort, it would be scheduled as 11 months with an average staffing level of 11 software developers ($11^2 = 121$). So, using both a COCOMO schedule equation and the square root rule of thumb would indicate that a 120 staff-month project could be scheduled as 11 to 12.5 months with an average staffing level of 10 or 11. A reasonable choice would be a 12 month project with an average staffing level of 10 people.

In the various COCOMO models the sensitivity of average staffing level to variations in the schedule is determined by the SCED cost driver; it is used to adjust estimated effort for schedules that differ from those calculated by the COCOMO schedule equation. Multiplier values of the SCED cost driver are listed in Table 6.4 and illustrated in Figure 6.14.

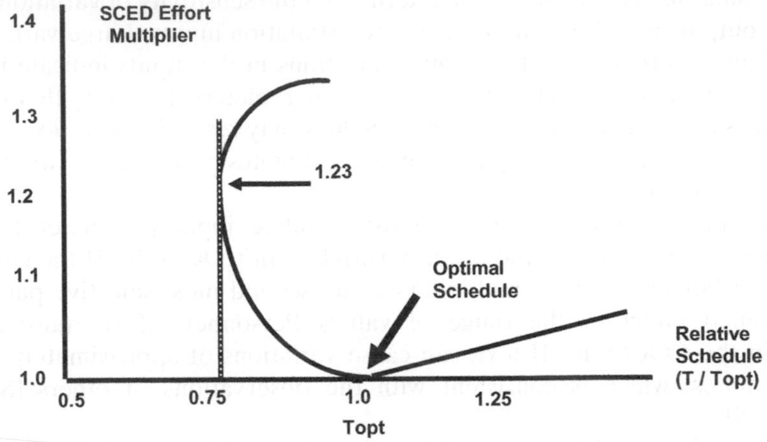

FIGURE 6.14 SCED effort multiplier

In Figure 6.14, T_{opt} is the schedule duration calculated by the COCOMO schedule equation (which is derived from historical data for past projects). T_{opt} is optimal in the sense that the minimum amount of effort will be required for a project of duration T_{opt}; durations that are both longer and shorter than T_{opt} will require more effort than the optimal duration. Longer durations require increased effort, and incur increased cost in a linear manner because of the costs of personnel and facilities on a permonth basis. A schedule of 1.6 T_{opt}, for example, would require a 10% increase in effort (SCED = 1.1). In the example above, a project of 12 months, 10 FTE average-staffing, if extended to 19 months (1.6 × 12) would require 7 FTE average-staffing (120 × 1.1)/19.

As illustrated in Figure 6.14, the effort penalty for compressing the schedule is more severe than the penalty for extending the schedule. If the schedule in the example were compressed from 12 months to 9 months (0.75 T_{opt}) the effort would be increased to 147 staff-months (120 × 1.23) and the required average staffing would be 16.4 (an increase of 64%). Note that a linear increase of average staffing would result in average staffing of 13.3 (10/0.75). The additional increase to 16.4 (1.23 × 13.3) is necessary to compensate for the decreased productivity of each individual caused by the increased effort devoted to communication and coordination among a larger group of people.

Note that the SCED cost driver in Figure 6.14 indicates that the schedule cannot be compressed more than 25% of T_{opt} (i.e., to 75% of the minimum-effort schedule). The 75% limit is based on the observation that only 4 of 63 projects in the COCOMO81 data set were able to successfully compress their schedules below the 75% limit; these 4 projects were small (total effort of 6, 7, 8, and 15 staff-months) and had low required reliability, high personnel capability, and good use of modern programming practices.

The upper portion of SCED in Figure 6.14 (not included in the COCOMO models) indicates that excessive effort (adding too many people to a project) will extend the schedule. This is consistent with Brook's law [Brooks95]: *Adding manpower to a late software project makes it later.*

Returning to Step 11 in the estimation procedure, the considerations above allow you to conduct sensitivity analyses of effort estimates and effort-schedule combinations; you can thus determine the input values to which your estimate is particularly sensitive, and determine the penalty to be paid for departing from an "optimal" schedule that minimizes total project effort.

As stated previously, the original SLIM model uses the following equation for calculating the minimum development time, T_d, for a software project:

$$T_d = \left(\frac{K}{C}\right)^{0.33},$$

where T_d is in years, K is in staff-years (the total area under the Norden–Rayleigh curve, and C is a constant in the range of 14 to 15. Converting years to months, staff-years to staff-months, and letting $C = 14.5$ results in

$$T_d = 2.15(E)^{0.33},$$

where T_d is in months and E is effort in staff-months.

For the example project above, the minimum schedule duration for a 120 staff-month project would be

$$T_d = 2.15(120)^{0.33} \sim 2.15 \times 5 = 10.75 \text{ months.}$$

This value is comparable to the 9 month minimum-time schedule estimated in COCOMO. The SLIM estimation model imposes severe effort penalties for schedule compression and, in contrast to the COCOMO models, computes decreased effort for longer schedule durations. The effort–schedule relationship in the SLIM model indicates that effort is proportional to schedule duration to the –4 power:

$$E \sim T^{-4}.$$

According to this relationship, decreasing the schedule from 12 months to 9 months in the example project would increase the effort from 120 staff-months to 370 staff-months ($0.75^4 = 0.32$; $120/0.32 = 370$) with an average staffing level of 41 personnel (370/9) and extending the schedule to 18 months would decrease effort from 120 staff-months to approximately 24 staff-months ($1.5^4 = 5.06$; $120/5.06 \sim 24$) with an average staffing level of 1.3 personnel (24/18).

You can use the Monte Carlo simulation technique to conduct sensitivity analyses of the tradeoff between effort and schedule using the SLIM estimation tool or using a spreadsheet programmed with regression equations using Crystal Ball. The results you obtain from estimation methods and tools should always be subjected to a reasonableness check: estimation tools and methods are aids; they are not panaceas. Recall that the goal of estimation is to determine, at a high level of confidence, a set of parameters that will allow you to successfully delivering an acceptable product within the estimated schedule and budget.

Steps 13, 14, and 15 of the estimation procedure are concerned with documenting the estimate. Step 13 (document risk factors exposed by the estimation process) provides information to be included in the documented estimation; also it can be used when preparing the risk management plan (see Chapter 9). The estimation procedure may have revealed, for example, that the requirements are too vague to support an accurate estimate, or that the schedule constraint results in unacceptable risk to successfully completing the project within the constrained duration, or that the software developers do not have sufficient knowledge of the new development environment to successfully use it on the project.

Step 14 (prepare a plan for updating the estimate at periodic intervals and as aperiodic events occur) is concerned with preparing a plan to keep the estimate current as understanding of the project grows, and as conditions change. Many organizations update project estimates on a monthly basis. Changes in the requirements, reduction of the budget, or loss of a key person are examples of aperiodic events that would warrant revision of your estimate.

Step 15 (prepare and implement a plan for baseline retention of estimation data, the documented estimate, and ongoing updates to the estimate) is concerned with version control of documented estimates, the data on which each estimate is based, and updated versions of the estimate that are created periodically and aperiodically. As with all revisions to all baselined work products, the following information should be recorded for each version of an estimate:

- the date of the revision,
- the reasons for the revision,
- the data used to make the revision, and
- the elements changed

Baseline control of documented estimates removes ambiguity as to which estimate is the current one and creates an audit trail of how and why the project changed over time.

The final step in the estimation procedure (document the estimate using a standard template for estimates) should be based on a standard template for recording estimates that is used throughout your organization. The template should provide for recording the information listed and discussed in the following section.

6.12 A TEMPLATE FOR RECORDING ESTIMATES

Questions to be answered when making estimates are typically of the form:

- effort: how much work will be needed?
- schedule duration: how long will it take?

- resources: what kinds of skill levels, tools, and other resources are needed? what quantities are needed? when will they be needed and for how long?
- allocations: how should effort and schedule be allocated to the various work activities?
- milestones: what progress indicators should be observed when conducting the project? when should they occur?
- quality: what are the estimated quality attributes of the product (pre-delivery and post-delivery defects, reliability, safety)?
- cost: how much will it cost to do the project?
- risk: what are the potential problems in these estimated factors?
- confidence level: how confident are you in the overall estimate?
- resources needed to improve the estimate

Various levels of probability for various combinations of the parameters can be determined by PERT analysis (Chapter 5), by risk analysis (Chapter 9), by Monte Carlo simulation (this chapter), and by subjective evaluation (this chapter).

Your organization should have a standard template for recording estimates. It should support recording and reporting of the following information:

- project identifier
- version number and date of the estimate
- total estimated effort
- total estimated schedule
- name(s) of the estimator(s)
- rationale for the estimate (why is this estimate being made? feasibility, initial estimate, periodic update, aperiodic update, etc.)
- elements changed (for updates to an estimate)
- amount of time and effort spent in making the estimate
- estimation methods and tools used
- the basis of estimation for each method or tool used (industry averages, expert judgment, local historical data, etc.)
- a list of assumptions made for each method or tool used
- a list of constraints observed in making the estimates
- a list of inputs used for each method or tool used (e.g., size, PI, MBI, adjustment factors for SLIM)
- estimation data provided by each estimation method or tool (e.g., total effort, schedule, project milestones, effort for various project activities by project phase, estimated pre-release and post-release defects, estimated reliability at product delivery, total life cycle costs)
- a range of estimates for effort, schedule, resources, cost, and quality attributes with associated probabilities for each method or tool used
- risk factors for the project
- the estimator's level of confidence in the accuracy of the estimate (0 to 10; low, medium, high)
- information, resources, and time needed to make an improved estimate

6.13 KEY POINTS OF CHAPTER 6

- A project estimate is a projection from past to future, suitably adjusted to account for differences between past and future.
- All estimates are based on a set of assumptions that must be realized and a set of constraints that must be satisfied.
- Projects must be re-estimated periodically as understanding grows and aperiodically as project parameters change.
- Size is the primary variable in most software estimation models.
- The most popular size measures are lines of code and function points.
- External size measures (ESMs) can be developed for each application area.
- Estimation models can be categorized as pragmatic, theory-based, and regression-based.
- Theory-based and regression-based estimation models can be calibrated using local data.
- Software estimation tools provide a variety of capabilities.
- Estimates should be prepared using at least two different methods.
- Estimates should be documented using a standard template.
- SEI, ISO, IEEE, and PMI provide frameworks, standards, and guidelines for project estimation techniques (see Appendix 6A to this chapter).

REFERENCES

[Albrecht79] Albrecht, A. J. Measuring application development productivity. *Proceedings of the IBM Application Development Symposium*, Monterey, California, October 1979, pp. 83–92.

[BOEHM81] Boehm, B. *Software Engineering Economics*. Prentice Hall, 1981.

[Boehm87] Boehm, B., and W. Royce. TRW IOC Ada COCOMO: Definitions and Refinements. *Proceedings of the Third International COCOMO Users Group*. Software Engineering Institute, 1987.

[Boehm02] Boehm, B. et al. *Software Cost Estimation with COCOMO II*. Prentice Hall, 2000.

[Brooks95] Brooks, F. *The Mythical Man-Month*. Addison Wesley, 1995.

[CMMI06] SEI. *CMMI® Models and Modules*. http://www.sei.cmu.edu/cmmi/models/, 2006.

[DeMarco99] DeMarco, T., and T. Lister. *Peopleware*, 2nd ed. Dorset, 1999.

[Fairley02] Fairley, R. Making accurate estimates. *IEEE Software*. 19 (November–December): 61–63.

[Fairley07] Fairley, R. The influence of COCOMO on software engineering education and training. *Journal of Systems and Software* 80 (August 2007): pp. 1201–1208.

[Forrester61] Forrester, J. W. *Industrial Dynamics*. Pegasus Communications, 1961.

[HAMID91] Abdul-Hamid, T. K., and Madnick, S. E. *Software Project Dynamics*. Prentice Hall, 1991.

[IEEE1058] IEEE Std 1058™–1998. *IEEE Standard for Software Project Management Plans*. Engineering Standards Collection. IEEE Product: SE113. Institute of Electrical and Electronic Engineers, August 2003.

[IEEE12207] IEEE/EIA 12207.0/.1/.2. *Industry Implementation of International Standard ISO/IEC 12207:1995 Standard for Information Technology–Software Life Cycle Processes*. Engineering Standards Collection. IEEE Product: SE113. Institute of Electrical and Electronic Engineers, August 2003. [IFPUG] www.ifpug.org.

[Jalote02] Jalote, P. *Software Project Management in Practice*. Addison Wesley, 2002.

[Jones86] Jones, T. C. The SPR feature point method. Software Productivity Research, Inc., 1986.

[Jones02] Jones, C. Software cost estimation in 2002. *Crosstalk*. Software Technology Support Center, June, 2002.

[Norden63] Norden, P. Useful tools for project management. *Operation Research in Research and Development*, edited by B. V. Dean. Wiley, 1963.

[PMI04] PMI. *A Guide to the Project Management Body of Knowledge*, 3rd ed. (PMBOK® Guide) Project Management Institute, 2004.

[Putnam92] Putnam, L., and W. Myers. *Measures for Excellence*. Yourdon Press, 1992.

[Sack68] Sackman, H., W. Erikson, and E. Grant. Exploratory Experimental Studies Comparing On-line and Off-line Performance. *Communication of the ACM*. 11 (January 1968). pp. 93–105.

[Symons88] Symons, C. R. Function point analysis: Difficulties and improvements. *IEEE Transactions in Software Engineering*. 14 (January 1988). pp. 2–11.

URLs

[COSMIC1] www.cosmicon.org.

[COSMIC2] www.cosmicon.com/advantagecs.asp.

[Costar] www.softstarsystems.com.

[Crystal] www.decisioneering.com.

[IFPUG] www.ifpug.org

[Madachy01] www-rcf.usc.edu/~madachy/sd/sd.html.

[PRICE] www.pricesystems.com/products/true_s_price_s.asp.

[USC] http://sunset.usc.edu/research/COCOMOII/index.html.

EXERCISES

6.1. In making an estimate, an adjustment factor is typically applied to account for the relative complexity of the product. Explain the meaning of "relative complexity."

6.2. Estimation principle 1 indicates that historical data of some type is necessary to makes estimates. Explain how you might go about making an estimate for a new type of system for which there is no historical data.

6.3. Explain the difference between an assumption and a constraint.

6.4. Briefly explain how you could derive a conversion factor from function points to lines of code.

6.5. List the ways in which external size measures are superior to lines of code for measuring product size.

6.6. List the ways in which the steps in the sidebar "Developing an External Size Measure" could have been used to develop the function point measure of product size.

6.7. Briefly explain the difference between an estimation rule of thumb and an estimation analogy.

6.8. Explain how the SLIM estimation model accounts for the factors listed in Figure 6.1; that is, how are product attributes, project constraints, past experiences, adjustment factors, and assumptions accounted for in the SLIM model?

6.9. In relation to Table 6.3, the text states that the joint probability of completing the project in 24 months with 500 staff-months of effort is roughly 81% (0.87×0.93). What assumption is involved in making this statistical calculation?

6.10. The SLIM estimation tool computes the minimum time, maximum effort estimate. In addition the maximum time and minimum effort can be specified as constraints.

a. Briefly explain why you might want to constraint the maximum time for a project.

b. Briefly explain why you might want to constraint the minimum effort for a project.

6.11. Explain how the COCOMO81 estimation model accounts for the factors listed in Figure 6.1; that is, how are product attributes, project constraints, past experiences, adjustment factors, and assumptions accounted for in COCOMO81?

6.12. The exponent b in the effort-size equation of regression-based estimation models is sometimes calculated to be greater than 1 (diseconomy of scale) and sometimes calculated to be less than 1 (economy of scale).

a. What factors would explain why b is greater than 1 for some sets of historical data?

b. What factors would explain why b is less than 1 for some sets of historical data?

6.13. In many estimation models the exponent in the equation that relates schedule duration to effort is in the range of 0.3 to 0.5. For example, the square root relationship (i.e., exponent = 0.5) states that a project of size 16 would require 4 units of duration while a project of size 25 would require only 5 units of duration. What factors would explain this relationship; that is, why do projects requiring more effort take proportionally less time than projects requiring proportionally more effort?

6.14. Which of the cost drivers listed in Table 6.4 might not affect an estimate (i.e., would have effort multiplier values of 1) when adjusting for the differences in effort and schedule duration for projects in a stable organization that develops Web-based client-server software?

6.15. List, and briefly explain three additional cost drivers you might add to Table 6.4 to explain the differences in effort and schedule duration for some software projects.

6.16. Using Table 6.4, calculate the variation in an effort estimate that can be caused by first setting all of the personnel attributes to Very Low and then setting them to Very High.

6.17. In Figure 6.14 the SCED effort multiplier for compressing the schedule to 75% of T_{opt} is 1.23; however the required increase in personnel is 1.64. Show by calculation, and explain in words, why there is a difference between the increase in effort and the increase in personnel.

6.18. In the text the term "full-time equivalent" (FTE) is used. What is the meaning of full-time equivalent?

6.19. When calibrating an estimation model, you should try to find a realistic set of parameters for the model that produces acceptably small variations between estimated values and actual values for completed projects.

a. What is an "acceptably small" variation?

b. What is the meaning of "a realistic set of parameters?"

APPENDIX 6A

FRAMEWORKS, STANDARDS, AND GUIDELINES FOR ESTIMATION

6A.1 ESTIMATION GOALS AND PRACTICES OF THE CMMI-DEV-v1.2 PROJECT PLANNING PROCESS AREA

CMMI-DEV-v1.2 includes estimation as specific goal 1 (SG 1) of the Project Planning process area. SG 1 has 4 specific practices [CMMI06]:

SG 1 Establish estimates

- SP 1.1 Estimate the scope of the project
- SP 1.2 Establish estimates of work product and task attributes
- SP 1.3 Define project life cycle
- SP 1.4 Determine estimates of effort and cost

Related process areas in the CMMI Models are:

- requirements development,
- requirements management,
- risk management, and
- technical solution.

In most cases the requirements (product features and quality attributes) are specified and a schedule, a set of resources, and a budget are estimated, as indicated by the specific practices listed above. But sometimes the constraints are a schedule, a set of resources, and a budget (time, effort, other resources, and money), and the product features and quality attributes that can be developed within those constraints are estimated.

6A.2 ISO/IEC AND IEEE/EIA STANDARDS 12207

Section 7.1.2.1 of 12207.0 [IEEE12207] states that management plans must include:

- schedules for completion of the tasks,
- effort estimates,
- resources needed to accomplish the tasks, and
- costs of executing the plans.

Annex G.9 of 12207.0 states that a management process should:

- define the scope of work, and
- identify, size, estimate, and plan the tasks and resources needed to accomplish the work.

6A.3 IEEE/EIA STANDARD 1058

Subclause 5.5.1 of IEEE Standard 1058–1998 for Software Project Management Plans indicates that an estimation plan should be an element of a project plan [IEEE1058]. According to 1058 the subclause must specify:

- cost and schedule for the project;
- methods and tools used to make the estimate;
- the basis of estimation; and
- frequency of, and ways in which periodic re-estimates will be made.

6A.4 THE PMI BODY OF KNOWLEDGE

The PMBOK® Guide of the Project Management Institute includes estimation as an element of the Project Time Management and Project Cost Management knowledge areas [PMI04]:

Project time management
- activity resource estimation
- activity duration estimation
- schedule development

Project cost management
- cost estimation
- cost budgeting

7

MEASURING AND CONTROLLING WORK PRODUCTS

When you can measure what you are speaking about, and express it in numbers, you know something about it; but when you cannot measure it, when you cannot express it in numbers, your knowledge is of a meagre and unsatisfactory kind; it may be the beginning of knowledge, but you have scarcely in your thoughts advanced to the state of Science, whatever the matter may be.

—Lord Kelvin

7.1 INTRODUCTION TO MEASURING AND CONTROLLING WORK PRODUCTS

Managing a software project involves planning and estimating, measuring and controlling, coordinating and leading, and managing risk. One reason you should make plans and estimates for your project is to provide objective targets against which progress of the work and quality of the work products can be determined. Progress is measured by periodically determining the current status of each attribute and comparing its current status to planned status. Project status is typically measured and reported weekly, bi-weekly, or monthly.

Determining project status involves determining the relationships among the project attributes (expended effort, schedule, and cost, and the current status of the work products) in addition to the status of each attribute individually. It is entirely possible to make good schedule progress while expending more resources than planned, or to make good cost and schedule progress while making the wrong product features or producing poor-quality work products. Project status is documented in progress reports.

Managing and Leading Software Projects, by Richard E. Fairley

The purpose of a progress report is to indicate which project factors are as planned and which need to be investigated for possible corrective action. You should, for example, monitor both effort and personnel cost. If, in a given reporting period, effort is as planned but personnel cost is higher than planned, you are using more expensive (more highly skilled) software developers than planned; perhaps the work is more difficult than anticipated or perhaps the work to be done by highly skilled, and expensive, designers is taking longer than planned.

Conversely, if, in a given reporting period, effort is as planned but personnel costs are lower than planned, it may be that you have been unable to acquire the needed skill levels (not good) or perhaps the work is easier than planned and highly skilled (highly paid) personnel are not needed (good). If effort and cost are both less than planned, this may indicate that you have not been able to acquire the planned number of software developers and, as a result, schedule progress is slower than planned. Or, it may be that effort and cost are higher than planned because of a desire to accelerate schedule progress. Other costs should also be measured and compared to plan. Travel cost may be higher (or lower) than planned; equipment costs may similarly deviate from plan. In any case, you will need to investigate these deviations from plan.

Project control is exerted by applying corrective action when one or more dimensions of progress deviate from plan by more than an acceptable amount or when the relationships among project attributes becomes unbalanced; for example, a delay of two days in achieving a major milestone may not require corrective action but being two weeks late may constitute an unacceptable delay for which corrective action must be taken. Similarly a 2% overrun of allocated memory for an incremental build of embedded software may be acceptable but a 20% overrun is probably not.

Depending on the nature of the deviation from plan, corrective action may involve one or more of

- extending the schedule,
- adding more resources,
- using superior resources,
- improving various elements of the development process,
- improving the technology, and/or
- de-scoping the product.

Resources to be improved, added, or replaced include people (being mindful of Brooks's law), software components (e.g., re-engineering a component to improve performance), hardware components (e.g., more memory, a faster processor), and software tools (e.g., a language processor or testing tool).

Descoping the product can be gracefully accomplished if you have prioritized the requirements and if you are using an iterative development process by which you have implemented the most important features first. If the delivery date is constrained, you may find it is acceptable to deliver a subset of highest priority capabilities on schedule with delivery of a subsequent full-feature version scheduled for a later, negotiated date.

Of course, you must be mindful of the trade-offs involved in corrective actions; for example, changing the testing process or adding a new testing tool may increase the number of detected defects over the long term, but it may have an unacceptable impact on your schedule, which results from the time required to learn and assimilate the new process or tool.

The workflow model depicted in Figure 1.1 (Chapter 1), and repeated here as Figure 7.1, illustrates the roles of measurement and control in the workflow model of software projects. The feedback loops of measuring, reporting, replanning, and controlling are highlighted in Figure 7.1.

The relationship between corrective action and risk management is examined Chapter 9. In brief, a risk is a potential problem—a problem that hasn't happened yet but has a nonzero probability of happening; if that happens, its impact will be negative on achieving a successful outcome. In risk management, potential problems are identified, objective indicators are monitored, and a predetermined plan of corrective action is initiated when a risk indicator crosses a predetermined threshold (the problem trigger).

When you plan, estimate, measure, and control a software project, you are practicing *institutionalized* risk management. Risk management is institutionalized because, through experience, we have learned that systematic planning, estimating, measuring, and controlling a software project increases the probability of a successful outcome; put differently, it is better to plan, estimate, measure, and control than to not do so. Measurement and control of effort, schedule, cost, product features, and quality attributes is thus a form of risk management; however, there are other aspects of risk management, as explained in Chapter 9, that augment the systematic planning, estimation, measurement, and control you should practice on your software projects.

It is possible, although not highly probable, that you may be able to delivery an acceptable product without planning, estimating, measuring, or controlling. The cost of planning, estimating, measuring, and controlling, like the cost of risk management, is an investment you make to increase the probability of success. Like risk

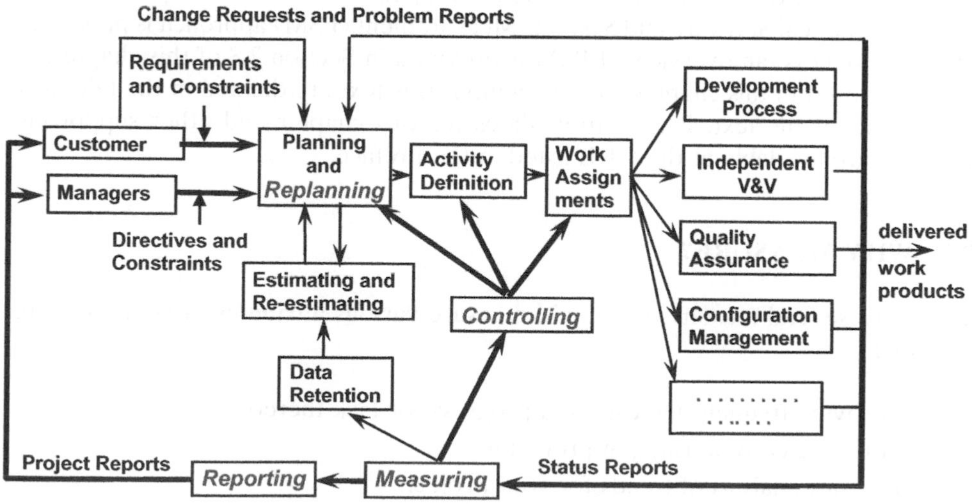

FIGURE 7.1 A workflow model for software projects with emphasis on measuring, reporting, replanning, and controlling

management, the amount you invest in planning, estimating, measuring, and controlling must be balanced against the cost of failing to deliver an acceptable product on schedule and within budget.

7.2 OBJECTIVES OF THIS CHAPTER

This chapter presents methods and techniques for measuring and controlling work products. Measurement and control of effort, schedule, and cost are presented in Chapter 8. After reading this chapter and completing the exercises you should understand:

- measures and measurement scales;
- product measures for different kinds of work products;
- the role of configuration management in measurement and control of work products;
- the roles of inspections, walkthroughs, and developer testing;
- complexity measures for software;
- reliability and availability measures;
- the defect detection and repair process;
- ways to document and analyze defects and defect repairs;
- guidelines for choosing product measures; and
- sources of standards and guidelines for measurement and control.

The four sets of standards and guidelines for managing project presented in this text, namely the CMMI-DEV-v1.2 process framework, the ISO/IEEE standard 12207, IEEE standard 1058, and the PMI Body of Knowledge address measurement and control of work products to varying degrees. Aspects of measurement and control in these documents are presented in Appendix 7A to this chapter. In addition the Practical Software and Systems Measurement (PSM) approach is presented in the Appendix; an overview of PSM is provided in Section 7.8 of this chapter.

Terms used in this chapter and throughout this text are defined in the Glossary at the end of the text. Presentation slides for this chapter and other supporting material are available at the URL listed in the Preface.

7.3 WHY MEASURE?

There are several reasons you should measure various attributes of your software projects:

- to provide frequent indicators of progress (or lack thereof),
- to provide early warning of problems,
- to permit analysis of trends for your project,
- to allow estimates of the final cost and completion date of your project, and
- to build a data repository of project histories for your organization.

The frequency of measurement may vary from daily, for example, in counting the number of user stories implemented by way of an Agile development process; to weekly, for example, in counting the number of use case scenarios implemented using an Incremental-build development process; to monthly, for example, in counting the number of design elements implemented in a Waterfall process. Teams may meet briefly each day to review progress and problem areas; team leaders and you, the project manager, may meet on a weekly basis to review the project and meet each month to plan the details of the coming month's work. You, the project manager, and some of your key personnel may meet with upper management and with customers on a monthly basis to review progress and identify problem areas.

Frequent measurement of status provides early warning of problems when actual status does not match planned status. Early identification of problems is desirable because problems are easier to fix when identified early, namely, before defects in work products can propagate into subsequent work products. Collection of status information on a periodic basis supports forecasting of trends in project attributes such as defects, cost, and schedule. If, for example, your project is determined to be two weeks behind schedule, and if the project is estimated to be half completed, and if progress continues at the present rate, the project will be four weeks late in completion. The "ifs" in the previous example are factors to be continuously monitored and updated.

As indicated in Chapter 6, all estimates are projections from the past to the future, suitably adjusted to account for differences between past and future. Estimates based on local data will be more accurate than estimates based on rules of thumb or industry averages. An important reason for measurement is thus to build a data repository on which estimates for future projects can be based. In addition analysis of project data collected across your organization may reveal common, recurring problems that need to be addressed at the organizational level. For example, analysis might show that for most projects, a large percentage of total defects are in the interfaces among code modules. Improving training and tools for the design of interfaces could significantly reduce total defects in the organization's software products.

7.4 WHAT SHOULD BE MEASURED?

The attributes you measure and control depend on the success criteria for your project: reliability and performance of the delivered software may be the most important success criteria, or it may be that controlling the schedule and cost of the project are uppermost. However, it is difficult to imagine a project for which some level of measurement and control over each of the following attributes is not important for a successful outcome:

- effort: amount of work expended for various work activities
- schedule: achievement of objectively measured milestones
- cost: expenditures for various kinds of resources, including effort
- progress: work products completed, accepted, and baselined
- product features: requirements implemented and demonstrated to work

- quality attributes of the product: defects, reliability, availability, response time, throughput, and others as specified
- risk: status of risk factors and mitigation actions

Typically the process attributes (effort, schedule, cost, and progress) are balanced against product attributes (features and quality attributes). Among the process attributes, schedule may (or may not) be more important than effort or cost, and security may be a more important product attribute than performance. Depending on the relative importance of the various process and product attributes, more effort may be expended on measuring and controlling some attributes than on measuring and controlling others.

Product and process measures are, or should be, by-products of the procedures, methods, tools, and techniques used to develop software; if not, the development and management processes must be improved. Excessive time, effort, and cost spent in obtaining, analyzing, and acting on product and process measures is a symptom of ineffective development and management processes.

7.5 MEASURES AND MEASUREMENT

A *measure* is the symbol assigned to some attribute of a real-world phenomenon; for example, using integer or real number symbols to measure temperature. *Measurement* is the process of mapping some attribute of a real-world phenomenon to a set of symbols for which well-defined operations are specified; for example, mapping temperature to a Celsius, Fahrenheit, or Kelvin measurement scale. Different kinds of measurement scales permit different kinds of operations; for example, 40 degrees Celsius or Fahrenheit is hotter than 20 degrees Celsius or Fahrenheit because the relational operation "hotter than" (i.e., greater than) is permitted, but we cannot say 40 degrees is twice as hot as 20 degrees on these scales because ratio operations are not valid for these measures (more later).

There are five commonly used measurement scales: nominal, ordinal, interval, ratio, and absolute. These scales provide a hierarchy of permitted operations. The hierarchy, based on the characteristics of each scale, is presented in Table 7.1.

A *nominal* scale assigns items to groups or categories. You might, for example, list the number of personnel in each of several categories: analysis and design, implementation, testing, user training, and so forth. Or, you might list the number of installations of your systems by region or country. The number of items in each category can be counted to provide frequency distributions among categories but no ordering of the items within a category is implied. For example, your project might have 12 implementers and 5 testers; you can say there are 7 more implementers than testers but nothing can be said about the rankings of skill levels of the implementers or the testers if you are using a nominal scale.

Measures based on symbols that form an ordered sequence, such as (Low, Medium, High) form *ordinal* scales. Skill levels or program complexity might be measured using the symbols (Low, Medium, High) with the permitted transitive relational operations of less than, greater than, and equal ($<$, $>$, $=$) defined on the set {Low, Medium, High}. The intervals between adjacent symbols are not specified for ordinal measures, and there is no objectively determined zero element; thus we

TABLE 7.1 Hierarchy of measurement scales

Scale	Characteristics
Nominal	Frequency distributions among measurement categories
Ordinal	Ordering within categories; arbitrary intervals among measures
Interval	Equal intervals among measures; arbitrarily determined zero element
Ratio	Equal intervals among measures; objectively determined zero element
Absolute	Similar to ratio but with uniqueness of measures

cannot say that a program of High complexity is 3 or 5 or 10 times more complex than a program of Low complexity if we are using an ordinal scale. However, transitive relational operations can be applied if the symbols form an ordered sequence, so a program of Low complexity is less complex than Medium, which is less complex than High, and two programs of Medium complexity are of comparable complexity. By the transitivity property, module *A* is less complex than module *C* if module *A* is less complex than module *B* and module *B* is less complex than module *C* or if module *B* is of equal complexity to module *C* (note the precedence among the "and" and "or" operators in this sentence). The value Low, Medium, or High might be determined for a program or a module using subjective criteria.

When using an ordinal scale, elements within a category are ordered. Symbols higher in the ordering indicate larger values but the intervals between the symbols cannot be assumed to be equal. For example, a software developer rated High in ability is not necessarily 3 times as capable as a developer rated Low in ability. The zero point in an ordinal scale, if it exists, is chosen arbitrarily; for example, an ability scale of (1, 2, 3) equated to Low, Medium, High could equally be scaled as (0, 4, 6); see the sidebar "Misuse of measurement scales" on the dangers of using integers as the measures of an ordinal measurement scale.

Measures based on symbols that have equal intervals between any two adjacent symbols but having an arbitrarily determined zero element form *interval* scales. In an interval measurement scale a unit of measure represents the same magnitude of a factor across the full range of the scale. For example, on the Celsius or Fahrenheit temperature scale the difference between 30 and 40 degrees is the same as the difference between 50 and 60 degrees (10 degrees in each case). However, the zero point on these scales does not denote the absence of temperature (i.e., is not objectively determined) and ratios cannot be formed. Thus a temperature of 60 degrees Celsius or Fahrenheit is not twice as hot as a temperature of 30 degrees.

Daniel Fahrenheit invented the mercury thermometer in 1714 after discovering that mercury has a linear expansion/contraction factor over a wide range of temperatures, thus making it a suitable element for constructing glass thermometers with linear markings on the glass. Mr. Fahrenheit established three points on his measurement scale: 0 °F was determined as the temperature of a mixture of salt, ice, and water; 32 °F was determined as the temperature at which water freezes without salt; and 96 °F was determined to be the bodily temperature of a healthy adult person. A fourth point on the scale, 212 °F, was later established as the boiling point of water at sea level. This point on the Fahrenheit scale recalibrated the temperature of a healthy adult to be 98.6 °F. Mr. Fahrenheit could just as readily have assigned the number 10 to his zero element and added 10 to the other calibration points.

Zero degree Fahrenheit is thus an arbitrary value, so 0 °F does not indicate the absence of temperature.

The numbers used as calibration points on the Celsius temperature scale are similarly arbitrary. Mr. Celsius established 0 °C as the boiling point of water and 100 °C as the freezing point. The measurement scale was later inverted to the now-familiar scale with 0 °C as the freezing point and 100 °C as the boiling point of water at sea level. The Fahrenheit and Celsius temperature scales are interval measurement scales because the intervals between measures are equidistant, but the zero element does not denote the absence of the phenomenon being measured, namely temperature.

In measurement theory, measures that have equal intervals between any two adjacent symbols and a zero element that denotes absence of the quantity being measured form a *ratio* scale. On measurement scales that uses integer and real-number measures, for example, and that have objectively determined zero values, the relational operations and the arithmetic operations are permitted and ratios can be formed, as in the measurement of the number of statements in a computer program. Because the measure of program size is in integer units of equal intervals with an objectively zero element (the absence of statements), it can be said that a program of 100 statements is twice as large as a program of 50 statements and the size of the combined programs is 150 statements.

Note that temperature measured in Kelvin (K) forms a ratio measurement scale because the zero element is an objectively determined value; temperature in Kelvin is a measure of the kinetic energy associated with the motion of atoms and molecules. The zero point of the Kelvin temperature scale is the temperature at which all movement at the atomic level ceases, meaning the absence of temperature. Thus 0 K is an objective measure and 200 K is twice as hot as 100 K (i.e., the kinetic energy of the atoms is twice as much).

An *absolute* measurement scale is one for which ratios are allowed (equal intervals plus an objectively determined zero element that denotes absence of the phenomenon) plus uniqueness of the measures. For example, measuring defect density as an integer number of defects per line of code by measuring total number of defects and dividing by the number of lines of code forms a ratio measurement scale because defects per line of code can be converted to defects per thousand lines of code by the transformation:

$$\frac{\text{D}}{\text{KLOC}} = \left(\frac{\text{D}}{\text{LOC}}\right) \times 1000.$$

If, for some reason, monotonic transformation of D/LOC were disallowed, the measurement scale would be an absolute one. Measuring program size in function points and disallowing any transformations, for example, into lines of code, would form an absolute measurement scale. Stated in another way, identity is the only transformation allowed for an absolute measurement scale.

Ordinal, ratio, and absolute scales are the most commonly used measurement scales in software engineering. Program complexity, as measured by (Low, Medium, High), is an example of an ordinal measurement scale. Measuring the size of a program as an integer number of function points and performing transformations of function points to lines of code forms a ratio measurement scale because there are equal intervals in both measures, and a program having no function points or lines of code has size zero. Measuring program size in function points and disallowing any transformations forms an absolute measurement scale.

You must have well-defined rules for determining the mapping from the phenomena of interest to the measures you use, such as measuring the phenomenon of program size using the counting rules for counting function points or an algorithm to count lines of code. Also it is important that the measures you use be applied uniformly throughout your organization so that different projects can be compared along different dimensions and so that trends across the organization can be determined. As the saying goes, you want to compare apples to apples (i.e., defects to defects) and not apples to oranges by mistakenly thinking the oranges are also apples (i.e., mistakenly comparing defects in one product to requirements changes in another product).

If you are counting lines of code, for example, you want each project to count in the same way:

- do semicolons delimit "lines?"
- do end-of-line symbols delimit lines?
- do you include comments?
- do you count a library routine as the 1-line "include" statement or as the equivalent lines of code in the body of the included routine?
- how do you count unmodified lines of code that are reused from other software programs?

How do you count defects?

- what constitutes a defect (e.g., a syntax error during compilation? a system crash during system validation)?
- do you have a way of categorizing defects (e.g., data, calculation, interface)?
- how do you characterize the severity of defects (e.g., minor, major, catastrophic)?

A *direct measure* is obtained by applying your measurement rules directly to the phenomenon of interest; for example, counting the lines of code in a computer program using well-defined counting rules. An *indirect measure* is obtained by combining direct measures using operations appropriate to that measurement scale. For example, the number of function points in a program is an indirect measure that is determined by applying the function point counting rules to determine the unique (integer) number of inputs, outputs, files, interfaces, and queries in the program; multiplying each by an integer complexity factor; and adding the results together. Tables 7.3 and 7.4 provide examples of direct and indirect measures used in software engineering.

Note in Table 7.3 that "number of defects fixed" could be measured as a "progress" measurement or as "quality" measurement, or both, and that "weeks taken to achieve a milestone" could be used to measure "progress" or "time," or both.

MISUSE OF MEASUREMENT SCALES

You must take care that the measurement scales you use are appropriate to the situation and are appropriately used. For example, a subjective determination of (Low, Medium, High) may be a sufficient characterization of program complexity for your purposes, based on your criteria for determining the complexity rating of a program or module, but you cannot add, subtract, multiply, or divide these symbols. Unfortunately, this is sometimes done by equating Low to 1, Medium to 2, and High to 3 or some other ascending numeric values. To equate Low to 1 and High to 3 and to then apply arithmetic operations implies that a program module of High complexity is 3 times as complex as a module of Low complexity.

My favorite example of misusing measurement scales is the way in which classes and professors are rated by student evaluations in many schools. In these cases an ordinal scale is often used and treated as if it were a ratio scale. For example, students are often asked to rate various attributes of a class or the instructor by comparing the class or instructor to other classes or instructors they have had on a scale of (Much Worse, Worse, Same, Better, Much Better). These ratings are then equated to (1, 2, 3, 4, 5). This implies that a professor who receives a rating of Much Better (equated to 5) is rated as 1.67 better than a professor that receives a rating of Same (equated to 3).

Objective criteria are not provided to determine the ratings, so each student applies his or her subjective rating based on their likes, dislikes, past experiences, and the grade they expect to receive in the class. Students' individual ratings are then (incorrectly) added together and the sum is divided by the number of responses to produce the professor's average rating for each attribute measured. Worse still, all the averaged responses are averaged together to provide an overall "rating" of the class or professor. Using this nominal scale, it is incorrect to say, for example, that Professor Fairley's overall rating for all response categories is 4.2, nor can you say Professor Fairley is 80% as effective as Professor Willshire, who received an overall rating of 4.7.

TABLE 7.2 Responses to a course evaluation survey

Compared to other instructors you have had, was you instructor:	Much Worse	Worse	Same	Better	Much Better
Knowledgeable?				5	10
Well prepared?				4	11
Responsive to questions?				3	12
Were her/his assignments relevant?			7	5	3
Were her/his exam questions appropriate?			9	6	
Were graded materials returned in a timely manner?			4	11	

The correct way to present nominal data is to list in a table, a histogram, or a pie chart the number of responses at each rating level for each attribute assessed as, for example, in Table 7.2. The number of total responses at each rating level can be counted and the (less than, same as, and greater than) relational operators can be used to compare categories; for example, Professor Fairley received more Excellent ratings for responsiveness to questions than for relevant assignments. In addition the integer ratio scale can be used to compare the number of responses in each category and to compute percentages; for example, 67% of responses were Excellent for knowledgeable of the material. But it is incorrect to say that an Excellent rating is 5/4 better than a Good rating.

We use ordinal scales when we do not have an objective, agreed-on, method of determining the intervals between and ratios among the individual values of the measure being used. The evaluative measures of a Low complexity program combined with a High complexity program, for example, will result in a High complexity rating, based on the transitive properties of the (Low, Medium, High) complexity measure; High complexity is more complex that Medium or Low complexity, but we cannot say by how much: the complexity rating is not 4 (1 + 3).

TABLE 7.3 Some direct measures

Measurements	Direct Measures
Software size	Lines of code
Number of personnel by category	Number of programmers; number of testers
Progress	Number of requirements baselined; number changed; number of modules baselined; number of defects found; number of defects fixed; weeks to achieve a milestone
Resource usage	CPU cycles used; memory bytes used
Time	Weeks taken to achieve a milestone
Quality	Number of defects fixed; computer response time

TABLE 7.4 Some indirect measures

Measurement	Indirect Measures
Size	Function points
Productivity	Lines of code developed per developer-month; function points implemented per programmer-week
Production rate	Lines of code per month; function points per week
Testing rate	Tests conducted per staff-day
Defect density	Defects per thousand lines of code; defects per function point
Defect efficiency	Number of defects fixed per staff-day
Defect effectiveness	Number of defects detected/total defects
Requirements stability	Current number/initial number; current number/most recent number
Cost performance index	Actual cost/budgeted cost

Categorizing a measure depends on your desired use of the measure; and a measure may fit into more than one category.

Also note that size measured as lines of code is a direct measure (Table 7.3) and that size measured as function points is an indirect measure (Table 7.4). As indicated in Table 7.4, productivity is the amount of output produced per unit of resource, whereas production rate is the total amount of output in a given time period. An effective process is one that accomplished tasks with minimal expenditure of resources. In Table 7.4 "number of defects fixed per staff day" could be used as a productivity measurement and/or as a measure of efficiency of defect fixing. The measure of effectiveness in Table 7.4 (number of defects detected during design review/total defects) might count total defects as those detected prior to release of a product or delivery of a system to a customer, or perhaps number of defects found during development and the first 6 months (or 12 months) of operational use. The cost performance index in Table 7.4 is an element of earned value tracking, which is discussed in Chapter 8.

7.6 MEASURING PRODUCT ATTRIBUTES

You should verify that each work product, as it is developed, is complete, correct, and consistent with respect to other work products. You should also validate that each work product is fit for its intended use in its intended environment. In addition each kind of work product (operational requirements, technical specifications, architectural design, detailed design, implemented code, test plans, test results, etc.) provides unique opportunities to periodically measure the quantity and quality of the work product. The following sections indicate some aspects of quantity and quality that can be measured and compared to specified or expected values for different kinds of work products. Selection and tailoring of product measures is discussed in a later section of this chapter.

7.6.1 Measuring Operational Requirements and Technical Specifications

As discussed in Chapter 3, there are three kinds of operational requirements and four kinds of technical specifications:

The operational requirements include:

- operational feature,
- quality attributes, and
- design constraints.

The technical specifications, which are derived from the operational requirements, include:

- primary requirements,
- derived requirements,
- quality attributes, and
- design constraints.

Design constraints and quality attributes, as stated in the operational requirements, may be vague and imprecise but they must be stated in the technical specifications in a manner that permits objective verification. The characteristics of operational requirements and technical specifications are presented in Chapter 3.

Operational requirements are often documented using a numbered list of statements such as:

5. The ATM terminals shall offer a "quick cash" option to customers.

In contractual terms, "shall" indicates a contractually binding requirement; terms such as "should" or "may" can be used to indicate nonbinding requirements; for example, desired properties expressed as design goals may be stated using "should" or "may."

Counting the number of "shalls" is one way to measure the number of requirements; however, some requirements may be less precise or less detailed than others. To account for this, each of the "shalls" should be assessed on a measurement scale (e.g., Low, Medium, High) to indicate the degree to which each requirement satisfies the *decomposition criteria* presented in Section 5.3 of this text namely:

- the requirement is sufficiently precise and detailed that areas of uncertainty, complexity, and risk are identified;
- estimates of effort, schedule, and resources needed to implement the requirement can be made with confidence; and
- opportunities for reuse of existing components that can be used to satisfy the requirement are identified.

If you assess an Essential or Desirable requirement to be Low in satisfying the decomposition criteria, you should further decompose that requirement. For example, the operational requirement that states:

3.0 The Automated Teller System shall provide the features, performance, and quality attributes typically provided by such systems.

would be rated Low by the decomposition criteria.

Some requirements imply quality measures. The precision of these requirements can be assessed by assigned ratings that indicate the level of quantification. A rating of Low quantification would indicate that the requirement is stated in a vague, imprecise, and/or ambiguous manner, and a rating of High would indicate that the requirement is stated in a precise and unambiguous manner. Requirements rated Low on the quantification scale are categorized as design goals, as in:

3.6. The customer terminals in the Automated Teller System shall provide good response time.

while a quantified requirement would be rated High in precision of expression, as in:

> 3.6. The customer terminals in the Automated Teller System shall provide an average response time of 2 seconds and a maximum response time of 5 seconds for balance inquiries; and an average response time of 5 seconds and a maximum response time of 15 seconds for withdrawal and deposit requests. All of these response times shall be measured when 50 terminals are concurrently active and the server is running at an average load factor of 80%. Averages are to be determined for a 1-hour period of operation.

A Medium rating on the quantification scale would indicate that the quantification is incomplete or impractical. For example, requirement 3.6 would be rated Medium if the last two sentences were not present. A requirement stating "the system shall be 100% reliable" would likewise be rated Low in quantification, even though it is precisely stated, because it is infeasible. Requirements rated Low or Medium on the quantification scale require additional work.

The level of quantification can also be used to access the adequacy of a requirement as a basis for test planning. Operational requirement 4, above, would be rated Low as a basis for test planning while primary requirement 3.6 would be rated High. A requirement would be rated Medium in adequacy for test planning if either the functionality to be tested or quantification of a quality attribute to be achieved, as stated, was weak.

If assessment of the decomposition criteria, precision of expression, and adequacy for test planning are stated as an ordered triplet, requirement 3.6 would receive a rating of (Medium, High, High) or (M, H, H). Requirements that receive a Low rating in decomposition criteria, precision of expression, or basis for test planning must be further decomposed and/or quantified. You might decide, in addition, that all Essential requirements must receive a High rating in each of the three dimensions, especially if the system is safety-critical or mission-critical.

With respect to technical specifications, primary requirements should be categorized as Essential, Desirable, or Optional. Derived requirements are, by definition, Essential because they are necessary to support primary requirements. Similarly design constraints are categorized, by definition, as Essential once it is determined that the design constraints are, in fact, essential. Design goals are primary requirements for which objective validation criteria cannot be, or have not been, stated. Each design goal should be categorized as Desirable or Optional, depending on the importance of the goal. Requirements can thus be measured in several different ways, as indicated in Table 7.5.

Operational requirements can be assessed and measures determined by joint reviews between your customer/user representative (who is a knowledgeable and appropriate spokesperson) and software engineers who are skilled in requirements elicitation and requirements development. Technical requirements can be assessed and measured by internal reviews.

Some assessment ratings may be labeled TBD (to be determined) in initial meetings; the status of all TBDs must be documented, reviewed periodically, resolved in a timely manner, and tracked to closure.

Other measures that can be used to determine the status of requirements development are listed in Table 7.6.

ASSESSING USE CASES

Use cases are a popular mechanism for specifying the operational features of a system or product [Kulak03]. Each use case specifies a well-defined and self-contained user feature. In the ATM example, the validation, balance inquiry, withdrawal, and deposit features should thus be expressed as separate use cases. Use cases can "use" other use cases; for example, a withdrawal request use case would make use of a balance inquiry use case to determine that there are sufficient funds in the account before dispensing the requested amount. A template for documenting use cases, with an example, is presented in Figure 7.2.

Scenarios are key elements of use cases. Each scenario specifies a sequence of interactions between an external entity (a use case "actor") and the system. Each use case provides a primary scenario (e.g., the withdrawal scenario) and one or more secondary scenarios. Each secondary scenario specifies an alternative action to be taken, for example, the scenario to be enacted when the user fails to enter a correct PIN during the user validation process.

Sequence diagrams and state diagrams are the most commonly used mechanisms for specifying scenarios. A sequence diagram can be used to specify a single scenario. A state diagram can be used to document multiple scenarios; each path through the state diagram specifies a scenario of operation, as illustrated in Figure 7.3.

The notation used in Figure 7.3 is based on UML [Rumb05]. The names of states are provided in the nodes of the diagram. The "dotted" arrow indicates the entry point to the sate diagram (i.e., the idle state). Expressions on the arrows are of the form *xx*[*yy*]/*zz*, where *xx* is the trigger for taking that path, provided *yy* is

Use case ID: ATM #34
User case name: authorize transaction
Actor that initiates the use case: bank customer
Other actors, if any: none
Statement of purpose:
this use case documents the way bank customers log onto an ATM and prepare to conduct a transaction
Preconditions that must be true before this use case can be "executed":
customer has a valid bank card and PIN
Primary scenario to describe the main action of the use case:
sequence diagrams, state diagrams, or narratives can be used; see the example of a state diagram in Figure 7.3
Postconditions that must be true after this use case is "executed":
customer is logged-on OR customer received a sorry message
Alternative scenarios for exception handling:
incorrectly entered PIN; invalid account number; not enough money in the account; not enough money in the machine, etc.
Comments: this use case belongs to ATM Validation Processing

FIGURE 7.2 A template for documenting, and an example of a use case

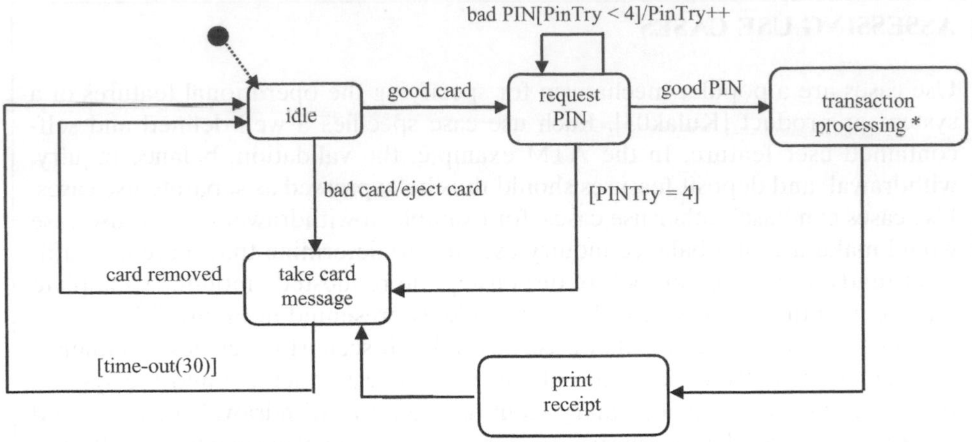

FIGURE 7.3 State diagram for the use case in Figure 7.2

true. If *yy* is absent it is taken to be true. *zz* is the action to be taken while traversing that path. Each of *xx, yy*, and *zz* is optional. An arrow with a blank expression indicates a path to be taken as soon as the activities in the preceding state are completed. The star (*) on the transaction processing state in Figure 7.3 indicates that transaction processing is defined in a subordinate (nested) state diagram.

The adequacy of use cases can be measured using an ordered triple to indicate:

1. the level of granularity specified in the use case,
2. the level of detail in the primary and secondary scenarios, and
3. the sufficiency of the number of secondary scenarios in specifying alternatives to the primary scenario.

The use case in Figures 7.2 and 7.3 might be rated as (Medium, High, Low), indicating that the use case is of appropriate granularity (M), the level of detail in the primary scenario is very good (H), but some secondary scenarios are missing (L).

Use cases rated High in granularity (excessive detail) should be examined for merging into other use cases and use cases with Low ratings for granularity (insufficient detail) should be examined for decomposition into two or more use cases. Use cases rated Low for level of detail in the primary scenario or Low for adequacy of secondary scenarios should be reworked. Operational scenarios assessed as Medium or High in level of detail, and Medium or High in sufficiency of secondary scenarios provide good bases for generating test scenarios. Those assessed as Low do not.

Use cases specify user features. Quality attributes and design constraints that apply to an individual use case can be specified in the comments section of the use case. Those that apply to multiple user cases can be specified separately.

TABLE 7.5 Ways to measure requirements

- By the number of "shalls" in the operational requirements;
- By the number of technical specifications in each of the Essential and Desirable categories;
- By the number of derived requirements in the Essential category;
- By the number of design constraints in the Essential category;
- By the number of design goals in the Desirable and Optional categories;
- By the degree to which each technical requirement satisfies the decomposition criteria for requirements, measured on a scale of (Low, Medium, High);
- By the degree of quantification of quality attributes, measured on a scale of (Low, Medium, High); and
- By the measure of suitability of each requirement as a basis for test planning, measured on a scale of (Low, Medium, High).

TABLE 7.6 Some product measures for requirements activities

- Number of requirements baselined versus number planned during this reporting period and cumulatively
- Number of use cases developed versus number planned during this reporting period and cumulatively
- Number of use cases reviewed and accepted as adequate during this reporting period and cumulatively
- Number of requirements-based test cases and test scenarios generated versus number planned during this reporting period and cumulatively
- Number of prototypes developed and reviewed versus number planned during this reporting period and cumulatively
- Number of *CRs and *DRs for baselined requirements submitted, number accepted, number rejected, and number deferred during this reporting period and cumulatively
- Number of requirements defects by defect category and severity level
- Number of CRs and DRs for baselined requirements completed and closed during this reporting period and cumulatively
- Number of CRs and DRs for requirements still open from this reporting period and from previous reporting periods
- Amount of time required to close each CR and DR for baselined requirements
- Status of traceability matrices (see Table 3.6 in Section 3.4.4)
    - from operational requirements to technical specifications
    - from technical specifications to test cases and test scenarios

*CR: Change Request;
*DR: Defect Report.

7.6.2 Measuring and Controlling Changes to Work Products

Reporting the measures listed in Table 7.6 requires a change control process:

1. When selected work products, including requirements, satisfy objective acceptance criteria, they are placed under version control, and thus become baselines (i.e., baselined work products). The status of baselines is periodically reported to indicate trends in changes.
2. If it is later found that a baselined work product is not an adequate baseline, it is updated, and the reason for updating it (requirements change or defect) plus the time and effort required are reported.

Acceptance of a work product as a baseline does not mean the work product is perfect, but that it is an adequate basis for further activities that depend on, or make use of the baselined work product. If it is later found that baselined work products of a particular kind are not adequate baselines, the acceptance criteria for that kind of work product must be strengthened.

Satisfaction of the acceptance criteria for technical specifications is determined by:

- inspecting and reviewing the traceability matrices,
- establishing the sufficiency of requirements-based test plans,
- examining the number of TBD design goals that remain to be translated into technical specifications,
- examining the measures in Table 7.5, and
- other criteria discussed above.

Satisfaction of the acceptance criteria for technical specifications is determined by requirements engineers and other appropriate stakeholders who are qualified to assess the completeness, correctness, and consistency of the specifications.

In general, a baselined work product is changed, and a new version generated, for one of two reasons:

1. because factors that affect the work product have changed; or
2. because the work product is found to be incomplete, incorrect, or inconsistent.

Change Requests (CR) are used to document requests for changes to baselines of type 1 and Defect Reports (DR) are used to document requests for changes of type 2. No change can be made to a baselined work product without an approved CR or DR that authorizes the change; otherwise baseline control of work products will not be effective. Tables 7.7 and 7.8 provide templates for CRs and DRs.

Configuration management (CM) is the mechanism used to implement change control. Elements of CM include a change control process, a version control tool, and a Change Control Board (CCB). The CCB consists of stakeholders who have the authority to approve, defer, or deny CRs and DRs. Members of the requirements CCB should include:

- you (the project manager),
- your software architect,
- the customer,
- a user representative, and
- a representative of the organization that will maintain the operational system.

In some cases the marketing department may be the customer and the user representative. For embedded systems projects your software project maybe subordinate to, and part of, the larger program; your software CCB may include a system engineer or program manager as your customer. In this case you (the software project manager) and/or your software architect should be a member of the system-

TABLE 7.7 Template for a change request

Change request number:
Submitter:
Date submitted:
Disposition:
___Accept ___Defer ___Deny ___Duplicated
Priority (if accepted):
___High ___Medium ___Low
Baselines added (names, version numbers):
Baselines modified (names, version numbers):
Staff-hours to make change:
Date new and modified baselines approved:
Acceptance sign-off:
Date closed:
Personnel notified of change:

level CCB. As a rule, the CCB should include the primary stakeholders but should not be so large that it becomes an unwieldy decision-making group.

The workflow of a change control process was presented in Chapter 3; Figure 3.5 is repeated here as Figure 7.4. The initial baseline of a work product is established

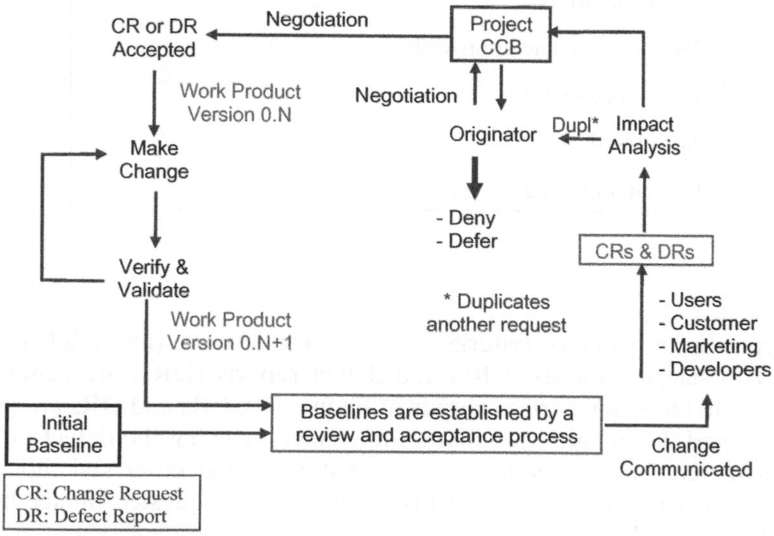

FIGURE 7.4 Workflow of a change request process

TABLE 7.8 Template for a defect report

Defect report number:
Submitter:
Date opened:
Brief description of the failure:
Severity level:
___Major ___Minor ___Inconvenience
Priority for fixing:
___Immediate ___ASAP ___Defer
Phase in which the mistake was made:
___Rqmts ___Design ___Imple. ___Verif. ___Valid.
Phase in which the mistake was found:
___Rqmts ___Design ___Imple. ___Verif. ___Valid. ___Ops
Kind of mistake:
___Incomplete ___Incorrect ___Inconsistent
___Other (specify):
How mistake was detected:
___Inspection ___Review ___Test ___Demo.
___ Other (specify):
Baselines modified to fix mistake (names, version numbers):
Staff-hours to fix:
Date new baseline approved:
Acceptance sign-off:
Date closed:
Personnel notified of change:

by satisfying the acceptance criteria for the work product (lower left corner of Figure 7.4). Change requests (CRs) and defect reports (DRs) are generated by various stakeholders (lower right corner of Figure 7.4). CRs and DRs are analyzed for urgency and the impacts of making the change or fixing the defect on factors such as cost, schedule, technology, users, customer, and other stakeholders are assessed. The originator of the request is notified if the requested change has been previously submitted.

The CCB may accept the CR or DR for action on a specified schedule, perhaps after making adjustments to other project factors, or they may negotiate with the originator of the request, which may result in denial of the request or deferral of action until a later date. For example, a Change Request for an additional feature might be denied or deferred until a future release of the system.

Some negotiation with one or more team leaders may be required to schedule the developers and other resources make the changes. The baselined work product to be modified (version 0.N in Figure 7.4) is checked out from the version control system. The modified work product is verified for completeness, correctness, and consistency and validated to ensure that it will satisfy its intended use in its intended environment.

Having satisfied its acceptance criteria, the new baseline of the work product is checked in to the version control system and becomes version 0.N + 1. All relevant stakeholders are notified of the new baseline.

Small changes to a requirements baseline (or other work product baselines), over time, indicate a stable project. Large changes, especially those that result in large amounts of rework without compensating changes in the effort and schedule constraints, are cause for concern.

The baseline control process described above is presented within the context of requirements management; however, baseline control (i.e., a change control process, a version control tool, and a CCB) is a fundamental tool for measuring and controlling all work products of a software project.

7.6.3 Measuring Attributes of Architectural Design Specifications

Design is the process of synthesizing a system[26] to optimize specified design criteria while satisfying specified constraints. The process of software design includes architectural design and detailed design. Architectural design is concerned with synthesizing a set of components, specifying the structural and behavioral relationships among the components, and specifying the interfaces to the software's environment. The implemented design should result in a product that satisfies the technical specifications and constraints and achieves, to the extent possible, the design goals for the system or product.

Detailed design is concerned with specifying the interface, algorithms, data structures, internal behavior, and exception handling mechanisms of each software component to be built or modified. Detailed design is part of implementation (along with coding of modules, code documentation, integration of modules to form components, inspections and code reviews, and testing by the implementers). Measures for implementation are presented in the following section.

Software architectures have several kinds of relationships among the elements of the architecture, which result in different views of the architecture including the [Bass03]:

- Decomposition,
- Deployment,
- Uses,
- Class,
- Layer,

[26] A *system* is a collection of interacting components that exists within and interacts with an environment.

- Command and Control, and
- Implementation views.

Other structural views are also possible.

The decomposition view of software structure, for example, is the view of hierarchical relationships among components, it is embedded in the work breakdown structure, as described in Chapter 5 of this text. This is the primary view that you, as the project manager, should use to plan, organize, and control your project.

The deployment view illustrates the relationships among components deployed on different elements of the system hardware, as for example, in the deployment of software components in the client-server architecture of an automated teller system. The deployment view is useful in assessing the impact of component placement on performance and security. The deployment view would indicate, for example, whether customer access is to be validated by maintaining a copy of customer IDs and passwords in each ATM or whether the validation data is kept on the server. Keeping the validation data on each ATM will improve performance, by reducing the number of accesses to the server, but might make the system more vulnerable to unauthorized access to account information.

The behavior of a system is determined by the sequential and concurrent activations of system components at run time. Activity diagrams, Petri nets, sequence diagrams, and state diagrams are commonly used mechanisms for documenting the behavioral aspects of software at the architectural level. Interfaces to the environment can be documented by tailoring and using a standard template, such as that provided in [Bass03].

An important task for you, as project manager, and your software architect(s) is to determine which views, representations of behavior, and interface attributes will be provided in the documentation of the system architecture. Some attributes of work products that can be measured during the architectural design phase, or phases,[27] are listed in Table 7.9.

As indicated in Table 7.9, updates to requirements status indicators should be reviewed periodically during architectural design (and throughout the development process). Small changes to the requirements baseline, increasing numbers of design goals converted to technical specifications, and growing numbers of requirements-based test scenarios indicate a stable project for which design can proceed with confidence. Conversely, large changes to the requirements baseline (especially without compensating changes to effort and schedule constraints), increasing numbers of design goals, and lack of requirement-based test scenarios indicate an unstable project for which design proceeds at the risk of large amounts of rework based on instability of the requirements.

Architectural design specifications provide the first opportunity to assess the impact of design decisions on the quality attributes of the product to be developed. Quality-attributes scenarios can be used to assess the design for such attributes as ease of changing the software for postulated changes in requirements and for the availability, performance, security, testability, and usability of software [Bass03].

The architectural design specification is baselined (i.e., placed under version control) when appropriate stakeholders determine that the specification, or a

[27]A *work phase* is characterized by the work activities accomplished and work products produced. Various phases of work, including design, may be repeated multiple times in an iterative development process.

TABLE 7.9 Some product measures for architectural design

- Updates to requirements *CRs, *DRs, and other requirements status indicators
- Number of design elements in the architectural design baseline versus number planned in this reporting period and cumulatively
- Number of quality-attribute scenarios prepared versus number planned in this reporting period and cumulatively
- Number of quality-attribute scenario walkthroughs and reviews versus number of planned in this reporting period and cumulatively
- Number of design-based test cases generated versus number planned in this reporting period and cumulatively
- Number of design-baseline CRs and DRs submitted, number accepted, number rejected, and number deferred during this reporting period and cumulatively
- Number of design defects by defect category and severity level
- Number of design-baseline CRs and DRs completed and closed during this reporting period and cumulatively
- Number of design-baseline CRs and DRs still open from this reporting period and from previous reporting periods
- Amount of time required to close design–baseline CRs and DRs
- Status of traceability matrices
    - Requirements to design components
    - Components to test cases

*CR: Change Request;
*DR: Defect Report.

significant part of it, satisfies objective verification and validation criteria for acceptance. Acceptance criteria for a design specification typically involve applying:

- traceability analyses,
- reviews,
- walkthroughs,
- inspections, and
- completion of revisions based on quality-attribute scenarios.

A defect in the architectural design specification results when the baselined specification is found to be incomplete, incorrect, and/or inconsistent with respect to the operational requirements and the technical specifications:

- the operational features,
- quality attributes,
- design constraints,
- primary requirements, and
- derived requirements.

In addition the design specification must be validated, that is, determined to be fit for its intended use as a basis for implementation and testing planning. Note that a design specification can be verified to be complete, consistent, and correct with respect to the requirements, but it might not be valid if it is expressed in a notation (e.g., UML) that is unfamiliar to the implementers and testers because it would not be fit for its intended use in its intended environment.

A defect in the architectural design specification may be caused by a defect in the baselined requirements or by a mistake in preparing the design specification. As discussed subsequently, it is important to identify the sources of defects.

7.6.4 Measuring Attributes of Software Implementation

Implementation of software includes:

- detailed design of modules;
- coding of modules;
- code documentation;
- integration of modules to form components; and
- inspections, code reviews, and testing by the implementers.

In many cases, existing software modules and components are modified or used without being coded in entirety. The amount of implementation to be accomplished depends on the amount of reuse of existing software.

Detailed design is concerned with specifying the algorithms, data structures, internal behavior, interfaces, and exception handling mechanisms of each software module to be built or modified. The amount of detailed design to be accomplished depends on the familiarity of the implementers with the algorithm(s) and the complexity of code to be implemented. You will probably not need a detailed design specification to guide implementation of your tenth variation on the merge-sort algorithm. However, detailed design will likely save time and effort, and improve the quality of the implementation if you are implementing complex data compression and encryption algorithms for the first time.

Coding is concerned with implementing design specifications (architectural and detailed design specs). The code must satisfy the requirements and optimize the design criteria and design goals for the product or system being implemented. As indicated in Section 5.3, requirements for features and quality attributes should be allocated to each element of the work breakdown structure to provide guidance to the implementers and testers. The implementation techniques chosen may be determined by the requirement to enhance reliability at the expense of performance, for example, by embedding run-time assertions in the code, or the chosen implementation technique may maximize performance at the expense of increased memory usage, for example, by creating tables of frequently used values to avoid computing the values on each usage. Some attributes of work products that can be measured during the implementation phase, or phases, are listed in Table 7.10.

As indicated in Table 7.10, completion of detailed design, coding, and unit testing of modules can be forecasted by tracking the rate of progress and comparing it to the estimated number of modules to be written or modified. If, for example, the current rate of progress is 5 modules per week, and 50 modules remain to be completed, implementation will be completed in 10 week, at the current rate of progress. Of course, the estimates of completion should be updated weekly because the rate of progress may vary from week to week.

TABLE 7.10 Some product measures for software implementation

- Updates to requirements *CRs and *DRs, architectural design CRs and DRs, and other requirements and design status indicators
- Number of modules baselined versus number planned in this reporting period and cumulatively
- Complexity measures for modules, components, subsystems, and system
- Number of code inspections conducted versus number planned during this reporting period and cumulatively
- Number of code-baseline CRs and DRs submitted, number accepted, number rejected, and number deferred during this reporting period and cumulatively
- Number of code-baseline CRs and DRs completed and closed during this reporting period and cumulatively
- Number of code-baseline CRs and DRs still open from this reporting period and from previous reporting periods
- Amount of time required to close code-baseline CRs and DRs
- Cumulative density of discovered defects by defect category and severity level, based on total defects and total lines of baselined code
- Forecast for completion of detailed design, coding and developer testing
- Status of traceability matrices:
  - from baselined modules and components to architecture
  - from test cases specified to modules and components
  - from test cases successfully completed to modules and components

* CR: Change Request;
* DR: Defect Report.

Code Inspections The number of code inspections conducted versus the number planned during a reporting period, and cumulatively, are measures cited in Table 7.10. A code inspection is a form of peer review conducted by the peers of the person who developed the code. In general, a peer is one who has equal status or standing with others who perform similar tasks. A code inspection is accomplished by a small team of software developers (typically 3 to 5). Managers (including you, the project manager), customers, user representatives, and others are excluded from participating. Peer reviews are thus free of the social and political pressures that result when participants of differing ranks or standings are present.

With respect to code inspections, your job as project manager is to:

- provide training in the inspection process, if needed;
- allow adequate time in the schedule to prepare for and conduct the inspections;
- review the results; and
- make improvements in your inspection and development processes as indicated by the reported trends found during inspections.

In particular, the inspection process requires that you, as project manager, schedule sufficient time for the preparation, meeting, rework, and follow-up activities of inspections.

The team leader of each small software team is responsible for the work products generated by the team, and she/he should participate in inspections of the code developed by their teams. Team leaders are technical contributors and are, or should be, regarded as team members and not as having superior rank. If your project is small (i.e., 5 or fewer software developers) and you are the project manager, software architect, and team leader, you should participate in inspections. You (the project manager) are excluded from participation on larger projects; otherwise, candid discussions and self-corrective actions will not occur.

As shown in the sidebar, inspections are the most efficient and most effective mechanism known to find and fix defects early in the development process. In most cases inspections require less effort and find more defects than testing. However, the inspection process is labor-intensive and may appear to be an inefficient use of personnel resources (but not as labor-intensive as testing per defect found and corrected). You and your organization can counter the appearance of inefficiency of inspections by analyzing inspection data and comparing it to similar data from testing (e.g., effort per defect found and fixed). There is something wrong with your inspection process if your data do not show inspections to be efficient and effective because inspections have been found to be both efficient and effective in many situations by many organizations.

Some organizations have found that unit testing following inspection of code modules is not cost-effective because very few defects are found by unit testing after inspection and repair. In these organizations, software modules are integrated into the evolving product after a developer fixes the defects found during an inspection. However, inspections do not remove the need for integration testing and independent verification and validation of an evolving system, since the dynamics of interactions among system components under various operational scenarios may expose defects that cannot be found by inspections. The defects that have been found and fixed by inspections make integration testing, verification, and validation more efficient. The inspection process is illustrated and discussed in the accompanying sidebar.

Walkthroughs Walkthroughs and inspections are two types of work product reviews. The purpose of an inspection is to find defects and to collect data for later analysis on the kinds and numbers of defects and the effort required to fix them. Participation in inspections is limited to a small number of people; typically 2 to 4. The purpose of a walkthrough is to communicate and review technical issues to a (perhaps large) group of people. Defects may be discovered during a walkthrough, but defect detection is not (should not be) the primary purpose of a walkthrough; communication is (or should be) the primary purpose of a walkthrough. Some of the distinctions between inspections and walkthroughs are listed in Table 7.11.

You should use both inspections and walkthroughs as appropriate: inspections to find defects and walkthroughs to communicate technical issues. Table 7.12 lists various kinds of reviews and the purposes for which they are conducted.

Developer Testing The "developer tests" cited in Table 7.10 (forecast for completion of detailed design, coding, and developer testing) are designed to validate the features and quality attributes of each module. Developer tests are prepared by the software developers in conjunction with preparation of the detailed design and the code. Developer testing may require development of test harnesses to simulate the environment in which the module will operate. If you are using an iterative

INSPECTIONS

There are four roles to be played in an inspection:

1. the moderator role to convene and lead the meeting,
2. the developer role for the developer that generated the work product,
3. the reader role for presenting the material to the group by paraphrasing it, and
4. the recorder role to record defects and other areas of concern.

The recorder role is essential because defects found during an inspection are not fixed at that time and concerns to be investigated are not pursued during the inspection; they are recorded for follow-up actions. A single individual can play more than one role. The only exclusion is that the developer must not play the reader role. Two is thus the minimum number of people who can conduct an inspection: one person can play the roles of moderator and reader, and the developer can play the roles of developer and recorder. More typically, each of four people is assigned a role and participate in the inspection; each member of an inspection team is an inspector.

The six phases of workflow for the software inspection process are illustrated in Figure 7.5. Planning involves the moderator and the developer. They review the material and determine whether it is ready for inspection, identify necessary related materials, solicit participants, and schedule the meeting. This typically requires 2 to 4 hours. The overview session is optional; it is held if the participants need an orientation to the material to be inspected. The overview session, if held, typically requires ½ to 1 ½ hours.

Each participant must spend 2 to 3 hours preparing: reviewing the material and, using a standard form, recording defects, possible defects, and areas of concern for discussion during the inspection meeting.

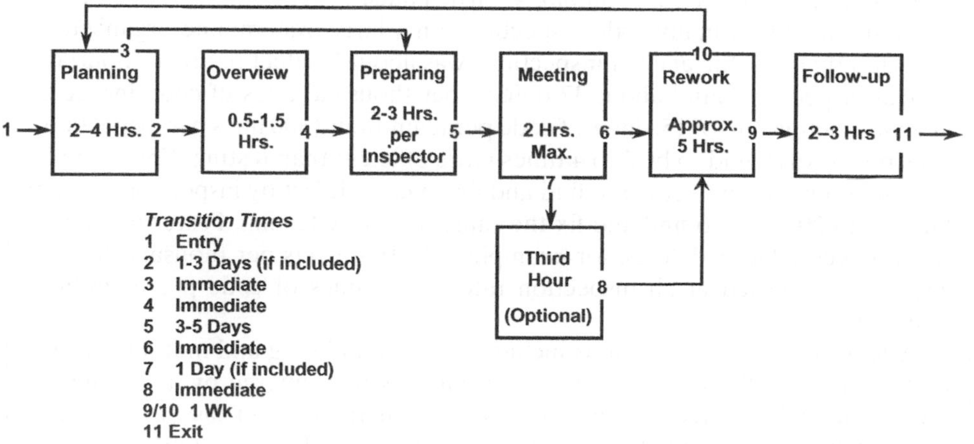

FIGURE 7.5 The inspection process

At the start of the inspection meeting, the moderator records the time spent by each participant in preparing for the meeting; these data are the source of the times listed in Figure 7.5 [Bush88]. If one or more of the participants has not prepared, that person or persons are excused from the meeting, and the moderator determines whether the meeting should be postponed or whether to proceed without that person or persons.

During the inspection meeting, the reader paraphrases small blocks of material (i.e., code for a code inspection, design for a design inspection, requirements for a requirements inspection, test scenario for a test plan inspection) and asks each participant, in turn and including herself or himself, if they see any problems or have any concerns. The recorder records, on a standard form, the defects, issues, and concerns voiced during the meeting.

It is important that the meeting be limited to not more than 2 hours because participants will become tired after 2 hours of concentrated activity and because participants can schedule the remainder of their work day, and thus are more likely to be willing participants if they know the meeting has a definite starting and ending time. With some experience, you and your organization will learn the optimal amount of material that can be inspected in a 2-hour meeting: too much material makes the process ineffective because defects and concerns will be overlooked; too little material makes the process inefficient because time is wasted.

The third hour is not an extension of the 2-hour meeting. It is an option that can be used for informal discussions among some or all of the participants, after a break or perhaps the next morning over coffee.

Rework is accomplished by the developer of the material in consultation with others as appropriate; this activity typically requires approximately 5 hours. The developer, or the inspection team, can request another inspection after rework is completed if the rework is substantial. However, this seldom happens in practice because the moderator and developer should not schedule an inspection until they agree that the material is ready to be inspected.

The moderator and developer conduct the follow-up meeting to agree that all defects and concerns have been addressed and that all of the reporting forms have been completed. An inspection requires about 2 weeks of elapsed time and 30 to 40 hours of total effort among 4 participants.

In an analysis of many code inspections on a large system, one organization reported that the efficiency of inspections was about 1 defect per team-hour; the typical inspection found about 37 defects per thousand lines of code inspected at an inspection rate of 150 lines of code per team-hour (300 lines per inspection). This result was found to be 2 to 4 times more efficient than testing. For example, if it takes 5 hours on average to find and fix a major defect by inspection it might take 10 to 20 hours to find and fix the same defect by testing. Faster inspection rates detected fewer defects; for example only 10 defects per thousand lines of code were detected at an inspection rate of 500 lines of code per team-hour [Russell91].

Added benefits of inspections include the team building and mutual learning that occurs, and the detection of defect patterns that emerge by analyzing the records of kinds of defects found during inspection. In the latter case, for example, it might become evident that a large percentage of defects found are in the interfaces among modules. This might indicate that the detailed design of interfaces prior to coding will substantially reduce defects. Procedures for conducting inspections and the associated recording forms are contained in Appendix 7B of this chapter.

development process (recommended) the current version of the evolving software can be used as the test harness for unit testing of modules under development (which will be integrated into the evolving product and will provide the test harness for the next iteration of implementation). If you are using an agile development process, the test cases are written before the code is written (always a good idea).

Another of the implementation measures in Table 7.10 is complexity of modules, components, subsystems, and system. The following section presents some complexity measures for software code.

7.6.5 Complexity Measures for Software Code

As discussed in Chapter 1, complexity is one of the inherent characteristics of computer software. Complex software is difficult to understand, difficult to document, difficult to test, difficult to modify, and as a consequence, difficult to reuse. Conversely, you can conclude that software that is difficult to understand, difficult to document, difficult to test, difficult to modify and/or difficult to reuse is, by definition, complex. Three commonly used measures of software complexity are

TABLE 7.11 Distinction between inspections and walkthroughs

Inspections	Walkthroughs
Purpose: to find defects	Purpose: to communicate
Training of participants	No training of participants
Assigned roles: moderator, reader, recorder, developer	No assigned roles
Names of participants recorded	Names of participants (usually) not recorded
Developer does not present	Developer typically presents
Record keeping	No record keeping
Analysis of inspection results	No analysis of the walkthrough results

TABLE 7.12 Various kinds of reviews and their purposes

Kind of Review	Purpose
Inspection	To find defects and document discovery and the repair processes
Walkthrough	To review work products and communicate issues
Team	To review progress and plan work activities
Project	To review progress, process and product constraints, and confront risk factors
Customer	To review progress, constraints, and risk factors
Department	To review portfolios of projects, identify and confront common risk factors, assess status of budgets and customers, and confirm/revise mission statement

cyclomatic complexity, the COCOMO complexity cost driver, and coupling and cohesion.

Cyclomatic Complexity Cyclomatic complexity is a measure from graph theory. When applied to source code, it is a measure of the number of linearly independent paths through the code. It is applied to software by computing the structural complexity of a module's control flow graph and can also be used to compute the complexity of collections of modules. Figure 7.6 depicts a control flow graph in which the nodes represent groups of sequentially executed statements and the edges represent flow of control among statement nodes. The dark nodes contain statements that invoke other modules (more on this later). As indicated in Figure 7.6, the formula for computing cyclomatic complexity of a control flow graph is

$$C = E - N + 2,$$

where E is the number of edges and N is the number of nodes in the control flow graph; the entry and exit edges are not counted.

As a rule of thumb, modules that have complexity measures greater than 10 or 12 are generally considered to be too complex; they are difficult to understand, difficult to document, difficult to test, and difficult to modify. Measures of cyclomatic complexity taken before and after software is modified can be used to control software entropy, which is the tendency of software to become more complex as it undergoes modification [Belady76]. In some cases software systems have been retired because they have become so complex, through a series of modifications, that they can no longer be modified without creating unacceptable numbers of new defects. Modules for which the complexity measure becomes too large can be further modified to reduce complexity and thereby avoid excessive entropy. This is a form of preventative maintenance for software.

Cyclomatic design complexity of a collection of modules is computed by retaining only the nodes of each module (and the associated edges) that contain statements that invoke, or are invoked by other modules. Design complexity is computed by computing the cyclomatic complexity of each resulting module and combining those complexities using the formula

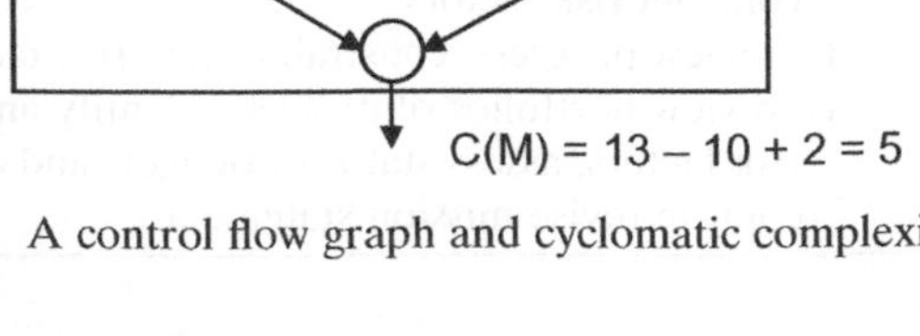

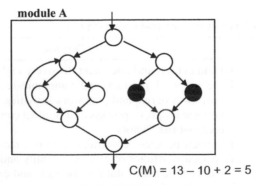

FIGURE 7.6 A control flow graph and cyclomatic complexity calculation

$$DC(S) = \sum DC(M_j) - N + 1,$$

where $DC(M_j)$ is the design complexity of module j and N is the number of modules.

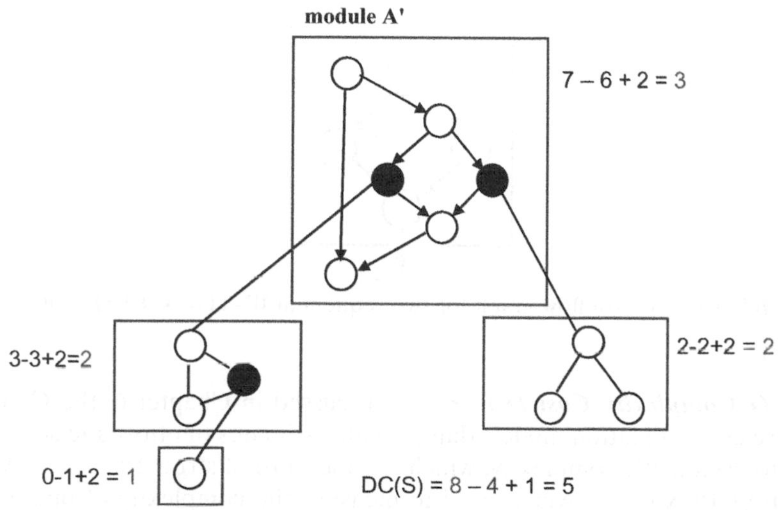

FIGURE 7.7 Cyclomatic design complexity

In Figure 7.7, module A′ is the pruned version of module A in Figure 7.6. The other modules in Figure 7.7 are those invoked by module A. Collections of modules that have design complexities greater than 40 or 50 are considered to be too complex. In such cases the system should be separated into two or more subsystems, each of acceptable complexity, that communicate through a single, well-defined interface. A complex system might be decomposed, for example, into user interface, database, computational, and communication subsystems with well-defined interfaces among the subsystems.

The fact that the cyclomatic complexity of a section of source code is the count of the number of linearly independent paths through a module (or any section of code) can be used as a guideline for test planning because the cyclomatic complexity measure is an upper bound on the number test cases required to achieve branch coverage and a lower bound on the number of test cases required to achieve total path coverage. For example, the number of test cases to achieve branch coverage of two sequential IF–THEN–ELSE statements, as depicted in Figure 7.8 is 2. The number of test cases to achieve path coverage is 4. The cyclomatic complexity number is 3.

The cyclomatic complexity metric for software was developed by Tom McCabe in 1976 [McCabe76]. The McCabe Company markets tools to calculate the cyclomatic complexity of modules and systems written in various programming languages [www.mccabe.com]. Some development tool sets also incorporate cyclomatic complexity calculators.

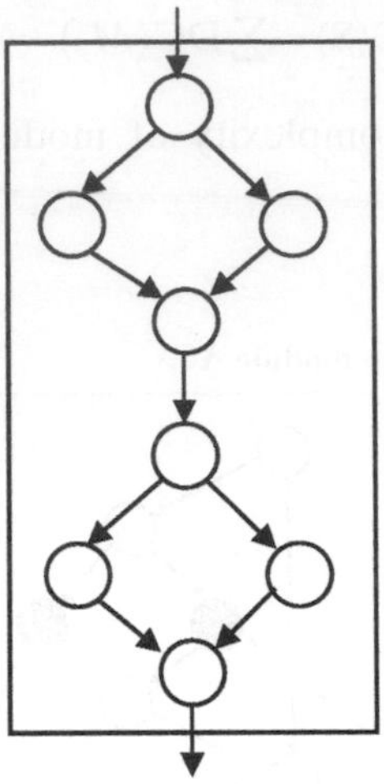

FIGURE 7.8 Control flow graph for two sequential IF–THEN–ELSE statements

COCOMO Complexity Cost Driver As discussed in Chapter 6, the COCOMO models are cost estimation models that provide estimates of effort and schedule. In contrast to cyclomatic complexity, which is a measure of structural complexity, the COCOMO CPLX cost driver is used to measure the complexity of operations to be performed by a module or a collection of modules. In COCOMO, the value of CPLX is used to increase or decrease an effort estimate.

Determining the value of CPLX is based on evaluation of the complexity of five kinds of operations a program typically performs:

- control operations,
- computational operations,
- device dependent operations,
- data management operations, and
- user interface management operations.

A table is provided to select a value for each of the five elements; for example, a program estimated to have control operations that involve mostly straight-line code with a few non-nested structured programming operators such as DOs, CASEs, and IF–THEN–ELSEs and simple procedure calls or simple scripts would be rated Very Low in complexity (0.73). A program estimated to have multiple resources to be scheduled with dynamically changing priorities and with distributed real-time control would be rated extra high in complexity (1.74) [Boehm2000]. The range of effort multiplier values for CPLX is thus

$$0.73 \leq \text{CPLX} \leq 1.74.$$

The value of CPLX for each of the five complexity factors is estimated from the requirements and from the design, if it is available; or, it can be determined from the source code for purposes of software maintenance. The numeric value of the dominant complexity factor, or factors, among the five factors is used as the effort multiplier for CPLX in the effort estimation equation. A CPLX value greater than 1 indicates that the code is, or is estimated to be, more complex than the typical product and thus the project will require more effort than the typical project; a value less than 1 indicates that the code is, or is estimated to be, less complex than the typical product and the project will require less effort than the typical one. CPLX, like cyclomatic complexity and coupling and cohesion, can be applied to existing code to determine the difficulty of understanding, documenting, testing, and modifying the code.

Coupling and Cohesion Coupling and cohesion are measures of the relationships among modules (coupling) and the relationships among elements within modules (cohesion) [Myers74]. Coupling is measured on a scale of Weak to Strong; Weak coupling is less complex than Strong coupling. Weak coupling is desirable because it promotes ease of understanding, ease of documentation, ease of testing, ease of modification, and ease of reuse; that is to say, it results in desirable complexity of coupling among a group of modules. Some levels of coupling are listed in Table 7.13. Message coupling, as in object-oriented software, and communication by passing of parameters, in both object-oriented and functionally structured software, are the preferred methods of coupling.

The stronger, and less desirable, measures of coupling (stamp, control, common, and content) are undesirable because the effect of making a change may ripple beyond the module being changed. For example, if a data structure is changed in a system that exhibits stamp or common coupling, all modules that directly access the data structure will have to be changed.

Cohesion is a measure of the relationships among the statements within a module, on a scale of Strong to Weak. Strong cohesion is desirable because it indicates that all of the statements in a module are contributing to the same purpose. Strong cohesion reduces complexity because each module can be given a short, simple name that indicates its purpose. This allows humans to build up mental models of collections of modules by, as psychologists say, "chunking" of information. For example, if a module named "quicksort" does only quick-sorting of data communicated by input and output parameters (data coupling), the internal details of the module do not have to be recalled when reasoning about the program in which the quicksort module is embedded. In addition highly cohesive modules have no unexpected or surprising side effects. You would be quite surprised if, within the quicksort module,

TABLE 7.13 Some measures of coupling complexity

Kind of Coupling (Weak to Strong)	Explanation
Message coupling	Request for service
Data coupling	Passing of parameters
Stamp coupling	Two modules directly access the same data structure(s)
Control coupling	Modules pass flags to control execution paths of other modules
Common coupling	All modules directly access the same data structure(s)
Content coupling	Modules directly access the internal details of other modules

TABLE 7.14 Some measures for software cohesion

Kind of Cohesion (Strong to Weak)	Explanation
Object cohesion	Each method in an object has functional cohesion and supports the single, well-defined purpose of the object
Functional cohesion	All elements in a function support a single, narrowly defined concept
Sequential cohesion	Output of some elements provide inputs to the following elements in a module
Communication cohesion	All elements in a module use the same input data but for different purposes
Temporal cohesion	The only relationship among elements is that they are executed as a group
Coincidental cohesion	No meaningful relationships among the elements in a module

you found a command to launch a guided missile. Needless to say, that module would not be highly cohesive.

Some levels of cohesion are listed in Table 7.14. Object cohesion, as in object-oriented software and functional cohesion, in both object-oriented and functionally structured software, are the preferred levels of cohesion.

The weaker, and less desirable, measures of cohesion (sequential, communication, temporal, and coincidental) result in increased complexity because they make a module difficult to understand, document, test, modify, and reuse. Weak coupling (message and data) and strong cohesion (object and functional), taken together, result in software that contains reusable modules, and is easy to understand, document, test, and modify because the ripple effect of changes is reduced, as compared to collections of modules that have strong coupling and weak cohesion.

7.6.6 Measuring Integration and Verification of Software Units

In the Waterfall development model, the unit of software to be integrated and verified is the collection of components for the entire system. Integration of system components thus occurs at the end of the development process, as indicated in Figure 2.8. In an iterative process, integration and verification (plus validation) of software units occurs on a cyclic basis, as indicated in Figure 2.10; in an iterative process the software units are growing subsets of the entire system. In any case, software integration and verification is concerned with:

- integrating system components into larger units;
- verifying that the larger units are implemented as designed; and
- verifying that the units are complete, correct, and consistent with respect to their functional and quality requirements.

Some product measures that can be obtained during software integration and verification are listed in Table 7.15.

TABLE 7.15 Some measures for software integration and verification

- Updates to requirements, design, and code *CRs and *DRs, and other status indicators
- Number of modules successfully integrated and verified versus number planned during this reporting period and cumulatively
- Defect density for each component, each subsystem, and the total system
- Number and percentage of design-based tests passed during this reporting period and cumulatively
- Number and percentage of design-based tests failed; during this reporting period and cumulatively
- Number of integration-baseline CRs and DRs submitted, number accepted, number rejected, and number deferred during this reporting period and cumulatively
- Number of integration-baseline CRs and DRs closed during this reporting period and cumulatively
- Number of integration-baseline CRs and DRs still open from this reporting period and from previous reporting periods
- Amount of time required to close integration-baseline CRs and DRs
- Status of traceability matrices:
  - from software units to successfully completed design-based test cases and test scenarios
  - from software units to successfully completed requirements-based test cases and test scenarios
- Forecast for completion of integration and verification

*CR: Change Request;
*DR: Defect Report.

You should monitor updates to CRs and DRs for requirement, design, and code baselines plus other product status indicators to determine whether those changes are in scope or out of scope for your process parameters (effort, other resources, budget, schedule, technology) and adjust those parameters as necessary. Other measures in Table 7.15 allow you to determine whether you are making adequate progress as measured by comparing planned progress to actual progress.

7.6.7 Measuring System Verification and Validation

System verification is concerned with determining that the system to be delivered is correct, complete, and consistent with respect its technical specifications and operational requirements when operated in the development environment. System validation is concerned with determining the degree to which the delivered system satisfies its intended purpose when operated by its intended users in its intended operational environment. The processes, methods, and techniques are similar in each case. However, system verification typically occurs in the development environment, whereas system validation typically occurs in the operational environment and involves real users. You (the project manager), your designated development personnel, user representatives, and customer should witness the tests and demonstrations in both cases.

Some product measures for system verification and validation are listed in Table 7.16. You can use these measures to forecast completion of system verification and system validation. Commonly used techniques for system V&V are testing, demonstrations, reviews, and traceability analysis.

TABLE 7.16 Some measures for system verification and validation

- Updates to requirements, design, code, and integration *CRs and *DRs, and other status indicators
- Number and percentage of scenario-based functional tests and demonstrations executed successfully during the present reporting period and cumulatively
- Number and percentage of scenario-based functional tests and demonstrations failed during the present reporting period and cumulatively
- Number and percentage of quantitative tests passed during the present reporting period and cumulatively
- Number and percentage of quantitative tests failed during the present reporting period and cumulatively
- Estimates of system reliability and availability
- Cumulative DR density (DRs per size unit)
- Number of system-baseline CRs and DRs submitted, number accepted, number rejected, and number deferred during this reporting period and cumulatively
- Number of system-baseline CRs and DRs closed during this reporting period and cumulatively
- Number of system-baseline CRs and DRs still open from this reporting period and from previous reporting periods
- Amount of time required to close system-baseline CRs and DRs
- Forecast for completion of system verification
- Forecast for completion of system validation

*CR: Change Request;
*DR: Defect Report.

Scenario-based tests and demonstrations are intended to assess the degree to which the system provides the necessary features, functionality, and quality attributes including exception handling and degraded operation. Testing and demonstration of features and functionality in a system specified by use cases, for example, would exercise all of the primary and secondary scenarios in the use cases. The secondary scenarios should cover exceptions and exception handling, for example, by testing the response when a customer fails to enter the correct PIN in an Automated Teller System. Degraded operation might include testing and demonstration of specified operational capabilities of ATM terminals, such as the response of ATMs when the server or the communication channel is down.

The difference between a test and a demonstration is as follows: a test is designed by specifying the test environment, the input stimuli, and the expected outcome of the test. For example, a functional test of a square-root function should return 3 when the input is 9, 3.1622 … (to a specified degree of resolution) when the input is 10, and so forth. The square-root value to be returned for negative numbers would also be tested for conformance to the specification, provided that the specification includes the outcomes for negative numbers.

A demonstration is conducted by specifying the environment and input stimuli, but the outcome cannot be predicted in advance. Acceptability of the result is determined by human judgment. Acceptability of a user interface, for example, is determined by representative users; the level at which a chess playing program performs is determined by chess masters. System level demonstrations should be confirmations of previous demonstrations of prototypes and demonstrations of incremental progress during software development; there should be no surprises in system-level demonstrations.

Quantitative system tests are derived from the quantitative attributes stated in the primary requirements, derived requirements, and design constraints. These tests are primarily concerned with verifying and validating the quality attributes of the system such as performance under various specified conditions, mean time to failure, mean time to repair, and availability.

Attributes such as ease of learning and ease of use, as measured by specific, predetermined experiments may also be assessed. Quantitative attributes based on stress testing may also be performed; as for example, testing the response time of ATM terminals when 100 terminals are concurrently active and the server is running at 90% CPU usage.

7.7 MEASURING AND ANALYZING SOFTWARE DEFECTS

Software defects, when encountered during operation of a system or product, result in failures. A failure occurs when software does not satisfy its user needs, customer expectations, or technical specifications (primary requirements, derived requirements, design constraints) when it is operated by its users, as intended in its intended operational environment. Some failures are more serious than others; a system crash is more serious than an incorrect error message and incorrectly computed results may constitute a more serious failure than a system crash.

Incorrectly computed customer balances in an Automated Teller System, for example, may result in serious problems for users or for the financial institution, depending on the nature of the defect that causes the failure. A system crash from which recovery is possible using a transaction log (after the defect that caused the crash is fixed) may cause inconvenience during the outage but causes no long-term harm. A type mismatch in a software interface that causes an undetected error in navigational computations (as in a Mars orbiter that crashed into the surface of Mars) is more serious than an in-flight software failure from which the system can reboot itself, or for which a software patch can be uploaded.

Software defects are caused by human mistakes. Unlike physical artifacts, software does not wear out or break from repeated usage. Human mistakes are of two kinds:

- error of omission (not doing something that should have been done) and
- error of commission (doing something incompletely, incorrectly, or inconsistently).

Table 7.17 lists some reasons humans make mistakes. Most of the mistakes made during software development and modification are caused by problems in communication and coordination, and by lack of knowledge, skill, or appropriate tools, but some are caused by human fallibility. Mistakes in communication and coordination can be reduced by better work processes. Mistakes of fallibility can be reduced, for example, by not requiring excessive overtime, which results in mental fatigue, which in turn results in mistakes.

RELIABILITY, AVAILABILITY, MEAN TIME TO FAILURE, AND MEAN TIME TO REPAIR

Table 7.16 indicates that estimates of system reliability and availability can be made during system verification and validation. System reliability is defined by three attributes:

1. The system will perform specified operations
2. Under stated conditions
3. For a specified period of time

A reliability rating R is the probability that a system will be reliable (i.e., will perform specified operations under stated conditions for a specified period of time). If the reliability rating for a system states that the system will operate for 5 minutes (wall-clock time) between failures, where failure means a system crash, with 80% probability ($R = 0.8$), and if the system satisfies this (absurd) requirement (i.e., it operates without a system crash for 5 minutes or more, 80% of the time), the system will be said to be reliable. Mission-critical systems often have reliability ratings on the order of 0.999995 over periods of time extending up to several years. Redundant hardware and software is required to meet such stringent reliability requirements.

Mean Time To Failure (MTTF) is the average amount of time a system is operational between failures. Mean Time To Repair (MTTR) is the average amount of time it takes to return a failed system to operational status. Availability is the probability a system will be available when needed.

Availability can be expressed as

$$A = \frac{\text{MTTF}}{\text{MTTF} + \text{MTTR}}.$$

If MTTF = 80 hours and MTTR is 20 hours then $A = 0.8$, assuming failures are uniformly distributed in time. It might be that an ATM system has an availability requirement of 0.9 from 6:00 AM until 11:59 PM each day with no availability requirement from 12:00 AM until 5:59 AM. Upgrades, account reconciliations, and other kinds of maintenance activities could thus be scheduled during late night hours.

Systems that have extremely high availability requirements typically employ multiple hardware processors with concurrent operation and majority voting of the processors (as in the case of the NASA space shuttle's on-board computers) or with hot standby processors (as in the case of the New York stock exchange).

As is the usual case when dealing with statistics, the deviations as well as the mean values should be stated and validated. Users of a system with MTTF = 80 hours having a standard deviation of 2 hours would probably rate it higher in availability than a system having MTTF = 80 hours and a standard deviation of 40 hours even if MTTF was the same for both systems (80 hours) and MTTR was the same for both systems (e.g., 4 hours).

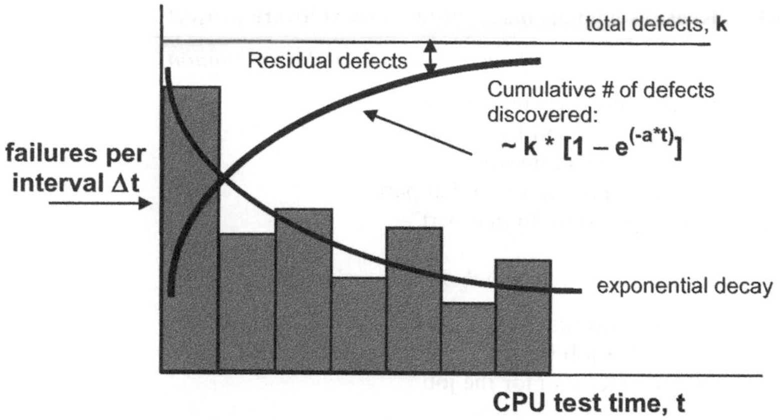

FIGURE 7.9 A reliability growth model

Reliability growth during system testing can be approximated as illustrated in Figure 7.9. During system testing the number of defects found per unit of testing interval typically decreases in an exponential manner; defects that are easy to find are quickly exposed while fewer of the difficult ones are found per testing interval. If each defect results in a failure (i.e., a departure from specified or desired behavior), the exponential decay curve in Figure 7.9 is an inverse measure of MTTF. For example, if 16 defects are found during an 8-hour day of testing, the average number of defects per test hour is 2 on that day and the MTTF is 30 minutes for that day. The reciprocal of the defect curve is thus a reliability growth curve. The remaining test time required to achieve a specified value of MTTF can be estimated by extrapolating the reliability growth curve.

The exponential and logarithmic Poisson models of reliability growth are presented in [Mala97]. Other models can be found on the Internet.

As a project manager you should analyze defects and, to the extent possible, endeavor to reduce mistakes. Of course, humans do make mistakes (we are not automatons), so the probability of producing defect-free software for large, complex systems is close to zero.

Defects are counted as mistakes discovered during the process of accepting work products to be baselined or mistakes discovered after a work product is baselined. Mistakes found and corrected prior to initial baselining of a work product are not counted as defects:

> Defects are mistakes found during baseline acceptance of work products, and mistakes found in baselined work products.

When a defect is discovered, a Defect Report is prepared and used to track repairing of the defect (i.e., correcting of the mistake that created the defect). Figure 7.10 illustrates the process of defect detection and repair. The DR template in Table 7.8, repeated here as Table 7.18, can be used to record defect information throughout

TABLE 7.17 Reasons humans make mistakes on software projects

Failures of communication and coordination
• "I didn't receive the necessary information"
• "The information changed and I wasn't told"
• "I misinterpreted the correct information"
• "I didn't know I was supposed to do that part"
• "I thought I was supposed to do that part"
Lack of skill and tools
• "I didn't know how to do that job"
• "I have never done that job before"
• "I didn't have the correct tool for the job"
Human fallibility
• "I was tired, sick, troubled, ..."
• "My child, husband, wife, was sick"
• "I was thinking about my upcoming vacation"
• "I was distracted by a phone call"
• ...

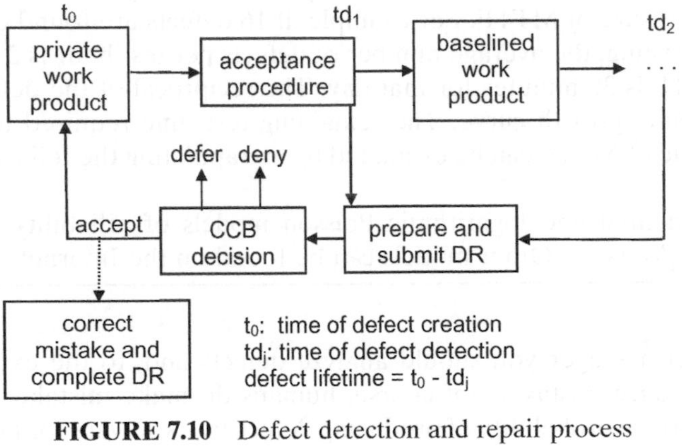

FIGURE 7.10 Defect detection and repair process

the development phases of your project and to record defects throughout the maintenance life cycle of a software product or system. Information from completed DRs can be analyzed, as discussed below.

As indicated in Table 7.18, Defect Reports (DRs) are used to record:

- dates of opening and closing the defect report,
- a brief description of the failure caused by the defect,
- how the defect was detected,
- staff-hours spent in fixing the defect,
- phase in which the mistake was made that created the defect,

TABLE 7.18 Template for a defect report

Defect report number:
Submitter:
Date opened:
Brief description of the failure:
Severity level:
___Major ___Minor ___Inconvenience Priority for fixing:
___Immediate ___ASAP ___Defer
Phase in which the mistake was made:
___Rqmts ___Design ___Imple. ___Verif. ___Valid.
Phase in which the mistake was found:
___Rqmts ___Design ___Imple. ___Verif. ___Valid. ___Ops Kind of mistake
___Incomplete ___Incorrect ___Inconsistent
___Other (specify):
How mistake was detected:
___Inspection ___Review ___Test ___Demo.
___Other (specify):
Baselines modified to fix mistake (names, version numbers):
Staff hour to fix:
Date new baseline approved:
Acceptance sign-off:
Date closed:
Personnel notified of change:

- phase in which the defect was discovered and corrected,
- baselined work products modified to fix the mistake,
- sign-off by a responsible party to certify the modified work product successfully passed its acceptance criteria,
- date the new baseline was entered into the version control system, and
- personnel notified of the change.

Data for Defect Reports can be captured during the inspection–review–testing process of initial baseline acceptance and during configuration management check-out and check-in procedures for modifying baselined work products. Data entry is facilitated by displaying electronic templates that are completed by software developers and maintainers during check-out and check-in.

Your organization should have criteria for categorizing the severity level of a defect, for example:

- a Major defect must be fixed immediately because the defect may cause a ripple effect into other work products that depend on this work product (e.g., a Major defect would be incorrect statement of a requirement that would create defects in the design documentation, code, and test plans);
- a Minor defect must be fixed in the near future but it will not propagate into other work products (e.g, a mistake in a test scenario that must be corrected before it is used would be classified as a Minor defect);
- an Inconvenient defect will not affect the operational behavior of the system but might create an inconvenience for the users (e.g., a user interface feature that requires the user to enter a sequence of control characters rather than selecting a clickable item).

Other categorizations of severity level are possible. For example a Catastrophic defect in a mission-critical system might result in loss of several lives and/or catastrophic loss of property, a Significant defect might result in loss of a single life or significant loss of property; a Serious defect might result in serious injury or serious loss of property, and a Minor defect might result in minor injury or minor loss of property.

The template presented in Table 7.19 can be used to report the aging of open defect reports by severity level. You and your organization should have goals for closing defect reports within specified period of time; for example, major defects must be fixed within 24 hours, minor defects within 3 days, and inconvenient defect within 5 days.

A report can also be generated to indicate the total number of open defects, the number of newly reported defects, and the number carried forward from the previous reporting period, as in Table 7.20.

The format of Defect Reports in Table 7.18 includes entries for recording the development phase during which the mistake was made and the development phase in which the defect was found. These data can be used to prepare a report using the template illustrated in Table 7.21. Table 7.22 provides a partial legend for the entries in Table 7.21, which should be sufficient to explain the remaining entries. In Table 7.21 verification and validation defects, for example, are defects found in V&V work products such as traceability matrices, reports from inspection meetings, and in test cases, test scenarios, test environments, and test plans.

TABLE 7.19 Template for reporting defect aging by severity level

Defect Type	Open <1 day	Open <3 days	Open <5 days	Open >5 days
# major defects				
# minor defects				
# inconvenience defects				

TABLE 7.20 Template for reporting defects by reporting period

Defect Type	Total Number	Newly Reported	Carried Forward
Major defects			
Minor defects			
Inconvenient defects			

TABLE 7.21 Template for defect matrices

	Activities: Rqmts.	Design	Imple.	Verif.	Valid.	Ops.	Totals
Defects: Rqmts.	RDr	RDd	RDi	RDve	RDva	RDo	Σ RqD
Design		DDd	DDi	DDve	DDva	DDo	Σ DeD
Imple.			IDi	IDve	IDva	IDo	Σ ImD
Verif.				VEve	VEva	VEo	Σ VeD
Valid.					VAva	VAo	Σ VaD
Totals:	Σ RqT	Σ DeT	Σ ImT	Σ VeT	Σ VaT	Σ VaO	TOTAL

TABLE 7.22 A partial legend for Table 7.21

Defect	When Found
RDr	Requirements defects found during requirements acceptance for baselining
RDd	Requirements defects found during a design activity
RDi	Requirements defects found during an implementation activity
RDve	Requirements defects found during a verification activity
RDva	Requirements defects found during a validation activity
ΣRqD	All requirements defect found during all software development activities
ΣImT	Defects of all kinds found during an implementation activity
TOTAL	Defects of all kinds found during all software development activities and operation

Defect data presented in the format of Table 7.21 can be used to determine, for example, the percentage of requirements defects found during design:

$$\left[\frac{\text{RDd}}{\sum \text{RqD}}\right] \times 100,$$

or, for example, the percentage of design defects that "escape" the design process and are discovered subsequently:

$$\left[1 - \left(\frac{\text{DDd}}{\sum \text{DeD}}\right)\right] \times 100.$$

Table 7.23 provides an example of a defect matrix for a completed project. The 20 total operations (Ops) defects are the defects that have been found by users

TABLE 7.23 An example of a defect matrix for a completed project

Phases When Defects Found:	Rqmts.	Design	Imple.	Verif.	Valid.	Ops.	Totals
Defects: Rqmts.	50	25	13	6	3	3	100
Design		60	30	15	8	7	120
Imple.			80	40	20	10	150
Verif.				6	3	0	9
Valid.					7	0	7
Totals:	50	85	123	67	41	20	386

during the first 6 months of operation. If, as in Table 7.23, the number of requirements defects found during requirements activities was 50, the number found during design was 25, the number found during implementation was 13, the number found during verification was 6, the number found during validation was 3, and the number found by users during the first 6 months of operation was 3, it would be apparent that:

1. the acceptance criteria for baseline acceptance of requirements must be improved for other present and future projects (50% of requirements defect found during development escaped the requirements verification process);
2. detection of requirements defects must be improved in subsequent development phases (roughly 50% of remaining requirements defects were detected at each subsequent stage of development; more should have been detected during the design phase);
3. defect detection effectiveness at each stage of development was about 50%; and
4. roughly 5% of total defects escaped the development process and were found by users during the first 6 months of operation (20/386; a result of the 50% effectiveness at each stage).

Other analyses are possible. In Table 7.23, 3% of requirements defects escaped the development process and were found by users (3 of 100). Also note that the acceptance criteria for implemented code are only 53% effective (80 of 150 implementation defects we found during the implementation activity; 70 escaped). Overall, roughly 7% of implementation defects escaped the development process (10 of 150).

Analysis of Table 7.23 might also reveal that of the 60 design defects found during design activities, 40 were the result of the 25 requirements defects that escaped into the design process and another 20 design defects were created during the design activity. Similarly analysis might show that of the 80 implementation defects found during implementation, 50 were caused by the 43 requirements and design defects on which implementation was based and the other 30 were created during implementation. These and similar analyses can identify areas for improvement of development processes, procedures, methods, tools, and techniques across the development process.

As noted above, effectiveness of defect detection in Table 7.23 is approximately 50% at each phase of development (25 of 50 requirements defects escape into design; 12 requirements defects are found during design and 13 escape into implementation; and so forth). It is not unreasonable that the acceptance criteria for a work product should find 70% to 80% of the defects in the work product prior to baselining it (it is unreasonable to expect that 100% of the defects in a work product will be found prior to baselining it).

If 70% of requirements defects are found at each of five development stages (requirements, design, implementation, verification, and validation), then only 0.073% of the 100% of requirements defects will remain to be found by users ($[1 - 0.3^5] \times 100$). The overall effectiveness of finding requirements defects during software development is thus 99.927%. By similar reasoning, 0.24% of design defects should escape the development process, and 0.81% of implementation defects should be released to users. This (simple) analysis is based on the assumption of a linear, Waterfall development process. An iterative development process should do much better than indicated because of the repeated opportunities to update baselined work products on successive iterations.

The example in Table 7.23 is for a completed project and a system that has been in operation for six months. You can prepare similar defect matrices during software development that are updated at each reporting interval. The evolving matrix can be analyzed for developing trends and compared to expectations, based on results from similar past projects at similar stages of development.

7.8 CHOOSING PRODUCT MEASURES

Earlier sections of this chapter have presented many possibilities for measuring the attributes of work products. Chapter 8 presents methods and techniques for measuring and controlling your work processes. It is possible, although not highly probable, that you may be able to delivery an acceptable product on schedule and within budget without any planning, estimating, measuring, or controlling of your work processes and work products. As stated earlier, the cost of planning, estimating, measuring, and control, like the cost of risk management, is an investment you make to increase the probability of success. The amount you invest in planning, estimating, measuring, and controlling depends on the criticality of delivering an acceptable product within the project constraints, and the cost of failure to do so.

Given the multiple constraints that you will typically encounter in managing a software project, you will never have enough time to do a thorough and complete job of measuring and controlling work products or work processes (or anything else; i.e., system engineering, requirements engineering, design, development, review, testing, project planning, estimating, and other project activities). In the case of measuring and controlling requirements, for example, you may decide that the Essential requirements should receive the most attention, and perhaps only a subset of the Essential requirements judged to be critical to product success will be controlled at the level of detail indicated above. As a general guideline, however, it is true that most problems encountered in software development are caused by insufficient time and effort spent on requirements and design, so that the time and effort spent on these endeavors is well spent.

Some aspects of measurement and control may be prescribed by your organization; for example, all projects may be required to report, at prescribed intervals, project attributes such as:

- product size,
- defects,
- effort spent on various project activities
- corrective rework of work product baselines, and
- schedule progress in achieving prescribed milestones.

Both current values and trends over time should be reported and analyzed.

Goals–Questions–Metrics (GQM) is an approach that can be used to determine the measurements that should be made on a software project [Basili94]. GQM arrives at a set of metrics by answering the following questions:

Goals: what do you wish to achieve?

Questions: what questions should be answered to assure that you achieve your goals?

Metrics: what data should be collected and analyzed to answer the questions?

Suppose, for example that one of your goals is to reduce defects:

Goal: reduce defects during software development

Questions:

how many defects are introduced during software development?

what percentage of total defects found during software development is introduced in each phase of software development?

what percentage of total defects found during software development is found in each phase of software development?

what kinds of defects are found in each phase of software development?

by what percentage should defects found during software development be reduced in the next 12 months?

Metrics:

total number of defects found during software development

percentage of total defects introduced in each phase of software development

percentage of total defects found in each phase of software development

kinds of defects found in each phase of software development

These metrics can be determined using the techniques and formats presented in this section. The kinds of defects found might be categorized as incorrect, incomplete, interface, logic, and so forth; see the checklist in Appendix 7B for an example of kinds of defects.

The next step in reducing defects would be to find the answers to the following kinds of questions and to take the appropriate actions:

what kinds of mistakes are being made that result in the predominant kinds of defects?

what kinds of actions should be taken first to reduce the predominant kinds of mistakes?

what kinds of actions should be taken subsequently to reduce the less prominent kinds of mistakes?

If you are fortunate to work in a well-managed organization, there will be templates, tailoring guidelines, and personnel to help you design a plan of measurement and control for your work products and work processes.

7.9 PRACTICAL SOFTWARE MEASUREMENT

Additional guidance for choosing and implementing software measures is provided on the Web site for and in the publications of Practical Software and Systems Measurement [PSM]. *Technical Measurement A Collaborative Project of PSM, INCOSE, and Industry* provides an introduction to Practical Software Measurement [Roed05]. The report is a collaborative effort between the PSM (Practical Software and Systems Measurement) and INCOSE (International Council on Systems Engineering) organizations. As stated in the report, technical measures include Measures of Effectiveness (MOEs), Key Performance Parameters (KPPs), Measures of Performance (MOPs), and Technical Performance Measures (TPMs).

- MOEs are measures of success that are independent of the particular solution used to achieve the operational objectives. An objective measure used to determine that a system is easy to learn and easy to use (or not), for a specified group of users, is an example of an MOE.
- MOPs provide insight into the performance of a specific system. Examples of MOPs are measurement of response time and throughput for a particular system.
- TPMs measure attributes of a system to determine how well a system, or some elements of a system, satisfy specified requirements. Measuring the amount of memory used versus the amount of memory allocated, as in Figure 7.11, is an example of TPM.
- KPPs are a critical subset of the performance parameters representing the most critical capabilities or characteristics. Measures of performance that are related to Essential requirements are examples of KPPs.

The relationships among MOEs, MOPs, TPMs, and KPPs as illustrated in the report, and are reproduced here in Figure 7.12.

Additional information concerning Practical Software and Systems Measurement is included in Section 5 of Appendix 7A to this chapter.

7.10 GUIDELINES FOR MEASURING AND CONTROLLING WORK PRODUCTS

The following guidelines are offered to assist you in developing and executing a plan of measurement and control of your work products:

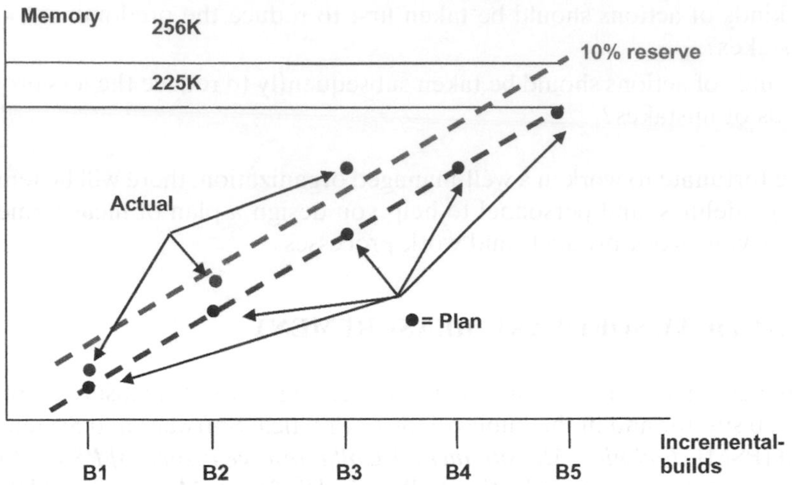

FIGURE 7.11 Technical Performance Measurement of memory usage

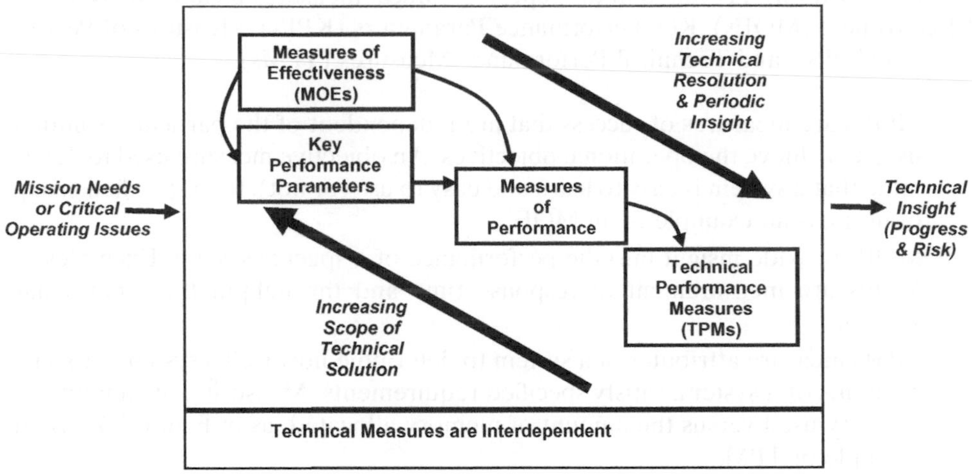

FIGURE 7.12 Relationship of the technical measures [Roed05]

G1: Configuration management of work-product baselines, based on objective acceptance criteria for work products, is essential.

G2: Time and effort spent on system engineering, requirements engineering, and design is time and effort well spent.

G3: Time and effort spent on prototyping, development of scenarios, inspections, and reviews of requirements and design is time and effort well spent.

G4: Time and effort spent on traceability among work products is time and effort well spent.

G5: Time and effort spent on developing and executing system-level verification and validation plans, based on the operational requirements and technical specifications, is time and effort well spent.

G6: Time and effort spent in finding and fixing defects as early as possible is time and effort well spent.

G7: Time and effort spent on collecting and analyzing defect data, and taking corrective action based on the analysis is time and effort well spent.

Guidelines for developing process measures are discussed in next chapter.

7.11 ROLLING-WAVE ADJUSTMENTS BASED ON PRODUCT MEASURES AND MEASUREMENT

As discussed in Chapter 5, evolution of detailed plans, based on current status, is known as the rolling-wave approach to planning. Rolling-wave planning acknowledges that it is impossible to develop plans at the level of detail indicated throughout this chapter during the initial planning phase of a project.

Examples of work activities that might be adjusted based on measures and measurements of software products include:

- remaining number of use cases to be developed,
- remaining number of scenarios to be generated,
- remaining number of prototypes to be constructed,
- remaining number of test scenarios to be generated,
- remaining number of inspections and unit tests to be conducted, and
- remaining number of integration and system tests to be conducted.

Adjustments that might be made to maintain a balance among requirements, effort, schedule, cost, and technology are discussed in Chapter 8.

7.12 KEY POINTS OF CHAPTER 7

- Periodic measurement of product attributes permits comparison of actual status to planned status.
- Control (corrective action) is exerted when actual status differs from planned status by more than a predetermined acceptable amount.
- Product and process measures are, or should be, a by-product of the procedures, tools, and techniques used to develop software, if not the development process must be modified.
- A measure is a mapping from a phenomenon of interest to a symbol.
- Different measurement scales permit different kinds of operations on the measures.
- Each work product should be verified and validated; in addition specific attributes of each kind of work product can be measured.
- Version control of work product baselines is necessary for measurement and control of work products.
- Inspections are the most cost-effective technique known to find defects in work products, especially in requirements and design when they are easily corrected.

- Inspections are used to find defects; walkthroughs are used to communicate technical issues.
- Software that is hard to understand, hard to document, hard to verify and validate, and hard to modify is too complex.
- Cyclomatic complexity, the COCOMO CPLX cost driver, and coupling and cohesion are three measures for software complexity.
- A reliability rating is the probability that a system will not fail to perform its intended functions within its intended environment for a stated period of time.
- An availability rating is the probability a system will be available for use when needed.
- Defects are the result of human mistakes; defects in an operational system cause departures from specified or expected behavior or results.
- Software failures result when defects are detected during the operation of a system by its intended users within its intended environment.
- Systematic record keeping of the defect detection and repair process permits analysis of defect containment and escape during the various phases of software development.
- The time, effort, and cost of measuring and controlling work products, like the time, effort, and cost of risk management, is an investment you make to provide early warning of problems and increase the probability of success.
- Like risk management, the amount you invest in measurement and control of work products depends on the criticality of delivering an acceptable product within the project constraints, and the cost of failing to do so.
- SEI, ISO, IEEE, PMI, and PSM-INCOSE provide frameworks, standards, and guidelines for measuring and controlling product attributes (see Appendix 7A to this chapter).
- Procedures and forms for conducting software inspections are contained in Appendix 7B to this chapter.

REFERENCES

[Basili94] Basili, V., G. Caldiera, and H. D. Rombach. The goal question metric approach. *Encyclopedia of Software Engineering*. Wiley, 1994, pp. 528–532.

[Bass03] Bass, L., P. Clements, and R. Kazman. *Software Architecture in Practice*, 2nd ed. Addison Wesley, 2003.

[Belady76] Belady, L., and M. Lehman. A model of large program development. *IBM Systems Journal* 15 (3): 225–252, 1976.

[Boehm00] Boehm, B., C. Abts, A. Brown, S. Chulani, B. Clark, E. Horowitz, R. Madachy, D. Reifer, and B. Steece. *Software Cost Estimation with COCOMO II*. Prentice Hall, 2000.

[Bush88] Bush, M. Inspection results at JPL. *Proceedings of 10th International Conference on Software Engineering*. IEEE Computer Society Press, 1998.

[IEEE1058] IEEE Std 1058™–1998. *IEEE Standard for Software Project Management Plans*. Engineering Standards Collection, IEEE Product: SE113. Institute of Electrical and Electronic Engineers, August 2003.

[IEEE12207] IEEE/EIA 12207.0/.1/.2. *Industry Implementation of International Standard ISO/IEC 12207:1995 Standard for Information Technology—Software Life Cycle Processes*. Engineering Standards Collection. IEEE Product: SE113. Institute of Electrical and Electronic Engineers, August 2003.

[Kulak03] Kulak, D., and E. Guiney. *Use Cases: Requirements in Context*, 2nd ed. Addison Wesley, 2003.

[McCabe76] McCabe, T. A complexity measure. *IEEE Transactions on Software Engineering* 2 (December 1976): 308–320.

[Mala97] Mala, Y. K., and J. Denton. What do the software reliability growth model parameters represent? *Proceedings of the 8th International Symposium on Software Reliability Engineering*. IEEE Press, November 1997.

[Myers74] Myers, G., and L. Constantine. Structured design. *IBM Systems Journal* 13 (February 1974): 115–139.

[PMI04] PMI. *A Guide to the Project Management Body of Knowledge*, 3rd ed. (PMBOK® Guide). Project Management Institute, 2004.

[Roed05] Roedler, G. J., and C. Jones. *Technical Measurement: A Collaborative Report of PSM, INCOSE, and Industry.* INCOSE-TP-2003-020-01, Version 1.1 (27 December 2005). Available at http://www.psmsc.com/Downloads/Technology Papers/TechnicalMeasurementGuide_v1.0.pdf.

[Rumb05] Rumbaugh, J., I. Jacobron, and G. Booch. *The Unified Modeling Language Reference Manual*, 2nd ed. Addison Wesley, 2005.

[Russell91] Russell, G. Experience with inspection in ultralarge-scale developments. *IEEE Software* vol. 8, No. 1. (January 1991). pp. 25–31.

URLs

[PSM] www.psmsc.com/Prod_TechPapers.asp

[SEI06] www.sei.cmu.edu/publications/documents/06.reports/06tr008.html

EXERCISES

7.1. CMMI-DEV-v1.2 lists two related process areas in the Monitoring and Controlling process area:

Project Planning, and

Measurement and Analysis.

Access the CMMI Web site at http://www.sei.cmu.edu/publications/documents/06.reports/06tr008.html, review the Monitoring and Controlling process area, and briefly explain how each of the two related process areas is related to Monitoring and Controlling.

7.2. People who play different roles in a software project need differing kinds of status reports concerning product attributes. For each of the following, list and briefly explain the kinds of product status reports that would be useful to them (assume an iterative development process):

a. customer

b. project manager

c. designers

d. programmers

e. testers

7.3. Section 7.2 lists five attributes of software projects to be measured and controlled: effort, schedule, cost, product features, and quality attributes of the product. List three other attributes of a software project that might be important to measure and control. Briefly explain why they might be important and how they might be used.

7.4. In Section 7.5 measurement of temperature is used to illustrate the difference between interval and ratio scales.

a. Celsius and Fahrenheit scales have zero values. Why are they not ratio scales?

b. Provide an example of an interval scale not mentioned in the text that is not a ratio scale. If you scale has a zero element, briefly explain why the zero element does not make it a ratio scale.

c. Provide an example of a ratio scale not mentioned in the text. Briefly explain why the zero element of your scale makes it a ratio scale.

7.5. Use the Internet to find a set of rules for counting lines of code. Briefly explain the rules.

7.6. Tables 7.3 and 7.4 list some direct and some indirect measures for software projects.

a. List the direct and indirect measures for product attributes in the tables.

b. List the direct and indirect measures for process attributes in the tables.

c. List and briefly explain three addition direct product measures that might be used in a software project.

d. List and briefly explain 3 additional indirect product measures that might be used in a software project.

7.7. Briefly explain why lines of code is a direct measure of product size. Briefly explain why function points is an indirect measure of product size.

7.8. Figure 7.3 illustrates the state diagram for the use case in Figure 7.2.

a. List the states of the state diagram that provide the primary scenario for the use case.

b. Provide names for and list the states of 3 secondary scenarios in the state diagram.

c. Name and briefly explain a missing secondary scenario that should be added to the state diagram.

7.9. In Section 7.6.2 it is stated that the CCB must have the authority to accept, defer, or deny a Change Request or a Defect Report.

a. Briefly state a circumstance under which a CCB might defer a Change Request

b. Briefly state a circumstance under which a CCB might deny a Change Request

c. Briefly state a circumstance under which a CCB might defer a Defect Report

d. Briefly state a circumstance under which a CCB might deny a Defect Report

7.10. Tables 7.6, 7.9, and 7.10 include "number of defects by category and severity level" for requirements, architectural design, and implementation, respectively.

a. List three different categories of defects for requirements.

b. List three different categories of defects for architectural design.

c. List three different categories of defects for implementation.

7.11. In the sidebar on inspections it is stated that the developer of the material being inspected (i.e., the author) should never be the reader. Briefly explain why this is a good rule.

7.12. Refer to Figure 7.6.

a. How many test cases will be required to obtain branch coverage?

b. How many test cases will be required to obtain path coverage? (*Hint*: Let N be the number of traversals of the loop.)

c. What is the cyclomatic complexity number of the graph? What is the relationship of the answers to a and b to the cyclomatic complexity of the graph?

7.13. Select a program of your choosing (or a program chosen by your instructor).

a. Construct a control flow graph for one of the modules in the program.

b. Calculate the cyclomatic complexity number for one of the modules in the program.

c. Construct the design flow graph for the program.

d. Calculate the design complexity of the program.

e. Assess and assign a value of Very Low, Low, Nominal, High, or Very High to each of the five complexity factors used to determine CPLX in a COCOMO II model for the program. Briefly explain why you chose the values you assigned to each of the five factors. (*Hint*: See Table II-15, page 31, at ftp://ftp.usc.edu/pub/soft_engineering/COCOMOII/cocomo99.0/modelman.pdf.)

f. Assess and assign a value of Low, Medium, or High to the cohesion of each module in the program. Briefly explain why you chose your assigned values.

g. Assess and assign a value of Low, Medium, or High to the coupling of each module in the program. Briefly explain why you chose your assigned values.

7.14. A system having an MTTF of 80 hours with as standard deviation of 2 hours would probably be rated higher in reliability than a system having an MTTF of 80 hours and a standard deviation of 40 hours. Briefly explain why this would be true.

7.15. The workflow model in Figure 7.11 indicates that every defect found during acceptance of a work product or found in a baselined work product should be reported using a Defect Report. Briefly explain a circumstance under which a DR might not be filed for a detected defect. Briefly explain the problems that might be created by not filing a DR.

7.16. Refer to Table 7.23.

a. What percentage of total defects were design defects?

b. What percentage of defects found by users (Ops) were requirements defects?

APPENDIX 7A

FRAMEWORKS, STANDARDS, AND GUIDELINES FOR MEASURING AND CONTROLLING WORK PRODUCTS

7A.1 THE CMMI-DEV-v1.2 MONITORING AND CONTROL PROCESS AREA

> The purpose of Project Monitoring and Control is to provide an understanding of the project's progress so that appropriate corrective actions can be taken when the project's performance deviates significantly from the plan.

The specific goals and specific practices of Monitoring and Control in CMMI-DEV-v1.2 are [SEI06]:

SG 1 Monitor project against plan
- SP 1.1 Monitor project planning parameters
- SP 1.2 Monitor commitments
- SP 1.3 Monitor project risks
- SP 1.4 Monitor data management
- SP 1.5 Monitor stakeholder involvement
- SP 1.6 Conduct progress reviews
- SP 1.7 Conduct milestone reviews

SG 2 Manage corrective action to closure
- SP 2.1 Analyze issues
- SP 2.2 Take corrective action
- SP 2.3 Manage corrective action

There are two related process areas in the CMMI-DEV-v1.2:

1. Project Planning and
2. Measurement and Analysis.

The Project Planning process area is covered in appendixes to Chapters 5 and 6 of this text.

The specific goals and specific practices of Measurement and Analysis are:

SG 1 Align measurement and analysis activities
- SP 1.1 Establish measurement objectives
- SP 1.2 Specify measures
- SP 1.3 Specify data collection and storage procedures
- SP 1.4 Specify analysis procedures

SG 2 Provide measurement results
- SP 2.1 Collect measurement data
- SP 2.2 Analyze measurement data
- SP 2.3 Store data and results
- SP 2.4 Communicate results

7A.2 ISO/IEC AND IEEE/EIA STANDARDS 12207

ISO/EIC and IEEE/EIA Standards 12207 include Supplier Monitoring as an element of the acquirer's acquisition process and Execution and Control as a supplier activity [IEEE12207]. The acquirer's monitoring activity is specified in section 5.1.4 of 12207.0, Supplier monitoring. Section 5.1.4.1 indicates that the acquirer will monitor the supplier using the Joint Review Process and the Audit Process, plus the Verification Process and the Validation Process as necessary.

The Supplier's Execution and Control activities (section 5.2.5) include monitoring and controlling progress and the quality of work products throughout the project life cycle. This iterative activity should include monitoring of technical performance, costs, and schedules and the reporting of project status. In addition problems should be identified, recorded, analyzed, and resolved.

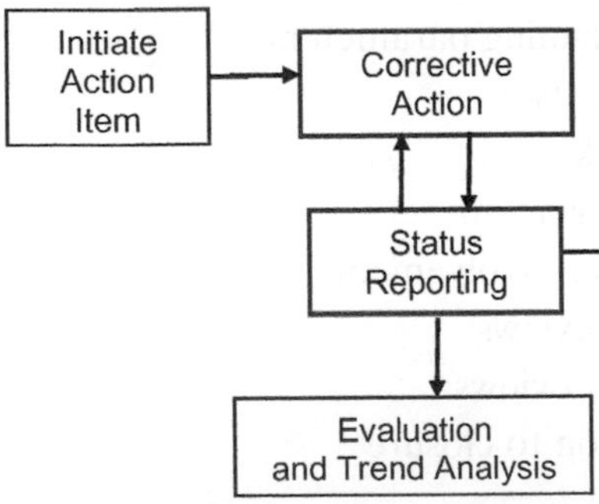

FIGURE 7A.1 Closed loop problem resolution

Section 6.8 of 12207.0, Problem Resolution states that the problem resolution system should:

- be closed loop,
- contain a scheme for categorizing and prioritizing problems,

- include a trend analysis procedure, and
- provide for evaluation of problem resolutions and dispositions.

The closed loop nature of problem resolution is illustrated in Figure 7A.1 of this Appendix.

7A.3 IEEE/EIA STANDARD 1058

Clause 5.3 of IEEE Standard 1058-1998 for Software Project Management Plans (SPMPs) indicates that plans for controlling the following attributes of a project should be included in your project plan [IEEE1058]:

- requirements
- schedule
- budget
- quality

In addition SPMPs that conform to IEEE 1058 will contain a Metrics collection plan and a Reporting plan. The Risk Management plan is contained in clause 5.4.

7A.4 THE PMI BODY OF KNOWLEDGE

The PMI Body of Knowledge (PMBOK®) includes the following chapters related to measuring and controlling a project [PMI04]:

- Chapter 5 Project Scope Management
- Chapter 6 Project Time Management
- Chapter 7 Project Cost Management
- Chapter 8 Project Quality Management
- Chapter 9 Project Human Resource Management
- Chapter 10 Project Communication Management
- Chapter 11 of PMBOK® covers Project Risk Management.

7A.5 PRACTICAL SOFTWARE AND SYSTEMS MEASUREMENT (PSM)

The report *Technical Measurement: A Collaborative Report of PSM, INCOSE, and Industry* is the result of a collaborative effort between the PSM (Practical Software and Systems Measurement) and INCOSE (International Council on Systems Engineering) organizations [Roed05]. The report provides guidance for choosing and implementing technical measures for software and systems projects. An introduction to Practical Software and Systems Measurement is presented in Section 7.8 of this chapter.

APPENDIX 7B

PROCEDURES AND FORMS FOR SOFTWARE INSPECTIONS

7B.1 CONDUCTING A SOFTWARE INSPECTION

There are five (or six) steps to an inspection:

1. Conduct a short Planning Meeting to assign team roles and schedule a time and place for the Inspection Meeting. (Optional step: Have a walkthrough of the document to be reviewed, led by the author, if necessary to familiarize participants.)
2. Prepare for the Inspection Meeting by using a Checklist and completing a *personal* Individual Preparation Log.
3. Team members attend the Inspection Meeting, limited to 2 hours.
4. Team members assist the author, as requested in follow-up activities.
5. After rework, the moderator and author meet to prepare the inspection summary report.

A flow diagram for the inspection process is illustrated in Figure 7B.1.

Details of each step follow:

Step 1

The moderator and author meet to plan the inspection: who should participate; what materials should be distributed to the participants and available for their reference; is the author's material ready for inspection?

Step 2

Have a Planning Meeting for your team to distribute inspection materials and to assign roles to the team members. The author should provide an overview of material to be reviewed, and if necessary to familiarize the participants. Also a time and place for the Inspection Meeting is scheduled. The Review Meeting should be held a few days after the Planning Meeting to allow time for Individual Preparation, but not so long that everyone forgets their preparation. The Inspection Meeting should be planned for 2 hours.

There are four team roles for the four team members. One person will be the *Moderator*, whose job is to be the chairperson of the Inspection Meeting and to prepare the final Review Package *with the help of the Author*. Another person will be the *Reader*, whose job is to paraphrase the document being reviewed during the Inspection Meeting. One person will be *Recorder*. The Recorder's role is to record on an Inspection Defect List defects discovered during the Inspection Meeting. The Author of the document to be reviewed attends the meeting to listen and answer questions. All team members are Document Inspectors.

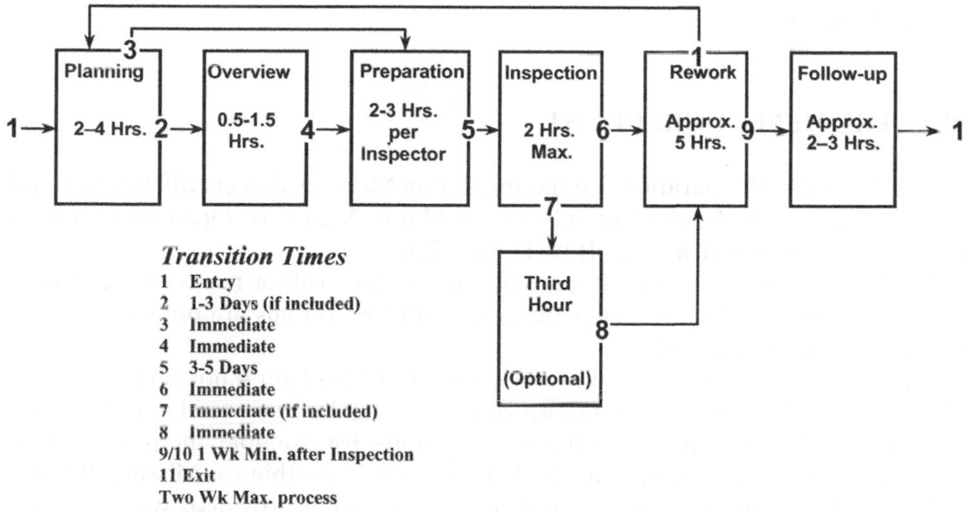

FIGURE 7B.1 Flow diagram for the inspection process

Step 3

Individual Preparation: Each person should plan to spend 2 to 3 hours preparing for the Inspection Meeting by studying the document to be inspected and recording discovered defects on an Individual Preparation Log. A Defect Checklist should be used during individual preparation.

Step 4

The Inspection Meeting: During the Inspection Meeting, the Reader will present the document by paraphrasing (summarizing) it. All team members, including the Moderator, Reader, Recorder, and Author, will contribute the defects they found during individual preparation and will (perhaps) discover new defects. *See the instructions for conducting an inspection meeting in 7B.3.* Defects will be recorded by the recorder on the Inspection Defect List and each defect will be categorized in four ways: (1) by Finders' initials; (2) as Major, Minor, or Open Issue;

(3) as Missing, Wrong, or Extra; and (4) by Defect Type. *See the included Inspection Defect List for more information.*

Step 5

Follow-up: After the meeting, the Author will correct the defects found during the inspection, with assistance if requested. This should be finished in two or three days.

Step 6

Preparing the Inspection Report: After the defects are corrected, the Author and Moderator prepare the Review Package. The Review Package includes a Cover Sheet, the Inspection Defect List, Individual Preparation Logs, and the Inspection Summary Report.

7B.2 THE DEFECT CHECKLIST

During Individual Preparation and the Inspection Meeting, defects will be classified in four ways: (1) by Finders' initials; (2) as Major, Minor, or Open Issue; (3) as Missing, Wrong, or Extra; and (4) by Defect Type.

The Finders' Initials are for traceability in case the Author needs to speak with the Finder(s) of a defect at a later time. The Finders' Initials are *not* for counting who found the most defects.

A Major defect is one that will cause serious problems later if not corrected now; a Minor defect is one that must be corrected, but it can be corrected later. An Open Issue is something that needs further investigation—for example, the possibility of a mistake in another document or whether to classify something as Missing, Wrong, or Extra. Missing means some needed information is not provided; Wrong means the information is incorrect, and Extra means the information is unnecessary. Extra could be requirements for features the users don't need, or information that belongs in another document, such as schedule and budget information or personnel assignments.

The Defect Checklist is different for different types of documents. An example checklist for Code Inspections is:

- C1. Functionality—implementation of the design in the code
- C2. Logic—inputs, outputs, loop tests, branch tests, nesting, calls and returns among modules
- C3. Data Usage—declarations, initializations, assignments and uses
- C4. Interfaces—matching of argument lists and other interfaces, return codes
- C5. Clarity—comment blocks, commenting, variable names, indentation, white space
- C6. Maintainability—ease of understanding, traceability to detailed design, coupling and cohesion, change history in the comments header block
- C7. Syntax—use of symbols and punctuation (note: a clean compile should be inspected)

C8. Files—declarations, opening, closing
C9. Style—use of comment headers and in-line comments, guidelines for coding style
C10. Other—defects that are not of the listed defect types

Types of Open Issues include:

O1: Questionable changes to the design in the code
O2: Packaging of the code modules
O3: Other open issues

Checklists should be tailored to the needs of the particular project and organization.

7B.3 CONDUCTING AN INSPECTION MEETING

1. The Moderator first states the purpose of the meeting and describes the document to be reviewed. The Moderator then asks each person how much time they spent preparing for the Review Meeting and ensures that everyone is prepared. If someone is not prepared, that person is excused or the meeting is rescheduled.
2. The Moderator asks the Reader to begin. The Reader presents a brief overview of the document and paraphrases the first section. The Moderator asks if there are any comments on that section. Each team member uses their Individual Preparation Log to contribute comments. (*If there are several comments, the Moderator asks each person, in turn, to contribute one comment.*) The Moderator leads a team discussion to determine whether the comment is to be accepted as a defect. If so, the initials of the Finder(s) is recorded, and the defect category is decided by the team: (Missing, Wrong, Extra); (Major, Minor, Open Issue); and Defect Type. The recorder enters the information on an Inspection Defect List and make additional notes as necessary. Before continuing, the Moderator asks if there are any additional comments. This continues until all comments are discussed. The Moderator then asks the next person if they have a defect to contribute; this continues until all defects are recorded for that section of the document.
3. The Moderator then asks the Reader to present the next section and the process described in step 2 is repeated until the review of the document is finished.
4. After the document review is finished, the Moderator collects the Inspection Defect List from the Recorder and reviews it with the team to be sure the team agrees on the defects discovered *and* to be sure that the defects are described in a way that everyone (especially the author, who will correct them) can understand them.
5. The team helps the Moderator prepare the Inspection Summary Report.

6. The Moderator then collates the Review Package, which includes the Cover Sheet, the Individual Preparation Logs, the Inspection Defect Lists, and the Inspection Summary Report.

Everyone must remember that the purpose of the Meeting is to find defects, *not* to fix them. It is the Moderator's job to maintain a productive meeting and to finish the meeting in two hours. The Moderator must keep the meeting moving, but not so fast that Major defects are missed.

The Author of the document receives a copy of the Inspection Defect List at the end of the meeting. The Author and other team members are assigned Action Items to be completed within one week. The Author might ask some team members to spend an informal "third hour" following the Review Meeting to help the Author, *but only if the author asks for help*.

After the Author has fixed the Major defects (and maybe the Minors also), she meets with the Moderator to verify that the Major defects have been fixed and to complete the Summary Report. The Moderator also checks on the status of any Open Issues and generates official Action Items for any remaining work to be done before submitting copies of the Summary Report to the Software Architect and the Chief Moderator. This meeting should occur within 5 to 10 days following the inspection meeting.

INDIVIDUAL PREPARATION LOG

Name____________________

Project ____________________ Date Package Received___________

Inspection Type: e.g., *Software Code* Completion Date_________________

PREPARATION TIME	Date	Time Spent
	______________	______________
	______________	______________
	______________	______________
	______________	______________

TOTAL HOURS & MINUTES: _________

DEFECTS/OPEN ISSUES

#	Location (line number)	Type & Description
1	__________________	______________________________
		______________________________
2	__________________	______________________________
		______________________________
3	__________________	______________________________
		______________________________
4	__________________	______________________________
		______________________________
5	__________________	______________________________
		______________________________
6	__________________	______________________________
		______________________________
7	__________________	______________________________
		______________________________
8	__________________	______________________________
		______________________________

NOTE: Add more pages as needed

INSPECTION REPORT COVER SHEET

Inspection ID #______________________ Inspection Date:__________

Project:___________________________

Moderator:___________________ Phone No:___________

e-mail:______________

Component:_______________________

Is this a Re-inspection? _____yes _____no

Inspector	Phone No.	Role	Inspection Type
__________	______	__________	System Requirements:____
__________	______	__________	Software Requirements:___
__________	______	__________	Architectural Design:____
__________	______	__________	Detailed Design:________
__________	______	__________	Source Code:__________
__________	______	__________	Test Plan:____________
__________	______	__________	Test Results:__________
__________	______	__________	Other:______________

Size of Work Product Inspected: _________________

Reference

Documents:____

____

____

Comments

____

____

____

____

____

Is a Re-inspection after rework recommended? _____yes _____no

INSPECTION DEFECT LIST
(for use by recorder and author)

Project:______________________ Moderator:______________

Component:____________________ Recorder:______________

Inspection Type:_______________ Inspection ID #__________

Defect #	Location	Defect Type #	Classification	Finder's Initials	Date Corrected**
#1	________	_____	Major Minor Open / Missing Wrong Extra	________	________
Description:________					
#2	________	_____	Major Minor Open / Missing Wrong Extra	________	________
Description:________					
#3	________	_____	Major Minor Open / Missing Wrong Extra	________	________
Description:________					
#4	________	_____	Major Minor Open / Missing Wrong Extra	________	________
Description:________					
#5	________	_____	Major Minor Open / Missing Wrong Extra	________	________
Description:________					
#6	________	_____	Major Minor Open / Missing Wrong Extra	________	________
Description:________					
#7	________	_____	Major Minor Open / Missing Wrong Extra	________	________
Description:________					
#8	________	_____	Major Minor Open / Missing Wrong Extra	________	________
Description:________					
#9	________	_____	Major Minor Open / Missing Wrong Extra	________	________
Description:________					
#10	________	_____	Major Minor Open / Missing Wrong Extra	________	________
Description:________					

Inspection ID #__________

Page__________ of __________ pages

Defect #	Location	Defect Type #	Classification	Finder's Initials	Date Corrected**
#11	________	______	Major Minor Open / Missing Wrong Extra	________	________

Description:____

Defect #	Location	Defect Type #	Classification	Finder's Initials	Date Corrected**
#12	________	______	Major Minor Open / Missing Wrong Extra	________	________

Description:____

Defect #	Location	Defect Type #	Classification	Finder's Initials	Date Corrected**
#13	________	______	Major Minor Open / Missing Wrong Extra	________	________

Description:____

Defect #	Location	Defect Type #	Classification	Finder's Initials	Date Corrected**
#14	________	______	Major Minor Open / Missing Wrong Extra	________	________

Description:____

Defect #	Location	Defect Type #	Classification	Finder's Initials	Date Corrected**
#15	________	______	Major Minor Open / Missing Wrong Extra	________	________

Description:____

Defect #	Location	Defect Type #	Classification	Finder's Initials	Date Corrected**
#16	________	______	Major Minor Open / Missing Wrong Extra	________	________

Description:____

Defect #	Location	Defect Type #	Classification	Finder's Initials	Date Corrected**
#17	________	______	Major Minor Open / Missing Wrong Extra	________	________

Description:____

Defect #	Location	Defect Type #	Classification	Finder's Initials	Date Corrected**
#18	________	______	Major Minor Open / Missing Wrong Extra	________	________

Description:____

Defect #	Location	Defect Type #	Classification	Finder's Initials	Date Corrected**
#19	________	______	Major Minor Open / Missing Wrong Extra	________	________

Description:____

Defect #	Location	Defect Type #	Classification	Finder's Initials	Date Corrected**
#20	________	______	Major Minor Open / Missing Wrong Extra	________	________

Description:____

Note: Re-inspection following rework is recommended if more than 20 defects are found.

To be completed after Re-work:

Specified completion date for rework:____________

Actual completion date for rework:______________

Time spent by Author in Re-work:______________ (hours)

INSPECTION SUMMARY REPORT

Inspection ID #______________________ Inspection Date:__________

Project:______________________________ Moderator:______________

Component:_________________________ Phone No:_____________

Is this a Re-Inspection?_____yes _____no e-mail:________________

Inspection Type:

System Requirements:___ Software Requirements: ___ Architectural Design: ___

Detailed Design: ___ Source Code___ Test Plan: ___ Test Results: ___ Other: ___

Size of Work Product:____________

Total Person-Hours Expended (m.n):

	Planning	Overview	Individual Preparation	Meeting	Rework	Follow-Up	Third-Hour	Total
Inspectors								
Moderator								
Author(s)								

MAJOR DEFECTS

Number of Missing Type Defects Detected:_______ Number Corrected:_______

Number of Wrong Type Defects Detected:________ Number Corrected:_______

Number of Extra Type Defects Detected:_________ Number Corrected:_______

TOTAL MAJOR DEFECTS:__________________

MINOR DEFECTS

Number of Missing Type Defects Detected:_______ Number Corrected:_______

Number of Wrong Type Defects Detected:________ Number Corrected:_______

Number of Extra Type Defects Detected:_________ Number Corrected:_______

TOTAL MINOR DEFECTS:__________________

Open Issues:

Issue:_____________________________ Assignee:__________________

Issue:_____________________________ Assignee:__________________

Issue:_____________________________ Assignee:__________________

8

MEASURING AND CONTROLLING WORK PROCESSES

You can see a lot just by looking.
—Yogi Berra

8.1 INTRODUCTION TO MEASURING AND CONTROLLING WORK PROCESSES

An introduction to measures, measurement, and control is presented in Chapter 7, Sections 7.1 and 7.2. Those sections should be read as background material for this chapter.

There are several reasons to measure various attributes of your work processes:

- to provide frequent indicators of progress,
- to provide early warning of problems,
- to permit analysis of trends for your project,
- to allow estimates of the final cost and completion date of your project, and
- to build a data repository of project histories for your organization.

The workflow model for software projects depicted in Figure 1.1 (Chapter 1) and repeated as Figure 7.1 illustrates the roles of measurement and control in software projects. Measuring, reporting, replanning, and controlling are highlighted in Figure 7.1. Measurement of project status involves determining the current values and cumulative values of various project attributes. As related in Chapter 7, it is

Managing and Leading Software Projects, by Richard E. Fairley

difficult to imagine a project for which some level of measurement and control over each of the following attributes is not important to assure a successful outcome:

- effort: amount of work expended for various work activities
- schedule: achievement of objectively measured milestones
- cost: expenditures for various kinds of resources, including effort
- progress: work products completed, accepted, and baselined
- product features: requirements implemented and demonstrated to work
- quality attributes of the product: defects, reliability, availability, response time, throughput, and others as specified
- risk: status of risk factors and mitigation activities

Measured values of these project attributes are compared to planned or specified values for each measurement interval specified in your project plan. Control is exerted when actual values deviate from planned or specified values by more than an acceptable amount; being two days late in achieving a major milestone may be acceptable, being two weeks late is probably not acceptable, but being two months late is certainly not acceptable.

Depending on the relative importance of the various process and product attributes of your project, more effort may be expended on measuring and controlling some attributes than on measuring and controlling others. Performance and reliability of the delivered software may be the most important product criteria or it may be that controlling schedule and cost of the project needed to deliver a minimally acceptable product are uppermost. However, it is difficult to imagine a project in which some level of control over effort, schedule, cost, product features, and the specified quality attributes of the product do not all contribute to a successful outcome, although some attributes may be more or less important than others.

Typically the process attributes (effort, schedule, and cost) are balanced against product attributes (features and quality attributes). Among the process attributes, schedule may be more important than effort and cost, and safety may be a more important product attribute than reliability. Measurement and control of effort, schedule, cost, and progress are covered in this chapter. Managing the risk factors related to product and process attributes is covered in Chapter 9.

Effort, cost, and schedule have common attributes, and each has unique attributes. The common attributes of effort, schedule, and cost to be measured and controlled include the amount and percentage of each that you are spending on various project activities, including project management, analysis, and design and implementation, as well as verification, validation, and other supporting activities. You should compare measured values to planned values and expected values, the latter being derived from historical data and local rules of thumb.

For example, projects in your organization might typically spend 5% to 10% of total effort on measurement and control of project attributes. If you are spending more, or less, you should determine why this is the case and apply corrective action as appropriate. It may be, for example, that you are spending 15% to 20% of effort on measurement and control because your organization is converting from a Waterfall development process to Iterative development and your project is the first one to implement the new approach; the amount of effort you are spending on measurement and control is thus appropriate.

On the other hand, if you are spending less than 5% of effort on measurement and control, it may be that you are not spending enough time on measurement and control or that your (large) project does not have enough personnel assigned to your project management group to do an effective job of measuring and controlling.

Relationships among effort, schedule, and cost should also be measured and controlled. For example, it may be that you expect to spend 30% of effort and 40% of your schedule on requirements and design. If significantly more or less of either is being spent, you should determine the reasons and take corrective action, as indicated. The relationship between effort and personnel cost should also be measured and controlled. If, in a given reporting period, effort is as planned but personnel cost is higher than planned, you are using more expensive (more highly skilled) software developers than planned. The cost overrun may, of course, be because the work is more difficult than anticipated or because the work to be done by highly skilled analysts and designers is taking longer than planned.

Conversely, if, in a given reporting period, effort is as planned but personnel costs are lower than planned, it may be that you have been unable to acquire the needed skill levels or that the work is easier than planned and the highly skilled (highly paid) personnel are not needed. If effort and cost are both less than planned, this may indicate that you have not been able to acquire the planned number of software developers, so schedule progress is slower than planned. Or, it may be that effort and cost are higher than planned because of a desire to accelerate schedule progress.

Other costs should also be measured and compared to plans. Travel cost may be higher (or lower) than planned; equipment costs may similarly deviate from plan. In any case, you will need to investigate these deviations from plan.

Possibilities for corrective action, when actual values of project attributes are not as planned or expected, include:

- extending the schedule,
- adding more resources,
- using superior resources,
- improving various elements of the development process, and/or
- de-scoping the product requirements.

Resources that might be improved, added, or replaced include:

- people (be mindful of Brooks's law when adding people),
- software components (e.g., re-engineering a software component to improve performance),
- hardware components (e.g., more memory, a faster processor), and
- software tools (e.g., a language processor or testing tool).

You should never use the following techniques to "get a project back on track:"

- excessive levels and durations of overtime;
- reduction or elimination of planned verification and validation activities;
- reduction or elimination of planned user documentation, training aids, and so forth; or
- reduction or elimination of any planned activity that would reduce the features or quality attributes of the system to be delivered without the customer's consent.

8.2 OBJECTIVES OF THIS CHAPTER

This chapter presents methods and techniques for measuring and controlling work processes (measurement and control of work products were presented in Chapter 7). After reading this chapter and completing the exercises you should understand how to:

- measure and analyze original effort, evolutionary rework, and avoidable rework;
- use work packages to track effort, schedule, and work products;
- use binary tracking to avoid the 90% complete syndrome, and to thus accurately determine the status of effort, schedule, and work products, and to estimate effort and schedule to complete a project;
- use earned value reporting, based on binary tracking, to provide succinct and accurate reports of effort, schedule, and work progress; and
- use earned value techniques to forecast estimated actual cost and estimated completion date for software projects.

As related in Chapter 7, CMMI-DEV-v1.2, ISO/IEEE Standard 12207, IEEE Standard 1058, and the PMBOK Guide of PMI all provide guidance for measurement and control of software projects. See Appendix 7A in Chapter 7.

Terms used in this chapter and throughout this text are defined in the Glossary at the end of the text. Presentation slides for this chapter and other supporting material are available at the URL listed in the Preface.

8.3 MEASURING AND ANALYZING EFFORT

As illustrated in Figure 8.1, there are three categories of effort [Fairley05]:

- original work,
- evolutionary rework, and
- avoidable rework (retrospective and corrective).

Original work is the effort expended in establishing initial baselines of work products (e.g., requirements, design, code, test plans). Evolutionary rework is the effort you spend to change baselined work products in ways that add value to an

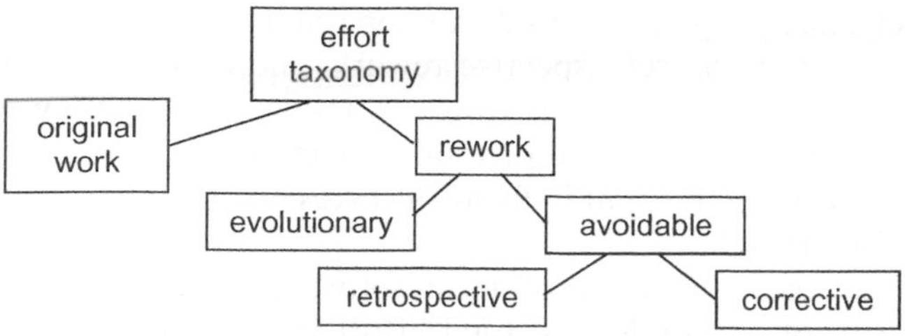

FIGURE 8.1 A taxonomy of project effort

evolving product or system. For example, the design and some of the code may have to be reworked because of a change in requirements that results from analysis of a competitor's new product or from a change of mission for a customer's mission-critical system.

Avoidable rework is rework required to make changes to baselined work products developed during original work or evolutionary rework. In principle, avoidable rework (as the name implies) is work that should not have to be done. Because humans are not infallible, some small amount of avoidable rework is, unavoidable. As indicated in Figure 8.1, there are two kinds of avoidable rework: retrospective and corrective. Retrospective rework occurs in Waterfall development, for example, when the code has to be reworked because defects found during software verification make it an unsuitable basis for system validation. Retrospective rework occurs in iterative development when a baselined work product has to be reworked to accommodate the needs of a subsequent iteration. In iterative development, for example, an interface in baselined code might have to be redesigned and recoded to provide a basis for the code of the next iteration that is to be integrated into the growing product baseline. Excessive amounts of retrospective rework may indicate the need for more attention to the design of interfaces, for example.

Corrective rework occurs when a defect discovered in a baselined work product is corrected. Because corrective rework is the result of defects made by human mistakes, and because humans are human, a certain amount of avoidable rework is to be expected. A large percentage of total effort devoted to avoidable rework, like a high fever in a sick person, is a problem in itself; more significantly, it is an indicator of other serious problems. In the case of software projects, unacceptably high levels of avoidable rework are a symptom of inefficient and ineffective work processes.

Refactoring of software during iterative development provides an example of the distinctions among evolutionary rework, retrospective rework, and corrective rework. Evolutionary rework occurs when refactoring of existing software is done to accommodate new requirements that could not be foreseen in an iterative development process. Retrospective rework occurs when a foreseen feature needed as a basis for the current iteration is not included in the previous iteration and thus has to be added now. Retrospective rework usually requires more effort than would have been required to include the needed feature during the previous iteration. Corrective rework occurs in an iterative development process when mistakes are discovered in work products that have been reviewed, tested, and accepted.

Unfortunately, many organizations do not separately measure and report original work, evolutionary rework, retrospective rework, and corrective rework, and are thus unaware of how project resources are being spent. In many organizations, avoidable rework is 50% and more of total project effort; in these organizations, half or more of effort is thus spent in fixing mistakes made by the software developers [Basili94], [Boehm01].

Avoidable rework is the bane of most software development organizations. Avoidable rework of 5% or less of total effort is attained in the best software organizations; 20% or less avoidable rework is achievable and should be a goal for all software organizations, including yours [Fairley05].

Because software development is effort-intensive, reducing avoidable rework improves the productivity and morale of the workers and the quality of work products. Because avoidable rework consumes project resources that could be devoted to original work or evolutionary rework, reducing avoidable rework improves productivity. Because software developers can spend their time doing high-quality original work and evolutionary rework rather than correcting mistakes, their morale improves. Because a certain percentage of defects will escape the development process and be found by users, reducing avoidable rework also improves the quality of the delivered software. If, for example, avoidable rework during development corrects 200 defects and an additional 5% of development defects are found by users during the first year of operation, the users will find approximately 10 defects during the first year. On the other hand, if avoidable rework fixes 20 defects during software development, users will find 1 defect.

The amounts of, and ratios among, the four kinds of work (original work, evolutionary rework, retrospective rework, corrective rework) should be separately measured, analyzed, and reported periodically. Measurement may reveal that large amounts of evolutionary rework are being performed without appropriate changes to the baselined plan for effort and schedule, or that corrective rework is a significant fraction of total effort. Because evolutionary rework is value-adding, it should not be a problem for you, the project manager, provided corresponding adjustments are made to plans for effort, schedule, and other resources needed to accommodate the changes. Evolutionary rework can be a big problem when value-adding changes to the product or system are mandated without corresponding adjustments to other project attributes. Avoidable rework is always a problem.

You can measure the amount of effort for each kind of work by tracking:

- work packages for original work from your WBS,
- effort resulting from change requests for evolutionary rework, and
- effort resulting from defect reports for retrospective rework and corrective rework.

Your configuration management system can provide the data needed to produce the status reports (see Chapters 3 and 7).

Work packages (presented in Chapter 5) are a mechanism for documenting the tasks in a work breakdown structure. Original work can be tracked by augmenting the work package templates, as indicated in Table 8.1, to include fields for recording actual amounts of effort, schedule, and resources expended, and actual work

TABLE 8.1 A work package template augmented to report planned versus actual outcomes

Task ID:	≪WBS number≫
Task identifier:	≪WBS name≫
Task description:	≪brief description≫
Estimated duration:	≪days or weeks≫
Resources needed:	
Personnel:	≪numbers of people needed to complete this task≫
Skills:	≪personnel skills needed to complete this task≫
Tools:	≪software and hardware needed≫
Travel:	≪to where? for how long?≫
Other:	≪other resources needed to complete this task≫
Predecessor tasks:	≪to be completed before this task can begin≫
Successor tasks:	≪can be started after this task is completed≫
Work products:	≪outputs of this task≫
Baselines:	≪work products to be placed under version control≫
Risk factors:	≪potential problems for this task≫
Acceptance criteria:	≪for the work products of this task≫
Starting date:	*planned* ____________ *actual* ____________
Ending date:	*planned* ____________ *actual* ____________
Personnel:	*planned* ____________ *actual* ____________
Other resources:	*planned* ____________ *actual* ____________
Work products:	*planned* ____________ *actual* ____________

products produced. Because each work package produces one or more work products that are placed under baseline control after they satisfy their acceptance criteria, templates for recording actual values can be provided as part of the check-in process to the configuration management system. A work package that uses binary tracking is not closed (i.e., a task is not completed) until the work products satisfy their acceptance criteria and the augmented values are provided. Then the actual results can be compared to planned results for each completed task and for collections completed of tasks.

8.4 MEASURING AND ANALYZING REWORK EFFORT

Rework matrices, similar in format to the defect matrix presented in Chapter 7, can be used to record and analyze rework effort. A template for rework matrices is presented in Table 8.2 and an example of a corrective rework matrix is presented in Table 8.4; the matrix is for a system that has been in operation for 12 months. Note that copies of the template in Table 8.2 can be used to separately report evolutionary, retrospective, and corrective rework.

Table 8.3 provides a partial legend for the entries in Table 8.2, and these descriptions should be sufficient to explain the remaining entries. The phase "a particular kind of rework" in Table 8.3 means one of evolutionary rework, retrospective rework, or corrective rework.

TABLE 8.2 A template for rework matrices

Kind of Rework: ___ evolutionary ___ retrospective ___ corrective

Work Product:	Rqmts.	Design	Imple.	Verif.	Valid.	Ops.	Totals
	Phase When Rework Occurs:						
Rqmts.	RRr	RRd	RRi	RRve	RRva	RRo	Σ RqR
Design		DRd	DRi	DRve	DRva	DRo	Σ DeR
Imple.			IRi	IRve	IRva	IRo	Σ ImR
Verif.				VEve	VEva	VEo	Σ VeR
Valid.					VAva	VAo	Σ VaR
Totals	Σ RqT	Σ DeT	Σ ImT	Σ VeT	Σ VaT	Σ VaO	TOTAL

TABLE 8.3 A partial legend for Table 8.2

Rework	Kind of Rework
RRr	A particular kind of rework of requirements during requirements acceptance for baselining
RRd	A particular kind of rework of requirements during a design activity
RRi	A particular kind of rework of requirements during an implementation activity
RRve	A particular kind of rework of requirements during a verification activity
RRva	A particular kind of rework of requirements during a validation activity
ΣRqR	All requirements rework of a particular kind during all software development activities
ΣImT	All rework of a particular kind during an implementation activity
TOTAL	All rework of a particular kind during all software development activities

TABLE 8.4 Rework effort in staff-hours for a hypothetical, but realistic, software product

Rework Reported: ___ evolutionary ___ retrospective ___×___ corrective ___ total

Kind of Rework:	Rqmts.	Design	Imple.	Verif.	Valid.	Ops.	Totals
	Phase When Rework Occurs:						
Rqmts.	200	150	130	120	138	300	1038
Design		360	299	300	365	701	2025
Imple.			800	800	920	1000	3520
Verif.				60	150	0	210
Valid.					70	0	70
Totals:	200	510	1229	1280	1643	2001	6863

Table 8.4 provides an example of a rework-effort matrix for a hypothetical but realistic software product during development and the first 12 months of operation.

Note, for example, the large amount of rework effort in Table 8.4 required to correct requirements defects that were not found during requirements work activities (1038–200: ~80%). Also note that the 3 requirements defects found by users (Table 8.5) requires more effort than the 50 found during review of the requirements

(300 staff-hours vs. 200). On the other hand, the largest percentages of rework effort was for defects found by users; 29% of all corrective rework occurred during the first 12 months of system operation (2001/6863). Assuming a work month is 152 staff-hours and that a work-year consists of 11 staff-months per person, maintenance fixes during the first year required approximately 1.2 FTE personnel (2001/[11*152]).

An alternative approach to determining rework effort can be based on a defect matrix such as the one illustrated in Table 8.5 and an exponential rework model such as the one depicted in Figure 8.2.

Figure 8.2 is normalized to 1 staff-hour to fix a defect that is found during requirements work activities, 1.5 staff-hour to fix the defect during design, 2.5 staff-hour to fix it during implementation, 5 staff-hour during software verification, 10 staff-hour during system validation, and 25 staff-hours if found by users (i.e., during operation of the system). Figure 8.2 is realistic but should be verified or corrected using your local historical data. Many organizations report even greater exponential growth in effort required to fix defects.

If it takes more (or less) than 1 staff-hour to fix a defect that is found during a requirements phase, the effort to fix the defect should be multiplied by that factor. For example, if it takes 4 staff-hours to fix a requirements defect during requirements acceptance, it will 100 staff-hours to fix it if found by users (4×25).

TABLE 8.5 An example of a defect matrix for a completed project

	Phases When Defects Found:						
Kinds of Defects:	Rqmts.	Design	Imple.	Verif.	Valid.	Ops.	Totals
Rqmts.	50	25	13	6	3	3	100
Design		60	30	15	8	7	120
Imple.			80	40	20	10	150
Verif.				6	3	0	9
Valid.					7	0	7
Totals:	50	85	123	67	41	20	386

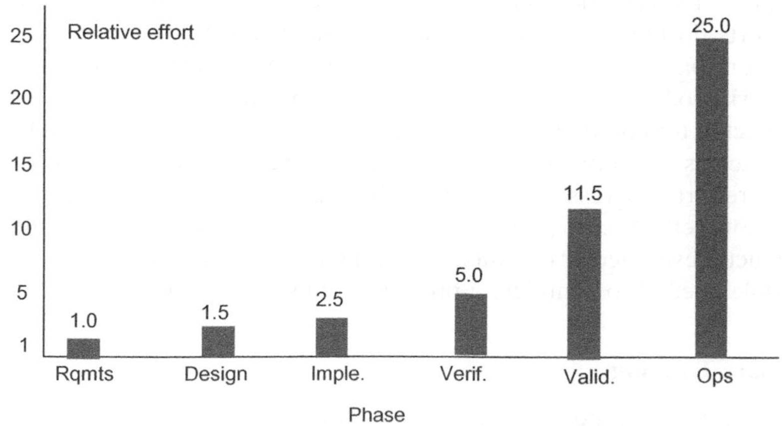

FIGURE 8.2 Relative effort to fix a defect

TABLE 8.6 Exponential growth of the effort multiplier to fix a defect for a hypothetical, but realistic, organization

Work Phase	Effort Multiplier for Rqmts. Defects	Effort Multiplier for Design Defects	Effort Multiplier for Imple. Defects	Effort Multiplier for Verif. Defects	Effort Multiplier for Valid. Defects
Requirements	1				
Design	1.5	1			
Implementation	2.5	1.66	1		
Verification	5	3.33	2	1	
Validation	11.5	7.6	4.6	2.3	1
Operations	25	16.7	10	5	2.17

Multiplication factors to fix other kinds of defects in subsequent phases are listed in Table 8.6, which is based on Figure 8.2.

The results based on Tables 8.5 and 8.6 are in Table 8.4, assuming it takes, on average, 4 staff-hours to fix a requirements defect during the requirements phase, 6 staff-hours to correct a design defect during design, and 10 staff-hours to correct an implementation defect during implementation, a verification defect during verification, and a validation defect during validation. You can easily develop a spreadsheet program to record defect data and perform the desired rework calculations.

The relative values in Table 8.6 and the example in Table 8.4 make it apparent that effort spent in finding and fixing defects as early as possible is effort well spent. The patterns of values in Table 8.4 indicate where process improvement efforts to reduce rework should be concentrated.

8.5 TRACKING EFFORT, SCHEDULE, AND COST; ESTIMATING FUTURE STATUS

As illustrated above, the basic mechanisms for tracking effort, schedule, and cost of software projects are work packages for original work, and change requests and defect reports for rework; change requests document evolutionary rework and defect reports document avoidable rework (retrospective and corrective). Recall that each work package, change request, or defect report must produce one or more tangible work products that can be verified using objective acceptance criteria. Data can be collected for completed work and detailed analysis of various kinds of work activities, such as corrective rework, can be performed. These mechanisms can also be used to report progress at coarser levels of granularity by providing summary reports of total effort, cost (personnel cost plus other costs) and schedule for the work products developed or modified. These data can then be used to estimate effort and schedule needed to complete a project, as illustrated below.

8.5.1 Binary Tracking

Binary tracking is the fundamental technique for accurately tracking project status; the concept was termed "binary deliverables" by Tom DeMarco [DeMarco82]. Each work package, change request, and defect report produces one or more work products that must satisfy objective acceptance criteria before the new version(s) become baselines. A task (a work package for original work, a change request, or a defect report) is counted as 0% complete until the associated work product satisfies its acceptance criteria. The work product is then counted as 100% complete; tracking is thus binary.

Binary tracking helps to avoid the 95% complete syndrome of software projects. Tracking progress on a "guesstimate" basis often results in projects that are reported to be 95% complete for long periods of time. Binary tracking, as depicted in Figure 8.3, where each "X" represents progress based on binary tracking of work packages, provides accurate tracking of actual progress. Also note in Figure 8.3 that actual progress deviates from planned progress early in the project. Corrective action should have been taken no later than the second month of the project.

Figure 8.3 illustrates the maxim of binary tracking:

> It is better to be 100% complete with 90% of the work, and know it is true (binary tracking at month 10), than to think you are 90% complete with 100% of the work, and hope it is true (the guesstimate at month 5).

Because binary tracking does not give credit for work in progress, the accuracy of binary tracking can be improved by tracking at finer levels of granularity. Figure 8.4 illustrates binary tracking of work packages in a work breakdown structure. As illustrated, tasks (the leaf nodes of the WBS) are counted as 0% complete or 100% complete. Percentage completions for higher level activities are calculated based on percentages of completion of subordinate tasks and activities. For simplicity of presentation, each work package in Figure 8.4 is assumed to require equal amounts of effort. Accuracy can be improved by weighting each task by relative amount of effort, perhaps on a scale of 1 to 5.

Work packages 3.1.2, 3.2.2, and 3.2.3 in Figure 8.4 may be 70% or 80% complete (or 95%) but by binary tracking no credit is given until the associated work products satisfy their acceptance criteria.

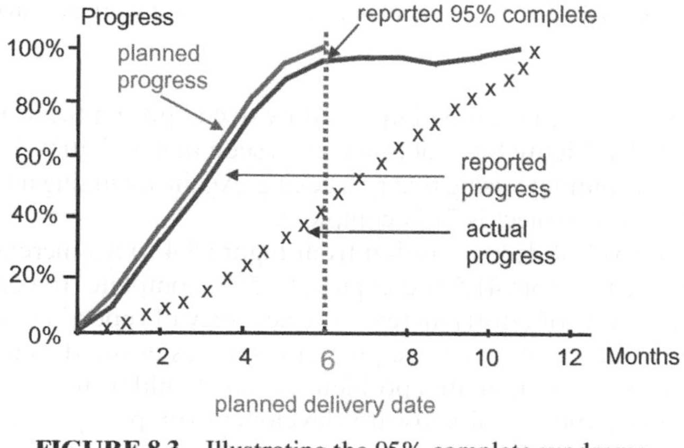

FIGURE 8.3 Illustrating the 95% complete syndrome

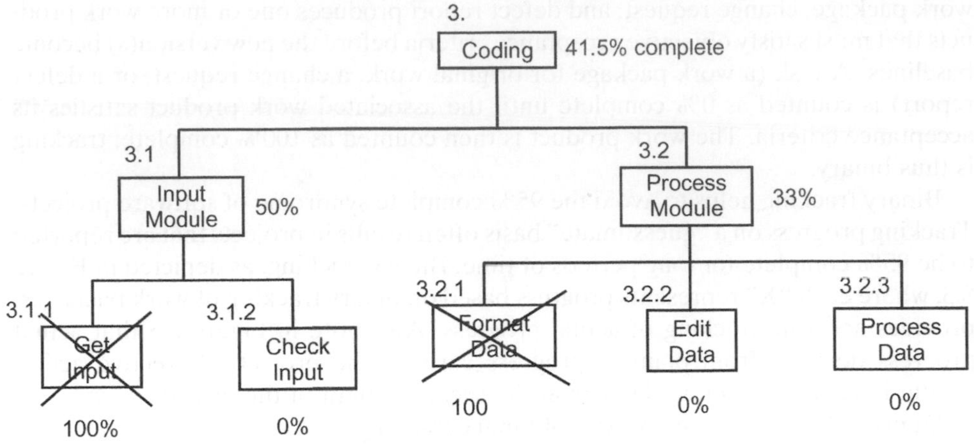

FIGURE 8.4 Binary tracking of work packages

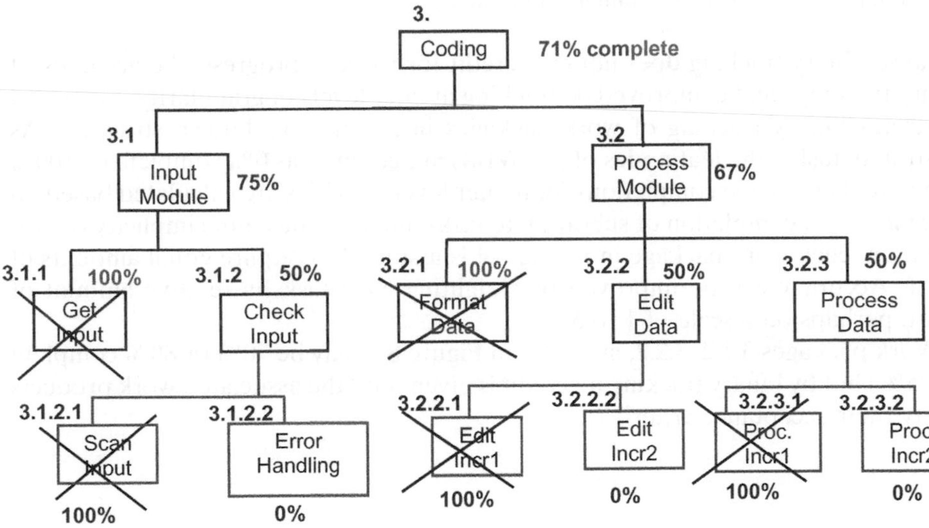

FIGURE 8.5 Increased detail in binary tracking of work packages

The accuracy of tracking can be improved by decomposing the work into small tasks, as illustrated in Figure 8.5, where it can be seen that activities 3.1.2, 3.2.2, and 3.2.3 are each 50% complete using binary tracking. Again, assuming all tasks require equal effort, the same project is 71% complete.

Increasing the level of decomposition from Figure 8.4 to 8.5 increased the accuracy of status reporting from 41.5% complete to 71% complete. In general, smaller tasks (i.e., smaller units of effort) increase the accuracy of reporting but at the risks of micromanagement and of excessive project resources devoted to measuring and controlling. To avoid these potential problems, tasks should be not smaller than one staff-week of effort. Individual software developers (or pair programmers, as in Agile development) may decompose their work into small units, for example, by completing several iterations on a work product during a weekly cycle, but for purposes of measuring and controlling, tasks should not be smaller than one staff-week.

After the associated work product satisfies its acceptance criteria, a work package, change request, or defect report is closed and never reopened. Subsequent modifications of work products are documented in new change requests and defect reports.

The upper limit on task size is determined by considerations of risk. Recall that fundamental purposes of measurement and control are to provide frequent demonstrations of progress and early warning of problems when progress is not as planned or expected. If a task is scoped to require a large amount of effort, and completion of the task is not as planned, early warning of problems will not be obtained. A rule of thumb is:

> each task in your software project should require between 1 staff-week and 1 staff-month of effort.

Because effort is the product of people and time, a 2 staff-week task might be accomplished by 2 people in one week, thus providing a weekly measure of progress, which is highly desirable.

Suppose that your project is scoped to require 5 people for 12 months (5 person-years of effort). If each task in the project requires 2 staff-weeks of effort, the project would consist of 120 tasks (or 240 tasks if each task is of 1 staff-week of effort); 120 tasks would, on average, be 10 tasks to be completed each month (2 tasks per staff member per month). As discussed in Section 5.2, planning at this level of detail is best accomplished in an incremental, rolling-wave manner.

Larger projects (e.g., 10 people for 12 months, 20 people for 24 months, or 200 people for 30 months) should be organized into teams of 5 or fewer staff-members per team, as discussed in Chapter 1 and illustrated in Figure 1.3. It is the duty of each team leader, working with her or his team members, to negotiate weekly tasks, assure that acceptance criteria for work products are satisfied, and use binary tracking to report progress (or lack thereof) to the project manager and other appropriate stakeholders.

8.5.2 Estimating Future Status

Table 8.7 provides an example of using binary tracking to determine project status. The table indicates that 270 of 300 baselined requirements are sufficiently covered by the product architecture. Detailed design specifications for 750 modules of the architecture have been baselined, 500 code modules have been coded, verified, and accepted as baselines, 200 modules have been successfully integrated and baselined, and the code for 43 requirements has been validated and baselined (i.e., the code has been shown to satisfy its intended purpose in its intended environment).

Clearly, the product is being developed in an iterative manner because code for 20% of the requirements has been validated and design of 30 requirements remain to be completed. The "percentage complete" column is accurate because binary tracking of work products is being reported. Work based on the remaining 30 requirements may be 80% or 90% completed but we do not count them as progress measures until they are 100% complete.

TABLE 8.7 Example of project status using binary tracking

Status	Percentage Complete
270 of 300 requirements traced to design	90%
750 of 1000 modules designed and accepted	75%
500 of 1000 modules coded and accepted	50%
200 of 1000 modules integrated	20%
43 of 300 requirements validated	14%

TABLE 8.8 Percentage of effort for various work activities

Work Activity	Percentage of Development Effort
Architectural design	17%
Detailed design	26%
Coding and unit testing	35%
Integration and verification	10%
Validation	12%

Table 8.8 is used to determine the overall percentage completed for the project. The table contains typical percentages of effort for various types of work activities in the organization where the project is being conducted.

From Tables 8.7 and 8.8 it can be determined that 17% of the work is 90% complete (architectural design), 26% of the work is 75% complete (detailed design), and so forth. Combining the two tables provides the overall percentage completed for the project:

$$(90\times 0.17)+(75\times 0.26)+(50\times 0.35)+(20\times 0.10)+(14\times 0.12)=56\%\text{ complete.}$$

The project is 56% complete, and thus 44% of the work remains to be completed.

Suppose the project is at the end of its seventh month and 75 staff-months of effort has been expended thus far. If 75 staff-months is 56% of total project effort, the remaining 44% will require 60 staff-months of effort ([44/56] × 75). Average staffing level has been approximately 11 software developers (75/7); 60 staff-months of remaining effort using 11 software developers will require roughly 5.5 additional months (60/11). It is therefore estimated that the project will require a total schedule of 12.5 months (7 + 5.5). The project could be completed in 11 months if 4 more software developers could be added in a manner that did not violate Brooks's law. It is highly unlikely that the project could be completed in 9 months total time (another 2 months) by adding 19 software developers (60/2 = 30; 30 = 11 + 19).

A caution: The calculations above assume that the remaining work to be done for each task is at the same level of granularity and difficulty as work completed, and that a constant rate of progress will prevail for the remaining work activities. It may be that the most difficult parts are completed, meaning the 30 remaining requirements are all simple and the project is more than 56% complete. Conversely, the 30 remaining requirements may be the most complex ones and the project is less than 56% complete.

The accuracy of the estimate to complete can be improved. First, be sure that the decomposition criteria for requirements are satisfied. Recall that each requirement should be decomposed until:

- complexities and risk factors are exposed;
- opportunities for reuse are identified; and
- effort to implement the requirement can be estimated.

Then weighting factors (e.g., on a scale of 1 to 5) based on estimated effort can be applied to each remaining requirement. It may be, for example, that some requirements are estimated to require 3 times or 5 times the amount of effort compared to some of the other requirements. If a requirement is estimated to be a "20" in relative effort compared to other requirements on a scale of 1 to 5, that requirement clearly needs to be decomposed into a set of smaller, derived requirements. Remaining effort to complete the project can be calculated more accurately using the weighting factors.

8.6 EARNED VALUE REPORTING

Binary tracking of work packages for original work, change requests for evolutionary rework, and defect reports for avoidable rework (retrospective and corrective) can be used to produce earned value (EV) reports. The EV approach for reporting work package completions is as follows (change requests and defect reports can be tracked in a similar manner):

1. Using a rolling-wave approach, specify the planned cost and duration in the work package for each task to be completed during the coming month.
2. When a task is completed, credit the planned cost (effort plus other costs) for the task as its "earned value" (i.e., *earned value* is the planned cost that is "earned back" when a task is completed).
3. For all tasks completed to date, compare the sum of the earned values (i.e., the planned cost for all of the tasks) to the sum of the actual costs for the tasks.
4. For all tasks completed to date, compare the number of tasks that should have been completed to those that have been completed.

If the cumulative actual cost to complete all tasks to date is greater than the planned cost for those tasks (step 4), the project is over budget; conversely, if actual cost is less than planned cost, the project is under budget. Similarly, if fewer tasks have been completed to date than planned for completion the project is behind schedule; if more tasks have been completed than planned the project is ahead of schedule (step 5). Binary tracking assures that the work as reported to be complete is actually complete because the work products have passed their acceptance criteria. The terminology of earned value is summarized in Table 8.9.

From the formulas in Table 8.9, it can be seen that a CPI > 1 means the actual cost is greater than the budgeted cost and a SPI > 1 means the project is behind

TABLE 8.9 Earned value terminology

Term	Definition	Explanation
BCWP	Budgeted Cost of Work Performed	Cumulative amount of the budget for all tasks completed to date (i.e., the earned value)
ACWP	Actual Cost of Work Performed	Actual cost of all tasks completed to date
BCWS	Budgeted Cost of Work Scheduled	Planned cost of all tasks scheduled for completion to date
BAC	Budget Actual Cost	Planned cost of the total project
SCD	Scheduled Completion Date	Planned completion date of the project
EAC	Estimated Actual Cost	Estimated actual cost of the project based on progress to date
ECD	Estimated Completion Date	Estimated completion date based on progress to date
CV	Cost Variance	CV = ACWP – BCWP
SV	Schedule Variance	SV = BCWS – BCWP
CPI	Cost Performance Index	CPI = ACWP / BCWP
SPI	Schedule Performance Index	SPI = BCWS / BCWP
CVC	Cost Variance at Completion	CVC = EAC – BAC
SVC	Schedule Variance at Completion	SVC = ECD – SCD
	where	EAC = BAC * CPI and ECD = SCD * SPI

schedule; conversely, a CPI < 1 and an SPI < 1 would mean that the project is under budget and under schedule. Other combinations of CPI and SPI are of course possible.

A caution: the formulas for CPI, SPI, EAC and ECD in Table 8.9 are sometimes inverted, as in

$$\text{CPI} = \frac{\text{BCWP}}{\text{ACWP}},$$

$$\text{SPI} = \frac{\text{BCWP}}{\text{BCWS}},$$

which makes

$$\text{EAC} = \frac{\text{BAC}}{\text{CPI}}$$

and

$$\text{ECD} = \frac{\text{SCD}}{\text{SPI}}.$$

In this case CPI < 1 and SPI < 1 would mean a project is over budget and behind schedule. Both sets of formulas produce the same values of EAC and ECD if they are consistently applied.

An example of an earned value report is provided in Figure 8.6. In this example, the project is over budget because, by the formulas in Table 8.9, the CPI is greater than 1 (i.e., $A > C$) and behind schedule because the SPI is greater than 1 (i.e., $B > C$). All 8 combinations of *A*, *B*, and *C* are possible, as illustrated in Table 8.10. The relationship among *A*, *B*, and *C* in column 1 of Table 8.10 is illustrated in Figure 8.6.

Cost performance and schedule performance indexes can be used to calculate the estimated actual cost and estimated completion date using the formulas in Table 8.9. An example is provided in Figure 8.7. Because the CPI and SPI will vary from one reporting period to the next, the EAC and ECD will also vary from period to period. For example, a project may be over budget but ahead of schedule in one reporting period, back on planned budget and schedule in the next, or on budget but behind schedule in the next reporting period.

The examples in Figures 8.6 and 8.7 are exaggerated for the purposes of illustration. On a well-run project, the ACWP and BCWP lines will closely track the BCWS

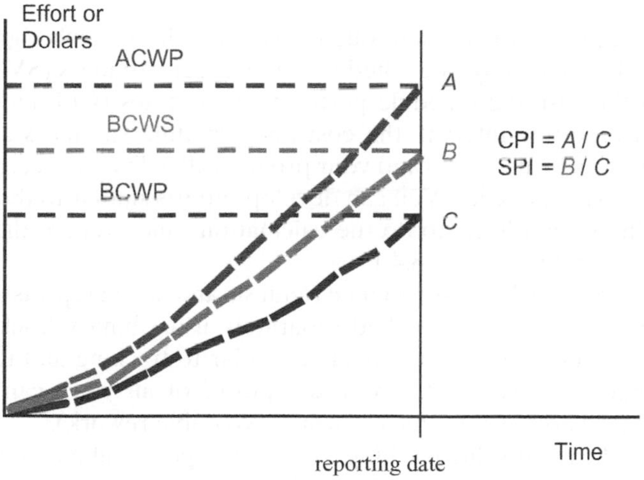

FIGURE 8.6 An example of earned value reporting

TABLE 8.10 Earned value relationships

Orientation: / Condition:	*A* *B* *C*	*A* *C* *B*	*B* *A* *C*	*C* *A* *B*	*B* *C* *A*	*C* *B* *A*
Cost overrun	X		X		X	
Cost savings		X		X		X
Schedule delay	X	X	X			
Schedule advance				X	X	X

A: ACWP; *B*: BCWS; *C*: BCWP

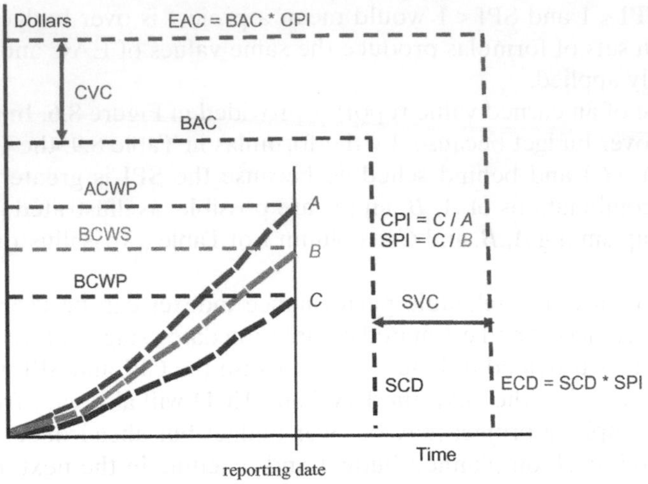

FIGURE 8.7 Earned value projections of Estimated Actual Cost and Estimated Completion Date

line, meaning the project will remain roughly on schedule and on budget throughout the project. Said another way, the schedule and budget variances (SV and CV) will be near 0 and the cost and schedule performance indexes (CPI and SPI) will be near 1 in each reporting interval; the cost and schedule variances at completion (CVC and SVC) will be near zero and your project will deliver an acceptable system on schedule and within budget. You can develop reports similar to those in Figures 8.6 and 8.7 using spreadsheets to do the calculations and prepare the graphs (see also the control panel in Section 8.4.1).

The status of work packages for change requests and defect reports (evolutionary and avoidable rework) can be tracked separately using binary tracking and presented as earned value reports in a manner similar to tracking and reporting progress of original work. Alternatively, a composite of all work can be reported together (original work, evolutionary rework, avoidable rework).

An example of earned value tracking follows: Suppose that a certain project has just completed the third month of a 12-month schedule. The planned budget for the project is $500,000. According to the project plan, $40,000 of the budget should have been completed in the first three months; $50,000 has been completed. It has cost $60,000 to complete the work to date. Thus:

SCD = 12 months
EAC = $500,000
BCWP = $50,000
BCWS = $40,000
ACWP = $60,000

Using the formulas in Table 8.9, project status at the end of month 3 is found to be:

$$\text{CPI} = \frac{\$60{,}000}{\$50{,}000} = 1.2,$$

$$\text{SPI} = \frac{\$40{,}000}{\$50{,}000} = 0.8,$$

and the EAC and ECD are

$$\text{EAC} = \$500{,}000 \times 1.2 = \$600{,}000,$$

$$\text{ECD} = 12 \times 0.8 = 9.6 \text{ months}.$$

Although binary tracking and earned value reporting are presented here for an integrated set of work activities, as occur in a software project, the techniques can be used to track activities that are not well integrated. For example, you can use this approach to good advantage during the maintenance phase of the software life cycle when various change requests and defect reports are processed on an individual basis. Cumulative values of actual cost and time can be compared to budgeted values for, say, all maintenance activities month by month on an annual basis.

In summary, EV reports are a concise way of presenting:

1. the current status of cost (effort plus other costs), schedule, and progress on work products;
2. trends over time; and
3. ongoing (e.g., monthly) estimates of the final cost of a project (EAC) and the delivery date of the system (ECD) based on the ongoing current status of your project.

Earned value reporting based on binary tracking provides accurate measures of work products completed because work products are not counted as complete until they satisfy objective acceptance criteria and become baselines that are placed under version control. Subsequent changes to baselined work products are initiated by change requests and defect reports, which are also accepted, baselined, and tracked using data that are tracked in a binary manner based on objective acceptance criteria.

Necessary conditions for accurate earned value reporting are as follows:

1. Specification of work packages for original work, change requests, and defect reports to be completed during the next month, updated monthly in a rolling-wave manner.
2. Iterative development and baseline acceptance of work products at frequent intervals to provide demonstrations of progress and early warning of problems.
3. Version control of baseline work products.
4. Binary tracking based on objective acceptance criteria for work products.
5. Accurate reporting of effort and time required to complete work packages, change requests, and defect reports.

6. Standard methods, tools, and formats across the organization for capturing and reporting earned value status.
7. Use of earned value status to forecast estimated actual cost and estimated completion date.

For earned value reporting to be effective, effort and time (item 5) must be accurately reported. Time cards prepared on a weekly basis (e.g., each Friday afternoon) are not acceptable because the amount of time you spend on various work activities during the week will not be accurately recalled. Pleasant tasks will be recalled as being much shorter than was actually required; unpleasant or difficult tasks will be recalled as taking much longer than actually required, or perhaps they will not be reported.

Alternatives to weekly time cards include:

1. electronic templates, completed at the end of each day or at intervals during the day;
2. templates for recording work activities that are generated for each work package, change request, or defect report assigned to each software developer; and
3. templates attached to the version control system that require entry of data on check-in of accepted work products.

An alternative to automated data collection is to have a nonthreatening person, (e.g., a clerical worker) collect the data manually from each software developer on a daily basis, enter it into a spreadsheet, and generate earned value reports based on composite data on a weekly basis.

It is the responsibility of each team member to report time and effort data for each task in a timely manner; it is the responsibility of each team leader to ensure that accurate time and effort data are being entered by the team members. It is the responsibility of quality assurance personnel to periodically audit the reporting system to ensure that time and effort data are accurate and timely.

The smallest level of granularity in effort to be reported should be in the range of 2 to 4 work-hours. Said differently, the amount of time spent on each of the 2 to 4 most significant tasks that occupy an 8-hour work day should be reported. If, for example, you close 6 defect reports in one day, you should report the time spent on each. However, in general, your project is not well organized if your staff members work on more than 4 distinct tasks per day, on average.

Lawyers and accountants, when working for clients, often report their time in 15 minute increments. This level of granularity is not necessary for software projects. Recall that the reasons for measuring various attributes of software projects are to provide frequent indications of progress and early warning of problems, to permit analysis of trends, to allow estimates of final cost and completion date of your project, and to build a data repository of completed project. These goals can be achieved by reporting effort in units of 2 to 4 hours at the end of each day, or periodically throughout the day. This level of detail is sufficient to satisfy the purposes of measurement while avoiding the tedium and interruption to work activities inherent in more detailed reporting.

A final caution on collecting and reporting project data (both product and process): reporting of project data should be at the level of teams (3 to 5 individuals) and projects (aggregations of teams). Data should *never* be related to individuals, except in private meetings where the emphasis should be "what can I do, as your project manager (or team leader) to help you do a better job?" and not "how could you be so stupid as to have made so many mistakes?" Nothing will kill a measurement program faster or more effectively than public disclosure of data related to individual productivity and individual quality of work.

Because of the myriad factors that influence productivity and quality of software, individuals may be incorrectly credited or blamed for exceeding or failing to meet expectations. For example, Joe Programmer may have the lowest productivity, as measured in lines of code or function points produced per week, or defect reports closed per week. This may be because Joe, being the best programmer in your group, was given the most difficult parts or it may be that Joe thinks carefully and writes concise, but readable and correct, code that requires fewer lines than the more verbose and defect-prone code written by others. Or it is possible that Joe, while excellent at some kinds of tasks, was mistakenly assigned a task for which he had no experience or aptitude.

8.7 PROJECT CONTROL PANEL©

The Project Control Panel© (PCP) is an MS Excel spreadsheet tool for entering project status data and preparing visual representations of the data; a copy of the tool can be downloaded by clicking on the referenced link [PROJCP] The original version of PCP was developed under the auspices of the Software Project Managers Network (SPMN); it is now administered by the Integrated Computer Engineering (ICE) Directorate of the American Systems Corporation.

Figure 8.8 illustrates the PCP display. Five categories of project data are displayed: Progress (which includes Earned Value, Productivity, and Completion), Risk, Change, Staff, and Quality. Each element in Figure 8.8 has a corresponding worksheet for entering data and viewing expanded displays. The corresponding worksheets can be accessed by clicking on the display or by clicking on the worksheet bar at the bottom of the PCP workbook. The displays in Figure 8.8 are generated by Visual Basic code that uses the data from the worksheets to generate the displays. All items in the control panel display can thus be modified and tailored to suit the needs of each project and/or each organization by modifying the Visual Basic code.

The upper left corner of the display contains the dates of the reporting period and the earned value presentation. The reporting period can be selected to be "weekly" or "monthly." The BCWP line illustrates the BCWS and the BAC; the project is behind schedule because the BCWP is less than the BCWS. The ACWP line indicates that the project is over budget because the BCWP is less than the ACWP. The EAC is projected on the ACWP line, and as can be seen, the EAC is greater than the BAC, based on the CPI value of 0.8 displayed to the right of the EV displays (the CPI is calculated as ACWP/BCWP and EAC is calculated as BAC/CPI; thus a CPI less than 1 indicates that the project is currently over budget).

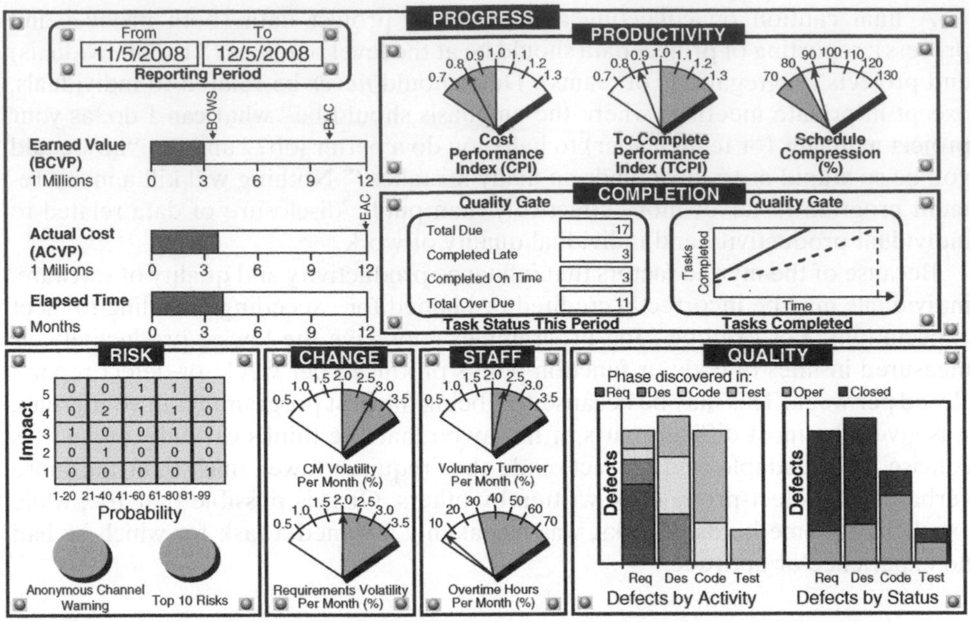

FIGURE 8.8 Display from the Project Control Panel© [PROJCP]

The Elapsed Time display shows the end date for the current reporting period. Data for earned value calculations can be imported from Microsoft Project.

The To-Complete Performance Index (TCPI) gauge measures the same ratio for the remainder of the project that CPI measures up to the end of the current reporting period. TCPI is calculated as

$$\frac{BAC - BCWP}{EAC - ACWP}.$$

It is used in conjunction with the CPI gauge. According to the control panel users' manual, which can be downloaded from the referenced Web site:

> *If TCPI is much greater than CPI, then the project team is anticipating an efficiency improvement to make it more effective in meeting cost estimates in the future than has been the case to date. The estimated total cost of the project (EAC) can therefore be calibrated by comparing TCPI with CPI. Always question claims of future productivity improvement that results in a 20 percent or greater increase in TCPI over CPI to ensure they are based on sound reasoning. This is especially true of "silver bullets" like new tools, languages, or methodologies that may actually decrease productivity due to training and start-up costs. The redline on this gauge [TCPI] should be about 20 percent above the current value of the CPI gauge to show the relationship and warning level between the two gauges.*

The Schedule Compression gauge in Figure 8.8 shows the ratio of the Estimated Completion Date (ECD) for this project compared to the "nominal" schedule, which is computed as

$$\text{Nominal calendar months} = 2.5 \times (\text{person-months})^{1/3}.$$

Recall from Chapter 6 that the relationship between schedule and effort is typically involves an exponent in the range of 0.33 to 0.5. The users' manual for the control panel notes that a Schedule Compression ratio less than 80% of the Nominal schedule indicates a high-risk schedule; this is indicated by the shaded portion of the Schedule Compression gauge. The 80% value is consistent with the schedule compression values in the SLIM and COCOMO estimation tools.

The Quality Gate displays in Figure 8.8 are based on binary tracking of task completions. Total Due is the total number of tasks that should have been completed during the current reporting period plus any overdue tasks from previous reporting periods. Completed On Time shows the number of tasks that were completed as scheduled. Completed Late includes tasks scheduled for completion during the current reporting period that were completed late plus any overdue tasks from previous periods that were completed in the current period. Total Overdue is the total number of tasks for all previous reporting periods plus the current period that were overdue at the end of the current reporting period:

$$\text{Total Overdue} = \text{Total Due} - (\text{Completed on Time} + \text{Completed Late}).$$

Total Overdue indicates the number of tasks that must be completed to get the project back on schedule.

The Quality Gate Tasks Completed graph shows the cumulative number of tasks planned for completion by the end of the current reporting period (the solid line) and the actual number completed (the dashed line). The horizontal distance between the two lines indicates the current slippage in schedule to date, which is similar to the horizontal distance between BCWS and BCWP in Figures 8.6 and 8.7.

The RISK area in Figure 8.8 shows, in the table, the number of risk factors that have been identified in each of the Consequence/Probability cells. Risk exposure is the product of Probability × Impact (see Chapter 9); thus the risk factors in the lower left corner of the table have the lowest risk exposures and those in the upper right corner have the highest exposure. Clicking on the "Top 10 Risks" button displays a worksheet that shows the name of the risk factor, its probability, impact, and risk exposure.

The Anonymous Channel Warning button displays a red light when an anonymous warning of a potential problem (a risk factor) or an anonymous warning of a real problem has been received. The red light switches off when all anonymously reported risk factors and problems have been dealt with. Unfortunately, the culture in some organizations does not provide an atmosphere in which individuals feel that it is okay to report risk factors and problems. The anonymous reporting channel allows them to raise issues without fear of retribution.

The CHANGE area in Figure 8.8 indicates the percentage of Configuration Management Volatility and Requirements Volatility per Month. CM Volatility is calculated as the ratio of baselined work products (i.e., configuration items) that have been modified (or replaced) and rechecked into the configuration management system during the last reporting period divided by the total number of baselined configuration items. As indicated in Figure 8.8, a threshold value of 2% is an indicator of excessive change.

Requirements Volatility per Month is calculated by dividing the sum of new, changed, and deleted requirements specified during the current reporting period by the total number of requirements at the end of the reporting period.

The shaded areas indicate that the threshold for both gauges in CHANGE is set at 2%. It should be noted that the shaded areas for all of the gauges in Figure 8.8 can be reset as desired.

The STAFF area in Figure 8.8 indicates percentages of Voluntary Turnover per Month and Overtime Hours per Month. Voluntary Turnover per Month is the number of project members leaving the project during the current reporting period (i.e., the current month) when they are still needed on the project divided by the number of staff at the beginning of the reporting period. The percentage of Overtime Hours per Month is calculated by dividing the total number of overtime hours worked by all project members by the total number of hour worked on a 40 hour per week schedule. According to the control panel users' manual the target range should be less than 10% (i.e., less than 4 hours overtime per week per staff member, on average); when the overtime rate approaches 20% (8 hours overtime per week per person, on average) there is a high risk of future high Voluntary Turnover.

The QUALITY area of Figure 8.8 is concerned with defects by activity and the Open/Closed status of known defects. The Defects by Activity graph displays the number of defects detected for the development phases of requirements, design, code, and test. The horizontal axis of Defects by Activity indicates the phases in which defects were discovered. The color coding of each bar graph indicates the number of defects of each kind found in each development phase; for example, the left-most bar graph indicates that most requirements defects were found during requirements work activities, some were found during design, some during coding, and some during testing. The Defects by Activity graph reports similar data as in Table 8.4 in this chapter, but with the axes interchanged.

The Defect Status graph indicates the number of defect reports that are open (i.e., the defect is yet to be fixed) and the number that have been closed (i.e., the defect has been fixed and the modified work has been accepted as a new version of the baselined work product).

The next to last worksheet in the Project Control Panel provides an example of tailoring of the spreadsheet display. The c21b users' manual (downloadable from the referenced Web site) provides instruction on how to modify the Visual Basic code to modify and create new displays. For example, you might want to have new spreadsheets and gauges (or a different control panel) to record data about software inspections. You might display the average rate of software inspections and the average inspection efficiency.

The former display might show the rate of inspection checking by dividing the average number of logical document pages (or function points or lines of code) inspected per inspection meeting by the average number of work-hours spent by inspection team members during the last reporting period; the display would show pages (or some other measure) inspected per staff-hour. The latter display (average inspection efficiency) would display the number of defects found by all inspections during the previous reporting period divided by the total number of work-hours expended on inspections.

The inspection displays could be monitored over time to determine increases or decreases in inspection rates and inspection efficiency. Similar displays could be developed for testing effort and defects found during testing. Comparisons of rates and efficiencies of code inspections versus testing could be readily be made within reporting periods and cumulatively over reporting periods.

8.8 KEY POINTS OF CHAPTER 8

- The purposes of process measurement are to provide frequent indications of progress, to provide early warning of problems, to permit analysis of trends in your project, to allow estimates of the final cost and completion date of your project, and to build a data repository of project histories for your organization.
- The primary dimensions of work to be measured and controlled are effort, schedule, and cost for each of the various work processes.
- Measurement of effort, schedule, and cost must be related to tracking of work products produced using binary tracking.
- The amount of effort, time, and money you invest in measurement and control is determined by considerations of risk: what is the potential impact of not doing enough? what is the potential impact of doing too much?
- Possibilities for corrective action, when actual values of project attributes are not as planned or expected, include extending the schedule, adding more resources, using superior resources, improving various elements of the development process, and/or de-scoping the product requirements.
- Possibilities for corrective action that should never be used include excessive amounts and durations of overtime; reduction or elimination of planned verification and validation activities; reduction of planned user documentation, training aids, and so forth; and reduction, without agreement of the customer, of any planned activity that would reduce the specified features or quality attributes of the system or product to be delivered.
- Rolling-wave planning by team leaders and project managers, with detailed plans for the coming month in the range of one to two staff-weeks per task, provides sufficient granularity for accurate tracking of progress.
- Binary reporting of work packages is the only technique known to us that avoids the 95% complete syndrome of software projects.
- Earned value reporting based on binary tracking of completed work packages provides concise reports of actual versus planned cost, schedule, and work completed.
- Reporting of time spent on tasks at intervals of 2 to 4 hours each day by each individual is sufficiently accurate for most software projects.
- Productivity and quality data should be reported at the level of teams and projects but never at the level of individual contributors.
- The following techniques, when used together, can provide accurate status information and accurate forecasts for software projects: rolling-wave elaboration of work plans documented in work packages, change requests, and defect reports; iterative development with frequent demonstrations of progress; baseline control of work products; tracking and analysis of rework by kind

(evolutionary, retrospective, corrective); binary tracking of work packages, change requests, and defect reports; and earned value reporting.

- Summary displays, such as the one provided by a control panel, can provide succinct status reports for software projects.

REFERENCES

[Basili94] Basili, V., and S. Green. Software process evolution at the SEL. *IEEE Software* (July 1994): 58–66.

[Boehm01] Boehm, B., and V. Basili. Software defect reduction top 10 list. *Computer* (January 2001): 135–137.

[DeMarco82] DeMarco, T. *Controlling Software Projects*. Yourdon Press, 1982.

[Fairley05] Fairley, R. E., and M. J. Willshire. Iterative rework in software development: The good, the bad, and the ugly. *IEEE Computer* (September 2005). Vol. 38, No. 9. pp 34–41.

[IEEE1058] IEEE Std 1058™–1998. *IEEE Standard for Software Project Management Plans*. Engineering Standards Collection. IEEE Product. SE113. Institute of Electrical and Electronic Engineers, August 2003.

[IEEE12207] IEEE/EIA 12207.0/.1/.2. *Industry Implementation of International Standard ISO/IEC 12207:1995 Standard for Information Technology—Software Life Cycle Processes*. Engineering Standards Collection. IEEE Product: SE113. Institute of Electrical and Electronic Engineers, August 2003.

URLs

[PROJCP] http://www.iceincusa.com/16CSP/content/software/tools/cntrlpnl/cpnlrgt.htm

EXERCISES

8.1. Why is it important to include objective measures of work products completed when tracking effort, schedule, and cost?

8.2. CMMI-DEV-v1.2 lists two related process areas for Project Monitoring and Control: Project Planning, and Measurement and Analysis.

Access the Web site Access the CMMI Web site at http://www.sei.cmu.edu/publications/documents/06.reports/06tr008.html, review the Project Monitoring and Control process area, and briefly explain how each of the two related process areas is related to Project Monitoring and Control.

8.3. People who play different roles in a software project need differing kinds of status reports concerning process attributes. For each of the following, list and briefly explain the kinds of process status reports that would be useful to them (assume an iterative development process):

a. Customer

b. Project manager

c. Designers

d. Programmers

e. Testers

8.4. IEEE Standard 1058 specifies, in clause 5.3, that at minimum, requirements, schedule, budget, and quality should be measured and controlled in a software project. List three additional attributes of a software project that might be measured and controlled. Briefly explain why it might be important to measure and control each of them.

8.5. Briefly explain the differences among budget, cost, and price for a software project.

8.6. Software work consists of original work, evolutionary rework, retrospective rework, and corrective rework. Give a brief, specific example of each kind of work.

8.7. Refer to Table 8.4.

a. What percentage of total effort was spent on fixing design defects?

b. What percentage of effort to fix defects found by users (Ops) was spent on fixing requirements defects?

8.8. Suppose that the remaining effort to complete the work in Table 8.7 is as follows:

Weighting of 4 for each of the remaining 30 requirements

Weighting of 3 for each of the remaining 250 modules to be designed and accepted

Weighting of 1 for each of the 500 modules to be coded and accepted

Weighting of 2 for each of the remaining 800 modules to be integrated

Weighting of 1 for each of the remaining 257 requirements to be validated

a. What is the percentage of completion for the project?

b. How many months remain to complete the project, assuming the project has just ended its seventh month and 77 staff-months of effort have been expended?

8.9. Using the formulas in Table 8.9, develop a spreadsheet program to compute the following factors for a software project:

Cost variance (CV)

Schedule variance (SV)

Cost performance index (CPI)

Schedule performance index (SPI)

Estimated actual cost (EAC)

Estimated completion date (ECD)

Cost variance at completion (CVC)

Schedule variance at completion (SVC)

8.10. Apply the spreadsheet program developed in Exercise 8.9 to compute the values listed in the exercise.

a. Use the following set of data: BCWP = \$40K, ACWP = \$50K, and BCWS = \$60K. Assume that BAC = \$200K, SCD = 12 months, and that the project is at the end of the third month of a 12-month schedule.

b. Verify the correctness of your spreadsheet by performing the calculations by hand; show your work.

8.11. Repeat Exercise 8.10 with the following data:

> After 6 months a project has completed \$60K of its planned budget. The plan was to complete \$50K of the planned budget. The cost for the work completed is \$45K. The project is planned for 10 months and the total budget is \$100K.

8.12. Briefly explain how work packages, binary tracking, and earned value reporting can be used to good advantage during the maintenance phase of the software life cycle when various change requests and defect reports are assigned to individuals and processed on an individual basis. Assume there is an annual budget for maintenance activities.

8.13. Briefly explain why data related to productivity and quality should be made public within software organizations at the team and project levels. Briefly explain why data related to productivity and quality should never be reported at the level of individual project members.

8.14. Download a copy of Project Control Panel© from the referenced Web site [PROJCP].

a. Enter the earned value data from Exercise 8.10, and compare the results to your hand calculations.

b. Follow the instructions in the cp21b users' manual to modify the control panel display in some interesting ways.

APPENDIX 8A

FRAMEWORKS, STANDARDS, AND GUIDELINES FOR MEASURING AND CONTROLLING WORK PROCESSES

See Appendix 7A (Chapter 7) for an overview of the measurement and control elements of CMMI-DEV-v1.2, ISO/IEEE Standard 12207, IEEE 1058, and the PMI Body of Knowledge.

9

MANAGING PROJECT RISK

> When a software project is successful, it is not because there were no problems but because the problems were overcome.
>
> —Paul Rook

9.1 INTRODUCTION TO MANAGING PROJECT RISK

The goal of risk management is to identify and mitigate potential problems with sufficient lead time to prevent adverse impacts on project factors, such as budget, schedule, resources, and cost, and on product features and quality attributes. If unattended, potential problems can become real problems that may lead to crisis situations. For software projects, a crisis is a "show-stopper" that halts or seriously impedes progress. You do not want to be the manager of, or a member of, a project that is in a crisis situation; risk management can help you mitigate potential problems and avoid crises.

Informally, it can be said that risk is the chance a bad thing might happen and the associated consequences should the bad thing happen. More formally, the chance of a bad thing happening is expressed as the probability of occurrence. The bad thing that might happen is a potential problem that hasn't happened yet but, if it occurs, will have a negative impact on one, some, or all of budget, schedule, resources, cost, product features, and quality attributes. The consequences of the negative impact could be loss of human life, property, information, money, reputation, late delivery of an unacceptable product, unacceptable cost, or your job.

Risk is thus characterized by probability p, where $0 < p < 1$, and potential loss L. For software projects, the potential loss is usually expressed on an ordinal scale of

TABLE 9.1A Quantitative determination of risk exposure levels

Potential Impact	$L = 25$	$L = 50$	$L = 75$	$L = 100$
Probability				
$p = 0.25$	6.25	12.5	18.75	25
$p = 0.5$	12.5	25	37.5	50
$p = 0.75$	18.75	37.5	56.25	75
$p = 0.90$	22.5	45	67.5	90

TABLE 9.1B Qualitative determination of risk exposure levels

Potential Impact	Low	Medium	High	Very high
Probability				
Low	Low	Medium	High	Medium
Medium	Low	High	High	High
High	Medium	High	Very high	Very high
Very high	Medium	High	Very high	Extremely high

(Low, Medium, High), or in monetary units, or in dimensionless units of utility.[28] In mission-critical situations, risk may be expressed as the potential for loss of human life or the potential for significant loss of information or property. Both characterization (probability and potential loss) are important. If $p = 0$, it means that the potential loss will never become a real loss; if $p = 1$, it means that the loss has already occurred or will occur with certainty. If the potential loss is negligible there is no reason for concern. If the potential loss is great, effort may be exerted to reduce the impact or the probability even if the probability of occurrence is already very low.

Risk exposure (RE) is the product of probability and potential loss:

$$\text{RE} = p * L.$$

A risk factor having probability $p = 0.25$ of occurrence and potential loss of $L = \$100{,}000$ has a risk exposure of \$25,000.

Quantitative values of probability and potential loss can be used to determine levels of risk exposure, as in Table 9.1*a*. It is not always possible to quantify the probabilities and potential impacts of risk factors. In those cases risk exposure is characterized in a qualitative manner using an ordinal measurement scale. Risk exposure is then determined by combinations of probability and potential impact, as in Table 9.1*b*.

[28] Utility is a dimensionless unit of measure, usually on a scale of 0 to 100, of relative value within a given context. A glass of water, for example, has much greater utility to a person lost in the desert than to a person in the comfort of her or his home.

Risk is the probability something bad will happen and the associated loss if the bad thing does happen. Conversely, it can be said that opportunity is the probability something good will happen, with an associated gain if it happens. Viewing opportunity as the converse of risk is mirrored in the sayings: "one person's risk is another's opportunity" and "you see the glass as half-empty, but I see it as half-full."

A risk-averse organization, or individual, will typically choose lower risk alternatives while a risk-taking organization, or individual, will typically choose higher risk alternatives because high-risk situations typically have high gains, if successful, but high losses if unsuccessful. Some organizations pursue opportunity management, which involves assessing potential gains to be made and the risk involved, and being prepared to take advantage of situations, should potential gains overcome the potential for losses in the judgment of project stakeholders.

9.2 OBJECTIVES OF THIS CHAPTER

This chapter presents methods and techniques for managing risk factors in your software projects. After reading this chapter and completing the exercises you should understand:

- the terminology of risk management for software projects
- the role of conventional project management techniques in managing generic risk factors for software projects
- methods and techniques used to identify, analyze, prioritize, and mitigate project-specific risk factors
- risk mitigation strategies of avoidance, transfer, acceptance, immediate action, and contingency plans and actions
- contents of risk management plans
- top-N risk tracking and reporting
- format, content, and use of risk registers
- crisis management for software projects
- risk management at the organizational level
- joint risk management with customers and subcontractors

Because projects, in general, and software projects, in particular, are characterized by many uncertainties (i.e., they are inherently high-risk endeavors), each of the frameworks, standards, and guidelines presented in this text (CMMI-DEV-v1.2, ISO/IEEE Standard 12207 , IEEE Standard 1058 , and PMBOK) include processes and recommended practices for risk management. The relevant aspects of these standards and guidelines are contained in Appendix 9A of this chapter. In addition an overview IEEE/EIA Standard 1540-2001 for Life Cycle Processes—Risk Management is presented in Appendix 9A. Terms specific to risk management are defined in Appendix 9B to this chapter and in [Fairley05].

Additional terms used in this chapter and throughout this text are defined in the Glossary at the end of the text. Presentation slides for this chapter and other supporting material are available at the URL listed in the Preface.

9.3 AN OVERVIEW OF RISK MANAGEMENT FOR SOFTWARE PROJECTS

Software projects are inherently risky endeavors because achieving a successful outcome (i.e., delivering an acceptable product on time and within budget) involves establishing and maintaining a balance among many technical, organizational, social, and political constraints, any or all of which may change as a project evolves. Each potential problem for a software project is called a risk factor because it represents a threat to a successful outcome. Table 9.2 lists some commonly occurring kinds of risk factors for software projects.

The risk of inadequate calendar time may result from:

- committing to a bad estimate,
- customer or management compression of a schedule without a corresponding adjustment to resources and/or requirements,
- addition of requirements without corresponding adjustments to schedule and resources, or
- reduction in planned resources without corresponding adjustments.

The risk of insufficient funds to conduct a project may involve lack of enough money in the budget to carry out all of the necessary work activities (perhaps caused by a bad estimate or by agreeing to a "mandated" budget), or it may involve not receiving the money in a timely manner. In the latter case, for example, the customer who is paying for a project may delay incremental payment of funds or your management may defer allocation of needed funds until next fiscal quarter or fiscal year.

Lack of adequate requirements management can create may different kinds of potential and real problems. As indicated in Table 9.2, requirements may be infeasible because:

TABLE 9.2 Some commonly occurring risk factors for software projects

Risk Factors	Examples
Schedule	Inadequate calendar time
Budget	Insufficient funds when needed
Requirements	Infeasible, unstable, incorrect, incomplete, inconsistent
Personnel	Recruitment, ability, retention
Process	Inefficient and/or ineffective procedures
Resources	Host and target machines; supporting organizations
Technology	Platform and domain
Geography	Multiple development sites
External factors	Vendors and subcontractors
Operational risks	Missing features, inadequate performance
Quality	User and customer dissatisfaction
Maintenance	Corrections, missing features

- your organization lacks skill and/or experience in the application domain;
- the requirements may be constantly changing and fail to stabilize after a reasonable amount of time;
- they may be incorrectly state user needs and customer expectations;
- they may be incomplete, thus requiring the software engineers to "fill in the blanks" as they think best (and which may be wrong); or
- they may be inconsistent, which can result in failure of various product features to interact correctly.

Other requirements-based risk factors arise from requirements creep and "gold plating," as termed by Boehm [Boehm91]. Requirements creep, as the name implies, occurs when requirements increase over time without compensating adjustments to schedule, resources, budget, and technology. Requirements creep is the result of ineffective requirements management.

Gold plating occurs when features and quality attributes that are not cost-effective (as determined by users and customers) are included. Gold plating often occurs when software developers add features that are not specified in the requirements and are not needed to support primary requirements (i.e., they are not derived features).

Personnel risks include:

- recruitment risk: potential inability to recruit the necessary numbers of personnel;
- ability risk: potential lack of the necessary skills and abilities among project personnel; and
- retention risk: the potential for loss of project personnel.

Work processes have the potential to be inefficient and/or ineffective. An inefficient work process requires more effort, time, resources, and money than an efficient one. An ineffective work process fails to achieve the desired results. A work process can be effective but inefficient; that is, it can produce the desired result but at an inordinate cost or an excessive amount of time. An (absurdly) efficient process that is ineffective is one that does little work and produces no results. Clearly, work process should be both efficient and effective to reduce risk of project failure.

There are two kinds of resource risk factors:

1. risk factors in physical assets such as processor speed and memory capacity, which can occur in the host machine used to develop software and in the target machine on which the software will be operated; and
2. risk factors in supporting organizations such as configuration management and independent testing on which you must rely but over which you have no direct control.

Risk factors in technology include risks in the platform technology used to develop software, such as networks, workstations, operating systems, compilers, debuggers, database tools, and testing tools, plus risks in the technology of the user/customer domain.

Risk factors in the customer domain may arise because your organization and your project personnel are not sufficiently familiar with factors in the customer domain such as accounting practices, tax laws, the physics of interplanetary navigation, or critical patient care. Or, the technology of the user/customer domain may be immature and thus beyond the known capabilities of computer science and software engineering. Examples of the latter situation include comprehensive diagnosis of human diseases using automated DNA analysis or automatic discrimination of friend and foe in missile defense.

Globalization and Internet technology have resulted in the increasing use of multiple development sites for software projects. Risk factors created by developing software at multiple sites include increased difficulties of communication when face-to-face meetings are not possible, plus the difficulties created by differing time zones and differing cultures of the team members.

External risk factors are created when your project depends on the performance of vendors and subcontractors. Risk factors in procuring components from vendors and subcontractors may result in failure of a vendor or subcontractor to deliver a satisfactory component, or components, on time and within budget.

A vendor may:

- fail to make the requested modifications to a software package you have licensed,
- fail to release a next version that contains features you need in a timely manner,
- release a next version that is not compatible with the present version, or
- discontinue support of the package.

Risk factors in subcontracting include potential problems in communication between you and your subcontractor, and potential problems internal to the subcontractor (i.e., the risk factors in Table 9.2).

Operational risks are risk factors that may become problems if you fail to include all the required features or quality attributes in the delivered system or product, thus rendering the system or product unusable or less useful than envisioned. Quality risk factors are potential problems that will become real problems if users and/or customers are dissatisfied with the performance or results produced by the delivered system.

User dissatisfaction may arise from factors such as:

- lack of system availability (i.e., frequent crashes),
- production of erroneous results, or
- difficulty of learning and use.

It is possible for user needs to be fulfilled but not customer expectations, and vice versa. For example, the users of an Automated Teller System (you and I) may be satisfied with the system, but the customer (the financial institution) may not satisfied because the reports produced by the system are difficult for financial personnel to use and sometimes erroneous.

Risk factors for software maintenance include the potential need for excessive numbers of maintainers to find and fix defects in the delivered software, and the need to add features that should have been included in the delivered software but were not. The 12 factors itemized in Table 9.2 are some commonly occurring risk factors for software project but the list is not exhaustive; there are many kinds of things that have the potential to go wrong in a software project.

The overall risk for your software project is the total set of risk factors that have been identified as potential problems for that project. Managing project risk involves mitigating each identified risk factor individually and dealing with the interactions among risk factors. It may be, for example, that avoiding the problem of a schedule overrun by reducing planned verification activities creates the risk of unacceptable product quality, or that violating the principles of coupling and cohesion to avoid the problem of exceeding available memory creates a risk for code maintainability.

In general, risk factors in the following areas, and the trade-offs among them, must be identified and confronted:

- cost
- schedule
- resources
- product objectives
  - product features
  - quality attributes
- assumptions
- constraints

In addition risk factors in areas such as the platform technology, domain technology, and communication and coordination with customers, users, and acquirers must be managed.

9.4 CONVENTIONAL PROJECT MANAGEMENT TECHNIQUES

The conventional techniques of project management presented in this text can be thought of as *institutionalized* risk management. Over time it has become apparent that applying conventional techniques such as:

- planning and estimating
- managing requirements,
- preparing work breakdown structures,
- establishing schedule networks, and

and measuring progress using techniques such as:

- iterative development,
- binary tracking, and
- earned value reporting,

improve the chance of success by reducing risk exposure. In other words, it is better to do conventional project management than to not do it.

Risk management augments conventional project management techniques. Explicit management of assumptions and constraints, for example, is a key element of risk management. As described previously in this text (Chapter 4) assumptions are conditions that you assume will be true but cannot verify during planning. You might assume, for example, that sufficient numbers of personnel who have the necessary skills will be available when needed. Or, you might assume that product complexity will not be a problem because you expect to have software developers who are familiar with this kind of system. Assumptions are potential problems (risk factors); assumptions proved to be false create real problems.

Constraints are externally imposed conditions that your project must satisfy (i.e., factors that are beyond your control as project manager). They are limitations that have been imposed on project attributes such as:

- the schedule,
- budget,
- available resources,
- software to be reused,
- technologies to be used, and
- interfaces to other systems.

Constraints can be categorized as design constraints and process constraints. A design constraint might require reuse of existing components or building specified interfaces to another system. A process constraint might limit the money, resources, and/or time available to conduct the project. More restrictive constraints create risk factors having higher probabilities of becoming problems that will impede delivering an acceptable product within schedule and budget.

Risk factors created by project constraints can sometimes be avoided by modifying the constraints. Process constraints (schedule, budget, resources) and product constraints (features and quality attributes) should be examined. Some constraints may be essential to a successful outcome. Others, on closer examination, may be relaxed or removed. An operational requirement for "near instantaneous response time" may be acceptably satisfied with a 5-second response time rather than the stated requirement for a 2-second response time, for example. The increased response time may significantly decrease the probability that a risk factor will become a problem.

Risk management augments conventional project management in (at least) three ways. First, you can actively manage assumptions and constraints by:

- explicitly itemizing them,
- identifying the associated risk factors,
- prioritizing the risk factors,
- tracking risk indicator metrics,
- periodically reviewing the risk factors, and
- pursuing mitigating actions as necessary.

Second, you can:

- set threshold values for the risk indicator metrics and other project parameters (e.g., schedule performance index, cost performance index, requirements volatility) and
- prepare responses (i.e., develop mitigation plans) to be initiated if those thresholds are violated.

You, your customer, and your managers may tolerate a 2-day delay in achieving a major project milestone but you and they may agree, in advance, that a delay of more than 2 weeks in achieving a major milestone will trigger mitigating actions. Or, you may agree that a memory overrun of more than 10% on any weekly build-demonstration cycle will trigger a mitigating action.

As indicated throughout this text, there are acceptable and unacceptable ways to compensate for problems in a software project. Acceptable methods include:

- increasing the schedule,
- increasing the budget,
- applying more resources,
- applying better resources,
- reducing the requirements; and
- improving the work processes.

Unacceptable methods include:

- requiring excessive overtime;
- reducing verification and validation activities; and
- reducing user, customer, support, and maintenance aids and documentation.

The third way in which risk management augments conventional project management is by using a systematic approach to identify, analyze, prioritize, and mitigate specific risk factors for your project, during initial planning and on an ongoing basis. You may be using the conventional methods, tools, and techniques presented in this text to plan and estimate, measure and control, and lead and direct your project, but if you are not doing systematic risk management, you may fail to identify and respond to specific risk factors with sufficient lead time to avoid crisis situations.

Identified risk factors must be prioritized because some risk factors, and some interactions among risk factors, may have larger probabilities and/or greater potential impact than others and thus should receive more attention and resources. Risk mitigation strategies must be devised. In some cases, risk mitigation involves taking immediate action to reduce the probability and/or potential impact of an identified risk factor. In other cases, risk mitigation involves tracking a risk indicator and taking action if (when) a potential problem becomes a real problem (i.e., when a trigger value crosses a predetermined threshold—the problem trigger). In some cases, decisions about how to deal with identified risk factors may be deferred until the situation is better understood.

TABLE 9.3 Risk factors and risk management techniques

Risk Factors	Risk Management Techniques
Personnel shortfall	Staff with top talent; match jobs to skills; make key-personnel agreements; provide cross-training; pre-schedule key personnel
Unrealistic schedule and/or budget	Multiple estimation techniques; design to cost and schedule; incremental development; software reuse; requirements scrubbing
Developing the wrong software functions	Organization analysis; mission analysis; developed Concept of Operations; conduct user surveys; prototyping; early development of user manuals
Developing the wrong user interface	Prototyping; scenarios; user-task analysis; user characteristics (user classes, work loads, work styles)
Gold plating	Requirements scrubbing, prototyping; cost-benefit analysis; designing to cost and schedule; traceability
Continuing stream of requirements changes	Change control boards; setting a high threshold for changes; information hiding (to ease changes); incremental development (to defer changes to later increments)
Shortfalls in externally furnished components	Benchmarking of potential components; inspections; reference checking; compatibility analysis
Shortfalls in externally performed tasks	Reference checking of potential subcontractors; pre-award audits; award-fee contracts; competitive design or prototyping; team building
Real-time performance shortfalls	Simulation; benchmarking; modeling; prototyping; instrumentation; tuning
Straining computer science capabilities	Technical analysis; cost-benefit analysis; prototyping; reference checking

In cases where the correct course of risk management is uncertain,[29] and in cases where a mitigating action is not apparent, you should place identified risk factors on a watch list that is reviewed at frequent intervals; risk mitigation actions are then initiated as appropriate. Techniques for prioritizing risk factors and strategies for mitigating project risk are discussed later in this chapter.

Software projects often have risk factors that are unknown during initial planning but become apparent later in a project. It is not uncommon to allocate a contingency reserve to be used when unknown risk factors appear later in a project. The amount of money in the contingency reserve may range from 10% to 50% or more of the project budget, depending on the level of uncertainty during initial planning.

Many of the conventional techniques of project management can be used to manage risk factors. Table 9.3 lists some of the techniques that can be used to manage the risk factors listed by Boehm in his top-10 list of risk factors for software projects [Boehm91]. The following sections present techniques for risk identification, analysis and prioritization of risk factors, and risk mitigation strategies.

[29] Uncertainty results from lack of knowledge or information; it is often the root cause of a risk factor.

9.5 RISK IDENTIFICATION TECHNIQUES

As indicated in the various standards and guidelines for risk management, project risk factors must be identified as they develop. Risk factors should be identified, analyzed, prioritized, and mitigation plans developed, to the extent possible, during initial project planning, but risk factors must also be identified, analyzed, prioritized, and mitigated on a continuous, ongoing basis. Some potential problems will not materialize; for example, the hardware you need is delivered on schedule, so the risk of late delivery does not become a problem. Other unforeseen risk factors will arise as the project evolves; for example, your software architect tells you she may be moving to another city for personal reasons, but she is not certain she will and she is not sure when she will move, if she does.

Some risk factors thought to be settled may re-emerge. For example, a former risk of failure to achieve consensus on the layout of the user interface that was previously achieved may now re-emerge because some new users who have recently joined the users' organization are saying they want major changes. This re-institutes the risk of late product delivery based on lack of consensus among the users.

Some techniques for identifying risk factors are listed in Table 9.4. In general, any technique you use to identify potential problems for your project can be used for risk identification.

9.5.1 Checklists

Checklists are often used to identify risk factors. They can be used by individuals, in group meetings, or as aids to those participating in a Delphi process (see Chapter 6). The risk taxonomy developed at SEI is one of the best-known checklists for risk identification [Carr93]. The taxonomy is a three-level hierarchy of commonly occurring risk factors for software projects. Table 9.5*a* lists the top two levels of the hierarchy. Table 9.5*b* lists some of the second-level and third-level elements in the hierarchy. The report that contains the full taxonomy and other aspects of risk identification and risk management can be accessed at the URL cited in [Carr93].

TABLE 9.4 Some techniques for identifying risk factors

- Checklists
- Brainstorming
- Expert judgment
- SWOT analysis
- Assumptions analysis
- Constraints analysis
- Lessons-learned files
- Cost modeling
- Schedule analysis
- Requirements triage
- Assets inventory
- Trade-off analysis

TABLE 9.5A Top levels of the SEI risk taxonomy [Carr93]

Top-Level Elements	Second-Level Elements
A. Product engineering (technical aspects of the work)	A.1. Requirements A.2. Design A.3. Code and unit test A.4. Integration and test A.5. Engineering specialties
B. Development environment (methods, procedures, and tools to be used)	B.1. Development process B.2. Development system B.3. Management process B.4. Management methods B.5. Work environment
C. Program constraints (contractual, organizational, and operational factors that are outside the control of local management)	C.1. Resources C.2. Contract C.3. Program interfaces

TABLE 9.5B Some second- and third-level elements of the SEI risk taxonomy [Carr93]

Second-Level Elements	Third-Level Elements
A.1. Requirements	A.1a. Stability A.1b. Completeness A.1c. Clarity A.1d. Validity A.1e. Feasibility A.1f. Precedent A.1g. Scale
B.1. Development process	B.1a. Formality B.1b. Suitability B.1c. Process control B.1d. Familiarity B.1e. Product control
B.3. Management process	B.3a. Planning B.3b. Project organization B.3c. Management experience B.3d. Program interfaces
B.5. Work environment	B.5a. Quality attitude B.5b. Cooperation B.5c. Communication B.5d. Morale
C.1. Resources	C.1a. Schedule C.1b. Staff C.1c. Budget C.1d. Facilities

9.5.2 Brainstorming

Brainstorming is a widely used technique for generating lists of risk factors. The rules of brainstorming are "anything goes" (excluding distasteful racial, ethnic, religious, or sexual comments) and "no criticisms allowed." Criticism and critiquing occur in a later analysis session.

It is quite easy for a group of individuals to generate long lists of risk factors in a one or two hour brainstorming session. The group is usually restricted to 10 or fewer people so that everyone has an opportunity to participate. A round-robin, one idea in each turn, process provides everyone the opportunity to participate. A second session, held after a break, can be used to discuss and prioritize the risk factors using a ranking method such as open voting by show of hands, allocating a total number of points to the risk factors, or a Delphi process (see Chapter 6).

9.5.3 Expert Judgment

Expert judgment relies on the expertise and memories of past experiences among a selected group of experts. The biases (both optimistic and pessimistic) of the consulted experts should be taken into account when discussing risk factors and problems in past projects. The Delphi process can be used in conjunction with expert judgment to reduce biases among the experts (see Chapter 6).

9.5.4 SWOT

SWOT stands for strengths, weaknesses, opportunities, and threats. Four lists are prepared, one for each of S, W, O, and T. Checklists, brainstorming, and expert judgment can be used to facilitate a SWOT session. As in the case of brainstorming, free association of ideas should be encouraged. After a break in the meeting, the results of the SWOT exercise can be examined to identify risk factors in each of the four categories. A SWOT analysis can identify opportunities as well as risk factors.

9.5.5 Analysis of Assumptions and Constraints

An assumption is a situation or an event that is believed to be true, or believed will be true but which cannot be verified at the present time, or which you are unwilling to verify at this time. For example, it might be assumed that the requirements will not be modified without corresponding adjustments being made to schedule, resources, budget, and technology as necessary to maintain an acceptable probability of delivering a satisfactory product, on time and within budget. Or, it might be assumed that the hardware will be delivered as scheduled and will be available when needed.

Constraints are external conditions imposed on the development process and/or the deliverable product. As discussed previously, constraints should be examined for necessity and for possibilities of flexibility. It might be, for example, that the scheduled delivery date cannot be extended but some of the lower priority requirements could be deferred for inclusion in a second version of the product.

Assumptions and constraints for both the process and the product should be explicitly enumerated and examined for risk factors. An assumption that later proves to be false is a potential problem (a risk factor) that becomes a real problem when proved false. A constraint that might not be satisfied is a risk factor that becomes a problem if the constraint is not satisfied.

The results of checklist analysis, brainstorming, expert judgment, SWOT analysis, and other risk identification techniques should be examined for implicit assumptions and implied constraints. Those assumptions and constraints should be made explicit and analyzed as risk factors.

9.5.6 Lessons-Learned Files

Lessons-learned files are (or should be) prepared as a project termination activity for each project. A lessons-learned file should indicate:

- what went right in the project,
- what went wrong in the project,
- what could have been done better,
- root causes for both successes and failures, and
- recommendations for future projects.

Risk factors identified and confronted throughout the life cycle of the project should be included in the lessons-learned. You should consult the lessons-learned files within your organization when planning a project. You should also speak with project managers, software architects, team leaders, project members, and customers (to the extent possible) to understand social and political risk factors that may not be stated in lessons-learned files.

9.5.7 Cost and Schedule Modeling

Cost and schedule modeling can be used in several ways to identify and assess risk factors for your project. Recall, from Chapter 6, that an estimate is a projection from past to future, suitably adjusted to account for differences between past and future. The past is summarized by calibration of the cost model using historical data from past projects. The future is summarized by a size estimate based on the requirements. The adjustment factors account for differences between the "typical" past project and the future one caused by differences in factors such as product attributes, project attributes, personnel attributes, and technology factors.

The first way a cost and schedule estimation model can be used to identify risk factors is to examine the cost model(s) used:

- Is it (are they) appropriate, and appropriately calibrated for your kind of project?
- Does the scope of activities estimated match the scope of your project?
- Is the calibration data based on industry averages or local projects?
- Is the calibration recent or ancient?

A second way to identify risk factors using cost and schedule models is to examine the assumptions and constraints on which the estimate is based, and to do explicit management of assumptions and constraints, as described above. Some of the estimation parameters may be constrained (e.g., project duration and/or total cost); other estimation parameters are assumptions that cannot be verified during initial planning (e.g., adjustment factors that reflect the assumption of availability of adequate numbers of skilled personnel).

A third way of using cost and schedule models to identify risk factors is to do "what-if" analysis and sensitivity analysis of the estimate(s) produced by the model(s). What-if analysis involves varying the input parameters to a model and observing the outputs in a "what-if this were the case" manner:

- what if estimated size is bigger (or smaller) than assumed?
- what if the skill levels and experience of the software developers was higher (or lower)?
- what if other estimation parameters are not as assumed?

Sensitivity analysis is concerned with determining which input parameters produce large variations in estimated values for correspondingly small changes in those input parameters. For example, the combined effect of the personnel cost drivers in the COCOMO models exert the second strongest influence on estimated values, after estimated size. The effort-schedule trade-off in the SLIM model is very sensitive to the schedule duration (effort varies with the inverse fourth power of schedule in SLIM).

Analysis of the project's activity network can be used to identify risk factors associated with the project schedule. An activity network, such as the one illustrated in Figure 9.1, can be analyzed to determine:

- accuracy of estimated task durations on the critical path,
- paths that are "almost critical," and
- fan-in and fan-out at project milestones.

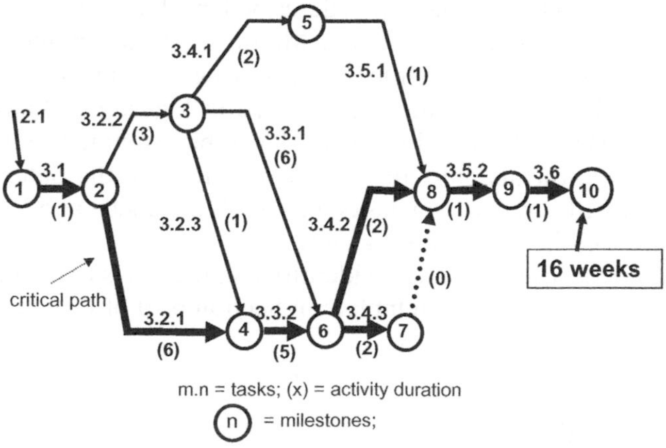

FIGURE 9.1 A critical-path activity network

Because the critical path (or paths) determine the overall project schedule, it is essential that estimates for the durations of tasks on the critical path be as accurate as possible. Multiple critical paths, as in Figure 9.1, present a risk factor because slippage in the schedule for either task 3.4.2 or 3.4.3 will delay completion of the project.

Because software projects are dynamic entities, a path that is "almost critical" can become the determinant of project completion if that path takes longer than estimated. In Figure 9.1, for example, the estimated duration to reach milestone 6 on the critical path is 12 weeks. The durations for tasks 3.1, 3.2.2, and 3.3.1 indicate the duration to reach milestone 6 is 10 weeks. Those tasks must be monitored closely determine that they do not use more than 2 weeks of slack time; otherwise, a contingency plan must be invoked.

The fan-in at a project milestone is determined by the number of incoming arrows that are incident on the milestone. Milestone 6 in Figure 9.1 has a fan-in of 2 and milestone 8 has a fan-in of 3. Because successor tasks cannot start until all predecessor tasks are completed, delay in completing any predecessor tasks that exceeds the scheduled time to reach the milestone will delay the start of predecessor tasks. Critical-path tasks 3.4.2 and 3.4.3 will be delayed if the path for tasks 3.1, 3.2.2, and 3.3.1 takes more than 12 weeks.

Fan-out is determined by the number of arrows leaving a milestone node. The fan-out is 3 at milestone 3 in Figure 9.1. Because none of the successor tasks can start until the predecessor tasks are completed, delay in any of the predecessor tasks will delay the start of all successor tasks. In Figure 9.1, for example, delayed completion of tasks 3.1 and 3.2.2 will delay the start of tasks 3.2.3, 3.3.1, and 3.4.1.

Milestones having high fan-in and/or high fan-out thus represent areas of potential problems in the schedule network, especially if they are on the critical path or a "near-critical" path. It may be possible to redesign the schedule network to reduce the fan-in and fan-out at high-risk milestones, provided that the work products produced by predecessor tasks are available when needed. Other options include preparing contingency plans and closely monitoring the predecessor and successor tasks, and redesigning the schedule network by extending the schedule to reduce fan-in and fan-out.

The fourth way a schedule network can be used to manage risk factors is to use the Monte Carlo method of estimation, as described in Chapter 6, to produce ranges of estimates with associated probabilities. Monte Carlo techniques can be used produce estimates of the probabilities of achieving various project milestones, including the completion milestone, as illustrated in Figure 9.2 [Fairley94]. Work packages for the tasks in the schedule network can be examined to determine risk factors associated with availability of needed resources on the dates needed, risk factors associated with predecessor tasks and work products, and the risk factors explicitly documented in the work packages.

Still another way to use estimates to identify risk factors is to examine the items documented using the estimation template in Section 6.10 of Chapter 6:

- when was the estimate made?
- who made the estimate?
- how much time and effort was spent in making the estimate?

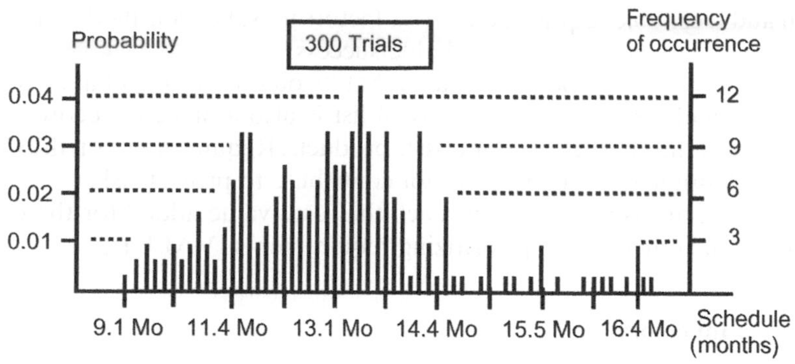

FIGURE 9.2 A Monte Carlo estimate of project completion date

- what estimation methods and tools were used?
- what was the basis of estimation for each method and tool used (industry averages, expert judgment, local historical data, etc.)?
- how were differences in the estimates reconciled?
- what assumptions were made for each method or tool used?
- what constraints were observed in making the estimates?
- what inputs were used for each method or tool used (e.g., size, PI, MBI, adjustment factors)?
- what are the probability levels for effort, schedule, resources, cost, and quality attributes for each method or tool used?
- what other estimation data was provided by the estimation methods and tools (e.g., project milestones, effort for various project activities, estimated pre-release and post-release defects, estimated reliability at product delivery, total life cycle costs)
- what risk factors were identified for the project?
- what is the estimator's (estimators') level of confidence in the accuracy of the estimate (0 to 10; low, medium, high)?
- what information, resources, and time do the estimators need to make an improved estimate?

9.5.8 Requirements Triage

Requirements triage is the process of determining which requirements a product should satisfy given the time and resources available [Davis03]. In Chapter 3, this was described as the process of prioritizing requirements into Essential, Desirable, and Optional categories. Risk management can be applied to requirements triage to determine that time and resources are sufficient to provide a very high level of probability that the Essential requirements can be implemented.

Desirable requirements must be prioritized and the time and resources needed to implement them must be negotiated with project stakeholders, perhaps at decreased probability of success for the lower priority requirements. In both cases

(Essential and Desirable requirements) risk factors must be identified and mitigated to provide the necessary levels of probable success.

Optional requirements specify features that "would be nice to have" if there is sufficient time and resources. The Optional list is also a place to record ideas for future releases of the product and for future products. Requirements on the Optional list are, by definition, optional and do not contribute to project risk.

Value engineering is a similar approach that uses value added for the customer versus cost as the criterion for prioritizing requirements [VALUE].

9.5.9 Assets Inventory

Assets are organizational resources that can be applied software projects. Another way to identify risk factors is to do an inventory of assets within your organization and to determine the quantities and qualities of assets that are available to your software project. Examples of organizational assets are listed in Table 9.6.

TABLE 9.6 Examples of organizational assets

- Project managers
- Requirements engineers
- Software architects
- Development team leaders
- Software developers
- Software testers
- Software development processes
- CM personnel, procedures, and tools
- QA personnel, procedures, and tools
- Analysis and design tools
- Testing tools
- Integrated development environments
- Workstations
- Local area networks
- Printers
- Quiet work spaces
- Private meeting rooms

Each type of asset can be analyzed for strengths and weaknesses in quantity and quality. Mitigation strategies can be developed to mitigate risk factors associated with assets. For example, you might determine that, for your project, there are insufficient software developers who have adequate experience using the Java programming language. Your mitigation process might involve providing training for your developers, hiring skilled developers, or subcontracting the work to an organization that has the necessary capabilities.

9.5.10 Trade-Off Analysis

Trade-off analysis is concerned with identifying permissible trade-offs and the risk factors associated with the trade-offs. It may be permissible to increase resources to maintain schedule progress but not permissible to de-scope any Essential requirements. In this case the risk factors to be identified are those related to availability of additional resources when (if) needed and the potential problems of implementing all the Essential requirements within the schedule constraint using reasonable amounts of resources.

9.6 RISK ANALYSIS AND PRIORITIZATION

Risk analysis is concerned with assessing the probabilities, potential impacts, and time frames of likely occurrence of identified risk factors. Prioritization ranks risk factors by probability, impact, and/or time frame when a potential problem might become a real problem. Ideally you will be able to perform quantitative risk analysis by assigning numeric values to probabilities and potential impacts for each identified risk factor, using a ratio scale, so that numerical risk exposure (i.e., the product of probability and potential impact) can be computed for each risk factor.

In some cases, you may be able to quantify probabilities and impacts by examining past projects, by consulting individual experts within your organization, or by using the Delphi method to obtain group consensus. Experts may differ in their assessments. If so, you can use their ranges of values to assess the ranges of risk exposures for various risk factors. In other cases, you may try "what-if" analysis that involves specifying various values of probability and impact for different risk factors and calculating the resulting risk exposures.

In other cases, you may not be able to quantify probabilities and impacts, so you may have to conduct risk analysis using a qualitative ordinal scale and assigning values such as Low, Medium, High, and Very High to the probability and potential impact of each identified risk factor. Risk exposure is then determined using Table 9.1. The ordinal values can be obtained by analyzing historical data, by consulting experts, by a Delphi process, or by what-if analysis.

Some organizations convert ordinal scales to ratio scales by assigning numeric values to probabilities and potential impacts as indicated in Table 9.7. In this case all involved parties must bear in mind the pitfalls of converting an ordinal scale to a ratio scale and thereby placing too much emphasis on the resulting values. For example, the involved parties may not agree as to what constitutes a Medium probability or impact as compared to a High probability or impact and the corresponding numeric values may be misleading.

TABLE 9.7 Ratio-scale equivalents of ordinal symbols

	Ordinal Value	Approximate Ratio-scale Value
Probability	Very low	0.10
	Low	0.25
	Medium	0.50
	High	0.75
	Very high	0.90
Impact	Very low	10
	Low	25
	Medium	50
	High	75
	Very high	90

In addition to the assessment of probability and impact, the time frame in which the risk factor might become a problem must be assessed. The risk of having insufficient personnel for work activities scheduled three months hence, for example, provides sufficient time to make arrangements. As the time for the work to commence draws nearer, the probability that a staffing risk will become a staffing problem becomes higher. According to Table 9.1, the risk exposure of having insufficient personnel for tasks scheduled in the coming week will be Very High, assuming that the probability is Very High and the Impact is High. As mentioned earlier, the goal of risk management is to identify and mitigate potential problems with sufficient lead time to avoid crisis situations. If you do not find the needed personnel during the present week you may well be in a crisis situation next week.

Risk factors can be prioritized using risk exposures (probability × potential impact) and the time frames of probable occurrence. Suppose, however, that two risk factors have equal risk exposures and similar time frames of occurrence. For example, suppose risk factor *A* has probability of 0.25 and potential impact of 75 on a utility scale of 100, and that risk factor *B* has probability of 0.75 and potential impact of 25. Both have risk exposures of 18.75. Assuming there are insufficient resources to effectively mitigate both *A* and *B*, which should receive the mitigation resources?

Suppose, for example, that if risk factor *A* becomes a problem it will negatively impact response time for the primary users of the system (i.e., customers of an Automated Teller System) and risk factor *B* will negatively impact response time for secondary users of the system (i.e., operational personnel who maintain the ATS). In this case resources probably would be allocated to mitigating risk factor *A*. Risk factor *B* would be placed on a watch list. Additional resources may have to be found, or existing resources reallocated to mitigate risk factor *B*, if it later becomes apparent that the risk exposure for *B* has increased to an unacceptable level.

This example illustrates an important point about risk management: risk management decisions are based on objective factors, such as risk exposure, and also on subjective factors that involve social and political considerations.

9.7 RISK MITIGATION STRATEGIES

Risk mitigation is concerned with developing and implementing strategies to handle risk factors. Mitigation is usually concerned with reducing either the probability of occurrence of a potential problem or reducing the impact of the potential problem, should it become a real problem. Mitigation strategies must be developed for the risk factors that have been identified, analyzed, and prioritized. As indicated in Table 9.8, mitigation strategies include avoidance, transfer, acceptance, immediate action, and contingent action.

9.7.1 Risk Avoidance

Risk avoidance is concerned with changing the situation to reduce the probability of a potential problem to an acceptable level. If a timing constraint in a real-time system is of concern, perhaps the timing constraint can be relaxed or perhaps a

TABLE 9.8 Risk mitigation Strategies

Strategy	Approach
Avoidance	Change the project or the product
Transfer	Reallocate the requirement(s)
Acceptance	Watch list
Immediate action	Reduce probability and/or impact
Contingent action	Delayed action, if warranted

faster hardware processor can be used; if there is insufficient time to complete the project, perhaps the schedule can be extended, thus avoiding the risk of late delivery.

As mentioned above, risk factors are often created by project constraints and can sometimes be avoided by modifying the constraints. Process constraints (schedule, budget, resources), product constraints (features and quality attributes), and technology constraints (processor speed, available memory) should be examined. Some constraints may be essential to a successful outcome. Others, on closer examination, may be relaxed or removed.

9.7.2 Risk Transfer

Risk transfer involves reallocating the requirements that created the risk factor to another system component or another organizational unit that can better handle the risk factor. Data compression, for example, may have to be implemented in a special purpose chip if the data compression algorithm cannot be executed rapidly enough in software. Or, you may decide to use a subcontractor for certain parts of your project if your project team does not have the necessary expertise to implement those parts.

Care must be taken that transfer of a risk factor does not create other unacceptable risks. The time and expense required to design and develop a special purpose chip may create unacceptable risks to cost and schedule. Managing a subcontractor may represent a greater risk to success than the learning curve required for your team, and your project will fail if the subcontractor fails to deliver acceptable components within an acceptable time frame.

9.7.3 Risk Acceptance

Risk acceptance is the third strategy for mitigating a risk factor. Acceptance involves acknowledging the risk factor but taking no action at the present time other than placing the risk factor on a watch list. Although risk acceptance does not result in a specific mitigation activity, each risk factor on a watch list is frequently re-examined on a periodic basis to determine if the level of probability, impact, or time frame has become prominent enough to warrant additional mitigation activities (e.g., avoidance, transfer, immediate action, or contingent action).

A watch list thus serves as a constant reminder to re-examine risk factors that may become more serious as your project progresses. Project staffing for example, might be sufficient for the next 3 months, but a concern for future staffing might result in placing staffing issues on the watch list. If staffing issues have not been resolved as the time of need approaches, an immediate action plan might be developed and implemented to acquire the needed staff members.

9.7.4 Immediate Action

Immediate actions are mitigation activities that are undertaken now to reduce the probability that a potential problem (i.e., a risk factor) will become a real problem, and/or actions to reduce the impact of a potential problem should it become a become real problem. Immediate actions are specified in immediate action plans. Suppose, for example, that your project team has insufficient skill in using the Java programming language. You might implement an immediate-action training plan to improve their skills and thereby reduce the risk of delivering an unacceptable product and/or overrunning the delivery schedule.

Documentation of an immediate-action plan includes:

- an identifier,
- the individual who is responsible for seeing that the plan is executed,
- responsibilities of others involved in implementing the plan,
- a description of the risk factor to be mitigated,
- the actions to be completed,
- the resources needed,
- the planned duration of the indicated actions,
- the progress milestones to be achieved, and
- the success criteria that will indicate successful completion of the planned activities.

An example is provided in Table 9.9.

You will never have enough time, money, or resources to perform adequate mitigating actions for all identified risk factors. Risk factors that have the highest priorities, as determined by risk exposures and subjective factors, should receive the majority of your limited resources.

One way to determine investment strategies is to calculate and compare risk leverage factors (RLF) for various investment strategies for your highest priority risk factors. RLF is calculated by calculating the risk exposure before mitigation, the risk exposure after mitigation, and dividing the difference by the cost of mitigation:

$$\text{RLF} = \frac{\text{RE}_{\text{before}} - \text{RE}_{\text{after}}}{\text{cost of mitigation}}.$$

Suppose, for example, that you are considering an investment of \$25,000 to reduce the probability from 0.4 to 0.1 of a risk factor with potential impact of \$500,000. Risk exposure before mitigation is \$200,000 (0.4 × \$500,000), risk exposure after mitigation would be \$50,000 (0.1 × \$500,000), and the cost of mitigation is estimated to be \$25,000. The RLF is thus

TABLE 9.9 Example of an immediate-action plan

- *Action plan number and name:* AP#3, Java Training
- *Responsible party:* Sue Smith
- *Other responsible parties:* Joe Williams will set up the workstations; as-yet unidentified instructor will deliver the course.
- *Risk factor to be mitigated:* lack of sufficient Java skill
- *Actions to be completed:* training class and lab exercise for 20 programmers
- *Responsible party:* Sue Smith
- *Resources needed:* instructor, classroom with work stations, release time for attendees
- *Duration of this action:* 4 weeks
- *Milestones for this action:*
  Week 1: find instructor, reserve classroom, identify attendees
  Week 2: load software on computers, obtain/reproduce class materials
  Week 3: conduct 5-day class
  Week 4: complete lab project (1/2 time, 4 days)
- *Success criteria for this action:* 19 of 20 attendees successfully complete the lab project

$$\text{RLF} = \frac{200{,}000 - 50{,}000}{25{,}000} = 6.0.$$

Larger risk leverage factors indicate better investment strategies.

There is no guarantee, of course, that the investment will reduce the probability from 0.4 to 0.1, nor is it certain that the risk factor will become a problem if it is not mitigated. The probability is "only 40%." However, $500,000 would be a severe financial loss to your organization and a severe loss of reputation for you. If you do not spend $25,000 to mitigate the risk factor and the problem occurs, you will be criticized. If you do spend $25,000 and the problem does not occur, you (and others) will never know if it would have occurred without spending $25,000.

In this regard investing in risk mitigation is akin to investing in insurance. You may be one of the fortunate ones who has never had a serious auto accident. It could be said that you have wasted a lot of money paying for auto insurance (especially if you are my age). However, the potential financial impact created by not buying insurance is so great that most rational people will continue to buy insurance, even though the probability of an accident based on historical evidence is low, and even if it were not required by law.

9.7.5 Contingent Action

Contingent actions are specified in contingency plans that are prepared for potential problems for which no immediate actions are warranted. If, for example, you are pursuing an incremental development strategy, lack of sufficient memory or inadequate response time may become a problem later, but for now, there is sufficient memory and the response time is acceptable. These kinds of risk factors become problems when objective risk indicators (objective measures) cross predetermined thresholds (the problem triggers).

Figure 9.3 (repeated from Chapter 7) provides an example of tracking allocated memory versus memory used in an embedded system project. The risk factor is lack

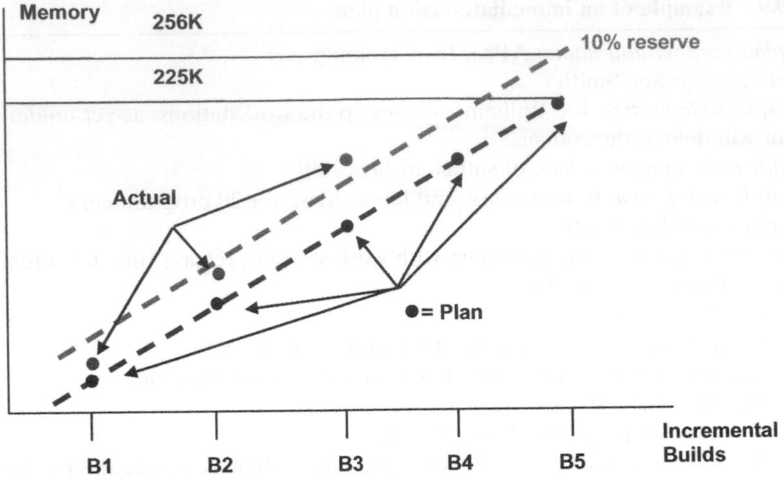

FIGURE 9.3 Illustrating a 10% memory threshold for risk management

of sufficient memory to implement the required software. The system is being implemented in a series of weekly incremental builds. Memory is allocated to each successive build of the system and the cumulative amount of memory used for each demonstrated build is compared to the allocated amount. As indicated in Figure 9.3, 10% of memory is held in reserve. The software will fit in the available memory if this margin is never exceeded.

In Figure 9.3, actual memory used in incremental builds B1 and B2 exceed the allocated amount planned but not by more than 10%. Build B3, however has caused actual memory used to exceed the 10% threshold. This is the trigger for invoking a contingency plan (see Table 9.11). One of the common failures of risk management is to "wait and see" whether the situation will improve without invoking the contingency plan.

Spontaneous improvement in a bad situation almost never happens. Recall that the purpose of risk management is to identify potential problems with sufficient lead time to avoid crisis situations. Although there is lots of memory still available after build B3, there is still a lot of functionality to be implemented. The trend, based on builds B1, B2, and B3, indicates that successively more memory is being used than was planned on each build. Now is the time to invoke the contingency plan to avoid the crisis of memory overrun.

A template for contingency plans is presented in Table 9.10. As indicated, a contingency plan specifies:

- the risk indicator to be measured;
- the frequency of measurement;
- the threshold value for contingent action (i.e., the problem trigger), the contingent-action plan; and
- the specified duration for the contingent actions to resolve the problem.

TABLE 9.10 Template for a contingency plan

Contingency plan number and name: CP#1 [name]

- *Responsible party:* [your name]
- *Risk factor to be mitigated:* [brief description]
- *Risk indicator(s) to be tracked:* [brief description]
- *Frequency of measurement:* [include units of time]
- *Threshold value(s) for contingent action(s):* [include units of measure]

Contingency action plan

- *Actions to be completed:* [brief description]
- *Responsibilities:* [list of who will do what]
- *Resources needed:* [list them]
- *Milestone for this action:* [frequency of progress measurement]
- *Success criteria for this action:* [how will we know when the problem is solved?]
- *Maximum duration of this action:* [when will we declare a crisis?]

TABLE 9.11 Example of a contingency plan

Contingency plan number and name: memory CP #5

- *Responsible party:* John Smith
- *Risk factor to be mitigated:* lack of sufficient memory in the microprocessor
- *Risk indicator to be measured:* planned versus actual memory used in successive incremental builds
- *Frequency of measurement:* weekly measurement of memory usage for successive incremental builds
- *Threshold value:* 10% over plan on any incremental build

Contingency action plan

- *Actions to be completed:* re-engineering of the software to fit within allocated memory
- *Responsibilities:* Joe Williams and Sue Smith will attempt to rectify the memory overrun; they will be released from all other duties and receive paid overtime
- *Resources Needed:* an additional target machine will be flown in overnight from San Jose
- *Milestones for this action:* no objective milestones; brief stand-up status meetings will be held at 11:00 AM and 6:00 PM each day
- *Success criteria for this action:* memory usage reduced to not more than 5% over allocated amount
- *Maximum duration of this action:* 7 days

A project enters crisis mode if the contingent actions do not achieve the success criteria specified in the plan within the specified duration.

The contingency plan for the risk factor in Figure 9.3 is presented in Table 9.11. Exceeding the 10% margin provides the trigger for activating the contingency plan. Figure 9.3 indicates that the contingency plan should be activated because incremental build B3 has exceeded the cumulative memory allocation for the build.

As discussed in Chapter 7, measuring attributes of a system to determine how well the system or some elements of the system satisfy specified requirements is known as Technical Performance Measurement (TPM). Measuring the amount of memory used versus the amount of memory allocated, as in Figure 9.3, is an example of TPM.

9.8 TOP-*N* RISK TRACKING AND RISK REGISTERS

Risk factors, the priorities among them, and their status can be displayed on top-*N* lists, where *N* is roughly 10. Different levels of your project and in your organization should have different lists. The top-*N* list is limited to roughly 10 risk factors because you, your project members, and your organization will not have the resources or time to effectively deal with more than 10 significant risk factors at any given level of the project (team, subsystem, project). You, your organization, and your customer should seriously consider re-scoping, or perhaps canceling your project if you have identified more than 10 significant risk factors (i.e. risk factors having High or Very High risk exposures as indicated in Tables 9.1*a* and 9.1*b*).

As illustrated in Table 9.12, each risk factor is ranked, its ranking in the previous reporting period is indicated, and the status of risk mitigation is indicated. Ranking is determined by consensus among those who will be affected if the risk factor becomes a problem. A risk factor may move up or down in the ranking based on periodic reassessment of the risk factor and the criticality of other risk factors. Both objective and subjective considerations should be taken into account in ranking the risk factors.

As indicated in Table 9.12, entry number 7 is a new risk factor in the top-*N* list. The last two entries are risk factors that were closed during the past week. If you were the project manager of the project in Table 9.12, you would be (should be) thinking about plans for contingent actions if the current actions fail to satisfactorily resolve the indicated risk factors in the indicated time frames.

Organizations that use top-*N* lists often have different lists of risk factors at different levels in the organization. Each team within a project has its list, each project has its list, each supporting organization has its list, and departments in which software projects are conducted have their lists. Project teams identify risk factors and pursue mitigation actions that are within the scope of their responsibility and authority. Risk factors that cannot be mitigated within the team are moved upward to the project level. Risk factors that can be mitigated within a project or a supporting organization are mitigated at that level. Risk factors that cannot be mitigated within a project or a supporting organization are reported upward and provide inputs to the department's top-*N* list.

Many organizations that use top-*N* lists update the lists on a weekly basis and post the lists in publicly accessible work spaces. This facilitates communication about potential problems and, in the words of a colleague, "decriminalizes" risk, which is to say that it becomes acceptable to discuss potential problems, their probabilities, their impacts and time frames, and mitigation strategies. Weekly updating of top-*N* lists ensures that ongoing, continuous risk management will occur. Use of top-*N* lists can have a revolutionary, positive effect on software projects and the culture of the work place within an organization.

Top-*N* risk tracking can be incorporated into a Risk Register, which is a table that can be implemented as a spreadsheet used to manage risk factors. As indicated in Table 9.13, each row of a Risk Register table includes the following items:

TABLE 9.12 Example of a top-*N* risk report ($N = 8$)

Project:	www					
Date:	xx/yy/zz					
Rank This Week	Rank Last Week	Weeks on List	Risk Factor	Potential Impact	Mitigating Action	Time Frame for Resolution
1	4	2	Replacement for sensor-control team leader	Delay in completion of coding; lower quality code	Meeting with department manager on Monday	Immediate
2	6	2	Requested changes in the user interface	Delayed delivery date	Assigned 2 additional people	Must complete changes by next Friday
3	2	5	Compiler bugs	Delay in completing the coding of hardware drivers	Validation tests in progress	New release must be validated by this Friday
4	3	6	Availability of work stations for system test	Cost and schedule delay	Meeting with customer and department manager on Wednesday	Must have work stations installed within one month
5	5	3	Definition of hardware test-bed	Delay of system integration	Review meeting scheduled for next Tuesday	Definition must be available by end of this month

TABLE 9.12 ***(Continued)***

Project:	www					
Date:	xx/yy/zz					
Rank This Week	Rank Last Week	Weeks on List	Risk Factor	Potential Impact	Mitigating Action	Time Frame for Resolution
6	1	3	Impact of fault-tolerance requirements on performance	Could require major change to the hw/sw architecture	Prototype demonstration scheduled for one week from Thursday	As soon as possible
7	—	1	Specification of telecommunications interface not completed	Delayed procurement of hardware subsystem	Meeting to consider alternatives scheduled for Wednesday	Must complete the specification by end of this month
8	8	4	Unavailability of technical writer/editor	Poor quality manuals	HR has placed ad with job agency	Needed as soon as possible
—	7	4	CM person needed	Inadequate support for increasing workload	Experienced CM person has joined the project	Resolved
—	9	5	Interface to the data base	Time and effort to implement a new interface	Resolved in the latest demonstration	Resolved

TABLE 9.13 Elements of a risk register

Risk factor identifier
Revision number and revision date
Responsible party
Risk category (schedule, resources, cost, technical, other)
Description
Status (closed, action, monitored)
If closed: date of closure and disposition (disposition: avoided, transferred, removed from watch list, immediate action or contingent action completed, crisis managed)
If active: action plan number or contingent-action plan number and status of the action (status: on plan; or deviating from plan plus risk factors in completing the plan)
If monitored: the following items apply:

- Top-*N* rank
- Previous rank
- Weeks on the list
- Potential impact
- Current action
- Time frame for resolution
- Relationship to other risk factors
- Related contingency plan

As indicated in Table 9.13, the responsibility for managing each risk factor should be assigned to an appropriate person. Responsibilities include:

- assuring that a mitigation plan is developed for the risk factor,
- tracking the risk indicator metric (or metrics),
- implementing and tracking the progress of action plans and contingency plans, and
- reporting status to designated parties.

The status of a risk factor can be Closed, Action, or Monitored:

- A Closed risk factor is one that did not happen (e.g., the hardware was delivered on time) or one for which a mitigation activity has successfully reduced the probability of occurrence and/or the potential impact to acceptable levels;
- Active status of a risk factor indicates that an immediate-action plan or a contingent-action plan has been invoked and is currently in progress; and
- A Monitored risk factor is one that is being tracked on a watch list or is being monitored by one or more risk indicator metrics. If a risk indicator crosses a predetermined threshold value, a contingent-action plan will be initiated and status will be changed from monitored to active.

Various kinds of reports can be generated from a risk register. For example, a list of all Closed, Active, or Monitored risk factors can be generated. Or, all of the risk factors for which particular individuals are responsible. Or, only the Top-*M* in the list of risk factors.

Different risk registers should be used at different levels of your organization. Each team should maintain a risk register that is updated weekly. The project team members should meet with you, the project manager, on a weekly basis to update the register, or with their team leaders who meet with you in turn. Items to be included in the project register are those risk factors that individual teams cannot handle and those that will have an impact beyond the individual team, should those risks become problems.

The department in which your project occurs should have a risk register that is updated on a weekly, bi-weekly, or monthly basis. Items in the department's risk register include those risk factors that cannot be handled at the project level or that are better handled at the department level. Similarly you and your customer, and you and your subcontractors (if any), should maintain jointly managed risk registers that are updated on a periodic basis, either monthly or quarterly depending on the duration and criticality of the project.

Each version of each risk register should be identified by number, date, type (team, project, department, customer, or subcontractor). Each version should be under version control to provide traceability and a historical log. As indicated above, using publicly displayed top-*N* risk lists and risk registers can have a positive, revolutionary effect on project and organizational communication.

Risk Radar is software tool that based on Microsoft Access that can be used to implement a risk register. Many of the items in Risk Radar are similar to those listed in Table 9.13, although Risk Radar uses a somewhat different format. Sample screen shots from Risk Radar can be seen at http://www.iceincusa.com/Content/RRFlyer.pdf. A free demo copy of Risk Radar can be downloaded from http://www.iceincusa.com/Products.aspx?p=Products_RiskRadar.

9.9 CONTROLLING THE RISK MANAGEMENT PROCESS

Like all processes of software engineering, the risk management process must be tailored to fit the needs of each of your projects. In a small project consisting of a single development team (5 or fewer developers), a weekly updated risk register in the form of a single spreadsheet is sufficient. You, as project manager, software architect, and team leader, would be the keeper of the risk register and control the risk management process.

Like all processes the risk management process becomes more complex in larger projects that involve multiple development teams and that may involve multiple departments, multiple customers, and multiple subcontractors. In these cases each risk factor should be documented using a risk reporting form, such as the one illustrated in Table 9.14.

Each reported risk factor is analyzed and controlled by a Risk Management Board (RMB), which is similar in operation to a Change Control Board (see Section 3.4.5). Your project RMB should be headed by you, the project manager, and should include your software architect, your team leaders, and representatives of the CM, QA, support, and maintenance functions. You should have separate RMBs to jointly manage acquirer-supplier risk factors that have the potential to affect relations with

TABLE 9.14 Format of a risk reporting form

Risk report number:
Submitter: [name and contact information]
Risk category: [schedule, resources, cost, technical, other]
Severity level:
Description:
Potential impact:
Time frame:
Recommended disposition: [avoid, transfer, accept, immediate action, contingent action]

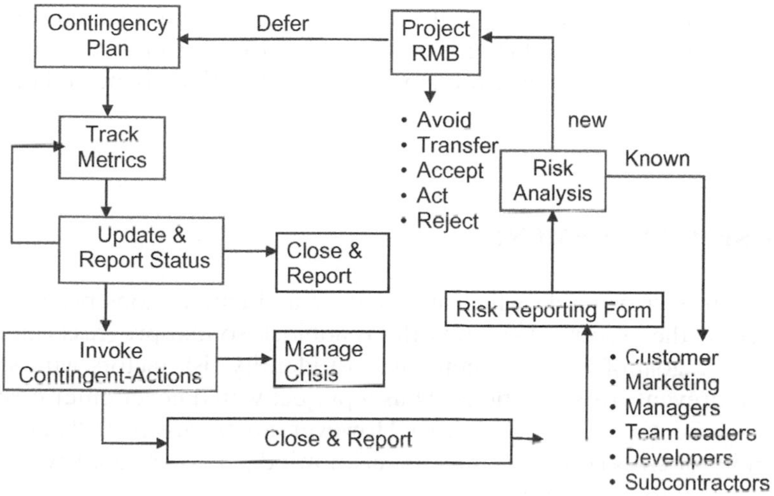

FIGURE 9.4 Process flow for controlling the risk management process

your customer and to jointly manage risk factors with your subcontractor(s), if any (see Section 9.11 and 9.12).

As indicated in Figure 9.4, items of concern to project stakeholders are reported using risk reporting forms. Items are analyzed by a risk analyst (you, on a small project; perhaps by a staff assistant on larger projects). The submitter is notified if the risk factor is already known and is being handled. Otherwise, the analyst reviews the risk report, adds her or his concurrence or other recommendations, and forwards the report to the RMB.

The RMB takes action (or directs others to take action) to:

- avoid,
- transfer,
- accept the risk factor and place it on a watch list,
- develop and execute an immediate-action plan ("Act" in Figure 9.4), or
- develop a contingency plan and monitor the risk factor ("Defer" in Figure 9.4);

or the RMB may decide to reject the risk report.

In all cases other than rejection of the risk report, a new item is entered in the appropriate risk register (team, project, department, customer, subcontractor). Like all important work products, the risk register is placed under version control to prevent unauthorized changes and provide a historical log of risk management activities.

If the decision is to monitor the risk factor, a contingency plan is developed (see Tables 9.10 and 9.11), one or more risk indicator metrics are tracked, and status is reported on a periodic basis. At some point the entry in the risk register may be closed because the risk did not materialize, or a risk indicator metric may trigger contingent actions because the metric crossed a predetermined threshold value.

Contingent actions may successfully handle a risk factor that has become a problem. In that case the risk factor is closed in the risk register. Or, the contingent actions may fail to overcome the problem in the specified time frame and the project enters crisis mode.

9.10 CRISIS MANAGEMENT

A project enters crisis mode when an event or a situation stops progress. Crisis management is the process of clearing the roadblock so that progress can resume. Recall that the goal of risk management is to identify risk factors with sufficient lead time to prevent crisis situations. Thus a project would never enter crisis mode if risk management were 100% effective. However, no process is 100% effective, so the possibility of crisis situations must be acknowledged. There are several ways a project can get into crisis mode:

- failing to systematically identify, prioritize, and mitigate potential problems;
- identifying potential problems but taking no mitigating actions;
- unforeseen and unforeseeable situations and events; and
- failure of a contingent-action plan to solve the problem in the allocated time frame.

It could be, for example, that no one foresaw lack of sufficient memory would be a problem, or perhaps the possibility of insufficient memory was discussed but no mitigating actions were taken (including failure to put the risk factor on a watch list), or perhaps the contingent-action plan, as executed by Joe and Sue, failed to solve the problem within the 7 days allocated to fixing the problem.

Guidelines for managing crisis situations include:

- acknowledging the situation,
- allocating sufficient resources,
- seeking creative solutions,
- reviewing status frequently, and
- setting a “drop-dead” date.

A project in crisis mode is in jeopardy of failure. Appropriate stakeholders, including the customer and upper level managers, must be notified; painful as that may be. A drop-dead date for the project must established by those stakeholders. Because the project is in jeopardy, all available resources that can be productively used must be allocated to overcome the crisis even if other work activities must be temporarily halted. Creative solutions should be explored but not to the extent that progress is overcome by "analysis paralysis." Status should be reviewed on a daily, or even twice daily basis, in short status meetings with participants limited to those directly involved in attempting to overcome the crisis (e.g., 15 to 30 minute stand-up meetings).

If the crisis is overcome within the allocated time for crisis management, schedules, budgets, and work plans must be revised to account for the time and resources spent on crisis management.

The last guideline, setting a "drop-dead" date, is particularly important to force decisive action when a crisis cannot be overcome within a specified time frame; otherwise, a project may languish in crisis mode far beyond a reasonable decision point. The resulting decision at the drop-dead date will be to:

1. cancel the project or
2. significantly re-scope it.

If the project is canceled a termination plan must be prepared and executed. The plan must include a redeployment plan for the project members and may require difficult negotiations with the customer, who may be internal or external to your organization. If the project is re-scoped, the requirements and a project plan must be developed for the (new) project.

In any case (successfully overcoming the crisis, canceling the project, or significantly re-scoping it), the staff members who have made extraordinary contributions in attempting to overcome the crisis must be rewarded for their efforts. The reward may take the form of a couple of days off to catch up on sleep and to see family members plus a letter or e-mail of appreciation (the recommended reward), or a dinner for the family, or conference travel, or some combination of these.

9.11 RISK MANAGEMENT AT THE ORGANIZATIONAL LEVEL

Most of the processes, methods, and techniques presented in this chapter are concerned with managing risk factors at the level of individual projects. Managing risk factors in your software projects will be easier, and more likely to be successful, if risk management is supported at the organizational level of the organization in which your project is conducted. Communications with senior managers and customers that are based on risk management will enable them to understand the competitive, financial, and strategic options for systems, products, and product suites.

Factors that result in successful risk management at the organizational level include [Fairley96]:

- explicit definition of development and management practices,
- communication based on risk management,
- risk reporting to senior managers, and
- a corporate policy for risk management of software projects.

At the corporate level risk management policies should require, for all projects:

- risk management plans developed at the planning stage of a project and incorporated into the overall project plan;
- project-specific tailoring of the development process and the risk management methods, tools, and techniques to be used; and
- explicit review of risk factors on a regular, ongoing basis.

As indicated earlier in this chapter, uniform risk management processes throughout the organizational unit is a level 3 process area in the staged representation of CMMI-DEV-v1.2.

9.12 JOINT RISK MANAGEMENT

Some risk factors may require mitigation strategies that involve an external customer, your organization (the supplier), and you (the project manager). For example, reducing risk factors created by ambiguous operational requirements may require greater involvement of representative users; mitigation of technical risk factors may require increased allocation of resources (i.e., money) from the customer, increased involvement with a hardware group, or de-scoping of the requirements. Effective risk management at this level requires a great deal of trust and cooperation between the customer and the supplier (your organization). On the other hand, if there is no trust or cooperation between acquirer and supplier the project will probably fail in any case.

Similarly risk factors that arise in using subcontractors should be jointly managed by you (the subcontractor's customer) and the subcontractor (your supplier). Each subcontract should require the subcontractor to practice internal and joint risk management.

9.13 KEY POINTS OF CHAPTER 9

- A risk factor is a potential problem that becomes a real problem when an objectively measured risk indicator crosses a predetermined threshold.
- Risk factors are characterized by probability of occurrence and potential loss.
- Project risk is the set of risk factors that have the potential to negatively impact a software project.
- Most standards and guidelines for software project management include risk management as a key process.
- Conventional project management techniques for planning and estimating, measuring and controlling, and leading and directing software projects are institutionalized techniques used to manage generic risk factors.

- Risk management techniques are used to identify, analyze, prioritize, and mitigate project-specific risk factors.
- Risk mitigation strategies include avoidance, transfer, acceptance, immediate action, and contingent action.
- Successful risk mitigation reduces the probability and/or the loss of a potential problem to acceptable levels.
- Managing risk factors in your software projects will be easier, and more likely succeed, if risk management is supported at the organizational level of the organization in which your project is conducted.
- You and your customer, and you and your subcontractors (if any), should engage in joint risk management.

REFERENCES

[Boehm91] Boehm, B. W. Software risk management: Principles and practices. *IEEE Software* (January 1991). vol. 8, No. 1. pp 32–41.

[Carr93] Carr, M. J., et al. *Taxonomy-Based Risk Identification*. www.sei.cmu.edu/pub/documents/93.reports/pdf/tr06.93.pdf, 1993.

[CMMI06] SEI. CMMI® *Models and Modules*. http://www.sei.cmu.edu/cmmi/models/, 2006.

[Davis03] Davis, A. The art of requirements triage. *IEEE Computer* (March 2003). Vol. 32, No. 3. pp 42–49.

[Fairley94] Fairley, R. E. Risk management for software projects. *IEEE Software* (May 1994). vol. 11, No. 3, pp 57–67.

[Fairley96] Fairley, R., and P. Rook. Risk management for software development. *IEEE Tutorial on Software Engineering*. IEEE Computer Society, 1996. pp 387–400.

[Fairley05] Fairley, R. E. Software risk management glossary. *IEEE Software* (May/June 2005). Vol. 22, No. 3, pp 101.

[IEEE1058] IEEE Std 1058™–1998. *IEEE Standard for Software Project Management Plans*. Engineering Standards Collection. IEEE Product: SE113. Institute of Electrical and Electronic Engineers, August 2003.

[IEEE12207] IEEE/EIA 12207.0/.1/.2. *Industry Implementation of International Standard ISO/IEC 12207:1995 Standard for Information Technology—Software Life Cycle Processes*. Engineering Standards Collection. IEEE Product: SE113. Institute of Electrical and Electronic Engineers, August 2003.

[IEEE1540] IEEE Std 1540™–2001. *IEEE Standard for Software Life Cycle Processes—Risk Management*, Engineering Standards Collection. IEEE Product: SE113. Institute of Electrical and Electronic Engineers, August 2003.

[PMI04] PMI. *A Guide to the Project Management Body of Knowledge*, 3rd ed. (PMBOK® Guide). Project Management Institute, 2004.

[VALUE] http://www.value-eng.org/.

EXERCISES

9.1. CMMI-DEV-v1.2 lists three related process areas in the risk management process area: project planning, project monitoring and control, and decision analysis and resolution. Access the CMMI Web site at http://www.sei.cmu.edu/publications/documents/06.reports/06tr008.html. Review the risk management process area, and briefly explain how each of the three related process areas is related to risk management.

9.2. Table 9.1 lists some commonly occurring risk factors for software projects. List three additional risk factors that can occur in software projects and provide an example of each one.

9.3. One of the risk factors listed by Boehm in [Boehm91] is straining computer science capabilities; that is, attempting to implement software for which the algorithms are not known. Give three examples not mentioned in this text of areas where a customer might request features that would strain computer science capabilities. Briefly explain each.

9.4. In Section 9.1 it is stated that one might create a risk to maintainability by violating the principles of coupling and cohesion in order to avoid the problem of exceeding available memory.

a. Briefly explain how memory usage could be reduced by violating the principles of coupling and cohesion.

b. Briefly explain how violating those principles could create a maintainability risk.

9.5. Excessive overtime is an unacceptable method for overcoming problems in a software project.

a. Briefly explain how much overtime is excessive, in your opinion.

b. Briefly explain three risk factors for project success that are created by excessive overtime.

9.6. Software projects often have risk factors that are not apparent during initial planning of a software project. Give three examples of risk factors not mentioned in this text that might not be apparent during initial planning of a software project. Briefly explain each.

9.7. Select one risk management technique (avoid, transfer, accept, act, defer, reject) for each of the risk factors listed in Table 9.2 (10 total). Briefly explain how each of the risk management techniques you selected can be used to manage risk factors for software projects. Select each of the six techniques at least once.

9.8. In Section 9.2 an example is given of a risk factor that will become a problem if your software architect leaves your company. Briefly explain 3 techniques you might use to mitigate the problems that would be created if she leaves. Note that she has not yet left and that she may not leave.

9.9. Prepare a spreadsheet to implement a risk register using the format in Table 9.13. Populate the spreadsheet with some risk factors from Exercises 9.7 and 9.8, and/or some hypothetical risk factors. Hand in your spreadsheet program and a printed listing of the output from it.

APPENDIX 9A

FRAMEWORKS, STANDARDS, AND GUIDELINES FOR RISK MANAGEMENT

9A.1 THE CMMI-DEV-v1.2 RISK MANAGEMENT PROCESS AREA

The CMMI-DEV-v1.2 process framework includes risk management as a process area at level 3 in the staged representation and as a project management process area in the continuous representation. As stated in CMMI-DEV-v1.2[30]:

> The purpose of Risk Management (RSKM) is to identify potential problems before they occur so that risk handling activities can be planned and invoked as needed across the life of the product or project to mitigate adverse impacts on achieving objectives.

The specific goals and specific practices of risk management in the CMMI process models are:

SG 1 Prepare for risk management
- SP 1.1 Determine risk sources and categories
- SP 1.2 Define risk parameters
- SP 1.3 Establish a risk management strategy

SG 2 Identify and analyze risks
- SP 2.1 Identify risks
- SP 2.2 Evaluate, categorize, and prioritize risks

SG 3 Mitigate risks
- SP 3.1 Develop risk mitigation plans
- SP 3.2 Implement risk mitigation plans

Process areas related to risk management in the CMMI models are:

[30] CMU/SEI-2006-TR-008, page 432.

- Project Planning,
- Project Monitoring and Control, and
- Decision Analysis and Resolution.

9A.2 ISO/EIC AND IEEE/EIA STANDARDS 12207

Appendix G, Section G.10, of IEEE/EIA Standard 12207.0 (management process) includes the following objectives:

- determine the scope of risk management to be performed for the project;
- identify risks to the project as they develop;
- analyze risks and determine the priority in which to apply resources to mitigate those risks;
- define, implement, and assess appropriate risk mitigation strategies; and
- define, apply, and assess risk metrics to measure the change in the risk state and the progress of the mitigation activities.

The scope of risk management includes the activities to be performed, which are listed in Annex L of IEEE/EIA 12207.2 :

- risk planning
- risk identification
- risk analysis
- risk mitigation
- risk tracking and control

IEEE/IEA Standard 12207.2 , Section L.2 (risk planning), states that a risk management plan should be developed and that the plan should include methods of performing risk management, ways in which risk management activities will be documented and reported, those responsible for risk management activities, and ways in which risk factors and their status will be communicated to other organizations, such as the acquirer and subcontractors. It is also noted that the risk management plan may be part of the project management plan.

Section l.1 of Annex L in 12207.2 emphasizes that risk management is part of the overall management process and is not a replacement for other project management activities (i.e., risk management augments conventional project management).

9A.3 IEEE/EIA STANDARD 1058

Subclause 5.4 of IEEE Standard 1058-1998 for software project management plans (risk management plan) states that risk management plans shall specify:

- processes and procedures that will be used to identify, analyze, prioritize, and mitigate project risk factors, both initially and throughout the life cycle of the project;

- methods that will be used to track the various risk factors;
- methods of evaluating changes in the levels of risk factors; and
- plans for responding to changes.

In addition a risk management plan should specify who will be responsible for the various aspects of risk management, how often risk factors will be reviewed, the review process, and who will be involved. Also the plan should specify how risk status will be reported and to whom.

Risk factors that should be considered include potential problems in:

- acquirer-supplier relationship;
- contractual factors;
- technological factors;
- size and complexity of the product;
- development and target environments;
- personnel acquisition, skill levels, and retention;
- schedule and budget; and
- acquirer acceptance of the product.

Section 5.4 of Appendix B in Chapter 4 of this text poses a set of questions to be addressed in preparing a risk management plan.

9A.4 THE PMI BODY OF KNOWLEDGE

Chapter 11 of the *Guide to the PMI Project Management Body of Knowledge* (PMBOK) is concerned with risk management. The introduction to Chapter 11 states that the objectives of project risk management are to increase the probability and impact of positive events, and decrease the probability and impact of events adverse to the project.

Topics addressed in Chapter 11 of PMBOK include:

- Risk Management Planning,
- Risk Identification,
- Qualitative Risk Analysis,
- Quantitative Risk Analysis,
- Risk Response Planning, and
- Risk Monitoring and Control.

According to PMBOK, the distinction between quantitative and qualitative risk management is determined by the degree to which objectively derived numbers can be assigned to probabilities and impacts of potential problems, as illustrated in Tables 9.1*a* and 9.1*b* of this chapter.

9A.5 IEEE STANDARD 1540

Although risk management is mentioned throughout ISO/IEC and IEEE/EIA Standards 12207 , they do not contain an explicit risk management process. IEEE Standard 1540–2001 is the *IEEE Standard for Life Cycle Processes—Risk Management* [IEEE1540].

According to IEEE 1540, the procedures that implement the risk management process should specify:

- frequency at which risks are to be reanalyzed and monitored,
- type of risk analysis required (quantitative and/or qualitative),
- measurement scales to be used to estimate risk likelihood and consequences,
- types of risk thresholds to be used,
- types of measures used to track and monitor the state of the risks,
- how risks are to be prioritized for treatment,
- which stakeholder(s) perspectives the risk management process supports, and
- risk categories to be considered.

The standard contains 5 annexes (i.e., appendixes):

- Annex A: risk management plan
- Annex B: risk action request
- Annex C: risk treatment plan
- Annex D: application of risk management in the IEEE/EIA 12207 series
- Annex E: annotated bibliography

The outline for risk management plans in Annex A of IEEE Standard 1540 contains the following items to be included in the risk management plan for each project:

- policies and guidelines to be followed
- responsibilities for risk management
- risk management orientation and training
- costs and schedules for risk management
- a description of the risk management process
  - risk analysis
  - risk monitoring
  - risk treatment
- risk management process evaluation
  - capturing risk information
  - assessing the risk management process
  - generating lessons learned

- risk communication
  - documentation and reporting
  - coordination of risk management with stakeholders
  - coordination of risk management with interested parties
- change procedures and history

APPENDIX 9B

SOFTWARE RISK MANAGEMENT GLOSSARY

Contingency plan A plan for dealing with a risk factor, should it become a problem.

Continuous risk management The process of analyzing the progress of a planned activity, project, or program on a periodic, ongoing basis and handling identified risk factors; includes developing options and fallback positions to permit alternative solutions to reduce the impact if a risk factor becomes a problem.

Crisis A critical state of affairs in which a decisive, undesirable outcome is impending.

Crisis management Steps to take when a contingency plan doesn't solve the associated problem.

Problem A negative situation to overcome. A risk factor becomes a problem when a risk metric (an objective measure) crosses a predetermined threshold (the problem trigger).

Risk The probability of incurring a loss or enduring a negative impact.

Risk acceptance Acknowledgment of a risk factor's existence along with a decision to accept the consequences if the corresponding problem occurs; *also called risk assumption.*

Risk analysis The process of examining identified risk factors for probability of occurrence, potential loss, and potential risk-handling strategies.

Risk avoidance A course of action that removes a risk factor from further consideration (e.g., by changing the requirements, extending the schedule, or transferring the cause of the risk factor to another domain).

Risk exposure The product of probability times potential loss for a risk factor; usually on a ordinal scale (e.g., Low, Medium, High) or expressed on a ratio scale in monetary units or utility.

Risk factor A potential problem that would be detrimental to a planned activity, project, or program, characterized by the probability of problem occurrence

($0 < p < 1$) and a potential loss (of life, money, property, reputation, etc) should the problem occur. Both probability and potential loss might change over time.

Risk handling A course of action taken in response to a risk factor; includes risk acceptance, risk avoidance, risk transfer, and risk mitigation.

Risk identification An organized, systematic approach to determining the risk factors associated with a planned activity, project, or program.

Risk leverage factor (*rlf*) *rlf* (*reb* – *rea*)/*rmc*, where *reb* is risk exposure before risk mitigation, *rea* is risk exposure after risk mitigation, and *rmc* is the risk mitigation activity's cost. A larger *rlf* indicates a better mitigation strategy.

Risk management An organized process for identifying and handling risk factors; includes initial identification and handling of risk factors as well as continuous risk management.

Risk metric An objective measure associated with a risk factor to be mitigated.

Risk mitigation A course of action taken to reduce the probability of and/or potential loss from a risk factor; includes executing contingency plans when a risk metric crosses a predetermined threshold (when a risk factor becomes a problem).

Risk reduction Reducing the probability and/or potential impact of a risk factor; might involve research, prototyping, and other means of exploration.

Risk transfer Transferring responsibility for managing a risk factor to another organization or functional entity better able to mitigate the risk factor.

Risk trigger The predetermined threshold value of a risk metric that triggers invocation of a contingency plan when the risk metric crosses the threshold.

Root-cause analysis Determination of a potential problem's (a risk factor's) underlying cause or causes.

Uncertainty The result of not having accurate or sufficient knowledge of a situation; often the root cause of a risk factor.

Utility A measure of value within a given context, often measured on a scale of 0 to 100.

10

TEAMS, TEAMWORK, MOTIVATION, LEADERSHIP, AND COMMUNICATION

If your actions inspire others to dream more, learn more, do more, and become more, you are a leader.

—John Quincy Adams

10.1 INTRODUCTION

The three key assets for software projects are people, processes, and technology. To succeed, you must have the correct number of people who have adequate skills and are motivated to do their best work. Processes include procedures for accomplishing the work and coordinating work activities. Technology includes the infrastructure, methods, hardware, software tools, and other equipment needed to develop the product. People are the most important asset; people of outstanding ability and motivation can often overcome inadequate processes and technology, but excellent processes and technology cannot compensate for lack of ability and motivation. Also salaries for project members are typically the largest component of project costs.

In addition to individual ability and motivation, software projects require closely coordinated teamwork. Teams are essential because the variety of skills possessed by different team members are needed and because no one is interested in waiting 10 years for 1 person to complete a 10 person-year project that could be completed in 1 year by 10 people. In addition the synergy that occurs when team members work together in a collaborative manner often results in a product superior to the one that would have resulted from the efforts of several individuals working in isolation. Software developers must be individual contributors as well as willing and enthusiastic team members.

Because software development and modification are intellectual efforts, close coordination of your team's (or teams') efforts is essential. Unfortunately, some software engineers with outstanding technical skills are not interested in being, nor are psychologically suited to be, members of a cohesive team.

Too often software organizations are guilty of suboptimizing the productivity of a team by catering to the idiosyncrasies of technically skilled but socially inept individuals. In some cases it may be necessary to remove a disruptive team member for the greater good of the team, the project, and the organization.

This chapter is concerned with issues of teamwork, motivation, and leadership styles for software projects. These factors exert a strong influence on the morale of individuals and teams, and as a result, on productivity, production rate, product quality, and customer satisfaction.

10.2 OBJECTIVES OF THIS CHAPTER

After reading this chapter and completing the exercises you should understand:

- managing versus leading,
- the nature of teams and teamwork,
- techniques for maintaining morale and motivation,
- personality styles, and
- the 5-layer behavioral model of software development.

The standards and guidelines presented in each of the preceding chapters, namely, CMMI-DEV-v1.2, ISO/IEEE Standard 12207, IEEE Standard 1058, and the PMI Body of Knowledge, address people issues to a limited degree. Other guidelines for leading and directing individual and team efforts include the people CMMI, the team software process (TSP) which is based on the personal software process (PSP), and the dos and don'ts in the text *Peopleware*. A summary of these guidelines is provided in Appendix 10A to this chapter.

Terms used in this chapter and throughout this text are defined in Appendix A to the text. Presentation slides for this chapter and other supporting material are available at the URL listed in the Preface.

10.3 MANAGING VERSUS LEADING

Your duties, as project manager, include managing the project and leading the project personnel. Managing is concerned with making plans and estimates, collecting and analyzing project and product data, reporting progress, controlling the development process and the work products, and identifying and mitigating risk factors. Leading is concerned with communicating with your project personnel and other stakeholders, coordinating the work activities, and maintaining morale.

Good managers are not necessarily good leaders, and good leaders are not necessarily good managers. Managing is an analytical activity, whereas leading involves human relations. Different personality traits and different skill sets are required for

TABLE 10.1 Some attributes of effective leaders

- Listens carefully
- Delegates authority
- Facilitates teamwork
- Coordinates work activities
- Facilitates communication
- Speaks with individuals on a daily basis
- Says "thank you" when warranted
- Coaches and trains
- Maintains enthusiasm
- Reconciles differences
- Resolves conflicts
- Indoctrinates newly assigned personnel
- Helps employees develop career plans and achieve their professional objectives
- Reassigns, transfers, and terminates personnel as necessary

managing and for leading. Some excellent managers are poor leaders and some excellent leaders are poor managers.

An effective leader is a good listener who listens for, hears, and responds to the subtext as well as the main text of a conversation; is a facilitator who provides the catalyst for effective teamwork; is a coach who provides guidance and encouragement; and is an enthusiast who believes in the project team and the goals of the project. Attributes of effective leaders are listed in Table 10.1.

To be an effective project manager, you must identify those activities of managing and leading for which you have an aptitude and which you enjoy doing. You must then find ways to compensate for the other work activities that you do not enjoy and for which you do not have the aptitude. As Tom DeMarco has said, "Find out what you are not good at and don't do it." [31]

You may find, for example, that you are an excellent leader who easily establishes good working relationships with others and that others enjoy working with you, but that you do not enjoy preparing earned value reports or analyzing defect data. In this case you and your organization may find it cost-effective to delegate the analytical tasks to a designated person who will work with you on those tasks which, for you, are unappealing. That person might be a staff assistant working with you on a part-time or full-time basis, depending on the scope of your project or, the person might be someone whom you are mentoring and preparing to become a project manager.

Or it may be, by dint of your personality and skill set, you are an excellent manager but less capable as a leader. You may find that your technical leader (i.e., software architect) is the de facto leader of the software developers to whom they look for technical decisions and guidance. This can be a very effective arrangement, provided that you and your technical leader have a close working relationship, a clear understanding of your realms of responsibility, and the ability to work out your differences in private, thus presenting a united front.

The division of responsibilities between you, as project manager, and your technical leader are as follows:

[31] Private conversation.

- You are responsible for delivering an acceptable product on schedule and within budget.
- Your technical leader is responsible for leading the project team to achieve the "acceptable product" part of the equation, within the constraints of schedule and budget.

As Fred Brooks observed, you, the project manager, are akin to the movie producer who is responsible for the overall project. Your technical leader is akin to the movie director who is responsible for the content of the product [Brooks95]. The most successful movies (and software projects) are those in which the producer and director have a harmonious working relationship. The failures are often the result of incompatibilities in viewpoints and personality conflicts between producer (project manager) and director (technical leader). Your software developers and support personnel are the actors and stage hands who work to develop an acceptable product within the constraints of schedule, budget, and technology.

In the best case you will find that you are effective as both a manager and a leader. On small projects you may function as both manager and technical leader or, on small projects, you (the producer) and your technical leader (the director) may work simultaneously together on two or more small projects, thus applying your separate skill sets in the most beneficial way.

You may find some management tasks are unpleasant because you do not have the training, tools, or organizational infrastructure to do your tasks in an efficient and effective manner. One of the ironies of software organizations (and of engineering organizations in general) is that the best technical people are often selected to be project managers without benefit of training, apprenticeship, or mentoring in management and leadership. If you are fortunate enough to receive proper support from your organization, you can become effective in areas you formerly regarded as your weaknesses.

10.4 TEAMS AND TEAMWORK

One of your primary tasks as a leader is to foster a teamwork atmosphere within your project. A team is a group of individuals working in a cooperative and coordinated manner to achieve shared objectives and goals. A group of people working together is not a team if they do not have a cooperative attitude and share common objectives and goals. Team members are individuals who have individual goals, agendas, motivations, desires, aptitudes, and attitudes; but to be a team, the individual members must also have a shared vision and shared work products. Each member must be willing to subordinate some of their individual goals to the shared goals of the team; better yet, individual goals should be aligned with team goals. In return, rewards (and penalties) should be for the project team as a whole, and for subteams as appropriate, but never for individual project members.

Coalescence of individuals into cohesive teams seldom happens spontaneously. Factors that contribute to team formation include the personalities of the individuals and the social and cultural conditions in the organization [Katzen93]. Some factors that contribute to efficient and effective software teams are listed in Table 10.2.

TABLE 10.2 Factors that contribute to efficient and effective software engineering teams

- Appropriate number of people
- Correct skill mixture
- Good tools
- Adequate training
- Respect for one another
- Respect for managers and leaders
- Willingness to be team members
- Shared ownership of the work products
- Good communication skills
- Good communication channels
- Good working environment
- Having some fun together

One of your primary responsibilities, as project manager, is to facilitate the conditions listed in Table 10.2 so that your project members will coalesce into a team, or teams. Your project team(s) must have a sufficient number of people who have the necessary skills, tools, and training to achieve the project objectives within the constraints of schedule, budget, requirements, and technology.

In many organizations team members are selected by applying for, and being interviewed for, membership in the project team. The applicant may be an employee of the organization or a potential new hire from outside the organization. In the former case (a present employee), personnel throughout the organization are allowed to apply for jobs that constitute lateral transfers at the same skill level or that constitute promotions to positions such as lead designer, leader of a development team, leader of the testing team, or tester to developer. Applicants are not accepted without the approval of the appropriate persons, including you (the project manager), your lead designer, and the present team members who would work with the applicant, and the applicant's present manager.

Respect, as is often said, must be earned. You, the project manager, must work to earn the respect of your project team members by exhibiting:

- competence,
- ability,
- integrity, and
- concern for their welfare.

Every project member must likewise exhibit these characteristics to earn and keep the respect of other team members.

You may find some individuals have no interest in being members of a team. These so-called lone wolves should be removed from your project team. If this is not possible, you must find tasks they can perform in relative isolation from the rest of the team; they should not receive special perquisites and rewards that result from the team's efforts. As the saying goes, "one rotten apple can spoil the barrel;" one uncooperative individual can destroy a project team.

A key indicator of an effective team is shared ownership of the work products. While each individual is responsible for her or his work assignments and work products, shared ownership of work products is evident when project members are willing to help one another. Conversely, dysfunctional groups are characterized by an unwillingness of individuals to help others, perhaps because excessive schedule pressure, excessive overtime, and/or competition among team members that does not reward cooperation.

Good communication skills, good communication channels, and a pleasant physical environment are all conducive to team coalescence. Finally, having some fun together is the glue that can bond a team; however, the "fun" activities must be carefully selected. Not everyone enjoys bowling or paintball.

Other techniques that contribute to team coalescence include:

- conducting off-site planning and review meetings that include sufficient time for informal socializing,
- arranging for team members to participate together in off-site training courses,
- providing pizza or cookies to celebrate achievement of project milestones, and
- organized social events such as attending baseball games or "family days" at amusement parks.

In their text *Peopleware*, Tom DeMarco and Tim Lister describe a "jelled team" as "a group of people so strongly knit that the whole is greater than the sum of the parts" [DeMarco99]. Jelled teams thus exhibit synergy in their work activities. In their text, DeMarco and Lister describe the attributes of jelled teams, which include:

- low turnover of team members,
- a strong sense of identity with the team,
- a sense of elitism,
- joint ownership of the product,
- willingness to help one another, and
- obvious enjoyment of the work and of one another.

DeMarco and Lister then introduce the concept of "teamicide," which is "sure fire ways to inhibit formation of teams and disrupt project sociology." Teamicide techniques include:

- defensive management,
- mindless bureaucracy,
- physical separation of team members,
- fragmentation of time,
- unrealistic schedules,
- lack of sufficient time to produce quality work products,
- clique control, and
- excessive overtime.

TABLE 10.3 Some antidotes for teamicide

Teamicide Practice	Antidote
Defensive management	Trust your team members until proved otherwise; fix personnel problems as they occur
Mindless bureaucracy	Use cost-effective procedures and paperwork; demonstrate the benefit of them to all involved parties
Unrealistic deadlines	Set deadlines that have a reasonable probability of being met
Physical separation	Provide group workspaces and opportunities for casual interactions
Fragmentation of time	Assign people to one task at a time, and to one team at a time; avoid "firefighting" assignments
Clique control	Allow team members to work together for extended periods of time
Quality reduction	Don't compress schedules without de-scoping the requirements; don't add requirements without extending the schedule
Excessive overtime	Avoid it!

Avoiding teamicide is a necessary condition for building and maintaining jelled teams. Table 10.3 lists some antidotes for teamicide.

For many organizations, physical separation of different teams is a reality in the age of globalization. In these cases the work must be carefully partitioned so that geographically separated teams can pursue their work activities in relative isolation from other teams.

You, as project manager, must develop trust between you and your team members and foster trust among your team members. Trust, like respect, must be earned by exhibiting:

- honesty,
- candor,
- sincerity, and
- follow-through

on agreements and commitments in your interactions with your team members.

A common area of mistrust by team members is concern for how productivity and quality data collected from individual team members will be used. Data collected from individuals should always be consolidated, analyzed at the level of small teams, and aggregated among small teams as needed for purposes of analysis and reporting. You must do everything in your power to prevent association of individuals with the collected data. Nothing will kill trust faster than disclosure or use of data promised to be held in confidence.

You, as project manager, must avoid the temptation to "be one of the boys (or girls)" by joining in on programming, testing, and review activities unless you are the manager/technical-leader of a small project (5 or fewer people) where you are a technical contributor.

When data indicate that an individual's performance is not up to expectations, you should hold a private meeting with the individual. The goal and tone of the meeting should be to determine the conditions that are causing inadequate performance and to help the individual develop an action plan that will remedy those conditions. Remedies may include one or more of:

- training,
- mentorship,
- better tools,
- clarification of responsibilities,
- reassignment of duties within the project, or
- reassignment to another project or department.

Poor performance may require that you and the individual work with your human resources department to resolve the issue (perhaps personality differences make you, in the view of the individual, the problem to be resolved).

The leaders of small teams (3 to 5 members) are responsible for monitoring the productivity and quality of output of their team members, and for working with their members to apply corrective actions for deficiencies in performance. On larger projects, it may be necessary for the team leader and you, the project manager, to work privately with team members that are not performing, or cannot perform up to expectations. Team members, team leaders, and others who prove to be untrustworthy and who do not improve must be removed from your project.

Other teamicide techniques listed in Table 10.1 include mindless bureaucracy and unrealistic deadlines. Mindless bureaucracy is sometimes truly mindless but is often perceived as mindless based on lack of understanding, because:

> What is productive for the team or the project is not always viewed as productive by individuals.

Completing defect reports and recording time and effort spent on each task, for example, may detract from time available to write code or run test cases; however, these data are essential for effective measurement and control of a project. Each individual must see tangible results from the "paperwork" that are beneficial to them, to the project, to the organization, and to the customers. For example, analysis of defect data may result in better processes, methods, and/or tools that reduce rework and overtime.

You must ensure that each team member understands the purpose and benefits of each element of "paperwork," you must provide feedback to the team members based on the data they provide, and you must incorporate into their schedules sufficient time to complete the necessary paperwork. If the time is not well spent, you must either eliminate that aspect of paperwork or make it an effective mechanism for the project. If you cannot justify, and demonstrate to your project members, the purpose, benefits, and value of the time spent preparing requested data, you should not ask your project members to report it. For example, explaining to team members that accurate reporting of overtime work-hours can be of benefit them by providing you the data you need to convince your managers and customer that the schedule needs to be extended.

Managers and customers often set unrealistic deadlines in the belief that unrealistic deadlines will encourage workers to achieve greater productivity in an effort to meet the deadlines. This is a wrong-headed, Machiavellian, Theory X approach to managing people [Mach13], [McGreg85]. It is wrong-headed for several reasons:

1. it engenders cynicism among project members,
2. it results in poor quality work products,
3. it results in job dissatisfaction because team members are not allowed to produce quality work products, and
4. it results in excessive overtime in attempting to meet unrealistic schedules

Excessive overtime results in mental fatigue and burnout, which demoralizes workers and results in mistakes that show up as defects in the work products. Excessive overtime also leads to voluntary turnover of personnel, which is disruptive to progress, as it is expensive and time-consuming to replace personnel. You must resist the pressure from your managers and customer to set unrealistic deadlines.

As indicated in Table 10.3, physical separation is another technique of teamicide to be avoided. Team members must be co-located because software engineering is an intellect-intensive, teamwork activity. Team members developing common work products must be within physical proximity of one another so that continuous ad hoc communication is possible. E-mail and conference calls are useful but they are not substitutes for face-to-face discussions and meetings. Physical separation of team members is a major issue for geographically dispersed projects. These projects are most successful when work activities are partitioned in a manner that requires little communication among the partitioned teams. Learning about other cultures can be helpful, as can exchange of personnel between and among geographically disperse project teams. Investing in one or more face-to-face meetings, even when expensive travel is involved, is a worthwhile investment.

Opportunities for casual interactions must be created. Organizations have noted declines in team cohesion, productivity, and quality of work products when opportunities for casual interactions such as the communal coffee pot or the afternoon tea break are discontinued.

Fragmentation of time among multiple job assignments or projects is another teamicide technique to be avoided. Assignment to multiple projects prevents team members from working together over extended periods of time to learn one another's idiosyncrasies, to regard work products as shared artifacts, and to build trust with one another.

A related issue is disruption of an individual's concentrated flow of thought processes. *Flow* (or "being in the zone") is a mental state in which a person is fully immersed in what he or she is doing; it is characterized by effortlessness of activity and a loss of sense of time. The concept of flow was proposed by psychologist Mihály Csíkszentmihályi in 1975 and has been widely referenced across a variety of fields. Many of the intellect-based work activities of software development are best accomplished by concentrated mental effort that occurs when one is "in the flow" or "in the zone." In their text *Peopleware*, DeMarco and Lister indicate that it takes approximately 15 minutes to enter in the state of flow;[32] if you are interrupted by phone calls and other people every 15 or 20 minutes you will never enter the state of mental flow needed for full concentration on the task at hand.

DeMarco and Lister observe that small offices with doors that can be closed, perhaps shared by two or three people, provide better opportunities to perform concentrated work than do the ubiquitous carrel spaces of modern office buildings. This author once observed an organization that had a policy of "quiet hours" from 1:30 to 3:30 each work day. During this time phone calls were diverted and no meetings were scheduled. The resulting quiet atmosphere allowed individuals to enter the flow and perform concentrated mental work. Other techniques include erecting a small flag or a sign that indicates "I'm busy just now" and/or wearing noise-canceling headphones.

Clique control is yet another teamicide technique sometimes used by insecure and distrustful managers who fear rebellions by united team members. At other times detrimental clique control is the unintended consequence of rotating staff members among job assignments in the belief that constant job rotation broadens the skill sets of workers and injects new thinking into projects. You and your organization should work with each software engineer to develop and implement career plans that will provide the depth and breadth of skills that are beneficial to the organization and are in line with the individual's career goals. However, these growth plans should be implemented at intervals that do not disrupt continuity of the current job assignment or team membership.

Quality reduction is a major teamicide technique to be avoided. One of the major frustrations of software developers is not being allowed sufficient time to produce work products that have the features and quality attributes their personal creeds and senses of responsibility demand. Quality reduction occurs when a schedule is compressed without compensating actions such as descoping the requirements or increasing the resources. Quality reduction can also occur because of virtual schedule compression. This happens when new requirements are added and no compensating actions are taken; as a result more work must be done in the available time. Quality reduction must be avoided if team cohesiveness and individual morale are to be maintained. On the other hand, you (the project manager or manager/team leader) must guard against "gold plating," which occurs when software developers add features or improve quality attributes (e.g., performance) beyond what is needed to satisfy the requirements, users' needs, and customer's expectations.

Excessive overtime is the final item in Table 10.3. Overtime is time worked beyond the obligated time commitment, which is typically 8 work-hours per day. Because software development and modification are intellect-intensive activities, it is not reasonable to expect that software engineers can be intellectually productive on a continuing basis when they work more than 8 hours per day, 5 days per week. Every software engineer and software manager knows there will be times when short bursts of overtime are required. However, more than 10% overtime per week (4 hours) or 10% per month (two 8-hour days) should be regarded as excessive. Short bursts of excessive overtime (i.e., 1 to 2 weeks' duration) must be compensated with time off to allow individuals to recharge physically, mentally, and emotionally.

[32] [DeMarco99], page 63.

In a simple phrase, the only way to deal with excessive overtime is to avoid it. To summarize the danger of teamicide, we quote DeMarco and Lister: "Most organizations don't set out to consciously kill teams. They just act that way."[33]

10.5 MAINTAINING MORALE AND MOTIVATION

It is your responsibility, as project manager and leader, to maintain the morale of your project team. Morale is evident when a project team exhibits confidence, cheerfulness, discipline, and willingness to perform assigned tasks. Morale is the outward manifestation of motivation. Maintaining morale is thus largely a matter of providing the environment and conditions in which project personnel are motivated to willingly perform their assigned tasks with confidence, cheerfulness, and discipline.

To motivate is to provide an incentive for performing an action. People can be motivated by fear and intimidation, which may take the form of fear of reprimand, fear of humiliation, or fear of losing one's job. This approach is not likely to produce the desired result of cheerfulness and willingness to confidently perform assigned tasks with discipline. A more positive approach is to create the conditions in which individuals can satisfy their psychological needs while pursuing their work activities. Individuals will thus derive satisfaction from their jobs and be motivated to do high-quality work in a timely manner.

TABLE 10.4 Psychological elements of job satisfaction

For psychological needs to be satisfied people need:

- To believe their work is important
- To have a continuing sense of achievement
- To receive recognition for their contributions
- To use a variety of skills
- To perform well defined tasks
- To have profession growth opportunities
- To have some autonomy
- To have pleasant social interactions

Some of the ways people find psychological satisfaction at work are listed in Table 10.4. It is probably true that most people, in order to derive psychological satisfaction from work, need to believe their work is important, to have a continuing sense of achievement (i.e., "closure" in psychological terms), and to receive recognition for their contributions. Other items listed in Table 10.4 vary in order of importance for different individuals.

The prevailing view is that those who work in marketing, sales, or human relations derive job satisfaction from social interactions, whereas software engineers prefer autonomy over social interactions (i.e., to be left alone to do their job in their own way). However, people are not so easily characterized or caricaturized. Some marketeers may prize autonomy to deal with customers in their own way over pleasant social interactions with office mates, and some software engineers may derive more

[33] *Ibid*, page 139.

satisfaction from performing well-defined tasks that contribute to their team's results than having a great deal of individual autonomy in performing those tasks.

In order to provide a positive work environment, you must understand which motivational factors are important to each individual and attempt, to the extent possible, to create those conditions for the individuals. Joe Tester may enjoy performing the well-defined tasks of debugging more than interacting with users, and Sue Analyst may enjoy interacting with users more than debugging code. If circumstances allow, each should be assigned to the tasks that permit them to satisfy their psychological needs.

TABLE 10.5 Factors that make software engineers happy at work

- A quiet place to work
- Challenging technical problems
- Autonomy in solving problems
- Ability to control own schedule
- A chance to learn new things and try new ideas
- Adequate computing facilities and software tools
- Competent technical leaders
- Communication with peers via electronic mail, bulletin boards, news groups, blogs, and technical conferences

Table 10.5 provides an anecdotal list of job satisfiers for software engineers. The lists in Tables 10.4 and 10.5 are not intended to be definitive but rather illustrative of factors that should be taken into consideration when creating a work environment in which workers can derive psychological satisfaction and thereby exhibit positive morale.

10.6 CAN'T VERSUS WON'T

As observed by Andy Grove, a founder and former CEO of Intel Corporation, workers who are not performing up to expectations either can't or won't [Grove95]. If a software developer wants to do a good job but can't, it may be because she or he lacks training, skill, experience, tools, time, or basic ability to do the job. When a person has the necessary prerequisites to do a good job but won't, it is because they lack motivation (or perhaps are perversely motivated to derail a project). Those who can't are unable, and those who won't are unwilling. Table 10.6 lists the four possible combinations and the resulting situation.

As indicated, unable and unwilling is a realistic situation because the person who is not qualified to do a job is unwilling to do it and should not be assigned to that

TABLE 10.6 Four combinations of can't and won't

Unable and unwilling	A realistic situation
Unable but willing	A dangerous situation
Able but unwilling	Lack of motivation
Able and willing	The best situation

job. Unable and willing is a dangerous situation because the person will most likely make serious mistakes in attempting to do a job for which he or she is not qualified. Able and unwilling is the situation in which a person is qualified to perform a task but refuses to do it, or will do it grudgingly and with lack of enthusiasm. Able and willing is the most desirable situation; the person has the ability and is willing to perform assigned tasks.

To be an effective leader, you must understand the personalities, skills, and motivations (or lack thereof) of each individual and respond as the situation requires. This approach is known as situational leadership [Hershey99]. Each of the can't versus won't situations listed in Table 10.6 can be dealt with using the techniques of situational leadership indicated in Table 10.7.

TABLE 10.7 Four situations and leadership styles

Can't versus Won't	Leadership Style
Unable and unwilling	Teaching plus selling
Unable but willing	Teaching plus reinforcing
Able but unwilling	Selling plus reinforcing
Able and willing	Reinforcing plus delegation

For those who are unable and unwilling, a teaching style is appropriate to enable them and a selling style is appropriate to motivate them. Teaching techniques include attending classes, reading papers, being mentored, and working with consultants. Selling techniques include anecdotes, testimonials of respected individuals, guest speakers, papers to be read, and classes. Teaching plus selling would be appropriate for individuals who do not have the training or experience to participate in software inspections, for example, and are skeptical of the value of inspections.

For those who are unable but willing, a teaching plus reinforcing style is appropriate; teaching to impart the skills, and reinforcing to channel their efforts in the desired ways. Reinforcing techniques include a combination of teaching, selling, and other techniques, such as attending workshops, being coached, and apprenticeship to increase ability to do the job. Teaching plus reinforcing would be appropriate for those individuals who are willing to give software inspections a try but lack the necessary skill.

Those who are able but unwilling must be motivated by creating the conditions under which they are willing to do the job with enthusiasm. Motivational techniques include selling and reinforcing, plus other techniques such as removing barriers that de-motivate the individual. Selling and reinforcing would be an appropriate approach for those individuals who have had bad experiences participating in poorly managed software inspections because the participants were not trained to do inspections. The de-motivating barrier could be removed by providing training and coaching.

The best situation is when individuals are able and willing to do the assigned job. The appropriate leadership style is reinforcement and delegation. Reinforcement will bolster their ability and delegation will strengthen their motivation. Delegation techniques include working with individuals to set goals, giving them the authority and autonomy to do the job in the way they think best, and establishing procedures for reporting progress and problems. Individuals who are able and willing to perform software inspections, for example, are candidates to become inspection moderators.

10.7 PERSONALITY STYLES

Personality is determined by the behaviors, mental traits, and emotions that distinguish one person from another; personality is what makes a person a person. Individuals will respond best when the leadership style you exhibit is compatible with their personality. If you are interacting with someone who is methodical and detail-oriented, he or she will respond positively to carefully thought-out, detailed plans. Conversely, if you are dealing with a creative "big picture" person, she or he will want to understand the scope of the work and the impact of his or her tasks on the overall outcome; these people will be impatient with detailed explanations.

Many different models of personality have been developed. Some of these models are useful to provide insight into ourselves and insight into how best to interact with others who have personality traits that differ from ours. The following sections briefly summarize three models of personality:

- Jungian personality traits,
- Myers–Briggs Type Indicators, and
- Wilson's Dimensions of Social Styles.

It must be emphasized that these models portray some aspects of personality and none are complete or comprehensive portrayals of human personality.

10.7.1 Jungian Personality Traits

A personality trait is a characteristic way in which a person perceives, feels, believes, or acts. One of the most comprehensive models of personality traits was developed by Carl Jung in the 1920s [Jung23]. He first distinguished between introversion and extroversion, which is determined by how one perceives his or her environment, makes decisions, and "recharges" her or his energy level. Introverts prefer the internal world of thoughts and feelings; a good time for an introvert is reading a book, working on a puzzle, or listening to music. Extroverts prefer the external world of things, people, and actions; they enjoy parties and social gatherings. The stereotype of a software engineer is the introverted nerd; extroversion is the stereotype of a salesperson.

Jung then defined four ways in which we deal with our surroundings, independent of whether we are introverts or extroverts. These four ways are sensing, thinking, intuiting, and feeling. A sensing person obtains knowledge of the world using his or her five senses and reacts to information as it is received from external sources.

A person who is predominately a thinker collects information and evaluates it in a logical manner before acting (or not acting) on the information. Decisions are made on a rational basis rather than by reacting to stimuli as does one who is predominately a sensing person. Thinkers are thus less spontaneous than sensers.

Intuiting is a perception of the world that occurs outside of conscious processes. Intuition is based on integrating large amounts of information in a subconscious manner rather than simply seeing, hearing, and reacting as is the case for the sensing person, or by logical reasoning processes, as is the case for the thinking person.

Feeling is the fourth way in which Jung observed that people deal with the world. Feeling involves evaluating information based on one's emotional responses to that information.

Jung observed that most individuals tend to be introverts or extroverts, and although all individuals use all four ways of dealing with the world (sensing, thinking, intuiting, feeling), most people predominately use one way most of the time, secondarily use another, and weakly use the other two. Predominant traits are compensated for, in the case of introverts who make excellent public presentations and extroverts whose jobs require extensive periods of individual effort. However, the introvert is most comfortable (i.e., in his or her "comfort zone") when not making public presentations and the extrovert is most comfortable when interacting with people rather than when developing software in an isolated environment.

Jung stressed that not everyone has a predominant trait. However, most researchers agree that introversion and extroversion and the four personality traits identified by Jung are universal across cultures, although the proportion of individuals that exhibit different predominant traits varies across different cultures. Wurster provides a comprehensive review of Jung's work and the associated MBTI personality types [Wurster93].

10.7.2 MBTI Personality Types

In the 1940s, Katharine Briggs and her daughter Isabel Briggs Myers developed the Myers–Briggs Type Indicator (MBTI) based on Jung's personality traits. It is one of the most widely used tests for evaluating personality styles.

The test involves answering approximately 100 questions. Several Web sites provide on-line, self-scoring version of the MBTI questionnaire; they can be found by using your favorite search engine to find "MBTI" links. Test results are evaluated on four scales:

- extroversion–introversion,
- sensing–intuiting,
- thinking–feeling, and
- judging–perceiving.

Based on results from thousands of MBTI tests, it has been determined that about 75% of test takers in the United States score as extroverts (25% introverts), and about 75% of test takers score on the sensing side of the sensing–intuiting scale. Although the thinking–feeling percentages are almost equal by gender, about 2/3 of men score on the thinking side of the thinking–feeling scale and about 2/3 of women score on the feeling side. Conversely, it can be said that 1/3 of men score on the feeling side and 1/3 of women score on the thinking side [Boeree06].

The fourth scale (judging–perceiving) is not one of Jung's dimensions. Myers and Briggs included it to indicate which of Jung's styles predominates and which is secondary in the test results. "Judging" does not imply that one is judgmental; those who score on the judging side of the judging–perceiving scale tend to be orderly and methodical. Those who score more toward the perceiving end of the scale are more flexible and spontaneous. If you score on the extrovert side of the extroversion–introversion scale and on the judging side of the judging–perceiving scale, your predominant style is thinker or feeler, depending on which side of the thinking–feeling scale your score is on and your secondary style is the other one. If you score as an introvert with a high judging score, your predominant style is sensing or intuiting, depending on which side of the sensing–intuiting scale your score lies on, and your secondary style is the other one.

Using the 16 combinations of extroversion–introversion, sensing–intuiting, thinking–feeling, and judging–perceiving, Myers and Briggs identified 16 personality styles. Most people who take the MBTI test fall somewhere within the 16 categories. However, some individuals place somewhere between two or three different styles.

The 16 MBTI personality styles are listed in Table 10.8, and abbreviated as

TABLE 10.8 MBTI styles and career choices

MBTI Personality Style	Predominant and Secondary Styles	Typical Career Choices
ENFJ	Extroverted feeling with intuiting	Therapists, teachers, salespersons
ENFP	Extroverted intuiting with feeling	Marketeers, advertisers, politicians, actors
ENTJ	Extroverted thinking with intuiting	Executives and administrators
ENTP	Extroverted intuiting with thinking	Analysts, entrepreneurs
ESFJ	Extroverted feeling with sensing	Service occupations involving personal contact
ESFP	Extroverted sensing with feeling	Performance arts, public relations
ESTJ	Extroverted thinking with sensing	Public service, volunteer organizations
ESTP	Extroverted sensing with thinking	Promoters, entrepreneurs
INFJ	Introverted intuiting with feeling	Therapists, ministers, general practitioner doctors
INFP	Introverted feeling with intuiting	Psychology, architecture, religion
INTJ	Introverted intuiting with thinking	Applied science, engineering
INTP	Introverted thinking with intuiting	Philosophy, mathematics, theoretical science
ISFJ	Introverted sensing with feeling	Nurses, librarians, teachers
ISFP	Introverted feeling with sensing	Arts and nature
ISTJ	Introverted sensing with thinking	Accountants, auditors, engineers
ISTP	Introverted thinking with sensing	Soldiers, technicians

- E: Extroversion; I: Introversion;
- S: Sensing; N: Intuiting;
- T: Thinking; F: Feeling;
- J: Judging; and P: Perceiving.

If you score as an ENFJ, for example, it indicates that your personality style is Extrovert with Feeling as your predominant style and Intuiting as your secondary style (because of the J score). If you score as an ENFP, it indicates that your personality style is Extrovert with Intuiting as your predominant style and Feeling as your secondary style (because of the P score). The distribution of personality styles among the North American population is as follows [Wideman98]:

- Extrovert: 75%; Introvert: 25%;
- Sensing: 75%; Intuitive: 25%;
- Thinking: 50%; Feeling: 50%;
- Perceiving: 50%; Judging: 50%.

Over time Myers, Briggs, and others have matched MBTI personality types with career choices, compatibility with the personality types of others, and many additional behavioral characteristics of individuals. Personality styles have been matched to occupations in which people having those personality types have successful and satisfying careers. Some of those occupations are indicated in the right-hand column of Table 10.8. The MBTI test is widely used in career counseling, but such use is not without controversy.

MBTI results indicate that more than 50% of software engineers are introverts, compared to about 25% in the general population. MBTI results also indicate that software engineers are predominately thinkers (80% to 90%) [McConnell99]. Software engineers are thus more attuned to logic and analytical reasoning and less concerned with human relations than the general population.

The most common personality types for software engineers are INTJ and ISTJ with an equal split between N (intuiting) and S (sensing) [McConnell99]. An INTJ might be your most creative designer, and an ISTJ might be your best programmer. When it is possible, your projects might benefit by including different personality types in the mix of personalities; N personalities are concerned with broad understanding of a situation and S personalities are concerned with deep exploration of narrow topics. Mixing them together can bring more viewpoints to solving problems. However, caution must be taken to avoid conflicts among distinctly different personality types; interactions between INTJs and ISTJs, for example, can lead to conflict.

Other observers believe that competent software engineers tend to fall into the NT and SJ classifications, for example: "NT types tend to visualize the complete solution to a problem, while SJ types tend to visualize the steps necessary to implement the solution." [Hardiman97].

Some researchers believe that your style as a project manager is most closely related to your position on the Judging–Perceiving scale of the MBTI profile [Hammer01]. If you are on the Judging side of the scale you will probably prefer to:

- set clear, measurable goals,
- break large tasks down into subtasks and proceed methodically,
- develop a time line with milestones to monitor progress carefully,
- come to closure quickly and be reluctant to change decisions,
- like to work in a structured environment,
- believe that a recipe for success is "Plan the work, then work the plan,"
- be motivated by achievement,
- want to achieve results on one project and then move on,
- establish rules for who makes decisions when, and
- trust their ability to organize the project to achieve the desired goal.

Many elements of this list (from [Hammer01]) reflect techniques presented in this text (e.g., work breakdown structures, critical paths, earned value), but this should not be interpreted to mean that you cannot succeed as a project manager if you are on the Perceiving side of the scale (see below).

Cautions for those project managers who are predominantly Judging include:

- confusing the plan with the project,
- missing opportunities by failing to adapt to new information,
- mistakenly assuming that everyone is as motivated by deadlines as you are,
- irritating others by continually reminding them of deadlines,
- making decisions without all the information you need,
- appearing rigid to others,
- limiting creativity or spontaneity that could prove valuable, and
- setting unrealistic time lines that don't account for human behavior.

If you are predominantly a Perceiver, you will probably:

- realize that a clear plan doesn't ensure that everything will go well;
- stay open to changing the plan as more information becomes available;
- find out what motivates others in addition to achievement of deadlines (e.g., autonomy, opportunity for learning new skills);
- develop ways to regularly scan the environment for new information or consult with someone who does this naturally (e.g., marketing or sales staff);
- allow people to work in their own ways while still holding them accountable for the final product;
- plan for spontaneity, for example, set a time period for brainstorming and then let the process emerge; and
- early in the process, seek feedback on the feasibility of time lines.

Most of the attributes on the perceiver list are also emphasized throughout this text (e.g., rolling-wave planning, iterative development, and ongoing risk management).

Clearly, all of the attributes of judging and perceiving are valuable personality traits for a project manager. Understanding your personality type can help you to compensate for traits that may not be natural for you and also help you to guard against overzealousness in the traits that are natural for you.

10.7.3 Dimensions of Social Styles

In the 1960s Larry Wilson introduced his model of social styles. According to the Wilson Learning Center's Web site (see [Wilson04]), the dimensions of social styles are useful for:

- first-line managers who have experienced interpersonal difficulties in the transition from employee to manager;
- managers at all levels who desire to improve their working relationships with managers, peers, direct reports, and internal or external customers;
- employees who wish to establish effective team working relationships;
- managers or team leaders who facilitate teamwork;
- salespeople or sales managers who work as a team;
- individuals who collaborate with others to reach innovative solutions; and
- all people in organizations who want to develop a better understanding of others and to adapt their behavior to have more effective interactions.

Social styles might be better named "communication styles;" it is based on the dimensions of assertiveness and responsiveness in communication, as illustrated in Figure 10.1. Assertiveness is on a continuous scale of ask-oriented to tell-oriented. Those who are ask-oriented are listeners; those who are tell-oriented are talkers. Responsiveness is on a scale of task-oriented to people-oriented. Those who are task-oriented have little time for personal interactions; the task comes first, people second. Those who are people-oriented believe that the task is best accomplished when people issues are addressed first.

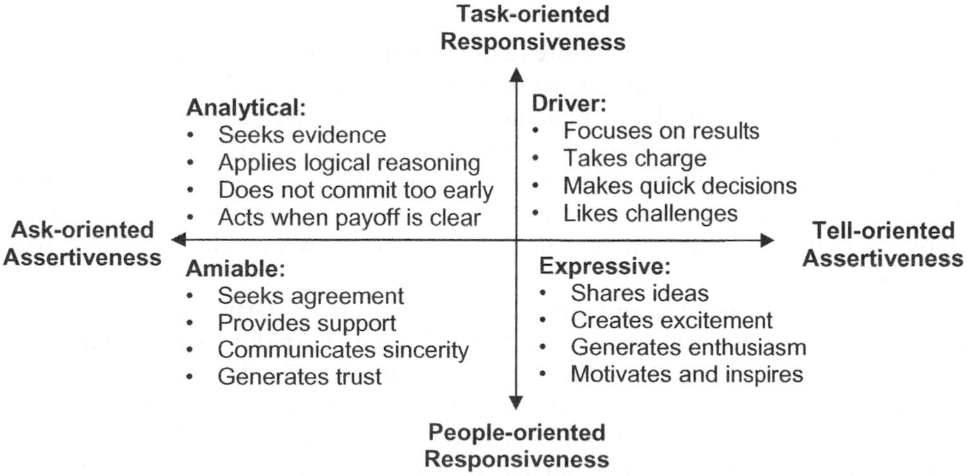

FIGURE 10.1 Dimensions of social styles [Wilson04]

The resulting four quadrants are labeled Driver, Expressive, Amiable, and Analytical. As indicated in Figure 10.1, Drivers exhibit no-nonsense behavior. They are task-oriented and tell-oriented; getting the task done is of higher priority than personal relations and a Driver will tell you how it is to be done rather than asking your opinion. Drivers quickly get to the point when dealing with others, and they may be regarded as brusque. They are results-oriented and are often workaholics. The tough, but fair, first sergeant is the stereotypical Driver, as is the no-nonsense project manager.

Expressives are also tell-directed, but personal relations come before tasks. They are enthusiastic, talkative, competitive, and creative. Expressives like to see everyone having a good time; they are the "life of the party." They prefer to start interactions with a conversation on a personal level before addressing the task to be done; however, they are more interested in telling you about their weekend than asking about yours, for example. Willy Lohman (the protagonist in "Death of a Salesman") is a stereotypical Expressive [Miller98], as is the project manager who develops a cordial relationship with the customer (who may be external to your organization or in your organization's marketing department).

Amiables share with Expressives the emphasis on personal relations. Amiables are quieter than Expressives and their assertiveness takes the form of asking rather than telling. An Expressive will tell you about their weekend, and Amiable will ask you about yours. Amiables are easy going and seek to minimize conflict whenever possible. They believe that the task will go smoother if people are comfortable with one another. The kindly shopkeeper who inquires about, and is genuinely interested in your family, is a stereotypical Amiable as is the project manager who is genuinely concerned about the welfare of his or her project members and takes an interest in their personal lives.

Analyticals, like Amiables, are ask-oriented, but as with Drivers the task comes before people. They are quiet and unassuming and do not seek social interactions. Analyticals exhibit competence and initiative to work through problems in a logical manner. The popular image of an accountant provides a stereotype of an Analytical social style. A project manager who is primarily concerned with schedule and budget data, defect reports, and earned-value tracking would be classified as an Analytical.

To make the four stereotypes more realistic, Wilson embedded the grid in Figure 10.1 in each of the four quadrants so that an individual might be an Amiable but more toward the Analytical style than the Expressive, or a Driver might be primarily a Driver with a secondary Driver style (the extreme upper right in Figure 10.1). Individuals who share common attributes of social styles are more compatible than those who share few attributes. A strong Amiable and a strong Driver do not have many shared personality traits, nor do a strong Analytical and a strong Expressive.

Stereotypes of conflict from Figure 10.1 include a strong Driver interacting with a strong Amiable, as in the case of the "brow-beaten" husband (Amiable) and the brow-beating wife (Driver), or the "slap-em-on-the-back" salesman (Expressive) interacting with a no-nonsense statistician (Analytical). In software projects the counterparts might be a project manager who is predominantly a Driver interacting with a laid-back but productive team leader or software developer (an Amiable) or an Analytical team member interacting with an Expressive project manager. In these cases interactions go better when each individual understands the communication style of the other and adjusts their behavior to accommodate the personality traits of their counterpart.

10.8 THE FIVE-LAYER BEHAVIORAL MODEL

In their paper, "A Field Study of the Software Design Process for Large Systems," Curtis, Krasner, and Iscoe presented a five-layer behavioral model of software development processes [Curtis88]. The model is depicted in Figure 1 of their paper and reproduced here as in Figure 10.2; it illustrates behavioral issues at the levels of individual, team, project, company, and business milieu. The model emphasizes psychological, social, and organizational processes at each level. Their goal was to understand how these processes affect software productivity and quality.

The individual level is concerned with cognitive and motivational processes of individual software developers. At the team level, cognitive and motivational processes interact with the social processes of the team; issues of communication and coordination arise within and among teams. At the organizational level, projects undertaken by the organization are determined by, and are affected by, corporate politics and corporate culture. At the business level, the organization in which projects are conducted interacts with other elements of the parent organization, with customer organizations, and may interact with subcontractor, vendor, and affiliate contractor organizations. Curtis et al. emphasize that problems in a layer of the model can promulgate into, affect, and be affected by other levels.

The size and structure of a project determines how much influence each layer has on the software development process. The higher layers of the model may exert little or no influence if you are doing a small project for an internal customer within your local organization. If you are doing a large project for an acquirer who represents multiple customers (or multiple customers without a single point of contact) and the project involves vendors and subcontractors, the higher levels of the model may exert a strong influence on how you organize and conduct your project.

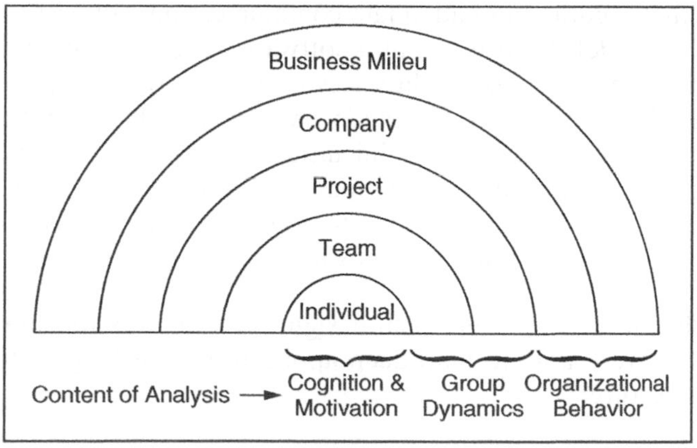

FIGURE 10.2 Five-layer behavioral model of software development [Curtis88]

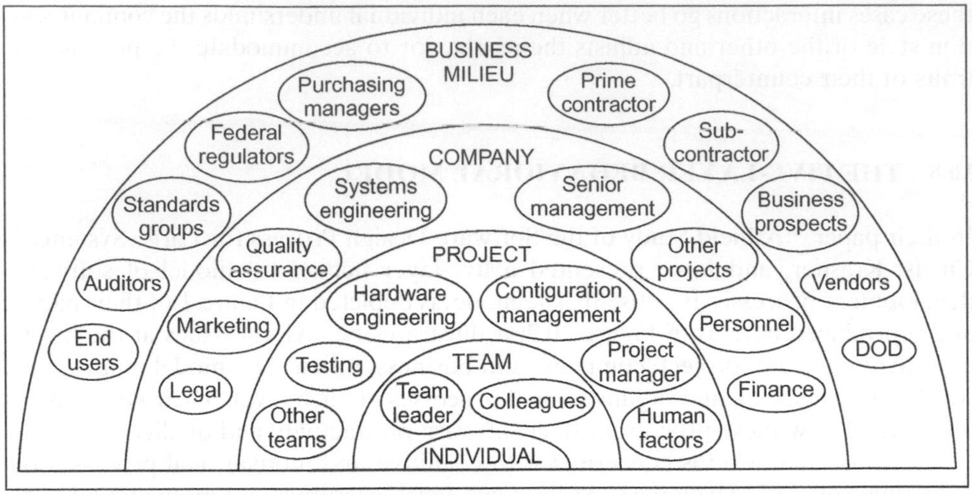

FIGURE 10.3 Layers of communication in the behavioral model [Curtis88]

Curtis et al. report on the results of studying 17 large projects across the 5 behavioral levels. They analyze three problems:

1. the thin spread of application domain knowledge,
2. fluctuating and conflicting requirements, and
3. communication and coordination breakdowns.

They investigated how these problems "affected software productivity and quality through their impact on cognitive, social, and organizational processes." [34]

Figure 6 in the Curtis et al. paper, reproduced here as Figure 10.3, illustrates the levels of communication from individual software engineer to business milieu. In the figure DOD is Department of Defense. Remoteness of communication is determined by the number of nodes information has to pass through in order to link two nodes. As these authors observe, the more nodes information has to traverse, the less likely it is that accurate and adequate communication will occur.

The five-layer model illustrates that a software developer communicates most frequently with team members, slightly less frequently with other project teams, much less often with corporate groups, and very seldom with external groups. Curtis et al. also considered communication difficulties caused by cultural differences and by geographic separation (and the accompanying differences in time zones).

Some of their findings, in each of the three areas studied are as listed below.

Thin spread of application domain knowledge:

- at the individual level, exceptional designers exerted extraordinary influence because they were able to map deep application knowledge into a computational architecture;

[34] From the abstract of [Curtis88].

- at the team level, substantial effort was spent coordinating a common understanding of both the application domain and how the system should perform within it;
- at the project level, time was spent to ensure that the development teams shared a common model of the system;
- at the company level, the cost of learning an application area was a significant corporate expense, and the time required for a new project member to become productive in an unfamiliar application domain ranged from six months to one year; and
- within the business milieu, common understanding of the application domain and the system architecture for large, complex systems developed by several companies was hindered by the organizational boundaries between and among the companies.

Fluctuating and conflicting requirements:

- at the business milieu level, fluctuations and conflicts among requirements usually resulted from market factors such as differing needs among customers, the changing needs of a single customer, changes in underlying technologies or in competitors' products, and misunderstandings of the application domain;
- at the company level, requirements problems also emerged from internal sources such as marketing, corporate politics, and management of product lines;
- at the project level, the design team often negotiated to reduce conflicts and limit requirements to those that could be implemented within schedule, budget, and technology constraints;
- at the team level, it was difficult to enforce those agreements across teams; and
- at the individual level, programmers often created a hidden source of requirements fluctuation when they added enhancements that were not required.

Communications and coordination:

- at the individual level, the need for extensive communication was not reduced by documentation;
- at the team level, teams spend considerable time defining terms, coordinating representational conventions, and creating channels for the flow of information;
- at the project level, artificial (often political) barriers to communication among project teams created a need for individuals to span team boundaries and to create informal communication networks;
- at the company level, organization boundaries hindered understanding of requirements, while temporal boundaries buried the design rationale; and
- at the business milieu level, no single group served as the sole source of requirements; organizational communications became crucial to managing projects.

In summary, aggregating the issues caused by the thin spread of application domain knowledge across behavioral levels points to the importance of managed learning (e.g., training classes and mentorship) as a major factor in productivity, quality, and costs. The communication and coordination processes within a project often became crucial in coping with the fluctuation of and conflict among requirements. Effective communication at all levels is crucial to all aspects of managing a project. As Curtis et al. put it:

> [T]hese problems have survived for several decades despite serious effort at improving software productivity and quality. We are not claiming to have discovered new insights for engineering management. Rather, we are trying to organize observations about the behavioral processes of large systems design to help identify which factors must be attacked to improve overall project performance.[35]

10.9 KEY POINTS OF CHAPTER 10

- Managing and leading are distinct activities; a competent project manager is good at both, or finds ways to compensate for his or her weaknesses.
- A team is a group of individuals working in a cooperative manner to achieve common, shared goals.
- Many organization do not intentionally kill teams, they just act that way; antidotes can be applied to overcome commonly occurring teamicide techniques.
- When people are not performing up to expectations, it is because they can't and/or because they won't.
- Your job as a leader is to create the conditions in which your followers can satisfy their psychological needs in their work environments.
- You and your personnel can communicate more effectively when each person understands and compensates for the personality styles of the others.
- The five-layer behavioral model illustrates problems of communication and coordination at the individual, team, project, company, and business milieu levels.

REFERENCES

[Boeree06] Boeree, G. C. Assessment. *Personality Theories*. http://www.ship.edu/%7Ecgboeree/jung.html, 2006.

[Brooks87] Brooks, F. W. No silver bullets: Essence and accidents of software engineering. *IEEE Computer* (April 1987) Vol. 20, No. 4. pp 10–19.

[Brooks95] Brooks, F. W. *The Mythical Man-Month*. Addison Wesley, 1995.

[CMMI06] SEI. *CMMI® Models and Modules*. http://www.sei.cmu.edu/cmmi/models/, 2006.

[35] Ibid, p. 1282.

[Curtis88] Curtis, B., H. Krasner, and N. Iscoe. A field study of the software design process for large systems. CACM. Vol. 31, No. 11, November 1988. pp 1259–1267.

[Curtis01] Curtis, B., W. Hefley, and S. Miller. *People Capability Maturity Model Guidelines for Improving the Workforce*. Addison Wesley, 2001.

[DeMarco82] DeMarco, T. *Controlling Software Projects*. Yourdon Press, 1982.

[DeMarco99] Demarco, T., and T. Lister. *Peopleware, Productive Projects and Teams*, 2nd ed. Dorset Publishing, 1999.

[Grove95] Grove, A. S. *High Output Management*. Vintage Books, 1995.

[Hammer01] Hammer, A. L. *Myers–Briggs Type Indicator Work Styles Report*. Consulting Psychologists Press. 2001. http://www.cpp.com/images/reports/smp261182.pdf.

[Hardiman97] Hardiman, L. T. Personality types and software engineers. *IEEE Computer* (October, 1997) Vol. 30, No. 10. pp 10.

[Hershey99] Hershey, P., and K. H. Blanchard. *Leadership and the One Minute Manager*. William Morrow, 1999.

[Hump97] Humphrey, W. S. *Introduction to the Personal Software Process*. Addison Wesley, 1997.

[Hump00] Humphrey, W. S. *Introduction to the Team Software Process*. Addison Wesley, 2000.

[IEEE1058] IEEE Std 1058™–1998. *IEEE Standard for Software Project Management Plans*. Engineering Standards Collection. IEEE Product: SE113. Institute of Electrical and Electronic Engineers, August 2003.

[IEEE12207] IEEE/EIA 12207.0/.1/.2, *Industry Implementation of International Standard ISO/IEC 12207:1995 Standard for Information Technology–Software Life Cycle Processes*, Engineering Standards Collection; IEEE Product: SE113, The Institute of Electrical and Electronic Engineers, Inc. August, 2003.

[Jung23] Jung, C. W. *Psychological Types*. Pantheon Books, 1923 (English translation H. Godwyn Baynes).

[Katzen93] Katzenbach, J., and D. Smith. *The Wisdom of Teams*. Harvard Business School Press, 1993.

[Mach13] Machiavelli, N. *The Prince*. Bantam classics, 1984.

[McConnell99] McConnell, S. *After the Gold Rush*. Microsoft Press, 1999.

[McGreg85] McGregor, D. *The Human Side of Enterprise*. McGraw-Hill. 1985.

[Miller98] Miller, A. *Death of a Salesman*. Penguin, [1949] 1998.

[PMI04] PMI. *A Guide to the Project Management Body of Knowledge*, 3rd ed. (PMBOK® Guide). Project Management Institute, 2004.

[Wideman98] Wideman, R. M. Project teamwork, personality profiles and population at large: Do we have enough of the right kind of people? *Proceedings of the 29th Annual Project Management Institute Seminar/Symposium,* Long Beach, CA, Project Management Institute 1998. Also available at http://www.maxwideman.com/papers/profiles/profiles.pdf.

[Wilson04] Wilson, L. *The Social Styles Handbook: Find Your Comfort Zone and Make People Feel Comfortable with You*, Wilson Learning Library, 2004. Also available at http://portalcenter.wilsonlearning.com.

[Wurster93] Wurster, C. W. *Myers–Briggs Type Indicator: A Cultural and Ethical Evaluation*. National Defense University, Washington, DC, 1993. Also available at http://www.ndu.edu/library/ic6/93S86.pdf.

EXERCISES

10.1. List and briefly explain three of the attributes of an effective leader listed in Table 10.1 that you have observed in a favorite teacher, manager, or other leader. List and briefly explain three attributes in Table 10.1 you have observed that were not present in an ineffective teacher, manager, or other leader.

10.2. List and briefly explain three of the techniques listed in Table 10.2 that you have observed or that you can imagine might realistically be important for a software development team.

10.3. List three additional teamicide techniques, in addition to those in Table 10.3, that you have observed or that you can imagine might realistically happen. Briefly state some antidotes for each of your three items.

10.4. List and briefly explain the three most important techniques in Table 10.4 that contribute or would contribute to satisfying your psychological needs at work. You may include factors that are important to you that are not listed in the table.

10.5. List and briefly explain three factors in Table 10.5 that make you, or would make you, happy at work. You may include factors that are important to you that are not listed in the table.

10.6. List and briefly explain a situation from your personal, academic or professional life for each of the four combinations listed Table 10.6. For each one, briefly explain which of the leadership styles in Table 10.7 was, or would be, most effective in helping you.

10.7. Locate and use a (free) on-line testing and scoring service for an MBTI evaluation. Briefly explain why the results do, or do not, reflect your image of yourself. Ask some friends if they think the results mirror your personality.

10.8. The social styles model depicted in Figure 10.1 can often be observed in the archetypes of personality (caricatures) played by characters in movies, television shows, and plays. Give an example of each of the four styles (Driver, Expressive, Amiable, Analytical) in characters from movies, television shows, or plays with which you are familiar. Briefly explain the aspects of personality observed in each of your example characters that place them in the selected category.

10.9. The five-layer behavioral model in Figure 10.2 was used to study three problems often observed in the design of large software-intensive systems: the thin spread of application domain knowledge, fluctuating and conflicting requirements, and problems in communications and coordination. Choose another problem in addition to the three in the model (such as rapidly changing technology or competitive changes in a competitor's product) that you have observed or that you can imagine could realistically happen. Briefly explain the impact of that problem at each of the five levels (individual, team, project, company, business milieu).

APPENDIX 10A

FRAMEWORKS, STANDARDS, AND GUIDELINES FOR TEAMWORK AND LEADERSHIP

10A.1 THE CMMI-DEV-v1.2 FRAMEWORK PROCESSES

The CMMI framework processes, including CMMI-DEV-v1.2 [CMMI06], continue to have a major positive impact on the discipline of software engineering, but the models are not panaceas. In particular, they do not address issue of expertise in application domains, specific software development methods and technologies, or personnel issues (e.g., selection, training, motivation, and retention). This appendix is concerned with other models and guidelines that have been developed to improve the ability and motivation of individuals and the effectiveness of teams and teamwork.

10A.2 ISO/IEC AND IEEE/EIA STANDARDS 12207

The 12207 standards for software life cycle processes covers five primary life cycle process areas, eight supporting process areas, and four organizational process areas [IEEE12207]. Organizational processes include the management, infrastructure, improvement, and training processes. The training process is concerned with ensuring that the correct numbers and kinds of personnel who have the necessary skills are available when needed. The training process is the only process area in 12207 that is concerned with people issues.

10A.3 IEEE/EIA STANDARD 1058

IEEE Standard 1058 for software project management plans includes a Staff Training Plan in Subclause 5.1.4, which is consistent with IEEE/EIA Standard 12207. This is the only section in 1058 that addresses issues of teamwork, motivation, and leadership [IEEE1058].

10A.4 THE PMI BODY OF KNOWLEDGE

The PMI Guide to the Project Management Body of Knowledge (PMBOK®) includes Human Resource Management (Chapter 9) and Communications Management (Chapter 10) [PMI04]. Topics covered in Chapter 9 of PMBOK are:

- Human Resource Planning
- Acquire Project Team
- Develop Project Team
- Manage Project Team

Topics covered in Chapter 10 are:

- Communications Planning
- Information Distribution
- Performance Reporting
- Manage Stakeholders

In addition section 2.3.2—Organizational Cultures and Styles discusses aspects of organizational cultures and factors that shape these cultures, such as:

- shared values, norms, beliefs, and expectations;
- policies and procedures;
- view of authority relationships; and
- work ethic and work hours.

10A.5 OTHER SOURCES OF INFORMATION

Four additional sources of information concerning individuals, teams, and leadership in software projects are:

- People CMM [www.sei.cmu.edu/cmm-p/]
- *Introduction to the Personal Software Process* [Hump97]
- *Introduction to the Team Software Process* [Hump00]
- *Peopleware: Productive Projects and Teams*, 2nd ed. [DeMarco99]

10A.5.1 The People CMM

The People Capability Maturity Model (People CMM) is sponsored by the Software Engineering Institute. According to the Web site, the People CMM is:

> [A] framework that helps organizations successfully address their critical people issues. Based on the best current practices in fields such as human resources, knowledge management, and organizational development, the People CMM guides organizations in improving their processes for managing and developing their workforces. The

People CMM helps organizations characterize the maturity of their workforce practices, establish a program of continuous workforce development, set priorities for improvement actions, integrate workforce development with process improvement, and establish a culture of excellence. Since its release in 1995, thousands of copies of the People CMM have been distributed, and it is used worldwide by organizations, small and large.

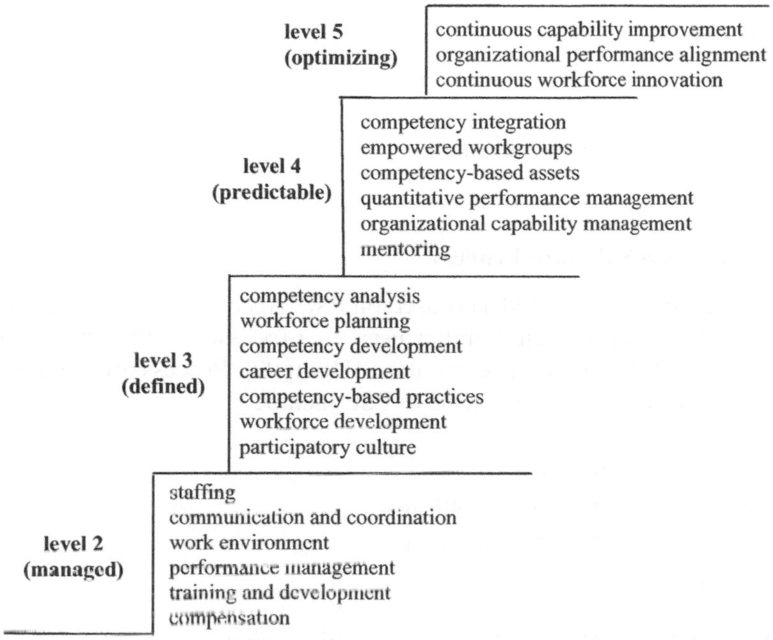

FIGURE 10A.1 Maturity levels of the People CMM

The People CMM is structured as a 5-level model, similar in structure to the staged representations of the CMMI models. The elements of the model are indicated in Figure 10A.1.

The book *People Capability Maturity Model Guidelines for Improving the Workforce* describes the People CMM and the key practices that comprise each of its maturity levels. It shows how to apply the model in guiding organizational improvements and includes case studies [Curtis01].

10A.5.2 The Personal Software Process

The Personal Software Process (PSP) is concerned with keeping records and learning from one's personal experiences. Forms are provided to allow recording of personal performance on software projects. By periodically analyzing the information, one learns how to better estimate personal productivity and to avoid mistakes (i.e., creation of defects).

The PSP addresses, at the level of individual software developers, many of the CMMI-DEV-v1.2 process areas and recommended practices, including:

- requirements development
- project planning
- project monitoring and control
- peer reviews
- measurement and analysis
- technical solution
- product integration
- verification
- validation
- risk management
- decision analysis and resolution

10A.5.3 The Team Software Process

The Team Software Process (TSP) is based on PSP. According to Humphrey, a team that practices TSP, where each member uses the processes of PSP, will function at Level 5 of the CMMI staged representation [Hump00]. Process areas incorporated into TSP in addition to those included in PSP include:

- requirements management
- process and product quality assurance
- software configuration management
- quantitative project management

PSP, TSP, and CMMI-DEV-v1.2 thus form a hierarchy:

- PSP is concerned with individual processes,
- TSP is concerned with team processes, and
- CMMI-DEV-v1.2 is concerned with processes at the project and organizational levels.

10A.5.4 Peopleware

The *Peopleware* text [DeMarco99] advances the premise that the root causes of most of the problems faced by project managers and software developers are organizational and managerial, not technical. The text is in six parts:

Part I: Managing the Human Resource
Part II: The Office Environment
Part III: The Right People
Part IV: Growing Productive Teams
Part V: It's Supposed to be Fun to Work Here
Part VI: Son of Peopleware

TABLE 10A.1 Teamicide techniques and examples

Teamicide Techniques	Examples
Defensive management	Lack of trusting your team members
Bureaucracy	Mindless procedures and excessive paper work
Physical separation	No group work space; no chances for casual interactions
Fragmentation of work time	Assigning people to multiple projects and teams
Phony deadlines	Unrealistic deadlines everyone knows cannot be met
Quality reduction	Compressing schedules without descoping the requirements
Clique control	Not allowing team members to stay together over extended periods of time
Excessive overtime	No time to help one another; fatigue and burnout
Demeaning aspects of motivational posters and plaques	Substitution of mindless phrases in place of providing concrete opportunities for individual motivation
An unanticipated aspect of overtime	Differing abilities of team members and willingness to work overtime

The sixth part of the second edition includes 8 additional chapters beyond those in the first edition of the text. For example, among the topics addressed in these additional chapters are of teamicide and "teamicide revisited." Teamicide is described as a way to "inhibit the formation of teams and disrupt project sociology." Table 10A.1 lists teamicide techniques and examples. Table 10.3 in this chapter lists some antidotes for teamicide.

At the end of Chapter 20, DeMarco and Lister conclude: "Most organizations don't set out to consciously kill teams. They just act that way."

11

ORGANIZATIONAL ISSUES

The achievements of an organization are the results of the combined effort of each individual.

—Vince Lombardi

11.1 INTRODUCTION TO ORGANIZATIONAL ISSUES

Because software is built and maintained by humans, and because organizations are composed of humans, software projects and the organizations that conduct software projects are complex social networks. The term *organization* is used to denote "an administrative structure in which people collectively manage one or more projects as a whole, and whose projects share a senior manager and operate under the same policies." [CMMI06].

At the organizational level:

- the corporate culture must be established and maintained;
- strategic goals must be determined and pursued;
- intellectual assets must be nurtured;
- software development processes must be established; and
- technical infrastructure, methods, tools, and techniques must be provided.

These organizational concerns are addressed in this chapter.

As a project manager within an organizational unit, you must establish communication channels among organizational entities, for example, between your software development group and the independent testing group, and between

Managing and Leading Software Projects, by Richard E. Fairley

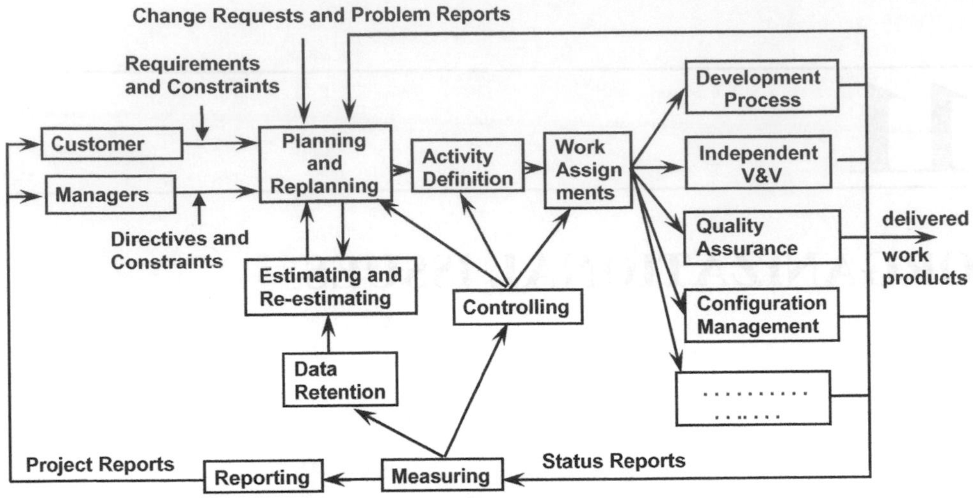

FIGURE 11.1 A workflow model for managing software projects

your project and the separate configuration management group (if there is one). Informal communication channels that are beneficial to the project must be encouraged and informal communication channels detrimental to the project must be discouraged.

You may, on one hand, want to encourage informal communication between software developers and system engineers in order to clarify and refine the software requirements. On the other hand, you may want to discourage informal communication between individual software implementers and end users because these communications can result in unauthorized requirements creep and may create false expectations among the users. Communication between users and developers should be limited to requirements elicitation sessions that involve representative users and software engineers who are skilled in requirements elicitation, and to technical interchange meetings between software developers, their team leaders or project manager, and users. The intent is not to discourage interactions but rather to ensure that the interactions occur in an orderly manner.

To facilitate communication internal to your project, a workflow model similar to Figure 1.1, repeated here as Figure 11.1, and a project structure similar to Figure 1.3, repeated here as Figure 11.2, should be established for your software project. The intent of a hierarchical structure, as in Figure 11.2, is not to discourage informal communication among developers in different teams, but to allocate the requirements and decompose the software architecture so that each team can pursue their work activities with high internal cohesion among the team members and loose couplings to other teams (see Chapter 4).

11.2 OBJECTIVES OF THIS CHAPTER

After reading this chapter and completing the exercises you should understand:

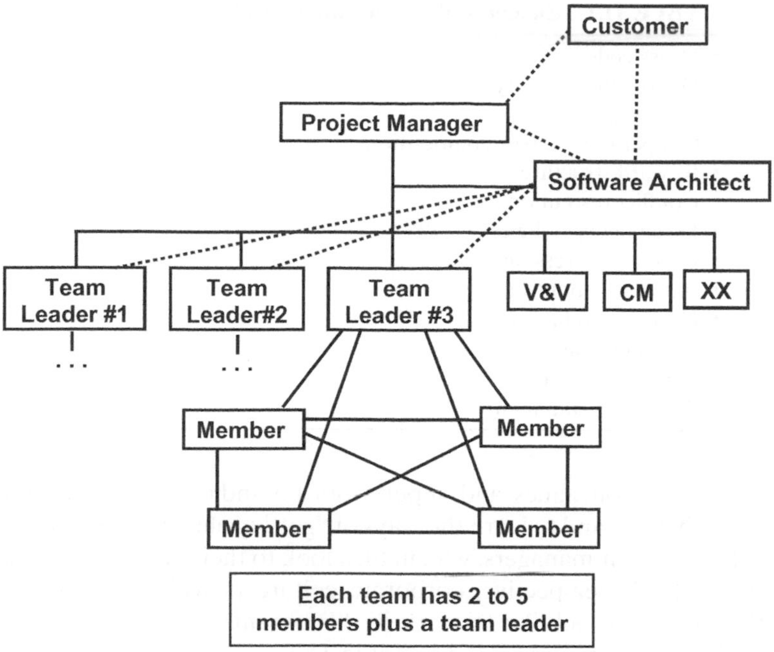

V&V: Verification and Validation
CM: Configuration Management
XX: other supporting processes

FIGURE 11.2 An organizational model for software projects

- the elements of corporate cultures,
- the importance of mission and vision statements,
- assessing and nurturing intellectual capital,
- key personnel roles,
- responsibility versus authority, and
- 15 guidelines for organizing and leading software engineering teams

The frameworks, standards, and guidelines presented in each of the preceding chapters, namely CMMI-DEV-v1.2, ISO/IEC and IEEE/EIA Standard 12207, IEEE/EIA Standard 1058, and the PMI Body of Knowledge address organizational issues to varying degrees. The relevant elements of these standards and guidelines are summarized in Appendix 11A of this chapter.

Terms used in this chapter and throughout this text are defined in Appendix A to the text. Presentation slides for this chapter and other supporting material are available at the URL listed in the Preface.

11.3 THE INFLUENCE OF CORPORATE CULTURE

Corporate culture is comprised of the beliefs, values, and behavior patterns that exist within an organization. Cultural norms flow from the top down. Individuals

TABLE 11.1 Elements of organizational culture

- Dress code
- Degree of formality
- Working hours
- Cooperation versus competition
- Reward structure
- Conflict resolution
- Disciplinary policies
- Career progression
- Attitudes about quality
- Customer relations
- Ethical behavior
- A vision statement
- A mission statement

look to their senior colleagues and supervisors for indicators of acceptable and unacceptable behaviors and to learn the ways of "getting ahead" in the organization. Supervisors look to their managers, who in turn look to their managers for guidance. From the individual's perspective, corporate culture provides the answer to the question "What does it feel like to work in this organization?" Some factors that determine cultural patterns are listed in Table 11.1.

Different organizations have different dress codes, ranging from formal attire at all times (e.g., neckties, jackets, dresses), to formal when meeting with customers and informal otherwise, to "business casual," to "dress-down" Fridays, to jeans-and-tee-shirts at all times. In a similar manner the degree of formality varies from first names throughout the organization to more respectful forms of address for supervisors and managers.

Some organizations are quite flexible in working hours, and others have strictly enforced times to be at work. In the case of flexible hours, some organizations require everyone to be present between 10:00 AM and 3:00 PM so that meetings can be scheduled during times when people are available to attend. Strictly enforced working hours may be based on the desires of higher level management or perhaps required by security considerations that dictate the facility must be locked down from 6:00 PM until 7:00 AM Monday through Friday and on weekends.

Some organizations encourage competition among individual contributors in the belief that the stress of competition improves productivity and quality of work. Other organizations encourage cooperation and teamwork in the belief that the synergy that results from cooperative teamwork improves productivity and quality of work. The reward structure in some organizations recognizes and rewards individual achievements, whereas other organizations encourage and reward team efforts.

The approaches to conflict resolution and disciplinary action vary from laissez faire to intervention and amelioration. Disciplinary actions vary from hands-off to well-defined procedures that include documentation of unacceptable behaviors, counseling sessions, probationary periods, and dismissal policies.

Some organizations have well-defined career ladders, career development plans for each employee, qualifications and procedures for advancing up a career ladder, and a human relations department that works with employees to advance each employee's career. Career advancement in other organizations is on an ad hoc basis.

Customer relations, attitudes about quality, vision statements, mission statements, and ethical behavior are interrelated elements of organizational culture. In contrast to conventional wisdom, the customer is not always right and not all customers are the right customers for an organization. Some organizations promulgate throughout the organization positive attitudes toward customers, quality, and ethics, whereas others are silent on these issues. Regard for customers, attitudes toward quality, and ethical behavior are often instilled by the mission statement and the vision statement of an organization. The mission and vision statements serve distinct purposes and should be clearly differentiated.

A mission statement defines the purpose and goals of an organization. For example,

> We provide information systems of highest quality to customers who value quality

is a mission statement.

Organizational values and ethical behavior must be aligned with the mission statement. If providing information systems of highest quality is the mission, concerns for quality must be reinforced and supported throughout the organization and ethical considerations must prevent delivery of software with known deficiencies. The phrase "to customers who value quality" indicates that the organization places value on these customers and must be selective in the customers it deals with if the mission statement is to be fulfilled; that is, customers who demand short schedules that sacrifice quality products should not be pursued.

In contrast, a vision statement has specific objectives and a time frame for achieving them. An example of a vision statement is

> We will be one of the top three providers of information systems for critical-patient care in the United States by 2010.

A mission statement and a vision statement, taken together, provide the basis for strategic planning and norms of organizational behavior.

Some organizations live by their mission and vision statements; others do not have them or have them but pay no attention to them.

11.4 ASSESSING AND NURTURING INTELLECTUAL CAPITAL

The primary assets of a software organization are the skills and abilities of the project managers, the software developers, and other software personnel. Human assets are termed intellectual capital [Stewart97]. Because people are corporate assets, they should be managed to maximize return on investment and not to minimize cost. Organizations that regard workers as costs to be minimized include fast food restaurants and many retail-sales organizations. In these cases workers are regarded as interchangeable, replaceable units; they are paid the minimum amount possible and are often replaced when they become eligible for increases in wages and benefits.

Organizations that regard people as assets systematically determine the skill levels needed, recruit the best candidates available, ensure that the workers have the processes, procedures, methods, and tools they need, and invest in training and career development activities for the workers. A litmus test of an organization's commitment to its intellectual capital is to observe what happens when times are tough. Unfortunately, many organizations stop investing in training and tools and reduce or cancel travel funds for workers to attend conferences and professional development seminars. These practices indicate that the organization's managers regard their software people as costs to be controlled rather than assets to be nurtured.

Table 11.2 lists some of the (direct and indirect) measures that organizations can use to assess their intellectual capital [Stewart97].

Like all elements of a well-run organization, intellectual capital should be assessed, weaknesses determined, and actions taken to improve the intellectual capital of your organization.

11.5 KEY PERSONNEL ROLES

Your key personnel are those project members who are assigned responsibilities and are given the authority to carry out those assignments by you, the project manager. If you are project manager, team leader, and software architect for a project of 5 or 6 members, every project member is a key person on your project. If you are project manager of a project consisting of multiple small teams (i.e., 5 or 6 members per team) your key personnel include the team leaders and the software architect (who may be you). It is the responsibility of your team leaders to coordinate the work activities of their team members, who are in turn their key personnel. Team leaders must be given the authority to make work assignments within their teams, and accept the responsibility of producing high-quality work products on schedule.

They, the team leaders, are responsible for the quantity, quality, and timeliness of the work products produced by their teams. Table 11.3 lists some key personnel roles for software projects. Note that process and product quality assurance, verification, and validation are not listed in Table 11.3. Quality assurance personnel are not project members, nor are they members of independent verification and validation groups because you, the project manager, do not have (should not have) authority to direct their work activities. The configuration manager for your project should be a member of your team, whether or not that person or persons reports directly to you or to another manager; either arrangement is acceptable provided that the goals and procedures of configuration management are satisfied. The software tester role is not a verification or validation role; it is the role that conducts independent testing within your project; this role could be shared among team members who test one another's code.

One of your first tasks as project manager is to determine the extent of your responsibilities and authority. You may, for example, have a great deal of autonomy in hiring and firing of your project personnel, or you may be constrained to use the personnel assigned to your project. You may work directly with an external customer and negotiate schedule, budget, and deliverables with the customer organization, or your customer may be a system engineering group or a marketing department within which you are in a subordinate position.

TABLE 11.2 Direct and indirect measures of intellectual capital

Measures of Intellectual Capital	Examples
• Measures of innovation	• New products or services delivered in the past 12 months • Numbers of patents and copyrights filed and obtained in the past 12 months • Percentage of sales attributable to new products or services
• Measures of employee attitudes	• On a scale of (Unhappy, OK, Very Happy), how happy are you with your job? • Compared to a year ago, are you happier, about the same, or less happy at work? • Do you understand how your job is of benefit to customers (not at all, a little, somewhat, etc.)
• Measures of experience, turnover, and tenure	• Essential personnel: percentage of employees whose expertise is essential to the business of the company • Average number of years experience among essential personnel • Rookie ratio: percentage of essential personnel with less than two years experience • Turnover among essential personnel • Average number of years of experience of all employees • Reasons people leave to accept jobs elsewhere
• Measures of education and training	• Degrees, by level, of essential personnel • Degrees being sought by essential personnel with corporate sponsorship • Nondegree courses being taken by essential personnel with corporate sponsorship • Average training hours per year for essential personnel
• Other measures	• Revenue generated per employee • Revenue generated per essential employee • Percentage of customers who challenge us • Which skills are most important in satisfying customer needs? • Which skills are most admired by other employees? • What are the most desired assignments by high-potential managers and workers? Where do they least want to work? What explains the differences? • What accounts for any differences between what customers value and what employees value? • What emerging technologies or skills could undermine the value of your organization's special knowledge and skills? • What percentage of essential personnel time is spent in activities of low value to your customer base? • What percentage of *all* employees' time is spent in activities of low value to your customer base? • What is the reputation of your company among experts in your field?

TABLE 11.3 Some key personnel roles for software projects

- Project manager
- Requirements engineer
- Software architect
- Team leader
- Software implementer
- Software tester
- Configuration manager

AUTHORITY AND RESPONSIBILITY

Responsibility is the obligation to perform the assigned tasks and duties of your job position. In a well-organized company, each organizational role has a job description that itemizes the primary duties of that role. The primary duties of a project manager, for example, are to:

- prepare and update estimates and plans;
- measure and control the work process and the work products;
- communicate, coordinate, and lead; and
- manage risk.

The primary duties of a software architect (i.e., lead designer) are itemized in Table 11.4.

TABLE 11.4 Responsibilities of the software architect role

- Interacts with requirements engineering personnel
- Develops design options and presents the trade-offs among them to decision makers
- Leads the design team
- Leads and coordinates the implementation team leaders
- Keeps the product vision
- Coordinates technical activities with other design teams, other disciplines, and other organizations

The responsibilities of team leaders are itemized in Table 11.5. Similar lists of duties should be included in the job descriptions for all of the roles to be played in your projects. In a well-managed organization, job descriptions will exist for each of the roles to be played. In a chaotic organization you might have to develop the job descriptions yourself.

Authority is the power to make the decisions that must be made in fulfilling one's responsibilities, and the power to implement those decisions, or to see that they are implemented. A CCB, for example, must have the authority to establish work-product baselines and to accept, reject, or defer change requests and defect reports. Each job description should include the authority vested in the job as well as the assigned responsibilities. An individual software developer, for example, has (or should have) the authority, within the constraints of the project's (or organization's) style guidelines, to implement code in the way she or he thinks will best satisfy the requirements, but he or she does not have the authority to change the requirements baseline for the product.

TABLE 11.5 Responsibilities of the team leader role

- Supervises personal and team processes
- Assures personal and team product quality
- Mentors and coaches team members
- Maintains team morale, energy, and drive
- Keeps management informed of progress and problems
- Coordinates work activities with other teams and groups
- Resolves problems and issues within his or her control
- Elevates problems and issues beyond his or her control

Authority can be delegated but responsibility cannot. You can, for example, delegate authority to your chief architect to negotiate requirements with the customer. However, you are still responsible, as project manager, for delivering an acceptable product within the constraints of schedule and budget. If your architect fails to successfully negotiate the requirements and your project fails, you will be responsible for the failure. And, of course, you deserve to share the credit for successful outcomes.

A common complaint among those who work in organizations is that they do not have the authority to carry out their responsibilities. Sometimes this is the result of the ineptitude of a manager who delegates authority insufficiently, sometimes it is based on the desire of a manager to exert control over every aspect of the work for which he or she is responsible (perhaps because of the manager's insecurity or perhaps because she or he does not trust the team members to carry out their assigned responsibilities), and sometimes those who complain about lack of authority mistakenly think their responsibilities are larger than they are in fact.

Personnel assignments are made by first identifying the roles that must be played. The roles to be played include project manager, software architect, software implementer, configuration manager, and others, as listed in Table 11.6. One person may play multiple roles as, for example, one person (you) playing the project manager, software architect, and team leader roles in a small project. One role may require multiple individuals as, for example, the implementer role or tester role. One individual may play different roles at different times, for example, as software designer and later as software tester.

Some roles, such as configuration manager, may be a part-time role for one of the software implementers on a small project, a full-time role on a larger project, or a role performed by a separate organizational entity. Some roles, quality

TABLE 11.6 Some software project roles

- Project manager
- Requirements engineer
- Software architect
- Team leader
- Implementer
- Tester
- Configuration manager
- Process and product quality assurer
- Independent verifier
- Independent validator
- Technical writer
- Trainer
- Installer
- System maintainer

assurance and independent verification and validation, for example, must be played by individuals from organizational entities separate from the project.

Having identified the roles to be played and the number of individuals needed to fill those roles, the next step is to state the qualification of individuals who will play the roles, when those individuals will be needed, and for how long. It may be, for example, that your software implementers must be proficient in using the Java programming language or that your configuration manager must be proficient in using a specific version control tool.

If, during initial planning, the names of those who will play the roles are known, they can be entered in the personnel assignment matrix, as in Table 11.7. If their names are not known, a personnel acquisition plan should be developed. The plan should state the roles to be played, the number of personnel needed to fill the roles, the job qualifications for the roles, and the dates when the roles must be filled.

TABLE 11.7 Assignment of individuals to roles

Role Person	PM	RE	SA	IT	CM	CCB
Joe S.		P		P		M
Sue W.	P					P
Bill P.	B	B			P	
Mai L.			P	B		M

PM: Project Manager; RE: Requirements Engineer; SA: Software Architect; IT: Independent Tester; CM: Configuration Manager; CCB: Change Control Board; P: Primary; B: Backup; M: Member.

Your human resources department or some other organizational entity may be of assistance in filling the roles, or you may be on your own in staffing your project, depending on the infrastructure of your organization and possibly on the conditions stated in the contract between the customer's organization and your organization. The personnel acquisition plan should be reviewed when developing the risk management plan to determine potential problems in acquiring the needed personnel.

In Table 11.7 note that each role, except for software architect and configuration manager, has a primary person and a backup person. Every role should have a backup person to fill in when the primary person is not available (for whatever reason). Note that Bill P. is backup for both project manager and requirements engineer roles; perhaps he is serving as an apprentice in these roles in preparation for becoming a project manager and/or requirements engineer. Joe S. is primary for both requirements engineering and independent testing which are compatible roles; Joe can develop requirements-based tests during requirements analysis and apply them as the implementers develop the code. Mai has no backup for the architect role and Bill has no backup for configuration management. These assignments should be made. The head of the CCB is Sue, the project manager. CCB members are Joe, the requirements engineer and Mai, the software architect.

If the project depicted in Table 11.7 is a small one all project members, except Joe, may be software implementers in addition to their other roles. If the project is a large one with multiple development teams, each team leader and his or her backup should be listed in the table.

11.6 FIFTEEN GUIDELINES FOR ORGANIZING AND LEADING SOFTWARE ENGINEERING TEAMS

This concluding section of the text is an updated version of a paper previously published by the author [Fairley93]. It summarizes many topics covered in the text and presents a few new ones.

11.6.1 Introduction to the Guidelines

Software, unlike other artifacts of engineering, is exclusively a product of the human intellect; our raw materials are the gray matter inside the human skull. As the size and complexity of software grows and as the demand for higher quality software and shorter development cycles increase, the ability of individual software engineers to work as members of teams, and the ability of the team leaders to direct the efforts of team members become more critical to success. This section presents 15 guidelines for organizing and leading software engineering teams.

There are several reasons that teams are more effective than a collection of individuals working alone. Scheduling and skill sets are primary reasons. Customers won't wait 5 years for one person to develop or modify a software product requiring 60 staff-months of effort. At the other extreme, it is not reasonable to assign 60 people for 1 month. We might scope a 60 staff-month project as a job for 5 people over 12 months or 6 people over 10 months, or using the square root rule 8 people for 8 months.

Teams are also needed to provide the variety of skills and aptitudes required to develop or modify a software system. In addition the synergy that occurs when team members work together in a collaborative manner often results in a product superior to the one that would have resulted from the efforts of several individuals working in isolation.

Organizing and coordinating the activities of individuals engaged in intellect-intensive teamwork is a relatively new kind of human endeavor. Over time we have learned how to organize agricultural and manufacturing activities to utilize the skills of multiple individuals, but we have not yet mastered the corresponding organizational and leadership techniques for intellect-intensive work teams.

To illustrate the problems of intellect-intensive teamwork, consider the difficulties that would arise if a group of individuals were to write a book as a team effort, and on a predetermined schedule and within a specified budget of staff-hours that could be devoted to the project. The problems encountered would be similar to those encountered by a group of software engineers working as a team (this analogy is repeated from Chapter 1).

Determining the type of book to write and documenting the requirements for the book in a clear, complete, and unambiguous manner are procedures analogous to specifying the requirements for a software system. Deciding on the structure of and relationships among chapters, sections, and (perhaps) volumes of the book is the analogue of architectural design in software. Specifying style, voice, tense, and page layout for each chapter is similar to detailed design of software.

Writing the chapters and checking spelling, syntax, and grammar is analogous to coding and unit testing of software modules. Merging the chapters corresponds to software integration. When the book is completed, the integrated text should flow smoothly, as if written by a single individual in a single session. An editor performs independent verification and makes suggestions for improvements to the product, both during development and upon completion of the book. The perceived value of the finished product is largely determined by reviews of critics and work of mouth among customers. If the book is popular, it may be updated and released through several editions following initial release.

Because there are no physical laws that govern book writing and no mathematical theories of how to write a book, a successful outcome for the team effort would depend on clearly defined goals, common understanding and acceptance of those goals, a common approach, adequate resources and calendar time, the skills of the individual contributors, and their ability to work as a cohesive team.

Over time we have observed a number of factors and developed a number of techniques that differentiate capable software teams from the less capable. We call these teams Software Engineering Teams (SETs). The following guidelines summarize our observations and explain our techniques for organizing and leading SETs. These techniques are equally applicable to the development of new software-intensive systems and modification (maintenance) of existing systems.

11.6.2 The Guidelines

1. Hire the best people you can find.

In the context of software engineering teams, "best" means people who have adequate technical skills *and* sufficient interpersonal skills to interact with other team members. Some software engineers have outstanding technical skills but are neither interested in being, nor psychologically suited to be members of cohesive teams. Too often organizations are guilty of suboptimizing the productivity of a team by catering to the idiosyncrasies of technically skilled but socially inept individuals. In some cases it may be necessary to remove a disruptive team member for the greater good of the team, the project, and the organization.

Hiring the best people you can find means you will probably have to pay more than the going rate for individuals within a given skill category. It has been repeatedly shown that programmer productivity varies by factors of 10:1 or more among individual programmers who have similar backgrounds and experiences. Simple economics would indicate that paying 10% to 20% more in return for a gain of 500% or 1000% is a bargain.

2. Treat people as assets rather than costs.

The first rule of business is to manage corporate assets to maximize return on investment in those assets; the second rule is to control costs. Unfortunately, many software organizations confuse the second rule with the first one and treat their software engineers as costs rather than assets. Companies that regard their software engineers as assets invest in the engineers by providing adequate compensation, a work environment that enhances productivity and quality of work, and a management environment that is supportive of software workers and work activities. The work environment for software engineers includes the social, cultural, and intellectual work environment; the automated development environment; and the physical workspace.

According to DeMarco and Lister [DeMarco99] the ability to divert phone calls and other interruptions, thereby preventing disruptions to thought patterns, is one of the most effective mechanisms for improving individual productivity. Co-locating team members engaged in a joint work activity in adjacent workspaces is essential. Providing private breakout areas where two or three individuals can converse without disturbing others is another example of a workspace factor that can improve the efficiency and effectiveness of individuals and teams. A policy of quiet hours during part of each working day can improve the intellectual work environment of software engineering teams. During quiet hours no phone calls are accepted, no meetings are held, and each team member works on individual tasks, as in a library environment.

3. Provide a balance between job specialization and job variety.

Many software engineers are motivated by apparently conflicting needs: the need to be recognized for their expertise within a subdiscipline, and the need to learn and apply new skills.

In the software field, tasks that are initially challenging can quickly become repetitive and boring. On the other hand, the organization often needs highly skilled specialists in various arcane technologies. It is reasonable to assign tasks to those who are best qualified to perform those tasks; however, new and challenging job assignments need also to be provided so that individual contributors do not become technically stagnant. Short-term productivity may benefit from prolonged and concentrated specialization by individuals, but in the long term the individual and the organization will both benefit from a judiciously chosen variety of job assignments for team members.

4. Keep team members together.

It takes time for team members to learn one another's work habits, aptitudes, skills, likes, and dislikes, and for team members to become comfortable with their team environment. On of the potential problems of matrix organizations is lack of team cohesion; project members drawn from functional homes for short periods of time often have more allegiance to their functional managers and their functional colleagues than to their project manager and project colleagues. Keeping a team together over extended periods of time and using explicit team-building techniques such as off-site planning and review meetings, team participation in training courses, and corporate-sponsored recreational activities are effective techniques for building a cohesive team. Weekly status meetings can be team-building experiences if properly conducted (see guideline 10).

5. Limit team size.

Closely coordinated, intellect-intensive teamwork is best accomplished by small teams. We have observed two types of cohesive software engineering teams, the first being the more common. This team structure consists of three to six team members plus a team leader, which results in a maximum team size of seven. If a team grows to eight or more, it is split into two teams of three to six members each plus team leaders. When a team grows larger than six or seven, it is difficult for team members to coordinate their work activities with each of the other team members. It is also impossible for the team leader to provide the necessary level of planning, coordination, and leadership.

Teams larger than seven may be a symptom of inadequate partitioning of the requirements and insufficient decomposition of the software architecture. The product should be structured as a collection of loosely coupled, highly cohesive elements, where each element can be implemented by a small team. The teams are then highly cohesive and loosely coupled.

The second team structure consists of 7 to 12 individuals plus a team leader. Within these larger teams, individual team members are more autonomous and tend to be more loosely coupled to other team members than in the 3 to 6 person teams. To be effective, these larger teams must satisfy some special conditions; namely:

- each team member must be a highly skilled and experienced professional;
- each team member must have a well-defined functional role; and
- everyone must have a clear understanding of his or her role, and the roles of the other team members.

In addition, each team member must have sufficient initiative and discipline to plan and organize his or her individual work activities and to communicate with the other team members and the team leader (see guideline 8).

These larger cohesive teams have been observed in domains such as telecommunications, process control, and systems engineering. Members of these teams are often highly skilled and experienced in their functional specialties, functional roles are clearly differentiated, and the role of each person is clearly understood by others. It must be emphasized that teams and project are placed at risk when teams larger than seven (six member plus leader) are utilized without the prerequisites of individual skill, experience, job specialization, and initiative.

6. Differentiate the role of the team leader.

In both types of teams, the team leaders plays the pivotal roles of:

- planning, negotiating, and coordinating work activities of the team members;
- setting performance goals for each team member;
- tracking progress of individuals and the team;
- updating plans;

- validating the work products produced by team members; and
- communicating with the project manager, the software architect, other elements of the project, the parent organization, and the customer organization.

Although the responsibilities are the same, the team leader's activities are somewhat different for teams of 3 to 6 than they are for teams of 7 to 12 (see guideline 8).

In all cases a team leader may assist a team member but never takes the initiative in generating work products—the job of a team leader is to plan and coordinate work activities, set performance goals, validate work products, monitor progress, advise and help team members, anticipate problems, and be spokesperson for the team. Given these roles of planner, coordinator, progress monitor, communicator, and quality control agent (see guideline 7), the leader of a software engineer team is not "management overhead" but rather is the catalyst that causes a group of individuals to coalesce into a cohesive, productive team.

The Chief Programmer Team is another type of cohesive software team [Baker72]. The primary distinction between our approach (SETs) and that of the Chief Programmer Team is that the SET leader does not generate the work products, nor is she or he required to be the technical guru (but a SET leader must be familiar with the application domain and must be competent in the software technologies being used).

In a cohesive SET, team members, individually and collectively, have the authority to make technical decisions and are responsible for the technical content of their work. In the Chief Programmer approach, the Chief Programmer makes all technical decision and generates most, if not all, of the software. Also it is difficult for the Chief Programmer to perform all of the necessary technical and managerial duties because of the heavy workload involved, and because of the variety of skills required to do both jobs well. In addition it is difficult to scale up the Chief Programmer technique to multiple-team projects; the techniques described in this chapter can be scaled to projects of arbitrary size (see guideline 14).

7. Make each team leader the team's quality control agent.

An important task for a team leader is specifying or tailoring the validation criteria for work products and determining that the work products satisfy those criteria. In teams of three to six, the team leader is the moderator of peer reviews (i.e., inspections) and determines that other quality engineering activities are conducted in an effective manner; for example, determining that unit-test completion criteria are satisfied.

In larger teams (7 to 12 members) the team leader does not usually validate all the work products generated by all team members, but rather assigns validation tasks, such as moderator duties for review teams, to team members in a "round-robin" manner so that everyone takes his or her turn. This is possible because each member in the larger teams has sufficient skills and experience to lead peer reviews and apply objective validation criteria to the work products generated by other team members. Each team member is trained to serve as moderator, reader, and recorder for formal peer reviews.

The leader thus does "real work," stays in close contact with the efforts of each team member, and takes responsibility for the quality of work products generated by the team. In software projects organized around SETs, the team leaders are thus the primary quality control agents for those projects. The role of the quality assurance group is then to advise the team leaders, analyze quality metrics data, recommend process improvements, and to ensure that the team leaders and their teams are fulfilling their responsibilities.

Note that on a small project (i.e., 6 or fewer team members) the team leader may also play the roles of project manager and software architect.

8. Decompose tasks into manageable units of work.

Lowest level tasks are sized to achieve a balance between micromanagement of individual team members and macromanagement of an entire team. At the level of job assignments for individuals, we recommend the "one-to-two" rule: one to two persons, one to two weeks, but not to exceed 80 staff-hours per task. The one-to-two rule thus brackets work tasks in a 40 staff-hour to 80 staff-hour range. A task assigned to one person for two weeks or two persons for one week would satisfy the one-to-two rule. Forty staff-hours of effort on the lower end avoids micromanagement of individuals who can plan and arrange their work activities week by week, perhaps on a flex-hour schedule. Eighty staff-hours on the upper end avoids macromanagement by forcing attention to detailed planning and monitoring of progress by team leaders and project managers.

In teams of three to six, the one-to-two rule provides a manageable workload for the team leader. For a team of five individual contributors, each working on a 40 staff-hour task, the team leader will, on average, have one completed task to validate and one new task to initiate each day. A team of three, each working on 80 staff-hour tasks, represents one-and-a-half tasks to validate and initiate each day; however, the tasks are twice as large to initiate and the work products to be validated are larger and/or more complex than 40-staff hour tasks and may require more effort per task.

In SETs of 7 to 12 members, the team leader delegates some duties. Each team member is responsible for generating and documenting 40 to 80 hour work plans, each of which generates a work product that is accepted by objective validation criteria, and for coordinating her or his plans with the team leader and other team members. However, the team leader is still responsible for reviewing, approving, and coordinating plans; setting performance goals; monitoring progress; optimizing the allocation of team members and other resources; ensuring that work products satisfy their validation criteria; communicating with the software architect, project manager, other elements of the organization, and customer entities; and assuring that individual team members are meeting their performance goals (see guideline 11).

9. Use an augmented rolling-wave approach to planning.

In software projects it is usually not possible, nor desirable, to plan work activities at the one-to-two staff-week level of detail more than one or two months in advance of the work to be accomplished. To plan at the one-to-two level of detail, one should adopt an augmented rolling-wave approach to detailed planning. The rolling-wave approach involves refining and revising plans on a monthly basis. The augmented rolling-wave approach to planning augments traditional rolling-wave planning by maintaining 3 levels of detail in the plan as illustrated in Figure 11.3.

The most detailed level is for the coming month, and is planned at the one-to-two (40 to 80 staff-hours) level of detail. The second, less detailed level of planning is

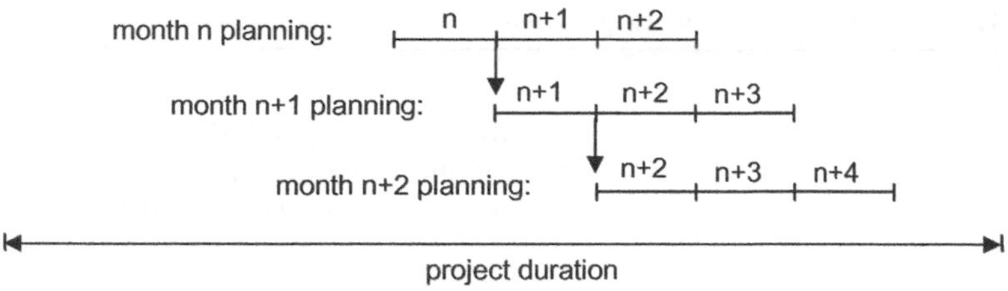

FIGURE 11.3 Augmented rolling-wave planning

for the subsequent month; this plan is as detailed as possible, but it will by necessity be less detailed than the coming-month version. The third level of detail is for the third subsequent month. Each of these levels of detail must be consistent with the overall constraints on effort, schedule, budget, and technology. On projects of long duration, it may be desirable to roll forward a six-month level of detail in addition to the one-month, two-month, and three-month levels of detail.

Each month the planning "wave" is rolled forward by updating each level of the plan in light of the evolving situation. We call this approach an augmented rolling-wave because we indicate three (or four) levels of detail in the plan. This prevents short-sighted focus on activities for the coming month to the exclusion of future, less well-defined, but foreseeable tasks.

10. Adopt a contractual model for task assignments.

Large work activities (requirements development, design, coding, testing) are decomposed into tasks of 40 to 80 staff-hours using the augmented rolling wave approach to planning. Each task is documented in a work package and each work package becomes a negotiated contract between the team leader and the individual(s) assigned to that work package.

Each work package provides a description of the task, the relationships of that task to other tasks and activities (i.e., hierarchical relationships between activities and tasks in the work breakdown structure; and precedence relationships among tasks in the schedule network); the planned duration of the task, the numbers and kinds of resources needed to accomplish the tasks, the work products to be produced, the risk factors that might create problems for successful completion of the task, and the acceptance criteria for the work products. Each work package must produce one or more tangible work products that must satisfy objective acceptance criteria. An example of a typical work package is presented in Table 11.8.

The Member_of and Preceded_by relations in Table 11.8 are used to impose a work breakdown structure and a schedule network on a collection of work packages. Member_of identifies the larger activity to which a work package belongs; the set of subordinate activities and tasks defines the larger activity. Preceded_by specifies the tasks and work products that must be completed before a work package can be initiated. The schedule network can be determined from the Preceded-by relationships of the work packages; the critical path that determines the duration of a project can be determined from the schedule network.

A collection of work packages can be analyzed for attributes such as completeness, consistency, critical path, collective resource requirements, and risk factors. The implementation status of tasks and their parent activities (pending/open/closed) can be determined by examining work package status. Personnel assigned and start date

TABLE 11.8 An example of a work package

Work package 3.2.2.1	
Activity_name:	DESIGN_INPUT_SUBSYSTEM
Description:	Specify the architectural structure of INPUT and develop the test plan for INPUT
Member_of:	3.2.2
Preceded_by:	3.1.1 and 3.1.2
Plan	
Planned_duration:	2 weeks
Resources_needed:	
Personnel:	1 senior telecomm designer
Skills:	must know the X25 protocol
Methods:	state-based OO design IEEE Std. 829 for test plan
Tools:	1 MACBOOK workstation; iLogix Prodigy
Travel:	None
Work_products:	Architectural spec for INPUT Test plan for INPUT
Acceptance_criteria:	Successful peer reviews of design and test plan Sign-off by chief architect
Risk_factors:	Telecomm designer not identified Schedule constraint
Responsible_party:	R. Fairley
Implementation	
Status:	(pending/open/closed)
Personnel_assigned:	(planned/actual)
Start_date:	(planned/actual)
Completion_date:	(planned/actual)
Work products generated:	(planned/actual)
Resources_consumed:	(planned/actual)
Legacy_comments:	
End 3.2.2.1	

can be determined and compared to plan for open work packages. The actual completion date, resources consumed, work products generated, and legacy comments can additionally be determined for closed work packages.

Assignment of work packages to individuals and estimates of time durations needed to complete tasks are negotiated by the team leader and each team member, subject to overall resource and scheduling constraints. Agreement on a work package between the team leader and a team member constitutes a contract for completion of one or more work products within the specified time duration that will demonstrably satisfy the acceptance criteria for those work products.

Binary tracking of deliverables can (and should) be used to track task completions [DeMarco82]. Binary tracking requires that a work package be credited as 0% complete until the associated work products satisfy their acceptance criteria; the work package then becomes 100% complete. Decomposing work packages to a granularity of 40 to 80 staff-hours and using binary tracking provide accurate information for an earned value reporting system [Webb03], which in turn provides a concise summary of project status and early warning of impending problems.

11. Set performance goals for the team and for each team member.

In their book, *The Wisdom of Teams*, Katzenbach and Smith observe that the most effective way to build a cohesive team is to set challenging performance goals for the entire team *and* for each member of the team. [Katzen93] The goals should be challenging but not impossible. DeMarco and Lister include impossible schedules (phony deadlines) as one of the "sure fire ways to inhibit formation of teams and disrupt project sociology." [DeMarco99] Other factors cited by Katzenbach and Smith that distinguish effective teams include having a meaningful purpose, a common approach, complementary skills, and mutual accountability.

It is important to set performance goals for each team member as well as for the entire team. This approach eliminates the possibility that collective team efforts might dilute individual accountability, initiative, and recognition. Elements of a performance goal include objective, measurable criteria, and a time frame for achievement of the goal. For example, a team goal might be to reduce schedule overrun from 20% to 10% in the next quarter by reducing the number of mistakes made (i.e., defects injected) and thus reducing corrective rework [Fairley05].

It is also important that team goals be discussed and negotiated in an open manner with the entire team, and that individual goals are discussed, negotiated, and reviewed in private with each individual. Goals should be challenging but not impossible. Progress toward goals should be monitored and corrective action taken if extrapolation of the current trend indicates that a goal will probably not be met within the specified time frame. Failure to achieve an ambitious goal should be regarded as an opportunity to learn from the experience and to improve future performance.

Performance is reviewed periodically (e.g., monthly) with the team and with each team member. Achievement of ambitious goals is celebrated, problems are identified, and impediments to better performance are identified. Team goals, progress toward those goals, and team achievements are displayed in a public manner. Review of individual performance is a confidential matter between the individual and the team leader. Team members who consistently fail to meet agreed-to goals should be counseled to determine the reasons they are unable to meet the goals and to develop courses of action that will enable the team member to improve his or her performance.

Setting of new goals is an ongoing process. This can be done in conjunction with the rolling-wave approach to planning and control (see guideline 9). Goals setting and performance measurement do not have to be, and should not be, Machiavellian [Mach13]. Attributes of cohesive teams include a collective sense of humor, healthy skepticism, and enjoyment of working together. These attributes facilitate collective setting of team goals.

12. Ensure daily interactions with each team member and among team members.

It is important that the team leader interact with each team member and that team members interact with one another on a daily basis. One mechanism for ensuring daily interaction is a 15 to 20 minute "stand-up" meeting in which each team member briefly reports on work accomplished the previous day, work in progress for the current day, and any issues that should be brought to the attention of other team members. Issues to be resolved between two or three individuals should be noted but handled apart from the team meeting. Issues that require the attention of the entire team should be scheduled for later in the day or perhaps the following day, depending on the urgency of the situation.

A daily forum provides an opportunity for the team leader to communicate any new information, report on the status of work in progress, to comment on the latest rumors, and to provide advance notice of upcoming events. It also provides an opportunity for team members to "pair-off" and discuss issues of mutual interest following the meeting.

Electronic mail, video conferencing, and groupware tools should never be used in place of daily "face-to-face" meetings. Electronic media can be effective communications mechanisms and should be fully utilized, but they should augment and not replace human contact among team members and between team members and the team leader. Team members who are on travel should speak, by phone, with their team leader on a daily basis. News of their activities should be communicated by the team leader to other team members during the daily stand-up meetings. An acting team leader should be designated when the official leader is absent and the acting and official team leaders should communicate, by phone, on a daily basis.

13. Conduct weekly status review meetings.

The team should meet each week to review project status and to assist the team leader in preparing a weekly status report and a list of action items for problems that have been newly encountered. The status report includes a summary of progress against the planned schedule and summarizes tasks completed during the past week, tasks to be initiated in the coming week, tasks to be completed in the coming week, and the status of risk factors and action items.

Problem status is categorized into problems solved during the past week, new problems that have surfaced in the past week, ongoing problems, and old problems thought to have been solved that have resurfaced. Risk factors are potential problems that might happen but haven't yet; a problem is a risk factor that has materialized. Risk factors are characterized by probability, impact, time frame, and mitigation activities. Mitigation activities are concerned with reducing the probability and/or the potential impact of a risk factor; they include avoidance, transfer, acceptance, immediate action, and contingent action. Problems and risk factors that cannot be, or should not be, handled by the team are brought to the team leader's weekly meeting with the project manager. In small projects, where the team leader is also the project manager, problems and risk factors that cannot be handled within the project are elevated to the project manager's weekly meeting with the department manager.

Based on the weekly review of resolved, new, continuing, and resurfaced problems, team members assist the team leader in developing the team's prioritized "top-N" problem list (where $N \leq 10$) [Boehm89]. Each problem on the top-N list has an associated action item that specifies the nature of the problem, the actions to be pursued, the responsible individual, and the scheduled closure date. Authority for decision making and resources to be applied are specified, as appropriate.

TABLE 11.9 Format of a weekly status report

Weekly status report

Date:
To:
From:
Work status:
  Tasks completed:
  Tasks to be initiated:
  Tasks to be completed:
Problem areas:
  Problems solved:
  New problems:
  Ongoing problems:
  Resurfaced problems:
Risk factors:
  Description of each:
  Probability, potential impact, timing of each:
  Recommended mitigation strategy for each:

Action items are entered into a tracking system and the status of each open action item is reviewed at the weekly status meeting. Action items are treated as discrepancy reports against the development process, as such they are tracked to closure in the same way problem reports (bug reports) are tracked against the product. It is important that team members agree on priorities among problems and the associate action items so that task priorities and allocation of resources are understood and supported by all.

An effective technique for weekly status reporting is to adopt a standard format for the reports, as in Table 11.9. Each team member submits, by electronic mail, his or her individual weekly report to the team leader and to all other team members on the afternoon before the weekly meeting. Everyone comes to the weekly meeting having reviewed all individual reports.

Weekly status reviews are limited to not more than two hours. Items that do not involve the entire team are handled separately. An effective technique is to schedule weekly reviews as working lunches. In one of my former jobs, I was fortunate to have funds available to purchase sandwiches and soft drinks for the Friday review meetings. These two-hour lunch meeting were so effective as status reviews *and as team-building* experiences that if (and when) I lead another team in the future, I will pay for the sandwiches (pizza, Chinese, ...) myself if necessary.

A recommended agenda for weekly status meetings and follow-up activities is presented in Table 11.10. Some re-negotiation of contracts with team members (item 4 of follow-up activities) may occur and may involve trading off of responsibilities among team members (with the team leader's concurrence). In a cohesive team, it is quite common for those individuals who are running ahead of schedule on their tasks to volunteer to help those who are running behind. Job sharing and willingness to help one another are key indicators of a cohesive software engineering team.

14. Structure large projects as collections of highly cohesive, loosely coupled small projects.

TABLE 11.10 Agenda and follow-up activities for weekly status meetings

Meeting agenda (2 hours)

1. Have lunch—avoid technical discussions (1/2 hour)
2. Review individual status reports
3. Review status of open action items
4. Generate a revised, collective top-*N* problem list
5. Generate a revised, prioritized list of action items
6. Generate a revised list of risk factors and mitigation strategies

Team leader's follow-up activities

1. Enter new action items into the tracking system
2. Re-prioritize existing action items as necessary
3. Generate work packages for new action items
4. Re-negotiate contracts with individual project members as necessary
5. Initiate risk mitigation strategies as necessary
6. Revise schedule and resource allocations as necessary
7. Report upward action items and risk factors that cannot be, or should not be, handled by the team

Projects requiring more than six team members plus a team leader (or 7 to 12 members in certain circumstances; see guideline 5) must use multiple teams. Figure 11.2 illustrates a project structure that can be tailored to fit the needs of projects ranging from 3 or 4 members to projects having hundreds of members. In the case of a small project (6 or fewer members), one person may play the roles of customer contact, project manager, software architect (i.e., lead designer), and team leader. On projects of medium size (7 to 50 members), multiple team leaders (6 or fewer members per team) report to a project manager; in addition they are members of the software architect's design team. On large projects (more than 50 members) the team leaders depicted in Figure 11.2 are managers of subsystems; each subsystem manager will have multiple teams and team leaders. Depending on the size and complexity of a subsystem, the manager may also be the software architect for that subsystem or may be assisted by a subsystem architect. On a large project the project manager may be assisted by one or more staff members, and the chief architect may head a design team consists of the subsystem architects.

Different teams and different subsystem groups may use different methods and tools, as appropriate within the overall framework of the project. Some teams might practice pair programming and other Agile development techniques while others might use an incremental development strategy with weekly builds and demos; some teams might use a state-based approach to design and implementation while others are using functional decomposition or object-oriented techniques.

The rule of thumb for structuring software projects, as with software itself, is to design a collection of highly cohesive, loosely coupled elements. In a 1968 article Mel Conway observed that the structure of a software product tends to resemble the structure of the team that develops it [Conway68]. Like many profound statements, this one is obvious once pointed out: the protocols and conventions worked out among team members and between teams become the interfaces among the software modules and subsystems developed by those team members and teams.

Conway's observation can be termed as "Conway's law" in order to introduce "Fairley's corollary:"

> To maximize efficiency and effectiveness, task assignments for project teams and for individual project members must be structured to reflect the desired product structure.

One technique for ensuring adherence to Fairley's corollary is to embed the product structure in the work breakdown structure (WBS) by partitioning the development tasks in the WBS in one-to-one correspondence with the software architecture.

Figure 11.4 illustrate a partial WBS in which the product structure is denoted by the work products that will result from completion of the corresponding work packages. The work packages are thus the specifications for the WBS elements; note that each element of the WBS is a verb phrase denoting an activity or task to be accomplished. Task assignment for teams and individuals are generated from the work packages.

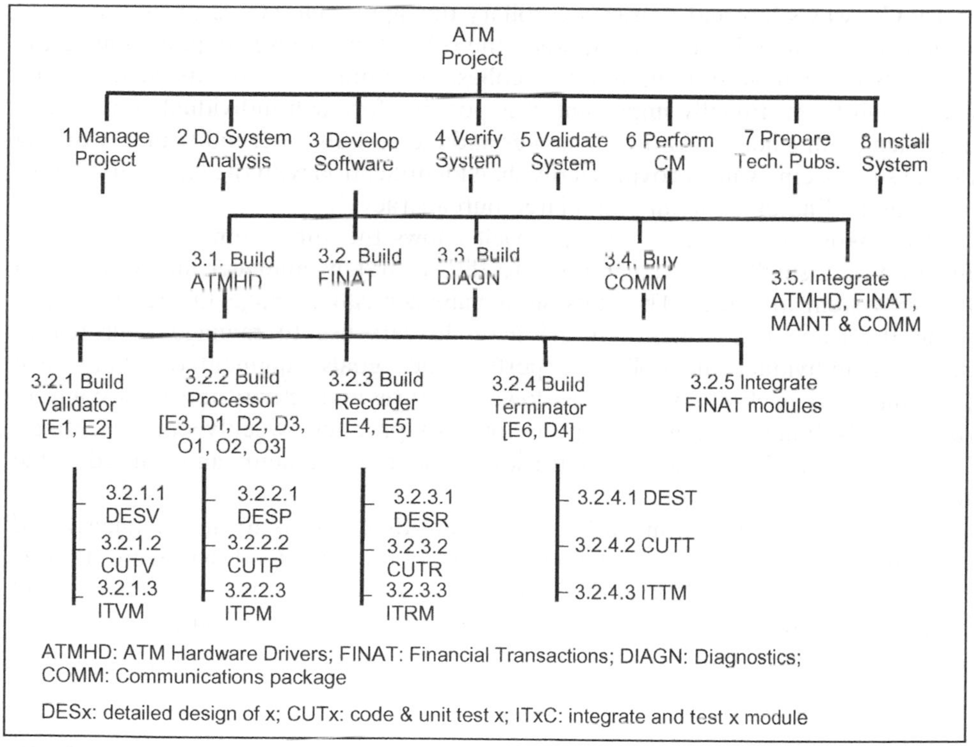

FIGURE 11.4 A partial work breakdown structure

For example, task 3.2.1.2, (code and unit test the validator) might be a 40-hour work package that becomes a contract with one individual team member for one week; the resulting work product would be the validator module. Use of process-oriented work breakdown structures and work packages to specify tasks ensures that the product structure will be reflected in the work assigned to teams and to individual team members, since each work package must generate one or more tangible work products that are accepted using objective acceptance criteria. Note that the requirements for the Validator, Processor, Recorder, and Terminator elements of the ATM are allocated to those modules as Essential (Ei), Desirable (Di), and Optional (Oi) requirements.

Aggregation of the work packages and work products completed by a team represent the contributions of that team to a larger project. The work package for a team is specified as a contract between the team and the larger project. That work package is then decomposed by the team leader, in consultation with the team members, into a collection of work packages and work assignments for individual team members, using the one-to-two decomposition rule and augmented rolling-wave planning.

Large systems (those requiring the effort of perhaps hundreds of people) should be partitioned so that no individual team member or team leader has to be aware of, or concerned about, the efforts of more than 25 or 30 other people who are working on the same subsystem. This might amount to five teams of six people plus team leaders; collectively the teams are responsible for developing a subsystem of the larger system.

By Conway's law and Fairley's corollary this approach will result in a product with loosely coupled interfaces between the subsystems, loose coupling among the elements of each subsystem, and high cohesion within the elements generated by each small team. Equally important, it is possible for each individual contributor, and each team leader to know the names and faces of all other individuals working on the subsystem, which provides individual identification with the larger effort thus avoiding feeling of anonymity in a large bureaucracy.

Perhaps most important, this approach allows the subsystem team leaders to function as a small team that reports to the subsystem manager and works with the subsystem architect. The subsystem manager can manage the team leaders using the same techniques that the team leaders use to manage their teams, including individual and collective performance goals, augmented rolling-wave planning, work packages, work breakdown structures and activity networks, contractual models, binary acceptance criteria for work products, weekly status meetings, top-*N* problem lists, action item tracking, risk management, and earned value reporting.

In turn, the subsystem managers are a team that reports to their manager and the subsystem architects are members of the chief architect's design team. Performance goals and work packages flow downward through the hierarchy; negotiated commitments, work products, and performance metrics flow upward. This way the described team techniques can be generalized from individuals to projects of arbitrary size.

15. Remember that organizations are nothing more than individuals and groups of individuals.

It is easy to forget this rule when you are in the midst of a software project. The techniques presented in this section make it possible to achieve a balance between the needs of individuals and the needs of organizations. Fred Brooks's famous observation—there are no silver bullets in software engineering—is by now a cliché, albeit an important one [Brooks87]. However, groups of individuals, working in small, well-organized and well-led teams are the "silver-plated" bullets of software engineering. The technical skills of individuals and the ability of individuals to function as members of cohesive teams engaged in intellect-intensive teamwork are the keys to success.

Every engineering discipline is dependent on people, processes, and technology. In software engineering people are the most important factor. Competent people and cohesive teams can overcome weak processes and poor technology. But excellent processes and outstanding technology can never compensate for inadequate skills or dysfunctional teams.

11.6.3 Summary of the Guidelines

This section has provided 15 guidelines for organizing and leading software engineering teams (SETs). The guidelines are summarized in Table 11.11. These guidelines can be, and should be, tailored to fit your particular situation. If you are involved in development of a large system the techniques described in guideline 15 can be applied. If you are involved in an agile project of 10 or fewer members the guidelines for using work packages to develop work breakdown structures and critical-path networks may not be appropriate. However, most of the guidelines are applicable to all kinds and sizes of software projects.

TABLE 11.11 Fifteen guidelines for organizing and leading SETs

1. Hire the best people you can find.
2. Treat people as assets rather than costs.
3. Provide a balance between job specialization and job variety.
4. Keep team members together.
5. Limit team size.
6. Differentiate the role of team leader.
7. Make the team leader the team's quality control agent.
8. Decompose tasks in manageable units of work.
9. Use an augmented rolling-wave approach to planning.
10. Adopt a negotiated contractual model for task assignments.
11. Set performance goals for the team and for each team member.
12. Ensure daily contact among team members.
13. Conduct weekly status review meetings.
14. Structure large projects as collections of highly cohesive, loosely coupled small projects.
15. Remember that organizations are nothing more than individuals and collections of individuals.

Do not be misled by the 15 easy steps to SETs. The guidelines presented here are by no means complete or comprehensive, nor are they foolproof. There are no physical laws or mathematical theories for building and maintaining cohesive software engineering teams. Interpersonal skills and goodwill are key ingredients of successful teams. Good intentions, alone, are not sufficient. The techniques presented in this section, when applied with common sense and within a supportive organization can produce gratifying results.

11.7 KEY POINTS OF CHAPTER 11

- Corporate culture is comprised of the beliefs, values, and behavior patterns that exist within an organization.
- A mission statement defines the purposes and goals of an organization.
- A vision statement has specific objectives and a time frame for achieving them.
- The primary assets of a software organization are the skills and abilities of the project managers, the team leaders, the software developers, and other software personnel.
- The first rule of business is to manage corporate assets to maximize return on investment in those assets; the second rule is to control costs. Unfortunately, many software organizations confuse the second rule with the first one and treat their software engineers as costs rather than assets.
- Your key personnel are those project members who are assigned responsibilities and are given the authority to carry out those assignments by you, the project manager.
- Responsibilities are (or should be) documented in job descriptions. Authority is the power to make the decisions that must be made in fulfilling one's responsibilities, and the power to implement those decisions.
- Authority can be delegated; responsibility cannot.
- The 15 guidelines for organizing and leading software engineering teams are by no means complete or comprehensive, nor are they foolproof. There are no physical laws or mathematical theories for building and maintaining cohesive software engineering teams.
- However, the 15 guidelines, when applied with common sense and within a supportive organization, can produce gratifying results.

REFERENCES

[Baker72] Baker, F. T. Chief programmer team management of structured programming. IBM Systems Journal. 11(1): 1972, pp. 56–73.

[Boehm89] Boehm, B. W. *Tutorial: Software Risk Management*. Computer Society Press, 1989.

[Brooks87] Brooks, F. W. No silver bullets: Essence and accidents of software engineering. IEEE Computer (April 1987). 20(4), pp. 10–19.

[CMMI06] SEI. *CMMI® Models and Modules*. http://www.sei.cmu.edu/cmmi/models/, 2006.

[Conway68] Conway, M. How do committees invent? Datamation (April): 1968. 14(2), pp. 28–31.

[DeMarco82] DeMarco, T. *Controlling Software Projects*. Yourdon Press, 1982.

[DeMarco99] Demarco, T., and T. Lister. *Peopleware*. Dorset Publishing, 1999.

[Fairley05] Fairley, R. E., and M. J. Willshire. Iterative rework in software development: The good, the bad, and the ugly. IEEE Computer (September 2005). 38(9), pp. 34–41.

[Fairley93] Fairley, R. E., Organizing and leading software engineering teams. *International Perspectives in Software Engineering*. Rocky Mountain Institute of Software Engineering, 1993.

[Hardgr05] Hardgrave, B. C., and D. J. Armstrong. Software process improvement: It's a journey, not a destination. Communication of the ACM. Vol. 48, No. 1, November, 2005. pp. 219–228.

[IEEE1058] IEEE Std 1058TM–1998. *IEEE Standard for Software Project Management Plans*. Engineering Standards Collection. IEEE Product: SE113. Institute of Electrical and Electronic Engineers, August 2003.

[IEEE12207] IEEE/EIA 12207.0/.1/.2. *Industry Implementation of International Standard ISO/IEC 12207:1995 Standard for Information Technology—Software Life Cycle Processes*. Engineering Standards Collection. IEEE Product: SE113. Institute of Electrical and Electronic Engineers, August 2003.

[Katzen93] Katzenbach, J. R., and D. K. Smith. *The Wisdom of Teams: Creating the High-Performance Organization*. Harper Collins, 2003.

[Mach13] Machiavelli, N. *The Prince*. Bantam Classics. 1984.

[PMI04] PMI. *A Guide to the Project Management Body of Knowledge*, 3rd ed. (PMBOK® Guide). Project Management Institute, 2004.

[Stewart97] Stewart, T. *Intellectual Capital*. Doubleday Publishing, 1997.

[Webb03] Webb, A. *Using Earned Value. A Project Manager's Guide*. Gower Publishing, 2003.

EXERCISES

11.1. Briefly summarize the ways in which each of the cultural factors in Table 11.1 applies to your school or work environment.

11.2. Find the mission and vision statements for your school or your work organization. Copy them into your answer for this exercise and briefly state how your school or work organization does or does not adhere to the mission statement and the vision statement. Provide some examples.

11.3. The term "essential personnel" is used in Table 11.2. Briefly explain your understanding of the difference between "essential personnel" and "nonessential personnel."

11.4. Provide another example, in addition to those in Table 11.2, of a measure that might be used to assess the level of innovation in a software organization. Briefly explain.

11.5. List and briefly explain five responsibilities of an individual software developer, similar to those in Tables 11.4 and 11.5.

11.6. The difference between responsibility and authority is explained in Section 11.5.

a. Provide and briefly explain a situation you have experienced or observed in your personal or professional life for which authority was or is commensurate with responsibility.

b. Provide and briefly explain a situation you have experienced or observed in your personal or professional life for which authority was or is not commensurate with responsibility.

11.7. At the end of Section 11.6 it is stated: "If the project depicted in Table 11.7 is a small one, all project members, except Joe, may be software implementers in addition to their other roles."

a. Briefly explain why Joe is excluded from being a software implementer.

b. Briefly explain how a small project might be organized so that Joe could be a software implementer.

11.8. Provide an example of a risk factor that could not be handled at the team level. Briefly explain. Provide an example of a risk factor that could be, but should not be, handled at the team level. Briefly explain.

11.9. For the 15 guidelines listed in Table 11.11,

a. List the ones you think would be easiest for a software organization to implement. Briefly explain your reasoning.

b. List the ones you think would be hardest for a software organization to implement. Briefly explain your reasoning.

APPENDIX 11A

FRAMEWORKS, STANDARDS, AND GUIDELINES FOR ORGANIZATIONAL ISSUES

11A.1 THE CMMI-DEV-v1.2 PROCESS FRAMEWORK

As stated on the SEI Web site, the Capability Maturity Model® Integration (CMMI) was developed by the Software Engineering Institute of Carnegie Mellon University to

> ... guide process improvement across a project, a division, or an entire organization. CMMI helps integrate traditionally separate organizational functions, set process improvement goals and priorities, provide guidance for quality processes, and provide a point of reference for appraising current processes.

(see http://www.sei.cmu.edu/cmmi/general/general.html).

The level 2 process areas in the staged representation of CMMI-DEV-v1.2 are concerned with processes that apply to individual projects. The level 2 processes are listed in Table 11A.1 [CMMI06]. It is possible for all of the projects in your organization to be at level 2 but for each project to accomplish the goals of the processes listed in Table 11A.1 in different ways. For example, different projects could achieve the goals of configuration management using different methods and tools.

At level 3 of the staged representation, all of the level 2 processes and the level 3 processes are conducted in uniform ways across the organization. Level 3 processes include development processes for individual projects and processes that apply at the organizational level. The processes for software and systems development are, or should be tailored from a common framework of processes within your organization that satisfy the goals of the level 2 and level 3 processes. The level 3 process areas that apply to individual projects are listed in Table 11A.2; those that apply at the organizational level are listed in Table 11A.3.

The organization training process is intended to promulgate the organizational processes throughout the organization, as well as to provide understanding of methods, tools, and techniques for all the level 2 and level 3 processes to all project

TABLE 11A.1 CMMI-DEV-v1.2 level 2 process areas

- Requirements management
- Project planning
- Project monitoring and control
- Supplier agreement management
- Measurement and analysis
- Process and product quality assurance
- Configuration management

TABLE 11A.2 CMMI-DEV-v1.2 level 3 process areas for projects

- Requirements development
- Technical solution
- Product integration
- Verification
- Validation
- Risk management

TABLE 11A.3 CMMI-DEV-v1.2 level 3 organizational process areas

- Organizational process focus
- Organizational process definition +IPPD
- Organization training
- Integrated project management +IPPD
- Risk management

members in all projects. Integrated project management ensures that all projects are managed to satisfy project goals and organizational goals in a uniform manner. IPPD (integrated process and product development) is included for projects that involve coordinated software and systems development. Note that risk management is listed at both the project level and the organizational level. Risk factors that cannot be handled at the project level and risk factors that have the potential to negatively impact the entire organization are handled at the organizational level.

Levels 4 and 5 in the staged representation of the CMMI process frameworks are concerned with collecting uniform data across all projects in your organization in order to:

- identify areas in need of improvement,
- make improvements in processes and technology, and
- assess the impact of improvement efforts.

The level 4 and level 5 processes are listed in Table 11A.4.

Level 4 is termed quantitatively managed, which denotes the use of uniformly collected, reported, and validated metrics across all projects in the organization; hence the two processes at level 4: organizational process performance and quantitative project management. Note that level 5 is termed optimizing and not

TABLE 11A.4 CMMI-DEV-v1.2 levels 4 and 5 processes

Level 4: quantitatively managed processes	• Organization process performance • Quantitative project management
Level 5: optimizing processes	• Organizational innovation • Causal analysis and resolution

optimized. Optimizing is meant to imply that improvements in productivity, quality, and customer satisfaction are always possible. As has often been said, the journey of process improvement is more important than the destination of achieving a particular maturity level [Hardgr05].

11A.2 ISO AND IEEE STANDARDS 12207

The 12207 standards for software life cycle processes cover five primary life cycle process areas, eight supporting processes, and four organizational processes [IEEE12207]. The primary life cycle processes are:

- acquisition,
- supply,
- development,
- operation, and
- maintenance.

The eight supporting process areas are.

- documentation,
- configuration management,
- quality assurance,
- verification,
- validation,
- joint reviews,
- audits, and
- problem resolution.

The organizational processes are the

- management,
- infrastructure,
- improvement, and
- training processes.

These processes integrate the customer and supplier processes at the level of individual projects and at the organizational level of customer and supplier.

11A.3 IEEE/EIA STANDARD 1058

The major sections (clauses) of IEEE Standard 1058 for software project management plans (SPMPs) include [IEEE1058]:

- project organization,
- managerial process plans,
- technical process plans,
- supporting process plans, and
- additional process plans.

As explained in Chapter 4, and emphasized throughout this text, the project plan for each project should be tailored from a standard organizational template for project plans, which could be based on IEEE 1058.

11A.4 THE PMI BODY OF KNOWLEDGE

Section I of the *Project Management Body of Knowledge*, 3rd ed. (PMBOK® Guide) covers the project management framework [PMI04]. Section I includes chapter 1 (Introduction) and chapter 2 (Project Life Cycle and Organization). Section 1.5.5 of PMBOK covers interpersonal skills. Topics listed include:

- effective communication,
- influencing the organization,
- leadership,
- motivation,
- negotiation and conflict management, and
- problem solving.

Topics presented in Chapter 2 of PMBOK include:

- organizational influences,
- organizational systems,
- organizational cultures and styles,
- organizational structure,
- the role of the PMO (project management office) in organizational structures, and
- the project management system.

GLOSSARY OF TERMS

See also Appendix B to Chapter 9 for definitions of terms specific to risk management. Italicized terms are defined in this glossary.

Acquirer The person or organization that is the primary point of contact between a *supplier* and a *customer* in a contractual situation. See also *Contract*.

Activity An element of work in a software *project*; higher level activities are decomposed into subordinate activities and *tasks*.

Allocation The *process* of parceling out a *monetary budget*, a *technology budget, system requirements, software requirements, effort* or any other quantity that can be subdivided and assigned to elements of a *process* or a *system*.

Architecture decomposition view (ADV) A hierarchical view of the elements in a software architecture. Each element of an ADV is named using a noun to denote the product-oriented nature of an ADV. See also *Work breakdown structure*.

Assumption A condition accepted as true but which cannot be verified at the current time or which would be too expensive to verify at the current time.

Authority The power to make and implement decisions that must be made to fulfill one's *responsibilities*.

Avoidable rework Work that in principle should not have to be done to a *baselined work product*. See also *Baseline, Retrospective rework*, and *Corrective rework*.

Baseline A *work product* that has satisfied its predetermined acceptance criteria and has been placed under version control. Baselines provide the basis for future work during software development and maintenance. Synonymous with *Baselined work product*.

Baselined work product A *work product* that has satisfied its predetermined acceptance criteria and has been placed under version control; a baselined work

Managing and Leading Software Projects, by Richard E. Fairley

product can be changed only if the change is in response to an approved *change request* or *defect report.* Synonymous with *Baseline.*

Binary tracking The practice of counting *work products* as 0% complete until they satisfy their predetermined acceptance criteria; they are then counted as 100% complete.

Change control board (CCB) The *stakeholders* who approve initial *baselines* and control *baselined work products.* See also *Change request* and *Defect report.*

Change request (CR) A documented request to change a *baselined work product* because of external factors such as a change to the requirements or a change to a hardware or software interface. See also *Defect report.*

COCOMO COnstructive COst MOdel; acronym for a family of estimation models.

Completion date The calendar date on which the software elements of a *software-intensive system* must be ready for delivery to a *customer* or ready for integration into a *system.*

Configuration management (CM) The *process* and mechanisms used to track and control *baselined work products*. See also *Change control board.*

Constraint A limitation imposed by external agents on some or all of the *operational domain, operational requirements, software requirements, project scope, monetary budget, technology budget, resources, completion date*, and *platform technology.*

Contract A statement of understanding between two or more parties. A contract may be informal or legally binding (i.e., formal). See also *Acquirer, Memo of understanding*, and *Statement of work.*

Corrective rework Work performed in response to a *defect report* for a *baselined work product*. See also *Rework, Avoidable rework, Evolutionary rework*, and *Retrospective rework.*

Crisis An event that halts or seriously impedes *progress.*

Critical path A shortest path through a *schedule network.*

Critical path method (CPM) The process of determining the set of (one or more) longest paths through a *schedule network*. See also *PERT.*

Customer (1) The person or organization that specifies the *operational requirements* for and the *constraints* on development of a *software system*, provides the *monetary budget*, and accepts the deliverable *work products* from an *acquirer* or a *supplier*. (2) The person or organization that evaluates a *software product* and purchases it from a *vendor* for one or more *users*; the customer may or may not be a user.

Defect A flaw in a *work product* that renders it incorrect, incomplete, and/or inconsistent. See also *Error* and *Failure.*

Defect report (DR) A documented report of a defect that has been found in a *baselined work product*. See also *Change request.*

Delphi technique An iterative estimation technique that relies on the judgments of multiple experts; each expert's estimates are provided individually, in isolation from the other experts.

Derived requirement (1) An elaboration of a *primary requirement*; (2) a *software requirement* added to support a primary requirement.

Design The process of synthesizing a *system* that optimizes specified design criteria while satisfying specified *constraints.*

Development phase A set of related *tasks* that produce one or more *work products*. Development phases can be interleaved, overlapped, and iterated as specified by the *development process* being used.

Development process The technical *process* used to develop the software elements of a *software-intensive system*; examples include the Waterfall, Incremental-build, Agile, Evolutionary, and Spiral development *processes.*

Development team A small group of individuals (3 to 5 persons) plus a team leader that is responsible for developing or modifying part or perhaps all of the software elements of a *software-intensive system.* See also *Project team.*

Domain technology The technological basis of the *operational domain.*

Earned value Cumulative value of the allocated *monetary budget* for all *tasks* completed. See also *Allocation* and *Binary tracking.*

Earned value tracking The *processes* of (1) comparing *earned value* to the actual cost of work performed and (2) comparing earned value to the budgeted cost of work scheduled. See Table 8.9 for the terminology and calculations of earned value tracking.

Effectiveness The characteristics of a *process* that facilitate incorporation of desired attributes in the resulting *work products.* See also *Efficiency.*

Efficiency The characteristics of a *process* that facilitate development of the associated *work products* without wasting time, effort, or other resources. See also *Effectiveness.*

Effort A measure of work computed as the product of people × time; typically measured in units of person-days, person-weeks, person-months, or person-years.

Embedded system A *system* contained within another system, as in the case of one or more digital devices and the associated software embedded in a larger system such as an airplane or a DVD player. See also *Software-intensive system.*

Error A human mistake that results in a software *defect.* See also *Failure.*

Evolutionary rework Work performed in response to an approved *change request* for a *baselined work product.* See also *Configuration management* and *Change control board.*

External size measure (ESM) A software *measure* determined by counting the numbers of unique inputs, outputs and passive interfaces for the software elements of a *software-intensive system.* See also *Function Point.*

Failure A situation that, when encountered in operation, renders a *software-intensive system* unable to produce the desired, expected, or required response. See also *Defect* and *Error.*

Fan-in The number of *tasks* that immediately precede another task in a *schedule network.*

Fan-out (1) The number of tasks that immediately succeed another task in a *schedule network*; (2) the number of activities or *tasks* emanating from another *activity* in a *work breakdown structure.*

Functional requirement A feature of a *software-intensive system* typically specified as an input/response pair. See also *Operational requirement, System requirement, Software requirement*, and *Quality attribute*.

Function Point A software *measure* determined by applying well-defined counting rules to determine the number of unique inputs, outputs, files, queries, and interfaces in the software elements of a *software-intensive system*.

Gantt chart (1) A task-Gantt chart is a graph that indicates the time in which each *task* in a software *project* is scheduled to occur; (2) a resource-Gantt chart is a graph that indicates when a particular *resource* will be needed to accomplish some of the tasks in the project *schedule*.

Goal An unquantified statement of intent or desired outcome. See also *Objective*.

Guideline A pragmatic statement of a practice that has been found to be effective in practical situations.

Impact analysis The *process* of assessing the need for and making necessary changes to *schedule, budget, resources,* technology, and *risk factors* commensurate with changes to baselined requirements. See also *Change request* and *Baselined work product*.

Inspection A formalized review *process* conducted by small teams (i.e., 2 to 5 people) for the purpose of finding *defects* in *work products*. See also *Walkthrough*.

Iterative development The *process* by which a *work product* is repeatedly elaborated to add value to the work product during each of the development iterations.

Measure (*n*) A symbol that is assigned to some attribute of a real-world phenomenon; the symbol must be from a set of symbols for which well-defined operations are specified. See also *Measurement* and *Metric*.

Measure (*v*) To assign a symbol to a real-world phenomenon; the symbol must be from a set of symbols for which well-defined operations are specified. See also *Measurement* and *Metric*.

Measurement The *process* of mapping some attribute of a real-world phenomenon to a symbol within a set of symbols for which well-defined operations are specified. See also *Measure* and *Metric*.

Memo of understanding (MOU) Specification of the *scope* of work activities to be performed on a software *project* for an internal *customer*; an MOU is typically an informal *contract*. See also *Statement of work*.

Metric A generic term used to denote *measure* and *measurement*.

Milestone A specified time within a *project schedule* by which specified *progress* should be achieved.

Monetary budget The money available to acquire and pay for the use of *resources*.

Monte Carlo estimation A statistical estimation method that uses samples from input probability distributions to produce output probability distributions.

Objective A quantified statement of a desired outcome to be achieved within a specified time frame. See also *Goal*.

Operational domain The environment in which delivered software will be used.

Operational requirement A statement of a need, desire, expectation, or *constraint* for a *software-intensive system* specified by a *user, customer, acquirer*, or other *stakeholder*.

Opportunity management The *process* of assessing potential gains to be made and the *risk factors* involved, and being prepared to take advantage of situations, should the potential for gains overcome the potential for losses in the judgment of *project stakeholders*. See also *Risk management*.

Original work Effort expended to develop initial *baselines* of *work products*. See also *Rework*.

PERT A statistical method used to determine the probability distributions for achieving various *milestones* in a *schedule*, including the end-date milestone. PERT is an acronym for Program Evaluation and Review Technique. See also *Critical path method*.

Platform technology The set of software tools, development environment, hardware, and operating system used to produce or modify the software elements of a *software-intensive system*.

Policy A statement of general principles to be observed throughout an organization. A policy may apply to managerial, technical, human resource, or other aspects of an organization.

Primary requirement A *software requirement* developed directly from an *operational requirement* or a *system requirement*. See also *Derived requirement*.

Procedure A set of *tasks* to be completed in accomplishing a *process*. See also *Technique*.

Process A way of accomplishing one or more work *activities* and *tasks*; typically involves, *procedures*, and the use of software tools.

Process engineering The *process* of developing and constantly improving *software engineering processes* to make them more *efficient* and more *effective*.

Process model A model of one or more elements of a software *project* that emphasizes work *activities* and the flow of *work products* among work activities.

Process standard A specified collection of *procedures* for conducting one or more work *activities* of a software *project*. See also *Process* and *Activity*.

Process framework A generic *process model* that can be tailored and adapted to fit the needs of particular projects and organizations.

Program A collection of *projects*, typically involving multiple technical disciplines, concerned with developing a complex *software-intensive system* consisting of hardware, software, and people elements. Diverse kinds of hardware elements, in addition to digital devices, may be included.

Progress A *measure* of *work products* completed, accepted, and *baselined*.

Project A group of coordinated work *activities* and *tasks* that utilizes *resources* to achieve specified *objectives* within a prescribed time frame.

Project management The collection of work activities concerned with planning and estimating, measuring and controlling, coordinating and leading, and managing *risk factors* for a software *project*.

Project manager The individual who is *responsible* for accomplishing *project management* and for delivering acceptable software elements of a *software-intensive system* on *schedule* and within the *monetary budget.*

Project risk The aggregated collection of identified *risk factors* for a software project.

Project team *Stakeholders* who are directly involved in development or modification of a *software-intensive system.* See also *Development team.*

Quality assurance The *process* of assuring that a software *project* is fulfilling its commitments to the planned software processes and *work products* as specified in the requirements, *software project management plan, supporting plans*, and any *policies, procedures, standards,* or *guidelines* to which the process or the product must adhere. Contrast to *Verification* and *Validation.*

Quality attribute A desirable characteristic of a *software-intensive system*; quality attributes include factors such as safety, security, reliability, and ease of modification. See also *Operational requirement, System requirement, Software requirement*, and *Functional requirement.*

Resource Any asset used in developing or modifying the software elements of a *software-intensive system*; resources include but are not limited to calendar time, *monetary budget, technology budget*, project personnel, other *stakeholders*, software to be reused, and *platform technology.*

Responsibility The obligation to perform the assigned tasks and duties of your job position in satisfactory manner. See also *Authority.*

Retrospective rework Work that could have been done sooner and must now be done to modify a *baselined work product.* See also *Rework, Avoidable rework*, and *Corrective rework.*

Rework Work performed to modify a *baselined work product.* See also *Evolutionary rework, Avoidable rework, Retrospective rework*, and *Corrective rework.*

Risk The aggregated collection of *risk factors* for a software *project.*

Risk exposure The product of probability × potential-impact for a *risk factor.*

Risk factor A potential problem that, should it become a real problem, will inhibit the ability to deliver acceptable software elements for a *software-intensive system* on *schedule* and within the *constraints* of the *monetary budget* and/or the *technology budget.* A risk factor is characterized by probability and potential impact.

Risk management The *process* of identifying risk factors, and developing and implementing *risk mitigation strategies* on a continuing basis. See also *Opportunity management.*

Risk mitigation strategies Different approaches to confronting identified *risk factors*; strategies include avoidance, transfer, acceptance, immediate action, and contingent action.

Rolling-wave planning The *process* of iteratively developing detailed plans on a monthly basis.

Schedule The time frame within which the software elements of a *software-intensive system* are to be built or modified. A schedule typically has intermediate *milestones.*

Schedule network An acyclic directed graph that indicates the ordering in time of the is-preceded-by and is-followed-by relationships among *tasks* in a software *project*.

Scope The extent of all work *activities* required to develop or modify the *work products* of a software *project*.

Software architect Chief designer of the software elements of a *software-intensive system*; also coordinator of the technical *activities* of the *development teams* for a software *project*.

Software engineering The engineering discipline concerned with developing and modifying software for digital devices.

Software-intensive system A *system* that includes one or more digital devices and the associated software. Software-intensive systems include *Software products, Software systems,* and *Embedded systems*. Some software-intensive systems *projects* are part of a *program*; some are stand-alone systems projects; others are *software-only projects*.

Software-only project A *project* concerned with developing software for which the hardware and operating system are provided by an off-the-shelf computer, no special-purpose hardware is needed, and no special training is required for users, operators, or operational support personnel. *Software requirements* for a software-only project are derived from the *operational requirements*. See also *Software-intensive system.*

Software-only system A *software-intensive system* for which there are no special hardware or human elements; the *platform technology* for developing a software-only system may be specified as a *constraint*. Software-only systems are often *software products.*

Software process A collection of *procedures* performed to develop or modify the software elements of a *software-intensive system.*

Software product Software built by a *vendor* for sale to multiple *customers*. See also *Software-only project.*

Software project management plan (SPMP) The controlling document for developing or modifying a *software-intensive system.*

Software requirement A statement that specifies a *functional requirement* or a *quality attribute* that a software component of a *software-intensive system* must, should, or might possess to satisfy the *operational requirements* and *system requirements*. Software requirements include *primary requirements, derived requirements,* design *constraints*, and design *goals*. See also *Objectives.*

Software system Software built by a *supplier* for a specific *customer* on a contractual basis. See also *Contract, Software-only project, Software product, and Software-intensive system.*

Software-intensive system A *system* that contains one or more digital devices and associated software; the *operational requirements, system requirements* and *constraints* for a software-intensive system may specify: (1) *functional requirements* and *quality attributes* that the hardware, software, and human elements of the system must possess or (2) the operational requirements may specify constraints on the *platform technology* plus functional requirements and quality attributes for a *software-only system*. Software-intensive systems include *software products, software systems*, and *embedded systems*.

Stakeholder Any individual who affects or is affected by development, operation, or maintenance of a *software-intensive system*. Stakeholders include *users, customers, acquirers*, managers, software project personnel, operations personnel, maintenance personnel, and others.

Standard A codification of practices and *procedures* that is usually developed and endorsed by a professional society or independent agency.

Statement of work (SOW) A specification of the *scope* of work activities to be performed on a software *project* for an external *customer*; the SOW is typically part of a legally binding *contract*. See also *Memo of understanding*.

Supplier A software development organization that develops or modifies a *software system* or the software elements of an *embedded system* for an individual *acquirer* subject to a legally binding *contract*.

Supporting process A *process* that supports the *tasks* of developing and modifying *work products*; supporting processes include but are not limited to *configuration management, quality assurance, verification*, and *validation*.

System A collection of interacting components that exist within and interact with an environment.

System requirements A document that specifies the *functional requirements* and *quality attributes* for a *system* that includes hardware, software, and (perhaps) operational personnel. System requirements are derived from *operational requirements; software requirements* are derived from *operational requirements* and *system requirements*.

Task (1) The smallest unit of management accountability in a software *project*; (2) a lowest level unit of work in a *work breakdown structure*. See also *Activity*.

Team A small group of individuals (typically 2 to 5) plus a team leader who work in a cooperative manner to achieve common objectives.

Technical performance measurement (TPM) The process of comparing planned to actual values of technical parameters such as performance, memory usage, or *system* throughput.

Technique The way in which an individual accomplishes a *procedure*; techniques are often idiosyncratic to the individual.

Technology budget The constrained technology available to support implementation of software; includes *constraints* on one or more factors such as memory space, execution time, and communication bandwidth.

Traceability matrix A two-dimensional table that indicates correspondences between elements of two *work products* such as *operational requirements* and *software requirements* or *system requirements* and associated test plans.

User An individual (or another system, as in the case of an *embedded system*) who will utilize a *software-intensive system* to perform her or his (or its) work activities or pursue his or her recreational activities.

Validation The *process* of determining the degree to which *work products* satisfy their intended purposes in their intended environments.

Vendor An organization that builds a *software product* for sale to multiple *customers.*

Verification The *process* of determining the degree to which *work products* satisfy the conditions placed on them by other *work products* and work *processes.* A verified work product is correct, complete, and consistent with respect to other work products and work processes.

Walkthrough A review *process* conducted for the purpose of communicating information among a group of project *stakeholders.* See also *Inspection.*

Work breakdown structure (WBS) A hierarchical decomposition of the work activities in a software *project.* The lowest level activities in the hierarchy are *tasks.* Each element of a WBS is named using a verb phrase to denote the *process*-oriented nature of a WBS. See also *Architecture decomposition view.*

Work package Specification of a *task* in a *work breakdown structure.* Work packages for *activities* are aggregates of the work packages for subordinate activities and tasks.

Work product Any document, in either electronic or printed form, produced by a software *project*; work products include the source code.

GUIDELINES FOR TERM PROJECTS

INTRODUCTION

This appendix describes some projects for which software project management plans can be prepared. Also include are a schedule for completing various sections of the plan, and a template for the final report. Each of the projects is large enough to be interesting and small enough to allow completion of a project plan in a quarter or semester course. For example, the projects described here would require on the order of 10 to 12 people on a 10 to 12 month schedule; that is, 100 to 144 staff-months of effort.

Students sometimes misunderstand the nature of a term project in a project management class. It must be emphasized to students that the term project does not involve development of any software but rather will require them to develop elements of a plan for developing the software. Some creativity may be required of the students to complete some elements of their project plans, for example, in describing the acquiring organization or the development process model to be used. The instructor can specify some of the elements of a hypothetical project for students who may not have the background or experience to complete those elements.

Also students sometime confuse development of the software for a system with development of hardware and software. The term project for a course in software project management should concentrate on a plan for developing software with the assumption that the necessary hardware and software development environment will be available.

Possibilities for term projects other than those described here include real projects that students with work experience are currently involved in, have been involved in, or will be involve in, as well as projects assigned by class instructors. Term projects

Managing and Leading Software Projects, by Richard E. Fairley

should be of sufficient size to warrant a significant planning effort but not so large to prevent development of a plan within the constraints of a quarter or semester length course.

Although it is common practice in software engineering courses for students to work in small teams, it is recommended that students work individually in preparing their project plans so that each student can gain experience in preparing artifacts such as work breakdown structures, schedule networks, and risk management plans.

The recommended schedule for completion of term projects requires weekly deliverables from the students. The chapters of the text are structured to allow instructors to cover the material needed to complete each weekly assignment in advance of the assignment. Instructors can provide feedback on the weekly deliverables and allow students to revise those deliverables in an iterative manner. Students' final reports can then contain the integrated results of the (perhaps revised) weekly deliverables. The following sections of this guideline describe topics for term projects, a schedule for preparing the project plans, and a template for the final report.

Additional guidance for term projects, some software tools, and an electronic version of the final report template can be found at the URL listed in the Preface to this text.

PROJECT DESCRIPTIONS

Project Plan for Developing the Software Elements of an Automated Teller Machine

Planning a software project for the software elements of an Automated Teller Machine is used as the running example in this text. A term project would involve collecting and augmenting the various elements of the ATM example from the text to produce a software project management plan.

Project Plan for Developing a Web-based Application

Various kinds of Web-based applications might form the basis for a term project. Examples include a video-rental service such as that provided by Netflix or Blockbuster, or a point-of-sale system for a large chain of retail stores, or a nationwide inventory control system for a wholesale distributor. Other examples are limited only by your imagination.

Project Plan for Developing the Software Elements of a Programmable Home Control Unit

A programmable Home Control Unit (HCU) integrates sensing and control of the various elements of a house or apartment, including but not limited to elements such as security, lighting, Web cams, entertainment system, appliances, heating and cooling, and irrigation. The HCU must be programmable to allow control of elements such as the heating and cooling system (by zones) and a security system (for a variable number of devices, individually controlled). Other elements an HCU might control refrigerator and oven, a lawn sprinkler system (by zones) and the lighting system (by electrical outlet). An HCU might include control of the home entertainment system (by individual device), and anything else you want to include (e.g., opening and closing blinds, automatic dispensing of pet food).

An HCU system would include a user interface having password protected modes of operation, including a system configuration mode that allows a trained technician to set the installation parameters, an adult mode, a child mode, and perhaps a vacation mode. The software would include a local area network to sense and control various devices, the software device drivers for the devices to be sensed and controlled, and a communication package to provide interfaces to a security company, to the local fire and police departments, and to the Internet. In the latter case you might, for example, call up on your cell phone and instruct your oven to turn on, or you might instruct a robot to remove a prepared meal from the refrigerator and place it in the oven. The range of possibilities for an HCU is limited only by your imagination.

Project Plan for Developing the Software Elements of a Driving System Simulator

A Driving System Simulator (DSS) is envisioned as a realistic simulator that would allow drivers to experience various driving situations in a simulated environment. The simulator would consist of a student cabin that contains the elements of a modern automobile (or truck or bus or race car). A projection system in the cabin would provide realistic front, side, and rear views. A sound system in the cabin would provide realistic sounds of driving. The cabin would be mounted on a hydraulic platform that would simulate the experience of driving on various kinds of roads under various kinds of weather conditions (e.g., normal, wet, slick, icy, snowy, and foggy conditions).

An instructor's station would permit creation, playback, and monitoring of driving scenarios as well as the ability to create obstacles and other emergency conditions during driving scenarios. A data repository would contain the driving scenarios and software to control the hydraulics, and would provide the ability to store and retrieve scripts, to retain records of student performance, and to generate various kinds of reports.

Your DSS might have various modes of operation, for example, novice student mode, advanced student mode, race driving mode, instructor mode, and maintenance and diagnostics mode. The project plan should include work activities to verify and validate that the system will be safe, secure, easy to use, and reliable.

Hardware for a DSS would include (1) the elements of a realistic simulator, including the usual features of an automobile: door, seat, steering wheel, windshield, side window, rear window, mirror displays, dashboard controls and indicators, stereo system, and anything else you might want to include; (2) the projection system hardware in the student cabin; (3) a hydraulic system on which the student cabin is mounted; (4) the instructor's work station; (5) the data repository hardware; (6) a local area network to support communication among the various elements of the hardware; (7) the server for the LAN and the software components of the DSS; and (8) any other hardware needed for the DSS.

You would assume that the hardware is available and provides the necessary capabilities. The term project would be to develop a project management plan for building, modifying, and perhaps purchasing (some of) the necessary software elements for a DSS.

A SCHEDULE FOR TERM PROJECTS

This eight-week schedule is suitable for a quarter length or semester length class. Week 1 of the project will most likely start in week 2 of the class. The eight-week schedule also allows time for slippage of deliverables should it be necessary or desirable to extend the schedule for the term project.

As indicated in Chapters 4 and 5 of the text, the various elements of a project plan for a student term project can be prepared at various levels of detail; for example, the WBS may be partially decomposed and a few work packages prepared rather than doing extensive decomposition of a WBS and preparation of extensive work packages.

Week 2 deliverables (due at the end of class week 2):

- system overview
  - a short description of the system to be built
  - primary features and quality attributes of the system
  - modes of system operation

Week 3 deliverables (due at the end of class week 3; see Chapters 2 and 3):

- a description of user classes and other stakeholders
  - classes of users
  - other stakeholders and their needs
- a set of operational requirements
  - partitioned into subsets of Essential, Desirable, and Optional requirements
  - prioritized as E1, E2, ... D1, D2, ... , O1, O2, ...
- the software development model to be used
  - such as Incremental-build, Evolutionary, Agile
- the software development environment to be used
  - such as Unix, Windows, Eclipse

Week 4 deliverables (due at the end of class week 4; see Chapter 5):

- an architectural breakdown structure (ADV) with allocated requirements
  - in both graphical and indented forms

Week 5 deliverables (due at the end of class week 5; see Chapter 5):

- a work breakdown structure (WBS) with allocated requirements
  - in both graphical and indented forms

Week 6 deliverables (due at the end of class week 6; see Chapter 6):

- estimates of effort, schedule, and cost to include an estimation summary sheet, a copy of the estimation spreadsheet results, and a summary table of effort, schedule, and cost

Week 7 deliverables (due at the end of class week 7; see Chapter 5):

- a schedule network, a milestone chart, a Gantt chart, and a staffing profile
    - prepared manually or using a software tool (e.g., Microsoft Project)

Week 8 deliverables (due at the end of class week 8; see Chapter 5):

- work packages for some WBS elements

Week 9 deliverables (due at the end of class week 9; see Chapter 9):

- some identified risk factors for the envisioned project and a mitigation strategy for each one
- the final report

A TEMPLATE FOR THE FINAL REPORT

Cover page

- to include course name and number, instructor, project name, preparer's name, and date of submission

Abstract

- intended purpose of this report (as if this were a real project for a real company)
- intended audience for this report
- summary of effort, schedule, and cost of this project

Section 1: System overview [the week 2 deliverable]
  1.1 Short description
  1.2 Primary features and quality attributes
  1.3 Modes of operation

Section 2: Users and other stakeholders [a week 3 deliverable]
  2.1 Classes of users
    2.1.1
    2.1.2
    etc.

2.2 Other stakeholders and their objectives
2.2.1
2.2.2
etc.

Section 3: Operational requirements [a week 3 deliverable]
3.1 Essential requirements (prioritized)
3.2 Desirable requirements (prioritized)
3.3 Optional requirements (prioritized)

Section 4: Development model and development environment [a week 3 deliverable]
4.1 Software development model to be used
4.2 Software development environment to be used

Section 5: Architectural breakdown structure (ADV) with allocated requirements [the week 4 deliverable]
5.1 Indented ADV
5.2 Graphical ADV

Section 6: Work breakdown structure (WBS) [the week 5 deliverable]
6.1 Indented WBS with allocated requirements
6.2 Graphical WBS with allocated requirements

Section 7: Estimates [the week 6 deliverable]
7.1 Estimation summary sheet (as in Figure 6.14)
7.2 Estimation spreadsheet
7.3 Summary table of detailed effort, schedule, and cost

Section 8: Schedule [the week 7 deliverable]
8.1 Schedule network
8.2 Milestone chart
8.3 Task-Gantt chart
8.4 Staffing profile

Section 9: Work packages [the week 8 deliverable]
9.1 Work package #1 [name]
9.2 Work package #2 [name]
etc.

Section 10: Risk analysis [the week 9 deliverable]
10.1 Identified risk factors and mitigation strategies
10.1.1 Risk factor #1 [name]
Brief description
Mitigation strategy with explanation
10.1.2 Risk factor #2 [name]
Brief description
Mitigation strategy with explanation
etc.

INDEX

Managing and Leading Software Projects, by Richard E. Fairley

Printed and bound by CPI Group (UK) Ltd, Croydon, CR0 4YY
27/10/2024
14580137-0003